Lecture Notes in Computer Science   15886

Founding Editors

Gerhard Goos
Juris Hartmanis

Editorial Board Members

Elisa Bertino, *Purdue University, West Lafayette, IN, USA*
Wen Gao, *Peking University, Beijing, China*
Bernhard Steffen, *TU Dortmund University, Dortmund, Germany*
Moti Yung, *Columbia University, New York, NY, USA*

The series Lecture Notes in Computer Science (LNCS), including its subseries Lecture Notes in Artificial Intelligence (LNAI) and Lecture Notes in Bioinformatics (LNBI), has established itself as a medium for the publication of new developments in computer science and information technology research, teaching, and education.

LNCS enjoys close cooperation with the computer science R & D community, the series counts many renowned academics among its volume editors and paper authors, and collaborates with prestigious societies. Its mission is to serve this international community by providing an invaluable service, mainly focused on the publication of conference and workshop proceedings and postproceedings. LNCS commenced publication in 1973.

Osvaldo Gervasi · Beniamino Murgante ·
Chiara Garau · Yeliz Karaca ·
Maria Noelia Faginas Lago · Francesco Scorza ·
Ana Cristina Braga
Editors

Computational Science and Its Applications – ICCSA 2025 Workshops

Istanbul, Turkey, June 30 – July 3, 2025
Proceedings, Part I

Editors
Osvaldo Gervasi
University of Perugia
Perugia, Italy

Beniamino Murgante
University of Basilicata
Potenza, Italy

Chiara Garau
University of Cagliari
Cagliari, Italy

Yeliz Karaca
University of Massachusetts
Worcester, MA, USA

Maria Noelia Faginas Lago
University of Perugia
Perugia, Italy

Francesco Scorza
University of Basilicata
Potenza, Italy

Ana Cristina Braga
University of Minho
Braga, Portugal

ISSN 0302-9743　　　　　　　ISSN 1611-3349　(electronic)
Lecture Notes in Computer Science
ISBN 978-3-031-97575-2　　　ISBN 978-3-031-97576-9　(eBook)
https://doi.org/10.1007/978-3-031-97576-9

© The Editor(s) (if applicable) and The Author(s), under exclusive license
to Springer Nature Switzerland AG 2026

This work is subject to copyright. All rights are solely and exclusively licensed by the Publisher, whether the whole or part of the material is concerned, specifically the rights of translation, reprinting, reuse of illustrations, recitation, broadcasting, reproduction on microfilms or in any other physical way, and transmission or information storage and retrieval, electronic adaptation, computer software, or by similar or dissimilar methodology now known or hereafter developed.
The use of general descriptive names, registered names, trademarks, service marks, etc. in this publication does not imply, even in the absence of a specific statement, that such names are exempt from the relevant protective laws and regulations and therefore free for general use.
The publisher, the authors and the editors are safe to assume that the advice and information in this book are believed to be true and accurate at the date of publication. Neither the publisher nor the authors or the editors give a warranty, expressed or implied, with respect to the material contained herein or for any errors or omissions that may have been made. The publisher remains neutral with regard to jurisdictional claims in published maps and institutional affiliations.

This Springer imprint is published by the registered company Springer Nature Switzerland AG
The registered company address is: Gewerbestrasse 11, 6330 Cham, Switzerland

If disposing of this product, please recycle the paper.

Preface

The compiled 14 volumes (LNCS volumes 15886–15899) consist of the peer-reviewed papers from the 68 Workshops of the 2025 International Conference on Computational Science and Its Applications (ICCSA 2025), which was held between June 30 – July 3, 2025 in Istanbul (Türkiye). The peer-reviewed papers of the main conference tracks are published in a separate set made up of three volumes (LNCS 15648–15650).

The conference was held in a hybrid form, with the large majority of participants in presence, hosted by Galatasaray University, Istanbul, Türkiye. We enabled virtual participation for those who did not attend the event in person due to logistical, political and economic problems, by adopting a technological infrastructure via open-source software (jitsi + riot) and a commercial Cloud infrastructure.

With the 2025 edition, ICCSA celebrated its 25th anniversary, a quarter of a century as a memorable moment that is harmoniously aligned with Istanbul, an extraordinary city located at the crossroads and acting as a bridge connecting Asia and Europe, representing different cultures, beliefs as well as lifestyles, which highlights its intercultural fabric.

ICCSA 2025 marked another fruitful and thought-provoking academic event in the International Conferences on Computational Science and Its Applications (ICCSA) conference series, previously held in Hanoi, Vietnam (2024), Athens, Greece (2023), Málaga, Spain (2022), Cagliari, Italy (hybrid with a few participants in presence in 2021 and completely online in 2020), whilst earlier editions took place in Saint Petersburg, Russia (2019), Melbourne, Australia (2018), Trieste, Italy (2017), Beijing, China (2016), Banff, Canada (2015), Guimaraes, Portugal (2014), Ho Chi Minh City, Vietnam (2013), Salvador, Brazil (2012), Santander, Spain (2011), Fukuoka, Japan (2010), Suwon, South Korea (2009), Perugia, Italy (2008), Kuala Lumpur, Malaysia (2007), Glasgow, UK (2006), Singapore (2005), Assisi, Italy (2004), Montreal, Canada (2003), and (as ICCS) Amsterdam, the Netherlands (2002) and San Francisco, USA (2001).

Computational Science constitutes the main pillar of most present research, industrial and commercial applications, and plays a unique role in exploiting ICT innovative technologies, and the ICCSA conference series has, accordingly, provided ample opportunities to researchers and industry practitioners to discuss new ideas, to share complex problems and their solutions, and to shape new trends in Computational Science. As the conference mirrors society from a scientific point of view, this year's undoubtedly dominant theme was large language models, machine learning and Artificial Intelligence (AI) and their applications in the most diverse technological, economic and industrial fields, amongst the others.

The ICCSA 2025 conference was structured in six general tracks covering the fields of computational science and its applications: Computational Methods, Algorithms and Scientific Applications – High Performance Computing and Networks – Geometric Modeling, Graphics and Visualization – Advanced and Emerging Applications – Information Systems and Technologies – Urban and Regional Planning. In addition, the conference consisted of 68 workshops, focusing on topical issues of utmost importance to science, technology and society: from new computational approaches for earth science, to mathematical methods for image processing, new statistical and optimization methods, several Artificial Intelligence approaches, sustainability issues, smart cities and related technologies, to name some.

In the Workshops' proceedings, we accepted 362 full papers, 37 short papers and 2 Ph.D. Showcase papers from total of 1043 submissions (Acceptance rate 38.4%). In the Main Conference Proceedings, we accepted 71 full papers, 6 short papers and 1 Ph.D. Showcase paper from 269 submissions to the General Tracks of the Conference (with an acceptance rate of 29.9%). We would like to convey our sincere appreciation to the workshops' chairs and co-chairs and program committee members for their diligent work, commitment and dedication.

The success and consistent maintenance of the ICCSA conference series in general, and of ICCSA 2025 in particular, rely upon the support of many people: authors, presenters, participants, keynote speakers, workshop chairs, session chairs, organizing committee members, student volunteers, Program Committee members, Advisory Committee members, International Liaison chairs, reviewers and other individuals in various roles. Thus, we take this opportunity to wholehartedly thank each and everyone.

We additionally wish to thank publisher Springer for their agreement to publish the proceedings, besides sponsoring part of the best papers awards and for their kind assistance and cooperation during the editing process.

We would cordially like to invite you to refer to the ICCSA website https://iccsa.org, where you can find the relevant details regarding this academic endeavor and event of ours.

June 2025

Osvaldo Gervasi
Yeliz Karaca
Beniamino Murgante
Chiara Garau

A Welcome Message from the Organizers

The International Conference on Computational Science and Its Applications (ICCSA) reflects a culmination of meticulous and dedicated efforts and academic endeavors toward the progress of science and technology.

One of the most noteworthy aspects of ICCSA is its fostering of a collective spirit, bringing together a plethora of participants from all over the world. Correspondingly, this merging power manifests itself in the 25th anniversary of ICCSA, which is a quarter of a century, in Istanbul, Türkiye, which connects and acts as a bridge between two continents, namely Asia and Europe. This unique location in the world hosts the 25th year of ICCSA at Galatasaray University, located on Çırağan Avenue by Istanbul's Bosphorus, which is an established international university bestowed with a distinctive past of teaching tradition, research and education exceeding five centuries.

Istanbul, having served as the capital city of four empires, namely the Roman Empire (330–395), the Byzantine Empire (395–1204 and 1261–1453), the Latin Empire (1204–1261) and the Ottoman Empire (1453–1922), is an exceptional city of the Republic of Türkiye founded by Mustafa Kemal Atatürk.

Situated at a strategic location along the historic Silk Road, Istanbul is at the core of extending rail networks which span across Europe and West Asia along with the only sea route between the Black Sea and the Mediterranean.

The cultural, historical and economic pulses of the country are evident in Istanbul whose rooted origins have embraced varying beliefs, lifestyles and populace, which highlights the city's mosaic quality with blended fabric in a constant harmonious flow. This has enabled cultures to grow and be nurtured, which is profoundly rooted in its urban culture.

Computational Science constitutes the main pillar of most present research, industrial and commercial activities besides manifesting a unique role in exploiting and addressing innovative Information and Communication Technologies. Thus, the 25-year-old ICCSA conference series provides remarkable opportunities to get acquainted with leading researchers, scientists, scholars, practitioners and many more while exchanging innovative ideas and initiating new partnerships, associations and bonds.

With the hosting of Galatasaray University, I would personally and on behalf of the Local Organizing Committee, with the members Emre Alptekin, Gülfem Işıklar Alptekin, Cengiz Kahraman, Abdullah Çağrı Tolga and Ayberk Zeytin, like to convey our sincere gratitude and thanks to everyone who exerted their efforts in and contributed to the realization of ICCSA 2025. With these notes and remarks, welcome to Istanbul!

Cordially yours,
On behalf of the Local Organizing Committee.

June 2025   Yeliz Karaca

Organization

Honorary General Chairs

Bernady O. Apduhan	Kyushu Sangyo University, Japan
Kenneth C. J. Tan	Sardina Systems, UK

General Chairs

Yeliz Karaca	University of Massachusetts, USA
Osvaldo Gervasi	University of Perugia, Italy
David Taniar	Monash University, Australia

Program Committee Chairs

Beniamino Murgante	University of Basilicata, Italy
Chiara Garau	University of Cagliari, Italy
Ana Maria A. C. Rocha	University of Minho, Portugal
A. Çağrı Tolga	Galatasaray University, Turkey

International Advisory Committee

Jemal Abawajy	Deakin University, Australia
Dharma P. Agarwal	University of Cincinnati, USA
Rajkumar Buyya	Melbourne University, Australia
Claudia Bauzer Medeiros	University of Campinas, Brazil
Manfred M. Fisher	Vienna University of Economics and Business, Austria
Pierre Frankhauser	University of Franche-Comté/CNRS, France
Marina L. Gavrilova	University of Calgary, Canada
Sumi Helal	University of Florida, USA & Lancaster University, UK
Bin Jiang	University of Gävle, Sweden
Yee Leung	Chinese University of Hong Kong, China

International Liaison Chairs

Ivan Blečić	University of Cagliari, Italy
Giuseppe Borruso	University of Trieste, Italy
Elise De Donker	Western Michigan University, USA
Maria Noelia Faginas Lago	University of Perugia, Italy
Maria Irene Falcão	University of Minho, Portugal
Robert C. H. Hsu	Chung Hua University, Taiwan
Yeliz Karaca	University of Massachusetts Chan Medical School, USA
Tae-Hoon Kim	Zhejiang University of Science and Technology, China
Vladimir Korkhov	Saint Petersburg University, Russia
Takashi Naka	Kyushu Sangyo University, Japan
Rafael D. C. Santos	National Institute for Space Research, Brazil
Maribel Yasmina Santos	University of Minho, Portugal
Anastasia Stratigea	National Technical University of Athens, Greece

Workshop and Session Organizing Chairs

Beniamino Murgante	University of Basilicata, Italy
Chiara Garau	University of Cagliari, Italy

Award Chair

Wenny Rahayu	La Trobe University, Australia

Publicity Committee Chairs

Elmer Dadios	De La Salle University, Philippines
Nataliia Kulabukhova	Saint Petersburg University, Russia
Daisuke Takahashi	Tsukuba University, Japan
Shangwang Wang	Beijing University of Posts and Telecommunications, China

Local Organizing Committee Chairs

Emre Alptekin	Galatasaray University, Turkey
Gülfem Işıklar Alptekin	Galatasaray University, Turkey
Cengiz Kahraman	İstanbul Technical University, Turkey
A. Çağrı Tolga	Galatasaray University, Turkey
Ayberk Zeytin	Galatasaray University, Turkey

Technology Chair

Damiano Perri	University of Perugia, Italy

Program Committee

Vera Afreixo	University of Aveiro, Portugal
Vladimir Alarcon	Northern Gulf Institute, USA
Filipe Alvelos	University of Minho, Portugal
Debora Anelli	Polytechnic University of Bari, Italy
Hartmut Asche	Hasso-Plattner-Institut für Digital Engineering Ggmbh, Germany
Nizamettin Aydın	İstanbul Technical University, Turkey
Ginevra Balletto	University of Cagliari, Italy
Nadia Balucani	University of Perugia, Italy
Socrates Basbas	Aristotle University of Thessaloniki, Greece
David Berti	ART SpA, Italy
Michela Bertolotto	University College Dublin, Ireland
Sandro Bimonte	CEMAGREF, TSCF, France
Ana Cristina Braga	University of Minho, Portugal
Tiziana Campisi	Kore University of Enna, Italy
Yves Caniou	Université Claude Bernard Lyon 1, France
Alessandra Capolupo	Polytechnic University of Bari, Italy
José A. Cardoso e Cunha	Universidade Nova de Lisboa, Portugal
Rui Cardoso	University of Beira Interior, Portugal
Leocadio G. Casado	University of Almería, Spain
Mete Celik	Erciyes University, Turkey
Maria Cerreta	University of Naples Federico II, Italy
Ta Quang Chieu	Thuyloi University, Vietnam
Rachel Chien-Sing Lee	Sunway University, Malaysia
Birol Ciloglugil	Ege University, Turkey
Mauro Coni	University of Cagliari, Italy

xii   Organization

Florbela Maria da Cruz Domingues Correia	Polytechnic Institute of Viana do Castelo, Portugal
Alessandro Costantini	INFN, Italy
Roberto De Lotto	University of Pavia, Italy
Luiza De Macedo Mourelle	State University of Rio De Janeiro, Brazil
Marcelo De Paiva Guimaraes	Federal University of Sao Paulo, Brazil
Frank Devai	London South Bank University, UK
Joana Matos Dias	University of Coimbra, Portugal
Aziz Dursun	Virginia Tech University, USA
Laila El Ghandour	Heriot-Watt University, UK
Rafida M. Elobaid	Canadian University Dubai, United Arab Emirates
Maria Irene Falcao	University of Minho, Portugal
Florbela P. Fernandes	Polytechnic Institute of Bragança, Portugal
Paula Odete Fernandes	Polytechnic Institute of Bragança, Portugal
Adelaide de Fátima Baptista Valente Freitas	University of Aveiro, Portugal
Valentina Franzoni	University of Perugia, Italy
Andreas Fricke	University of Potsdam, Germany
Raffaele Garrisi	Centro Operativo per la Sicurezza Cibernetica, Italy
Ivan Gerace	University of Perugia, Italy
Maria Giaoutzi	National Technical University of Athens, Greece
Salvatore Giuffrida	University of Catania, Italy
Teresa Guarda	Universidad Estatal Peninsula de Santa Elena, Ecuador
Sevin Gümgüm	Izmir University of Economics, Turkey
Malgorzata Hanzl	Technical University of Lodz, Poland
Maulana Adhinugraha Kiki	Telkom University, Indonesia
Clement Ho Cheung Leung	Chinese University of Hong Kong, China
Andrea Lombardi	University of Perugia, Italy
Marcos Mandado Alonso	University of Vigo, Spain
Ernesto Marcheggiani	Katholieke Universiteit Leuven, Belgium
Antonino Marvuglia	Luxembourg Institute of Science and Technology, Luxembourg
Michele Mastroianni	University of Salerno, Italy
Hideo Matsufuru	High Energy Accelerator Research Organization, Japan
Fernando Miranda	Universidade do Minho, Portugal
Giuseppe Modica	University of Reggio Calabria, Italy
Majaz Moonis	University of Massachusetts, USA
Nadia Nedjah	State University of Rio de Janeiro, Brazil
Paolo Nesi	University of Florence, Italy

Suzan Obaiys	University of Malaya, Malaysia
Marcin Paprzycki	Polish Academy of Sciences, Poland
Eric Pardede	La Trobe University, Australia
Ana Isabel Pereira	Polytechnic Institute of Bragança, Portugal
Damiano Perri	University of Perugia, Italy
Massimiliano Petri	University of Pisa, Italy
Telmo Pinto	University of Coimbra, Portugal
Alessandro Plaisant	University of Sassari, Italy
Maurizio Pollino	ENEA, Italy
Alenka Poplin	Iowa State University, USA
Marcos Quiles	Federal University of São Paulo, Brazil
Nguyen Huu Quynh	Thuyloi University, Vietnam
Albert Rimola	Universitat Autònoma de Barcelona, Spain
Humberto Rocha	University of Coimbra, Portugal
Marzio Rosi	University of Perugia, Italy
Lucia Saganeiti	University of L'Aquila, Italy
Francesco Scorza	University of Basilicata, Italy
Marco Paulo Seabra dos Reis	University of Coimbra, Portugal
Jie Shen	University of Michigan, USA
Francesco Tajani	Sapienza University of Rome, Italy
Rodrigo Tapia Mcclung	Centro de Investigación en Ciencias de Información Geoespacial, Mexico
Eufemia Tarantino	Polytechnic University of Bari, Italy
Sergio Tasso	University of Perugia, Italy
Ana Paula Teixeira	Universidade do Minho, Portugal
Yiota Theodora	National Technical University of Athens, Greece
Giuseppe A. Trunfio	University of Sassari, Italy
Toshihiro Uchibayashi	Kyushu University, Japan
Marco Vizzari	University of Perugia, Italy
Frank Westad	Norwegian University of Science and Technology, Norway
Fukuko Yuasa	High Energy Accelerator Research Organization, Japan
Ljiljana Zivkovic	Republic Geodetic Authority, Serbia

Workshops

Workshop on Advancements in Applied Machine-Learning and Data Analytics (AAMDA 2025)

Workshop Organizers

Alessandro Costantini	INFN, Italy
Daniele Cesini	INFN, Italy
Elisabetta Ronchieri	INFN, Italy
Barbara Martelli	INFN, Italy

Workshop Program Committee Members

Alessandro Costantini	Istituto Nazionale di Fisica Nucleare (INFN), Italy
Daniele Cesini	Istituto Nazionale di Fisica Nucleare (INFN), Italy
Elisabetta Ronchieri	Istituto Nazionale di Fisica Nucleare (INFN), Italy
Barbara Martelli	Istituto Nazionale di Fisica Nucleare (INFN), Italy
Luca Dell'Agnello	Istituto Nazionale di Fisica Nucleare (INFN), Italy

Advanced and Innovative Web Apps 2025 (AIWA 2025)

Workshop Organizers

Damiano Perri	University of Perugia, Italy
Osvaldo Gervasi	University of Perugia, Italy
Stelios Kouzeleas	International Hellenic University, Greece
Sergio Tasso	University of Perugia, Italy

Workshop Program Committee Members

David Berti	ART SpA, Italy
JungYoon Kim	Gachon University, South Korea
TaiHoon Kim	Zhejiang University of Science and Technology, China

Advanced Processes of Mathematics and Computing Models in Complex Data-Intensive Computational Systems (AMCM 2025)

Workshop Organizers

Yeliz Karaca	University of Massachusetts Chan Medical School and Massachusetts Institute of Technology, USA
Dumitru Baleanu	Lebanese American University, Lebanon
Osvaldo Gervasi	University of Perugia, Italy
Yudong Zhang	University of Leicester, UK
Majaz Moonis	University of Massachusetts Chan Medical School and Massachusetts Institute of Technology, USA

Workshop Program Committee Members

TaeHoon Kim	Zhejiang University of Science and Technology, China
Martin Bohner	Missouri University of Science and Technology, USA
Shuihua Wang	University of Leicester, UK
Khan Muhammad	Sungkyunkwan University, South Korea
Mahmoud Abdel-Aty	Sohag University, Egypt
Aziz Dursun	Virginia Polytechnic Institute and State University, USA
Kemal Güven Gülen	Namık Kemal University, Turkey
Akif Akgül	Hitit Üniversitesi, Turkey

Advanced Numerical Approaches for Assessment and Design of No-Tension Masonry Structures (ANAMS 2025)

Workshop Organizers

Antonino Iannuzzo	Universitá degli studi del Sannio, Italy
Carlo Olivieri	Universitá Telematica Pegaso, Italy
Andrea Montanino	CIMNE, Spain
Elham Mousavian	University of Edinburgh, UK

Workshop Program Committee Members

Pietro Meriggi	Roma Tre University, Italy
Francesca Perelli	University of Naples Federico II, Italy
Marialuigia Sangirardi	University of Oxford, UK
Sam Cocking	University of Cambridge, UK

Matteo Salvalaggio	University of Minho, Portugal
Vittorio Paris	University of Bergamo, Italy
Luigi Sibille	Norwegian University of Science and Technology, Norway
Natalia Pingaro	Politecnico di Milano, Italy
Martina Buzzetti	Politecnico di Milano, Italy
Generoso Vaiano	Pegaso Telematic University, Italy
Alessandra Capolupo	Politecnico di Bari, Italy
Amal Gerges	Università degli Studi di Cagliari, Italy
Fabian Orozco	National Autonomous University of Mexico, Mexico
Nathanael Savalle	Polytech Clermont and Université Clermont Auvergne, France
Luca Umberto Argiento	University of Naples Federico II, Italy
Bartolomeo Pantó	Durham University, UK

Unveiling the Synergies Between Air Quality and Climate PlAnning (AQCliPA 2025)

Workshop Organizers

Angela Pilogallo	University of L'Aquila, Italy
Luigi Santopietro	University of Basilicata, Italy
Filomena Pietrapertosa	IMAA CNR, Italy
Monica Salvia	IMAA CNR, Italy
Carlo Trozzi	IMAA CNR, Italy
Valeria Scapini	Central University of Chile, Chile

Workshop Program Committee Members

Lucia Saganeiti	IMAA-CNR, Italy
Lorena Fiorini	University of L'Aquila, Italy
Antonio Mazza	IMAA-CNR, Italy
Gabriele Nolè	IMAA-CNR, Italy
Carmen Guida	University of Naples "Federico II", Italy
Floriana Zucaro	University of Naples "Federico II", Italy
Sabrina Lai	University of Cagliari, Italy
Chiara Garau	University of Cagliari, Italy

Advancements in Spatial assessment of Socio-Ecological SystemS (ASSESS 2025)

Workshop Organizers
Daniele Cannatella	TU Delft, The Netherlands
Giuliano Poli	University of Naples Federico II, Italy
Eugenio Muccio	TU Delft, The Netherlands
Claudiu Forgaci	TU Delft, The Netherlands

Workshop Program Committee Members
Daniele Cannatella	TU Delft, The Netherlands
Giuliano Poli	University of Naples Federico II, Italy
Eugenio Muccio	University of Naples Federico II, Italy
Claudiu Forgaci	TU Delft, The Netherlands
Maria Cerreta	University of Naples Federico II, Italy
Maria Somma	University of Naples Federico II, Italy
Laura Di Tommaso	University of Naples Federico II, Italy
Sabrina Sacco	Politecnico di Milano, Italy
Piero Zizzania	University of Naples Federico II, Italy
Gaia Daldanise	CNR IRISS, Italy
Benedetta Grieco	University of Naples Federico II, Italy
Giuseppe Ciciriello	University of Naples Federico II, Italy
Marta Dell'Ovo	Politecnico di Milano, Italy
Francesco Piras	University of Cagliari, Italy
Diana Rolando	Politecnico di Torino, Italy
Stefano Cuntò	University of Naples Federico II, Italy
Ludovica La Rocca	University of Naples Federico II, Italy

Blockchain and Distributed Ledgers: Technologies and Applications (BDLTA 2025)

Workshop Organizers
Vladimir Korkhov	Saint Petersburg State University, Russia
Elena Stankova	Saint Petersburg State University, Russia
Nataliia Kulabukhova	Saint Petersburg State University, Russia

Workshop Program Committee Members
Adam Belloum	University of Amsterdam, the Netherlands
Dmitrii Vasiunin	Deutsche Telekom Cloud Services E.P.E., Greece
Serob Balyan	Osensus Arm LLC, Armenia
Suren Abrahamyan	Osensus Arm LLC, Armenia
Ashot Sergey Gevorkyan	NAS of Armenia, Armenia

Michal Hnatic	Univerzita Pavla Jozefa Šafárika v Košiciach, Slovakia
Michail Panteleyev	Saint Petersburg Electrotecnical University, Russia
Martin Vala	Univerzita Pavla Jozefa Šafárika v Košiciach, Slovakia
Nodir Zaynalov	Tashkent University of Information Technologies named after Muhammad al Khwarizmi, Uzbekistan
Michail Panteleyev	Saint Petersburg Electrotecnical University, Russia
Alexander Degtyarev	Saint Petersburg University, Russia
Alexander Bogdanov	St. Petersburg State University, Russia

Bio and Neuro Inspired Computing and Applications (BIONCA 2025)

Workshop Organizers

Nadia Nedjah	State University of Rio de Janeiro, Brazil
Luiza de Macedo Mourelle	State University of Rio de Janeiro, Brazil

Workshop Program Committee Members

Nadia Nedjha	State University of Rio de Janeiro, Brazil
Luiza de Macedo Mourelle	State University of Rio de Janeiro, Brazil
Luigi Maciel Ribeiro	State University of Rio de Janeiro, Brazil
Joelmir Ramos	Federal University of Rio de Janeiro, Brazil
Rogério Moraes	Brazilian Navy, Brazil
Marcos Santana Farias	Institute of Nuclear Energy, Brazil
Luneque Silva Jr.	Federal University of ABC, Brazil
Alan Oliveira	University of Lisboa, Portugal
Brij Bhooshan Gupta	Asia University, Taiwan

Computational and Applied Mathematics (CAM 2025)

Workshop Organizers

Maria Irene Falcão	University of Minho, Portugal
Fernando Miranda	University of Minho, Portugal

Workshop Program Committee Members

Fernando Miranda	University of Minho, Portugal
Graça Tomaz	Polytechnic of Guarda, Portugal
Helmuth Malonek	University of Aveiro, Portugal

Isabel Cacao	University of Aveiro, Portugal
João Morais	Autonomous Technological Institute of Mexico, Mexico
Lidia Aceto	University of Eastern Piedmont, Italy
Luís Ferrás	University of Porto, Portugal
M. Irene Falcão	University of Minho, Portugal
Patrícia Beites	University of Beira Interior, Portugal
Paulo Amorim	FGV EMAp, Brazil
Regina de Almeida	University of Trás-os-Montes e Alto Douro, Portugal
Ricardo Severino	University of Minho, Portugal

Computational and Applied Statistics (CAS 2025)

Workshop Organizer

Ana Cristina Braga	ALGORITMI Research Centre, LASI, University of Minho, Portugal

Workshop Program Committee Members

Adelaide Freitas	University of Aveiro, Portugal
Andreas Futschik	Johannes Kepler University Linz, Austria
Ana Cristina Braga	University of Minho, Portugal
Ângela Silva	University of Minho, Portugal
Arminda Manuela Gonçalves	University of Minho, Portugal
Carina Silva	Polytechnic Intitute of Lisbon, Portugal
Elisete Correia	University of Trás-os-Montes e Alto Douro, Portugal
Frank Westad	Norwegian University of Science and Technology, Norway
Isabel Natario	New University of Lisbon, Portugal
Irene Oliveira	University of Trás-os-Montes e Alto Douro, Portugal
Ivan Rodriguez Conde	University of Vigo, Spain
Joaquim Gonçalves	Instituto Politécnico do Cávado e do Ave, Portugal
Lino Costa	University of Minho, Portugal
Marco Reis	University of Coimbra, Portugal
Maria Filipa Mourão	Polytechnic Institute of Viana do Castelo, Portugal
Maria João Polidoro	Polytechnic Institute of Porto, Portugal
Martin Perez Perez	University of Vigo, Spain
Michal Abrahamowicz	McGill University, Canada
Vera Afreixo	University of Aveiro, Portugal

Werner G. Müller	Johannes Kepler University Linz, Austria
Bruna Silva Ramos	University Lusiada de Famalicão, Portugal
Inês Sousa	University of Minho, Portugal
Luís Miguel Rocha Matos	University of Minho, Portugal
Manuel Carlos Figueiredo	University of Minho, Portugal

Cyber Intelligence and Applications (CIA 2025)

Workshop Organizer

Gianni D'Angelo	University of Salerno, Italy

Workshop Program Committee Members

Gianni D'Angelo	University of Salerno, Italy
Francesco Palmieri	University of Salerno, Italy
Massimo Ficco	University of Salerno, Italy
Arcangelo Castiglione	University of Salerno, Italy

Computational Methods for Business Analytics (CMBA 2025)

Workshop Organizers

Cláudio Alves	Universidade do Minho, Portugal
Telmo Pinto	Universidade do Minho, Portugal

Workshop Program Committee Members

Abdulrahim Shamayleh	American University of Sharjah, United Arab Emirates
Ana Rocha	University of Minho, Portugal
Angelo Sifaleras	University of Macedonia, Greece
Cristóvão Silva	University of Coimbra, Portugal
José Valério de Carvalho	University of Minho, Portugal
Miguel Vieira	Universidade Lusófona, Portugal
Rita Macedo	Université de Lille, France
Ana Moura	Universidade de Aveiro, Portugal
Cristina Lopes	ISCAP, Portugal
Eliana Costa e Silva	Instituto Politécnico do Porto, Portugal

Computational Methods, Statistics and Industrial Mathematics (CMSIM 2025)

Workshop Organizers

Maria Filomena Teodoro	IST ID, Instituto Superior Técnico, Portugal
Marina Alexandra Pedro Andrade	ISCTE – Lisbon University Institute, Portugal
Paula Simões	University of Lisbon, Portugal
Teresa A. Oliveira	IST ID, Instituto Superior Técnico, Portugal

Workshop Program Committee Members

Amilcar Oliveira	Universidade Aberta and Universidade de Lisboa, Portugal
Victor Lobo	Escola Naval and NOVA IMS Almada, Portugal
António Pacheco	IST Universidade de Lisboa, Portugal
Eliana Costa	Escola Superior de Tecnologia e Gestão IPPorto, Portugal
Aldina Correia	Escola Superior de Tecnologia e Gestão IPPorto, Portugal
Fernando Carapau	University of Évora, Portugal
Ricardo Moura	Portuguese Naval Academy, Portugal
Ana Borges	Escola Superior de Tecnologia e Gestão IPPorto, Portugal
Cristina Lopes	ISCAP IPPorto, Portugal
Fernanda Costa	University of Minho, Portugal
Cabrita Carlos	IPBeja, Portugal
Maria Luísa Morgado	University of Trás os Montes e Alto Douro and University of Lisboa, Portugal
Rosário Ramos	Universidade Aberta, Portugal
Sofia Rézio	Iscal, Instituto Politécnico de Lisboa, Portugal
Matteo Sacchet	University of Turin, Italy
Marina Marchisio Conte	University of Turin, Italy
António Seijas-Macias	University of Coruña, Spain
Luís F. A. Teodoro	University of Glasgow, UK and University of Oslo, Norway
Christos Kitsos	University of West Attica, Greece
M. Filomena Teodoro	Universidade de Lisboa, Portugal
Marina A. P. Andrade	Instituto Universitário de Lisboa, Portugal
Paula Simões	Military Academy and Universidade Nova de Lisboa, Portugal
Teresa Oliveira	Universidade Aberta and Universidade de Lisboa, Portugal

Computational Optimization and Applications (COA 2025)

Workshop Organizers

Ana Rocha	ALGORITMI Research Centre, LASI, University of Minho, Portugal, Portugal
Humberto Rocha	ALGORITMI Research Centre, LASI, University of Minho, Portugal, Portugal

Workshop Program Committee Members

Florbela Fernandes	Polytechnic Institute of Bragança, Portugal
Clara Vaz	Polytechnic Institute of Bragança, Portugal
Ana Pereira	Polytechnic Institute of Bragança, Portugal
Filipe Alvelos	University of Minho, Portugal
Joana Dias	University of Coimbra, Portugal
Eligius M. T. Hendrix	University of Málaga, Spain
Emerson José de Paiva	Federal University of Itajubá, Brazil
Ana Paula Teixeira	University of Trás-os-Montes and Alto Douro, Portugal
Lino Costa	Universidade do Minho, Portugal

Coastal Cities Versus Inland Areas. Hypotheses for Sustainable Regeneration Through Ecosystem Services of 'Hooking' and Rehabilitation of Brownfield Sites (CoastalCities_VS_InlandAreas 2025)

Workshop Organizers

Celestina Fazia	Università di Enna Kore, Italy
Angrilli Massimo	University of Chieti-Pescara, Italy
Valentina Ciuffreda	University of Chieti-Pescara, Italy
Maurizio Oddo	Università di Enna Kore, Italy
Marcello Sestito	Università di Enna Kore, Italy
Clara Stella Vicari Aversa	University of Reggio Calabria, Italy

Workshop Program Committee Members

Alessandro Camiz	Università d'Annunzio, Italy
Thowayeb Hassan	King Faisal University, Saudi Arabia
Alessandro Barracco	Università Kore di Enna, Italy
Mario Morrica	University of Urbino, Italy
Mariana Ratiu	University of Oradea, Romania
Alanda Akamana	Mohammed VI Polytechnic University, Morocco
Kaoutare Amini Alaoui	Mohammed VI Polytechnic University, Morocco

Computational Astrochemistry 2025 (CompAstro 2025)

Workshop Organizers

Marzio Rosi	University of Perugia, Italy
Daniela Ascenzi	University of Trento, Italy
Nadia Balucani	University of Perugia, Italy
Stefano Falcinelli	University of Perugia, Italy

Workshop Program Committee Members

Dario Campisi	Università degli Studi di Perugia, Italy
Giacomo Giorgi	Università degli Studi di Perugia, Italy
Andrea Giustini	Università degli Studi di Perugia, Italy
Luca Mancini	Università degli Studi di Perugia, Italy
Albert Rimola	Universitat Autònoma de Barcelona, Spain
Gianmarco Vanuzzo	Università degli Studi di Perugia, Italy
Dimitrios Skouteris	Master-Tec, Italy
Piero Ugliengo	Università degli Studi di Torino, Italy
Franco Vecchiocattivi	Università degli Sudi di Perugia, Italy
Giacomo Pannacci	Università degli Studi di Perugia, Italy
Costanza Borghesi	Università degli Studi di Perugia, Italy
Marco Parriani	Università degli Studi di Perugia, Italy
Marta Loletti	Università degli Studi di Perugia, Italy
Fernando Pirani	Università degli Studi di Perugia, Italy
Andrea Lombardi	Università degli Studi di Perugia, Italy
Noelia Faginas Lago	Università degli Studi di Perugia, Italy
Paolo Tosi	Università di Trento, Italy
Cecilia Coletti	Università degli Studi Chieti-Pescara, Italy
Nazzareno Re	Università degli Studi Chieti-Pescara, Italy
Linda Podio	Osservatorio Astrofisico di Arcetri INAF, Italy
Claudio Codella	Osservatorio Astrofisico di Arcetri INAF, Italy
Gabriella Di Genova	Università degli Studi di Perugia, Italy

Computational Methods for Porous Geomaterials (CompPor 2025)

Workshop Organizers

Vadim Lisitsa	IPGG SB RAS, Russia
Evgeniy Romenski	IPGG SB RAS, Russia

Workshop Program Committee Members

Vadim Lisitsa	Institute of Petroleum Geology and Geophysics SB RAS, Russia
Evgeniy Romenski	Sobolev Institute of Mathematics SB RAS, Russia
Vladimir Cheverda	Sobolev Institute of Mathematics SB RAS, Russia
Tatyana Khachkova	IPGG SB RAS, Russia
Dmitry Prokhorov	IPGG SB RAS, Russia
Mikhail Novikov	Sobolev Institute of Mathematics SB RAS, Russia
Sergey Solovyev	Sobolev Institute of Mathematics SB RAS, Russia
Kirill Gadylshin	LLC RNBashNIPIneft, Russia
Olga Stoyanovskaya	Lavrentev Institute of Hydrodynamics SB RAS, Russia
Yerlan Amanbek	Nazarbaev University, Kazakhstan

Workshop on Computational Science and HPC (CSHPC 2025)

Workshop Organizers

Elise de Doncker	Western Michigan University, USA
Hideo Matsufuru	High Energy Accelerator Research Organization, Japan

Workshop Program Committee Members

Elise de Doncker	Western Michigan University, USA
Hideo Matsufuru	High Energy Accelerator Research Organization (KEK), Japan
Fukuko Yuasa	KEK, Japan
Issaku Kanamori	RIKEN, Japan
Hiroshi Daisaka	Hitotsubashi University, Japan
Norikazu Yamada	KEK, Japan
Naohito Nakasato	University of Aizu, Japan
Robert Makin	Western Michigan University, USA

Cities, Technologies and Planning 2025 (CTP 2025)

Workshop Organizers

Giuseppe Borruso	University of Trieste, Italy
Beniamino Murgante	University of Basilicata, Italy
Malgorzata Hanzl	Lodz University of Technology, Poland
Anastasia Stratigea	National Technical University of Athens, Greece
Ljiljana Zivkovic	Republic Geodetic Authority, Serbia
Ginevra Balletto	University of Trieste, Italy

Workshop Program Committee Members

Giuseppe Borruso	University of Trieste, Italy
Beniamino Murgante	University of Basilicata, Italy
Malgorzata Hanzl	Lodz University of Technology, Poland
Anastasia Stratigea	National Technical University of Athens, Greece
Ljiljana Zivkovic	Republic Geodetic Authority of Serbia, Serbia
Ginevra Balletto	University of Cagliari, Italy
Silvia Battino	University of Sassari, Italy
Mara Ladu	University of Cagliari, Italy
Maria del Mar Munoz Leonisio	University of Cádiz, Spain
Ahinoa Amaro Garcia	University of Las Palmas of Gran Canaria, Spain
Maria Attard	University of Malta, Malta
Enrico D'agostini	World Maritime University, Sweden
Francesca Krasna	University of Trieste, Italy
Brisol Garcia Garcia	Polytechnic University of Quintana Roo, Mexico
Tu Anh Trinh	UEH University, Vietnam
Giovanni Mauro	Università degli Studi della Campania, Italy
Maria Ronza	University of Naples Federico II, Italy
Massimiliano Bencardino	University of Salerno, Italy
Tomasz Bradecki	Silesian University of Technology, Poland
Dorota Kamrowska-Załuska	Gdańsk University of Technology, Poland
Iwona Jażdżewska	University of Lodz, Poland
Yiota Theodora	National Technical University of Athens, Greece
Apostolos Lagarias	University of Thessaly, Greece
George Tsilimigkas	University of the Aegean, Greece
Akrivi Leka	National Technical University of Athens, Greece
Maria Panagiotopoulou	National Technical University of Athens, Greece
Andrea Gallo	Ca' Foscari University of Venice, Italy
Francesca Sinatra	University of Trieste, Italy

Digital Transition: Effects on Housing Mobility, Market, Land Governance (DIGITRANS 2025)

Workshop Organizers

Fabrizio Battisti	University of Florence, Italy
Fabiana Forte	University of Campania, Italy
Orazio Campo	Sapienza University of Rome, Italy
Alessio Pino	Kore University of Enna, Italy
Carlo Pisano	University of Florence, Italy
Mariolina Grasso	Kore University of Enna, Italy

Workshop Program Committee Members

Fabrizio Battisti	University of Florence, Italy
Fabiana Forte	Università della Campania Luigi Vanvitelli, Italy
Orazio Campo	University of Rome "La Sapienza", Italy
Alessio Pino	Kore University of Enna, Italy
Carlo Pisano	University of Florence, Italy
Mariolina Grasso	Università Kore di Enna, Italy

Evaluating Inner Areas Potentials (EIAP 2025)

Workshop Organizers

Diana Rolando	Politecnico di Torino, Italy
Alice Barreca	Politecnico di Torino, Italy
Manuela Rebaudengo	Politecnico di Torino, Italy
Giorgia Malavasi	Politecnico di Torino, Italy

Workshop Program Committee Members

John Accordino	Virginia Commonwealth University, USA
Francesco Bruzzone	Università Iuav di Venezia, Italy
Maria Cerreta	Università degli Studi di Napoli Federico II, Italy
Maddalena Chimisso	Università degli Studi del Molise, Italy
Chiara Chioni	Università degli Studi di Trento, Italy
Annalisa Contato	Università degli Studi di Palermo, Italy
Cristina Coscia	Politecnico di Torino, Italy
Marta Dell'Ovo	Politecnico di Milano, Italy
Benedetta Di Leo	Università Politecnica delle Marche, Italy
Sara Favargiotti	Università degli Studi di Trento, Italy
Maddalena Ferretti	Università Politecnica delle Marche, Italy
Salvo Giuffrida	Università degli Studi di Palermo, Italy
Barbara Lino	Università degli Studi di Palermo, Italy
Umberto Mecca	Politecnico di Torino, Italy
Beatrice Mecca	Politecnico di Torino, Italy
Giuliano Poli	Università degli Studi di Napoli Federico II, Italy
Marco Rossitti	Politecnico di Milano, Italy
Alexandra Stankulova	Politecnico di Torino, Italy
Elena Todella	Politecnico di Torino, Italy
Asja Aulisio	Politecnico di Torino, Italy
Giulia Datola	Politecnico di Milano, Italy

Francesco Calabrò	Università degli Studi Mediterranea di Reggio Calabria, Italy
Valeria Saiu	Università degli Studi di Cagliari, Italy
Maria Rosa Trovato	Università di Catania, Italy

Econometric and Multidimensional Evaluation in Urban Environment (EMEUE 2025)

Workshop Organizers

Maria Cerreta	University of Naples Federico II, Italy
Carmelo Maria Torre	Polytechnic University of Bari, Italy
Pierluigi Morano	Polytechnic University of Bari, Italy
Simona Panaro	University of Naples Federico II, Italy
Felicia Di Liddo	University of Naples Federico II, Italy
Debora Anelli	University of Naples Federico II, Italy

Workshop Program Committee Members

Carmelo Maria Torre	Polytechnic University of Bari, Italy
Maria Cerreta	University of Naples Federico II, Italy
Pierluigi Morano	Polytechnic University of Bari, Italy
Francesco Tajani	Sapienza University of Rome, Italy
Simona Panaro	University of Naples Federico II, Italy
Felicia di Liddo	Polytechnic University of Bari, Italy
Debora Anelli	Sapienza University of Rome, Italy
Giuliano Poli	University of Naples Federico II, Italy
Maria Somma	University of Naples Federico II, Italy
Simona Panaro	University of Campania Luigi Vanvitelli, Italy
Laura Di Tommaso	University of Naples Federico II, Italy
Caterina Loffredo	University of Naples Federico II, Italy
Ludovica La Rocca	University of Naples Federico II, Italy
Sabrina Sacco	Politecnico di Milano, Italy
Piero Zizzania	University of Naples Federico II, Italy
Gaia Daldanise	CNR IRISS, Italy
Benedetta Grieco	University of Naples Federico II, Italy
Giuseppe Ciciriello	University of Naples Federico II, Italy
Marta Dell'Ovo	Politecnico di Milano, Italy
Daniele Cannatella	TU Delft University, The Netherlands
Eugenio Muccio	University of Naples Federico II, Italy
Sveva Ventre	University of Naples Federico II, Italy

Governance of Energy Transition: Environmental, Landscape, Social and Spatial Planning (ENERGY_PLANNING 2025)

Workshop Organizers
Mara Ladu	University of Cagliari, Italy
Ginevra Balletto	University of Cagliari, Italy
Emilio Ghiani	University of Cagliari, Italy
Alessandra Marra	University of Salerno, Italy
Roberto De Lotto	University of Pavia, Italy
Balázs Kulcsár	Chalmers University of Technology, Sweden

Workshop Program Committee Members
Riccardo Trevisan	University of Cagliari, Italy
Marco Naseddu	University of Cagliari, Italy
Giuseppe Borruso	University of Trieste, Italy
Andrea Gallo	University of Trieste, Italy
Francesca Sinatra	University of Trieste, Italy
Maria Attard	University of Malta, Malta
Tu Anh Trinh	UEH University Ho Chi Minh City, Vietnam
Marcello Tadini	University of Eastern Piedmont, Italy
Luigi Mundula	University for Foreigners of Perugia, Italy
Silvia Battino	University of Sassari, Italy
Maria del Mar Munoz Leonisio	University of Cádiz, Spain
Anna Richiedei	University of Brescia, Italy
Michele Pezzagno	University of Brescia, Italy
Federico Mertellozzo	University of Firenze, Italy
Marco Mazzarino	IUAV University Venice, Italy

Ecosystem Services in Spatial Planning for Climate Neutral Urban and Rural Areas (ESSP 2025)

Workshop Organizers
Sabrina Lai	University of Cagliari, Italy
Francesco Scorza	University of Basilicata, Italy
Corrado Zoppi	University of Cagliari, Italy
Beniamino Murgante	University of Basilicata, Italy
Carmela Gargiulo	University of Naples Federico II, Italy
Floriana Zucaro	University of Naples Federico II, Italy

Workshop Program Committee Members

Alfonso Annunziata	University of Basilicata, Italy
Ginevra Balletto	University of Cagliari, Italy
Ivan Blečić	University of Cagliari, Italy
Giuseppe Borruso	University of Trieste, Italy
Barbara Caselli	University of Parma, Italy
Maria Cerreta	University of Naples Federico II, Italy
Chiara Garau	University of Cagliari, Italy
Carmen Guida	University of Naples Federico II, Italy
Federica Isola	University of Cagliari, Italy
Francesca Leccis	University of Cagliari, Italy
Federica Leone	University of Cagliari, Italy
Silvia Rossetti	University of Parma, Italy
Luigi Santopietro	University of Basilicata, Italy
Carmelo Torre	Polytechnic of Bari, Italy

The 15th International Workshop on Future Information System Technologies and Applications (FiSTA 2025)

Workshop Organizers

Bernady O. Apduhan	Kyushu Sangyo University, Japan
Rafael Santos	Brazilian National Institute for Space Research, Brazil

Workshop Program Committee Members

Agustinus Borgy Waluyo	Monash University, Australia
Andre Ricardo Abed Grégio	Federal University of Paraná, Brazil
Eric Pardede	La Trobe University, Australia
Kai Cheng	Kyushu Sangyo University, Japan
Ching-Hsien Hsu	Asia University, Taiwan
Fenghui Yao	Tennessee State University, USA
Yusuke Gotoh	Okayama University, Japan
Alvaro Fazenda	Federal University of São Paulo, Brazil
Kazuaki Tanaka	Kyushu Institute of Technology, Japan
Tengku Adil	MARA Technological University, Malaysia
Toshihiro Yamauchi	Okayama University, Japan
Yasuaki Sumida	Kyushu Sangyo University, Japan
Earl Ryan Aleluya	MSU-Iligan Institute of Technology, Philippines
Cherry Mae G. Villame	MSU-Iligan Institute of Technology, Philippines
Anton Louise De Ocampo	Batangas State University, Philippines
Krishnamoorthy Ranganthan	Chennai Institute of Technology, India

Flow Management in Urban Contexts (FMUC 2025)

Workshop Organizers
Alessio Pino	Kore University of Enna, Italy
Giovanna Acampa	Kore University of Enna, Italy

Workshop Program Committee Members
Giovanna Acampa	University of Florence, Italy
Alessio Pino	Kore University of Enna, Italy
Mariolina Grasso	Università Kore di Enna, Italy
Fabrizio Battisti	University of Florence, Italy
Fabrizio Finucci	Roma Tre University, Italy
Antonella G. Masanotti	Roma Tre University, Italy
Daniele Mazzoni	Roma Tre University, Italy

Geographical Analysis, Urban Modeling, Spatial Statistics 2025 (Geog-And-Mod 2025)

Workshop Organizers
Beniamino Murgante	University of Basilicata, Italy
Giuseppe Borruso	University of Trieste, Italy
Hartmut Asche	University of Potsdam, Germany
Rodrigo Tapia McClung	CentroGeo, Mexico
Andreas Fricke	University of Potsdam, Germany

Workshop Program Committee Members
Giuseppe Borruso	University of Trieste, Italy
Beniamino Murgante	University of Basilicata, Italy
Hartmut Asche	University of Potsdam, Germany
Rodrigo Tapia-McClung	Centro de Investigación en Ciencias de Información Geoespacial (CentroGeo), Mexico
Andreas Fricke	University of Potsdam, Germany
Malgorzata Hanzl	Lodz University of Technology, Poland
Anastasia Stratigea	National Technical University of Athens, Greece
Ljiljana Zivkovic	Republic Geodetic Authority of Serbia, Serbia
Ginevra Balletto	University of Cagliari, Italy
Silvia Battino	University of Sassari, Italy
Mara Ladu	University of Cagliari, Italy
Maria del Mar Munoz Leonisio	University of Cádiz, Spain
Ahinoa Amaro Garcia	University of Las Palmas of Gran Canaria, Spain
Maria Attard	University of Malta, Malta

Enrico D'agostini	World Maritime University, Sweden
Francesca Krasna	University of Trieste, Italy
Brisol García García	Polytechnic University of Quintana Roo, Mexico
Tu Anh Trinh	UEH University, Vietnam
Giovanni Mauro	Università degli Studi della Campania, Italy
Maria Ronza	University of Naples Federico II, Italy
Massimiliano Bencardino	University of Salerno, Italy
Andrea Gallo	Ca' Foscari University of Venice, Italy
Francesca Sinatra	University of Trieste, Italy
Salvatore Dore	University of Trieste, Italy

Geogames for Sustainable Development (Geogames 2025)

Workshop Organizer

Alenka Poplin	Iowa State University, USA

Workshop Program Committee Members

Alenka Poplin	Iowa State University, USA
Bruno Amaral de Andrade	Portucalense University, Portugal
Brian Tomaszewski	Rochester Institute of Technology, USA
Deepak Marhatta	Tribhuvan University, Nepal
Alessandro Plaisant	University of Sassari, Italy
David Schwartz	Rochester Institute of Technology, USA
Silvia Rossetti	University of Parma, Italy
Floriana Zucaro	University of Naples Federico II, Italy
Alfonso Annunziata	University of Basilicata, Italy
Reza Askarizad	University of Cagliari, Italy
Chiara Garau	University of Cagliari, Italy
Tanja Congiu	University of Sassari, Italy

Geomatics for Resource Monitoring and Management (GRMM 2025)

Workshop Organizers

Alberico Sonnessa	Politecnico di Bari, Italy
Eufemia Tarantino	Politecnico di Bari, Italy
Alessandra Capolupo	Politecnico di Bari, Italy

Workshop Program Committee Members

Umberto Fratino	Politecnico di Bari, Italy
Valeria Monno	Politecnico di Bari, Italy

Antonino Maltese	Università degli studi di Palermo, Italy
Athos Agapiou	Cyprus University of Technology, Cyprus
Michele Mangiameli	Università di Catania, Italy
Angela Gorgoglione	Universidad de la República de Uruguay, Uruguay
Roberta Ravanelli	University of Liège, Belgium
Ester Scotto di Perta	Università degli studi di Napoli Federico II, Italy
Giacomo Caporusso	CNR, Italy
Andrea Montanino	International Centre for Numerical Methods in Engineering of Barcelona, Spain
Antonino Iannuzzo	Università degli studi del Sannio, Italy
Alessandro Pagano	Politecnico di Bari, Italy
Francesco Di Capua	Università degli Studi della Basilicata, Italy
Albertini Cinzia	CNR-IREA, Italy
Alessandra Saponieri	Università degli studi del Salento, Italy
PierFrancesco Recchi	Università degli studi di Napoli Federico II, Italy
Vincenzo Totaro	Politecnico di Bari, Italy
Stefania Santoro	CNR Water Research Institute, Italy
Francesco Bimbo	University of Foggia, Italy
Cristina Proietti	Istituto Nazionale di Geofisica e Vulcanologia, Italy
Carla Cavallo	University of Salerno, Italy
Gaetano Falcone	Università degli Studi di Napoli Federico II, Italy
Valeria Belloni	Sapienza University of Rome, Italy
Alessandra Mascitelli	University of Chieti-Pescara, Italy

HERitage and CLIMAte neutrality. Resilient approach for nature centered/based sustainable cities (HERCLIMA 2025)

Workshop Organizers

Celestina Fazia	Università di Enna Kore, Italy
Angrilli Massimo	University of Chieti-Pescara, Italy
Clara Stella Vicari Aversa	University of Reggio Calabria, Italy
Dorina Camelia Ilies	University of Oradea, Romania
Mariana Ratiu	University of Oradea, Romania

Workshop Program Committee Members

Alessandro Camiz	Università d'Annunzio, Italy
Mario Morrica	University of Urbino, Italy
Thowayeb Hassan	King Faisal University, Saudi Arabia
Alessandro Barracco	Università Kore di Enna, Italy
Kaoutare Amini Alaoui	Mohammed VI Polytechnic University (UM6P), Morocco

Mariana Ratiu	University of Oradea, Romania
Valentina Ciuffreda	Università Chieti-Pescara, Italy

International Workshop on Information and Knowledge in the Internet of Things (IKIT 2025)

Workshop Organizers

Teresa Guarda	Universidad Estatal Península de Santa Elena, Ecuador
Luis Enrique Chuquimarca Jimenez	Universidad Estatal Península de Santa Elena, Ecuador
Gustavo Gatica	Universidad Andrés Bello, Chile
Filipe Mota Pinto	Polytechnic Institute of Leiria, Portugal
Arnulfo Alanis	Instituto Tecnológico de Tijuana, Mexico
Luis Mazon	Universidad Estatal Península de Santa Elena, Spain

Workshop Program Committee Members

Arnulfo Alanis	Instituto Tecnológico de Tijuana, Mexico
Bruno Sousa	University of Coimbra, Portugal
Carlos Balsa	Instituto Politécnico de Bragança, Portugal
Filipe Mota Pinto	Instituto Politécnico de Leiria, Portugal
Gustavo Gatica	Universidad Andrés Bello, Chile
Isabel Lopes	Instituto Politécnico de Bragança, Portugal
José-María Díaz-Nafría	Universidad a Distancia, Spain
Maria Fernanda Augusto	BiTrum Research Group, Spain
Maria Isabel Ribeiro	Instituto Politécnico Bragança, Portugal
Modestos Stavrakis	University of the Aegean, Greece
Simone Belli	Universidad Complutense de Madrid, Spain
Walter Lopes Neto	Instituto Federal de Educação, Brazil

International Workshop on territorial Planning to integrate Risk prevention and urban Ontologies (IWPRO 2025)

Workshop Organizers

Beniamino Murgante	University of Basilicata, Italy
Roberto De Lotto	University of Pavia, Italy
Elisabetta Maria Venco	University of Pavia, Italy
Caterina Pietra	University of Pavia, Italy

Workshop Program Committee Members

Stefano Borgo	Consiglio Nazionale delle Ricerche ISTC, Italy
Valentina Costa	Università di Genova, Italy
Hamid Danesh Pajouh	Middle East Technical University, Turkey
Ilaria Delponte	Università di Genova, Italy
Lorena Fiorini	Università de L'Aquila, Italy
Veronica Gazzola	Politecnico di Milano, Italy
Ghazaleh Goodarzi	Islamic Azad University, Iran
Michele Grimaldi	Università degli Studi di Salerno, Italy
Alessandra Marra	Università degli Studi di Salerno, Italy
Naghmeh Mohammadpourlima	Åbo Akademi University, Finland
Francesca Pirlone	Università di Genova, Italy
Silvia Rossetti	Università di Parma, Italy
Bahareh Shahsavari	University of Minnesota, USA
Ilenia Spadaro	Università di Genova, Italy
Maria Rosaria Stufano Melone	Politecnico di Bari, Italy

Regional Connectivity, Spatial Accessibility and MaaS for Social Inclusion (MaaS 2025)

Workshop Organizers

Mara Ladu	University of Cagliari, Italy
Ginevra Balletto	University of Cagliari, Italy
Gianfranco Fancello	University of Cagliari, Italy
Tanja Congiu	University of Sassari, Italy
Patrizia Serra	University of Cagliari, Italy
Francesco Piras	University of Cagliari, Italy

Workshop Program Committee Members

Marco Naseddu	University of Cagliari, Italy
Italo Meloni	University of Cagliari, Italy
Giuseppe Borruso	University of Trieste, Italy
Andrea Gallo	University of Trieste, Italy
Francesca Sinatra	University of Trieste, Italy
Maria Attard	University of Malta, Malta
Tu Anh Trinh	UEH University, Vietnam
Marcello Tadini	University of Eastern Piedmont, Italy
Luigi Mundula	University for Foreigners of Perugia, Italy
Silvia Battino	University of Sassari, Italy
Brunella Brundu	University of Sassari, Italy
Veronica Camerada	University of Sassari, Italy

Maria del Mar Munoz Leonisio	University of Cádiz, Spain
Anna Richiedei	University of Brescia, Italy
Michele Pezzagno	University of Brescia, Italy
Marco Mazzarino	IUAV University Venice, Italy

The Development of Urban Mobility Management, Road Safety and Risk Assessment (MANTAIN 2025)

Workshop Organizers

Antonio Russo	Università degli Studi di Enna, Italy
Corrado Rindone	University of Reggio Calabria, Italy
Antonio Polimeni	University of Messina, Italy
Florin Rusca	Politehnica University of Bucharest, Romania
Grigorios Fountas	Aristotle University of Thessaloniki, Greece
Antonio Comi	University of Rome Tor Vergata, Italy

Workshop Program Committee Members

Massimo Di Gangi	University of Messina, Italy
Orlando Marco Belcore	University of Messina, Italy
Antonio Polimeni	University of Messina, Italy
Socrates Basbas	Aristotle University of Thessaloniki, Greece
Claudia Caballini	Polytechnic of Torino, Italy
Efstathios Bouhouras	Aristotle University of Thessaloniki, Greece
Stefano Ricci	Sapienza University of Rome, Italy
Marina Zanne	University of Lubljana, Slovenia
Kh Md Nahiduzzaman	Mohammed VI Polytechnic University, Morocco
Alexsandra Deluka Tibljaš	University of Rijeka, Croatia
Guilhermina Torrao	Aston University, UK

Multidimensional Evolutionary Evaluations for Transformative Approaches (MEETA 2025)

Workshop Organizers

Maria Cerreta	University of Naples Federico II, Italy
Giuliano Poli	University of Naples Federico II, Italy
Maria Somma	University of Naples Federico II, Italy
Gaia Daldanise	CNR IRISS, Italy
Ludovica La Rocca	University of Naples Federico II, Italy

Workshop Program Committee Members

Maria Cerreta	University of Naples Federico II, Italy
Giuliano Poli	University of Naples Federico II, Italy
Maria Somma	University of Naples Federico II, Italy
Laura Di Tommaso	University of Naples Federico II, Italy
Sabrina Sacco	Politecnico di Milano, Italy
Piero Zizzania	University of Naples Federico II, Italy
Gaia Daldanise	CNR IRISS, Italy
Benedetta Grieco	University of Naples Federico II, Italy
Giuseppe Ciciriello	University of Naples Federico II, Italy
Marta Dell'Ovo	Politecnico di Milano, Italy
Daniele Cannatella	TU Delft, The Netherlands
Eugenio Muccio	University of Naples Federico II, Italy
Francesco Piras	University of Cagliari, Italy
Diana Rolando	Politecnico di Torino, Italy
Sveva Ventre	University of Naples Federico II, Italy
Caterina Loffredo	University of Naples Federico II, Italy
Ludovica La Rocca	University of Naples Federico II, Italy
Simona Panaro	University of Campania Luigi Vanvitelli, Italy

Building Multi-dimensional Models for Assessing Complex Environmental Systems (MES 2025)

Workshop Organizers

Vanessa Assumma	University of Bologna, Italy
Caterina Caprioli	Politecnico di Torino, Italy
Giulia Datola	Politecnico di Milano, Italy
Federico Dell'Anna	University of Bologna, Italy
Marta Dell'Ovo	Politecnico di Milano, Italy
Marco Rossitti	Politecnico di Milano, Italy

Workshop Program Committee Members

Vanessa Assumma	Università di Bologna, Bologna
Caterina Caprioli	Politecnico di Torino, Italy
Giulia Datola	DAStU Politecnico di Milano, Italy
Federico Dell'Anna	Politecnico di Torino, Italy
Marta Dell'Ovo	Politecnico di Milano, Italy
Marco Rossitti	Politecnico di Milano, Italy
Francesca Torrieri	Politecnico di Milano, Italy
Mariarosaria Angrisano	Università Telematica Pegaso, Italy
Maksims Feofilovs	Riga Technical University, Latvia

Danny Caprini	Politecnico di Milano, Italy
Giulio Cavana	Politecnico di Torino, Italy
Sebastiano Barbieri	Politecnico di Torino, Italy
Marta Bottero	Politecnico di Torino, Italy
Francesco Cosentino	Politecnico di Milano, Italy
Silvia Ronchi	Politecnico di Milano, Italy
Chiara Mazzarella	TU Delft, Netherlands
Marco Volpatti	Politecnico di Torino, Italy
Chiara D'Alpaos	Università degli Studi di Padova, Italy
Alessandra Oppio	Politecnico di Milano, Italy
Alessia Crisopulli	Politecnico di Milano, Italy
Domenico D'Uva	Politecnico di Milano, Italy
Giorgia Malavasi	Politecnico di Torino, Italy
Rubina Canesi	Università degli Studi di Padova, Italy
Elena Todella	Politecnico di Torino, Italy
Beatrice Mecca	Politecnico di Torino, Italy
Giulia Marzani	University of Bologna, Italy
Isabella Giovanetti	University of Bologna, Italy
Lucia Petronio	University of Bologna, Italy
Franco Corti	University of Padova, Italy
Salvatore De Pascalis	Politecnico di Milano, Italy
Valeria Vitulano	Politecnico di Torino, Italy
Lorenzo Diana	Università degli studi di Napoli Federico II, Italy
Maksims Feofilovs	Riga Technical University, Latvia
Marco De Luca	Politecnico di Torino, Italy
Ilaria Cazzola	Politecnico di Torino, Italy
Andrea De Toni	Politecnico di Milano, Italy
Eugenio Muccio	University of Naples Federico II, Italy
Giuliano Poli	University of Naples Federico II, Italy
Francesco Sica	University "La Sapienza" of Rome, Italy
Elena Di Pirro	Università degli Studi del Molise, Italy
Riccardo Alba	Università di Torino, Italy
Irene Regaiolo	Università di Torino, Italy
Francesca Cochis	Università di Torino, Italy

Modelling Liveable Cities: Techniques, Methods, Challenges, and Perspectives Behind the 'X-Minute' City (MLC 2025)

Workshop Organizers

Federico Mara	University of Pisa, Italy
Valerio Cutini	University of Pisa, Italy
Alessandro Araldi	Université Côte d'Azur, France

Flávia Lopes — Chalmers University of Technology, Sweden
Giovanni Fusco — Université Côte d'Azur, France

Workshop Program Committee Members

Simone Rusci — University of Pisa, Italy
Lorena Fiorini — University of L'Aquila, Italy
Chiara Di Dato — University of L'Aquila, Italy
Francesco Zullo — University of L'Aquila, Italy
Alfonso Annunziata — University of Basilicata, Italy
Beniamino Murgante — University of Basilicata, Italy
Alessandro Araldi — Universitè Côte d'Azur, France
Chiara Garau — University of Cagliari, Italy
Giampiero Lombardini — Università di Genova, Italy
Flavia Lopes — Chalmers University of Technology, Sweden
Giovanni Fusco — Universitè Côte d'Azur, France

Mathematical Methods for Image Processing and Understanding 2025 (MMIPU 2025)

Workshop Organizers

Ivan Gerace — Università degli Studi di Perugia, Italy
Gianluca Vinti — Università degli Studi di Perugia, Italy
Arianna Travaglini — Università degli Studi della Basilicata, Italy

Workshop Program Committee Members

Ivan Gerace — University of Perugia, Italy
Gianluca Vinti — University of Perugia, Italy
Arianna Travaglini — University of Basilicata, Italy
Marco Baioletti — University of Perugia, Italy
Marco Donatelli — University of Insubria, Italy
Anna Tonazzini — C.N.R. Pisa, Italy
Muhammad Hanif — Ghulam Ishaq Khan Institute of Engineering Sciences and Technology, Pakistan
Francesco Marchetti — University of Padua, Italy
Wolfgang Erb — University of Padua, Italy
Danilo Costarelli — University of Perugia, Italy
Francesco Santini — University of Perugia, Italy
Valentina Giorgetti — University of Perugia, Italy

Mobility Opportunities Bridging Inequalities: Social Inclusion and Gender Equity Initiatives Strategies Against Fragmentation and Complexity of Mobility (MOBIL-EGI 2025)

Workshop Organizers

Tiziana Campisi	University of Enna Kore, Italy
Guilhermina Torrao	Aston University, UK
Socrates Basbas	Aristotle University of Thessaloniki, Greece
Tanja Congiu	University of Sassari, Italy
Stefanos Tsigdinos	National Technical University of Athens, Greece
Florin Nemtanu	Politehnica University of Bucharest, Romania

Workshop Program Committee Members

Massimo Di Gangi	University of Messina, Italy
Orlando Marco Belcore	University of Messina, Italy
Francesco Russo	Mediterranean University of Reggio Calabria, Italy
Alexandros Nikitas	University of Huddersfield, UK
Marilisa Nigro	Rome Tre University, Italy
Kh Md Nahiduzzaman	Mohammed VI Polytechnic University, Morocco
Efstathios Bouhouras	Aristotle University of Thessaloniki, Greece
Antonio Comi	University of Rome Tor Vergata, Italy
Edouard Ivanjko	University of Zagreb, Slovenia
Osvaldo Gervasi	University of Perugia, Italy
Beniamino Murgante	University of Basilicata, Italy
Chiara Garau	University of Cagliari, Italy

MOdels and indicators for assessing and measuring the urban settlement deVElopment in the view of NET ZERO by 2050 (MOVEto0 2025)

Workshop Organizers

Lorena Fiorini	University of L'Aquila, Italy
Lucia Saganeiti	CNR-IMAA, Italy
Angela Pilogallo	CNR-IMAA, Italy
Alessandro Marucci	University of L'Aquila, Italy
Francesco Zullo	University of L'Aquila, Italy

Workshop Program Committee Members

Ginevra Balletto	University of Cagliari, Italy
Giuseppe Borruso	University of Trieste, Italy
Chiara Garau	University of Cagliari, Italy

Beniamino Murgante University of Basilicata, Italy
Giulia Desogus University of Cagliari, Italy
Ljiljana Zivkovic Republic Geodetic Authority, Serbia
Luigi Santopietro University of Basilicata, Italy
Ilaria Delponte University of Genoa, Italy
Carmen Guida University of Naples Federico II, Italy
Chiara Di Dato University of L'Aquila, Italy

5th Workshop on Privacy in the Cloud/Edge/IoT World (PCEIoT 2025)

Workshop Organizers

Lelio Campanile Università degli Studi della Campania Luigi Vanvitelli, Italy
Mauro Iacono Università degli Studi della Campania Luigi Vanvitelli, Italy
Michele Mastroianni Università degli Studi di Foggia, Italy

Workshop Program Committee Members

Arcangelo Castiglione Università degli Studi di Salerno, Italy
Maria Ganzha Warsaw University of Technology, Poland
Daniel Grzonka Cracow University of Technology, Poland
Antonio Iannuzzi Università degli Studi Roma Tre, Italy
Armando Tacchella Università degli Studi di Genova, Italy
Biagio Boi University of Salerno, Italy
Marco De Santis University of Salerno, Italy
Fiammetta Marulli Università degli Studi della Campania "L. Vanvitelli", Italy
Christian Riccio Università degli Studi della Campania "L. Vanvitelli", Italy
Luigi Piero Di Bonito Università degli Studi di Napoli Federico II, Italy

Preserving Our Past: Spatial and Remote Sensing Technologies for Cultural Heritage in a Changing Climate (POP 2025)

Workshop Organizers

Maria Danese CNR-ISPC, Italy
Nicola Masini CNR-ISPC, Italy
Rosa Lasaponara CNR-IMAA, Italy

Workshop Program Committee Members

Maria Danese	CNR-ISPC, Italy
Nicola Masini	CNR-ISPC, Italy
Rosa Lasaponara	CNR-IMAA, Italy
Dario Gioia	CNR-ISPC, Italy
Giuseppe Corrado	Università degli Studi della Basilicata, Italy
Canio Sabia	CNR-ISPC, Italy

Processes, methods and tools towards RESilient cities and cultural and historic sites prone to SOD and ROD disasters (RES 2025)

Workshop Organizers

Elena Cantatore	Polytechnic University of Bari, Italy
Dario Esposito	Polytechnic University of Bari, Italy
Alberico Sonnessa	Polytechnic University of Bari, Italy

Workshop Program Committee Members

Elena Cantatore	Politecnico di Bari, Italy
Dario Esposito	Politecnico di Bari, Italy
Alberico Sonnessa	Politecnico di Bari, Italy
Valeria Belloni	Sapienza University of Rome, Italy
Michela Ravanelli	Sapienza University of Rome, Italy
Silvano Dal Sasso	University of Basilicata, Italy
Francesco Chiaravalloti	CNR - IRPI, Italy
Roberta Ravanelli	University of Liège, Belgium
Alessandra Mascitelli	University of Chieti-Pescara, Italy
Francesco Di Capua	University of Basilicata, Italy
Gabriele Bernardini	Università Politecnica delle Marche, Italy
Vito Domenico Porcari	University of Basilicata, Italy
Carmen Rosa Fattore	University of Basilicata, Italy
Stefania Santoro	Water Research Institute, Italy

Scientific Computing Infrastructure (SCI 2025)

Workshop Organizers

Vladimir Korkhov	Saint Petersburg State University, Russia
Elena Stankova	Saint Petersburg State University, Russia
Nataliia Kulabukhova	Saint Petersburg State University, Russia

Workshop Program Committee Members

Adam Belloum	University of Amsterdam, the Netherlands
Dmitrii Vasiunin	Deutsche Telekom Cloud Services E.P.E., Greece
Serob Balyan	Osensus Arm LLC, Armenia
Suren Abrahamyan	Osensus Arm LLC, Armenia
Ashot Sergey Gevorkyan	NAS of Armenia, Armenia
Michal Hnatic	Univerzita Pavla Jozefa Šafárika v Košiciach, Slovakia
Michail Panteleyev	Saint Petersburg Electrotecnical University, Russia
Martin Vala	Univerzita Pavla Jozefa Šafárika v Košiciach, Slovakia
Nodir Zaynalov	Tashkent University of Information Technologies named after Muhammad al Khwarizmi, Uzbekistan
Michail Panteleyev	Saint Petersburg Electrotecnical University, Russia
Alexander Degtyarev	Saint Petersburg University, Russia
Alexander Bogdanov	St. Petersburg State University, Russia

Ports and Logistics of the Future - Smartness and Sustainability (SmartPorts 2025)

Workshop Organizers

Andrea Gallo	Università degli Studi di Trieste, Italy
Gianfranco Fancello	University of Cagliari, Italy
Giuseppe Borruso	Università degli Studi di Trieste, Italy
Enrico D'agostini	World Maritime University, Sweden
Silvia Battino	Università degli Studi di Sassari, Italy
Veronica Camerada	Università degli Studi di Sassari, Italy

Workshop Program Committee Members

Giuseppe Borruso	University of Trieste, Italy
Beniamino Murgante	University of Basilicata, Italy
Ginevra Balletto	University of Cagliari, Italy
Silvia Battino	University of Sassari, Italy
Mara Ladu	University of Cagliari, Italy
Maria del Mar Munoz Leonisio	University of Cádiz, Spain
Ahinoa Amaro Garcia	University of Las Palmas of Gran Canaria, Spain
Maria Attard	University of Malta, Malta
Enrico D'agostini	World Maritime University, Sweden
Francesca Krasna	University of Trieste, Italy

Tu Anh Trinh	UEH University - Ho Chi Minh City, Vietnam
Giovanni Mauro	Università degli Studi della Campania, Italy
Maria Ronza	University of Naples Federico II, Italy
Massimiliano Bencardino	University of Salerno, Italy
Andrea Gallo	Ca' Foscari University of Venice, Italy
Francesca Sinatra	University of Trieste, Italy
Salvatore Dore	University of Trieste, Italy
Veronica Camerada	University of Sassari, Italy
Brunella Brundu	University of Sassari, Italy
Gianfranco Fancello	University of Cagliari, Italy
Marcello Tadini	University of Eastern Piedmont, Italy
Marco Mazzarino	IUAV University Venice
José Ángel Hernández Luis	University of Las Palmas de Gran Canaria, Spain
Marco Naseddu	University of Cagliari, Italy
Maurizio Cociancich	Adriafer, Italy
Giovanni Longo	University of Trieste, Italy
Luca Toneatti	University of Trieste, Italy
Martina Sinatra	University of Cagliari, Italy
Enrico Vanino	University of Sheffield, UK
Patrizia Serra	University of Cagliari, Italy
Agostino Bruzzone	University of Genoa, Italy
Marco Petrelli	University of Roma 3, Italy

Smart Transport and Logistics - Smart Supply Chains (SmarTransLog 2025)

Workshop Organizers

Francesca Sinatra	University of Trieste, Italy
Maria del Mar Munoz	Universidad de Cádiz, Spain
Brunella Brundu	University of Sassari, Italy
Patrizia Serra	University of Cagliari, Italy
Salvatore Dore	University of Trieste, Italy
Marco Naseddu	University of Cagliari, Italy

Workshop Program Committee Members

Giuseppe Borruso	University of Trieste, Italy
Beniamino Murgante	University of Basilicata, Italy
Ginevra Balletto	University of Cagliari, Italy
Silvia Battino	University of Sassari, Italy
Mara Ladu	University of Cagliari, Italy
Maria del Mar Munoz Leonisio	University of Cádiz, Spain
Ahinoa Amaro Garcia	University of Las Palmas of Gran Canaria, Spain

Maria Attard	University of Malta, Malta
Enrico D'agostini	World Maritime University, Sweden
Francesca Krasna	University of Trieste, Italy
Tu Anh Trinh	UEH University, Vietnam
Giovanni Mauro	Università degli Studi della Campania, Italy
Maria Ronza	University of Naples Federico II, Italy
Massimiliano Bencardino	University of Salerno, Italy
Andrea Gallo	Ca' Foscari University of Venice, Italy
Francesca Sinatra	University of Trieste, Italy
Salvatore Dore	University of Trieste, Italy
Veronica Camerada	University of Sassari, Italy
Brunella Brundu	University of Sassari, Italy
Gianfranco Fancello	University of Cagliari, Italy
Marcello Tadini	University of Eastern Piedmont, Italy
Marco Mazzarino	IUAV University Venice
José Ángel Hernández Luis	University of Las Palmas de Gran Canaria, Spain
Marco Naseddu	University of Cagliari, Italy
Maurizio Cociancich	Adriafer, Italy
Giovanni Longo	University of Trieste, Italy
Luca Toneatti	University of Trieste, Italy
Martina Sinatra	University of Cagliari, Italy
Enrico Vanino	University of Sheffield, UK
Patrizia Serra	University of Cagliari, Italy
Agostino Bruzzone	University of Genoa, Italy
Marco Petrelli	University of Roma 3, Italy

Smart Tourism (SmartTourism 2025)

Workshop Organizers

Silvia Battino	University of Sassari, Italy
Francesca Krasna	University of Trieste, Italy
Ainhoa Amaro	University of Las Palmas de Gran Canaria, Spain
Maria del Mar Munoz	University of Cádiz, Spain
Brisol García García	Polytechnic University of Quintana Roo, Mexico
Marta Meleddu	University of Sassari, Italy

Workshop Program Committee Members

Giuseppe Borruso	University of Trieste, Italy
Beniamino Murgante	University of Basilicata, Italy
Gianfranco Fancello	University of Cagliari, Italy
Mara Ladu	University of Cagliari, Italy

Martina Sinatra	University of Cagliari, Italy
Salvatore Dore	University of Trieste, Italy
Marco Mazzarino	IUAV University Venice, Italy
Veronica Camerada	University of Sassari, Italy
Brunella Brundu	University of Sassari, Italy
Maria Attard	University of Malta, Malta
Ginevra Balletto	University of Cagliari, Italy
Giovanni Mauro	University degli Studi della Campania, Italy
Salvatore Lampreu	University of Sassari, Italy
Maria Ronza	University of Naples, Italy
Massimiliano Bencardino	University of Salerno, Italy

Sustainable evolution of long-Distance frEight and paSsenger Transport (SOLIDEST 2025)

Workshop Organizers

Francesco Russo	University of Reggio Calabria, Italy
Andreas Nikiforiadis	Democritus University of Thrace, Greece
Orlando Marco Belcore	University of Messina, Italy
Antonio Comi	University of Rome Tor Vergata, Italy
Tiziana Campisi	Kore University of Enna, Italy
Aura Rusca	Politehnica University of Bucharest, Romania

Workshop Program Committee Members

Massimo Di Gangi	University of Messina, Italy
Orlando Marco Belcore	University of Messina, Italy
Antonio Polimeni	University of Messina, Italy
Socrates Basbas	Aristotle University of Thessaloniki, Greece
Efstathios Bouhouras	Aristotle University of Thessaloniki, Greece
Marina Zanne	University of Ljubljana, Slovenia
Marilisa Nigro	Rome Tre University, Italy
Edoardo Marcucci	Molde University College, Norway
Eugen Rosca	Polytechnic University of Bucharest, Romania
Kh Md Nahiduzzaman	Mohammed VI Polytechnic University, Morocco
Beniamino Murgante	University of Basilicata, Italy
Chiara Garau	University of Cagliari, Italy

Sustainability Performance Assessment: Models, Approaches, and Applications Toward Interdisciplinary and Integrated Solutions (SPA 2025)

Workshop Organizers

Francesco Scorza	University of Basilicata, Italy
Sabrina Lai	University of Cagliari, Italy
Francesco Rotondo	Università Politecnica delle Marche, Italy
Jolanta Dvarioniene	Kaunas University of Technology, Lithuania
Michele Campagna	University of Cagliari, Italy
Corrado Zoppi	University of Cagliari, Italy

Workshop Program Committee Members

Federico Amato	University of Lausanne, Switzerland
Ferdinando Di Carlo	University of Basilicata, Italy
Maddalena Floris	University of Cagliari, Italy
Federica Isola	University of Cagliari, Italy
Giuseppe Las Casas	University of Basilicata, Italy
Federica Leone	University of Cagliari, Italy
Giampiero Lombardini	University of Genoa, Italy
Federico Martellozzo	University of Florence, Italy
Alessandro Marucci	University of L'Aquila, Italy
Ana Clara Moura	Universidade Federal de Minas Gerais, Brazil
Beniamino Murgante	University of Basilicata, Italy
Silviu Nate	Lucian Blaga University of Sibiu, Romania
Anastasia Stratigea	National Technical University of Athens, Greece
Francesco Zullo	University of L'Aquila, Italy
Luigi Santopietro	University of Basilicata, Italy
Benedetto Manganelli	University of Basilicata, Italy

Specifics of Smart Cities Development in Europe (SPEED 2025)

Workshop Organizers

Chiara Garau	University of Cagliari, Italy
Katarína Vitálišová	Matej Bel University, Slovak Republic
Marco Fanfani	University of Florence, Italy
Anna Vaňová	Matej Bel University, Slovak Republic
Kamila Borsekova	Matej Bel University, Slovak Republic
Paola Zamperlin	University of Florence, Italy

Workshop Program Committee Members

Claudia Loggia	University of KwaZulu-Natal, South Africa
Francesca Maltinti	University of Cagliari, Italy
Alessandro Plaisant	University of Sassari, Italy
Alenka Poplin	Iowa State University, USA
Silvia Rossetti	University of Parma, Italy
Gerardo Carpentieri	University of Naples Federico II, Italy
Carmen Guida	University of Naples Federico II, Italy
Floriana Zucaro	University of Naples Federico II, Italy
Anastasia Stratigea	National Technical University of Athens, Greece
Yiota Theodora	National Technical University of Athens, Greece
Giovanna Concu	University of Cagliari, Italy
Paolo Nesi	University of Florence, Italy
Emanuele Bellini	University of Roma Tre, Italy
Mana Dastoum	Polytechnic University of Madrid, Spain
Barbara Caselli	University of Parma, Italy
Martina Carra	University of Brescia, Italy
Alfonso Annunziata	University of Basilicata, Italy
Elisabetta Venco	University of Pavia, Italy
Caterina Pietra	University of Pavia, Italy
Enrico Collini	University of Florence, Italy
Luciano Alessandro Ipsaro Palesi	University of Florence, Italy

Smart, Safe, and Healthy Cities (SSHC 2025)

Workshop Organizers

Chiara Garau	University of Cagliari, Italy
Gerardo Carpentieri	University of Naples Federico II, Italy
Carmen Guida	University of Naples Federico II, Italy
Tanja Congiu	University of Sassari, Italy
Martina Carra	University of Brescia, Italy
Alenka Poplin	Iowa State University, USA

Workshop Program Committee Members

Rosaria Battarra	Istituto di Studi sul Mediterraneo, Italy
Barbara Caselli	University of Parma, Italy
Francesca Maltinti	University of Cagliari, Italy
Romano Fistola	Università degli Studi di Napoli Federico II, Italy
Alessandro Plaisant	University of Sassari, Italy
Silvia Rossetti	University of Parma, Italy
Marco Fanfani	University of Florence, Italy
Reza Askarizad	University of Cagliari, Italy

Floriana Zucaro	University of Naples Federico II, Italy
Anastasia Stratigea	National Technical University of Athens, Greece
Yiota Theodora	National Technical University of Athens, Greece
Giovanna Concu	University of Cagliari, Italy
Francesco Zullo	University of L'Aquila, Italy
Paola Zamperlin	University of Florence, Italy
Vincenza Torrisi	University of Catania, Italy
Tiziana Campisi	University of Enna Kore, Italy
Katarína Vitálišová	Matej Bel University, Slovakia
Tazyeen Alam	University of Cagliari, Italy
Mana Dastoum	Polytechnic University of Madrid, Spain
Martina Carra	University of Brescia, Italy
Alfonso Annunziata	University of Basilicata, Italy
Elisabetta Venco	University of Pavia, Italy
Caterina Pietra	University of Pavia, Italy

Smart and Sustainable Island Communities (SSIC 2025)

Workshop Organizers

Chiara Garau	University of Cagliari, Italy
Anastasia Stratigea	National Technical University of Athens, Greece
Yiota Theodora	National Technical University of Athens, Greece
Giovanna Concu	University of Cagliari, Italy

Workshop Program Committee Members

Milena Metalkova-Markova	University of Portsmouth, UK
Tarek Teba	University of Portsmouth, UK
Alenka Poplin	Iowa State University, USA
Gerardo Carpentieri	University of Naples Federico II, Italy
Carmen Guida	University of Naples Federico II, Italy
Floriana Zucaro	University of Naples Federico II, Italy
Silvia Rossetti	University of Parma, Italy
Barbara Caselli	University of Parma, Italy
Martina Carra	University of Brescia, Italy
Alfonso Annunziata	University of Basilicata, Italy
Maria Panagiotopoulou	National Technical University of Athens, Greece
Apostolos Lagarias	University of Thessaly, Greece
Paola Zamperlin	University of Florence, Italy
Vincenza Torrisi	University of Catania, Italy
Giuseppina Vacca	University of Cagliari, Italy
Roberto Minunno	Curtin University, Australia
Marco Zucca	University of Cagliari, Italy

Elisabetta Venco	University of Pavia, Italy
Caterina Pietra	University of Pavia, Italy
Pietro Crespi	Politecnico di Milano, Italy

From STreet Experiments to Planned Solutions (STEPS 2025)

Workshop Organizers

Silvia Rossetti	Università degli Studi di Parma, Italy
Angela Ricciardello	Kore University of Enna, Italy
Francesco Pinna	Università degli Studi di Cagliari, Italy
Chiara Garau	Università degli Studi di Cagliari, Italy
Tiziana Campisi	Kore University of Enna, Italy
Vincenza Torrisi	University of Catania, Italy

Workshop Program Committee Members

Martina Carra	University of Brescia, Italy
Barbara Caselli	University of Parma, Italy
Tanja Congiu	University of Sassari, Italy
Gabriele D'Orso	University of Palermo, Italy
Matteo Ignaccolo	University of Catania, Italy
Md Kh Nahiduzzaman	Mohammed VI Polytechnic University, Morocco
Muhammad Ahmad Al-Rashid	University of Malaya, Malaysia
Alessandro Plaisant	University of Sassari, Italy
Marianna Ruggieri	University of Enna Kore, Italy
Michele Zazzi	University of Parma, Italy

Sustainable Tourism Evaluations: approaches, methods and indicators (STEva 2025)

Workshop Organizers

Mariolina Grasso	Università Kore di Enna, Italy
Fabrizio Finucci	Roma Tre University, Italy
Daniele Mazzoni	Roma Tre University, Italy
Antonella G. Masanotti	Roma Tre University, Italy
Giovanna Acampa	University of Florence, Italy

Workshop Program Committee Members

Giovanna Acampa	University of Florence, Italy
Fabrizio Finucci	Roma Tre University, Italy
Mariolina Grasso	"Kore" University of Enna, Italy

Alberto Marzo	Ministero della Cultura, Italy
Antonella G. Masanotti	Roma Tre University, Italy
Daniele Mazzoni	Roma Tre University, Italy
Rocco Murro	Sapienza University of Rome, Italy
Claudio Piferi	University of Florence, Italy
Alessio Pino	"Kore" University of Enna, Italy
Nicoletta Setola	University of Florence, Italy
Laura Calcagnini	Roma Tre University, Italy
Antonio Magarò	Roma Tre University, Italy
Janos Ghyerghyak	University of Pécs, Hungary
Ágnes Borsos	University of Pécs, Hungary
Fabrizio Battisti	University of Florence, Italy

Sustainable Development of Ports (SUSTAINABLEPORTS 2025)

Workshop Organizers

Tiziana Campisi	University of Enna KORE, Italy
Giuseppe Musolino	University of Reggio Calabria, Italy
Efstathios Bouhouras	Aristotle University of Thessaloniki, Greece
Elen Twrdy	University of Ljubljana, Slovenia
Elena Cocuzza	University of Catania, Italy
Aura Rusca	Politehnica University of Bucharest, Romania

Workshop Program Committee Members

Massimo Di Gangi	University of Messina, Italy
Orlando Marco Belcore	University of Messina, Italy
Antonio Polimeni	University of Messina, Italy
Claudia Caballini	Polytechnic of Torino, Italy
Gianfranco Fancello	University of Cagliari, Italy
Marina Zanne	University of Lubljana, Slovenia
Stefano Ricci	Sapienza University of Rome, Italy
Beniamino Murgante	University of Basilicata, Italy
Chiara Garau	University of Cagliari, Italy

Theoretical and Computational Chemistry and Its Applications (TCCMA 2025)

Workshop Organizers

Noelia Faginas Lago	Università di Perugia, Italy
Andrea Lombardi	Università di Perugia, Italy
Marcos Mandado Alonso	University of Vigo, Spain

Workshop Program Committee Members

Noelia Faginas-Lago	University of Perugia, Italy
Andrea Lombardi	University of Perugia, Italy
Marcos Mandado	University of Vigo, Spain
Angeles Peña	University of Vigo, Spain
Luca Mancini	Universiy of Perugia, Italy
Massimiliano Bartolomei	CSIC, Spain
Cecilia Coletti	University of Chieti-Pescara, Italy
Iñaki Tuñón	Universidad de Valencia, Spain
Albert Rimola Gilbert	Universitat Autònoma de Barcelona, Spain
Stefano Falcinelli	University of Perugia, Italy
Dario Campisi	University of Perugia, Italy
Ernesto García Para	University of the Basque Country, Spain
Giacomo Giorgi	University of Perugia, Italy
Tomás González Lezana	IFF CSIC, Spain
Enrique M. Cabaleiro Lago	Universidade de Santiago de Compostela, Spain
Aurora Costales	Universidad de Oviedo, Spain
Angel Martin	Universidad de Oviedo, Spain
Jose Manuel	University of Vigo, Spain
Annarita Laricchiuta	CNR ISTP Bari, Italy
Fernando Pirani	University of Perugia, Italy

Transport Infrastructures for Smart Cities (TISC 2025)

Workshop Organizers

Francesca Maltinti	University of Cagliari, Italy
Mauro Coni	University of Cagliari, Italy
Benedetto Barabino	University of Brescia, Italy
Nicoletta Rassu	University of Cagliari, Italy
James Rombi	University of Cagliari, Italy

Workshop Program Committee Members

Francesco Pinna	University of Cagliari, Italy
Chiara Garau	University of Cagliari, Italy
Mauro D'Apuzzo	University of Cassino, Italy
Roberto Minunno	Curtin University, Australia
Tiziana Campisi	University of Enna Kore, Italy
Roberto Ventura	Universiy of Brescia, Italy
Alessandro Plaisant	University of Sassari, Italy
Massimo Di Francesco	University of Cagliari, Italy

Vincenza Torrisi   University of Catania, Italy
Paola Zamperlin   University of Florence, Italy

Transforming Urban Analytics: The Impact of Crowdsourced Mapping and Advanced AI Techniques on Future Cities (Tr-UrbAna 2025)

Workshop Organizers

Ayse Giz Gulnerman Gengec	Ankara Hacı Bayram Veli University, Turkey
Müslüm Hacar	Tildiz Technical University, Turkey
Himmet Karaman	Istanbul Technical University, Turkey

Workshop Program Committee Members

Beniamino Murgante	University of Basilicata, Italy
Abdulkadir Memduhoğlu	Harran University, Turkey
Zeynel Abidin Polat	İzmir Katip Çelebi University, Turkey
Güzide Miray Perihanoğlu	Van Yüzüncü Yıl University, Turkey
Tugba Memisoglu Baykal	Ankara Hacı Bayram Veli University, Turkey

From structural to TRAnsformative-change of City Environment: challenges and solutions and perspectives (TRACE 2025)

Workshop Organizers

Pierluigi Morano	Polytechnic University of Bari, Italy
Maria Rosaria Guarini	Sapienza University of Rome, Italy
Francesco Sica	Sapienza University of Rome, Italy
Francesco Tajani	Sapienza University of Rome, Italy
Marco Locurcio	Polytechnic University of Bari, Italy
Debora Anelli	Polytechnic University of Bari, Italy

Workshop Program Committee Members

Felicia di Liddo	Politecnico di Bari, Italia
Valeria Saiu	Università di Cagliari, Italia
Emma Sabatelli	Sapienza Università di Roma, Italia
Antonella Roma	Sapienza Università di Roma, Italia
Giuseppe Cerullo	Sapienza Università di Roma, Italia
Lucia della Spina	Università di Reggio Calabria, Italia
Alejandro Segura de la Cal	Politecnico di Madrid, Spain
Yilsy Nuñez	Politecnico di Madrid, Spain
Gabriella Maselli	Università di Salerno, Italy
Maria Rosa Trovato	Università di Catania, Italy

Manuela Rebaudengo	Politecnico di Torino, Italy
Pierfrancesco De Paola	Università di Napoli Federico II, Italy
Daniela Tavano	Università della Calabria, Italy
Maria Saez	University of Granada, Spain
Paola Amoruso	LUM "Giuseppe Degennaro" University, Italy

Temporary Real Estate management: Approaches and methods for Time-integrated impact assessments and evaluations (TREAT 2025)

Workshop Organizers

Chiara Mazzarella	TUDelft, The Netherlands
Hilde Remoy	TUDelft, The Netherlands
Maria Cerreta	University of Naples Federico II, Italy

Workshop Program Committee Members

Chiara Mazzarella	TU Delft, The Netherlands
Hilde Remoy	TU Delft, The Netherlands
Maria Cerreta	University of Naples Federico II, Italy
Maria Somma	University of Naples Federico II, Italy
Simona Panaro	University of Campania Luigi Vanvitelli, Italy
Laura Di Tommaso	University of Naples Federico II, Italy
Caterina Loffredo	University of Naples Federico II, Italy
Ludovica La Rocca	University of Naples Federico II, Italy
Sabrina Sacco	Politecnico di Milano, Italy
Piero Zizzania	University of Naples Federico II, Italy
Gaia Daldanise	CNR IRISS, Italy
Benedetta Grieco	University of Naples Federico II, Italy
Giuseppe Ciciriello	University of Naples Federico II, Italy
Marta Dell'Ovo	Politecnico di Milano, Italy
Daniele Cannatella	TU Delft, The Netherlands
Eugenio Muccio	University of Naples Federico II, Italy
Sveva Ventre	University of Naples Federico II, Italy

Supporting the Transition to Ecological Economy in Cities Regeneration: Circular Model Tools for Reusing Architecture and Infrastructures (TReE 2025)

Workshop Organizers

Mariarosaria Angrisano	Pegaso University, Italy
Giulio Cavana	Politecnico di Torino, Italy
Francesca Buglione	CNR-ISPC, Italy

Antonia Gravagnuolo   CNR-ISPC, Italy
Piera Della Morte   Pegaso University, Italy

Workshop Program Committee Members
Giulia Datola   Politecnico di Milano, Italy
Vanessa Assumma   University of Bologna, Italy
Marco Volpatti   Politecnico di Torino, Italy
Sebastiano Barbieri   Politecnico di Torino, Italy
Caterina Caprioli   Politecnico di Torino, Italy
Marta Dell'Ovo   Politecnico di Milano, Italy
Federico Dell'Anna   Politecnico di Torino, Italy
Elena Todella   Politecnico di Torino, Italy
Danny Casprini   Politecnico di Milano, Italy
Grazia Neglia   Università Telematica Pegaso, Italy
Francesca Nocca   Università degli Studi di Napoli Federico II, Italy
Giulio Cavana   Politecnico di Torino, Italy
Francesca Buglione   CNR-IPSC, Italy
Marco Rossitti   Politecnico di Milano, Italy
Jhon Escorcia   Politecnico di Torino, Italy
Beatrice Mecca   Politecnico di Torino, Italy
Sara Biancifiori   Politecnico di Torino, Italy

Urban Digital Twins and Data Spaces: Shaping the Future of Sustainable Cities (TwinAbleCities 2025)

Workshop Organizers
Dessislava Petrova Antonova   Sofia University, GATE Institute, Bulgaria
Beniamino Murgante   University of Basilicata, Italy
Senthil Rajendran   RMSI, Bahrain
Tiziana Campisi   Kore University of Enna, Italy
Mila Koeva   University of Twente, The Netherlands

Workshop Program Committee Members
Dessislava Petrova-Antonova   Sofia University, Bulgaria
Mila Koeva   The University of Twente, The Netherlands
Beniamino Murgante   University of Basilicata, Italy
Senthil Rajendran   RMSI, Bahrain
Tiziana Campisi   Kore University of Enna, Italy

Urban Regeneration: Innovative Tools and Evaluation Model (URITEM 2025)

Workshop Organizers
Fabrizio Battisti	University of Florence, Italy
Giovanna Acampa	University of Florence, Italy
Orazio Campo	Sapienza University of Rome, Italy
Melania Perdonò	University of Florence, Italy

Workshop Program Committee Members
Fabrizio Battisti	University of Florence, Italy
Giovanna Acampa	University of Florence, Italy
Orazio Campo	University of Rome "La Sapienza", Italy
Melania Perdonò	Università degli Studi di Firenze, Italy

Urban Space Accessibility and Mobilities (USAM 2025)

Workshop Organizers
Chiara Garau	DICAAR, University of Cagliari, Italy
Alessandro Plaisant	University of Sassari, Italy
Barbara Caselli	University of Parma, Italy
Mauro D'Apuzzo	University of Cassino and Southern Lazio, Italy
Gabriele D'Orso	University of Palermo, Italy
Matteo Ignaccolo	University of Catania, Italy

Workshop Program Committee Members
Mauro Coni	University of Cagliari, Italy
Martina Carra	University of Brescia, Italy
Tiziana Campisi	University of Enna Kore, Italy
Tanja Congiu	University of Sassari, Italy
Francesca Maltinti	University of Cagliari, Italy
Silvia Rossetti	University of Parma, Italy
Barbara Caselli	University of Parma, Italy
Angela Pilogallo	University of L'Aquila, Italy
Lorena Fiorini	University of L'Aquila, Italy
Reza Askarizad	University of Cagliari, Italy
Francesco Pinna	University of Cagliari, Italy
Aime Tsinda	University of Rwanda, Rwanda
Youssef El Ganadi	International University of Rabat, Morocco
Marco Migliore	University of Palermo, Italy
Alessio Salvatore	Italian National Research Council, Italy
Giuseppe Stecca	Italian National Research Council, Italy

Paola Zamperlin	University of Florence, Italy
Vincenza Torrisi	University of Catania, Italy
Gerardo Carpentieri	University of Naples Federico II, Italy
Carmen Guida	University of Naples Federico II, Italy
Floriana Zucaro	University of Naples Federico II, Italy
Alfonso Annunziata	University of Basilicata, Italy
Elisabetta Venco	University of Pavia, Italy
Caterina Pietra	University of Pavia, Italy
Tazyeen Alam	University of Cagliari, Italy
Valerio Cutini	University of Pisa, Italy

UX Mobility 2025: Placing User Experience at the Center of Urban Mobility: Methods and Frameworks (UXM 2025)

Workshop Organizers

Carmen Guida	Università degli Studi di Napoli Federico II, Italy
Gerardo Carpentieri	Università degli Studi di Napoli Federico II, Italy
Federico Messa	Systematica srl, Italy
Lamia Abdelfattah	Systematica srl, Italy

Workshop Program Committee Members

Rosaria Battarra	Istituto di Studi sul Mediterraneo CNR, Italy
Romano Fistola	Università degli Studi di Napoli Federico II, Italy
Lucia Saganeiti	IMAA-CNR, Italy

Virtual Reality and Augmented reality and applications (VRA 2025)

Workshop Organizers

Damiano Perri	University of Perugia, Italy
Osvaldo Gervasi	University of Perugia, Italy
Chau Ma Thi	University of Engineering and Technology, Vietnam National University, Hanoi, Vietnam
Paolo Nesi	University of Florence, Italy
Pierfrancesco Bellini	University of Florence, Italy

Workshop Program Committee Members

David Berti	ART SpA, Italy
JungYoon Kim	Gachon University, South Korea

TaiHoon Kim	Zhejiang University of Science and Technology, China
Marcelo de Paiva Guimares	Federal University of São Paulo, Brazil
Sergio Tasso	University of Perugia, Italy

Workshop on Advanced and Computational Methods for Earth Science Applications (WACM4ES 2025)

Workshop Organizers

Luca Piroddi	University of Cagliari, Italy
Patrizia Capizzi	University of Palermo, Italy
Marilena Cozzolino	University of Molise, Italy
Sebastiano D'Amico	University of Malta, Malta
Chiara Garau	University of Cagliari, Italy
Giuseppina Vacca	University of Cagliari, Italy

Workshop Program Committee Members

Andrea Angelini	CNR ISPC, Italy
Ilaria Barone	Università degli Studi di Padova, Italy
Patrizia Capizzi	University of Palermo, Italy
Luigi Capozzoli	CNR, Italy
Alberto Carletti	University of Cagliari, Italy
Emanuele Colica	University of Malta, Malta
Marilena Cozzolino	Università del Molise, Italy
Sebastiano D'Amico	University of Malta, Malta
Chiara Garau	University of Cagliari, Italy
Luciano Galone	University of Malta, Malta
Peter Iregbeyen	University of Malta, Malta
Mariano Lisi	Basilicata Aerospace Cluster CLAS, Italy
Raffaele Martorana	Università di Palermo, Italy
Paolo Mauriello	Università del Molise, Italy
Veronica Pazzi	University of Florence, Italy
Raffaele Persico	Università della Calabria, Italy
Luca Piroddi	University of Cagliari, Italy
Sina Saneiyan	Binghamton University, USA
Mercedes Solla	Universidade de Vigo, Spain
Deodato Tapete	ASI, Italy
Giuseppina Vacca	University of Cagliari, Italy
Enrica Vecchi	University of Cagliari, Italy

Sponsoring Organizations

ICCSA 2025 would not have been possible without the tremendous support of many organizations and institutions, for which all organizers and participants of ICCSA 2025 express their sincere gratitude:

Galatasaray University, Istanbul, Türkiye
(https://gsu.edu.tr/en)

African Mathematical Union
(https://www.africanmathunion.org/)

Springer Nature Switzerland AG, Switzerland
(https://www.springer.com)

The University of Massachusetts, USA
(https://www.umass.edu/)

University of Perugia, Italy
(https://www.unipg.it)

University of Basilicata, Italy
(http://www.unibas.it)

Monash University, Australia
(https://www.monash.edu/)

Kyushu Sangyo University, Japan
(https://www.kyusan-u.ac.jp/)

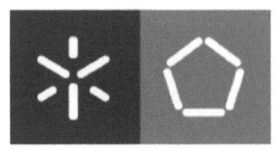

University of Minho, Portugal
(https://www.uminho.pt/)
Venue
ICCSA 2025 took place in: **Galatasaray University, Istanbul, Türkiye**

Additional Reviewers

Reviewers
The review tasks for each workshop have been carried out by the workshop Organizers and the members of the workshop Program Committee.

Plenary Lectures

Sky Safe with GAI and Post-quantum Computing

Elizabeth Chang

Professor of Cyber Security and Head of Discipline, University of the Sunshine Coast, Australia

Abstract. Professor Chang's talk in this presentation has two distinct parts. To start, she will introduce the landscape of cybersecurity development, attacks, threats, and vulnerabilities, as well as state-of-the-art cyber protection, cyber defence, and cyber incident prevention. This is followed by a discussion of the impact of Generative AI (GAI) and quantum-safe cryptographic computing, highlighting the major issues and challenges in research, education, and training. In conclusion, she will present a vision for Sky Safe solutions, aiming to achieve cyber resilience that supports business and economic stability, enhances human capabilities, and promotes environmental sustainability.

Disaster Preparedness and Risk Profiling in the Digital Era from Earth Observation Lens

Jagannath Aryal

Department of Infrastructure Engineering, University of Melbourne, Australia

Abstract. Natural hazards which turn into disasters result in severe losses of lives, infrastructure, and property. Disasters such as earthquakes and landslides and their impacts on transportation safety, infrastructure resilience, and displacement of people to new places are challenges. To address such challenges, earth observation data and intelligent methods can provide potential solutions in developing decision support systems. This talk will present the state of the art in Earth observation for disaster resilience using intelligent methods. In the Earth observation space, digitalisation has revolutionised the way we map, monitor, and develop decision support systems. Global case study examples covering earthquake-induced landslides from the Himalayan region will cover the digital capabilities. The digital capabilities will embrace object recognition, interpretation, and their accurate and precise capture to integrate into digital models. The developed digital models from representative case studies can be leveraged in other jurisdictions in profiling risks to protect lives and infrastructure and creating disaster preparedness in the era of digital age and digital economy.

Intelligent Image Enhancement for Real-World Applications in Adverse Atmospheric Conditions

Khan Muhammad

Department of Global Convergence, Sungkyunkwan University, South Korea

Abstract. The adverse impacts of atmospheric conditions such as haze, fog, and low-light environments pose significant challenges for real-world applications reliant on computer vision, including autonomous driving, surveillance, and remote sensing. This keynote explores cutting-edge advancements in intelligent image enhancement, drawing insights from two pivotal studies. The first introduces HazeSpace2M, a comprehensive dataset and novel classification-guided dehazing framework that improves image clarity across diverse atmospheric conditions, addressing the gap between synthetic and real-world dehazing performance. The second focuses on LoLI-Street, a benchmark for low-light image enhancement tailored to urban environments, extending beyond enhancement to enable robust object detection and scene understanding. Taken together, these contributions demonstrate how integrating domain-specific datasets, advanced algorithms, and performance benchmarks can significantly elevate the reliability of computer vision systems under challenging weather and lighting conditions. Attendees will gain valuable insights into the methodologies, datasets, and practical applications driving innovation in this field, with implications for research and industry alike.

In Memory of Carmelo Torre

Unfortunately, Professor Carmelo Torre, one of the cornerstones of the ICCSA Conference, passed away last December, leaving everyone stunned and deeply saddened. His loss has created a profound void within our academic community. Carmelo was not only a respected scholar and dedicated contributor to the success and growth of ICCSA, but also a generous colleague, mentor, and friend to many. His intellectual rigor, warm personality, and unwavering commitment to advancing research will be remembered with great admiration. As we continue the work he helped shape, we honor his legacy and the indelible mark he left on all of us. Carmelo Torre graduated in engineering at the Polytechnic of Bari with a thesis on urban planning under Dino Borri's guidance. He began his research career by collaborating with Franco Selicato. During his PhD at the University of Naples Federico II under Luigi Fusco Girard, he specialized in real estate market analysis and multi-criteria evaluation methods. He explored the social impacts of urban transformations with his lifelong friend Maria Cerreta. His first ICCSA participation was in Perugia in 2008, in the session Geographical Analysis, Urban Modeling, Spatial Statistics. Instantly captivated by the conference, his charisma enabled him to involve various Italian scientific communities, including those in real estate and statistics. ICCSA became a yearly commitment for him, where he valued the high editorial quality of the proceedings and the dynamic post-presentation discussions and debates he passionately and expertly enriched. In 2012, alongside Maria Cerreta and Paola Perchinunno, he organized the workshop Econometrics and Multidimensional Evaluation in the Urban Environment (EMEUE), fostering dialogue on critical topics. His influence steadily grew, drawing numerous research groups to ICCSA and establishing real estate and assessment as one of the conference's leading fields. A pillar of ICCSA, he was involved across all facets of the event. Torre's contributions to academic discourse were marked by intellectual rigor and innovative thinking. His conference interventions consistently challenged conventional wisdom, offering insights transcending disciplinary boundaries. Beyond the conference, he passionately advocated for equity and social justice. His left-leaning ideology, though firm, earned respect from those with differing views, thanks to his sincerity and loyalty. He was creative, generous, and always willing to help, even at a personal cost. Despite battling illness, he maintained his characteristic optimism, warmth, cheerfulness, and commitment, supported by his partner, Caterina Rinaldo. His legacy lives on in his ideas, dedication, and unmatched generosity.

Contents – Part I

Workshop on Advancements in Applied Machine-Learning and Data Analytics (AAMDA 2025)

Anomaly Detection for Vietnam Railway Using Unsupervised Learning Based on IoT Device Data Monitoring Railway Level Crossings 3
   Ngo Anh Tuan, Nguyen Nhu Hai Linh, Pham Van Hiep, Vu Thu Diep, and Phan Duy Hung

Aging-Based Weighting for Session Classification in User Behavior Analysis 16
   Nail Taşgetiren, Ilgın Şafak, and Mehmet S. Aktaş

Improving the Cloud Provider Ranking in the INDIGO PaaS Orchestration System Using AI Techniques 35
   Luca Giommi, Giovanni Savarese, Gioacchino Vino, Domingo Ranieri, Alessandro Costantini, and Giacinto Donvito

Artificial Intelligence for Detecting Cultural Heritage Issues on Overtourism Literature: A Topic Modeling Application 51
   Laura Claudia Verdesca, Elisabetta Ronchieri, and Alessandro Costantini

Towards Smarter Vegetation Health Clustering: Insights from Fractal Dimension, NDVI, and LST Metrics Derived via Remote Sensing Landsat Dataset 70
   Suhad A. Yousif, Venus W. Samawi, Nadia M. G. Al-Saidi, and Yeliz Karaca

Repository-Level Code Understanding by LLMs via Hierarchical Summarization: Improving Code Search and Bug Localization 88
   Amirkia Rafiei Oskooei, Selcan Yukcu, Mehmet Cevheri Bozoglan, and Mehmet S. Aktas

Enhancing Industrial Time Series Anomaly Detection Through Graph Modeling and a Hybrid VAE-GAN Approach 106
   Giovanni Zurlo, Roberto Cornali, and Elisabetta Ronchieri

Understanding Signal Feature Impact in CNN-Based Modulation Classification with Realistic Datasets 124
   Bruno M. S. Teixeira, Thalles M. Moreira, João Rodrigo Faria, Fábio D. L. Coutinho, Samuel S. Pereira, and Arnaldo S. R. Oliveira

Advanced Processes of Mathematics and Computing Models in Complex Data-Intensive Computational Systems (AMCM 2025)

Empirical Analysis for Future Excellence Tourism Policies: The Case of Arzachena (Sardinia, Italy) 139
   Brunella Brundu, Sonia Malvica, and Donatella Carboni

Data-Driven Time Series Modeling with Hurst Exponent for Nonlinear Indexes' Forecasting by Artificial Neural Networks 152
   Yeliz Karaca and Osvaldo Gervasi

Fractal and Multifractal Analysis in Cancer Diagnosis and Segmentation with MRI Data 165
   Bengü Karaca and Fatma Aslan-Tutak

A Review of Artificial Intelligence's Impact on Cybersecurity in the Big Data Era 182
   Esra Çakir and A Çağrı Tolga

Facial Stress and Fatigue Recognition via Emotion Weighting: A Deep Learning Approach 193
   Amirkia Rafiei Oskooei, Eren Caglar, Sehmus Yakut, Yusuf Taha Tuten, and Mehmet S. Aktas

Apache Spark Implementation of the Constrained K-Means Clustering Algorithm 212
   Nguyen Quang Huy, Vu Thu Diep, and Phan Duy Hung

Computational Linguistics and Media News: Linguistic Features and Lexical Choices with Time-frequency Statistical Analysis 226
   Ahu Dereli Dursun

Arabic Sign Language Recognition Using Image-Based Deep Learning and Edge User-Centered Interface 243
   Ahmad Alzu'bi, Amjad Albashayreh, and Lojin Bani Younis

Comparing Emerging Technologies in Image Classification: From Quantum to Kolmogorov 260
   Fabio Napoli, Mariarosaria Castaldo, Stefano Marrone, and Lelio Campanile

Analyzing the Impact of Visual and Listing Features in Real Estate Listings 274
   Serra Nur Bayrak, Gülfem Işıklar Alptekin, Günce Keziban Orman, and Afra Arslan

Advanced Numerical Approaches for Assessment and Design of No-Tension Masonry Structures (ANAMS 2025)

Toward a Unified Approach to Torsion-Shear Constraints in Convex Limit
Analysis of Masonry 289
    Elham Mousavian

Experimental and Numerical Study of SRG-to-Masonry Joints 302
    Salvatore Verre, Sam Cocking, Alessio Cascardi, Raimondo Luciano,
    Francesco Fabbrocino, and Carlo Olivieri

Geometrical Proportioning of Masonry Arch Bridges 314
    Michela Monaco

The Effects of Localised Damage on the Structural Stability of Masonry
Arches 325
    Luciana Di Gennaro, Mariateresa Gaudagnuolo, and Giorgio Frunzio

Seismic Performance of Irregular Buildings Through the CASS Method 338
    Andrea Montanino and Francesco Fabbrocino

FE Upper Bound Limit Analysis for Automated Identification of Collapse
Mechanisms in Masonry Structures 354
    Martina Buzzetti, Natalia Pingaro, and Gabriele Milani

Airy-Based Form-Finding of Purely Compressed Masonry Shells Under
Vertical and Horizontal Loads 368
    Sam Cocking, Luigi Sibille, Sigrid Adriaenssens, Americo Cunha Jr,
    Francesco Fabbrocino, and Carlo Olivieri

Insights into the Collapse of the Asciello Masonry Bridge in Benevento 381
    Antonino Iannuzzo, Giuseppe Matarazzo, Concetta Cusano,
    Mario Ferraro, and Giuseppe Maddaloni

FEMANOLA v3.0 as a Tool to Predict Settlement-Induced Cracks
in Masonry Walls 396
    Natalia Pingaro and Gabriele Milani

International Workshop on Territorial Planning to integrate Risk Prevention and Urban Ontologies. (IWPRO 2025)

Leveraging Gamification to Strengthen Social Resilience and Climate
Resilience 413
    Naghmeh Mohammadpourlima, Mikael Nygård, and Mehdi P. Heris

Digital Twin as a Tool for Participatory Cultural Heritage Regeneration:
The Case of Pavia Historical Urban Center in Italy 428
  Minqing Ni, Tiziano Cattaneo, and Lyu Ji

Author Index 441

Workshop on Advancements in Applied Machine-learning and Data Analytics (AAMDA 2025)

Anomaly Detection for Vietnam Railway Using Unsupervised Learning Based on IoT Device Data Monitoring Railway Level Crossings

Ngo Anh Tuan[1], Nguyen Nhu Hai Linh[2], Pham Van Hiep[2], Vu Thu Diep[3], and Phan Duy Hung[1](✉)

[1] FPT University, Hanoi, Vietnam
tuan23mse13141@fsb.edu.vn, hungpd2@fe.edu.vn
[2] Hanoi Railway Signal and Telecom, JSC, Hanoi, Vietnam
{linh.nnh,hiep.phv}@hasitec.vn
[3] HaNoi University of Science and Technology, Hanoi, Vietnam
diep.vuthu@hust.edu.vn

Abstract. In Vietnam, the railway industry has always been of interest to society, with its scale constantly expanding and upgrading. According to statistics, there are approximately 10,000 railway level crossings across the nation. At railway level crossings, system of protective equipment is deployed to ensure traffic safety. The operational data of these protective devices is collected and transmitted to the data center for monitoring and management. We developed and evaluated machine learning (ML) models to detect potential anomalies in crossing operations and identify potential safety risks. The system analyzes real-time sensor data including magnetic sensors, barrier status monitors, power supply indicators, and environmental sensors from multiple crossing locations. By using one class support vector machine (OCSVM) models to exploit the collected data, with the dual objectives of early detection of potential risks as well as the stable operation of the equipment we achieved 96% accuracy. This research proposes a methodology for improving the quality of management as well as the application of science and technology in the digital transformation and modernization of the railway industry in Vietnam.

Keywords: Railway Level Crossing · Railway Safety · Unsupervised Learning · SVM One Class · Anomaly Detection

1 Introduction

1.1 Problem and Motivation

At railway level crossings in Vietnam, a comprehensive system of devices and sensors is deployed to ensure safety operations. The core infrastructure includes six magnetic sensors strategically positioned along the tracks, these magnetic sensors function by counting the pulses generated each time a train wheel axle passes over the sensor location, with two sensors placed one to five kilometers before the crossing point for early train detection, and two sensors at the intersection to confirm train presence. The system also incorporates barrier gates equipped with traffic light signals, powered by both AC and DC supplies to ensure operational reliability. The IoT infrastructure continuously collects various parameters from these devices (Fig. 1).

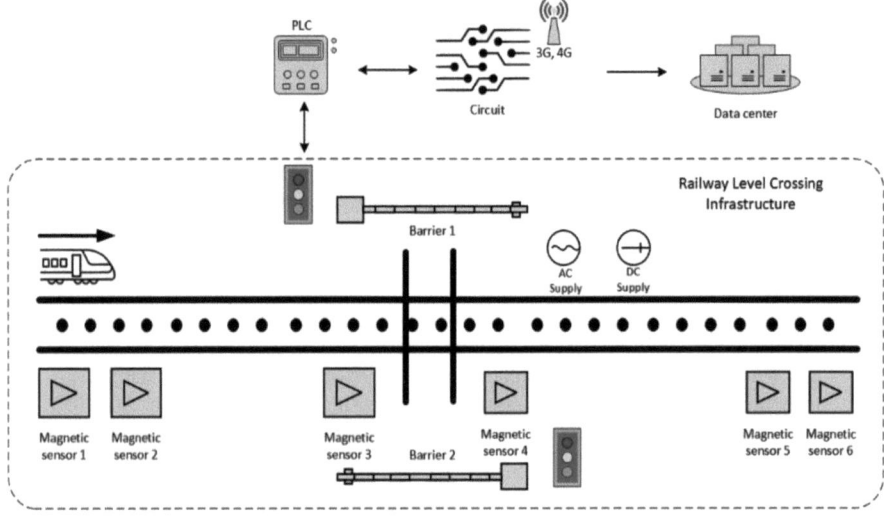

Fig. 1. System Architecture

The crossing protection devices are connected to a PLC (Programmable Logic Controller), which controls the operation of the entire infrastructure. Sensor data is sent to the PLC, and circuits collect it through indirect interfaces with the PLC. The processed data is then transmitted to the server through a Wi-Fi module, which connects to 3G/4G access points for reliable data transmission to centralized data centers.

Despite the centralized collection of sensor data from railway level crossings, its current application is limited to displaying information at monitoring centers, with incident response decisions still heavily dependent on human operators. This manual approach faces significant challenges as monitoring centers are responsible for supervising numerous level crossings simultaneously. The high volume of real-time data from thousands of crossing points creates a substantial cognitive load for operators, potentially leading to delayed response times and increased risk of oversight in critical situations.

The monitoring of level crossings faces numerous challenges due to the inability to comprehensively define all safety-affecting scenarios. The railway system extends throughout Vietnam with diverse operating conditions, and the message structure reveals over 40 different sensor parameters that must be monitored simultaneously. The combinations of these parameters create an extensive anomaly space, and many potentially dangerous situations have never occurred, making it impossible to pre-label them for traditional analysis methods.

Furthermore, the data exhibits complex temporal relationships. Train detection follows a specific sequence (approaching, passing through, and departing the crossing) that must trigger synchronized responses from barrier movements, light signals, and sound alerts. Any desynchronization in this sequence could indicate a potential safety risk that might be overlooked in manual monitoring.

We have recognized the potential to develop unsupervised learning models to detect these hidden risks. Unlike supervised learning methods that require extensively labeled training data, unsupervised learning can identify patterns and detect anomalies by leveraging the inherent structure of the data itself without explicit programming. This approach is particularly valuable for railway crossing safety where normal operational patterns can be learned, allowing deviations that may indicate potential safety issues to be automatically flagged for operator attention.

Therefore, there is a pressing need for automated systems that can not only collect data but also intelligently process and identify potential anomalies, supporting operators in making more timely and informed decisions.

1.2 Related Works

Statistics from 1990 to 2020 show that even countries with developed railway infrastructure such as China and Japan face significant challenges [1]. Both countries, along with many others [1, 2], continue to experience railway accidents due to environmental factors, poor management, and other challenges.

The complexity of railway safety management varies significantly across different economic contexts. Research on transport policy and management across low, middle, and high-income Asian countries demonstrated that while technological solutions are important, the effectiveness of safety measures heavily depends on the local context and management capabilities [3]. This is particularly relevant for Vietnam's railway system, where the railway infrastructure is outdated compared to global standards.

In the context of railway management, proactive safety is always the first priority [4]. Traditional monitoring methods often fail to detect potential risks before they develop into accidents. Railway safety systems must integrate risk management with real-time monitoring capabilities, indicating that advanced technologies such as Machine Learning [5] can play a crucial role in enhancing safety measures. The integration of ML technologies offers promising solutions for enhancing railway safety systems through improved risk detection and management capabilities [6–8]. The deployment of IoT devices at these crossings generates an exceptionally large volume of data [9]. Machine learning excels at identifying subtle patterns in large, complex datasets that may not be apparent through traditional statistical analysis [10].

To build a machine learning model with high accuracy, data preprocessing and feature extraction play a crucial role, as sensors at railway level crossings typically have different measurement scales [11, 12]. Normalization methods such as min-max scaling or Z-score are particularly important for magnetic sensors used in train detection, where environmental conditions can significantly affect raw measurements, requiring normalization to maintain consistent detection thresholds across different locations and weather conditions [13]. Additionally, dimensionality reduction helps significantly improve system performance. Methods such as Principal Component Analysis (PCA) or t-SNE are effective in reducing data complexity for railway systems with extensive data [14].

The One-Class Support Vector Machine (OCSVM) algorithm is particularly well suited to the problem of anomaly detection at railway crossings, as data in this area is often unlabeled. OCSVM is highly sensitive to rare and unusual data patterns [15], such as incidents with very low occurrence frequencies. This makes OCSVM particularly useful for safety monitoring at crossings, where severe anomalies may not have been present in historical data. However, the ability to detect these anomalies early is key to preventing accidents and ensuring safe operations.

2 Contribution

Our study proposes data filtering and normalization methods, thereby building a highly reliable training dataset that is suitable for the characteristics of the railway industry [26].

This research serves as a foundation for future approaches to processing data collected from devices at railway crossings via the Internet of Things (IoT) infrastructure. The proposed method demonstrates the ability to efficiently integrate and analyze multiple data streams, thereby supporting the early detection of potential safety-related risks and system operation anomalies.

This research offers valuable insights into the challenges and solutions associated with implementing smart monitoring systems in railway networks in developing countries where infrastructure and management capacity are limited. These insights are particularly important for countries facing similar issues in infrastructure development and modernization, providing a practical application framework that can be flexibly adapted to different operational contexts considering local technological and managerial constraints.

The remainder of this paper is organized as follows. Section 2 describes the methodology. Section 3 discusses experimental results. Finally, Sect. 4 provides conclusion and future works.

3 Methodology

Our method presents a comprehensive approach to detect anomalies at railway crossings. Raw data from IoT devices at these crossings is stored in our data center. The system processes this data through two parallel preprocessing threads:

- The first preprocessing thread prepares data specifically for the Modeling Module, where we employ a One-Class SVM machine learning model to establish reliable anomaly detection capabilities.
- The second preprocessing thread focuses on preparing data for real-time analysis, directly feeding into the Real-time Processing Module. This module leverages a sliding window technique to continuously sample incoming data, enabling immediate anomaly detection and prediction during railway crossing operations.

Our proposed overall architecture is illustrated as Fig. 2.

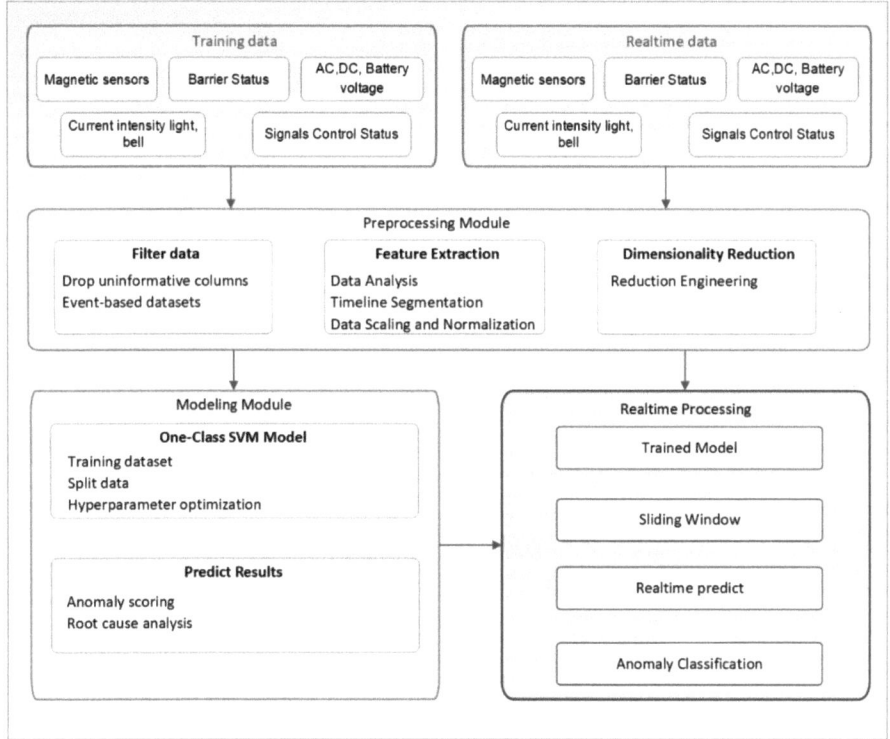

Fig. 2. Architecture overview

3.1 Preprocessing Module

Filter Data

Raw data will be filtered to remove unnecessary information fields. Each train passing through a level crossing will be a set containing valuable information collected from IoT devices over time. Information about these fields is described in Table 1.

Feature Extraction

The data will be normalized and feature vectors will be extracted from the dataset of each train crossing event. The methods implement:

Min-max scale. For magnetic sensor data, which increases gradually over time and has unchanging peak values, using the maximum and minimum values method will significantly improve model performance [16, 17]. With threshold is the train detection threshold the transformation formula is:

$$X\_normalized = \frac{X - Threshold}{X\_max - Threshold}$$

Peak Difference Analysis (PDA). PDA is typically used when we have two or more variables/series that are closely correlated. In our system, sensor pairs are deployed consecutively to backup each other, so monitoring the ΔX at peak values is critically

Table 1. Description of IoT Data

No	Field Name	Description	Value Range/Unit
1	time_stamp	Timestamp	ddMMyyyy_HHmmss
2	X1, X2 … X6	Magnetic sensor values	Integer values
3	S5	PLC control signal	0: Not operational 1: Ready 2: Controlling
4	S6, S7	Control signal for opening/closing barrier 1	Same as above
5	S9, S10	Control signal for opening/closing barrier 2	Same as above
6	C7, C8	Open/closed status of barrier 1	0: Undetermined 1: Opened/Closed
7	C13, C14	Open/closed status of barrier 2	Same as above
8	AI1	AC power voltage	220 V
9	AC2	DC power voltage	24 V
10	I1	Warning light current intensity	Blink. 0 to 2000mA
11	I3, I4	Yellow lights current intensity	Same as above
12	I5, I6, I7, I8	Red lights current intensity	Same as above
13	I9	Bell current intensity	Always on

important. By extracting peak features and calculating the differences, we can highlight sudden deviations that models based on raw values might overlook:

$$\Delta X = \frac{|\max(X\_norm_i) - \max(X\_norm_{i-1})|}{|t_i - t_{i-1}|}$$

t_i and t_{i-1} are the timestamps when peaks occur at sensors i and i-1.

This is especially useful for detecting anomalies [18] related to irregular train speeds.

Temporal Feature Extraction. Identifying time markers to include in the feature vector is very significant [19]. For our problem, there is a strong relationship between sensor values and timestamps.

For example, when a train is detected entering the level crossing (X1 > Threshold), the time interval from when the barrier closure control signal is given until the barrier is completely closed has a major impact on safety. We will analyze and incorporate these time intervals Δt into the feature vector:

$$t_{close} = \text{time}(C_{closed}) - \text{time}(S_{signal\_close})$$

Z-score. Is a powerful tool that can significantly improve the performance of models in anomaly detection tasks [20], especially when combined with min-max scaling, peak difference analysis, and Temporal Feature Extraction [21].

Apply Z-Score for each phase: train entering, train passing through, and train leaving the level crossing to enhance the sensitivity of anomaly detection when trains are running:

$$Z(X_{i,t}) = \frac{X_{i,t} - \mu_{i,t}}{\sigma_{i,t}}$$

- $X_{i,t}$ value of sensor X_i at time t in the train event
- $\mu_{i,t}$, $\sigma_{i,t}$ are mean value and standard deviation of sensor X_i at time t across multiple train events.

For example, to detect early mechanical degradation of the barrier system before failures occur, we can apply the formula.

$$Z(t_{close}) = \frac{t_{close} - \mu_{t_{close}}}{\sigma_{t_{close}}}$$

$\mu_{t_{close}}$ and $\sigma_{t_{close}}$ are the mean value and standard deviation of the barrier closing time.

Dimensionality Reduction

In this phase, after the data has been normalized using the aforementioned methods, we will proceed with dimensionality reduction to make the dataset more concise while still preserving the data characteristics. Common dimensionality reduction methods such as PCA (Principal Component Analysis), t-SNE (t-Distributed Stochastic Neighbor Embedding) or UMAP (Uniform Manifold Approximation and Projection) will be applied in this step

3.2 Modeling Module

At this phase, data is classified and anomaly levels are evaluated through unsupervised learning methods, where the One-Class SVM(OCSVM) model is selected to build the system. We choose OCSVM for anomaly detection in railway systems because:

- The data collected from railway systems are mainly normal operating cases, while anomalies are rare. OCSVM is specially designed for this imbalanced data, where normal data samples are the majority.
- One-class SVM can detect nonlinear relationships between features. This is important in this problem because the relationships between parameters such as magnetic sensor, Δt, and the states of the barriers are often nonlinear.

To implement One-Class SVM, the model is trained on a dataset representing normal operations to determine the boundary of standard behavior. The RBF (Radial Basis Function) kernel technique is used to better capture non-linear relationships between features. Hyperparameter tuning is applied to find optimal values for the hyperparameter pair (ν, γ), helping to balance between model sensitivity and specificity. Finally, a decision function is implemented to classify new observations, determining whether they belong to normal or anomalous behavior.

To evaluate the model, the first step is to extract normal operational data from various level crossings for training. Next, a synthetic anomaly dataset is generated with varying anomaly occurrence rates to assess the model's detection performance. Performance is then measured using precision, recall, F1-score, and AUC-ROC. Finally, a hyperparameter sensitivity analysis is conducted to ensure the model's stability and generalization capability

3.3 Realtime Processing

To deploy and apply trained models in production system, there is a huge challenge: there will be many incidents that are only detected when the train reaches a specific time point in the train running event chain. For each stage, we can detect different abnormalities. To solve this problem, we have implemented a method that combines Sliding Window and Dynamic Template.

Sliding Windows

Sliding Window technique plays an important role in detecting abnormalities by analyzing multivariate data series from real stages for the railway system, through analyzing multivariate data series from IoT points. This method is based on a number of defined technical characteristics, allowing to track statistical characteristics and correlations between sensors in each specific stage of the train passing event.

We can evaluate the similarity between windows and the standard template [22] using the formula:

$$\text{Eros}(A, B, w) = \sum_{i=1}^{n} w_i |\langle a_i, b_i \rangle| = \sum_{i=1}^{n} |\cos \theta_i|$$

$\langle a_i, b_i \rangle$ is the inner product between a_i and b_i,
w_i is a weight vector which is based on the eigenvalues of dataset.
$\cos \theta_i$ is the angle between a_i and b_i.

Dynamic Template

Applying the Dynamic Template allows early detection of anomalies without waiting for the event to complete in order to issue an alert [23]. Real-time data of train crossing events are continuously updated, while the standard template automatically adjusts when gradual changes occur. As a result, the system does not need to store the entire historical data, helping to optimize computational resources.

4 Experiments and Results

4.1 Data Collection

Our data was collected from the Hanoi-Hai Phong railway route, one of the busiest railway corridors in northern Vietnam. We selected 8 consecutive level crossings with the most stable operations to collect data over a 5-day period (from March 1 to March 5, 2025). These crossings were chosen because they have reliable infrastructure, creating favorable conditions for the research process.

For each day, the raw data is stored as a text file. After filtering the data, our dataset is transformed into CSV files, with a summary presented in Table 2.

Table 2. Summary of dataset

Total CSV files	40
Total train sessions	404
Total data rows	30561
Rows per event	75.46

4.2 Experiments

Since performance evaluation in unsupervised learning is crucial, all our collected data consists of train events operating under normal conditions (without incidents). This creates a major challenge known as class imbalance [24] in machine learning. To address the lack of incident data samples, we used historical error data, combined with simulated scenarios developed by railway experts, and integrate these samples into the original dataset. Table 3 summarizes the types of anomalies we simulated and the implementation methods used to generate these anomalies in our dataset.

Table 3. Anomaly types and implementation methods

Anomaly Type	Implementation Method
Barrier Malfunction	Extend closing time
Signal Control Delay	Increased time intervals
Power Instability	Voltage fluctuation
Sensor Detection Failure	Set sensor pair value

Barrier Malfunction errors are defined by the following process: find the first data point that satisfies the condition $C7 = 0$ and $C8 = 1$, then mark the next 10 consecutive records with values $C7 = 0$ and $C8 = 0$. The barrier closure time will be extended by the duration corresponding to the next 10 records, which results in a Barrier Malfunction.

The time from when the number of pulses counted by X1 or X6 exceeds the detection threshold (usually 7 pulses) until $S7 = 1$ and $S10 = 1$ is defined as the system reaction time. To generate the Signal Control Delay error, we update the value at the first time $S7 = 1$ and the next two records to 0, because this time interval is usually very short.

AC power typically has a threshold of 220V and DC power with a threshold of 24V usually operates very stably with a 5% error margin. We modify a few random records with a deviation higher than 10% to create the Power Instability error.

The magnetic sensors count pulses generated each time a train wheel axle passes, and at peak operation, the variation between sensors typically remains within an expected range of values. To simulate a Sensor Detection Failure scenario for a train event, we will set all X1 values after the pulse count reaches 30 to a fixed value of 30. Figure 3 illustrates the variation in magnetic sensor values for a normal train event and a simulated faulty train event.

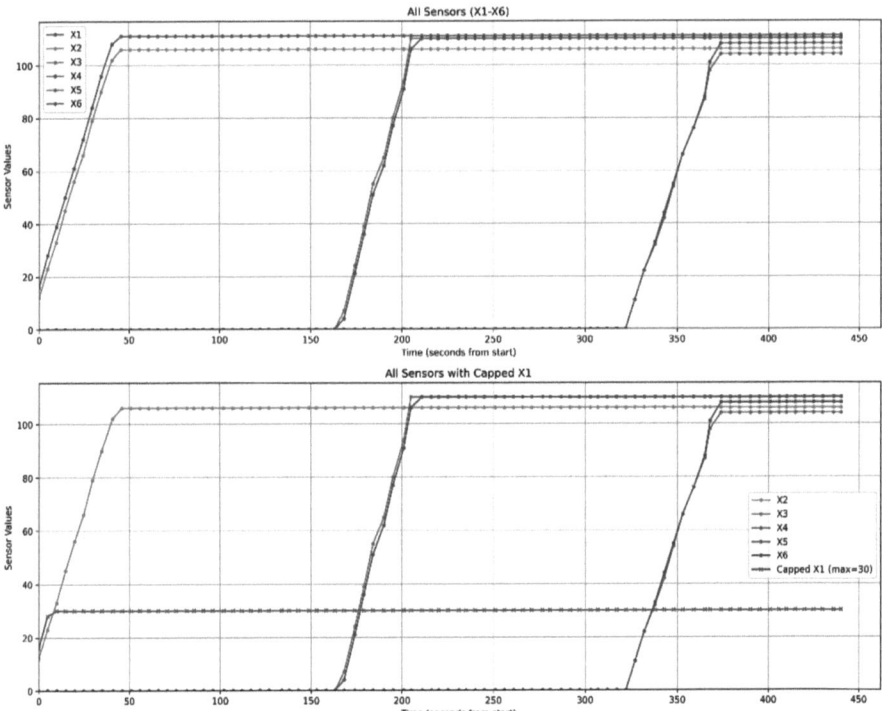

Fig. 3. Magnetic sensor values for a normal train event and a simulated faulty train event

4.3 Results

The characteristics of the dataset were collected under normal conditions, including 400 train events as described in Table 2. We divided the data into a training set and a testing set at a 50% ratio, with each set containing approximately 200 train events. From the training set, we proceeded to train the OCSVM model.

To evaluate the model based on metrics such as Accuracy, Precision, Recall, and F1-Score, our approach involves mixing different error ratios with our testing dataset, introducing anomalies at various proportions: 20% (40 samples), 10% (20 samples), 5% (10 samples), and 2% (4 samples) in a dataset of 200 samples. These ratios help evaluate our model's performance under both high anomaly density scenarios and more realistic conditions where anomalies are relatively rare. Testing with such varied ratios helps us gain deeper insights into how the model responds in different scenarios, while also helping identify the sweet spot [25] the point at which the model maintains effectiveness despite very low anomaly rates. This is particularly important in railway safety applications, where the cost of missing an incident (false negative) can be extremely high. Table 4 describes the metrics of the OCSVM model with default parameters $v = 0.5$, $\gamma = $ scale, kernel = rbf.

To increase the model's performance, we performed hyperparameter tuning as shown in Table 5. We achieved very good results during experimentation. Table 6 describes the results after tuning with $v = 0.01$, $\gamma = $ scale, kernel = linear.

Table 4. OCSVM default hyper params metrics

Sample error	Accuracy	Precision	Recall	F1-Score	ROC AUC
40	0.7865	0.8974	0.8642	0.8805	0.6173
20	0.7765	0.9429	0.8148	0.8742	0.5185
10	0.7952	0.9706	0.8148	0.8859	0.5185
4	0.8293	0.9855	0.8395	0.9067	0.5309

Table 5. Tuning OCSVM hyper params

Parameter	Tuning Range
nu	0.01, 0.05, 0.1, 0.2
gamma	scale, auto, 0.1, 0.01
kernel	rbf, linear

Table 6. Best metrics of OCSVM model

Sample error	Accuracy	Precision	Recall	F1-Score	ROC AUC
40	0.8989	0.9091	0.9877	0.9467	0.8519
20	0.9294	0.9518	0.9753	0.9634	0.8519
10	0.9398	0.9750	0.9630	0.9689	0.7160
4	0.9634	0.9875	0.9753	0.9814	0.8519

5 Conclusion and Future Works

This research has successfully developed an anomaly detection subsystem for railway crossings in Vietnam, applying unsupervised learning on IoT sensor data. The implementation of unsupervised learning not only helps reduce manual classification efforts but also enhances detection efficiency based on large-scale datasets.

This work establishes a foundation for future intelligent monitoring systems that can be adapted to different operational contexts while maintaining high reliability and performance. Our dataset, extracted in CSV format, can serve as a valuable reference resource for the community [26], supporting more effective research and development of models. This work can be applied to machine learning and data mining problems with tabular data [27–30].

In the future, there is significant potential for expanding this research. For instance, the system can be upgraded to monitor detailed train journeys as they pass through crossings. Additionally, after the preliminary classification, integrating another machine learning model to specifically identify each type of incident will help obtain accurately labeled data. This data, in turn, can be used to improve and retrain the original model, enhancing the reliability and efficiency of the entire system.

References

1. Cao, Y., An, Y., Su, S., Xie, G., Sun, Y.: A statistical study of railway safety in China and Japan 1990–2020. Accid. Anal. Prev. **175**, 106764 (2022)
2. Kyriakidis, M., Hirsch, R., Majumdar, A.: Metro railway safety: an analysis of accident precursors. Saf. Sci. **50**(7), 1535–1548 (2012)
3. Shah, S.A.R., Ahmad, N., Shen, Y., Pirdavani, A., Basheer, M.A., Brijs, T.: Road safety risk assessment: an analysis of transport policy and management for low, middle, and high-income Asian countries. Sustainability **10**(2), 389 (2018)
4. Bulakh, M., Okorokov, A., Baranovskyi, D.: Risk System and Railway Safety. IOP Conf. Ser. Earth Environ. Sci. **666**, 042074 (2021)
5. Alawad, H., Kaewunruen, S., An, M.: Learning from accidents: machine learning for safety at railway stations. IEEE Access **8**, 633–648 (2020)
6. Li, H., et al.: Improving rail network velocity: a machine learning approach to predictive maintenance. Transp. Res. Part C: Emerg. Technol. **45**, 17–26 (2014)
7. Thaduri, A., Galar, D., Kumar, U.: Railway assets: a potential domain for big data analytics. Procedia Comput. Sci. **53**, 457–467 (2015)
8. Paltrinieri, N., Comfort, L., Reniers, G.: Learning about risk: machine learning for risk assessment. Saf. Sci. **118**, 475–486 (2019)
9. Singh, P., Elmi, Z., Meriga, V.K., Pasha, J., Dulebenets, M.A.: Internet of things for sustainable railway transportation: past, present, and future. Cleaner Logistics Supply Chain **4**, 100065 (2022). https://doi.org/10.1016/j.clscn.2022.100065
10. Siddiqui, H.U.R., Saleem, A.A., Raza, M.A., Zafar, K., Munir, K., Dudley, S.: IoT based railway track faults detection and localization using acoustic analysis. IEEE Access **10**, 106520–106533 (2022). https://doi.org/10.1109/ACCESS.2022.3210326
11. Islam, U., et al.: A novel anomaly detection system on the internet of railways using extended neural networks. Electronics **11**(18), 2813 (2022). https://doi.org/10.3390/electronics11182813
12. Inan, M.S.K., Liao, K., Shen, H., Jayaraman, P.P., Georgakopoulos, D., Tang, M.J.: Deep-HeteroIoT: deep local and global learning over heterogeneous IoT sensor data. proceedings of the 20th EAI international conference on mobile and ubiquitous systems: computing, networking and services (2023)
13. Kumar, N., Krause, L., Wondrak, T., Eckert, S., Eckert, K., Gumhold, S.: Robust reconstruction of the void fraction from noisy magnetic flux density using invertible neural networks. Sensors **24**(4), 1213 (2024). https://doi.org/10.3390/s24041213
14. Lasisi, A., Attoh-Okine, N.: Hybrid rail track quality analysis using nonlinear dimension reduction technique with machine learning. Can. J. Civ. Eng. **48**(12), 1713–1723 (2021). https://doi.org/10.1139/cjce-2019-0832
15. Yang, K., Kpotufe, S., Feamster, N.: An efficient one-class SVM for anomaly detection in the internet of things. arXiv. https://arxiv.org/abs/2104.11146 (2021)
16. Mejri, N., Lopez-Fuentes, L., Roy, K., Chernakov, P., Ghorbel, E., Aouada, D.: Unsupervised anomaly detection in time-series: an extensive evaluation and analysis of state-of-the-art methods. Expert Syst. Appl. **256**, 124922 (2024)
17. Zhang, M., Xu, B., Wang, D.: An anomaly detection model for network intrusions using one-class SVM and scaling strategy. In: Guo, S., Liao, X., Liu, F., Zhu, Y. (eds.) Collaborative Computing: Networking, Applications, and Worksharing, pp. 280–291. Springer, Cham (2016). https://doi.org/10.1007/978-3-319-28910-6_24

18. Lee, B.S., Kaufmann, J.C., Rizzo, D.M., Haq, I.U.: peak anomaly detection from environmental sensor-generated watershed time series data. In: Lossio-Ventura, J.A., Valverde-Rebaza, J., Díaz, E., Alatrista-Salas, H. (eds.), Information Management and Big Data, pp. 156–170. Springer, Cham (2023). https://doi.org/10.1007/978-3-031-35445-8_11
19. Zhao, P., Chang, X., Wang, M.: A novel multivariate time-series anomaly detection approach using an unsupervised deep neural network. IEEE Access **9**, 109025–109041 (2021). https://doi.org/10.1109/ACCESS.2021.3101844
20. Tutivén, C., Vidal, Y., Insuasty, A., Campoverde-Vilela, L., Achicanoy, W.: Early fault diagnosis strategy for WT main bearings based on SCADA data and one-class SVM. Energies **15**(12), 4381 (2022). https://doi.org/10.3390/en15124381
21. Salam, A., et al.: Securing smart manufacturing by integrating anomaly detection with zero-knowledge proofs. IEEE Access **12**, 36346–36360 (2024)
22. Zhang, M., Xu, B., Gong, J.: An anomaly detection model based on one-class SVM to detect network intrusions. In: Proceedings of the 11th International Conference on Mobile Ad-hoc and Sensor Networks (MSN), pp. 102–107. IEEE (2015)
23. Lee, S., Park, D.: A real-time abnormal beat detection method using a template cluster for the ECG diagnosis of IoT devices. HCIS **11**(04) (2021). https://doi.org/10.22967/HCIS.2021.11.004
24. Hosseini, S.M., Shafique, A., Babaie, M., Tizhoosh, H.R.: Class-imbalanced unsupervised and semi-supervised domain adaptation for histopathology images. In: Proceedings of the 45th Annual International Conference of the IEEE Engineering in Medicine & Biology Society (EMBC), pp. 1–7. IEEE (2023)
25. Rufino, V.Q., et al.: Improving predictability of user-affecting metrics to support anomaly detection in cloud services. IEEE Access **8**, 198152–198167 (2020)
26. Tuan, N.A.: Vietnamese railway crossing IoT sensor data. Kaggle (2023). https://www.kaggle.com/datasets/ngtuan12/vietnamese-railway-crossing-iot-sensor-data
27. Hung, P.D.: Detection of central sleep apnea based on a single-lead ECG. In: Proceedings of the 5th International Conference on Bioinformatics Research and Applications (ICBRA '18). Association for Computing Machinery, New York, NY, USA, pp. 78–83 (2018)
28. Hung, P.D.: Central sleep apnea detection using an accelerometer. In: Proceedings of the 1st International Conference on Control and Computer Vision (ICCCV '18). Association for Computing Machinery, New York, NY, USA, pp. 106–111 (2018)
29. Dat, D.Q., Hung, P.D.: Improvement for time series clustering with the deep learning approach. In: Luo, Y. (eds.) Cooperative Design, Visualization, and Engineering. CDVE 2021. Lecture Notes in Computer Science(), vol. 12983. Springer, Cham (2021)
30. Minh, N.Q., Hung, P.D.: the system for detecting vietnamese mispronunciation. In: Dang, T.K., Küng, J., Chung, T.M., Takizawa, M. (eds.) Future Data and Security Engineering. Big Data, Security and Privacy, Smart City and Industry 4.0 Applications. FDSE 2021. Communications in Computer and Information Science, vol. 1500. Springer, Singapore (2021)

Aging-Based Weighting for Session Classification in User Behavior Analysis

Nail Taşgetiren[1](✉), Ilgn Şafak[2,3], and Mehmet S. Aktaş[4]

[1] Hepsiburada Research and Development Center, Istanbul, Turkey
nail.tasgetiren@hepsiburada.com
[2] Fibabanka R&D Center, Istanbul, Turkey
ilgin.safak@fibabanka.com.tr
[3] University of Jyväskylä, Jyväskylä, Finland
ilgin.i.safak@jyu.fi
[4] Yildiz Technical University, Istanbul, Turkey
aktas@yildiz.edu.tr

Abstract. Comprehending user behavior on e-commerce platforms is essential for augmenting customer interaction and refining recommendation algorithms. Clickstream data provides a significant resource for examining user navigation patterns; nevertheless, accurately describing and categorizing user sessions poses a challenge. This paper shows how to improve the accuracy of session-based classification using an embedding-based method combined with an aging-based weighting mechanism. The considered embedding methods, Word2Vec, Node2Vec, and LSTM Autoencoder, can turn session-based clickstream data into numbers. Furthermore, a dynamic weighting technique is introduced to emphasize recent interactions to improve classification performance. Our empirical assessment on an authentic e-commerce dataset reveals that the LSTM Autoencoder surpasses conventional embedding methods in capturing sequential dependencies. In addition, the age-based weighting technique markedly improves the classification accuracy, especially when used with deep learning models. A comparison of different classification algorithms, such as Random Forest, Logistic Regression, Gaussian Naive Bayes, and LSTM, shows that LSTM models are the best at finding correlations between events over time. The results also show the importance of temporal weighting in session-based clickstream analysis and provide a solid foundation for further research in behavioral analytics and personalized recommendation systems. This paper introduces an efficient method for clickstream-based user modeling that facilitates better user engagement in e-commerce systems.

Keywords: Clickstream data · E-commerce · Word2Vec · Node2Vec · LSTM Autoencoder · Aging-based weighting · User behavior modeling · Classification algorithms

---

A patent application related to this work has been filed by the author's institutions.

1 Introduction

The swift growth of digital commerce has led to an unparalleled collection of user interaction data. Comprehending and analyzing this data is essential for improving user experience, refining recommendation systems, and augmenting conversion rates. Clickstream data, which records users' consecutive interactions on e-commerce platforms, is one of the most effective sources for evaluating online user behavior [13,22]. However, traditional data embedding methods may not account for user interactions in time [18,23], even though they are good at turning raw clickstream data into structured formats. This constraint hinders their capacity to adapt to evolving user behavior over time.

To solve this problem, new time-sensitive embedding strategies use different weighting algorithms to better represent user interactions over time [10,35]. Aging-based weighting shows the user actions based on how recently they happened. This technique enhances predictive modeling by emphasizing new interactions and progressively diminishing the impact of previous activities, so it accurately reflects changing user preferences.

Standard embedding methods, such as Word2Vec [4] for sequence-based representations and Node2Vec [7] for graph-based representations, are useful for finding important patterns in user navigation data. Nevertheless, these may result in inadequate representations, as they do not consider changes in user behavior with time. On the other hand, sequence-to-sequence architectures like Long Short-Term Memory (LSTM) Autoencoders [19] have shown great success in modeling complex time-dependent interactions within sequential data. However, the incorporation of aging-based weighting into LSTM Autoencoders remains a mostly unexamined field, especially concerning the representation of e-commerce session data.

This paper presents an innovative aging (time)-sensitive weighting method in LSTM Autoencoder-based embedding representations for improving session-based user behavior modeling in e-commerce systems. This approach makes it easier to understand the temporal behavior of user activity more dynamically and flexibly. This method provides a more detailed and accurate picture of how sessions work, and improves the accuracy of classification tasks predicting user behavior. This paper is structured as follows: Sect. 2 provides an overview of the literature review. Section 3 presents the methodology. Section 4 describes the implementation and evaluation details of the proposed weighting methodology. The conclusions and future work are the focus of Sect. 5.

2 Literature Review

In data analytics, especially within e-commerce, the study of user interactions via clickstream data has become increasingly vital [2,34]. Traditional embedding methods, such as natural language processing (NLP) models like Word2Vec [4,26,29] and graph-based approaches like Node2Vec [7,17,38], map unstructured user activities into structured insights to the user behavior. However, as these methods do not account for the relative importance of different data points, they may lead to generalized and not sufficiently accurate conclusions in behavioral modeling. Recent research focused on graph embedding methods that use deep learning, specifically LSTM autoencoders [9,19,28]. [28] proposed to embed weighted graphs using LSTM autoencoders to get node-weight sequences and turn them into fixed-length vectors. [31] employs LSTM autoencoders to combine graph sequences from random walks, breadth-first search, and shortest paths. Both approaches exhibited efficacy in graph classification and similarity tasks. [6] classified graph embedding techniques into three groups: random walks, factorization methods, and deep learning approaches. They also launched GEM, an open-source Python library for graph embedding. [36] reviewed diverse deep learning techniques for graphs, encompassing graph recurrent neural networks, convolutional networks, autoencoders, reinforcement learning, and adversarial approaches while emphasizing their applications and prospective future trajectories.

Prior studies are mostly based on simplistic weighting strategies or using a particular data type. Some recent studies have investigated aging-based weighting for data embeddings in multiple areas. FedTime integrates data age into federated learning for smart home energy prediction, enhancing consumption projections [30]. [24] studies aging pathways to show how the hierarchical organization of brain networks changes with age by using hyperbolic embeddings of MEG data. The embedding of self-estimated residual age is used in a unified network architecture to demonstrate that face aging occurs continuously for each person [15]. However, the results of sentiment analysis algorithms and word embeddings often have age-biased problems [5]. These results show the importance of including age-related variables in data embeddings for different uses, such as energy forecasting, neuroscience, facial recognition, and language-based models.

Prior studies either solely employed temporal dynamics in language models or graph structures, or employed static weighting schemes. A method that has not received enough attention in the literature is the simultaneous addition of aging-based temporal weighting across several embedding paradigms. In this paper, three different embedding methods are considered to show how users navigate. These include a natural-language-based model (Word2Vec), a graph-based model (Node2Vec), and one that works with a sequence-to-sequence model (the LSTM Autoencoder). An aging-based weighting method with the LSTM Autoencoder enhances the accuracy of user session data modeling. To the best of our knowledge, this is the first study to combine Word2Vec, Node2Vec, and LSTM Autoencoder in a session-based classification approach that considers time when assigning weights. Embeddings and F1 scores are also employed in diverse data categorization tasks. Domain-specific word embeddings are better at recognizing named entities than general embeddings, even when the corpus size is small [37]. Furthermore, tabular embeddings have been created to improve the precision of column and tuple categorization in relational data, demonstrating significant enhancements in F-measure relative to models lacking embedding [12].

Recent studies have tackled various aspects of information systems, user behavior modeling, and data representation across diverse application domains. The authors of [1] proposed a scalable infrastructure with fault-tolerant, high-performance information services in distributed systems. The authors of [27] performed a systematic mapping of mobile application verification techniques, underscoring the importance of software quality. In the context of clickstream data, the authors of [20] investigated how user navigational behavior can be modeled using embeddings extracted from clickstream sequences, initially focusing on representation methods and later enhancing them with Pattern2Vec to capture more structural and sequential user behavior patterns [21]. Furthermore, the authors of [33] presented a provenance-aware data collection platform for scientific modeling, emphasizing traceability and transparency in simulation workflows. While these studies contribute to user modeling, provenance tracking, and system robustness, none directly combine aging-based temporal weighting with multiple embedding strategies (Word2Vec, Node2Vec, LSTM Autoencoder) for session-level classification, which is the novel focus of this study.

3 Methodology

This paper presents a novel approach to group user sessions with similar navigation patterns by using users clickstream data from a monitored e-commerce website. Figure 1 shows the proposed business process that consists of several modules, such as the embedding function module, the weighting function module, the weighted average-based vectorization module, and the classification module. Together, these tools properly analyze user session data, enabling the creation of user groups with similar behavior patterns.

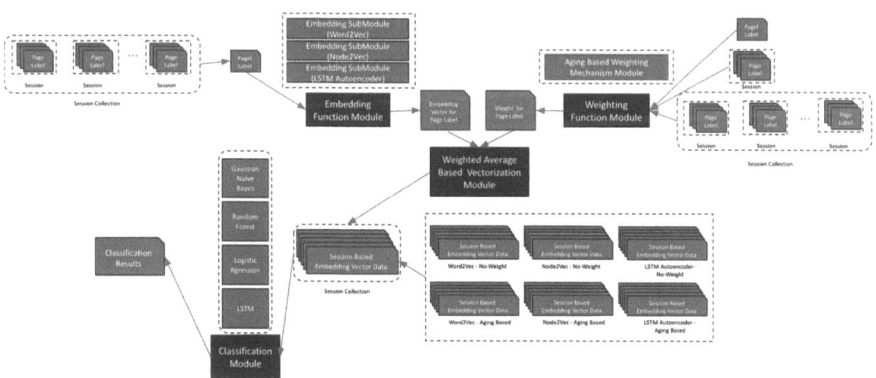

Fig. 1. Overview of the proposed business process

3.1 Embedding Function Module

The web log file provides extensive session information on user activities, with each click event monitored under a distinct sessionID. The embedding function module is an important part of this process since it uses different embedding techniques to encode session-based clickstream data into numerical vectors. This module contains a specific function for adaptively selecting the most appropriate embedding method to transform a page label into a numerical vector for precise and efficient data representation.

Word2Vec is an NLP-based embedding approach that generates vector representations for words. In this paper, page identifiers in the clickstream data are vectorized instead of words. The two fundamental architectures of Word2Vec are Continuous Bag of Words (CBOW) and Skip-Gram. The Skip-Gram technique was used in this paper to predict surrounding words (page IDs) that form the context of a specified target word (or page ID in this instance). Word2Vec lets you record the semantic links between web pages, bringing pages that are similar and close to each other in the resulting vector space. This approach makes it easier to model sequential interactions during user sessions and gives a good way to look at clickstreams.

In Word2Vec, each distinct token (such as a page ID in our dataset) is associated with a particular row in an embedding matrix. During the training phase, the model tries to find the best weights for this matrix so that tokens in similar situations are placed closer together in the vector space. This optimization aims to maximize the cosine similarity (or inner product) of adjacent embeddings while minimizing the similarity between randomly chosen embeddings. The CBOW model locates the target token by summing up the embedding vectors of adjacent tokens. Conversely, in the Skip-Gram paradigm, the target token infers the surrounding context tokens. Cosine similarity quantifies the alignment between vectors, resulting in related token vectors becoming more proximate. This method helps Word2Vec effectively capture the semantic and contextual links within sequential data, providing a strong representation to discover how users navigate.

Node2Vec elucidates the relationships among nodes by generating random walks within a graph, and provides a balanced exploration strategy by integrating Depth-First Search (DFS) and Breadth-First Search (BFS) algorithms. Random walks are stochastic systems characterized by probabilistic transitions among nodes. At each stage, a stochastic transition occurs from a specified node to the subsequent node, without following a fixed predetermined sequence. Two critical parameters govern the behavior of random walks: P (backward parameter) and Q (inside-outward exploration parameter). A high P value decreases the likelihood of retracing steps, so extending the walk and facilitating the exploration of a broader area inside the graph. A low P value increases the frequency of the random walk returning to the starting point, resulting in more localized movement. Similarly, a low Q value makes it more likely for the random walk to cover a larger area. A higher Q value makes it more likely for the walk to stay in a smaller area.

The LSTM Autoencoders follow sequence-to-sequence approach and excel in capturing complex temporal patterns and long-term dependencies. The LSTM autoencoder algorithm shows how nodes and their connections change over time in a network. Unlike Word2Vec or Node2Vec, the LSTM autoencoder doesn't use node identities (IDs) as input and doesn't have a separate layer that turns these IDs into embeddings. Each node is initially characterized by a distinct collection of attributes. These include fixed data like a node's degree and centrality, changing data about interactions like how often connections happen over time, or already calculated token embeddings if available. These attributes are represented in a time series format to capture temporal dependencies and trends.

For this method to work, the encoder packs sequential data into a small hidden state that holds both structural and temporal connections. The hidden state is then converted into an embedding vector containing the temporal dynamics of the node. The decoder subsequently reconstructs the original sequential data, maintaining both short-term and long-term dependencies. So, the LSTM autoencoder turns the nodes into numerical vectors that show their structural and temporal properties. The flexible design of the LSTM autoencoder allow to model sequential data effectively and to create meaningful representations that do not just rely on token embeddings.

NLP-based embedding methods are great at representing meaning linearly, while graph-based methods focus on learning about structural relationships. As for sequence-to-sequence approaches, they are successful in modeling sequence data changes over time.

3.2 Weighting Function Module

The weighting function module is a framework that calculates the suitable weight values for the data by implementing the specified weighting algorithm. This module uses aging-based weighting, which changes the importance of data items based on how they interact with each other over time. Unlike static weighting methods, aging-based weighting puts more weight on new interactions while decreasing the importance of older data over time. This method ensures that the weighting system adapts to changes in users behave over time. This improves the description of session-based interactions. These steps are activated according to the chosen weighting method, ensuring that the data is processed following the analytical framework.

Module for Weighted Session-Embedding Vector Calculation Aging-Based Approach. This module comprises code components that transform session-based clickstream data into numerical vectors via diverse embedding techniques. Traditional techniques assign equal significance to each page ID, but the aging-based weighting approach assigns weights to pages based on their visitation times during the session. This approach prioritizes more recently visited pages, hence effectively reflecting the session's dynamic character. This approach offers a robust mechanism for simulating the evolution of users' interests and browsing behaviors over time.

This paper uses an aging-based weighting approach to transform session-based clickstream data into numerical vectors. While each pageID has equal weight in traditional no-weight methods, the aging-based weighting method assigns more weight to pages visited more recently. Hence, the dynamic structure of the session over time is better represented.

We calculate the embedding vectors of sessions by utilizing various embedding vectors from each page. The aging-based weighting approach assigns a time-dependent weighting to each page. The mathematical representation of this method is given in (Eq. 1).

$$EV_{S_i} = \frac{\sum_{j=1}^{SessionLength_i} w_j EV_{P_j}}{\sum_{j=1}^{SessionLength_i} w_j}, \forall i \in 1, 2, \ldots, M \tag{1}$$

where;

(*) EV_{S_i}: Embedding Vector of Session i, and

(*) i is the index for the sessions in the log file (session-based clickstream data), and

(*) EV_{P_j}: embedding vector of the page ID of page j (p_j), and

(*) j is the index for the page ID in the Session i (S_i) and ranges from 1 to $SessionLength$ of (S_i), and

(*) $SessionLength_i$: Total number of page IDs in the Session i (S_i), and

(*) M is the total number of the sessions, obtained from the session-based clickstream data, and

(*) w_j: Aging-based weight assigned to the page p_j in Session i, computed as:

$$w_j = \frac{1}{Recency_j + 1} \tag{2}$$

where $Recency_j$ represents the recency value of the page p_j based on its timestamp in the session.

The aging-based weighting algorithm provides time-dependent weights depending on page visit times during the session. The vector representation of the session is created by giving more importance to newer pages while decreasing the influence of older pages. The page weights are inversely proportional to time as defined in Eq. 2, where the $Recency_j$ is calculated based on the time of the page visit. The overall vector representation of the session is made by normalizing the weighted sum of all the pages' embedding vectors. Newer pages are given more weight.

Session-based representation improved classification performance through age-based weighting. The efficacy of this methodology is assessed by comparing it with the no-weighting strategy.

3.3 Weighted Average-Based Vectorization Module

This module creates a numerical vector for each pageID using a chosen embedding technique. The weighted average vector components consist of the page weights within the session, and describe the session as a whole. This method makes it easier to see how pages are related in session-based clickstream data and to show sessions more meaningfully using numbers.

3.4 Classification Module

This module employs four distinct classification algorithms, which are essential in numerical data analysis and machine learning (ML) activities. They are designed to assign labels to data items based on predetermined classes. The considered classification algorithms are Gaussian Naive Bayes (GNB), Random Forest (RF), Logistic Regression (LR), and LSTM.

The GNB is a probabilistic classification model predicated on the assumption that the variables are independent of each other. Based on the assumption that the GNB classes have Gaussian (normal) distributions, Bayes' theorem is used to determine the likelihood of a data point belonging to a certain class. This rapid and computationally efficient model is particularly successful for short datasets and high-dimensional data.

RF is an ensemble learning technique based on decision trees. It aggregates the predictions by constructing numerous individual trees and identifying the most commonly observed class as the final prediction. RF can successfully predict complex relationships between data and uses sampling and random variable selection methods, like bagging, to keep overfitting to a minimum. This feature enables RF to deliver high accuracy and operate efficiently on extensive data sets.

LR is a statistical classification technique that effectively models linearly separable data. The model categorizes the data into two or more classes by computing a probability function based on the input variables. It standardizes the output values between 0 and 1 using the sigmoid activation function and generates a class prediction based on a specified threshold value. It is predominantly favored due to its simplicity, interpretability, and computing efficiency.

Finally, LSTM is a model for categorizing the output of Recurrent Neural Networks (RNN) and is very good at showing how things change over time. We engineered it to overcome the difficulties faced by conventional RNNs in acquiring long-term dependencies. LSTM can retain significant information over extended periods and discard extraneous information due to its gating processes. These properties render LSTM very proficient in time series analysis, sequential event forecasting, and text categorization jobs.

Each of the four methods possesses distinct advantages and disadvantages, necessitating selection based on the specific problem type. GNB is fast and needs little data. RF, on the other hand, is more accurate but may require high computing power for large datasets. Although LR is distinguished by its interpretability, it is constrained in its ability to describe nonlinear complicated interactions. LSTM, despite being one of the most effective techniques for sequential data, necessitates greater data and computational resources compared to alternative models.

3.5 Classification Results Evaluator Module

This module evaluates the efficacy of the employed categorization algorithms which determine the model's capability to accurately categorize data items. This paper employs four distinct evaluation metrics: Accuracy, Precision, Recall, and F1 Score.

Accuracy is a fundamental metric that assesses the precision of the model's predictions. It is defined as the ratio of accurately identified data points to the total number of data points. Nonetheless, it may not be adequate for skewed data sets.

Precision denotes the ratio of instances that the model identifies as positive. It is beneficial in situations where erroneous positive predictions are significant, particularly where the reduction of false positives is essential. Precision is a critical parameter for models aiming to achieve high-accuracy predictions.

The Recall measures the model's accuracy in identifying true positives. The ratio of genuine positives to the total number of true positives determines recall. This statistic is crucial, particularly in scenarios where incorrect negative predictions incur significant costs, as in essential domains like disease detection.

The F1 Score is a balanced metric combining Precision and Recall. It is defined as the harmonic mean of these two metrics, as shown in Eq. 3:

$$F1 = 2 \times \frac{\text{Precision} \times \text{Recall}}{\text{Precision} + \text{Recall}} \qquad (3)$$

The F1 Score serves as a robust evaluation metric when it is essential to optimize both Precision and Recall.

The four evaluation metrics discussed above offer a thorough assessment of the efficacy of categorization algorithms. Accuracy assesses overall performance, whereas Precision and Recall elucidate the nature of errors. The F1 Score is the most effective evaluation tool for imbalanced datasets. The determination of the appropriate measure in model selection is contingent upon the study's objectives and the data architecture.

4 Implementation and Evaluation of the Proposed Business Process

This section presents the dataset utilized in the study, along with the execution and assessment of the business process depicted in Fig. 1. The given dataset, data pretreatment steps, embedding methods, and classification algorithms were carefully considered during the business process to observe how well the aging-based weighting mechanism worked at reflecting user behavior. The results of this procedure were examined, the advantages and drawbacks of the suggested method were deliberated, and insights into its applicability in various circumstances were offered.

4.1 Dataset

The dataset included in this study has been meticulously chosen to facilitate a thorough assessment of the proposed methodology. The dataset provides a complete testing ground to see how well the aging-based weighting method shows and groups user behavior. This subsection delineates the size, structure, and fundamental characteristics of the dataset. The dataset is obtained from publicly available sources that provide important information about how users interact and browse the web. Such information makes it easier to evaluate the proposed method.

This study utilized dataset from the mobile application of a coffee chain, available on the Kaggle website [32], This dataset encompasses multiple variables, including 14-day user interactions, and offers a thorough foundation for evaluating user behavior. The dataset comprises 96,200 distinct clients, and their interactions with the application were monitored. A total of 296,100 sessions were documented during the study, creating a robust analytical framework for investigating user interaction patterns.

We established that each session of user exploratory activity may encompass between 1 and 11 page views. This data indicates that user interactions with the platform differ significantly. The users were found to spend a minimum of 1 s and a maximum of 1,349 s on a page. This data indicates that session durations can fluctuate significantly.

The dataset includes comprehensive information regarding the user activities. A total of 43,390,766 events was documented, yielding an average of 8.61 events per session. The maximum number of events documented in a session was established at 11. Furthermore, the dataset includes 46 extensive URLs, offering additional insights into users' interactions on the platform. The average session duration was determined to be 4,976.34 s; this sheds light on the evolution of user activity on the platform over time. Table 1 offers a comprehensive description of the dataset, facilitating a clearer observation of the evolution of user interactions over time.

To improve the reliability and accuracy of the classification results, we chose events that happened at least eight times for the embedding process. We established this criterion to mitigate the risk of brief sequences inadequately capturing significant patterns. By focusing on long interaction sequences, the model aimed to learn from a more stable dataset.

To get a better idea of how the session-based dataset is put together, the event statistics within the session was carefully studied. Consequently, sessions were classified based on the number of events they encompass. Five distinct groups were established: sessions with 1–6 events, those containing 7 events, those with 8 events, those encompassing 8–10 events, and those higher than 10 events. Figure 2 illustrates the distribution of the categories (number of sessions with n pages) within the dataset structure with the session length (number of pages n in a session). This study thus shows how the dataset is organized and what causes differences in session lengths and event frequencies.

Table 1. Dataset Features

	Dataset
Number of Distinct Customers	96.200
Number of Total Sessions	296.100
Number of Large-Scale URLs	46
Unique Event Count	46
Average Number of Events per Session	8,61
Maximum Number of Events per Session	11
Minimum Number of Events per Session	1
Total Number of Events	43.390.766
Time Period for the Dataset	14
Max. and Min. Visiting Page Count Per Session	Min = 1, Max = 11
Max. and Min. Time Spent on a Page	Min = 1 sec, Max = 1349 sec
Average Time Spent in Session	4.976,34 sec

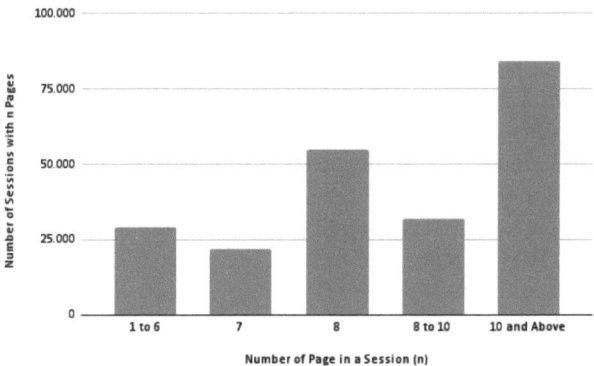

Fig. 2. Number of sessions with event counts for datasets

4.2 Implementation

The proposed method was executed with Python version 3.11.9. The Word2Vec, Node2Vec, and LSTM Autoencoder embedding techniques were implemented using the Gensim (4.2.0) [25], NetworkX [8], and Keras [11] packages, respectively. Apache Spark 3.2.3 [3,16] was employed in data processing and model training to handle large-scale datasets.

The implementation of the proposed approach involves multiple embedding and classification models, each requiring specific hyperparameter settings for optimal performance. Table 2 summarizes the key hyperparameters used in the Word2Vec, Node2Vec, and LSTM Autoencoder embedding techniques, as well as the settings for classification models. These parameters were determined based on prior research and fine-tuning experiments to achieve the best classification accuracy.

Table 2. Hyperparameter Settings for Embedding and Classification Models

Model	Parameter	Value	Description
Word2Vec	Vector Size	64	Dimensionality of word embeddings
	Window Size	5	Context window size
	Min Count	2	Minimum frequency threshold
Node2Vec	Walk Length	10	Number of nodes per walk
	Number of Walks	80	Walks per node
	P/Q Ratio	0.5	Return/In-out parameter
LSTM Autoencoder	Hidden Units	128	Number of LSTM neurons
	Dropout Rate	0.2	Regularization factor
	Batch Size	32	Number of samples per batch
Classification Models	Learning Rate	0.001	Step size for optimizer
	Epochs	20	Number of training iterations
	Optimizer	Adam	Optimization algorithm

We trained the Word2Vec model using the Gensim toolkit to create vector representations of session-based clickstream data within the framework of embedding approaches. The Node2Vec algorithm used graph-based random walks to figure out how the nodes were connected. We trained the node sequences and created vector representations using the Word2Vec model. The LSTM Autoencoder approach generated vector representations that incorporated temporal dependencies by acknowledging the sequential structure of the sessions.

Various ML and deep learning models were employed during the classification phase. We used the Scikit-Learn [14] module to run the GNB, RF, and LR models. Then, we used the results to group the session vectors into different categories. The LSTM-based classifier was developed and trained using the Keras package to analyze consecutive session data and more effectively capture user behavior over time.

We made a unique vector for each session by putting together embedding vectors that matched the PageIDs in that session. A method based on aging was used to give these embedding vectors more weight, which means that recent encounters were given more weight. Lastly, we got the total embedding vector for the session by taking the weighted average of these separate vectors.

This procedure was thoroughly tested to identify session-based user behaviors and model performance by using proposed methods with different classification algorithms.

Our classification task's target variable is a binary label that denotes user engagement (for example, whether or not a session resulted in a particular kind of interaction, like a purchase). The dataset had these labels predefined. To preserve class distribution, the data was stratified into training (80%) and testing (20%) sets.

Regularization strategies like dropout (used in LSTM) and early stopping were used during model training to avoid overfitting. Additionally, a separate holdout test set and stratified 5-fold cross-validation were used to confirm that the model performance was generalizable. Because preprocessing and embedding were rigorously limited to the training set during validation, there was no test set leakage.

4.3 Evaluation

In this section, we test how well the suggested aging-based weighting method works for representing sessions in e-commerce platforms. We tested the performance gains by comparing the aging-based weighting method to the old no-weight strategy using four classification algorithms: GNB, RF, LR, and LSTM. The comparison was made across three embedding methods: Word2Vec, Node2Vec, and LSTM Autoencoder.

4.4 Comparison of Weighting Mechanisms

The no-weight approach assumes uniform importance across all page visits within a session, whereas the aging-based strategy gives higher importance to more recent user actions, capturing the temporal relevance of interactions more realistically.

To go into more depth about the test, the following tables show the classification performance metrics for each embedding method and classifier combination:

- The results for Word2Vec embeddings can be seen in Table 3. It has been shown that aging-based scaling makes a big difference in how well classifiers work, especially GNB (F1: 0.4892 0.8455) and LSTM (F1: 0.7205 0.8763).
- The classification results for Node2Vec are shown in Table 4. It does a great job even without weighing. With aging-based weighting, on the other hand, all models get better than an F1 score of 0.99, showing that adding temporal context is useful.
- The measurements for the LSTM Autoencoder are shown in Table 5. Its performance is already very good, but it gets even better when aging-based weighting is used (e.g., LSTM: 0.9959 0.9999 F1 score).

4.5 Impact of Weighting Strategies on Classification Performance

The observed results can be summarized with the following key findings:

- Aging-based weighting makes classification much better across all models and embeddings, especially in measures like F1 score and Recall that are sensitive to class imbalance.
- No matter how the weights are set, the LSTM classifier always does the best, especially when paired with the LSTM Autoencoder encoding.

Table 3. Classification results using Word2Vec embeddings

Weighting	Metric	GNB	RF	LR	LSTM
No-Weight	F1 Score	0.4892	0.5364	0.5312	0.7205
	Accuracy	0.7038	0.6849	0.6839	0.7908
	Precision	0.9814	0.7461	0.7494	0.9131
	Recall	0.3258	0.4188	0.4114	0.5950
Aging-Based	F1 Score	0.8455	0.8722	0.8215	0.8763
	Accuracy	0.8758	0.8809	0.8586	0.9008
	Precision	0.9223	0.8184	0.9119	0.9587
	Recall	0.7806	0.9335	0.7474	0.8069

Table 4. Classification results using Node2Vec embeddings

Weighting	Metric	GNB	RF	LR	LSTM
No-Weight	F1 Score	0.8869	0.9716	0.9180	0.9776
	Accuracy	0.9074	0.9753	0.9294	0.9804
	Precision	0.9469	0.9724	0.9293	0.9752
	Recall	0.8341	0.9708	0.9069	0.9799
Aging-Based	F1 Score	0.9908	0.9913	0.9913	0.9924
	Accuracy	0.9917	0.9924	0.9924	0.9934
	Precision	0.9972	0.9899	0.9899	0.9887
	Recall	0.9845	0.9927	0.9927	0.9962

- When aging-based weighting and algorithms like RF and LR are used with Word2Vec and Node2Vec embeddings, the results are much better.
- GNB still doesn't work as well as other models because it relies on features not being related to each other and is sensitive to skewed distributions.

4.6 Effect of Embedding Methods

Evaluating different embedding approaches yields further insight into the modeling of user behavior:

- It turns out that LSTM Autoencoder is the best embedding method, working almost perfectly, especially when used with aging-based weighting (Table 5).
- Because it can keep structure relationships when users navigate (Table 4), Node2Vec gives good results, especially when used with ensemble-based classifiers.
- Word2Vec is widely used, but it doesn't work as well as it could because it can't model time or structure (Table 3).

Table 5. Classification results using LSTM Autoencoder embeddings

Weighting	Metric	GNB	RF	LR	LSTM
No-Weight	F1 Score	0.9952	0.9930	0.9940	0.9959
	Accuracy	0.9958	0.9939	0.9948	0.9964
	Precision	0.9907	0.9876	0.9927	0.9929
	Recall	0.9999	0.9985	0.9954	0.9989
Aging-Based	F1 Score	0.9976	0.9984	0.9992	0.9999
	Accuracy	0.9979	0.9985	0.9993	0.9996
	Precision	0.9955	0.9972	0.9987	0.9998
	Recall	0.9998	0.9996	0.9997	0.9999

Given that LSTM architectures naturally capture temporal patterns, the slight improvements in the LSTM Autoencoder model that were seen when aging-based weighting was added are in line with expectations. Even so, modest gains imply that weighting to emphasize time still adds complementary value.

4.7 Final Remarks on Aging-Based Weighting

The study shows that weighting based on age gives a more accurate and time-aware picture of user sessions. This is especially important in dynamic areas like e-commerce. The aging-based method makes the model more sensitive and flexible by giving more weight to recent events in user sessions. This leads to better personalization, more accurate session classification, and a better understanding of how users behave.

Our main goal was to improve classification accuracy, but we know that explainability is important for real-world use. Attention mechanism values can be added to LSTM models to make the temporal effect easier to understand. Ensemble models, like Random Forest, offer feature importance rankings. In the future, work will be done to incorporate these kinds of techniques to make things easier to understand.

5 Conclusion and Future Work

This paper proposes a novel strategy that combines an aging-based weighting mechanism with data embedding techniques to analyze user browsing activity on e-commerce platforms. The proposed method using embedding techniques such as Word2Vec, Node2Vec, and LSTM Autoencoder was observed to enhance the performance of classification algorithms. Using ML algorithms like GNB, RF, LR, and LSTM in experiments shows that the aging-based weighting method accurately describes user sessions and greatly improves classification performance.

Experimental results show that the aging-based weighting outperforms the no-weighting approach in accuracy, precision, recall, and F1 score, among other things. The LSTM-based model demonstrated superior performance due to its capacity to assess sequential user sessions. The RF and LR models performed well on some datasets, however, LSTM was observed to show the highest performance in predicting complex temporal connections.

The results of this study indicate that the aging-based weighting method enhances comprehension of users' evolving interaction patterns over time. It also notably enhanced categorization performance in scenarios when page content fluctuates and users regularly revisit specific pages. We also observed that this approach generates more significant representation vectors and enhances model correctness in web sessions with infrequent occurrences.

In the future, we intend to extend our work to cover hybrid methodologies underpinned by supervised learning techniques. This approach enables the development of proactive recommendation systems through user segmentation and the prediction of future user behaviors. The integration of the aging-based weighting mechanism with some other weighting algorithms to enhance tailored user experiences is a significant field for future research.

The proposed aging-based weighting framework can be applied to other domains that involve sequential interaction data, such as social media content engagement patterns, student learning activities on educational platforms, or patient visit logs in healthcare, despite the fact that this study is based on e-commerce data. This study offers a fundamental approach for time-sensitive behavior modeling, which can be useful in each of these domains.

As a result, using an aging-based weighting mechanism along with data embedding methods and ML can accurately model user navigation in e-commerce platforms. This approach establishes a robust basis for subsequent study and applications in e-commerce analytics.

Acknowledgments. This work was supported by Business Finland within the EUREKA CELTIC-NEXT project CISSAN (www.celticnext.eu). The authors would like to thank Hepsiburada R&D Center, Fibabanka R&D Center, the University of Jyvskyl and Yildiz Technical University management for their support.

References

1. Aktas, M.S., Fox, G.C., Pierce, M.: Fault tolerant high performance information services for dynamic collections of grid and web services. Futur. Gener. Comput. Syst. **23**(3), 317–337 (2007)
2. Bharathi, A.V., Rao, J.M., Tripathy, A.K.: Click stream analysis in e-commerce websites-a framework. In: 2018 Fourth International Conference on Computing Communication Control and Automation (ICCUBEA), pp. 1–5 (2018). https://api.semanticscholar.org/CorpusID:133605302
3. Caswell, T.A., et al.: matplotlib/matplotlib: Rel: v3. 5.0. Zenodo (2021). https://doi.org/10.5281/zenodo.5706396

4. Churc, K.W.: Word2Vec. Nat. Lang. Eng. **23**(1), 155–162 (2017). https://doi.org/10.1017/S1351324916000334
5. Diaz, M., Johnson, I., Lazar, A., Piper, A.M., Gergle, D.: Addressing age-related bias in sentiment analysis. In: Proceedings of the 2018 CHI Conference on Human Factors in Computing Systems, pp. 1–14. CHI 2018, Association for Computing Machinery, New York, NY, USA (2018). https://doi.org/10.1145/3173574.3173986
6. Goyal, P., Ferrara, E.: Graph embedding techniques, applications, and performance: a survey. Knowl. Based Syst. **151**, 78–94 (2018)
7. Grover, A., Leskovec, J.: node2vec: Scalable feature learning for networks. In: Proceedings of the 22nd ACM SIGKDD International Conference on Knowledge Discovery and Data Mining, pp. 855–864 (2016)
8. Hagberg, A., Swart, P., Chult, D.: Exploring network structure, dynamics, and function using networkX (2008). https://doi.org/10.25080/TCWV9851
9. Hamilton, W.L., Ying, R., Leskovec, J.: Representation learning on graphs: methods and applications. IEEE Data Eng. Bull. **40**, 52–74 (2017). https://api.semanticscholar.org/CorpusID:3215337
10. Kang, W.C., McAuley, J.: Self-attentive sequential recommendation. In: 2018 IEEE International Conference on Data Mining (ICDM), pp. 197–206 (2018). https://api.semanticscholar.org/CorpusID:52127932
11. Ketkar, N.: Introduction to Keras, pp. 97–111. Apress, Berkeley, CA (2017). https://doi.org/10.1007/978-1-4842-2766-4_7
12. Khan, R., Gubanov, M.N.: Towards tabular embeddings, training the relational models. In: 2020 IEEE International Conference on Big Data (Big Data), pp. 5724–5726 (2020). https://api.semanticscholar.org/CorpusID:232373210
13. Koehn, D., Lessmann, S., Schaal, M.: Predicting online shopping behaviour from clickstream data using deep learning. Expert Syst. Appl. **150**, 113342 (2020). https://api.semanticscholar.org/CorpusID:214300556
14. Kramer, O.: Scikit-Learn, pp. 45–53. Springer International Publishing, Cham (2016). https://doi.org/10.1007/978-3-319-33383-0_5
15. Li, Z., Jiang, R., Aarabi, P.: Continuous face aging via self-estimated residual age embedding. In: 2021 IEEE/CVF Conference on Computer Vision and Pattern Recognition (CVPR), pp. 15003–15012 (2021). https://api.semanticscholar.org/CorpusID:233481240
16. Van der Maaten, L., Hinton, G.: Visualizing data using T-SNE. J. Mach. Learn. Res. **9**(11), 2579–2605 (2008)
17. Mahdavi, S., Khoshraftar, S., An, A.: dynnode2Vec: scalable dynamic network embedding. In: 2018 IEEE International Conference on Big Data (Big Data), pp. 3762–3765 (2018). https://api.semanticscholar.org/CorpusID:54448357
18. Matsui, A., Ferrara, E.: Extracting fast and slow: user-action embedding with intertemporal information. ArXiv abs/2206.09535 (2022). https://api.semanticscholar.org/CorpusID:249888948
19. Nguyen, H.D., Tran, K.P., Thomassey, S., Hamad, M.: Forecasting and anomaly detection approaches using LSTM and LSTM autoencoder techniques with the applications in supply chain management. Int. J. Inf. Manage. **57**, 102282 (2021)
20. Olmezogullari, E., Aktas, M.S.: Representation of click-stream data sequences for learning user navigational behavior by using embeddings. In: 2020 IEEE International Conference on Big Data (Big Data), pp. 3173–3179 (2020)
21. Olmezogullari, E., Aktas, M.S.: Pattern2Vec: representation of clickstream data sequences for learning user navigational behavior. Concurr. Comput. Pract. Exp. **34**(9), e6546 (2022)

22. Padigela, P.K., Suguna, R.: A survey on analysis of user behavior on digital market by mining clickstream data (2020). https://api.semanticscholar.org/CorpusID:215831952
23. Rahmani, M., Caverlee, J., Wang, F.: Incorporating time in sequential recommendation models. In: Proceedings of the 17th ACM Conference on Recommender Systems, pp. 784–790. RecSys 2023, Association for Computing Machinery, New York, NY, USA (2023). https://doi.org/10.1145/3604915.3608830
24. Ramirez, H., et al.: Determining aging trajectories though hyperbolic embeddings of meg brain networks. Alzheimer's & Dementia **20** (2024). https://api.semanticscholar.org/CorpusID:275432018
25. Řehůřek, R., Sojka, P.: Software framework for topic modelling with large corpora. In: Proceedings of the LREC 2010 Workshop on New Challenges for NLP Frameworks, pp. 45–50. ELRA, Valletta, Malta (2010). http://is.muni.cz/publication/884893/en
26. Rong, X.: word2vec parameter learning explained. ArXiv abs/1411.2738 (2014). https://api.semanticscholar.org/CorpusID:2154019
27. Sahinoglu, M., Incki, K., Aktas, M.S.: Mobile application verification: a systematic mapping study. In: Gervasi, O., Murgante, B., Misra, S., Gavrilova, M.L., Rocha, A., Torre, C., Taniar, D., Apduhan, B.O. (eds.) ICCSA 2015. LNCS, vol. 9159, pp. 147–163. Springer, Cham (2015). https://doi.org/10.1007/978-3-319-21413-9_11
28. Seo, M., Lee, K.Y.: A graph embedding technique for weighted graphs based on LSTM autoencoders. J. Inf. Process. Syst. **16**, 1407–1423 (2020). https://api.semanticscholar.org/CorpusID:234352267
29. Sivakumar, S., Sarvani, L., Videla, Itnal, S., Kumar, R., Haritha, D.: Review on word2vec word embedding neural net. In: 2020 International Conference on Smart Electronics and Communication (ICOSEC), pp. 282–290 (2020). https://api.semanticscholar.org/CorpusID:222222773
30. Skianis, K., Giannopoulos, A., Gkonis, P., Trakadas, P.: Data aging matters: federated learning-based consumption prediction in smart homes via age-based model weighting. Electronics **12**(14) (2023). https://doi.org/10.3390/electronics12143054, https://www.mdpi.com/2079-9292/12/14/3054
31. Taheri, A.: Learning graph representations with recurrent neural network autoencoders (2018). https://api.semanticscholar.org/CorpusID:52235675
32. Tasgetiren, N.: Clickstream of a e-commerce dataset. https://www.kaggle.com/code/nailtasgetiren/clickstream-of-a-e-commerce-dataset (2024). Accessed 7 Mar 2025
33. Tufek, A., Gurbuz, A., Aktas, M.S.: Provenance collection platform for the weather research and forecasting model. In: 2018 14th International Conference on Semantics, Knowledge and Grids (SKG), pp. 17–24 (2018)
34. Wei, J., Shen, Z., Sundaresan, N., Ma, K.L.: Visual cluster exploration of web clickstream data. In: 2012 IEEE Conference on Visual Analytics Science and Technology (VAST), pp. 3–12 (2012). https://api.semanticscholar.org/CorpusID:552440
35. Zhang, Y., Xiong, Y., Li, D., Shan, C., Ren, K., Zhu, Y.: Cope: Modeling continuous propagation and evolution on interaction graph. In: Proceedings of the 30th ACM International Conference on Information & Knowledge Management (2021). https://api.semanticscholar.org/CorpusID:240230819
36. Zhang, Z., Cui, P., Zhu, W.: Deep learning on graphs: a survey. IEEE Trans. Knowl. Data Eng. **34**(01), 249–270 (2022)

37. Zhao, M., Masino, A.J., Yang, C.C.: A framework for developing and evaluating word embeddings of drug-named entity. In: Workshop on Biomedical Natural Language Processing (2018). https://api.semanticscholar.org/CorpusID:51877450
38. Zhou, D., Niu, S., Chen, S.: Efficient graph computation for Node2Vec. ArXiv **abs/1805.00280** (2018). https://api.semanticscholar.org/CorpusID:25752861

Improving the Cloud Provider Ranking in the INDIGO PaaS Orchestration System Using AI Techniques

Luca Giommi[1]( ), Giovanni Savarese[2], Gioacchino Vino[2], Domingo Ranieri[3], Alessandro Costantini[1], and Giacinto Donvito[2]

[1] INFN-CNAF, Viale Berti Pichat 6/2, 40127 Bologna, Italy
luca.giommi@cnaf.infn.it
[2] INFNSezione di Bari, Via Giovanni Amendola 173, 70126 Bari, Italy
{giovanni.savarese,gioacchino.vino,giacinto.donvito}@ba.infn.it
[3] ICSC, DAMA - Tecnopolo Data Manifattura Emilia-Romagna, Via Stalingrado 84/3, 40128 Bologna, Italy
domingo.ranieri@supercomputing-icsc.it

Abstract. The INFN Cloud platform's federation middleware is based on the INDIGO PaaS Orchestration system, which allows handling high-level deployment requests from users while orchestrating the deployment process across the IaaS platforms made available by the federated Cloud providers. Currently, the INDIGO PaaS Orchestrator determines which provider use for creating a deployment based on an ordered list of providers selected according to the user's group. This list is provided by the Cloud Provider Ranker (CPR) service, which applies a ranking algorithm using a limited set of metrics related to the user's request and the Service Level Agreements defined for the providers. The INDIGO PaaS Orchestrator submits the deployment to the first provider on the list and, in case of failure, moves to the next provider until the list is exhausted.

This contribution presents the ongoing activity aimed at improving the provider ranking system by leveraging a broader set of metrics and Artificial Intelligence (AI) techniques. In particular, we introduced Apache Kafka as a message broker to collect heterogeneous information, such as resource usage in federated providers, data on past deployments, and the resources requested by users for new deployments. We then developed the AI-ranker service, based on MLFlow, to replace the CPR, for training and inference of Machine Learning models using the messages read from specific Kafka topics. The ranked list of providers is generated by the AI-ranker by combining the prediction of deployment success/failure with the estimated deployment creation time.

Keywords: Artificial Intelligence · Cloud Computing · PaaS Orchestration System · Orchestrator · Cloud Provider Ranking

1 Introduction

The National Institute for Nuclear Physics (Istituto Nazionale di Fisica Nucleare, INFN) is the leading research institution in Italy specializing in nuclear, particle, theoretical, and astroparticle physics. INFN not only conducts and coordinates scientific research but also drives technological advancements in these fields. Additionally, it oversees the country's most extensive public computing infrastructure for scientific research, supporting more than 40 international collaborations.

In March 2021, INFN started the "INFN Cloud" initiative, designed to establish a federated Cloud infrastructure and provide a customizable portfolio of services tailored to the needs of scientific communities. This offering spans traditional Infrastructure as a Service (IaaS) solutions, alongside more advanced Platform as a Service (PaaS) and Software as a Service (SaaS) options, ensuring flexibility for various research requirements. At the core of INFN Cloud lies a middleware system based on the INDIGO PaaS Orchestration framework, which integrates interconnected open-source microservices. Among these, the INDIGO PaaS Orchestrator is responsible for handling deployment requests and managing resource provisioning across federated Cloud providers. By default, it selects a provider based on a prioritized list derived from user group memberships. This ranking is dynamically generated by the Cloud Provider Ranker (CPR), which applies an algorithm that considers a limited set of deployment metrics and the Service Level Agreements (SLAs) established for each provider. The Orchestrator initially attempts the deployment with the highest-ranked provider, and if unsuccessful, moves sequentially through the list until all options have been exhausted.

This paper presents an ongoing effort to enhance the Cloud provider ranking system by incorporating a more extensive set of metrics and leveraging Artificial Intelligence (AI) techniques. The objective is to improve the efficiency and accuracy of deployment decisions within the federated Cloud infrastructure by utilizing historical data. A key aspect of this approach is the integration of Apache Kafka [4] as a message broker, allowing for the continuous collection and processing of data from multiple sources. Among the collected information are real-time resource utilization metrics from federated Cloud providers and user-defined resource requirements for new deployment requests. To replace the existing CPR, we developed an advanced AI-driven ranking service called AI-Ranker [1]. Built on MLflow [17], AI-Ranker is designed to perform both training and inference of Machine Learning (ML) models by consuming structured messages from dedicated Kafka topics. By adopting this AI-based ranking approach, the system can dynamically adjust to evolving infrastructure conditions, improving decision-making and optimizing resource utilization across the federated Cloud.

The structure of the paper is as follows. Section 2 provides an overview of the INFN Cloud ecosystem, including its federated infrastructure and available services. Section 3 describes the INDIGO PaaS Orchestration system, outlining its components and workflow. Section 4 presents an initial attempt to leverage AI techniques to enhance the Cloud provider ranking mechanism. This process involved defining data sources, identifying the information to be collected, creating the dataset with data preprocessing, training the models, and evaluating their performance. Section 5 details the implementation of the Kafka-based service for data collection and aggregation, as well as the AI-Ranker service for training and inference of ML models. Finally, Sect. 6 summarizes the work and outlines future directions.

2 The INFN Cloud Ecosystem

To maximize the efficiency of available resources and expertise, INFN developed a national Cloud infrastructure for research, designed with three key principles in mind.

- **Federation of distributed infrastructures**: integrating existing infrastructures while transparently extending them to private Cloud providers when needed.
- **User-centric approach**: offering a dynamic set of tailored services to meet the specific needs of the scientific communities.
- **Building on past initiatives**: leveraging the results of various national and European Cloud projects in which INFN actively participated, such as the INDIGO-DataCloud project [25].

The INFN Cloud infrastructure is built on a core backbone, connecting at high speed the CNAF and Bari data centers, where the core Cloud services are hosted. This backbone connects to a network of loosely coupled federated sites, which currently include Cloud-CNAF, ReCaS-Bari, Cloud-Veneto, Cloud-INFN-Catania, and Cloud-Ibisco-Napoli. Moreover, INFN Cloud offers a broad range of services categorized into IaaS, PaaS and SaaS, allowing users to interact with the infrastructure at different levels.

- **SaaS (e.g., Notebook as a Service)**: ready-to-use solutions requiring no user customization.
- **PaaS (e.g., Virtual Machine (VM) or Kubernetes [15] cluster provisioning)**: configurable on-demand services, where users can, for example, select the OS and specify the compute resource flavor.
- **IaaS (e.g., starting and stopping VMs)**: direct infrastructure-level operations that users can execute as needed.

All services are accessible through a user-friendly interface, the INFN Cloud Dashboard [8], see Fig. 1. Advanced users can also interact with the platform programmatically through REST APIs, a command-line interface (CLI), and Python bindings.

The PaaS services available in the INFN Cloud portfolio of services are managed using an Infrastructure as Code (IaC) approach, ensuring automation, flexibility, and portability across different environments through a combination of:

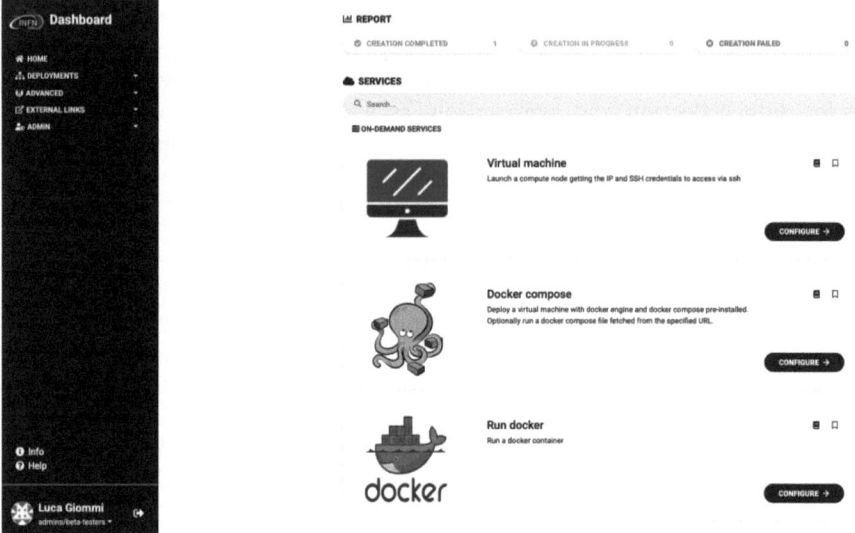

Fig. 1. The INFN Cloud dashboard. It allows users to access centralized services, instantiate PaaS services independently, and access IaaS solutions. The PaaS services available in the dashboard depend on the user group.

- **Topology and Orchestration Specification for Cloud Applications (TOSCA) templates** [29], used to model an application stack by defining its components, relationships, and deployment lifecycle;
- **Ansible roles** [2], which facilitate the automated configuration and management of virtual environments;
- **Docker containers** [5], employed to encapsulate high-level application software along with its dependencies and runtime environment;
- **Helm charts** [6], used to define, package, and manage the deployment of applications in Kubernetes clusters.

In INFN Cloud, each PaaS service is associated with a dedicated TOSCA template [30] that leverages extended INDIGO-DataCloud custom types [31]. A Lego-like approach has been adopted, leveraging modular and reusable components while utilizing the TOSCA service composition pattern.

3 The PaaS Orchestration System

The federation middleware of the INFN Cloud platform is built upon the INDIGO PaaS Orchestration system, which integrates a set of interconnected open-source microservices [3], see Fig. 2. These microservices establish an abstraction layer that facilitates seamless access to compute and storage resources provided by diverse and heterogeneous Cloud infrastructures. Currently in INFN Cloud, all the federated providers make available an instance of

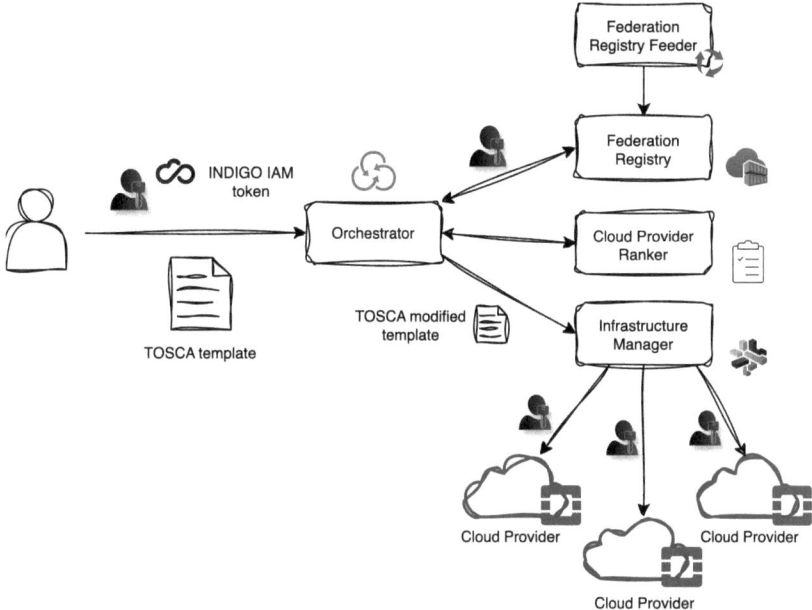

Fig. 2. High-level architecture and workflow of the PaaS Orchestration system. More details are provided in the text.

OpenStack [20] while the backbone provides two different OpenStack implementations, one at CNAF and one at INFN-Bari, which act as a single one with two regions. The core component of such a system is the INDIGO PaaS Orchestrator [21] which takes the information about the user's request in the form of a TOSCA template and interacts with the Federation Registry service to get information about the available providers and their capabilities (e.g. about flavors, images, and networks) [26]. The Federation Registry is populated by the Federation Registry Feeder that periodically contacts the OpenStack sites to collect information about the available resources. Then the CPR, using a limited set of deployment metrics and the SLAs established for each provider, gives to the Orchestrator an ordered list of providers where send the deployment request. The Orchestrator modifies and extends the TOSCA template submitted by the user and sends it to the Infrastructure Manager (IM) service [10] (the low-level orchestrator, at the IaaS level) that contacts the OpenStack site chosen by the Orchestrator for the provisioning of the resources. The Orchestrator tries the submission to the first provider in the list and, in case of failure, moves to the next provider until the list is exhausted.

Another essential component of the platform is the Authentication and Authorization Infrastructure, implemented through the INDIGO Identity and Access Management (INDIGO IAM) [7] service. This system governs authentication and authorization across all layers of INFN Cloud, including IaaS, PaaS, and SaaS services. To access the Orchestrator's APIs, a user must present a

JSON Web Token (JWT) [11] issued by the INFN Cloud INDIGO IAM service. This token contains a *groups* claim that specifies the INDIGO IAM groups the user belongs to. Each group corresponds to a scientific community, collaboration, or experiment and is mapped to dedicated OpenStack projects within the federated Cloud infrastructure. After a token exchange operation, the Orchestrator obtains a token from the INDIGO IAM service, which is then used in the request to the IM to access the IaaS-level services and create the required resources.

4 A First Study on Enhancing the Cloud Provider Ranking System with AI

To enhance the Cloud provider ranking mechanism of the PaaS Orchestration system, we adopted a Data Science approach and worked on integrating AI techniques. As a first step, we conducted an initial attempt to assess the feasibility of this approach and to explore the potential of the available data [16]. A key aspect of this work was to identify relevant information for the use case, determine where to find it, and establish methods for its collection. Below, we report the available data sources and the types of stored information.

- **Monitoring database**: contains information about resource usage over time, categorized by user group and by provider.
- **Rally** [24] **service**: provides data on simple tests periodically run on various providers, e.g. VMs creation.
- **Orchestrator Dashboard database**: stores information about all deployments.
- **Orchestrator logs**: maintain a complete history of all deployments.
- **Accounting**: offers aggregated data on resource usage over time, grouped by user and provider.
- **Orchestrator database**: tracks deployments that have not yet been deleted.

The last two sources were discarded, as their information was either already available in the other sources or considered superfluous. Then we defined the list of information to extract from the sources, that are: deployment ID, deployment creation time, provider name, user group, selected TOSCA template, resources requested by the user for the deployment (in terms of CPU, RAM, number of volumes, disk size of the volumes, number of VMs, floating IPs, request of GPU), quotas and resource usage by group and provider (in terms of CPU, RAM, number of volumes, disk size of the volumes, number of VMs, floating IPs), failure rate of simple tests run periodically on various providers, status of a deployment, creation/failure time of a deployment, average creation time of a deployment in the last month by deployment type and provider, deployment failure rate in the last month by deployment type and provider. Additionally, we included some static information obtained by contacting the administrators of the federated sites, i.e. bandwidth and overbooking for CPU and RAM.

The deployment type is determined by the name of the selected TOSCA template used to submit the deployment request. We grouped the templates into five categories based on different service types: single VM, which can be deployed with or without an external volume and on a private network or not; single VM with services, where the services can include Sync&Share, INDIGO-IAM, or Elasticsearch and Kibana; Docker, used for the Docker Run and Docker Compose services, with or without an external volume; K8s, which includes both simple Kubernetes clusters and configurations with Kafka, HTCondor, and Spark, deployed on a private network or not; Jupyter, which includes the Jupyter-Hub/Lab service on a single VM, on a private network or not, with or without Matlab installed, and the services used for the Jupyter-based platforms of the Cygno and ML_INFN experiments. See [9] for more details about the services offered by INFN Cloud.

A dataset was created with the aforementioned information collected from the corresponding data sources. In particular, a dump of the Orchestrator Dashboard database and the Monitoring database was made, Rally data was collected using the OpenSearch [19] tool, and Orchestrator logs were gathered by the SysLog server. We considered a time window of 6 months, from the 4th of August, 2023, to the 25th of January, 2024, with a total of 643 deployments. When constructing the dataset, an entry is added for each provider that was attempted for a deployment. For instance, if a deployment is submitted to four different providers, the dataset will include four entries. See Table 1 for the distribution of deployments that ended with success or failure by deployment type during this period.

Table 1. Distribution of deployments by outcome (success or failure) and deployment type within a specific time window. More details are provided in the text.

Deployment type	# of successes	# of failures
Single VM	137	67
Single VM with services	19	23
K8s	124	159
Docker	38	41
Jupyter	25	10
Total	**343**	**300**

The obtained dataset was cleaned by removing outliers, mapping strings to integers (e.g., deployments with the *CREATE_COMPLETE* status were mapped to 0, those with the *CREATE_FAILED* status to 1, while other deployment statuses were excluded), and eliminating redundant features based on the correlation matrix, using a 90% threshold.

Given the limited number of entries in the dataset, we decided to generate new features that aggregate information from multiple existing ones, replacing them. Specifically, we introduced features that measure the difference between the available quota of a resource and its current usage, further adjusted by subtracting the amount requested by the user. For example, we defined ram_diff as:

$ram\_diff = (quota\_ram - ram\_used) - requested\_ram$. Additionally, we introduced a new feature to represent deployment complexity, replacing the original deployment type feature. To define this, we analyzed the distribution of deployments based on their creation/failure times across different deployment types, as shown in Fig. 3. This analysis revealed two distinct categories with different behaviors: both peak at low time values but differ in tail length, one with a short tail and the other with a long tail. The first category (Single VM and Docker deployments) was assigned a complexity value of 0, whereas the second category (Single VM with services, K8s, and Jupyter deployments) was assigned a complexity value of 1.

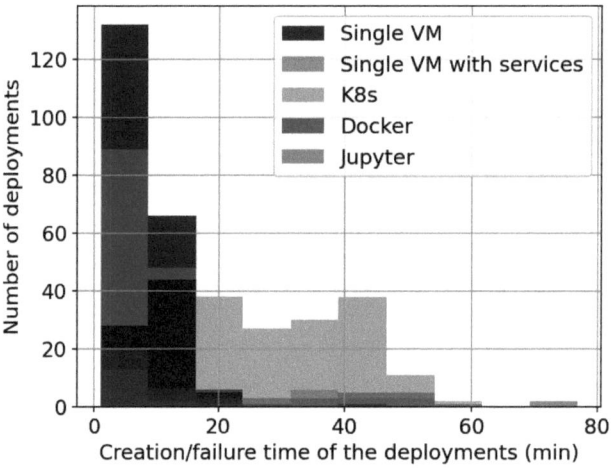

Fig. 3. Number of deployments by creation/failure time. More details are provided in the text.

Finally, after applying the aforementioned preprocessing steps, we defined eleven metrics as input features for the ML models. These features were normalized using the Min-Max normalization technique, which scales the data to the fixed range of $[-1, 1]$.

4.1 Model Design, Training, and Performance Evaluation

Two ML models were defined: one for classifying the deployment status (success/failure) and another for predicting the deployment creation/failure time using regression. For training, a sliding window approach with fixed-size data segments was adopted, where predictions were made on the subsequent time window. This process was iterated by shifting the windows along the time axis. A study was conducted to determine the optimal window size, resulting in the selection of 75 entries for training and 10 for performance evaluation. This configuration yielded the highest average accuracy of 0.692 for the Random Forest classification model. For the classification task, multiple ML models were evaluated using their default hyperparameters, specifically: Decision Tree, Random Forest, XGBoost, AdaBoost, and Neural Network. The Area Under the Curve (AUC) was then computed by aggregating predictions across all time windows, and the Receiver Operating Characteristic (ROC) curve was plotted (see Fig. 4). The highest AUC value (0.80) was achieved with the Random Forest model. For the regression task, different models were compared, highlighting the need for further improvements.

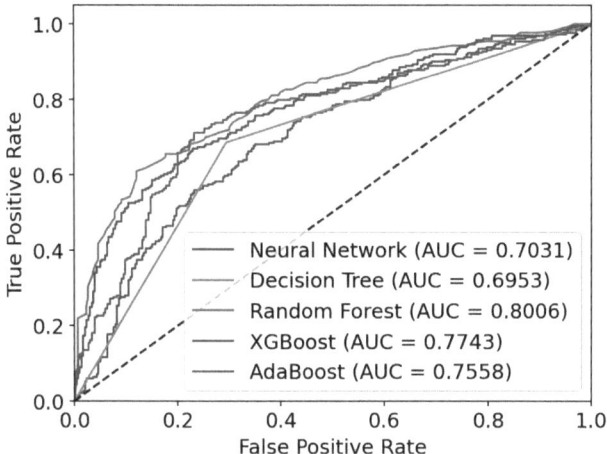

Fig. 4. ROC curves for the tested ML models.

5 Implementation of an AI-Based Service to Improve the Cloud Provider Ranking

The work presented in Sect. 4 served as a preparatory study to assess the feasibility of the proposed approach and to identify the available information and data sources. To enhance the Cloud provider ranking system and, consequently, improve the overall efficiency of the deployment process using AI techniques, we need to develop a service that can be integrated into the PaaS Orchestration system. The implementation consists of two main phases. The first phase focuses on introducing a service capable of collecting and aggregating heterogeneous information relevant to the use case, for which we selected Kafka as the core technology. The second phase involves the development of a service called AI-Ranker, dedicated to the training and inference of ML models, with MLflow as the core framework. In the following we provide details on both phases.

5.1 Data Collection and Aggregation Using Kafka

Apache Kafka is a distributed streaming platform designed for building real-time data pipelines and streaming applications. It provides a highly scalable, fault-tolerant, and durable mechanism for publishing and subscribing to streams of records. In Kafka, data is organized into queues called topics. Topics can be further divided into partitions, which are replicated across the cluster to ensure fault tolerance. A Kafka cluster can consist of a single node or multiple nodes (typically an odd number) to enhance fault tolerance. Actors that write data are called producers, while those that read data are called consumers. Kafka also offers features such as high-throughput and low-latency data processing, making it suitable for a wide range of applications, including log aggregation, stream processing, and event-driven microservices. Other technologies, such as RabbitMQ [23], can be used as alternatives to Kafka, as they provide similar key features, including fault tolerance, persistence, and ease of use. An internal evaluation determined that Kafka and RabbitMQ offer equivalent functionality. However, Kafka was preferred due to the existing expertise within the team with this technology.

In Fig. 5, we present the architecture of the Kafka-based service designed to collect and aggregate relevant information, make it available to the AI-Ranker service, and provide the Orchestrator with a sorted list of providers. The architecture consists of four main components: the Kafka cluster, the Kafka producers, the Kafka consumer, and the Kafka processors.

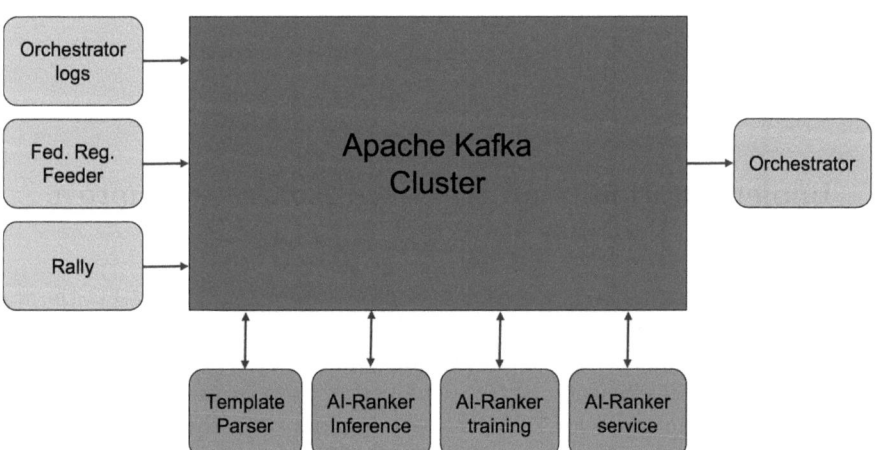

Fig. 5. Architecture of the Kafka-based service. At the center is the Kafka cluster, on the left are the producers, on the right is the Orchestrator as consumer, and below are the processors.

At the center is the Kafka cluster, which manages internal topics where messages are read and written. On the left are the producers, Kafka components responsible for collecting information and data from outside the cluster and writing it into specific topics. On the right is the Orchestrator as consumer. Below the Kafka cluster are the processors, which are responsible for transforming messages read from some topics and writing them back into other topics. Unlike producers and consumers, processors interact exclusively with Kafka. JSON was chosen as the message format because it is easily readable by both machines and humans. The Kafka components were developed in Python when implemented in-house and then containerized, otherwise official Docker images were used. Currently, the Kafka cluster consists of a single broker, and the microservices related to the different components run on the same machine where the Kafka cluster is deployed. In the following, details about the producers and processors are provided.

Orchestrator Logs Producer. Orchestrator logs contain information about the history of submitted deployments. To reduce the number of sources from which Kafka retrieves information, we decided to enrich the logs with data previously obtained from the Orchestrator Dashboard database. The Orchestrator sends its logs to the SysLog server, and to make them available to Kafka, we configured the local rsyslog service to forward them to an additional component that listens on a specific port for incoming logs (in syslog format) and forwards them to the *orchestrator-logs* Kafka topic.

Rally Producer. The Rally producer collects Rally test outputs, extracts the most relevant information, and sends it to the Kafka cluster in the *rally* topic. Currently, the component does not interact directly with Rally (although it will in the future) but only with its result output files. The producer is executed every 5 min and checks if new files are present in a specified folder. If new files are found, it imports all data related to the Rally test outcomes and extracts the most relevant information. After this step, it reads all messages present in the *rally* topic. In this way, any information not already present in the topic will be written to it, avoiding duplicate messages. Each message contains information about the provider where the test was executed, the final state of the test (either *finished* or *crashed*), a tag that provides more information about the type of test executed, and finally the timestamp.

Federation Registry Feeder Producer. The Federation Registry Feeder producer collects monitoring information from Cloud providers within the INFN Cloud federation, converts it into a JSON format, and writes messages to the *federation-registry-feeder* topic. Currently, the component executes this procedure periodically every 15 min. For each Cloud provider, it collects information about available projects, and for each project, it gathers data on state, resource usage, quotas, available flavors, and images.

Template Parser Processor. This component reads the user-submitted data, i.e. the TOSCA template and parameters, and validates it. This information is collected from the Orchestrator logs and stored in the *orchestrator-logs* Kafka topic. The validation of the template involves checking its compliance with the YAML format, verifying that the user has provided values for all required parameters, ensuring these values are consistent with the parameter types, and performing other necessary checks. Once validated and enriched with user-provided parameters, the template is written in JSON format to the *validated-template* Kafka topic.

AI-Ranker Inference Processor. This component starts its execution when a new message is read from the *validated-template* topic. It writes a message to the *ai-ranker-inference* Kafka topic with information about the validated template and details of all federated sites that can be used to deploy the service requested by the user. The latter information is retrieved from the *federation-registry-feeder* and *rally* topics. From the *rally* topic, the percentage of failed Rally tests over three periods is collected: one day, one week, and one month. When the inference component of the AI-Ranker service receives this message, it applies AI models to return a sorted list of federated sites that can be used by the Orchestrator for the deployment submission (see Sect. 5.2), which is then written to the *ranked-providers* topic. In this context, the inference component of the AI-Ranker service can be considered as an additional processor.

AI-Ranker Training Processor. The training-data processor collects information about the outcomes of deployment attempts in the federated sites from the *orchestrator-logs* topic, uses it to compute additional metrics, merges it with messages from the *ai-ranker-inference* topic regarding the selected provider(s), and writes the resulting data to the *ai-ranker-training* Kafka topic, which is consumed by the training component of the AI-Ranker. Specifically, for each federated site where the deployment was attempted, it computes the submission timestamp, the time spent to complete the deployment (in seconds), the number of failures, the failure reason (if any), and the cumulative time spent on failed attempts.

5.2 The AI-Ranker Service

During the design phase of the AI-Ranker to be integrated into the PaaS Orchestration system, we evaluated different technologies that could support the various phases of the ML lifecycle. In particular, we focused on Kubeflow [13] and MLflow, analyzing their strengths, differences, and limitations [14].

- **Kubeflow.** A Kubernetes-native platform designed to support end-to-end ML workflows, from data preprocessing and model training to hyperparameter tuning, serving, and monitoring. It provides a scalable and modular architecture where different components, such as Kubeflow Pipelines, Katib for

hyperparameter optimization, and KFServing for model deployment, work together to automate and streamline ML operations. By leveraging Kubernetes, Kubeflow ensures efficient resource allocation and workload distribution, making it particularly suitable for large-scale deployments and production environments with high computational demands. However, its complex setup and steep learning curve pose significant challenges, requiring in-depth knowledge of Kubernetes and additional infrastructure management efforts.
- **MLflow**. A lightweight, open-source platform designed to manage the ML lifecycle with a focus on experiment tracking, model versioning, and deployment. Unlike Kubeflow, MLflow is not tied to Kubernetes and can be deployed on any Cloud or local environment. It consists of four main components: MLflow Tracking (for logging experiments), MLflow Projects (for packaging and reproducing ML code on any platform), MLflow Models (for model versioning and deployment), and MLflow Registry (for managing different model versions). MLflow is particularly effective when used in combination with existing ML training workflows, providing a straightforward and easy-to-use interface for tracking and managing models. However, it lacks native support for complex pipeline orchestration and automated resource management. Additionally, MLflow's model serving capabilities are limited compared to those of Kubernetes-based solutions like KFServing, which offer more advanced scaling and inference optimizations.

Kubeflow and MLflow address different needs within the ML lifecycle: while Kubeflow is a powerful, MLOps framework suitable for large-scale and production-ready deployments, MLflow strengths are simplicity, flexibility, and model management. Since our use case does not involve complex pipelines or large datasets, is not intended to be used directly by large user communities, and aims to be deployable on any infrastructure without requiring a Kubernetes cluster, we chose MLflow as the core technology for our AI-Ranker service. This choice ensures easier integration into the PaaS Orchestration system, greater deployment flexibility, and a solution better suited to the scale and complexity of our needs.

We developed the AI-Ranker in three main components: training service, model registry service, and inference service, all based on the MLflow framework. The training and inference services are written in Python and containerized using Docker, while for the model registry service, we used the official MLflow Docker image. We employed Ofelia [18] as a job scheduler to trigger the training service at predefined intervals. Specifically, the actions performed by the training component are listed below.

- Reading of all messages in the *ai-ranker-training* Kafka topic.
- Preprocessing of the data, including outlier removal, normalization, and feature engineering.
- Training of ML models using the preprocessed data, with the option to perform k-fold cross-validation and select the best model based on performance metrics. Two types of ML models are used: classification models to predict

deployment success or failure, and regression models to predict deployment creation time. Currently, only ML models based on the scikit-learn library [27] are supported.
- Storing the (best) trained ML models in the MLflow model registry, along with relevant metadata, performance metrics, and artifacts (e.g. the scaler).

One of the advantages of MLflow is that it allows logging a wealth of information about training runs on the server, enabling us to track model performance, the hyperparameters used, training time, the features considered, and their importance. This information can be monitored through the MLflow UI, which provides a user-friendly interface for visualizing and comparing different training runs. An example is shown in Fig. 6.

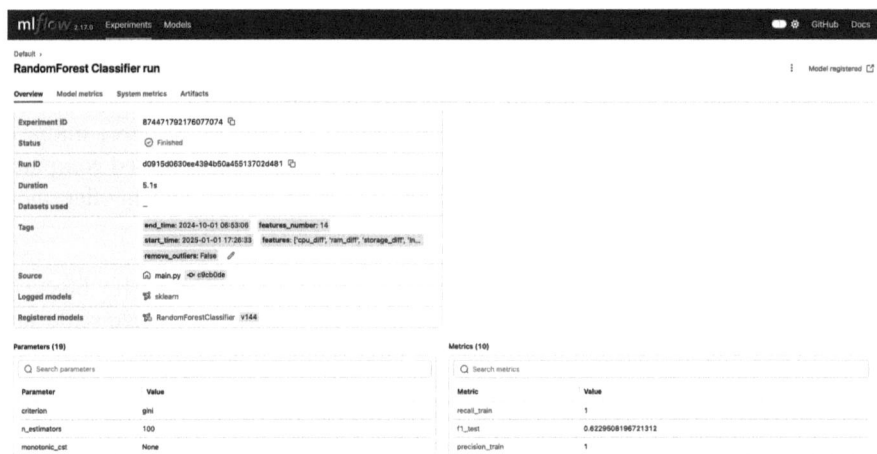

Fig. 6. Partial overview of the information saved in the MLflow registry after a training run.

The inference component of the AI-Ranker listens to the *ai-ranker-inference* Kafka topic, and when a new message is read, it performs the following actions:

- reads the message from the *ai-ranker-inference* Kafka topic;
- preprocesses the data;
- loads the classification and regression models from the MLflow model registry;
- performs inference using the loaded models and the preprocessed data;
- computes the ranking of providers by combining the predictions obtained from the two models, giving priority to those providers that offer the exact flavor(s) requested for the deployment;
- writes the ranked list of providers to the *ranked-providers* Kafka topic.

6 Conclusions and Outlook

In this paper, we presented the ongoing activity aimed at improving the Cloud provider ranking mechanism within the PaaS Orchestration system of the INFN Cloud platform. In Sect. 4, we described an initial study that helped us understand the available data sources and the information that can be extracted, as well as explore the potential use of AI techniques for this use case. The next step was to develop a service that could be integrated into the PaaS Orchestration system, as described in Sect. 5. The proposed solution involved the introduction of a Kafka-based service to collect, aggregate, and process relevant information from various sources, along with the development of the AI-Ranker service responsible for training and inference of ML models. Currently, the developed services are deployed in a pre-production environment, which helps assess the system's performance, determine if improvements are needed, and test their integration within the PaaS Orchestration system. In particular, for the Kafka-based service, the next steps should include implementing service monitoring, encrypting the messages exchanged between components, and expanding the cluster to three nodes to enhance fault tolerance and performance. For the AI-Ranker service, we plan to generate and store plots of the trained models' performance metrics in the MLflow server, integrate additional ML frameworks (such as Keras [12], TensorFlow [28], and PyTorch [22]), and allow users to upload the complete definition of the ML models to be used.

Acknowledgements. The work presented in this paper has been funded by the NextGenerationEU European initiative through the Italian Ministry of University and Research, PNRR Mission 4, Component 2 - TeRABIT: Investment 3.1, Project code IR0000022 - CUP I53C21000370006. The authors have no competing interests to declare that are relevant to the content of this article.

Disclosure of Interests. The authors have no competing interests to declare that are relevant to the content of this article.

References

1. AI-Ranker. https://github.com/infn-datacloud/ai-ranker. Accessed 04 Apr 2025
2. Ansible roles. https://docs.ansible.com/ansible/latest/playbook_guide/playbooks_reuse_roles.html. Accessed 04 Apr 2025
3. Antonacci, M., Salomoni, D.: Leveraging TOSCA orchestration to enable fully automated cloud-based research environments on federated heterogeneous e-infrastructures. PoS **ISGC&HEPiX2023**, 020 (2023). https://doi.org/10.22323/1.434.0020
4. Apache Kafka. https://kafka.apache.org. Accessed 04 Apr 2025
5. Docker containers. https://www.docker.com/resources/what-container/. Accessed 04 Apr 2025
6. Helm charts. https://helm.sh/docs/topics/charts/. Accessed 04 Apr 2025

7. INDIGO-IAM. https://indigo-iam.github.io/v/v1.11.0/docs/. Accessed 04 Apr 2025
8. INFN Cloud dashboard. https://my.cloud.infn.it. Accessed 04 Apr 2025
9. The INFN Cloud Use Cases Documentation. https://guides.cloud.infn.it/docs/users-guides/en/latest/index.html. Accessed 04 Apr 2025
10. Infrastructure Manager. https://github.com/grycap/im. Accessed 04 Apr 2025
11. JSON Web Tokens. https://auth0.com/docs/secure/tokens/json-web-tokens. Accessed 04 Apr 2025
12. Keras. https://keras.io. Accessed 04 Apr 2025
13. Kubeflow. https://www.kubeflow.org. Accessed 04 Apr 2025
14. Kubeflow vs MLFlow: which one to choose?. https://ubuntu.com/blog/kubeflow-vs-mlflow. Accessed 04 Apr 2025
15. Kubernetes. https://kubernetes.io. Accessed 04 Apr 2025
16. Giommi, L., Debiase, F., Savarese, G., Vino, G., Antonacci, M., Donvito, G., Costantini, A.: AI-based approach for provider selection in the INDIGO PaaS Orchestration System of INFN Cloud. In: Proceedings of the Conference on Computing in High Energy and Nuclear Physics 2024 (2025). Submitted, under review
17. MLflow. https://mlflow.org. Accessed 04 Apr 2025
18. Ofelia - a job scheduler. https://github.com/mcuadros/ofelia. Accessed 04 Apr 2025
19. OpenSearch. https://opensearch.org. Accessed 04 Apr 2025
20. OpenStack. https://www.openstack.org. Accessed 04 Apr 2025
21. Orchestrator. https://github.com/infn-datacloud/orchestrator. Accessed 04 Apr 2025
22. PyTorch. https://pytorch.org. Accessed 04 Apr 2025
23. RabbitMQ. https://www.rabbitmq.com. Accessed 04 Apr 2025
24. Rally. https://rally.readthedocs.io/en/latest/overview/overview.html. Accessed 04 Apr 2025
25. Salomoni, D., et al.: INDIGO-Datacloud: foundations and architectural description of a platform as a service oriented to scientific computing. CoRR arxiv:abs/1603.09536 (2016). http://arxiv.org/abs/1603.09536
26. Savarese, G., Antonacci, M., Giommi, L.: Federation-registry: the renovated configuration management database for dynamic cloud federation. In: International Symposium on Grids & Clouds (ISGC) 2024, p. 21 (2024)
27. scikit-learn. https://scikit-learn.org. Accessed 04 Apr 2025
28. TensorFlow. https://www.tensorflow.org/. Accessed 04 Apr 2025
29. TOSCA Simple Profile in YAML Version 1.1. http://docs.oasis-open.org/tosca/TOSCA-Simple-Profile-YAML/v1.1/csprd01/TOSCA-Simple-Profile-YAML-v1.1-csprd01.html. Accessed 04 Apr 2025
30. TOSCA templates. https://baltig.infn.it/infn-cloud/tosca-templates. Accessed 04 Apr 2025
31. TOSCA types. https://baltig.infn.it/infn-cloud/tosca-types. Accessed 04 Apr 2025

Artificial Intelligence for Detecting Cultural Heritage Issues on Overtourism Literature: A Topic Modeling Application

Laura Claudia Verdesca[ID], Elisabetta Ronchieri[(✉)][ID], and Alessandro Costantini[ID]

INFN CNAF, Viale Berti Pichat 6/2, Bologna, Italy
elisabetta.ronchieri@cnaf.infn.it

Abstract. Cultural heritage requires protection for preservation. Artificial Intelligence technologies present innovative methods to extract valuable insights from digital literature and understand complex themes in literary data.

This study applies artificial intelligence methods to cultural heritage literature in order to detect overtourism impacts on the preservation of cultural artifacts and historical sites.

Six different topic modeling techniques-Latent Dirichlet Allocation, Latent Semantic Indexing, Hierarchical Dirichlet Process, Non-Negative Matrix Factorization, Structural Topic Modeling, and Correlated Topic Modeling-have been used to determine topics.

The analysis reveals that overtourism is a multifaceted issue that significantly impacts cultural heritage. Many topics overlap across different models, such as overtourism and its impact, and cultural heritage and identity.

Keywords: Artificial Intelligence · Overtourism · Cultural Heritage · Topic Modeling

1 Introduction

Overtourism is a pressing global phenomenon characterized by an excessive number of tourists in popular destinations, leading to negative impacts on local communities, environments, and cultural heritage. As defined by [1], overtourism occurs when the volume of tourists exceeds the capacity of the infrastructure to accommodate them, resulting in strained resources and a decreased quality of life for residents. Cities, such as Venice, Barcelona, and Amsterdam, have experienced significant challenges due to the influx of tourists, leading to social conflicts, environmental degradation, and economic disparities [2].

Given the growing relevance of overtourism in tourism studies, it is crucial to conduct a comprehensive literature review to understand the underlying issues and trends with respect to cultural heritage. This study aims at identifying the key themes, challenges, and solutions presented in the existing research in order to develop effective management strategies. Furthermore, synthesizing the literature provides a solid foundation for future research and policy-making in sustainable tourism.

To systematically review the literature on overtourism, various topic modeling techniques have been employed, including Latent Dirichlet Allocation (LDA) [3], Latent Semantic Indexing (LSI) [4], Hierarchical Dirichlet Process (HDP) [5], Non-negative Matrix Factorization (NMF) [6], Structural Topic Modeling (STM) [7], and Correlated Topic Modeling (CTM) [8]. These techniques uncover latent themes and patterns in the literature, facilitating a deeper understanding of how overtourism is conceptualized and addressed in scholarly work. Furthermore, using multiple models ensures that the identified themes are consistent across different artificial intelligence (AI) technologies.

The `Gensim` Python library has been used to implement the LDA, LSI, HDP, and NMF models, while `Seaborn` and `Matplotlib` Python libraries have been employed for data visualization. In addition to Python, the R programming language has been essential in our analysis: the `stm` package in R has supported the implementation of the Structural Topic Model (STM), while the `topicmodels` package has been used to apply the Correlated Topic Model (CTM).

2 Dataset Definition and Preprocessing Phase

To develop the raw dataset, a systematic search has been conducted by using the keyword "overtourism" across two prominent databases: Scopus and Web of Science. This process has yielded 439 articles from Scopus and 471 articles from Web of Science. After removing duplicates, a comprehensive dataset of 698 articles has been defined. Further refinement has involved the removal of articles without abstracts, resulting in a final dataset of 662 articles suitable for analysis.

The earliest articles on overtourism in our dataset date back to 2017, highlighting that this issue has gained considerable attention in the past decade (see Fig. 1). The growing number of studies from a variety of journals underscores the multidisciplinary nature of overtourism, involving fields, such as environmental science, economics, urban planning, and social studies. This diversity of perspectives has enriched our understanding and has emphasized the complex, interconnected challenges of managing tourism sustainably.

A preprocessing pipeline has been defined to prepare the dataset for topic modeling analysis and includes several key steps for standardizing and cleaning the text data. First, all text has been converted into lowercase, ensuring consistency across words regardless of capitalization. Then, we have removed links, accented characters, and punctuation, reducing noise by eliminating irrelevant content and ensuring uniformity. Digits and single-character tokens have also been removed to further minimize extraneous data. Contractions have been expanded (e.g., "don't" has been transformed into "do not") to maintain semantic integrity. Next, tokenization has split the text into individual words or "tokens", enabling more precise text analysis. Stopwords, including both standard and

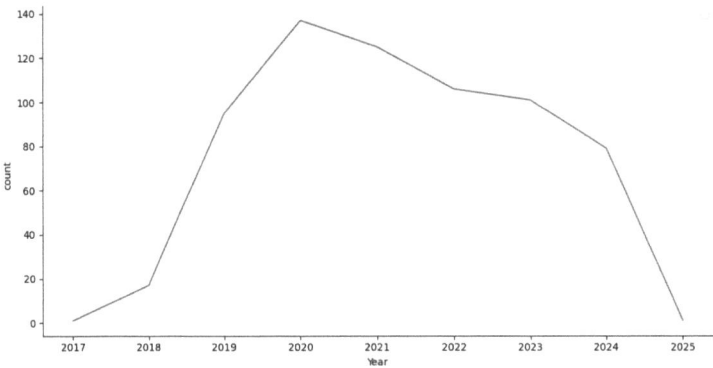

Fig. 1. Number of published papers per year - line chart showing the count papers from 2017 to 2025. The count increases from 2017, peaks around 2020, and then gradually declined towards 2025.

domain-specific terms, have been removed to concentrate on the core content. Finally, lemmatization has reduced words to their root forms, enhancing coherence by grouping variations of the same word. Together, these preprocessing steps have refined the text corpus, setting the stage for reliable and interpretable topic modeling results.

2.1 Initial Analysis

With the computations of unigrams and bigrams, we have identified the occurrence terms that have prominently emerged in the dataset:

- ***tourism***: A central term, as the concept of overtourism directly examines the negative aspects of excessive tourism in popular locations.
- ***destination***: Refers to the targeted places for tourism, often locations suffering from overtourism due to their appeal and limited capacity.
- ***heritage***: Indicates areas rich in cultural or natural heritage that are often highly vulnerable to degradation from overcrowding.
- ***negative impact***: Describes the adverse outcomes of overtourism on the environment, local infrastructure, and community well-being.
- ***sustainable tourism***: Highlights the need for tourism that balances economic benefits with environmental preservation and social equity, a solution often suggested for overtourism.
- ***tourism development***: Refers to the planning and growth of tourism infrastructure, which, if unregulated, can contribute to overtourism.
- ***community***: Denotes the local population whose lives and environment are affected by tourism influxes.
- ***quality of life***: Reflects the well-being of local residents, which can be negatively impacted by overtourism through increased congestion, noise, and other stressors.

– *local resident*: Refers to inhabitants of tourism hotspots who experience both the benefits and downsides of tourism, often advocating for measures to curb excessive tourism.

3 Topic Modeling Application

Each selected topic modeling technique has been applied to the preprocessed data to extract the appropriate themes and patterns. The quantitative evaluation of the models has been performed by computing the coherence score that measures how interpretable the topics are to humans: the higher the coherence score, the closer the words within a topic are. We have considered the UMass [9], and CV [10] coherence measures for LDA, LSI, HDP and NMF, while the semantic coherence measure [7], closely related to the UMass measure, for STM and CTM.

According to the training time, LSI has been the fastest model followed by NMF. LDA has requested a longer training time, while HDP has taken a moderate amount of time. STM and CTM have the highest training times due to their complexity.

3.1 LDA-Identified Topics in Overtourism Literature

Latent Dirichlet Allocation (LDA) have been applied to identify the major topics in the literature related to overtourism. The optimal number of topics have been identified by plotting the coherence score for models computed with topic numbers ranging from 1 to 15. The highest coherence score has been achieved with 8 topics, as the most suitable number as shown in Fig. 2.

Below there are the main themes, their associated key terms, and a description of each topic.

Topic 1 - Tourismphobia, Challenges to Local Identity and Heritage

- **Key terms:** *enterprise, business, tourismphobia, cultural, historical, resident, identity, sustainable*
- **Description:** This topic emphasizes the cultural and identity impacts of tourism, including the concept of "tourismphobia" and its challenges to local identity and heritage preservation.

Topic 2 - Sustainable and Innovative Tourism Strategies

- **Key terms:** *innovative, involvement, hospitality, tackle, strategy, sustainable, postcovid, stakeholder*
- **Description:** This topic focuses on the development of innovative and sustainable tourism strategies, particularly in the context of post-COVID-19 recovery efforts.

Topic 3 - New Smart Technology in Managing Events and Crises

- **Key terms:** *event, smart, host, crisis, covid, technology, sustainability, framework*

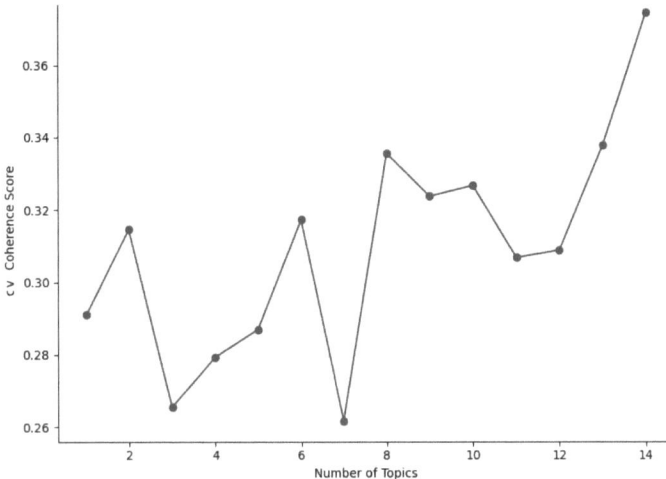

Fig. 2. CV coherence score for different numbers of topics identified with LDA - line chart showing the relationship between the number of topics and the coherence score.

– **Description:** This topic explores how technology and smart solutions contribute to managing events and crises, particularly within tourism contexts.

Topic 4 - Environmental Challenges in Tourism

– **Key terms:** *water, transport, climate, cruise, adaptation, season, traffic, heritage, unesco*
– **Description:** This topic discusses environmental issues in tourism, including the impacts on water resources, climate change, traffic, and UNESCO heritage sites.

Topic 5 - Urban Tourism Impact on Social Experiences and Communities

– **Key terms:** *city, resident, destination, tourist, urban, social, development, community*
– **Description:** This topic centers on urban tourism's social impacts, including resident experiences, community development, and the effects of increased tourist presence.

Topic 6 - Cruise Tourism and Environmental Impact

– **Key terms:** *cruise, water, port, venice, degrowth, policy, pollution, climate*
– **Description:** This topic focuses on the environmental implications of cruise tourism, especially concerning pollution, climate impact, and policy considerations in sensitive areas like Venice.

Topic 7 - Tourist Attraction Management and Resilience

- **Key terms:** *located, innovation, attraction, destination, resilience, service, transport, public*
- **Description:** This topic examines the management of tourism attractions with an emphasis on resilience, innovation, and public infrastructure to support sustainable tourism.

Topic 8 - Tourism Capacity and Management Techniques

- **Key terms:** *learning, technique, carrying capacity, tool, municipality, island, indicator, capacity*
- **Description:** This topic discusses strategies for managing tourism capacity, focusing on techniques and tools to ensure sustainability in areas with limited resources.

Wordclouds and barplots for the best 10 words in the topics we have unveiled are displayed in Figs. 3 and 4.

Fig. 3. Wordclouds visualization with eight topics identified with LDA - each topic contain a cluster of words varying in size, indicating their relevance.

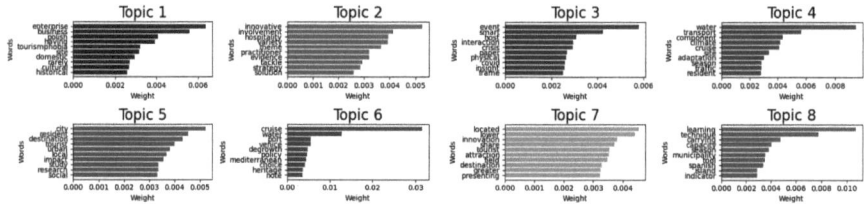

Fig. 4. Barchart plots for the best 10 words of each topic identified with LDA - the charts illustrate the weight of each word within its respective topic.

3.2 LSI-Identified Topics in Overtourism Literature

Latent Semantic Indexing (LSI) has been applied to identify main topics in the overtourism literature. The optimal number of topics have been determined by plotting the coherence score for models computed with topic numbers ranging from 1 to 15. The highest coherence score has been achieved with 6 topics, as the most suitable number as shown in Fig. 5.

Below there are the identified themes, their key terms, and a brief description of each topic.

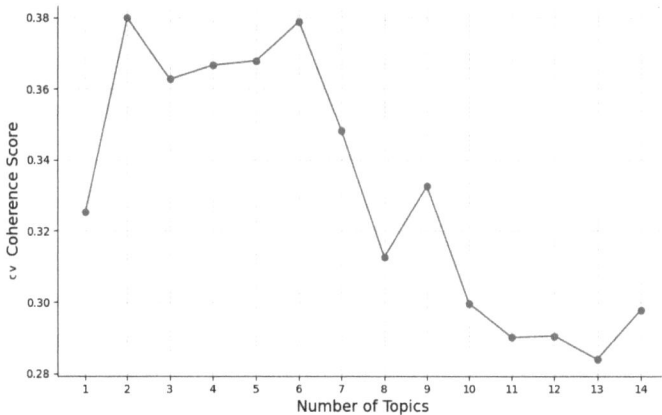

Fig. 5. CV coherence score for different numbers of topics identified with LSI - line chart showing the relationship between the number of topics and the c v coherence score.

Topic 1 - General Impact of Tourism and Development of a More Sustainable Approach

– **Key terms:** *impact, analysis, sustainability, model, policy, development, approach*
– **Description:** This topic broadly examines tourismâĂŹs impact, focusing on sustainability and the role of policies and models in guiding a sustainable approach within tourism studies.

Topic 2 - Urban Tourism and Resident Impact

– **Key terms:** *tourist, city, resident, impact, urban, social, development*
– **Description:** This topic tmphasizes the effects of tourism on urban areas and local residents, particularly the social impacts and challenges faced by cities with high levels of tourist activity.

Topic 3 - Urban Growth, Conflict, and Sustainability

– **Key terms:** *city, urban, growth, conflict, sustainable, problem, social*
– **Description:** This topic focuses on urban growth issues related to tourism, such as conflicts, sustainability, and social challenges emerging from increased tourism in city environments.

Topic 4 - Heritage and Cultural Tourism

– **Key terms:** *heritage, cultural, city, resident, development, pandemic*
– **Description:** This topic examines cultural and heritage tourism, discussing interactions with local development and community, as well as potential impacts stemming from the pandemic.

Topic 5 - Tourism Management and Development Models

- **Key terms:** *sustainable, model, approach, management, effect*
- **Description:** This topic covers tourism management strategies, focusing on sustainable approaches and development models aimed at managing tourism's impact on destinations.

Topic 6 - Community and Social Effects of Tourism

- **Key terms:** *community, effect, resident, social, impact, management*
- **Description:** This topic discusses the social and community-level effects of tourism, with an emphasis on local resident experiences and community-based management practices.

Wordclouds and barplots for the best 10 words in the topics we have unveiled are displayed in Figs. 6 and 7.

Fig. 6. Wordclouds for topics identified with LSI

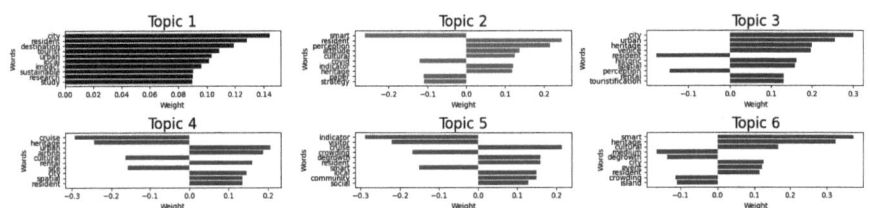

Fig. 7. Barplots for the best 10 words of each topic identified with LSI

3.3 HDP-Identified Topics in Overtourism Literature

The Hierarchical Dirichlet Process (HDP) model has revealed several key themes in the overtourism literature. In the following, each topic has been summarized with its key terms and description.

Topic 1 - Overview of Tourism and Local Impact

- **Key terms:** *tourist, destination, study, city, local, cultural, resident, impact, research*
- **Description:** This topic provides a broad overview of tourism, focusing on the relationships between tourists, local residents, and destinations, as well as the social and cultural impacts of tourism.

Topic 2 - Tourism Conditions and Quality Issues

- **Key terms:** *condition, impact, highlighted, suggests, quality, domestic, growing, tourist*
- **Description:** This topic emphasizes tourism conditions and challenges, including quality issues, the rise of domestic tourism, and increasing demands on tourism infrastructure.

Topic 3 - Tourism Patterns, Pricing, and Resident Dynamics

- **Key terms:** *resident, tourist, phenomenon, pattern, growth, attraction*
- **Description:** This topic discusses tourist behavior patterns, including pricing dynamics, tourism growth, and the interaction between tourists and local residents.

Topic 4 - Historical and Resilience-Focused Tourism

- **Key terms:** *position, context, historic, resilience, component, externality, stage*
- **Description:** This topic focuses on historical and resilience-oriented tourism, including the impact of tourism on heritage sites and efforts to manage externalities in historic areas.

Topic 5 - Tourism-Related Environmental Issues and Planning Concerns

- **Key terms:** *problem, decline, pollution, planning, model, cultural*
- **Description:** This topic examines environmental issues tied to tourism, including pollution, the decline of certain tourist locations, and the importance of strategic planning and modeling for sustainable management.

Topic 6 - Inclusivity in Tourism Development

- **Key terms:** *reaction, building, opportunity, inclusive, interview, evidence, historical*
- **Description:** This topic highlights inclusivity in tourism development, considering opportunities, stakeholder reactions, and community involvement based on historical evidence.

Topic 7 - Tourismphobia and Protection of Local Interests

- **Key terms:** *tourismphobia, planning, aspect, destination, protect, owner*

– **Description:** This topic focuses on "tourismphobia", or negative attitudes toward excessive tourism, and strategies to protect local interests and manage destinations effectively.

Topic 8 - Data Analysis and Innovation in Tourism Research

– **Key terms:** *analyse, data, innovative, primary, experiment, statistical*
– **Description:** This topic explores data-driven methods and innovation in tourism research, with a focus on data analysis, statistical techniques, and experimental approaches.

Wordclouds and barplots for the best 10 words in the topics we have unveiled are displayed in Figs. 8 and 9.

Fig. 8. Wordclouds for topics identified with HDP

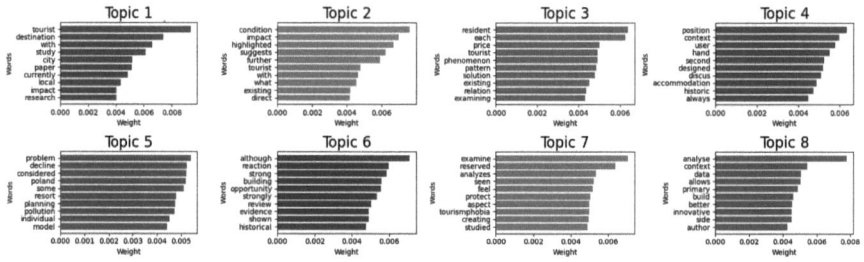

Fig. 9. Barplots for the best 10 words of each topic identified with HDP

3.4 NMF-Identified Topics in Overtourism Literature

The Non-Negative Matrix Factorization (NMF) model has uncovered several key themes within the overtourism literature. The optimal number of topics has been determined by plotting the coherence score for models computed with topic numbers ranging from 1 to 15. The highest coherence score was achieved with 10 topics, as the most suitable number as shown in Fig. 10.

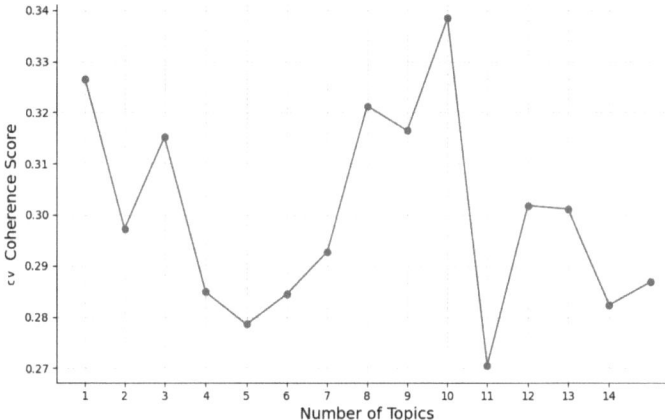

Fig. 10. CV coherence score for different numbers of topics identified with NMF

In the following, there is a summary of each topic, highlighting its key terms and description.

Topic 1 - Tourism Design, Experience, and Practical Implications

– **Key terms:** *experience, design, hospitality, visitor, methodology, practitioner*
– **Description:** This topic addresses the design and practical aspects of tourism, focusing on visitor experiences, industry practices, and methodological approaches.

Topic 2 - Urban Tourism and Housing Impact

– **Key terms:** *urban, conflict, gentrification, touristification, housing, congestion*
– **Description:** This topic focuses on the impacts of tourism in urban areas, particularly conflicts related to gentrification, housing shortages, and urban congestion.

Topic 3 - Environmental Issues and Rural Tourism

– **Key terms:** *medium, policy, rural, news, discourse, planning, behavior*
– **Description:** This topic examines media and policy discourse surrounding tourismâĂŹs environmental impact, particularly in rural settings.

Topic 4 - Cruise Tourism, Degrowth, and Technological Governance

– **Key terms:** *cruise, degrowth, smart, port, governance, technology*
– **Description:** This topic centers on cruise tourism, with a focus on degrowth strategies, technology integration, and governance.

Topic 5 - Seasonal Demand, Carrying Capacity, and Climate Concerns

– **Key terms:** *season, capacity, climate, crowding, park, demand*
– **Description:** This topic discusses seasonal demand, capacity management, and climate-related issues, particularly in high-traffic tourist areas.

Topic 6 - Post-Pandemic Tourism and Innovation

- **Key terms:** *sharing, economy, pandemic, sustainability, innovation, covid*
- **Description:** This topic explores the impacts of the COVID-19 pandemic on tourism, highlighting the sharing economy and sustainable innovations.

Topic 7 - Resident Attitudes and Cultural Impact of Tourism

- **Key terms:** *site, resident, cultural, survey, effect, crowding*
- **Description:** This topic addresses resident attitudes towards tourism, cultural impacts, and issues related to crowding and community responses.

Topic 8 - Heritage and Mass Tourism at UNESCO Sites

- **Key terms:** *heritage, cultural, unesco, site, venice, mass*
- **Description:** This topic focuses on heritage tourism and the challenges of managing mass tourism at UNESCO World Heritage Sites.

Topic 9 - Short-Term Rentals, Regulation, and Urban Impact

- **Key terms:** *rental, airbnb, regulation, pandemic, historic, population*
- **Description:** This topic examines the impact of short-term rentals on urban areas, with a focus on regulatory responses and effects on historic sites.

Wordclouds and barplots for the best 10 words in the topics we have unveiled are displayed in Figs. 11 and 12.

Fig. 11. Wordclouds for topics identified with NMF

3.5 STM-Identified Topics in Overtourism Literature

The Structural Topic Model (STM) analysis has revealed several key themes in the overtourism literature. A diagnostic of the model has been run with a range of topics between 2 and 10, including Held-out Likelihood, Residuals, and Semantic Coherence. The best balance between these metrics have been found at 6, as shown in Fig. 13.

Each topic is detailed below, including its focus, key words, and an explanation.

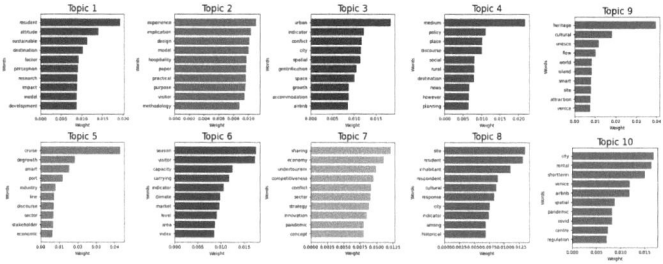

Fig. 12. Barplots for the best 10 words of each topic identified with NMF

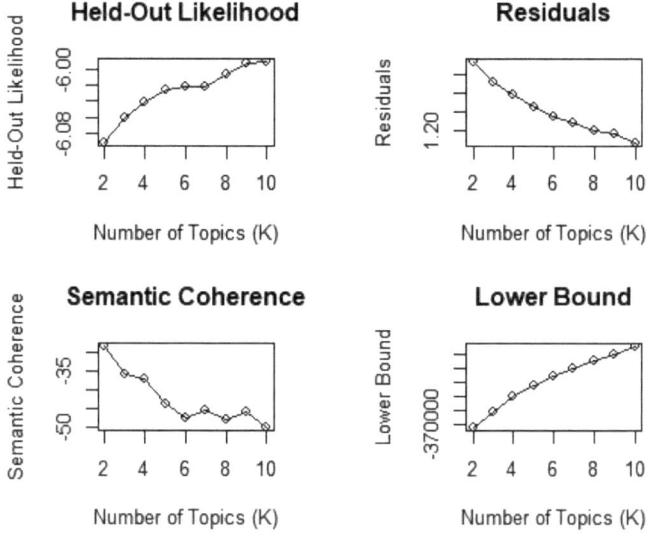

Fig. 13. Diagnostic values for different numbers of topics identified with STM

Topic 1 - Overtourism Analysis

- **Key Words:** *overtourism, tourism, urban, social, public policy, conflict, research, methodology, discourse, stakeholder, narrative, medium, analysis, interaction, space, network*
- **Description:** This topic explores the phenomenon of overtourism in urban settings, emphasizing social dynamics, conflicts, and public policy implications that arise when tourism reaches unsustainable levels. It highlights methodologies, discourse, and stakeholder engagement in urban tourism research.

Topic 2 - Sustainable Tourism: Overtourism and Undertourism

- **Key Words:** *overtourism, undertourism, sustainable development, innovation, economy, literature review, problem, concept, scientific, enterprise, solution, sharing, business, research, model*
- **Description:** This topic focuses on sustainable tourism practices, particularly regarding overtourism and undertourism. It discusses economic factors, innovation, and the literature addressing these challenges, highlighting sustainable development strategies for balanced tourism growth.

Topic 3 - Cultural Heritage and Tourism

- **Key Words:** *tourist, visitor, heritage, cultural, site, cruise, environmental analysis, UNESCO, traffic, attraction, location, natural, flow, park, season, index*
- **Description:** This topic examines the relationship between cultural heritage sites and tourism, focusing on visitor interactions and the environmental impacts. It emphasizes the importance of managing cultural and natural heritage, especially UNESCO sites, to preserve them for future generations.

Topic 4 - Community Engagement in Sustainable Tourism

- **Key Words:** *tourism, sustainable, destination, stakeholder, community, strategy, management, governance, resilience, planning, practice, finding, smart, approach, industry, crisis*
- **Description:** This topic discusses the role of local communities in sustainable tourism practices, with a focus on stakeholder involvement, governance strategies, and resilience. It explores how communities can address tourism challenges through smart planning and collaborative efforts.

Topic 5 - Urban Tourism Impacts on Housing

- **Key Words:** *city, tourism, urban, spatial, negative impact, rental, gentrification, pandemic, citizen, housing, short-term rental, touristification, concentration, analysis, life*
- **Description:** This topic examines the impacts of tourism in urban environments, particularly short-term rentals, gentrification, and the effects of the pandemic. It highlights the negative consequences of tourism concentration and discusses strategies to maintain balanced community dynamics.

Topic 6 - Relationship Between Tourists and Residents

- **Key Words:** *tourist, resident, perception, overtourism, crowding, satisfaction, attitude, survey, indicator, influence, significant, relationship, questionnaire, research, effect, local*
- **Description:** This topic explores residents' perceptions of overtourism and its effects on communities. It focuses on attitudes toward crowding, satisfaction, and public perception, using surveys to assess local views on tourism-related changes.

Wordclouds for the best 10 words in the topics we have unveiled are displayed in Fig. 14.

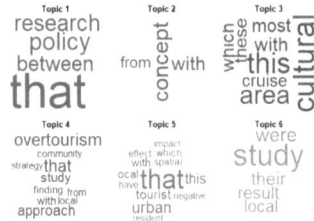

Fig. 14. Wordclouds for topics identified with STM

3.6 CTM-Identified Topics in Overtourism Literature

The following topics have been identified from the Correlated Topic Model (CTM) analysis, each providing insights into different aspects of overtourism and its impacts. The best number of topics is 6 based on the same metrics of STM, shown in Fig. 13.

Topic 1 - Overtourism Dynamics

- **Key Words:** *tourism, overtourism, destination, city, tourist, local, result, sustainable, effect, development, resident, analysis, research, covid, impact, future, negative, model, pandemic*
- **Description:** This topic examines the phenomenon of overtourism, where the volume of tourists overwhelms local resources and infrastructure. It explores the implications for urban environments, sustainability, and local residents, including the impact of events such as the COVID-19 pandemic on tourism patterns.

Topic 2 - Overtourism Impact on Local Communities

- **Key Words:** *study, social, overtourism, research, urban, tourist, finding, approach, paper, impact, local, policy, public, literature, area, sustainability, article, destination, community, factor*
- **Description:** This topic focuses on the social aspects of overtourism, examining how increased tourist activity affects local communities. It highlights the importance of understanding social dynamics, public policies, and community engagement for sustainable tourism management.

Topic 3 - Visitor Analysis in Tourism

- **Key Words:** *tourism, tourist, visitor, phenomenon, study, destination, analysis, flow, well, urban, area, impact, approach, model, result, research, future, sustainable, city, event*
- **Description:** This topic investigates tourist behaviors and their interactions with destinations, covering the impact of visitor flow on urban areas. It includes demographic insights, motivations, and overall tourist experience, helping to understand and manage tourism effectively.

Topic 4 - Sustainable Tourism Development

- **Key Words:** *tourism, destination, study, sustainable, research, based, management, development, space, indicator, growth, article, data, analysis, model, community, factor, economic, local, approach*
- **Description:** This topic covers sustainable tourism practices aimed at minimizing environmental impacts while maximizing social and economic benefits for communities. It discusses strategic management approaches and stakeholder roles in achieving sustainable tourism growth.

Topic 5 - Community Impact and Management

- **Key Words:** *impact, study, resident, community, tourism, negative, level, social, purpose, development, analysis, stakeholder, value, economic, perception, data, management, factor, result, finding*
- **Description:** This topic explores tourism's impact on local communities and the strategies used to manage these changes. It highlights the role of stakeholders in addressing social impacts and emphasizes community involvement in decision-making to address tourism challenges.

Topic 6 - Overtourism Research and Analysis

- **Key Words:** *overtourism, study, tourism, approach, research, paper, problem, resident, development, local, management, analysis, social, finding, concept, term, many, economic, data, result*
- **Description:** This topic focuses on research related to overtourism and its impacts, including methodologies, frameworks, and indicators to measure tourism effects. The aim is to inform policymakers and stakeholders about the challenges and mitigation strategies for overtourism.

Wordclouds for the best 10 words in the topics we have unveiled are displayed in Fig. 15.

Fig. 15. Wordclouds for topics identified with CTM

4 Discussion

The analysis of tourism-related themes has revealed several prominent topics that consistently emerge across various models (see Tables 1 and 2).

Table 1. Number of topics per modeling technique

Techniques	Number of Topics	Techniques	Number of Topics
LDA	8	NMF	10
LSI	6	STM	6
HDP	8	CTM	6

Table 2. Most common topics over modeling techniques

Topics	Modeling Techniques
Overtourism and its impact	LSI, HDP, STM, CTM
Cultural Heritage and Identity	LSI, HDP, NMF, STM
Sustainable Tourism Practices	LDA, LSI, HDP, NMF, STM CTM
Urban Dynamics and Challenges	LDA, LSI, HDP, STM, CTM
Community Perspective and Resident Impact	LSI, HDP, NMF, CTM
Economic Factors and Development	LSI, STM, HDP, NMF
Visitor Experience and Engagement	LDA, LSI, NMF, STM, CTM

Below there are the key themes:

1. **Overtourism and Its Impacts:** This theme highlights the social dynamics, community impact, and management strategies associated with overtourism. It emphasizes the negative consequences such as crowding, resident dissatisfaction, and the strain on local infrastructure, underscoring the urgency of addressing these issues.
2. **Cultural Heritage and Identity:** Many topics underscore the importance of cultural heritage and the identity of local communities affected by tourism. The relationship between tourism and the preservation of cultural and natural heritage, especially in relation to UNESCO sites, is a recurring concern that calls for protective measures and responsible tourism practices.
3. **Sustainable Tourism Practices:** Across all analyses, there is a strong emphasis on sustainable tourism strategies. This includes discussions around innovative solutions to mitigate tourismâĂŹs adverse effects, the role of stakeholders, and governance approaches that aim to achieve sustainable development while benefiting both tourists and local communities.
4. **Urban Dynamics and Challenges:** Urban tourism poses significant challenges, with several topics addressing the issues faced by cities due to tourism.

Concerns such as short-term rentals, gentrification, and social dynamics within urban environments highlight the necessity for comprehensive urban planning and management strategies to foster a balance between tourism and resident needs.
5. **Community Perspectives and Resident Impact:** The analysis frequently explores the perceptions and attitudes of residents toward tourism. It delves into how tourism impacts local communities, including social implications, quality of life, and the balance between tourism benefits and the challenges it brings, revealing the need for inclusive decision-making processes.
6. **Economic Factors and Development:** Economic aspects of tourism, particularly development challenges and the sharing economy, are frequently discussed in relation to overtourism. This theme examines the economic implications of tourism growth on local communities, emphasizing the importance of balancing economic benefits with sustainable practices that do not compromise local cultures and environments.
7. **Visitor Experience and Engagement:** Several topics address the experiences of tourists themselves, exploring their interactions with cultural sites. The significance of visitor satisfaction, and how it relates to the cultural and environmental context, is a key area of focus, suggesting that positive tourist experiences can enhance community support for tourism initiatives.

The analysis reveals that overtourism is a multifaceted issue that significantly impacts cultural heritage, community dynamics, and sustainable tourism practices. One of the critical insights is the interdisciplinary nature of tourism research; themes such as sustainability, cultural impact, and community perspectives are deeply interconnected. This interrelationship suggests that effective tourism management must consider multiple facets of tourism, recognizing that changes in one area can have ripple effects on others.

Moreover, the findings indicate a pressing need for informed policy-making and robust governance frameworks that incorporate the diverse experiences and needs of all stakeholders involved in tourism. Policymakers must engage with local communities, tourism businesses, and visitors to develop strategies that address the complex challenges posed by overtourism while ensuring the long-term viability of tourism as an economic driver.

Additionally, the recurring issues associated with overtourism and its management highlight areas ripe for future research. There is a significant opportunity to explore innovative solutions that support sustainable tourism while preserving local cultures and environments. Future studies could focus on the development of best practices for stakeholder engagement, community resilience, and sustainable tourism models that benefit both residents and tourists alike.

5 Conclusions

The application of topic modeling techniques successfully identified underlying themes within the reviewed literature. Many topics overlapped across different models, reflecting the complex and multidisciplinary nature of the subject.

The analysis underscores the need for comprehensive strategies and collaboration among stakeholders to address the challenges of overtourism effectively. By fostering a tourism model that prioritizes sustainability, respects cultural heritage, and considers the perspectives of local communities, it is possible to create a more equitable and responsible tourism industry that serves the interests of both visitors and residents.

In the future, a classifier will be developed to categorize new research publications into distinct thematic topics. The generated topic probability distributions from the modeling techniques will be used as input features for various classifiers. BERT-based embeddings will be also used to capture nuanced semantic information from abstracts.

Acknowledgments. The authors thank INFN for having funds this research with the Summer Student Internship Program.

Disclosure of Interests. The authors have no competing interests to declare that are relevant to the content of this article.

References

1. Doxey, G.V.: A causation theory of visitor-resident irritants: methodology and research inferences. In: Proceedings of 6th Annual Conference on Travel and Tourism Research Association, pp. 195–198 (1975)
2. Goeldner, C.R., Ritchie, J.: Tourism: Principles. John Wiley & Sons, Practices, Philosophies (2016)
3. Blei, D., Ng, A., Jordan, M.: Latent dirichlet allocation. J. Mach. Learn. Res. **3**, 601–608 (2001)
4. Papadimitriou, C.H., Tamaki, H., Raghavan, P., Vempala, S.: Latent semantic indexing: a probabilistic analysis. In: Proceedings of the Seventeenth ACM SIGACT-SIGMOD-SIGART Symposium on Principles of Database Systems, PODS '98, pp. 159–168 (1998)
5. Lee, D., Seung, H.: Learning the parts of objects by non-negative matrix factorization. Nature **401**, 788–791 (1999)
6. Teh, Y., Jordan, M., Beal, M., Blei, D.: Hierarchical Dirichlet processes. Mach. Learn., 1–30 (2006)
7. Roberts, M., et al.: Structural topic models for open ended survey responses. Am. J. Polit. Sci. **58**(4), 1064–1082 (2014)
8. Blei, D., Lafferty, J.: A correlated topic model of science. Ann. Appl. Stat. **1** (2007)
9. Mimno, D., Wallach, H., Talley, E., Leenders, M., McCallum, A.: Optimizing semantic coherence in topic models. In: Proceedings of the 2011 Conference on Empirical Methods in Natural Language Processing, pp. 262–272 (2011)
10. Roder, M., Both, A., Hinneburg, A.: Exploring the space of topic coherence measures. In: Proceedings of the Eighth ACM International Conference on Web Search and Data Mining, pp. 399–408 (2015)

Towards Smarter Vegetation Health Clustering: Insights from Fractal Dimension, NDVI, and LST Metrics Derived via Remote Sensing Landsat Dataset

Suhad A. Yousif[1], Venus W. Samawi[2(✉)], Nadia M. G. Al-Saidi[3], and Yeliz Karaca[4]

[1] Computer Science Department, Al-Nahrain University, Baghdad, Iraq
suhad.a.yousif@nahrainuniv.edu.iq
[2] Department of MIS/Smart Business, Isra University, Amman 11622, Jordan
venus.samawi@iu.edu.jo
[3] Department of Applied Sciences, University of Technology, Baghdad 10066, Iraq
nadia.m.ghanim@uotechnology.edu.iq
[4] University of Massachusetts Chan Medical School (UMASS), 55 Lake Avenue North, Worcester, MA 01655, USA
yeliz.karaca@ieee.org

Abstract. Vegetation plays a vital role in preserving the environment and mitigating the effects of climate change. Therefore, it is essential to identify areas of stress and non-vegetation factors to develop a plan to establish vegetation and combat desertification, which positively affects climate change and ensures a sustainable future. Remote sensing and satellite images have been used to identify vegetation areas and their density, which is a challenging problem. According to the literature, the Normalized Difference Vegetation Index (NDVI) is used in most studies to identify vegetation areas, while few utilize fractal dimensions and Land Surface Temperature (LST). Fractals are known for their effectiveness in identifying complex distribution patterns, such as vegetation areas in satellite images. This study will tackle the issue of categorizing the vegetation area into healthy, stressful, and non-vegetation regions based on satellite images. Two clustering methods are applied, namely K-means and threshold-based labelling, to categorize the vegetation area in the three aforementioned areas. The K-means and threshold-based labelling will be evaluated and compared based on the Silhouette score, Davies-Bouldin index (DBI), and Entropy metrics. The effect of selecting the proper features on clustering performance is also studied. The experimental results show that the threshold-based clustering method suits datasets with well-defined threshold boundaries between clusters. Conversely, the K-means clustering method provides flexibility for adaptive clustering with no pre-defined thresholds. Finally, it is worth noting that Fractal dimensions (FD) with threshold-based labelling achieve the best clustering results, making it crucial for detecting vegetation health and analyzing land surfaces.

Keywords: Clustering Vegetation Areas · K-means clustering · threshold-based Clustering · Normalized Difference Vegetation Index · Silhouette score · DBI · Entropy · Land Surface Temperature

1 Introduction

Vegetation is the lungs through which the Earth breathes. It limits global warming and plays a vital role in purifying the atmosphere of toxic gases and reducing climate change. Therefore, it is essential to focus on developing vegetation areas by specifically determining the distribution of the planet's cover to improve regions with poor vegetation. Developing vegetation areas and promoting smart farms play an important role in building a sustainable future [1–4]. To develop vegetation areas, it is important to categorize vegetation regions into healthy, stressed, and non-vegetation based on remote sensing [5, 6] or satellite images. Satellite images are images of the Earth's surface in different formats (e.g., multispectral, panchromatic, synthetic aperture radar images) [7].

One common method for vegetation detection is the NDVI [8]. Some studies combine NDVI, which uses the red and near-infrared (NIR) bands, with the enhanced vegetation index (EVI), which uses blue bands in addition to the red and near-infrared (NIR). Light detection and ranging (LiDAR) is an accurate method for obtaining three-dimensional (3D) surface information and is often used in vegetation studies. To extract the vegetation point set and describe the spatial morphological characteristics of different features in the LiDAR point cloud, 3D fractal dimensions [9] are used. The 3D fractal dimensions indicate the irregularity and roughness of land features [10–12]. Different types of features exhibit unique distribution and variation trends in their fractal dimensions. Therefore, fractals are used to improve detection accuracy in satellite images for vegetation detection. In 2023, Martinez and Labib [13] studied the NDVI values that respond to various vegetation types (trees and grass). They found a nonlinear relationship between the average NDVI and specific types. Additionally, increasing NDVI is relevant to varying vegetation changes. In their study, the assessment of NDVI is prioritized to improve urban health.

Satellite imagery is important in detecting land cover changes, especially in vegetation monitoring. This aspect has become increasingly important in scientific research because it addresses the challenges of stressed and uncultivated areas significantly affected by climate change. Therefore, mapping vegetation patterns is essential for tracking changes in vegetated areas and identifying non-vegetated, stressed, or healthy areas. Accurate vegetation detection is critical for various applications, including crop yield estimation, land cover and land use monitoring, urban growth assessment, and drought tracking [5]. Classification techniques, such as machine learning (ML) [14, 15], random forests (RF), support vector machine (SVM), gradient tree boosting (GTB), and classification and regression tree (CART) [16, 17], are used to classify satellite images into stressed, healthy, and non-vegetation areas. On the other hand, clustering techniques such as thresholding and K-means clustering are also used to categorize vegetation areas [6, 17, 18]. Recently, researchers have utilized Deep Learning (DL) to categorize vegetation areas [19]. In 2023, Kharat et al. [6] applied the RF classification and K-mean clustering methods to remote sensing data for recognizing land-cover types (vegetation, water, and soil). In their work, three metrics are used to evaluate the outcomes of K-means clustering: the Silhouette Score, Davies-Bouldin Index (DBI), and Calinski-Harabasz Index (CHI). Based on the Silhouette Score metric, the achieved clustering performance was 46%. On the other hand, the RF classifier achieved 88% accuracy. Ayhan et al. [19] studied DL and traditional vegetation detection approaches using DeepLabV3 + a custom CNN. The training and testing datasets were collected from different geographical locations, and the images are of different resolutions [20]. They introduced a new object-based method using NDVI and ML methods. Their technique was adopted for high-resolution airborne color images containing both RGB and NIR bands, as well as images containing only the RGB bands. Using two Kimisala test datasets, the researchers contrasted the performance of the DL methods with that of the object-based detection approach. All the result values confirm that NDVI-ML has better results than DL methods. Iryanti et al. [18] studied landslide risk in Garut using satellite-derived vegetation data, NDVI, and the K-means clustering method. They identify six landslide-prone areas, labelling NDVI grid codes 3 and 4 as potential zones due to sparse vegetation. Their analysis, based on data from NASA's Terra and Aqua satellites, maps high-risk points with GIS visualization. The K-means clustering method is chosen for its effectiveness with the limited dataset. The silhouette coefficient is used to assess the quality of clustering results. The resulting clusters are divided into three groups, with cluster one having a silhouette coefficient close to 1, indicating robust clustering.

Much research in the literature uses the NDVI to detect land cover, particularly vegetation areas, while few studies utilize fractal dimensions. Based on fractal theory, fractals serve as statistical measures of the irregularity and roughness of ground features. Fractal dimensions help to identify vegetation cover through its spatial morphology and offer valuable insights into the spatial complexity of ecosystems by focusing on complex distribution patterns. The main objective of this study is to detect vegetation cover areas by combining satellite images using the Natural Vegetation Index, fractal dimensions, and land surface temperature (LST) matrices. K-means clustering and threshold-based labelling are employed to analyze the Landsat remote sensing dataset and assess vegetation health. The analysis will categorize the vegetation areas into healthy, stressed, and non-vegetation. The performance of k-means and threshold-based labelling will be evaluated using the Silhouette Score, Davies-Bouldin Index, and Entropy. Based on these metrics, the effectiveness of the two clustering methods will be explored and compared. Additionally, selecting the appropriate feature or combination of features that influences the clustering of vegetation areas will be examined. In this research, K-means and thresholding methods are utilized as complements to each other since both of these methods have their useful aspects based on the treatment of vegetation species classification. Thresholding-based is suitable when interpretable, explicit conditions on the boundary are known for simplicity and interpretability, but K-means offers flexibility in overlapping or ambiguity in clusters. The joint use of these methods provides a solid approach to the classification of the health status of vegetation on satellite images.

The remainder of the paper is divided into three sections. Section 2 explains the study's methodology, including features, collection methods, and evaluation methods. Section 3 describes the dataset used. Section 4 presents the experimental results and evaluation. Finally, we conclude with Sect. 5.

2 Methodology

This study aims to categorize the vegetation area into healthy, stressful, and non-vegetation regions. Consequently, we develop a model consisting of three stages. The first is the feature extraction stage, where three features are extracted from the remote-sensing images. The clustering stage is performed using K-means and threshold-based labelling. Finally, there is the evaluation stage. In this section, the stages of the developed model are described.

2.1 Feature Extraction

Extracting features from Landsat Surface Reflectance Images (TIF format) datasets involves calculating key features that provide insights into vegetation health, land surface complexity, and thermal characteristics. NDVI represents vegetation health, where higher values indicate dense vegetation. FD quantifies the complexity of spatial patterns in the landscape, which can reflect structural diversity. LST is calculated from the thermal infrared band and highlights surface temperature variations critical for ecological and agricultural assessments. Together, these features provide a comprehensive understanding of environmental dynamics, enabling efficient classification and analysis of land cover and vegetation health. In this section, some background about the three features extracted from remote-sensing images used in this work is presented, along with samples of these extracted features.

Fractal Dimension (FD): Any object in real life has a degree of complexity. Some have a low degree, and other objects have a high degree that the topological dimension cannot describe. This complexity motivates mathematicians to find other techniques (methods) to calculate it, which is known as the fractal dimension (FD). The fractal dimension offers very important tools for describing and analyzing complex objects. It is frequently employed to characterize structures that exhibit irregularities or self-similarity across various scales. Studies show that the fractal dimension may provide information about ecosystems' spatial complexity by measuring vegetation distribution. Although there are several ways to calculate it, the box-counting method is the most straightforward and precise algorithm for estimating its value. It relates the number of boxes $N(\epsilon)$ needed to cover a shape with the side length of the box ϵ [12], so that FD is calculated using Eq. (1):

$$FD = lim_{\varepsilon \to 0} \frac{log N(\epsilon)}{log(1/\epsilon)} \qquad (1)$$

To analyze vegetation, the satellite images are partitioned into grids of varying sizes to count the number of nonempty cells in each grid [10, 11, 21]. To characterize the vegetation area, the digital images are divided into $N(\epsilon)$ distinct, non-overlapping grids of size ϵ. The FD value is constructed by stepwise decreasing of ϵ, whose regression line slope is given as in Eq. (2):

$$FD \approx \frac{\Delta log N(\epsilon)}{\Delta log \epsilon} \qquad (2)$$

In this work, we used the Fractal dimension to enhance the clustering method in vegetation analysis. It enhances the clustering accuracy by distinguishing between dense forests and fragmented landscapes. It also combines with machine learning models, such as K-means and threshold, to improve the classification of vegetation health states.

Normalized Difference Vegetation Index (NDVI): Remote sensing statistics are often used to assess the coverage, density, and health of vegetation in the Normalized Difference Vegetation Index (NDVI). The index uses vegetation's spectrum reflectance properties, particularly in the red and near-infrared (NIR) bands. Depending on the cellular makeup of the leaves, vegetation and leafy plants absorb the reddest light (R) for photosynthesis and reflect a sizable amount of near-infrared (NIR) light. It is computed using Eq. (3) [3, 13]:

$$NDVI = \frac{NIR - R}{NIR + R} \quad (3)$$

where

- NIR refers to the reflectance in the near-infrared band,
- R is the reflectance in the red band.

Its value ranges from -1 to $+1$, such that.

- If NDVI > 0.5: it indicates healthy and dense vegetation.
- If $0.2 <$ NDVI ≤ 0.5: it indicates sparse or stressed vegetation.
- If NDVI ≤ 0.2: it indicates that it signifies bare soil, water bodies, or non-vegetated areas.

The NDVI can be used for:

1. *Vegetable Health Assessment:* The NDVI has a direct correlation with plant productivity and chlorophyll content. Strong photosynthetic activity is indicated by higher NDVI values, while stress or degradation is indicated by lower values.
2. *Classification of Land Cover:* By differentiating between vegetated and non-vegetated areas, NDVI makes mapping land use and land cover easier.
3. *Temporal Analysis:* NDVI helps with studies of deforestation, desertification, and crop production prediction by allowing the tracking of seasonal and long-term vegetation changes.

The NDVI is calculated based on reflectance data from satellite sensors like Landsat or Sentinel-2. For instance:

- Bands 4 (Red) and 5 (NIR) are used by Landsat 8.
- Bands 4 (Red) and 8 (NIR) are used by Sentinel-2.

Typically, NDVI values are represented as heat maps or classified for aggregation into groups for clustering or statistical analysis. Correlating NDVI with other parameters like FD or LST improves the accuracy of vegetation classification. It is a strong index to study green vegetation on a large scale; due to its sensitivity to atmospheric content, soil background, and mixed pixels, which may require any sort of corrections or complementary indices.

Land Surface Temperature (LST): The temperature of the Earth's surface is represented by the Land Surface Temperature (LST), which is calculated from thermal infrared (TIR) data acquired by remote sensing. Understanding vegetation stress, urban heat islands, land-atmosphere interactions, and climate research all depend on LST. According to Planck's Law, LST is computed from the thermal radiation that the surface emits. Equation (4) provides the brightness L_λ at a given wavelength λ [22].

$$L_\lambda = \frac{2hc^2}{\lambda^5} \frac{1}{e^{\frac{hc}{\lambda kT}} - 1} \tag{4}$$

where:

- h is Planck's constant $(6.626 \times 10^{-34}\ \text{J} \cdot \text{s})$,
- c is the speed of light $(3 \times 10^8\ \text{m/s})$,
- k is Boltzmann's constant $(1.381 \times 10^{-\Upsilon}\ \downarrow \text{K})$,
- T is the temperature (K).

The top-of-atmosphere (TOA) radiance, which satellite sensors collect for LST estimation, needs to be adjusted for emissivity and atmospheric influences. The LST is calculated through the following three steps:

1. *Conversion to Spectral Radiance:* The calibration constants of the sensor are used to calculate the TOA spectral radiance L as in Eq. (5):

$$L = \frac{L_{\max} - L_{\min}}{Q_{\text{calmax}} - Q_{\text{calmin}}} (Q_{\text{cal}} - Q_{\text{calmin}}) + L_{\min} \tag{5}$$

where:
 Q_{cal} is the digital number,
 $L_{\max}, L_{\min}$ are sensor-specific radiance limits,
 $Q_{\text{calmax}}, Q_{\text{calmin}}$ are calibration values.

2. *Conversion to Brightness Temperature:* The inverse Planck function is used to determine the brightness temperature T_b as in Eq. (6).

$$T_b = \frac{K_2}{\ln\left(\frac{K_1}{L} + 1\right)} \tag{6}$$

where: K_1, K_2 The calibration constants are specific to the sensor, L is the spectral radiance.

3. *Surface Emissivity Correction:* Surface emissivity ϵ, is a gauge of a surface's ability to emit heat radiation (considered while calculating LST (see Eq. (7)).

$$LST = \frac{T_b}{1 + \left(\frac{\lambda_b}{hc}\right)\ln(\epsilon)} \tag{7}$$

where ϵ depends on land cover type (e.g., vegetation, soil, water).

The LST can be utilized for climate monitoring by monitoring long-term and seasonal temperature patterns, vegetation analysis by identifying thermal stress in plants, and urban heat island detection by identifying temperature anomalies in urban regions. A sample of the Landsat Surface Reflectance Dataset after feature extraction is illustrated in Table 1. Table 2 shows the preprocessing of the extracted Features.

Table 1. Sample of Landsat Surface Reflectance Dataset after Feature Extraction

File	NDVI	Fractal Dimension	LST
10000.tif	0.044197019	1.935009224	147.8502568
10001.tif	0.030440027	1.758902982	147.8973872
10002.tif	−0.11129284	1.817798437	147.8878181
10003.tif	−0.02735228	1.928295604	147.8711278
10004.tif	0.029509578	1.863981182	147.8735925
10005.tif	−0.03912205	1.913426392	147.8767818
10006.tif	−0.02609288	1.99312674	147.8746662
10007.tif	−0.01163762	1.948725655	147.8967401
10008.tif	0.021041805	1.951532602	147.896794
10009.tif	−0.03101563	1.910427572	147.8917216
10010.tif	−0.07040081	1.939831155	147.8970637
10011.tif	0.09750851	1.929277217	NAN
10012.tif	−0.1307911	1.942162104	147.8854531
10013.tif	0.003484572	1.869693652	147.8575551

2.2 Stage Two: Clustering of Vegetation Area

Threshold-Based Labeling Method: Using predetermined domain-specific thresholds, the threshold-based labelling is a clustering technique that groups data points into meaningful classes according to the attributes of individual features. This method starts by examining the values of a particular feature, like the NDVI, LST, or FD, and then clustering the data according to the mean feature values.

Table 2. Preprocessing of the Extracted Features

File	NDVI	Fractal Dimension	LST
10000.tif	0.496425	0.876778	0.039139
10001.tif	0.489106	0.796982	0.894325
10002.tif	0.413696	0.823668	0.720693
10003.tif	0.458357	0.873736	0.417845
10004.tif	0.48861	0.844594	0.462568
10005.tif	0.452095	0.866999	0.520438
10006.tif	0.459027	0.903112	0.482049
10007.tif	0.466718	0.882993	0.882583
10008.tif	0.484105	0.884265	0.883562
10009.tif	0.456408	0.86564	0.791523
10010.tif	0.435452	0.878963	0.888454
10011.tif	0.52479	0.874181	0.600507
10012.tif	0.403321	0.880019	0.677779

This method applied several steps:

1. *Feature-Based Clustering*: The input for clustering is a feature of interest (such as FD, LST, or NDVI). The feature data is divided using the K-means algorithm into a predetermined number of clusters, k, each of which contains data points with comparable feature values.
2. *Cluster Analysis:* The mean value of the feature within each cluster is calculated once the clusters have been created. This analysis reveals the underlying properties of the data by showing the central tendency of the feature within each cluster.
3. Threshold Assignment: The application of previously predetermined thresholds and domain expertise to label each cluster of data points with a label that has meaning and context.

    For example:

- The NDVI clusters are labelled as:

    - *Healthy vegetation* if the mean NDVI > 0.5.
    - *Stressed vegetation* if $0.2 <$ mean NDVI ≤ 0.5.
    - *Non-vegetated areas* if the mean NDVI ≤ 0.2.

- Based on LST, clusters are labelled based on temperature ranges:

    - *High Temperature* for mean values $> 30\ °C$.
    - *Moderate Temperature* for values between $15\ °C$ and $30\ °C$.
    - *Low Temperature* for values $\leq 15\ °C$.

- Based on Fractal Dimension, clusters are labelled as:
  - *Complex Structures* if the FD value exceeds 1.5.
  - *Simple Structures,* otherwise.

4. *Label Assignment:* Each feature's threshold values are mapped to its corresponding cluster, producing useful categorical labels that explain the physical or biological significance of the feature.

K-Means Clustering: Works perfectly well on datasets that have well-defined thresholds unique to the domain for any feature. Despite its simplicity, threshold-based labelling provides a realistic way to classify land surface elements, such as the status of vegetation, using predetermined thresholds and inspecting characteristics of clusters. Its main strength is described in *Algorithm_one,* which shows the transparency and the potential to provide perceptual labels that correspond to real-world phenomena that are indispensable for vegetation monitoring and ecological studies [23].

Algorithm_One: K-means Clustering with Meaningful Labeling
Input:

- Dataset D with features $F = \{NDVI, FD, LST\}$
- Number of clusters $k = 3$
- Predefined thresholds for each feature

Output:

- Dataset D' with cluster labels and meaningful descriptive labels.

Algorithm Steps:

1. Initialization: The feature values V_f is used to cluster the satellite images n the feature $f \in F$.
2. Clustering Process: The K-means algorithm is applied to split V_f into three clusters:
   a) Randomly initialize k centroids.
   b) Each data point in V_f is assigned to the nearest centroid using Euclidean distance.
   c) The centroid is recalculated as the mean of all data points in each cluster.
   d) Repeat steps 2.b and 2.c until centroids stabilize or maximum iterations are reached.
   e) Compute Cluster Statistics: For each cluster C_i ($i = 1,2,3$):
   f) Calculate the mean value μ_i of feature f in C_i.
3. Assign descriptive labels: Use μ_i and predefined thresholds to assign a descriptive label L_i to each cluster C_i:
   If $f = $ NDVI:

- $\mu_i > 0.5 \rightarrow L_i = $ "Healthy"
- $0.2 < \mu_i \leq 0.5 \rightarrow L_i = $ "Stressful"
- $\mu_i \leq 0.2 \rightarrow L_i = $ "Non-Vegetated"

If $f = \text{LST}$:

- $\mu_i > 30 \rightarrow L_i = $ "High Temperature"
- $15 < \mu_i \leq 30 \rightarrow L_i = $ "Moderate Temperature"
- $\mu_i \leq 15 \rightarrow L_i = $ "Low Temperature"
    If $f = $ Fractal Dimension:

    - $\mu_i > 1.5 \rightarrow L_i = $ "Complex Structures"
    - $\mu_i \leq 1.5 \rightarrow L_i = $ "Simple Structures"

4. Update Dataset: Add two columns to D for feature f:
    $Cluster_f$: Cluster labels (numeric).
    $Label_f$: Descriptive labels (textual).
5. Repeat steps 1–4 for each feature $f \in F$.
6. Output: The updated dataset D' where the cluster labels and descriptive labels are described for each feature.

This algorithm provides descriptive labels for each data point in the dataset, mapping the cluster assignments to intelligible categories. These indices are added in additional columns to be saved as labelled datasets, after which some statistical analyses are implemented to provide information like mean feature values within each cluster. These statistics are shown in a summary table that connects cluster means to the descriptive labels.

Environmental characteristics like vegetation health, structural complexity, and thermal characteristics are efficiently grouped into interpretable clusters by this K-means algorithm implementation. The method improves the dataset's usability for vegetation monitoring and land surface analysis by utilizing thresholds that are based on domain knowledge, offering researchers and practitioners useful information.

2.3 Stage Three: Evaluation Metrics

Silhouette Score: A statistical metric used to evaluate the quality of clustering by analyzing how accurately data points are allocated to their appropriate clusters. It measures how similar an object is to its cluster (cohesion) compared to other clusters (separation). The Silhouette score does not require previously classified data. This measure captures the clustering's variance, separation, and compactness [24]. The formula of the Silhouette score is illustrated in Eq. (8).

$$\text{Sil} = \frac{b - a}{\text{Maximum}(b, a)} \quad (8)$$

where a is the average distance within the same cluster, and b is the average distance to all other clusters. Better clustering is indicated by a value close to 1. Conversely, the worst-case scenario is represented by a value of -1, and the overlapping clusters are indicated by a value of 0.

Davies-Bouldin Index (DBI): The DBI is a commonly used metric to assess clustering performance. It measures the compactness and separation of clusters, with lower DBI values indicating better clustering outcomes. The average similarity of each cluster to the most comparable cluster is evaluated by DBI [25]. Equation (9) represents the DBI formula:

$$DBI = \frac{1}{k}\sum_{i=1}^{k} \max_{j \neq i}\left(\frac{S_i + S_j}{M_{ij}}\right) \quad (9)$$

where:
k: Total number of clusters,
S_i: Average intra-cluster distance for cluster i,
S_j: Average intra-cluster distance for cluster j,
M_{ij}: Inter-cluster distance between clusters i and j.

Entropy: A statistical metric that is used to express how diverse or unpredictable the label distribution is in each sample. In clustering, the entropy measures the homogeneity of the space (high entropy means no clustering, low entropy means high clustering) [26]. It reflects the unpredictability of assignments and assesses how equally the data points are divided among various labels or clusters in clustering or classification. The mathematical definition of entropy is represented in Eq. (10):

$$H = -\sum_{i=1}^{n} p_i \log_2 p_i \quad (10)$$

where:

- H: Entropy, which refers to the diversity in the distribution of clusters,
- k: The number of clusters,
- p_i: percentage of cluster i data points. It is computed as: $p_i = \frac{n_i}{N}$, where n_i represent the number of points in the cluster i, and N is the total number of data points.

3 Dataset Description

In this work, we adopted the Landsat Surface Reflectance dataset [27]. The dataset consists of 17,148 atmospherically corrected satellite images. Each frame (or: scene) covers an area of 185 km × 185 km (about 186 km × 186 km at the equator) of the Earth - in all possible global directions, including Africa, South America, North America, Europe, Asia, Indonesia, and parts of Antarctica (during daylight). The data used is a collection of spectral bands surface reflectance images from the Landsat satellite in raster format (pixel by pixel). These bands are designed to record in particular sets of wavelengths and are important for vegetation and land surface studies. The main spectral bands that have been used in the Landsat missions are shown in Fig. 1. The purpose of each band is:

- Blue (0.45–0.51 μm), detects shallow water penetration in coastal surveillance.

- Green (0.53–0.59 μm): sensitive to greenness of vegetation.
- Red (0.63–0.69 μm): (used in NDVI) to indicate vegetation health.
- Near-infrared (NIR) (0.85–0.88 μm): important for NDVI/EVI indices and biomass calculation.
- SWIR1/SWIR2 (1.56–2.29 μm): moisture and vegetation stress coverage.
- TIR (10.6–11.2 μm): developed to derive Land Surface Temperature (LST).

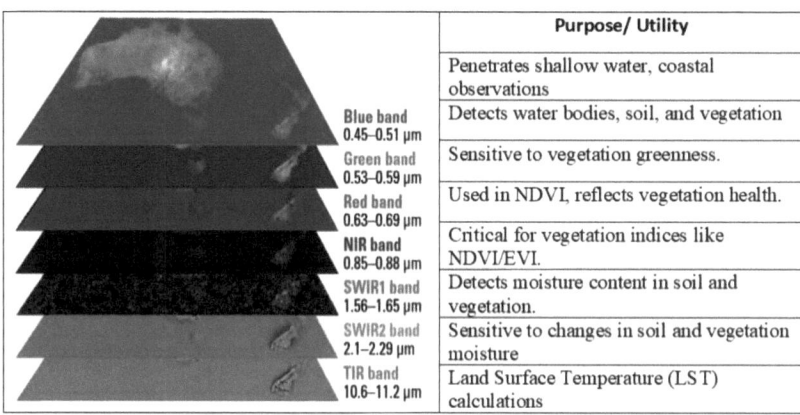

Fig. 1. Band Designations for Landsat Satellites

Computed bands allow us to calculate vegetation indices (e.g., NDVI), fractal dimensions, and LST, parameters important to our method for estimating vegetation health. Figure 2 provides an example of raster images (10000.tif, 10001.tif, and 10002.tif) from the dataset. These pictures illustrate how land cover, reflectivity level, and density of vegetation change over the different spectral bands, which may give a hint at the complex nature of the input data for unsupervised clustering.

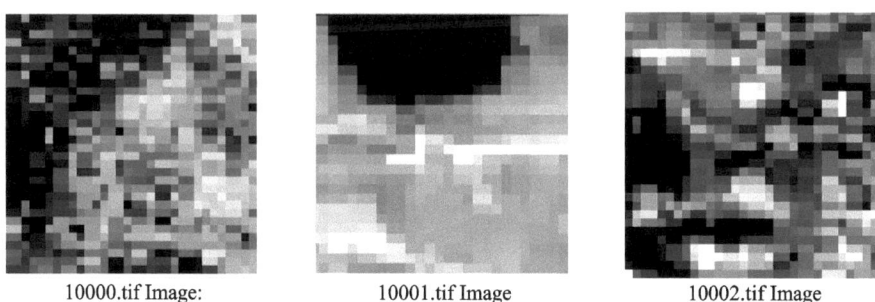

10000.tif Image: 10001.tif Image   10002.tif Image

Fig. 2. Sample from Landsat_Surface_Reflectance Dataset

4 Experimental Results and Analysis

The results of this study provide a comparative analysis of the two clustering techniques (threshold-based labelling and K-means clustering) after applying them to the Landsat Surface Reflectance dataset. The methods were evaluated based on their ability to cluster vegetation health and land surface characteristics using NDVI, FD, and LST features. To evaluate and compare the clustering performance of both methods (threshold-based labelling and K-means clustering), three measures are utilized, including the Silhouette score (shown in Eq. 8), the Davies-Bouldin index (DBI) using Eq. (9), and the Entropy metrics using Eq. (10). In this section, the key results are accompanied by data visualizations to illustrate the clustering performance and the assigned labels.

4.1 Threshold-Based Labeling Method Description

For threshold-based Labeling, the results illustrated in Fig. 3 show the clustering performance across all features. First, NDVI, the Silhouette Score, and the entropy metrics show relatively high performance, indicating a good balance of cluster cohesion and separation. The DBI is comparatively lower, suggesting relatively well-defined clusters. For FD, the Silhouette Score shows the best clustering performance. However, the DBI is significantly low, indicating superior clustering with minimal clustering overlap. Lastly, the entropy metric conveys good cluster labeling. For LST, the Silhouette Score indicates low performance compared with NDVI and FD methods. To sum up, the FD feature shows the best clustering performance overall with the highest Silhouette Score, the lowest DBI, and the entropy measures. LST gives the most informative threshold label (highest Entropy), and NDVI provides balanced metrics, but overall, NDVI does not outperform the other features under any single metric. The analysis demonstrates that some features are stronger than others, and thus, one should choose features based on the desired metrics in clustering applications.

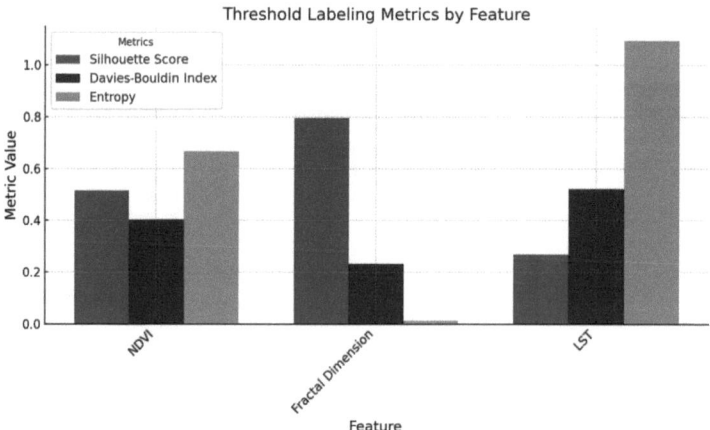

Fig. 3. Threshold Labeling Method: comparison

4.2 K-Means Clustering with Interpretable Clusters

The results illustrated in Fig. 4 show the clustering performance across all features using the K-means clustering. The clustering results of LST in terms of the Silhouette Score measure relatively low, indicating that the similarity of an object to its cluster (cohesion) compared to other clusters (separation) is poor. On the other hand, the DBI measures are relatively high, indicating high overlap and ill-defined cluster boundaries. Although the entropy is relatively low across features, it is considered medium, indicating that the elements within a cluster show average similarity. This confirms that LST has a low capacity in the cluster with a moderate ability to distinguish a clear cluster with cohesion.

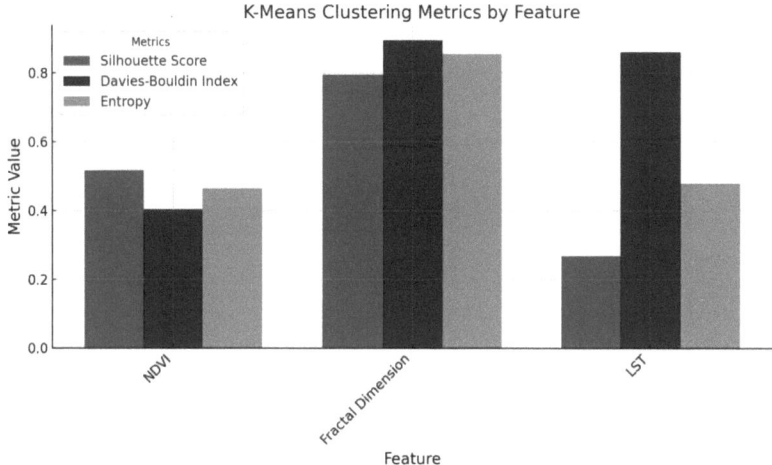

Fig. 4. Results of K-means Labels Across Features

The Silhouette Score for the FD is higher when compared to NDVI and LST (i.e., the clusters are more compact and separated for the FD). On the other hand, the DBI features the highest score among all and indicates high overlap and ill-defined cluster boundaries. The second fact is that the entropy is of high value, indicating a high changeability and diversity in cluster assignments [19]. These findings suggest that although FD is superior in cluster cohesion compared to NDVI, it has obvious difficulty in cluster separation. Thus, it cannot be recommended in the current study. The results for clustering are optimal for NDVI. It yields the best Silhouette Score overall features, indicating the best inter- and intra-cluster distance. The DBI is low, indicating well-separated and compact clusters. Entropy is moderate, which means there is a good amount of diversity of labels without over-mixing. The results showed that NDVI performed best with clear, cohesive, well-separated, meaningful clusters when K-means clustering is applied.

The comparison (K-means versus threshold-based labels) of clustering metrics, Silhouette Score, DBI, and entropy assesses both the cohesion and separation of clusters and the diversity of labels, as depicted in Fig. 5. This comparison highlights the importance of an appropriate selection of the features to be clustered and the right method fitting to the executed clustering. To sum up, K-means and threshold-based label methods showed the same behavior in terms of compactness and cohesion (Silhouette Score). However, threshold-based methods outperformed K-means regarding cluster separation (DBI) and informativeness (Entropy) for NDVI and LST. The metric should be chosen based on the clustering goal. If your priority is information gain maximization, threshold-based labels are better. However, if you need well-defined clusters, perhaps K-means is the most appropriate one. To sum up, for clustering vegetation health into three categories, K-means clustering with NDVI and threshold-based labels with FD as features would probably perform best regarding compactness and definition of clusters, which corresponds with the goals of this study.

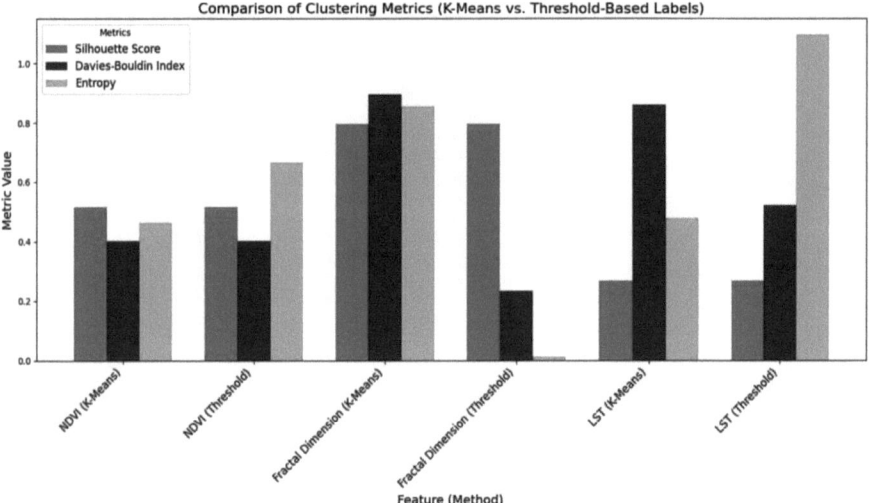

Fig. 5. Comparison of results between the two methods (K-means and threshold-based labels)

Figure 6 displays two scatter plots representing the clustering results of K-means and threshold-based labels by combining the features: NDVI, FD, and LST. The data points are color-coded based on their assigned clusters, with the color bar indicating cluster labels.

In terms of cluster boundaries, the clusters appear to be more cohesive and relatively separated in the feature space illustrated in Fig. 6(a), which represents K-means clustering. On the other hand, the threshold labeling clustering method shown in Fig. 6(b) depicts less cohesive clustering, and there is more overlap between clusters. Although the K-means method mathematically generates optimal clusters, the resulting cluster boundaries are less intuitive because they do not directly correspond to feature thresholds. Threshold-based clustering is easier to interpret, as cluster membership is explicitly attached to the feature ranges (e.g., NDVI < 0.3).

K-means clustering is well-formed and ensures reasonably separated clusters by defining boundaries that are updated based on variance in data. Therefore, it is a suitable method for identifying accurate vegetation health. It is also not explicit clustering

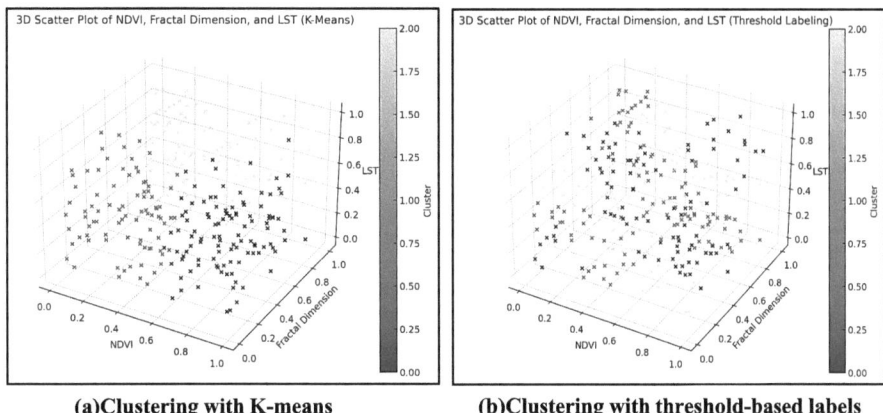

(a) Clustering with K-means   (b) Clustering with threshold-based labels

Fig. 6. Scatter plots of clustering results

because we are not minimizing inter-cluster but intra-cluster variance. On the other hand, threshold labelling is logical and easy to interpret, associating clusters with given ranges of features, but it is also not flexible and may lead to overlaps if the distribution of data is far from the thresholds. K-means grouping, on the one hand, is more appropriate for depth, accuracy, and precision, partly to cover the cons of threshold, on the contrary, where simplicity and replicability are far more important than precision.

5 Conclusion

This study is concerned with identifying vegetation health by clustering satellite images using NDVI, FD, and LST as features. We applied K-means and threshold-based labeling to Landsat remote sensing data to classify vegetation into healthy, stressed, and non-vegetation categories. Our findings reveal that threshold-based labeling creates cohesive and well-separated clusters for FD, as shown by high Silhouette and low DBI scores along with low entropy. In contrast, K-means clustering exhibits greater label diversity for NDVI and LST than FD due to their better entropy values. Both clustering methods yield similar Silhouette Scores for the three features (NDVI, FD, and LST), indicating effective cluster cohesion and separation. These results highlight the strengths of each method: threshold-based labeling is ideal for features with defined thresholds, while K-means allow for adaptability in cases without such limits. FD with Threshold-based labels demonstrates superior clustering results, offering clear and interpretable outcomes, which are crucial for evaluating vegetation health and analyzing land surfaces. This analysis offers important insights for researchers and practitioners in vegetation health monitoring and environmental data analysis, helping them choose the most suitable clustering technique based on specific datasets and objectives. In future work, since FD proves its effectiveness in detecting vegetation, we will investigate the performance of FractalNet to classify the vegetation in satellite images in terms of accuracy. We also aim to compare the performance of FractalNet with convolutional neural networks (CNNs) in terms of accuracy and processing speed.

Disclosure of Interests. The authors have no competing interests to declare in this study.

References

1. Hannah_Ospina.: Ensuring a sustainable future through plant health. NL Netherlands (2024). https://nlplatform.com/articles/ensuring-sustainable-future-through-plant-health#:~:text=Healthy%20plants%20play%20a%20crucial,and%20secure%20a%20sus-tainable%20future
2. Heeb, L., Jenner, E.: Climate-smart pest management: implementation guidance for policymakers and investors. (FAO) Practice Brief Climate-Smart Agriculture (2017). https://openknowledge.fao.org/server/api/core/bitstreams/fd66f08d-ea43-4bb8-8fa0-bda26d694840/content
3. Mehmood, K., et al.: Analyzing vegetation health dynamics across seasons and regions through NDVI and climatic variables. Sci. Rep. **14**(1), 11775 (2024). https://doi.org/10.1038/s41598-024-62464-7
4. Samawi, V.W: SMCSIS: An IoT-based secure multi-crop irrigation system for smart farming. Int. J. Innovative Comput. Inf. Control (IJICIC) **17**(4) (2021). http://www.ijicic.org/ijicic-170408.pdf
5. Gu, Z., Zeng, M.: The use of artificial intelligence and satellite remote sensing in land cover change detection: review and perspectives. Sustainability **16**(1), 274 (2024). https://doi.org/10.3390/su16010274
6. Kharat, V., Khatdeo, S., Kothe, H., Kshirsagar, R., Dixit, M., Balan, M.S.: Land cover clustering and classification of satellite images. In: First International Conference on Data Science and Advanced Computing (ICDSAC 2023), ITM Web Conf. 56. EDP Sciences (2023). https://doi.org/10.1051/itmconf/20235602004
7. Thwal, N.S., Ishikawa, T., Watanabe, H.: Land cover classification and change detection analysis of multispectral satellite images using machine learning. Image Sig. Process. Remote Sens. XXV **115510**, 11155 (2019). https://doi.org/10.1117/12.2532988
8. Khodadadi, N., et al.: Predicting normalized difference vegetation index using a deep attention network with bidirectional GRU: a hybrid parametric optimization approach. Int. J. Data Sci. Anal. (2024). https://doi.org/10.1007/s41060-0
9. Yang, H., Chen, W., Qian, T., Shen, D., Wang, J.: The extraction of vegetation points from LiDAR using 3D fractal dimension analyses. Remote Sens. **7**(8), 10815–10831 (2015). https://doi.org/10.3390/rs7081081
10. Yousif, S.A., Mohammed, A.J., Al-Saidi, N.M.G.: Texture images analysis using fractal extracted attributes. Int. J. Innovative Comput. Inf. Control **16**(4) (2020)
11. Yousif, S.A., Abdul-Wahed, H. ., Al-Saidi, N.M.: Extracting a new fractal and semi-variance attributes for texture images. In: AIP Conference Proceedings, vol. 2183, no. 1. AIP Publishing (2019)
12. Al-Azawi, R.J., Al-Saidi, N., Jalab, H.A., Ibrahim, R., Baleanu, D.: Image splicing detection based on texture features with fractal entropy (2021)
13. Martinez, A. D., Labib, S.: Demystifying normalized difference vegetation index (NDVI) for greenness exposure assessments and policy interventions in urban greening (2023). Environ. Res. **220** (2023). https://doi.org/10.1016/j.envres.2022.115155
14. Jehad, R., Yousif, S.A.: Fake news classification using random forest and decision tree (j48). Al-Nahrain J. Sci. **23**(4), 49–55 (2020)
15. Yousif, S.A., Samawi, V.W., Al-Saidi, N.M.: Automatic machine learning classification algorithms for stability detection of smart grid. In: 2022 IEEE 5th International Conference on Big Data and Artificial Intelligence (BDAI), pp. 34–39. IEEE (2022)

16. Kwan, C., Gribben, D., Ayhan, B., Li, J., Bernabe, S.: An accurate vegetation and non-vegetation differentiation approach based on land cover classification. Remote Sens. **12**(23), 3880 (2020). https://doi.org/10.3390/rs12233880
17. Ouchra, H., Belangour, A., Erraissi, A.: Comparison of machine learning methods for satellite image classification: a case study of casablanca using landsat imagery and google earth engine. J. Environ. Earth Sci. **5**(2), 118–134 (2023). https://doi.org/10.30564/jees.v5i2.5928
18. Iryanti, M., Nurjanah, R., Waslaluddin, Arifin, M.: Landslide mapping using K-means cluster by NDVI data in Garut, West Java, Indonesia. In: The 1st International Seminar on Physics and Its Application, Phys.: Conference Series 2900 012020. IOP (2024). https://doi.org/10.1088/1742-6596/2900/1/012020
19. Ayhan, B., et al.: Vegetation detection using deep learning and conventional methods. Remote Sens. **12**(15) (2020). https://doi.org/10.3390/rs12152502
20. Interior, U.D.: USGS science for a changing world. Landsat 8 acquired from the U.S (2023). https://www.usgs.gov/landsat-missions/landsat-8
21. Al-Saidi, N.M., Abdul-Wahed, H.Y.: Classification of remote sensing images via fractal descriptores. In: 2018 International Conference on Advance of Sustainable Engineering and its Application (ICASEA), pp. 99–104. IEEE (2018)
22. Li, Z.L., et al.: Satellite remote sensing of global land surface temperature: definition, methods, products, and applications. Rev. Geophys. **61**(1), e2022RG000777 (2023)
23. Yousif, S.A., Al-Dulaimy, A.: Clustering cloud workload traces to improve the performance of cloud data centers. In: Proceedings of the World Congress on Engineering, vol. 1, pp. 7–10 (2017)
24. Abdulhameed, T.Z., Yousif, S.A., Samawi, V.W., Al-Shaikhli, H.I.: SS-DBSCAN: Semi-supervised density-based spatial clustering of applications with noise for meaningful clustering in diverse density data. IEEE Access (2024)
25. Ros, F., Riad, R., Guillaume, S.: PDBI: a partitioning Davies-Bouldin index for clustering evaluation. Neurocomputing **528**, 178–199 (2023). https://doi.org/10.1016/j.neucom.2023.01.043
26. Joel, B.: Swartz, an entropy-based algorithm for detecting clusters of cases and controls and its comparison with a method using nearest neighbours. Health Place **4**(1), 67–77 (1998). https://doi.org/10.1016/S1353-8292(97)00026-9
27. Landsat_Surface_Reflectance Dataset. https://www.kaggle.com/datasets/reymas-ter/hwsd-landsat-processed

Repository-Level Code Understanding by LLMs via Hierarchical Summarization: Improving Code Search and Bug Localization

Amirkia Rafiei Oskooei[1,2](✉)[ID], Selcan Yukcu[1], Mehmet Cevheri Bozoglan[1], and Mehmet S. Aktas[2][ID]

[1] Intellica Business Intelligence Consultancy, R&D Center, Istanbul, Turkey
{amirkia.oskooei,selcan.yukcu,cevheri.bozoglan}@intellica.net
[2] Department of Computer Engineering, Yildiz Technical University, Istanbul, Turkey
amirkia.oskooei@std.yildiz.edu.tr, aktas@yildiz.edu.tr
https://www.intellica.net, https://www.yildiz.edu.tr

Abstract. Bug localization and semantic code search within large software repositories is a significant and time-consuming challenge for developers, particularly when dealing with bug reports from end-users who lack technical expertise. Traditional similarity-based code search methods struggle with the inherent domain and vocabulary mismatch between end-user reports and codebase semantics, while directly applying Large Language Models (LLMs) is hampered by their limited context windows and lack of repository-level understanding. To address these limitations, this paper introduces a novel, structure-aware methodology for creating repository-aware LLMs using hierarchical summarization. Our approach comprises a pre-processing phase that constructs an abstract repository tree, creates a context-aware LLM primed with project knowledge, and generates hierarchical summaries at project, directory, and file levels. The inference phase employs a top-down search strategy, guiding the LLM to progressively narrow down the search space from directory-level to file-level, effectively localizing bug-relevant code. This method mitigates the context window bottleneck and leverages LLMs' semantic understanding to overcome domain gap issues. Evaluated on a real-world dataset of Jira issues from a large-scale industrial project, our approach significantly outperforms both Flat Retrieval baselines and state-of-the-art LLM + Retrieval-Augmented Generation (RAG) systems, achieving a Pass@10 of 0.89 and Recall@10 of 0.33. The results demonstrate the efficacy of hierarchical summarization in enabling scalable, task-agnostic, and structure-aware repository-level code comprehension for improved bug localization and code search, particularly in scenarios involving non-technical end-user bug reports.

Keywords: Software Engineering · Large Language Models (LLMs) · Semantic Code Search · Automatic Program Repair · Defect Detection · Applied Machine Learning

1 Introduction

Locating and fixing bugs within codebases is a notoriously time-consuming and demanding task for software developers. This process typically necessitates a thorough review of the codebase, requiring developers to meticulously analyze potentially vast amounts of code to pinpoint the files or code segments responsible for a reported bug or defect. The challenge is amplified significantly in large code repositories, where the sheer volume of code can make bug localization feel like searching for a needle in a haystack.

Automated Program Repair (APR), encompassing Code Defect Detection and Repair, has long been a vital and actively researched area within software engineering. The promise of automated tools to identify and resolve bugs is highly attractive to developers seeking to improve efficiency and code quality. The rapid advancement of neural networks, driven by increased computational power and the explosion of large-scale datasets, has significantly propelled progress in this domain, offering new avenues for automating bug localization from issue reports.

For instance, early approaches to automated code search and bug localization have successfully employed language models like UnixCoder, CodeBERT, and ModernBERT. These encoder-only models operate by transforming both code and natural language into vector representations (embeddings). This embedding space enables the system to identify code files or segments that are semantically similar to a natural language query, such as a bug report from platforms like GitHub or Jira, by calculating a similarity score between the embeddings of query and code.

More recently, Large Language Models (LLMs), celebrated for their remarkable ability to understand and generate text, code, and visuals [14,19,24,26] thanks to their huge pre-training big data [23,28], have also been adopted for bug localization. While LLMs demand greater computational resources for both training and inference and are not as cost-effective as encoder-only models, their enhanced capabilities in understanding both codebase semantics and query content, coupled with their general intelligence, make them compelling alternatives.

Despite the increasing adoption of both encoder-only and LLM-based approaches for code search and bug localization, significant limitations persist. Similarity-based methods, which rely on embedding models to bridge natural language queries (bug reports) and code segments, often suffer from a "domain gap and vocabulary mismatch" problem, as shown in Fig. 1. This issue arises when the natural language query is poorly formulated or originates from a domain significantly different from the codebase itself. Consider, for example, an end-user reporting a graphical user interface issue, lacking any understanding of the underlying codebase or programming concepts. Their issue description, focused solely on UI functionality, may contain vocabulary and concepts that are semantically distant from the technical vocabulary of the codebase. Consequently, directly calculating similarity between embeddings of such end-user issue descriptions and code segments becomes ineffective. Developers are then forced to manually refine queries to bridge this gap, effectively requiring them to pre-analyze the codebase and understand the bug before even initiating an automated search.

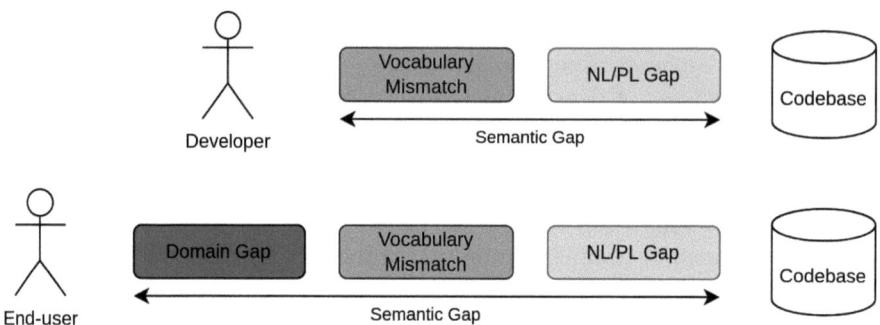

Fig. 1. Our approach in addition to vocabulary mismatch and NL/PL gap problems which are widely recognized and addressed in semantic code search, solves the issue of domain gap (the red box). (Color figure online)

LLMs, with their advanced semantic understanding, offer a potential avenue to mitigate the domain gap and vocabulary mismatch problem to some extent. However, even with their superior comprehension of natural language and code relationships, LLMs face their own set of challenges in bug localization, primarily stemming from **context window limitations**. This constraint becomes acutely apparent when dealing with large, enterprise-scale repositories containing hundreds or thousands of files. Prompting an LLM with the entirety of such a codebase is simply infeasible due to these context limits.

Furthermore, even when utilizing long-context LLMs capable of processing moderately sized repositories, simply feeding code files sequentially is insufficient for effective repository-level understanding. LLMs require a structured context that captures the intricate interconnectivity and functional relationships between files within the repository. Therefore, beyond merely addressing context window size, **pre-processing and structuring contextual information** becomes crucial to enable LLMs to truly comprehend code at the repository level.

To overcome these challenges, this paper introduces a **structure-aware, highly scalable, and task-agnostic approach** designed to empower LLMs with repository-level code comprehension, effectively creating **context-aware LLMs**. Our methodology centers around **hierarchical summarization**, representing expansive repositories as reduced-size, tree-structured prompts. This strategy effectively mitigates the context window limitations of LLMs while simultaneously leveraging their inherent strengths in semantic code search to address the domain gap and vocabulary mismatch problem prevalent in traditional similarity-based methods. This approach enables more effective code search and bug localization across diverse query types and large codebases.

In this study, our main objectives are:

1. To address the domain gap and vocabulary mismatch problem inherent in similarity-based code search approaches for bug localization, particularly when dealing with end-user bug reports.
2. To overcome the limited context window challenge faced by Large Language Models (LLMs) when applied to large-scale code repositories
3. To develop a scalable and task-agnostic approach that enables LLMs to effectively understand and reason about code at the repository level
4. To introduce a novel hierarchical summarization technique for representing large code repositories in a reduced-size format suitable for LLM prompting, while preserving essential structural and functional information.

This paper introduces a novel, hierarchical summarization methodology to enable repository-aware Large Language Models (LLMs). Our approach constructs a hierarchical tree of code summaries, significantly reducing the input size for LLMs while preserving crucial repository-level context. This addresses the LLM context window limitation and enables effective code understanding for downstream tasks. Specifically, we develop a context-aware LLM architecture for code search and bug localization, tackling the domain gap and vocabulary mismatch problem inherent in traditional similarity-based methods. Our hierarchical summarization allows the LLM to bridge the gap between natural language bug reports (even from end-users) and the codebase, effectively localizing bugs without requiring developers to manually craft specialized queries. Furthermore, this architecture forms a scalable and task-agnostic framework applicable to other software engineering tasks requiring repository-level code comprehension. A rigorous empirical evaluation on a real-world industry-level bug localization dataset demonstrates that our approach is highly effective. The results reveal that our method significantly surpasses the performance of both similarity-based and existing LLM-based methods, achieving quantifiable improvements in localization accuracy. This empirical evidence strongly validates the practical applicability of our technique for enhancing bug localization in complex, real-world software environments.

2 Related Works

To contextualize our proposed methodology, this section provides an overview of existing research in code search and bug localization, focusing on two dominant paradigms: similarity-based approaches and more recent Large Language Model (LLM)-driven techniques. We examine the core principles, strengths, and limitations of each category, highlighting how these prior works have attempted to address the challenges of bridging the gap between natural language queries and codebases. This review serves as a foundation for understanding the novelty and contributions of our hierarchical summarization approach, which aims to integrate the benefits of both paradigms while mitigating their respective drawbacks to achieve more effective repository-level code understanding for bug localization.

Similarity-based code search methods have long been a cornerstone in the field, leveraging the power of embedding spaces to bridge the gap between natural language queries and programming language code. These techniques, exemplified by models like CodeBERT [11], UniXcoder [12], and most recently ModernBert [31], encode both natural language queries and code snippets into a shared embedding space. Similarity metrics such as cosine similarity or dot product are then used to measure the semantic relatedness between queries and code. This approach effectively addresses the inherent Natural Language/Programming Language (NL/PL) gap by comparing queries and code in a semantically rich embedding space [8].

However, similarity-based methods are not without limitations. They often struggle with poorly formulated queries, such as vague or incomplete bug descriptions, and suffer from the vocabulary mismatch problem. For instance, end-user bug reports often use non-technical language that is semantically distant from the code's vocabulary, leading to poor retrieval performance. To mitigate these challenges, researchers have explored query expansion and augmentation techniques. Query expansion aims to broaden the scope of the original query by adding semantically similar terms, while query augmentation seeks to generate diverse query formulations to better capture the user's intent. Some studies have even leveraged LLMs to enhance similarity-based code search through query augmentation and expansion, as well as for flat retrieval using similarity calculation [16,17,30]. These hybrid approaches represent a significant step towards improving the robustness of similarity-based code search, but they still inherit some limitations, particularly in handling the domain gap and vocabulary mismatch problems when dealing with non-technical end-user bug reports.

In recent years, Large Language Models (LLMs) have emerged as powerful tools for various Software Engineering (SE) tasks, including repository-level code auditing [13], bug localization [25], code completion [32], and code question answering [6]. Unlike traditional similarity-based methods, LLM-driven approaches leverage the models' deep semantic understanding to directly process and reason about code and natural language queries. These methods have shown remarkable promise in tackling complex SE tasks at the repository level, offering several advantages over similarity-based techniques.

LLM-based approaches excel in semantic understanding, enabling them to bridge the domain gap and vocabulary mismatch that often plague similarity-based methods. For example, LLMs can effectively interpret non-technical end-user bug reports and relate them to the technical vocabulary of the codebase [18]. They also demonstrate superior context awareness, capable of processing and reasoning over long code sequences and complex inter-file dependencies [9,33]. Agentic workflows and planning have also recently received significant attention. CodePlan [5] introduces a neuro-symbolic framework that synthesizes multi-step plans of code edits, leveraging LLMs and combining incremental dependency analysis with adaptive planning for repository-level coding tasks. AutoCodeRover [34] proposes an autonomous program improvement approach that combines LLMs with sophisticated code search techniques, utilizing a stratified search strategy and test-based fault localization for effective GitHub issue resolution. REPOAUDIT [13] presents an autonomous LLM-agent for repository-level code auditing, employing an agent memory, data-flow analysis, and a validator to enable precise and efficient bug detection in real-world software systems.

However, LLM-based approaches also face challenges. Context window limitations remain a significant bottleneck, especially when dealing with large-scale code repositories [18,25]. Moreover, training and deploying LLMs for large codebases can be prohibitively expensive for many research groups and organizations, and inference latency can become a bottleneck for interactive developer workflows. While long-context LLMs offer expanded context windows, they may still struggle with massive repositories exceeding these limits [7]. Despite these challenges, LLM-based approaches represent a significant advancement in repository-level code understanding, offering a more robust and semantically aware alternative to traditional techniques.

The authors of [3] addressed dynamic information service reliability and scalability in distributed Grid environments, laying foundational work for system-level fault tolerance. The authors of [27] contributed a systematic examination of mobile application verification techniques, emphasizing formal and empirical evaluation methods. In the domain of behavioral modeling, the authors of [21,22] explored the use of embeddings for representing user interaction patterns in web environments. The authors of [29] proposed a provenance collection platform to ensure traceability in large-scale environmental simulations, while the authors of [4,20] developed collaborative and complexity-aware Grid platforms to support scientific computing and high-performance workflows. Although these works contributed significantly to distributed computing, provenance management, and user behavior modeling, none of them focus on repository-level code comprehension using hierarchical summarization or on bridging the semantic gap between natural language bug reports and codebases using LLMs, which is the central novelty of this study.

Our methodology, Repository-Level Code Understanding by LLMs via Hierarchical Summarization, uniquely synergizes the strengths of both similarity-based and LLM-based approaches while addressing their limitations. Like similarity-based methods, we leverage efficient retrieval techniques to navigate large codebases. However, unlike traditional similarity-based approaches that rely solely on embedding similarity, we incorporate LLMs to create a hierarchical summarization of the repository, enabling a more nuanced and context-aware representation of the codebase.

Similar to LLM-based approaches, we harness the semantic understanding capabilities of LLMs to bridge the domain gap and vocabulary mismatch problem. However, unlike existing LLM-based methods that often struggle with context window limitations, our hierarchical summarization significantly reduces the input size for LLMs, allowing them to process and reason over large codebases efficiently. Furthermore, our approach enhances the explainability of bug localization by providing structured, hierarchical summaries that facilitate both machine and human comprehension of the codebase, in contrast to the often opaque nature of embedding-based or end-to-end LLM approaches.

In essence, our methodology offers a novel, structure-aware approach to repository-level code understanding that combines the scalability of similarity-based methods with the semantic richness of LLMs. By leveraging hierarchical summarization, we overcome the context window bottleneck and domain gap challenges, enabling more effective and scalable code search and bug localization, particularly in complex, real-world software repositories.

3 Methodology

This research introduces a novel methodology for enhancing Large Language Model (LLM) performance in repository-level code understanding, specifically for the task of automated bug localization. Our approach centers on a two-phased system architecture encompassing a comprehensive pre-processing stage and an inference phase optimized for efficient and accurate bug localization within large codebases. The pre-processing phase focuses on transforming a raw code repository into a structured, LLM-interpretable format, while the inference phase leverages this structured representation to effectively guide the LLM in identifying bug locations based on natural language queries or bug reports. This methodology is designed to address key challenges in applying LLMs to large codebases, including context window limitations and the semantic gap between natural language bug reports and the technical vocabulary of source code.

3.1 Pre-processing Phase

The pre-processing stage is crucial for preparing the code repository and enabling effective LLM-based analysis. This phase consists of three key steps designed to create a hierarchical, context-rich representation of the codebase.

Step 1: Building Repository Tree. The initial step involves constructing an abstract **repository tree**, a hierarchical representation of the codebase tailored to project needs and not strictly bound by the physical file system structure. This abstract tree organizes the repository into three distinct levels: root, directory, and file, as shown in Fig. 2. While the depth of this tree can be adjusted to accommodate repositories with varying levels of nesting, for this study, we employ a depth of three, incorporating a single directory level beneath the root. This depth is strategically chosen to balance representational granularity with computational efficiency, particularly relevant for managing the complexity of large repositories. The flexibility to define the tree abstractly allows developers and stakeholders to structure the repository representation according to the logical modules and organizational principles most pertinent to the project's architecture and comprehension.

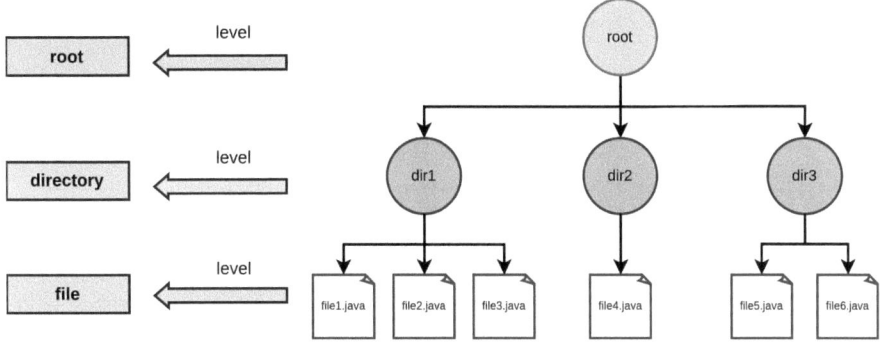

Fig. 2. The repository tree is an abstract tree created during the pre-processing phase that represents the codebase as file and directory level(s).

Step 2: Creating Context-Aware LLMs. To imbue the LLM with project-specific context, a crucial step is the creation of what we term a **"context-aware LLM."** This involves providing the LLM with a rich set of resources during the pre-processing phase to generate a comprehensive project summary. These resources, supplied by project stakeholders, include the raw codebase, project-specific rules and guidelines, README files, and project documentation. The repository tree, defined in the preceding step, also plays a vital role by illustrating the project's structural organization to the LLM. These resources collectively provide the LLM with essential information regarding the repository's general functionality, intended use cases, underlying technology stack, and overarching architecture. Specifically, to generate a detailed root-level project summary, these resources are input to a long-context LLM, capable of processing extensive textual information. The LLM then outputs a concise project summary in natural language. This project summary is subsequently integrated into the system-level prompts of any off-the-shelf LLM, effectively transforming it into a "context-aware LLM." Throughout this paper, the term "context-aware LLM" refers to an LLM that is systemically primed with this project summary and the aforementioned resources, enabling it to operate with an inherent understanding of the repository's structure, functionality, and architectural nuances.

Step 3: Building Knowledge Tree. Following the creation of the context-aware LLM and the definition of the repository tree, a **bottom-up** summarization approach is employed to generate concise, natural language summaries for each code file and directory within the repository. Starting at the leaf nodes of the repository tree (file level), the context-aware LLM is prompted to generate a summary for each code file (Fig. 3). These file-level summaries capture essential aspects of the code, including its functionality, imports, and interrelationships with other code components.

Subsequently, these file-level summaries are aggregated and provided as input to the context-aware LLM to generate directory-level summaries (Fig. 4). Each

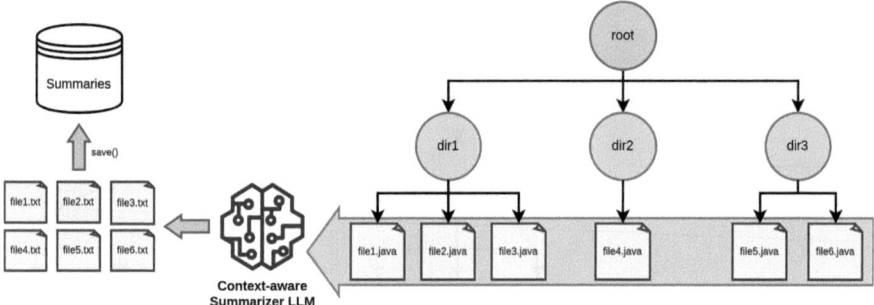

Fig. 3. Illustration of file-level summarization of repository tree using a context-aware LLM

directory-level summary concisely represents the collective functionality and purpose of all files contained within that directory.

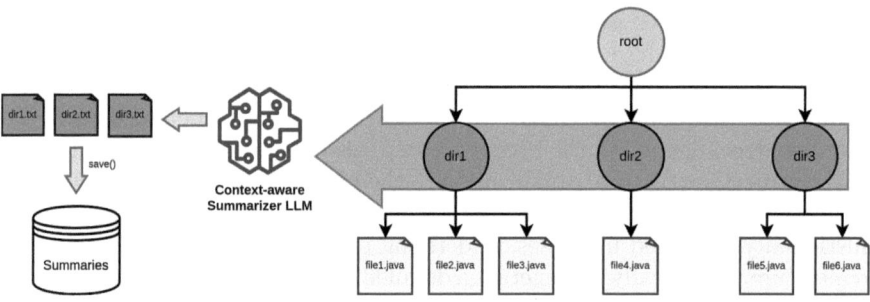

Fig. 4. Illustration of directory-level summarization of repository tree using a context-aware LLM

The culmination of this bottom-up summarization process is the creation of a **knowledge tree**. This knowledge tree mirrors the abstract repository tree structure defined earlier; however, instead of containing raw code files, each node in the knowledge tree is populated with a natural language summary, as shown in Fig. 5. At the root level, the node embodies the project-level summary. At the directory level, each node represents the directory's summary, encapsulating the responsibilities of the directory and its constituent files. At the file level, each node provides a summary of the file, detailing its attributes, methods, imports, and relationships with other files. Crucially, the context-aware nature of the LLM during the summarization process ensures that the generated natural language summaries are not only human-readable and understandable but also implicitly encode the interconnectedness and relationships between files within the larger repository context. This repository-level awareness, stemming from the LLM's initial exposure to the project's tree structure and comprehensive resources, results in high-quality, information-dense summaries that facilitate both machine and human comprehension of the codebase. While the knowledge tree provides a structured, hierarchical representation, it is important to acknowledge the presence of **implicit semantic connections** between nodes (as shown by orange arrows in Fig. 5), arising from the summaries' content, which explicitly mentions imports and file dependencies, further enriching the representation.

3.2 Inference Phase

The inference phase marks the operational stage of our methodology, where the hierarchically structured knowledge tree, generated during pre-processing, is leveraged for downstream tasks, specifically bug localization. In contrast to the bottom-up approach of the pre-processing phase, the inference phase adopts a **top-down** traversal strategy. Initiating from the root node representing the project-level summary, the context-aware LLM is tasked with progressively narrowing down the search space to identify the code components most likely implicated in a given bug report. The overall inference process is structured as a hierarchical search, assigning distinct responsibilities to the LLM at both the directory and file levels, executed in a top-down sequence. For bug localization, these responsibilities are defined as **"directory-level search"** and **"file-level search."** In the directory-level search stage (red arrows in Fig. 5), the context-aware LLM is provided with the bug description, which can originate from sources such as GitHub Issues or Jira bug reports, alongside the pre-computed directory summaries. The LLM's objective at this stage is to analyze these inputs and identify the **top-k directories** deemed most pertinent to the bug description, thus representing the most probable areas within the codebase where the bug might reside. Subsequently, the process proceeds to file-level search (blue arrows in Fig. 5). Here, the LLM is furnished with the file-level summaries of code files located within the top-k directories identified in the preceding directory-level search stage. The task at this level is to pinpoint the **top-n code files** within these selected directories that are most likely to be the source of the reported bug or defect.

This initial directory-level search plays a crucial role as a **filtering mechanism**. Instead of directly exposing the LLM to the entirety of code files within the repository, which would be computationally expensive and potentially overwhelm the model with irrelevant information, it strategically focuses the LLM's attention. By first identifying the most relevant directories, the system significantly mitigates the inherent **context window** limitations of LLMs. The subsequent file-level search then operates within a reduced search space, confined to the top-k directories. Furthermore, the file-level search benefits from the enriched context provided by file-level summaries. Rather than naively prompting the LLM with raw, unstructured code files devoid of explicit inter-file and intra-file relationship information, the system presents pre-processed, enhanced summaries. These summaries not only encapsulate the individual functionality of each file but also implicitly encode the critical interconnectivity and relationships between files, derived from the context-aware summarization process. This

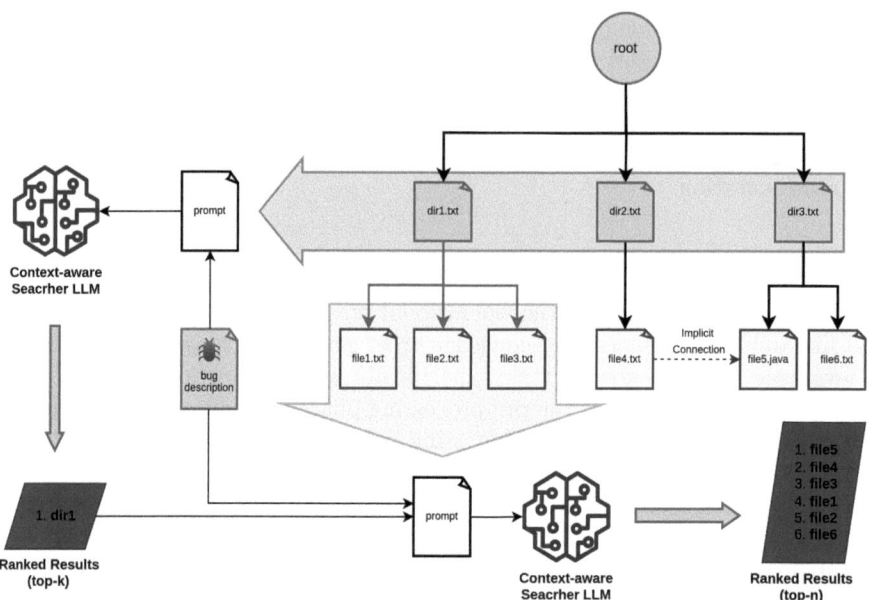

Fig. 5. The knowledge tree is traversed in a top-down manner by a context-aware LLM to identify the most relevant directories (red arrows) and rank the most relevant code files within that directory (blue arrows). (Color figure online)

strategic provision of pre-verified, ready-to-use information obviates the need for the LLM to expend computational resources on understanding the functionality of each code file and deciphering complex inter-file relationships during the inference phase. Instead, the LLM can efficiently focus its analytical capabilities on the core task of bug localization, leveraging the pre-processed knowledge to accurately pinpoint the most probable bug locations.

This hierarchical inference approach, in an abstract sense, draws parallels to the principles of **Chain-of-Thought (CoT)** prompting, a technique recognized for its effectiveness in enhancing LLM performance on complex tasks. CoT prompting advocates for decomposing a complex problem into a sequence of simpler sub-problems, guiding the LLM through a step-by-step reasoning process rather than directly presenting the entire problem at once. Analogously, our bug localization methodology implicitly embodies the spirit of CoT. During the pre-processing phase, we progressively build contextual knowledge: first, creating a context-aware LLM; second, utilizing this LLM to generate granular file-level summaries; and third, aggregating these summaries to form directory-level abstractions. In the inference phase, mirroring the step-by-step reasoning of CoT, the LLM is first tasked with identifying the most relevant directories and subsequently with pinpointing the most probable bug-causing files within those directories. This multi-phase, hierarchical, and step-wise approach inherently aligns with the theoretical underpinnings of CoT prompting, enhancing the efficiency and accuracy of bug localization by guiding the LLM through a structured reasoning process.

4 Experimental Study

To rigorously evaluate the efficacy of our proposed hierarchical summarization methodology for repository-aware bug localization, we conducted a comprehensive experimental study. This section details the experimental setup, including the dataset employed, the baseline methods chosen for comparison, the evaluation metrics utilized, and a discussion of the results obtained. Our study is designed to empirically validate the advantages of our approach in addressing the challenges of domain gap and context window limitations, as well as to assess its overall performance against established code search and bug localization techniques.

4.1 Dataset

For our experimental evaluation, we assembled a dataset of real-world Jira issues, representing bug reports, extracted from a large-scale, industry-level software project. The project's codebase, hosted in a private GitHub repository, provides a standardized solution for the rapid integration of partner products into an existing catalog system. Specifically, it empowers service providers to directly feed partner systems with technical product descriptions, streamlining the product integration process. This codebase is characterized by a microservice architecture and adheres to TM Forum standards, reflecting the complexity and architectural patterns typical of enterprise-level commercial software. The Jira issues within our dataset are particularly valuable as they are authored by end-users, not developers. This provenance introduces a significant domain gap and vocabulary mismatch between the natural language query (the Jira issue description) and the technical vocabulary of the codebase itself. Such end-user reported issues are recognized as among the most challenging for developers to effectively localize and resolve due to this semantic gap. Therefore, this case study provides an ideal benchmark to assess our methodology's capability to overcome the context window limitations of Large Language Models (LLMs), develop a scalable and task-agnostic approach for repository-level code understanding, and explicitly address the domain and vocabulary mismatch problem inherent in similarity-based bug localization, especially when dealing with non-technical end-user reports. The detailed statistics of our dataset are summarized in Table 1.

As indicated in the table, a single Jira issue often necessitates modifications across multiple code files. Solving a typical issue frequently requires developers to identify and modify several files, amplifying the complexity of the bug localization task. The automated system must therefore be capable of locating multiple relevant files within a substantial repository, akin to finding multiple needles within a haystack. This dataset, therefore, serves as a robust and realistic benchmark for evaluating the performance of our proposed system in real-world scenarios.

Table 1. Statistics of our datasest, consisted of queries and codes

Codebase	Repository	Language	Files	Java Files	Lines
	private	Java	743	474	95873
Query	Issue Type	Source	Reporter	Issues	Buggy Files
	Bug	Jira	End-users	9	86

4.2 Baselines

To provide a comparative performance analysis, we benchmarked our proposed methodology against established and state-of-the-art approaches in code search and bug localization. We selected similarity-based methods as a primary baseline, recognizing their widespread adoption and established presence in the field. We categorize this group of approaches as "Flat Retrieval", reflecting their fundamental retrieval-based nature. Specifically, we employed UnixCoder and ModernBERT to generate embeddings for each code file within our repository. Subsequently, we utilized the FAISS [10] library's efficient KNN (K-Nearest Neighbors) algorithm to retrieve the top-k code files most semantically similar to the natural language query (the bug description). As a further comparative baseline, we evaluated systems employing LLMs augmented with Retrieval-Augmented Generation (RAG). We selected Codeium [2] and Cursor AI [1], two state-of-the-art commercial tools widely adopted by developers for repository-level code understanding and "chatting with the codebase" functionalities. Both Codeium and Cursor AI offer capabilities to interact with an entire repository, rather than individual files, and both are understood to utilize RAG techniques to index the codebase and retrieve relevant code segments in response to user queries. While detailed, both systems are black-boxes and precise information regarding the proprietary methodologies employed by Codeium and Cursor AI is not publicly available, their widespread use and claims of RAG and context-aware approaches make them highly relevant benchmarks. Despite the lack of complete transparency in their implementation details, these tools represent the current state-of-the-art in commercially available, repository-aware code understanding systems, making them a compelling comparison point for our research. We term this comparative group "LLM + RAG." To ensure a fair and consistent comparison across LLM-based systems, we selected gpt-4o [15] as the underlying Large Language Model for both our proposed system and the "LLM + RAG" baseline systems, allowing us to isolate the impact of our hierarchical summarization methodology relative to standard RAG approaches.

4.3 Metrics

To quantitatively assess the performance of each approach, we adopted Pass@10 (indicates if at least one relevant file is in the top 10) and Recall@10 (measures the proportion of relevant files found in the top 10) as our primary evaluation metrics. The selection of these metrics is grounded in their established use within the code search and information retrieval domains, directly aligning with the nature of our bug localization downstream task. Furthermore, given that our benchmark dataset consists of issues that often require modifications across multiple code files, metrics like Recall@10 are particularly informative, indicating the extent to which the relevant files are successfully retrieved within the top-ranked results. Complementarily, Pass@10 provides a valuable measure of practical utility. It evaluates whether at least one file relevant to the bug is present within the top 10 retrieved files. In the context of large, enterprise-level repositories, even retrieving a single correct file within the top 10 results offers significant value to developers, effectively reducing their search space from thousands of files to a manageable set of just ten, thereby substantially accelerating the bug localization process.

4.4 Results

For the "Flat Retrieval" baseline, we directly queried the system using the raw Jira issue description as input. For the LLM-based approaches, including our system and the "LLM + RAG" baselines, we prompted the models with the raw Jira issue description, supplemented by a concise instruction explicitly requesting the models to return the top-10 files most relevant to the provided bug description. The quantitative results of this experimental evaluation, comparing the performance of our hierarchical summarization methodology against the baselines across the chosen metrics, are presented in Table 2.

Table 2. The results of experimental study using three different approaches

Approach	Model	Pass@10	Recall@10
Flat Retrieval	ModernBERT	0,22	0,11
Flat Retrieval	UnixCoder	0,22	0,14
LLM + RAG (Codeium)	gpt-4o	0.67	0.24
LLM + RAG (Cursor AI)	gpt-4o	0.67	0.26
Ours	gpt-4o	**0.89**	**0.33**

The results presented in Table 2 clearly demonstrate the superior performance of our proposed hierarchical summarization methodology compared to both Flat Retrieval and LLM + RAG baseline approaches across both Pass@10 and Recall@10 metrics. Specifically, our system, utilizing gpt-4o and hierarchical summarization, achieves a Pass@10 score of **0.89** and a Recall@10 score of **0.33**, significantly outperforming the best-performing baseline, LLM + RAG (Cursor AI), which achieves a Pass@10 of 0.67 and Recall@10 of 0.26. The Flat Retrieval baselines, using both ModernBERT and UnixCoder, exhibit considerably lower performance, with Pass@10 scores of 0.22 and Recall@10 scores of 0.11 and 0.14 respectively. These findings strongly suggest that our structure-aware, hierarchical approach effectively leverages the capabilities of LLMs for repository-level code understanding, leading to significantly improved bug localization accuracy. The substantial performance gains over both traditional similarity-based methods and contemporary LLM + RAG systems highlight the effectiveness of hierarchical summarization in addressing the challenges of domain gap and context window limitations inherent in bug localization within large code repositories, particularly when dealing with end-user reported issues.

5 Conclusion

This paper has presented a novel and effective methodology for enhancing Large Language Model (LLM) performance in repository-aware bug localization through hierarchical summarization. Our structure-aware approach addresses critical limitations of existing code search techniques, particularly the domain and vocabulary mismatch inherent in end-user bug reports and the context window constraints of LLMs when applied to large codebases. By introducing a hierarchical summarization technique, we enable the creation of context-aware LLMs capable of understanding and reasoning about code at the repository level, facilitating more accurate and scalable bug localization. Empirical evaluation on a real-world, industry-scale dataset demonstrates the significant performance gains achieved by our methodology compared to Flat Retrieval and LLM + RAG baselines, showcasing a substantial improvement in both Pass@10 and Recall@10 metrics. These results underscore the efficacy of hierarchical summarization in bridging the semantic gap and mitigating context window limitations, leading to more effective bug localization, especially for complex, enterprise-level software projects and user-reported issues. Furthermore, the task-agnostic nature of our approach suggests its potential applicability to a broader range of software engineering downstream tasks requiring repository-level code comprehension. Future work will focus on exploring further refinements to the summarization process, investigating dynamic adaptation of the hierarchical structure, and extending the evaluation to diverse codebases and downstream tasks to fully realize the potential of repository-aware LLMs in software engineering practice.

Acknowledgments. This manuscript underwent limited AI post-processing solely for enhanced readability and grammatical accuracy, with no alteration to its original content, conceptual framework, or research findings. This research was conducted as part of the R&D efforts within the TBTAK TEYDEB 1501 project, grant number 3240105, and gratefully acknowledges the support of **The Scientific and Technological Research Council of Turkey (TÜBTAK)**.

A Appendix

A.1 Prompts

Figure 6 illustrates sample prompt templates employed in this study. The left box presents a template used for generating code file summaries (file-level summaries) during the pre-processing phase. Conversely, the right box displays a sample prompt template designed for localizing buggy files within a specific directory (file-level search). It is important to note that these templates are provided as examples; the actual implementation utilized specific and optimized instructions tailored to our particular codebase.

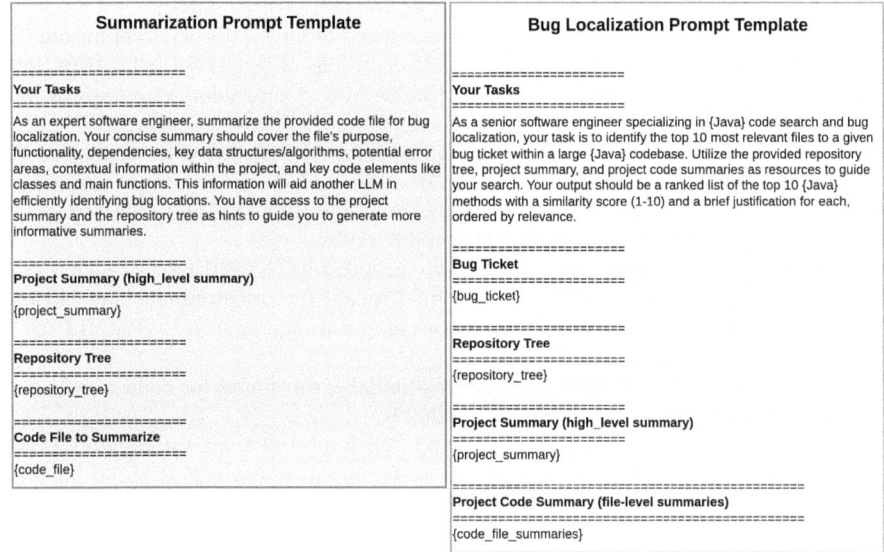

Fig. 6. Example prompt templates for summarizing code files (left) and localizing buggy code files (right)

A.2 Version Information

For code interaction, we utilized the Codeium v1.38 JetBrains extension, specifically its "Chat with Codebase" mode, released on February 13, 2025. Additionally, we employed Cursor IDE version 0.46.x, released on February 19, 2025, in its "Ask Codebase" mode.

References

1. Cursor - The AI Code Editor — cursor.com. https://www.cursor.com/en. Accessed 05 Mar 2025
2. Windsurf editor and codeium extensions — codeium.com. https://codeium.com/. Accessed 05 Mar 2025
3. Aktas, M.S., Fox, G.C., Pierce, M.: Fault tolerant high performance information services for dynamic collections of grid and web services. Futur. Gener. Comput. Syst. **23**(3), 317–337 (2007)

4. Aydin, G., Aktas, M.S., Sayar, A.: ServoGrid complexity computational environments CCE integrated performance analysis. In: 2005 6th International Workshop on Grid Computing (GRID), pp. 256–261 (2005)
5. Bairi, R., et al.: CodePlan: repository-level coding using LLMs and planning. In: Proceedings of the ACM on Software Engineering **1**(FSE), pp. 675–698 (2024)
6. Chen, J., et al.: CoreQA: uncovering potentials of language models in code repository question answering. arXiv preprint arXiv:2501.03447 (2024)
7. Chen, Y., et al.: When large language models confront repository-level automatic program repair: how well they done? In: Proceedings of the 2024 IEEE/ACM 46th International Conference on Software Engineering: Companion Proceedings, pp. 459–471 (2024)
8. Di Grazia, L., Pradel, M.: Code search: a survey of techniques for finding code. ACM Comput. Surv. **55**(11), 1–31 (2023)
9. Ding, Y., et al.: CoCoMIC: code completion by jointly modeling in-file and cross-file context. arXiv preprint arXiv:2212.10007 (2022)
10. Douze, M., et al.: The Faiss library. arXiv preprint arXiv:2401.08281 (2024)
11. Feng, Z., et al.: CodeBERT: a pre-trained model for programming and natural languages. Findings of the association for computational linguistics: EMNLP 2020 (2020)
12. Guo, D., et al.: UnixCoder: unified cross-modal pre-training for code representation. arXiv preprint arXiv:2205.07754 (2022)
13. Guo, J., Wang, C., Xu, X., Su, Z., Zhang, X.: RepoAudit: an autonomous LLM-agent for repository-level code auditing. arXiv preprint arXiv:2501.18160 (2024)
14. Huang, R., et al.: AudioGPT: understanding and generating speech, music, sound, and talking head. In: Proceedings of the AAAI Conference on Artificial Intelligence, vol. 38, pp. 23802–23804 (2024)
15. Hurst, A., et al.: GPT-4o system card. arXiv preprint arXiv:2410.21276 (2024)
16. Jain, S., Dora, A., Sam, K.S., Singh, P.: LLM agents improve semantic code search. arXiv preprint arXiv:2408.11058 (2024)
17. Li, H., Zhou, X., Shen, Z.: Rewriting the code: a simple method for large language model augmented code search. arXiv preprint arXiv:2401.04514 (2024)
18. Ma, Y., Yang, Q., Cao, R., Li, B., Huang, F., Li, Y.: How to understand whole software repository? arXiv preprint arXiv:2406.01422 (2024)
19. McKinzie, B., et al.: Mm1: methods, analysis and insights from multimodal LLM pre-training. In: European Conference on Computer Vision, pp. 304–323. Springer (2024). https://doi.org/10.1007/978-3-031-73397-0_18
20. Nacar, M.A., Aktas, M.S., Yuen, D.A.: VLAB: collaborative grid services and portals to support computational material science. Concurr. Comput. Pract. Exp. **19**(12), 1717–1728 (2007)
21. Olmezogullari, E., Aktas, M.S.: Representation of click-stream data sequences for learning user navigational behavior by using embeddings. In: 2020 IEEE International Conference on Big Data (Big Data), pp. 3173–3179 (2020)
22. Olmezogullari, E., Aktas, M.S.: Pattern2Vec: Representation of clickstream data sequences for learning user navigational behavior. Concurr. Comput. Pract. Exp. **34**(9) (2022)
23. Oskooei, A.R.: On the use of data parallelism technologies for implementing statistical analysis functions. In: The 14th International Workshop on Computer Science and Engineering (WCSE 2024), pp. 94–102 (2024)
24. Oskooei, A.R., Babacan, M.S., Yağcı, E., Alptekin, Ç., Buğday, A.: Beyond synthetic benchmarks: assessing recent LLMs for code generation. In: The 14th Inter-

national Workshop on Computer Science and Engineering (WCSE 2024), pp. 290–296 (2024)
25. Qin, Y., et al.: AgentFL: Scaling LLM-based fault localization to project-level context. arXiv preprint arXiv:2403.16362 (2024)
26. Rafiei Oskooei, A., Aktaş, M.S., Keleş, M.: Seeing the sound: multilingual lip sync for real-time face-to-face translation. Computers **14**(1), 7 (2024)
27. Sahinoglu, M., Incki, K., Aktas, M.S.: Mobile application verification: a systematic mapping study. In: Gervasi, O., et al. (eds.) ICCSA 2015. LNCS, vol. 9159, pp. 147–163. Springer, Cham (2015). https://doi.org/10.1007/978-3-319-21413-9_11
28. Shen, Z., et al.: SlimPajama-DC: understanding data combinations for LLM training. arXiv preprint arXiv:2309.10818 (2023)
29. Tufek, A., Gurbuz, A., Aktas, M.S.: Provenance collection platform for the weather research and forecasting model. In: 2018 14th International Conference on Semantics, Knowledge and Grids (SKG), pp. 17–24 (2018)
30. Wang, Y., et al.: You augment me: Exploring ChatGPT-based data augmentation for semantic code search. In: 2023 IEEE International Conference on Software Maintenance and Evolution (ICSME), pp. 14–25. IEEE (2023)
31. Warner, B., et al.: Smarter, better, faster, longer: a modern bidirectional encoder for fast, memory efficient, and long context finetuning and inference. arXiv preprint arXiv:2412.13663 (2024)
32. Zhang, F., et al.: RepoCoder: repository-level code completion through iterative retrieval and generation. arXiv preprint arXiv:2303.12570 (2024)
33. Zhang, W., et al.: GraphCoder: enhancing repository-level code completion via code context graph-based retrieval and language model. arXiv preprint arXiv:2406.07003 (2024)
34. Zhang, Y., Ruan, H., Fan, Z., Roychoudhury, A.: AutoCodeRover: autonomous program improvement. In: Proceedings of the 33rd ACM SIGSOFT International Symposium on Software Testing and Analysis, pp. 1592–1604 (2024)

Enhancing Industrial Time Series Anomaly Detection Through Graph Modeling and a Hybrid VAE-GAN Approach

Giovanni Zurlo[1]($\boxtimes$), Roberto Cornali[1], and Elisabetta Ronchieri[1,2]

[1] INFN CNAF, Viale Carlo Berti Pichat 6, 40127 Bologna, BO, Italy
{gzurlo,elironc,eronchie}@cnaf.infn.it
[2] Department of Statistical Sciences, University of Bologna, Via Belle Arti 41, 40126 Bologna, BO, Italy

Abstract. In mission-critical industries, early anomaly detection can make a difference between seamless operations and costly downtime. Traditional statistical methods often struggle with the complexity and high dimensionality of temporal dependencies, whereas Graph Neural Networks (GNNs) are emerging as a powerful tool for predictive maintenance, offering deeper insights into data from interconnected and distributed systems.

Building upon our previously proposed detection model integrating Generative Adversarial Networks and GNNs, we improve and adapt it to a new semi-supervised setting. By transforming multivariate time series into static graph structures, our method separately captures spatial and temporal dependencies. Within an adversarial framework, we train an autoencoder on these graph representations to learn the system's normal behavior. Anomalies are identified by analyzing the graph reconstruction errors and the discriminator scores.

We test our approach through a real-life case study on industrial data from a gas turbine generator. A preliminary comparison with the baseline production model shows that our approach achieves higher precision, reducing both the frequency and duration of false alarms. Additionally, we conduct an ablation study by introducing synthetic anomalies through systematic connectivity alterations, assessing both the model's robustness and the suitability of the graph representation algorithm.

By emphasizing interpretability alongside detection accuracy, this study investigates the potential of GNNs for advancing predictive maintenance in complex industrial systems.

Keywords: Graph Neural Networks · Generative Adversarial Networks · Anomaly Detection · Predictive Maintenance · Industrial Machinery

1 Introduction

In mission-critical industries, continuous operation exposes equipment to wear that can escalate into costly failures and downtimes. Preventive or reactive maintenance strategies have traditionally been used to mitigate these risks, relying on scheduled inspections and part replacements. However, these approaches are often inefficient, leading to unnecessary maintenance costs or unexpected failures. This has driven a shift toward more advanced, data-driven strategies that leverage real-time monitoring and predictive analytics to optimize maintenance operations.

The energy sector, in particular, relies on high-performance rotating machinery-such as turbines, compressors, and fans-having rotating mechanical parts that are exposed to enormous stress on a daily basis. The term "turbomachines" is conventionally adopted to refer to a specific class of these devices that extracts energy or imports energy from a continuously moving stream of fluid, either liquid or gas [32]. A turbomachine is a power or head-generating machine that employs the dynamic action of a rotating element, the rotor. The action of the rotor changes the energy level of the continuously flowing fluid through the machine. Damage to these types of systems not only causes economic loss but also a loss of reputation, therefore detecting and repairing them as early as possible is of utmost importance.

In modern industrial plants, almost all the installed equipment include IoT sensors for monitoring their behavior and remote-controlled actuators to regulate the operational profile and avoid undesired events. These IoT sensors provide real-time data on parameters such as temperature, vibration, pressure, and rotational speed. When paired with advanced analytics, machine learning algorithms, and historical data, these systems enable predictive maintenance-a proactive strategy that identifies potential failures before they occur. Predictive maintenance performs as a kind of trade-off between preventive and reactive. It leverages condition monitoring and anomaly detection to forecast wear patterns and detect irregularities. By analyzing trends and deviations from expected performance, maintenance teams can schedule repairs and replacements at optimal times, reducing unplanned outages and extending the life of the equipment. This not only minimizes costs but also enhances safety, reliability, and operational efficiency, making it a vital practice in modern industrial settings.

With the rise of deep learning and generative models, reconstruction-based anomaly detection methods have gained significant attention due to their ability to model complex data distributions. Unlike traditional statistical approaches, which often struggle with high-dimensional and nonlinear data, these methods leverage deep neural architectures to learn underlying patterns in time series data. Autoencoders, Variational Autoencoders (VAEs), and Generative Adversarial Networks (GANs) are among the most commonly used models in this category [4]. Their ability to learn a compressed representation of normal system behavior makes them particularly suitable for identifying deviations indicative of potential faults [27].

In this work, we build upon our previously proposed anomaly detection model, adapting it to a new semi-supervised setting [10]. While the original method operated in an unsupervised fashion due to the annotation cost and rarity of anomalies, we now leverage labeled instances to assess detection performance. Our model requires representing multivariate time series data as a static graph, highlighting relevant information while filtering noise. With Graph Neural Networks (GNNs) [38] we can model space and time relationships separately and enhance our results' interpretability by detecting anomalous edges explicitly. We apply this adapted approach to a new industrial domain, specifically to data from an oil and gas extraction plant, demonstrating its effectiveness and explainability in real-world anomaly detection tasks.

This paper is organized as follows: Sect. 2 summarizes some works related to this study. Sections 3.1, 3.2, 3.3 provide basic concepts on GANs, GNNs, and Graph Autoencoders. Section 4 introduces the anomaly detection model in use. Section 5 details our case study, with results and further speculations and finally Sect. 6 gives conclusions and future works.

2 Related Works

Traditionally, distance [5] and density-based techniques [39] have been widely used for detecting irregularities in time series data. With the advent of deep learning, neural network architectures including convolutional neural networks (CNNs), recurrent neural networks (RNNs), and transformers have demonstrated significant advantages in modeling time series data. Between 2020–2023, nearly 50% of newly introduced anomaly detection solutions were prediction-based methods leveraging these neural building blocks [4]. Prediction-based methods detect anomalies by measuring forecast and reconstruction errors, relying on the assumption that normal data are easier to predict, whereas unexpected anomalies lead to higher errors. These methods are most effective in semi-supervised settings, where the training set contains little to no anomalous data. Forecasting-based models predict future values based on past sequences, while reconstruction-based models learn normal behavior by encoding and reconstructing time series sub-sequences, using reconstruction errors as an anomaly score.

Autoencoders have been widely adopted for reconstruction-based anomaly detection [34,41], but they are prone to overfitting and struggle to regularize the latent space effectively, even with probabilistic algorithm variants. Generative Adversarial Networks (GANs) [17] have been introduced to address these issues by learning implicit distributions that generalize better. While a naive GAN formulation relies solely on discriminator loss, effective adaptations such as the Multivariate Anomaly Detection GAN (MAD-GAN) [27] and TadGAN [14] incorporate generator reconstruction loss into anomaly scoring. However, remapping data to the latent space during inference remains computationally expensive, representing a bottleneck for real-time applicability. A practical solution involves designing the generator and/or discriminator as an autoencoder to jointly leverage both reconstruction and discrimination capabilities [1,3].

Despite their success, models based on CNNs and RNNs struggle with explicitly capturing pairwise variables dependencies, such as spatial relationships in non-Euclidean spaces, which limits their expressiveness [22] and effectiveness in detecting complex anomalies [45].

Graph Neural Networks (GNNs) have recently gained traction for anomaly detection by modeling both inter-variable (relationships among different variables in a multivariate series) and inter-temporal (dependencies across time points) associations [7,12]. The idea of using graphs for time series anomaly detection dates back to the early 2000s; early approaches represented time points as graph vertices and detected anomalies using random walks [8,9]. However, these classical methods often struggle to learn informative representations and model fine-grained dependencies.

Within the industrial domain of application, [28] employs a cross-correlation graph-based encoder-decoder GAN (CCG-EDGAN) for anomaly detection in wind and steam turbines. Spatio-temporal GNNs have also been applied to condition monitoring of distributed systems of wind turbines [30] and photovoltaic panels [42], demonstrating the potential of graph-based models for the predictive maintenance of complex systems.

3 Preliminaries

3.1 Generative Adversarial Networks

Generative Adversarial Networks (GANs) are a class of deep learning models designed for generative tasks by employing a game-theoretic framework. Introduced by Goodfellow et al. [17], a GAN consists of two neural networks: a generator G_ϕ parametrized by ϕ, and a discriminator D_ψ which compete in a zero-sum game. The main motivation for the design of GANs is that the learning process requires neither approximate inference nor approximation of a partition function gradient [16]. The generator G_ϕ learns to map random noise $\mathbf{z}$ from a prior distribution $p_{prior}(\mathbf{z})$ to a data distribution $p_{data}(\mathbf{x})$, producing synthetic samples $G(\mathbf{z}, \phi) = \tilde{\mathbf{x}}$. The discriminator D_ψ, a binary classifier, distinguishes real samples $\mathbf{x}$ from generated ones $\tilde{\mathbf{x}}$ by estimating the probability $D(\tilde{\mathbf{x}}, \psi) \in [0, 1]$ that a given input is real. During training, G_ϕ is optimized to generate increasingly realistic samples to fool D_ψ, while D_ψ improves its ability to distinguish real from fake data. This process is governed by an adversarial loss $\mathcal{L}(\phi, \psi)$, where G_ϕ seeks to minimize it while D_ψ aims to maximize it. At equilibrium, G_ϕ generates samples that are indistinguishable from real data, thus D_ψ can be discarded.

GAN training is notoriously challenging, often suffering from non-convergence, instability, and mode collapse, where G_ϕ generates only a limited subset of the target distribution, leading to poor sample diversity [16]. Despite these challenges, GANs have been successfully applied to tasks such as image synthesis, style transfer, and data augmentation, showcasing their ability to produce highly realistic samples.

3.2 Graph Neural Networks

The success of Convolutional Neural Networks (CNNs) in computer vision has inspired the generalization of convolution operations to graph-structured data

[6]. This has led to the development of Graph Neural Networks (GNNs), with two primary approaches for defining convolutions on graphs: spatial-based and spectral-based methods [46]. **Spatial-based approaches** define convolution directly in the graph's vertex domain, mirroring the operation of traditional CNNs. The core idea is to compute the convolution for each vertex as a weighted average of its neighboring nodes, where the weights reflect the influence of these neighbors. A significant challenge in this approach lies in designing convolution operations that can handle neighborhoods of varying sizes while maintaining the weight sharing property characteristic of CNNs [20,43].

Spectral-based approaches, on the other hand, define graph convolutions as filters rooted in graph signal processing methodologies. From this perspective, a graph convolution can be seen as a technique to reduce noise in graph signals. This involves transforming the graph signals into the frequency domain using the eigen-decomposition of the graph Laplacian matrix, where eigenvalues represent frequencies and eigenvectors correspond to harmonics [6,35]. The graph Fourier transform decomposes the signal into its harmonic coefficients, and filters are defined as diagonal matrices that scale each frequency component.

However, the computational cost associated with calculating eigenvectors, especially for large graphs, prompted the development of more efficient methods. ChebNet [11] addressed this by approximating the spectral filter g_θ using Chebyshev polynomials $T_k(L)$ of the diagonal matrix of eigenvalues, up to the Kth order. The convolution of a graph signal x with this filter can be approximated as:

$$g_\theta \star \mathbf{x} \approx \sum_{k=0}^{K} \theta'_k T_k(L)\mathbf{x} \quad (1)$$

where $\star$ denotes the convolution operator, and $\boldsymbol{\theta}' \in \mathbb{R}^K$ are the Chebyshev coefficients.

The Graph Convolutional Network (GCN) module employed here simplifies Eq. (1) by limiting the approximation to the first order ($K = 1$), arguing that stacking multiple localized graph convolutional layers can create a deeper, yet parameter-efficient, architecture capable of capturing graph structure [24]. Approximating the largest eigenvalue $\lambda_{max} \approx 2$, the convolution operation in Eq. (1) becomes: $g_\theta \star \mathbf{x} = \theta(\mathbf{I} + \mathbf{D}^{-1/2}\mathbf{A}\mathbf{D}^{-1/2})\mathbf{x}$ where θ is a scalar Chebyshev coefficient. To address potential issues with exploding or vanishing gradients, a symmetric renormalization strategy is also introduced:

$$\mathbf{I} + \mathbf{D}^{-1/2}\mathbf{A}\mathbf{D}^{-1/2} \rightarrow \tilde{\mathbf{D}}^{-1/2}\tilde{\mathbf{A}}\tilde{\mathbf{D}}^{-1/2} \quad (2)$$

where $\tilde{\mathbf{A}} = \mathbf{A} + \mathbf{I}$ (adding self-loops) and $\tilde{\mathbf{D}}$ is the degree matrix of $\tilde{\mathbf{A}}$.

From a spatial perspective, the GCN can be reformulated as a form of neural message passing [15]. In this view, the hidden state of each node at the next layer is generated by aggregating and updating vector messages from its neighbors and itself using neural networks. Specifically, representations from the previous layer are aggregated across the neighborhood (including the node itself), a weighted average is taken, and then transformed by a weight matrix and an activation function to obtain the new representation of the node:

$$\mathbf{h}_i^{(l+1)} = \sigma \left(\sum_{j \in \mathcal{N}_i \cup \{i\}} \frac{\tilde{A}_{ij}}{\sqrt{\tilde{D}_{ii}\tilde{D}_{jj}}} \mathbf{h}_j^{(l)} \mathbf{W}^{(l)} \right) \quad (3)$$

where $\mathcal{N}_i$ denotes the set of neighbors of node i.

3.3 Graph Autoencoders

An autoencoder is an artificial neural network designed to learn a compressed representation (encoding) of input data while minimizing reconstruction loss. It consists of two components: an encoder and a decoder. The encoder maps input data to a lower-dimensional latent space, forcing it to retain only the most relevant information, while the decoder reconstructs the original data from this encoding. In the case of graph-structured data, this framework is referred to as a graph autoencoder (GAE). The entire network is trained jointly to optimize reconstruction accuracy.

A fundamental limitation of standard autoencoders in generative modeling is the structure of their latent space. The encoded representations may be discontinuous or highly clustered, making random sampling and smooth interpolation challenging. If a decoder is presented with an out-of-distribution latent vector (e.g., one sampled from a region where no training encodings exist), it is likely to generate unrealistic outputs.

Variational Graph Autoencoders (VGAEs) [25] address this issue by enforcing a continuous, well-structured latent space. Instead of outputting a single deterministic encoding, the encoder in a VAE produces two vectors: the mean vector and the standard deviation vector, which define a Gaussian distribution for each latent dimension. The actual encoding is then sampled from this learned distribution:

$$q(\mathbf{H} \mid \mathbf{X}, \mathbf{A}) = \prod_{i=1}^{N} q(\mathbf{h}_i \mid \mathbf{X}, \mathbf{A}), \quad q(\mathbf{h}_i \mid \mathbf{X}, \mathbf{A}) = \mathcal{N}(\mathbf{h}_i \mid \boldsymbol{\mu}_i, \mathrm{diag}(\boldsymbol{\sigma}_i^2)) \quad (4)$$

Here, $\boldsymbol{\mu} = \mathrm{GCN}_\mu(\mathbf{X}, \mathbf{A})$ and $\log \boldsymbol{\sigma} = \mathrm{GCN}_\sigma(\mathbf{X}, \mathbf{A})$ denote the outputs of GCN modules parameterizing the mean and standard deviation of the latent distribution. This so-called "reparameterization trick" [23] allows gradient-based optimization by re-expressing the stochastic sampling operation as a differentiable transformation.

In VAEs, the decoder reconstructs the graph by predicting its structure $\mathbf{A}$ from the latent embeddings $\mathbf{H}$:

$$p(\mathbf{A} \mid \mathbf{H}) = \prod_{i=1}^{N} \prod_{j=1}^{N} p(A_{ij} \mid \mathbf{h}_i, \mathbf{h}_j), \quad \text{where} \quad p(A_{ij} = 1 \mid \mathbf{h}_i, \mathbf{h}_j) = \sigma(\mathbf{h}_i^\top \mathbf{h}_j) \quad (5)$$

where A_{ij} are the elements of $\mathbf{A}$ and $\sigma(\cdot)$ is the sigmoid function. For attributed graphs, node features X can also be reconstructed using additional GCN layers.

This stochastic generation ensures that even for the same input, the sampled encoding varies slightly, exposing the decoder to different representations of the same data point and improving generalization.

However, unregularized autoencoders primarily focus on minimizing reconstruction loss and often ignore the global structure of the latent space, leading to degenerate identity mappings [33]. To address this, latent space regularization techniques enforce a structured prior distribution. One effective approach is adversarial regularization (AR), where an additional discriminator is trained to distinguish between true prior samples and latent encodings, encouraging the learned distribution to align with the prior [36].

4 Methodology

4.1 Graph Design

Representing a time series as a graph is a non-trivial task. In this work, we adopt a single-layer, observations-based nodes approach known as correlation network [44]. According to the taxonomy presented in [21], this method falls under the similarity-based heuristic approaches for time series mapping. Prior research highlights the importance of correlation structures in multivariate time series, as they provide critical insights into system behavior and anomaly detection [19] [29]. Changes in inter-variable correlations often indicate different types of anomalies, including point, contextual, and collective anomalies. Several alternative methods for mapping time series to graphs exist, as detailed in the comprehensive review of multivariate time series network representations [40].

In our approach, we construct graphs using correlation matrices, where each entry-representing a pair (time, signal)-is assigned as a node attribute. Two nodes are connected by an undirected edge if the correlation between their signals over the last $w = 100$ timestamps exceeds a threshold τ_c. Additionally, nodes corresponding to the same signal are connected by a directed edge if the autocorrelation between their timestamps surpasses a threshold τ_a (Fig. 1). The thresholds τ_c and τ_a are selected within stable ranges to prevent excessive sensitivity to minor fluctuations [44], with final values set to $\tau_c = 0.4$ and $\tau_a = 0.3$. If an edge is present, its weight is assigned based on the computed auto- or cross-correlation value. This design enables us to model temporal and inter-signal relationships separately, focusing on the most significant dependencies in the data.

The resulting graph is inherently signed, as negative edges naturally arise from negatively correlated signal windows. However, many graph neural network (GNN) architectures assume unsigned graphs, necessitating an additional preprocessing step. A few naive strategies include removing negative edges, ignoring edge signs, or binarizing the adjacency matrix A such that $A \in \{0,1\}^{N \times N}$ [13]. Instead, to retain correlation information while ensuring compatibility with the GCN module, we normalize the correlation values to the range [0,1] using:

$$\bar{\rho}_{ij} = \frac{\rho_{ij} + 1}{2} \tag{6}$$

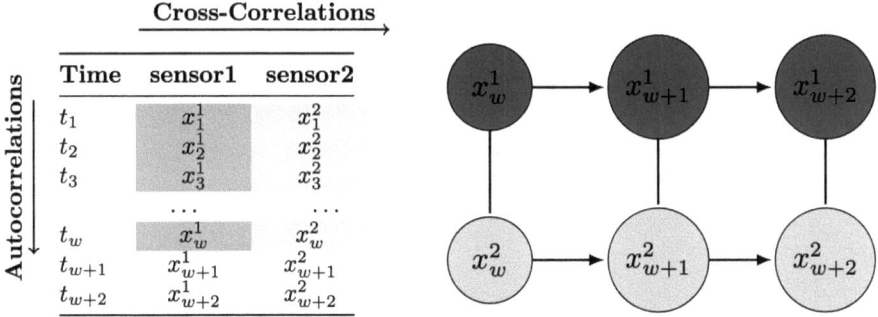

Fig. 1. The Correlation Network Approach

4.2 Model Architecture

The model introduced in [10] extends the AR-VGAE (described in Sect. 3.3) by incorporating an additional graph discriminator and refining the reconstruction process. Specifically, it adopts a Gaussian prior on the latent representations to enforce smoothness and structure in the learned embeddings. The variational Graph Encoder $Enc : \mathbf{x}_i|\mathbf{A} \rightarrow [\mu_i, \sigma_i]$ follows the inference model of Eq. (4) and is constructed using three shared GCN modules along with separate linear layers for $\boldsymbol{\mu}$ and $\boldsymbol{\sigma}$.

The Graph Decoder $Dec : \mathbf{h} \rightarrow \{\tilde{A}, \tilde{X}\}$ reconstructs both the topological structure $\mathbf{A}$ and node features $\mathbf{X}$. The attributed adjacency matrix is reconstructed using the standard VGAE approach via a sigmoid inner product (Eq. 5). For node feature reconstruction, the decoder incorporates three additional GCN layers to capture local node interactions effectively:

$$\tilde{\mathbf{x}}_i = GCN(\mathbf{h_i}|\tilde{\mathbf{A}}; \theta_\phi). \tag{7}$$

Together, these components form the VGAE part of the model, acting as a dual generator. Differently from the original implementation of [10], our autoencoder incorporates dropout layers with a 0.5 rate and use ReLU activations in all layers except the final ones, which use tanh and sigmoid functions to match the range of the output data.

The Regularizing Discriminator $D_r : \mathbf{h_i} \rightarrow r \in [0,1]$, introduced in [36] and discussed in Sect. 3.3, is implemented as a multi-layer perceptron (MLP) with a single output neuron and a sigmoid activation function. It serves as an adversarial classifier, distinguishing between latent codes sampled from the Gaussian prior and those produced by the Graph Encoder. This adversarial regularization ensures that the learned latent space remains structured and aligned with the prior, preventing degenerate solutions.

To further refine the generation process, [10] introduced a Graph Discriminator, $D_g : \tilde{\mathbf{x}}_i|\mathbf{A} \rightarrow r \in [0,1]$, to assess the authenticity of reconstructed nodes. This discriminator is a Graph Convolutional Network (GCN) with message-passing modules, a linear layer, and a sigmoid activation function,

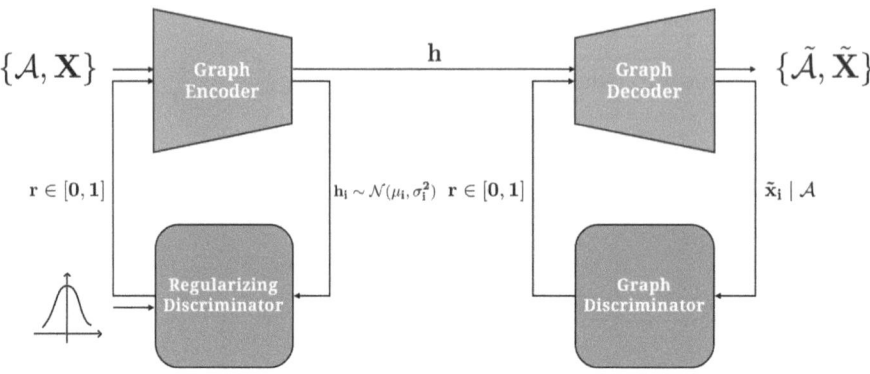

Fig. 2. Network Architecture of the Employed Model [10]

assigning a realness score between 0 and 1 to each decoded node. The complete architecture is illustrated in Fig. 2.

Previous studies indicate that dropout plays an important role in discriminator networks [16,37]. In particular, units should be randomly dropped while computing the gradient for the generator network to be followed. For our message-passing module of choice, we employ dropout as the primary source of stochasticity in the training process [24].

Overall, this AR-VGAE extension leverages both reconstruction-based anomaly detection and adversarially regularized embeddings, improving both interpretability and robustness in semi-supervised settings.

4.3 Model Training

The training of our model follows the adversarial learning framework of [10]. The objective is to simultaneously optimize the Graph Autoencoder for accurate reconstruction and the two discriminators for adversarial regularization and anomaly detection. Given the nature of our task, Wasserstein losses [2] are employed for both adversarial components, as they provide a more stable optimization process compared to standard GAN objectives. Specifically, one Wasserstein loss ensures a structured latent space by aligning it with a Gaussian prior, while the other improves the generation quality of reconstructed node features by encouraging realism in their distribution.

Unlike traditional adversarial training, where instability and mode collapse are major concerns, Wasserstein GAN with Gradient Penalty (WGAN-GP) [18] is adopted to enforce a local Lipschitz constraint on the discriminators. This regularization stabilizes training by penalizing large gradients, preventing the discriminators from becoming overly confident too quickly, which could otherwise disrupt the training dynamics of the encoder-decoder pair.

In addition to adversarial objectives, the Graph Autoencoder is optimized using an ℓ_2 reconstruction loss to directly minimize the discrepancy between original and reconstructed node features. This serves as an additional constraint, ensuring that even if the adversarial training introduces instabilities, the model retains a strong signal from the reconstruction task. By jointly optimizing adversarial and reconstruction losses, our approach balances reconstruction fidelity, latent space regularization, and adversarial discrimination.

While previous GAN work has used momentum to accelerate training, we adopt the Adam optimizer with tuned hyperparameters as in DCGAN [37]. We found the suggested learning rate of 0.001 to be too low, using 0.02 and 0.01 instead. Additionally, leaving the momentum term β_1 at the suggested value of 0.9 resulted in training oscillation and instability while reducing it to 0.5 helped stabilize training. In this way, we decrease the smoothness of the momentum, the exponentially weighted moving average of past gradients, to take care of the rapidly changing gradients because the generator and the discriminator compete with each other.

4.4 Anomaly Scores

Since a discriminator D_g is trained to distinguish fake data (i.e. anomalies) from real data with high sensitivity, a naive GAN-based anomaly detection approach might use the discriminator loss as the anomaly score. However, this method has limitations because the discriminator primarily serves to support the generator's learning rather than directly detect anomalies. To improve accuracy, it is now common practice to combine the generator's reconstruction errors with the discriminator loss when calculating the anomaly scores [14].

Our model generates both a critic score and a reconstructed attribute for each node in the input graph. This allows for a fine-grained examination of the model's predictions. The Graph Discriminator's scores on the real graph are low only if it cannot classify nodes as belonging to the real graph itself; we exploit this fact to identify nodes as anomalous. Node reconstruction errors are measured as the distance or dissimilarity between real and reconstructed attributes. Some methods calculate point-wise reconstruction errors, while others use time-aware interval-based errors, such as area difference [14].

In our case study, we compute the mean and standard deviation of sensor-wise reconstruction errors $RE(\mathbf{x})$, along with robust indices for the critic output $C(\mathbf{x})$. We then transform the z-scores $Z_{RE}(\mathbf{x})$ and $Z_C(\mathbf{x})$ to be non-negative by clipping or taking absolute values and shift them to have unit minimum. We explored two different methods to combine these into a single dataframe of anomaly scores. First, we take a convex combination $S(\mathbf{x}) = \alpha Z_C(\mathbf{x}) + (1 - \alpha) Z_{RE}(\mathbf{x})$ where α controls the relative importance of both terms. Alternatively, we tried to multiply the scores to emphasize high values $S(\mathbf{x}) = \alpha Z_C(\mathbf{x}) \odot Z_{RE}(\mathbf{x})$.

The scores obtained through this approach enable point-wise anomaly scoring by comparing values at each timestamp for each sensor. By applying an aggregation operation, such as a row-wise average or maximum, we can assess the operating conditions at the system level.

4.5 Two Phase Semi-supervised Approach

Our workflow consists of two-phases: (1) training a model exclusively on normal operating conditions data and (2) optimizing a decision threshold using labeled anomalies from the same training set:

1. During training, labeled anomalies are excluded to ensure that the model learns only normal operating conditions. This prevents the model from inadvertently adapting to anomalous patterns.
2. During inference, the decision threshold is adjusted to maximize precision or the generalized F_β score on the labeled anomalies.

While the F_1 score is commonly used for balancing precision and recall, prioritizing precision is more effective in scenarios where anomalies are rare or occur over short periods. The F_β score introduces a tunable parameter β to emphasize recall when necessary. By optimizing the threshold for high precision, we aim to minimize false positives while ensuring timely and reliable anomaly detection, thereby improving operational alerting systems [26].

Additionally to applying a single system-wide anomaly threshold, we experiment with a per-sensor approach, where each sensor is assigned an individual threshold τ_i. These thresholds are determined based on statistical dispersion of the anomaly scores, controlled by a tunable parameter σ (Eq. 8). Specifically, the anomaly threshold for each sensor is set as a function of its normal behavior scores $\mathbf{S}_{\mathrm{NOC}}$, ensuring adaptability across different sensors with varying signal characteristics. Once anomalies are detected at the sensor level, we aggregate the individual detections using an ensemble-like strategy, leveraging agreement among sensors to improve robustness.

$$\boldsymbol{\tau} = \boldsymbol{\mu}(\mathbf{S}_{\mathrm{NOC}}) + \sigma \cdot \boldsymbol{\sigma}(\mathbf{S}_{\mathrm{NOC}}) \tag{8}$$

5 Case Study

We trained our model using sensor data from a 10.5 MWe gas turbine generator, which provides self-generated electricity for an entire industrial plant. The training dataset consists of 55 covariates that monitor both performance and operating conditions. These include turbine and rotor speeds, multiple temperature readings (related to combustion, oil, bearings), fuel pressure and flow rates, and vibration levels in the bearings and gearbox. Additionally, electrical parameters such as generator amperage, voltage, frequency, and power output are available. The dataset spans 390 days of continuous multivariate time series data. Raw data were originally recorded at 30-second intervals, but for practical processing, first differences were taken and downsampled to 5-minute intervals. To account for operational status, we used the generator's power output as a discrete on-off parameter. Transient phases-including shutdown and ramp-up periods-were handled in the preprocessing pipeline. Specifically, for model training, we excluded data from 12 h before shutdown and 24 h post-ramp-up. However, during anomaly detection, we only removed the first 3 h after ramp-up to retain more operational data.

The trained model was validated using a separate test set from the same machine, covering 447 days of operation. This dataset includes a single anomaly event lasting 6 days, allowing us to assess the model's real-world performance.

5.1 Results

Experiments with various combination strategies revealed that the most effective approach involved computing a weighted sum of node reconstruction errors and critic scores with a very low weight for the latter. In the system-wise approach, these errors were aggregated at the system level using a mean. Overall, node attribute reconstruction errors emerged as the most critical anomaly indicator, highlighting the contextual nature of anomalies in the input graphs. Correlation heatmap analysis further confirmed that node reconstruction errors closely align with correlation patterns observed in the input data.

After fine-tuning the threshold and score combination strategy on the training set, our model repeatedly flags anomalies throughout the 7-day anomalous interval (Fig. 3). To enhance contextual relevance, we also apply a temporal aggregation logic, grouping consecutive point anomalies into anomaly segments. Specifically, point anomalies occurring within a 12-hour window are merged into a single anomalous event, ensuring that isolated detections do not overly fragment the results. With this aggregation strategy, the longest detected contextual anomaly falls within the actual confirmed anomaly. False positives are primarily associated with sudden large variations or transient periods; however, these are generally short-lived and could be effectively filtered through post-processing.

An individual analysis of scores revealed that only a few sensor-specific columns were effective in detecting the anomalous interval. The sensor-wise approach described in Sect. 4.4 mitigates the averaging effect of system-level aggregation, allowing key sensor contributions to be more distinctly highlighted when treated as an ensemble. However, this approach also increased the false positive rate (see Fig. 4).

We compared our model's scores to those generated by the existing anomaly detection system deployed at the plant (Fig. 5), using data available for a 175-day sub-interval. The baseline model relies on a more traditional reconstruction-based approach using principal component analysis (PCA) and kernel density estimation (KDE). For the performance comparison on raw scores, we used the baseline model's "Warning" threshold as a reference, since the "Alert" threshold did not provide valid metrics. To ensure consistency in the normalization, we set an arbitrary "Warning" threshold for our model while using the fine-tuned one as our reference "Alert". From a qualitative perspective, the baseline model offers broader anomaly detection coverage but also exhibits higher rate of false positives with varying durations, potentially leading to unnecessary alerts. Quantitatively, the baseline achieved a higher F_1 score of 0.249 ($F_{0.2} = 0.292$), but at the expense of lower precision (0.296 vs. 0.366 for our model) due to extended false positive intervals. This preliminary comparison suggests that differences between the two models may stem from operational preferences. Additionally, we are currently investigating whether certain discord patterns remain

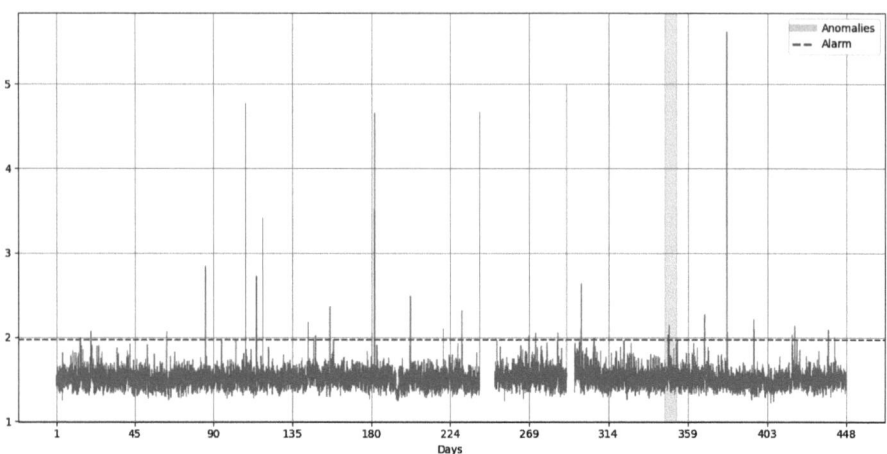

Fig. 3. Aggregated Anomaly Scores Across 55 Signals from the Examined Gas Turbine $Scores = (Z_{RE}, Z_C)$, $\alpha = 0.3$, $\tau = 1.995$, $smooth = 30\ min$, $gap = 12H$

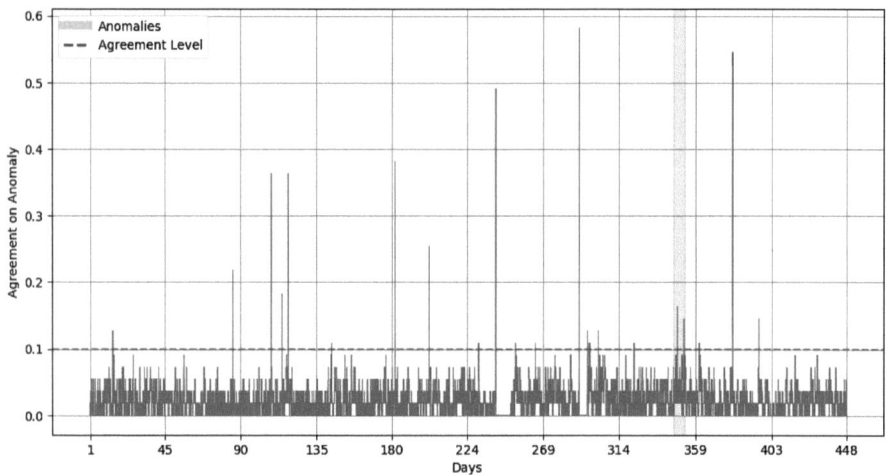

Fig. 4. Signal-wise Anomaly Agreement among Test Set Scores $Scores = (Z_{RE}, Z_C)$, $\alpha = 0.2$, $\sigma = 3.56$, $smooth = 30\ min$, $gap = 12H$

undetected by the baseline model (days 145–150 in Fig. 5). As an additional benchmark, we implemented a model that is architecturally similar to our proposed approach but operates directly on first-order differenced time series data rather than graph-structured inputs. This variant, inspired by [14], replaces the GCN modules in both the generators and critic with Bidirectional Long Short-Term Memory (BiLSTM) layers, making it more suited to sequential rather than relational modeling. While this baseline exhibited slightly broader coverage of the true anomaly interval, it achieved a lower $F_{0.2}$ score of 0.177 and an F_1 score of 0.14, primarily due to a higher false positive rate (precision = 0.216).

5.2 Ablation Study on Known Anomalies

In graph anomaly detection, we typically encounter two main types of anomalies: **Structural anomalies** manifest as nodes with unusual connectivity patterns. They often appear as densely connected clusters that deviate from the generally sparse connectivity of regular nodes in the graph. In **contextual anomalies**, node attributes significantly differ from their neighbors, regardless of their structural properties. Unlike structural anomalies, these could also be detected using traditional tabular outlier detection methods [31].

In real-world datasets, naturally occurring outlier nodes do not always fit neatly into the categories of structural or contextual anomalies. Their characteristics may not be explicitly defined, meaning they might not belong to either category or could exhibit characteristics of both. This ambiguity makes identifying organic outliers more challenging than detecting synthetic ones, which typically follow a predefined pattern [31].

We designed a benchmark to evaluate the robustness of our graph anomaly detection approach when faced with increasingly sparse structural anomalies. The experiment involves injecting synthetic structural patterns into a network-

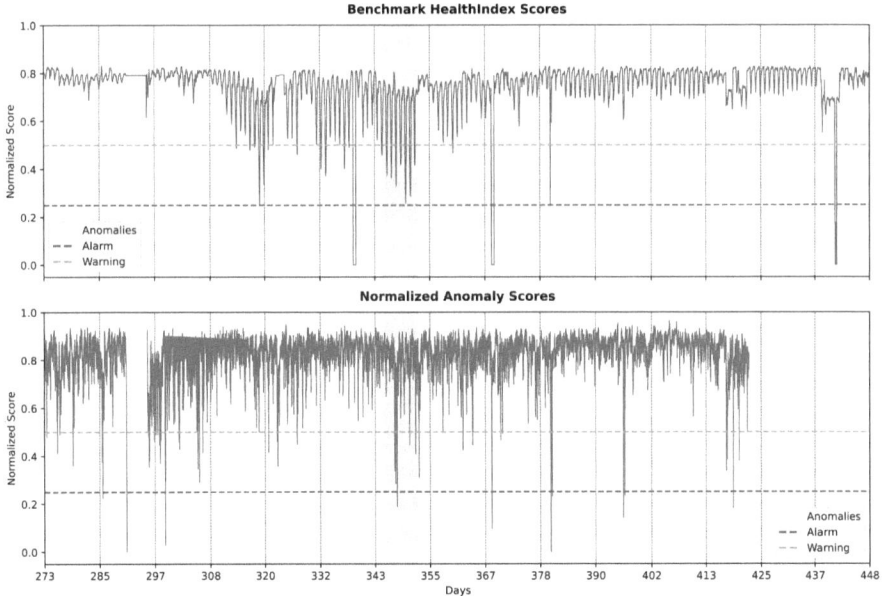

Fig. 5. Visual Comparison of the Test Set Anomaly Scores (Benchmark vs. Ours) Raw Benchmark achieved a precision of 0.296, recall = 0.214, F_1 = 0.249, F_β = 0.292. Our model resulted in a precision of 0.366, recall = 0.078, F_1 = 0.128, F_β = 0.210.

Table 1. Performance evaluation of the AD model on synthetically augmented anomalies. Results show detection metrics across different sparsification levels of injected cliques, controlled by edge dropout probability p. The F_β score and weight of the critic α are fine-tuned on the same set and reported alongside graph statistics. Added Edges represents the number of uncoalesced synthetic connections retained after dropout, while Total Edges indicates the final size of the coalesced graph structure.

p	.998	.9985	.999	.9995	1
$F_{0.2}$	.89	.88	.86	.77	.27
α	1	1	1	1	.4
Total Edges (Millions)	63	62.7	62.4	62.1	62
Added Edges (Millions)	1.24	.93	.62	.31	0

mapped test set and systematically reducing their connectivity to assess detection performance degradation. Starting from a baseline graph constructed following the procedure in Sect. 4.1, we introduce synthetic structural anomalies by embedding fully connected subgraphs (cliques) within a known anomaly period. To maintain consistency with the temporal windowing originally used, we generate 41 distinct cliques, each spanning up to 100 timestamps (same as w used for graph mapping). The edge attributes for these synthetic connections are sampled from the existing attribute distribution to ensure realistic features. The key experimental manipulation involves gradually degrading these anomalous patterns through a controlled edge dropout procedure. By randomly removing edges with increasing probability p, we systematically reduce the density of the injected patterns. This process creates a spectrum of anomalies that become progressively harder to distinguish from the normal graph structure mapping. Each resulting graph configuration is then evaluated using our trained model, which combines node reconstruction errors and critic scores to generate system-level anomaly scores. Detection performance is assessed through a grid search over different threshold values and critic scores weight (α), with results quantified using the F_β score (Table 1).

This methodology allows us to quantify exactly how sparse an anomalous pattern can become before it becomes less detectable, providing insights into the practical limitations of our graph-based anomaly detection approach. The findings have direct implications for real-world applications, where anomalous behavior often manifests not as perfectly dense structures, but as partial or shallow reconstructions of suspicious temporal patterns.

6 Conclusions

In this paper, we further investigated the approach proposed by [10], which integrates GANs, a reconstruction-based framework, and GNNs for effective and interpretable anomaly detection. We introduced several innovations: A sensor-wise anomaly detection approach shows promise, particularly when only a subset of signals exhibits anomalies. This method avoids system-wide aggregation by treating sensors as an ensemble of detectors. By setting individual thresholds, we can better preserve the role of key sensors in identifying anomalous intervals.

However, our findings also reveal certain limitations of the current model. Specifically, the model appears to over-rely on node attribute reconstruction errors as the primary anomaly indicator. The anomalies in our datasets are largely contextual, meaning that nodes exhibit deviations in their attributes compared to their neighbors, rather than unusual structural properties in the graph. This suggests that an effective model should prioritize attributes deviations over structural connectivity patterns when identifying anomalies.

We believe the full potential of this approach could be realized with a more advanced graph mapping algorithm—one that better captures contextual anomalies as structural deviations. Enhancing the representation of multivariate time series as graphs in a way that more effectively maps temporal contextual anomalies to structural ones could improve both anomaly detection performance and model interpretability. While our correlation-based graph construction allows for separate treatment of temporal and spatial relationships, it may not fully embed the structural intricacies of contextual anomalies.

In light of these observations, we are currently considering variants of our model using newer GNN modules that support signed graphs [13] or spatial-temporal graph mapping [21]. Until now, we have relied on conventional methods such as GCN, which are designed for unsigned graphs. However, disregarding the distinction between positive and negative links may introduce noise or lead to the loss of critical insights specific to signed graph data. By leveraging models explicitly designed for signed graphs, we aim to improve the model's ability to differentiate between various types of relationships, ultimately enhancing its anomaly detection capabilities.

Acknowledgments. The work presented in this paper is performed in the framework of the ICSC project – *Centro Nazionale di Ricerca in High Performance Computing, Big Data and Quantum Computing*, funded by the NextGenerationEU European initiative through the Italian Ministry of University and Research, PNRR Mission 4, Component 2: Investment 1.4, Project code CN00000013 - CUP I53C21000340006.

References

1. Akcay, S., et al.: GANomaly: Semi-supervised anomaly detection via adversarial training (2018). https://doi.org/10.48550/arxiv.1805.06725
2. Arjovsky, M., et al.: Wasserstein GAN (2017). https://doi.org/10.48550/ARXIV.1701.07875
3. Audibert, J., et al.: USAD: unsupervised anomaly detection on multivariate time series. In: Proceedings of the 26th ACM SIGKDD International Conference on Knowledge Discovery & Data Mining, pp. 3395–3404. KDD '20, Association for Computing Machinery, New York, NY, USA (2020)
4. Boniol, P., et al.: Dive into time-series anomaly detection: A decade review (2024). https://arxiv.org/abs/2412.20512

5. Breunig, M.M., et al.: LOF: identifying density-based local outliers. In: Proceedings of the 2000 ACM SIGMOD International Conference on Management of Data, pp. 93–104. SIGMOD '00, Association for Computing Machinery, NY, USA (2000)
6. Bruna, J., et al.: Spectral networks and locally connected networks on graphs (2014). https://arxiv.org/abs/1312.6203
7. Chen, Z., et al.: Learning graph structures with transformer for multivariate time-series anomaly detection in IoT. IEEE Internet Things J. **9**(12), 9179–9189 (2022). https://doi.org/10.1109/jiot.2021.3100509
8. Cheng, H., et al.: Detection and Characterization of Anomalies in Multivariate Time Series, pp. 413–424. https://doi.org/10.1137/1.9781611972795.36
9. Cheng, H., et al.: A robust graph-based algorithm for detection and characterization of anomalies in noisy multivariate time series, pp. 349–358 (2008). https://doi.org/10.1109/ICDMW.2008.48
10. Cornali, R., et al.: Graph neural network solutions for anomaly detection in time series. In: Proceedings of the 58th Hawaii International Conference on System Sciences, p. 997. HICSS'58 (2025). https://doi.org/10.24251/HICSS.2025.119
11. Defferrard, M., et al.: Convolutional neural networks on graphs with fast localized spectral filtering (2017). https://arxiv.org/abs/1606.09375
12. Deng, A., et al.: Graph neural network-based anomaly detection in multivariate time series. Proc. AAAI Conf. Artif. Intell. **35**(5), 4027–4035 (2021). https://doi.org/10.1609/aaai.v35i5.16523
13. Dinh, T.T., et al.: On the modelling and impact of negative edges in graph convolutional networks for node classification. In: NeurIPS 2023 Workshop: New Frontiers in Graph Learning (2023). https://openreview.net/forum?id=U0EPHUDrot
14. Geiger, A., et al.: TadGAN: Time series anomaly detection using generative adversarial networks (2020). https://doi.org/10.48550/arxiv.2009.07769
15. Gilmer, J., et al.: Neural message passing for quantum chemistry (2017). https://arxiv.org/abs/1704.01212
16. Goodfellow, I., et al.: Deep Learning. MIT Press (2016)
17. Goodfellow, I.J., et al.: Generative adversarial networks (2014). https://doi.org/10.48550/arxiv.1406.2661
18. Gulrajani, I., et al.: Improved training of wasserstein GANs (2017). https://doi.org/10.48550/arxiv.1704.00028
19. Hallac, D., et al.: Toeplitz inverse covariance-based clustering of multivariate time series data (2018). https://arxiv.org/abs/1706.03161
20. Hamilton, W.L., et al.: Inductive representation learning on large graphs (2018). https://arxiv.org/abs/1706.02216
21. Jin, M., et al.: A survey on graph neural networks for time series: Forecasting, classification, imputation, and anomaly detection (2024). https://arxiv.org/abs/2307.03759
22. Jin, M., et al.: Towards expressive spectral-temporal graph neural networks for time series forecasting (2025). https://arxiv.org/abs/2305.06587
23. Kingma, D.P., et al.: Auto-encoding variational bayes (2013). https://arxiv.org/abs/1312.6114
24. Kipf, T.N., et al.: Semi-supervised classification with graph convolutional networks. CoRR arxiv:abs/1609.02907 (2016). http://arxiv.org/abs/1609.02907
25. Kipf, T.N., et al.: Variational graph auto-encoders (2016). https://doi.org/10.48550/arxiv.1611.07308
26. Lavin, A., et al.: Evaluating real-time anomaly detection algorithms - the Numenta anomaly benchmark. CoRR arxiv:abs/1510.03336 (2015)

27. Li, D. et al.: MAD-GAN: Multivariate Anomaly Detection for Time Series Data with Generative Adversarial Networks, pp. 703–716. Springer International Publishing (2019). https://doi.org/10.1007/978-3-030-30490-4_56
28. Liang, H., et al.: Consistent anomaly detection and localization of multivariate time series via cross-correlation graph-based encoder decoder GAN. IEEE Trans. Instrum. Meas. **71**, 1–10 (2022). https://doi.org/10.1109/TIM.2021.3139696
29. Liang, H., et al.: Robust unsupervised anomaly detection via multi-time scale DCGANs with forgetting mechanism for industrial multivariate time series. Neurocomputing **423**, 444–462 (2021). https://doi.org/10.1016/j.neucom.2020.10.084
30. Liu, J., et al.: Condition monitoring of wind turbines with the implementation of spatio-temporal graph neural network. Eng. Appl. Artif. Intell. **121**(C) (2023). https://doi.org/10.1016/j.engappai.2023.106000
31. Liu, K., et al.: Bond: Benchmarking unsupervised outlier node detection on static attributed graphs (2022). https://arxiv.org/abs/2206.10071
32. Logan et al.: Handbook of Turbomachinery. Mechanical Engineering, CRC Press (2003). https://books.google.it/books?id=CNrKBQAAQBAJ
33. Makhzani, A., et al.: Adversarial autoencoders (2016). https://arxiv.org/abs/1511.05644
34. Malhotra, P., et al.: LSTM-based encoder-decoder for multi-sensor anomaly detection (2016). https://arxiv.org/abs/1607.00148
35. Ortega, A., et al.: Graph signal processing: Overview, challenges and applications (2018). https://arxiv.org/abs/1712.00468
36. Pan, S., et al.: Adversarially regularized graph autoencoder for graph embedding (2019). https://arxiv.org/abs/1802.04407
37. Radford, A., et al.: Unsupervised representation learning with deep convolutional generative adversarial networks (2016). https://arxiv.org/abs/1511.06434
38. Scarselli, F., et al.: The graph neural network model. IEEE Trans. Neural Networks **20**(1), 61–80 (2009). https://doi.org/10.1109/tnn.2008.2005605
39. Schölkopf, B., et al.: Support vector method for novelty detection. In: Proceedings of the 13th International Conference on Neural Information Processing Systems, pp. 582–588. NIPS'99, MIT Press, Cambridge, MA, USA (1999)
40. Silva, V.F., et al.: Time series analysis via network science: Concepts and algorithms. WIREs Data Mining and Knowledge Discovery **11**(3) (2021)
41. Su, Y., et al.: Robust anomaly detection for multivariate time series through stochastic recurrent neural network. In: Proceedings of the 25th ACM SIGKDD International Conference on Knowledge Discovery & Data Mining, pp. 2828–2837. KDD '19, Association for Computing Machinery, New York, NY, USA (2019). https://doi.org/10.1145/3292500.3330672
42. Van Gompel, J., et al.: Cost-effective fault diagnosis of nearby photovoltaic systems using graph neural networks. Energy **266**, 126444 (2023). https://doi.org/10.1016/j.energy.2022.126444
43. Velickovic, P., et al.: Graph attention networks (2018). https://arxiv.org/abs/1710.10903
44. Yang, Y., et al.: Complex network-based time series analysis. Phys. A: Stat. Mech. Appl. **387**(5 6), 1381–1386 (2008)
45. Zhao, H., et al.: Multivariate time-series anomaly detection via graph attention network (2020). https://arxiv.org/abs/2009.02040
46. Zhou, J., et al.: Graph neural networks: a review of methods and applications. AI Open **1**, 57–81 (2020). https://doi.org/10.1016/j.aiopen.2021.01.001

Understanding Signal Feature Impact in CNN-Based Modulation Classification with Realistic Datasets

Bruno M. S. Teixeira[1,2], Thalles M. Moreira[1,2], João Rodrigo Faria[1,2], Fábio D. L. Coutinho[1,2], Samuel S. Pereira[1,2], and Arnaldo S. R. Oliveira[1,2(✉)]

[1] Instituto de Telecomunicações, Aveiro, Portugal
[2] Departamento de Eletrónica, Telecomunicações e Informática, Universidade de Aveiro, Aveiro, Portugal
{bmteixeira,thallesmmoreira,jrfaria,fabiocoutinho,samuel.s.pereira, arnaldo.oliveira}@ua.pt

Abstract. Automatic Modulation Classification (AMC) plays a crucial role in modern communication systems by facilitating signal identification before demodulation. In recent years, Convolutional Neural Networks (CNNs) have been increasingly adopted for this task due to their inherent pattern recognition capabilities and robustness against noise, making them particularly suitable for the highly dynamic scenarios envisioned in future wireless communication systems. Regarding the model optimization process, the data characteristics are crucial in ensuring the model's readiness for real-world conditions. In the current literature, most open-access datasets primarily emphasize cumulative channel and hardware impairments introduced during signal transmission and reception. However, the influence of specific signal characteristics on CNN-based modulation classifiers remains underexplored. This paper addresses this gap by presenting an experimental dataset of M-ary Quadrature Amplitude Modulation (QAM) signals with diverse features, aiming to analyze their impact on CNN training performance. The results offer valuable insights into how factors such as the number of input samples, the number of examples per modulation order, and the oversampling ratio (OSR) affect model performance and generalization.

Keywords: automatic modulation classification · convolutional neural networks · experimental datasets · oversampling ratio · data features training impact

1 Introduction

Radio Frequency (RF) signal transmission, identification, and decoding have always played a crucial role in communication systems. Once the signal is received, down-converted, and digitized, the Digital Signal Processor (DSP)

modules play a pivotal role in processing the signal until demodulation. An essential step toward demodulation is the identification of the signal's modulation scheme, which is necessary to reconstruct the original signal and ensure it is ready for decoding and error correction [1].

Automatic Modulation Classification (AMC) enables the receiver to dynamically identify the modulation scheme of heterogeneous signals from diverse scenarios and environments [2]. Traditional AMC techniques often rely on decision theory and feature-based methods. The most commonly used approaches in each of these categories, as discussed in the literature, are maximum likelihood estimation and statistical signal properties, respectively. While these methods are effective in controlled environments, their performance degrades in dynamic and noisy conditions due to their intrinsic iterative nature and limited flexibility, which reduces their applicability in real-world scenarios [3]. To address this, classical machine learning (ML) classifiers like support vector machine (SVM) have been suggested in the literature, which offer a promising alternative by providing a feed-forward strategy and a more flexible approach compared to baseline methods. Despite these advances, classical ML saturates at 90 % accuracy on basic modulation sets (e.g., QPSK and 16-QAM) in AWGN channels at moderate SNR. Still, its performance deteriorates significantly when dealing with higher-order constellations or in the presence of fading and hardware impairments [4]. More recently, deep learning (DL)-based algorithms have garnered significant attention in the literature, particularly with the use of Convolutional Neural Networks (CNNs) [5].

CNN-based approaches have gained significant recognition across various scientific domains due to their inherent advantages, such as effective feature extraction, robustness to noise and input variations, and high classification accuracy. These make them strong candidates for AMC applications. Another crucial feature is the CNN architecture's independence from the input height and width, which is advantageous because this processing function is typically implemented in edge computing environments [6]. In these deployment scenarios, significant challenges arise for the hardware deployment of DL-based algorithms due to limited computational resources, strict latency requirements, and varying wireless conditions. Studies on CNN deployment have shown that, in environments that require a trade-off between energy consumption and computational resources, Field-Programmable Gate Arrays (FPGAs) are more appealing than Graphics Processing Units (GPUs) and Central Processing Units (CPUs). Due to their reconfigurability, FPGAs enable customized parallelism and dataflow architectures, resulting in lower latency and higher energy efficiency, especially in real-time or edge inference scenarios [7].

Furthermore, the dataset's representativeness in relation to the target scenario is crucial for optimizing a CNN-based classifier with the smallest possible number of learnable parameters. The dataset is used in the offline training process, allowing the CNN model to generalize the characteristics of the environment under consideration. Due to the relevance of this, various studies have utilized real-world-oriented datasets to demonstrate two key aspects: first, that CNN-based modulation classifiers are feasible even when considering channel and hardware impairments [8]; and second, that the CNN architecture can be optimized for the specific target scenario [5]. Nevertheless, the availability of these datasets obtained through experimental testbeds remains limited, constraining the study and proliferation of CNN-based classification estimators. Moreover, the literature still lacks a mature approach to introducing and adopting real-world scenario datasets in DL-based algorithms. This leads to skepticism regarding these algorithms for practical applications and prototyping wireless networks with such attributes.

With this in mind, this paper follows a complete workflow, from data generation to the prototyping phase of CNN-based classification estimators for edge implementation. An experimental dataset containing Quadrature Amplitude Modulation (QAM) with various signal features is generated to study its impact on CNN model training. The obtained training performance provides insights into the effects of factors such as the number of input samples, the number of examples per modulation order, and the oversampling ratio (OSR). This information, in turn, enables us to draw conclusions that will help optimize the model specifically for edge deployment by identifying trade-offs between these factors. Additionally, the entire dataset is made available to address the need for real-world-oriented implementations within the scientific community, aiming to foster the proliferation of various DL-based algorithms across the network stack[1].

The rest of the paper is structured as follows: Sect. 2 provides an overview of existing related work. Section 3 outlines the groundwork for implementation, while Sect. 4 provides the necessary details on the experimental setup used. Section 5 presents the obtained results and their subsequent discussion. Finally, the future work is explored in Sect. 6, followed by Sect. 7.

2 Related Work

Making Realistic datasets available has been a growing trend in the literature. This section provides an overview of datasets tailored for modulation recognition. With edge environments as the target deployment scenario, it is crucial to consider a key aspect: the complexity of the CNN-based model for modulation recognition. As mentioned earlier, reducing the number of learnable parameters by optimizing the model is essential, and to achieve this, understanding the impact of dataset characteristics is crucial. In addition to the effects of the radio frequency (RF) chain and the resulting RF impairments [3], as well as the channel conditions, we focus on isolating the impact of signal generation parameters on CNN model training, such as the OSR. This is crucial for recognizing any modulation, even if the signal has a different symbol rate or bandwidth. The literature on this matter is limited, and understanding how these parameters affect the performance of CNN-based modulation classification is vital.

---

[1] https://www.kaggle.com/datasets/brunomst/cabledamcdata.

Table 1. Open access datasets available in the literature.

Dataset	SNR	Size	Type	M-QAM	OSR	Roll-off	Citation
RML 2016.10a	$[-20,18]$	44,160	Synthetic	4, 16, 64	–	–	[2,9]
RML 2016.01b	$[-20,18]$	60,000	Synthetic	4, 16, 64	–	–	[2]
RML 2018.01a	$[-20,30]$	638,976	Synthetic	4, 16, 32, 64, 128, 256	–	(0.1,0.4)	[2,3,10]
HisarMod2019.1	$[-20,18]$	180,000	OTA	4, 16, 32, 64, 128, 256	2	0.35	[2]
Ours	30	24,576	Cabled	4, 16, 32, 64, 128, 256	6, 8, 10, 12	0.2	–

The available datasets targeting modulation classification with open access in the literature are displayed in Table 1, which includes data generation features such as the size in terms of samples per modulation, the obtained signal-to-noise ratio (SNR), the OSR value, the used roll-off filter, the works where it is used, and the type of dataset. As we are targeting QAM modulation for the envisioned model scenario, due to the verified complexity of achieving good performance with these algorithms in this case, along with the verified variance for this modulation [3], this table also provides information about the modulation order (M).

From Table 1, three different types of datasets are reported: synthetic, OTA, and cabled. Given the need to individualize the data generation features due to the gap found in the literature, the impact of channel impairments is minimized in the open-access dataset we provide. This helps create a dataset with a distinct nature, focusing more on data generation aspects rather than channel impairments. The inherent RF impairments from the transmission and reception RF chains are also present.

Typical datasets, such as Radio ML 2016.10a [9], primarily generated synthetic signals with simulated channel impairments, including multi-path fading, Doppler shift, symbol timing offset, and carrier frequency offset. A more detailed version, Radio ML 2018.01a [3], expanded the modulation variety and updated the channel impairments to include in-phase and quadrature component (IQ) imbalance, phase noise, and enhanced multi-path fading models. These improvements help reduce the gap between synthetic signals and real-world over-the-air (OTA) conditions. Regarding OTA datasets, the one provided in [2] is unique and stands as the most documented open-access dataset in the literature.

Nevertheless, the current open-access datasets in the literature exhibit a gap in dataset transparency or the range of data feature generation. Therefore, our provided open-access dataset aims to contribute by offering an alternative that enhances the existing datasets, improving transparency and expanding the variety of data features.

3 Workflow

This section outlines the workflow followed in this study, covering dataset organization, CNN architecture, and the training procedure. Figure 1 illustrates the overall workflow, which consists of three main steps: experimental data generation, training the CNN model, and prototyping the envisioned CNN for edge deployment.

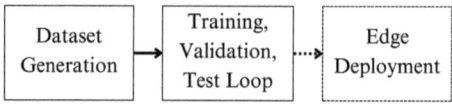

Fig. 1. Design workflow utilized in this work considering future edge deployment.

3.1 Dataset Organization

The different datasets adopted in this work contain various features with distinct value ranges. To establish a baseline comparison with our experimentally obtained dataset, we adopt the Radio ML 2018.01a dataset. This serves both as a validation for our code and a means to identify any missing data features in the existing dataset.

Figure 2 illustrates the various dimensions of the provided open-access dataset, including different OSR values, the number of samples per example, and the number of examples per modulation. The displayed organization mirrors the database structure to facilitate its usability.

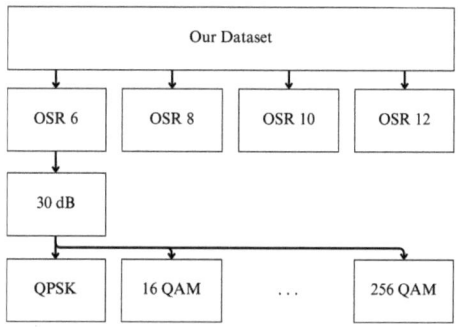

Fig. 2. Structure of the created dataset through the laboratory-acquired signals used in this study.

3.2 CNN Architecture

The CNN used in this study is based on the Deep Residual Network (ResNet) [11], well-known for its residual blocks. These blocks link the input of each block to its output, allowing the construction of deeper architectures while mitigating the vanishing gradient problem. Each residual block

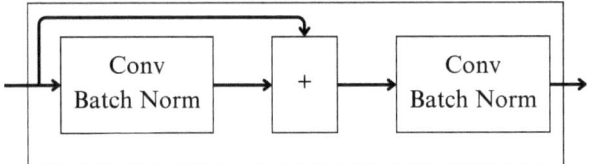

Fig. 3. Residual block structure.

typically consists of a convolutional layer (Conv), followed by batch normalization (BatchNorm), and finalized with a rectified linear unit (ReLU) activation layer as displayed in Fig. 3.

Table 2 presents the CNN architecture adopted in this work for $N_{classes} = 6$, corresponding to the number of modulation orders. This CNN consists of five residual blocks and is referred to as ResNet5. Note that $N_{samples}$ is integrated into the CNN structure to analyze its impact on model performance.

Table 2. CNN architecture details.

Layer	Output Dimensions
Input	$2 \times N_{samples}$
Conv	$16 \times N_{samples}$
Residual Block	$32 \times N_{samples}$
Residual Block	$64 \times N_{samples}$
Residual Block	$128 \times N_{samples}$
Residual Block	$256 \times N_{samples}$
Residual Block	$N_{classes} \times N_{samples}$
Flatten	$N_{classes} \times N_{samples}$
Fully Connected	$N_{classes}$
ReLU	$N_{classes}$

3.3 Training, Validation and Test Procedure

The CNN model optimization process is conducted on a machine equipped with an AMD Ryzen 9 7950X3D 16-Core Processor and an NVIDIA GeForce RTX 4080 SUPER GPU. Training is performed over 10 realizations to account for variations in weight initialization, with each realization consisting of 100 epochs. The PyTorch framework is used for model implementation, with the dataset divided into three subsets: 80% for training, 10% for validation, and 10% for testing.

Regarding the hyperparameter training, Table 3 provides a summary of them. The cross-entropy loss function is employed to compute training and validation losses. CNN weights are optimized using the Adam optimizer with a learning rate of 6 $times 10^{-5}$, ensuring efficient minimization of the training loss. The batch size is set to 256.

Table 3. Training hyper-parameters.

Processes	Num. of Epochs	Dataset Partition	Loss Function	Learning Rate	Optimizer	Batch Size
10	100	Train 80%, Validation 10%, Test 10%	Cross-Entropy	6e-5	Adam	256

4 Experimental Dataset Generation

This section provides an overview of the entire process, including data generation, transmission, reception, and pre-processing steps.

4.1 Signal Generation

The general process for signal generation is illustrated in Fig. 4. In the first step, a sufficient number of signals is generated to ensure that every sequence of bits in the transmitted signal is unique.

Fig. 4. Signal generation sequence.

A sampling frequency of 1.02 MHz is selected, as this value is evenly divisible by all considered OSR values. The Root Raised Cosine (RRC) filter is applied with a roll-off factor of 0.2, and 200 guard symbols are introduced to mitigate inter-symbol interference. During modulation, the adopted modulation orders (M) are 4, 16, 32, 64, 128, and 256, while the considered OSR values are 6, 8, 10, and 12. Consequently, the output signal for each configuration has a structure of 43 lines by 200,000 rows.

Table 4 provides a comprehensive description of the parameters used for each generation signal process.

4.2 Laboratorial Setup

The experimental setup for the signal acquisition process is shown in Fig. 5. As previously mentioned, the transmitted signal consists of 200,000 samples and is loaded into the Vector Signal Generator (VSG), specifically the SMA100J model.

Table 4. Dataset parameters.

Parameters	Values
Roll-off Factor	0.2
SNR	30 dB
Guard Symbols	200
OSR	6, 8, 10, 12
Bit Precision	32-bit floating-point
Number of samples	25,165,824 complex samples
Modulations	4QAM, 16QAM, 32QAM, 64QAM, 128QAM, 256QAM

The VSG is programmed to operate at a center frequency of 500 MHz with a transmission power of -66 dBm, resulting in an approximate SNR of 30 dB. The VSG is directly connected to the Vector Signal Analyzer (VSA) via a coaxial cable. The VSA is configured to operate at the same center frequency, with a sampling rate of 1.02 MHz and a capture length of 100,000 samples.

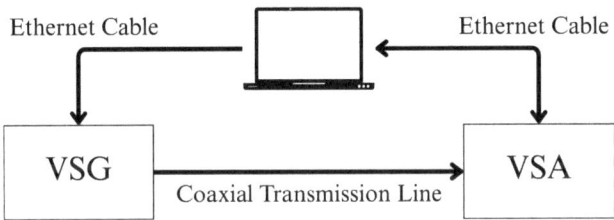

Fig. 5. Connection diagram between VSG, VSA and the computer.

After confirming the correct setup of both devices, a query is executed to retrieve samples from the VSA buffer. The received signal is then tested through a demodulation process. A new query is performed if the signal fails any of the tests. Otherwise, the next signal is loaded into the VSG for transmission. The query buffer size required careful consideration, as longer queries are more prone to errors. To accommodate larger sample buffers, the device reduces precision per sample. Given this, a query length of 100,000 samples is selected to ensure that each query remains smaller than the loaded signal, maintains the uniqueness feature, and prevents any loss of precision in the retrieved data. A picture of the laboratory setup is shown in Fig. 6.

4.3 Data Pre-processing

To feed the experimental data into the ResNet5 model for optimization, we adopt the same dataset organization as in the Radio ML 2018.01a. In our provided

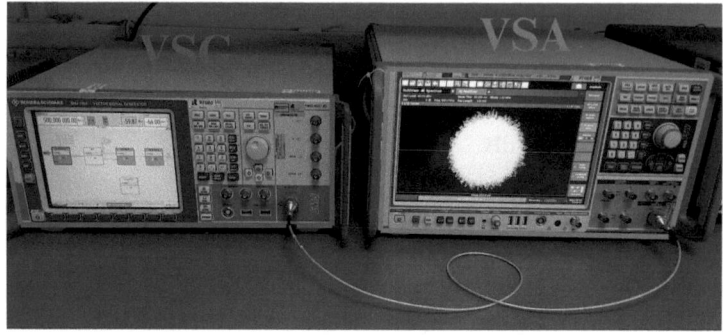

Fig. 6. Picture of the laboratory dataset acquisition setup.

dataset, the data in the .h5 file format is divided into the /X group, which contains the input data with a structure of $(N_{examples} \times N_{classes}, 2, 1, N_{samples})$, and the target output /Y with a structure of $(N_{examples} \times N_{classes}, N_{samples})$.

Therefore, it is necessary to prepare the received signal in the proper dataset structure. First, signal normalization is performed, followed by restructuring the data into variable dimensions, ensuring each example corresponds to a one-shot solution.

Radio ML 2018.01a Comparison. To perform the baseline comparison, it is necessary to individualize the 30 dB QAM modulations from the Radio ML 2018.01a dataset. It is important to note that this dataset is not normalized. However, we cannot perform normalization due to the lack of information relative to the signal generation, the maximum value in each example may not correspond to a constellation maximum, and normalizing it will introduce error.

5 Results and Discussion

In this section, we present and discuss the results of the modulation classification using the ResNet5 model with a batch size of 256, considering the training process over 100 epochs with 10 realizations to account for variations in weight initialization. The primary metric used for optimization is test accuracy, as it directly reflects the model's performance. In our experimental dataset, OSR values of 6, 8, 10, and 12 are considered. Additionally, to analyze the impact of data features on the ResNet5 model, different values for the number of samples per example, $N_{samples}$ equal to 512, 1024, 2048, and 4096, as well as the number of examples per modulation order, $N_{examples}$ of 512, 1024, 2048, and 4096, are considered. Note that, as a result of shortening or increasing $N_{samples}$, an inverse adjustment is applied to $N_{examples}$ to preserve the overall amount of data.

In Fig. 7, the test accuracy results are presented to compare the performance between the synthetic Radio ML 2018.01a dataset-denoted as *Baseline* in the figure legend-and the dataset proposed in this work. The primary objective is to observe the general training behavior and assess the potential impact of the missing OSR value. However, it is essential to note that the Radio ML 2018.01a dataset includes a variety of hardware and channel impairments, which necessitates caution when concluding the influence of OSR. From the results, the OSR value of the *Baseline* dataset appears to lie between OSR = 10 and OSR = 12, based on the observed accuracy trends. Additionally, it is noticeable that for every first epoch, the accuracy of each OSR configuration in our dataset is significantly higher than that of the *Baseline*, with all OSR values showing relatively close performance. This behavior may be attributed to the lack of normalization in the *Baseline* dataset and the presence of hardware and channel impairments included in its generation process.

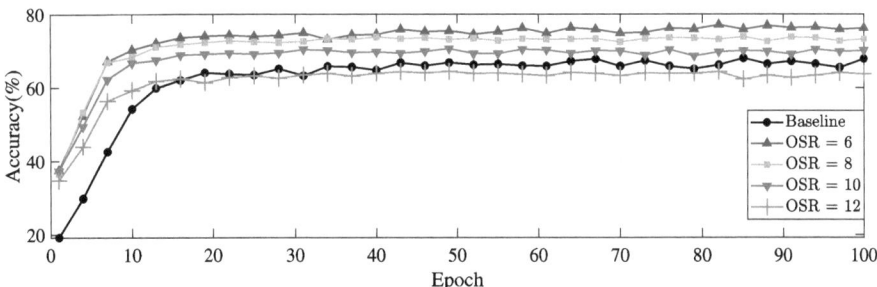

Fig. 7. Comparison of test accuracy across various OSR values from our experimental dataset and the RadioML 2018.01a dataset.

Figure 8 shows the impact of the sample size ($N_{samples}$) in the classification test accuracy for (a) $OSR = 6$ and (b) $OSR = 12$. It is noticeable that in the $OSR = 6$ scenario, the final accuracy improves, particularly for lower $N_{samples}$ values, which correspond to higher $N_{examples}$. This suggests that reducing the sample length improves performance, as the higher density of complementary data points between signal samples, due to the lower OSR, leads to a reduction in helpful information per sample by a factor of the OSR.

In Fig. 9, the impact of the number of examples per modulation ($N_{examples}$) on classification test accuracy is presented for (a) $OSR = 6$ and (b) $OSR = 12$. For a small number of examples, both OSR configurations yield similar accuracy. However, as the number of examples increases, accuracy improves for both, but not at the same rate. For $OSR = 6$, the accuracy difference between the lowest and highest number of examples is approximately 20%, while for $OSR = 12$, the improvement is only around 10%. Interestingly, despite $OSR = 12$ having double the oversampling of $OSR = 6$, it does not translate into higher classification accuracy, revealing an inverse relationship between OSR and classification performance in this scenario.

Figure 10 illustrates the impact of (a) $N_{examples}$ and (b) $N_{samples}$ on the obtained test accuracy for the different OSR values considered in this study. Given the significance of data volume in the training process, increasing the

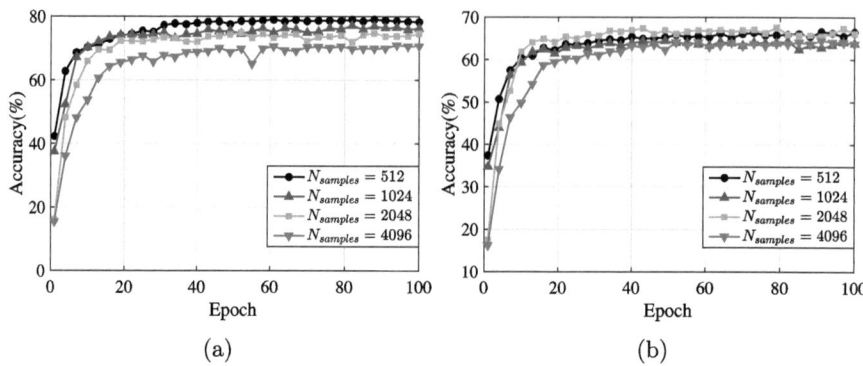

Fig. 8. Impact of the $N_{samples}$ in the obtained test accuracy considering (a) $OSR = 6$ and (b) $OSR = 12$.

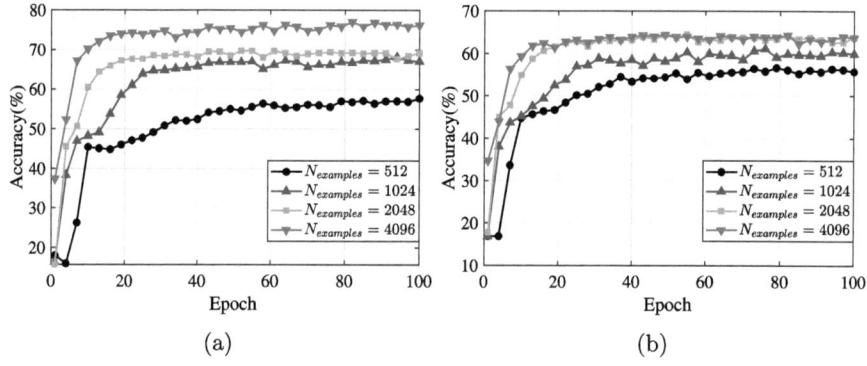

Fig. 9. Impact of the $N_{examples}$ in the obtained test accuracy considering (a) $OSR = 6$ and (b) $OSR = 12$.

number of examples would generally lead to improved model accuracy. However, when focusing on the effect of $N_{examples}$, it is observed that for higher OSR values, the accuracy does not increase linearly with the number of examples. On the other hand, increasing $N_{samples}$ leads to a consistent decrease in test accuracy across all OSR values. This suggests that while larger input sequences may carry more data, they do not necessarily contribute positively to the learning process, possibly due to redundancy or overfitting effects. Consequently, a trade-off between $N_{examples}$ and $N_{samples}$ must be considered when targeting a specific OSR value for edge deployment.

6 Way Forward

This paper aims to fill the gap in publicly available datasets of telecommunication modulations, the variation of OSR with real measurements. This is necessary to recognize any real-world signal with precision clearly. However, a fully

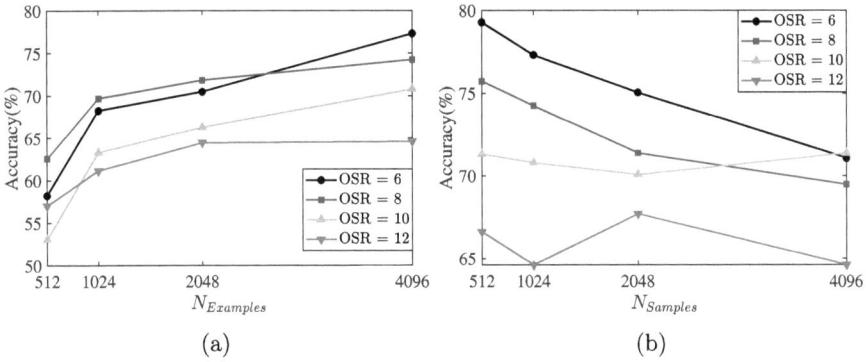

Fig. 10. Impact of the (a) $N_{examples}$ and (b) $N_{samples}$ in the obtained test accuracy for different OSR values.

autonomous signal recognition system needs more than just knowing the modulation. For that, carrier frequency, bandwidth, or symbol rate are also important. The inclusion of multiple ORS attempts to equip our ML algorithm with the ability to recognize any modulation, even if the signal has a different symbol rate or bandwidth; however, it does not enable us to determine the values for these parameters.

In our vision, this dataset must be extended to accommodate the integration of these parameters, carrier frequency, and bandwidth. Furthermore, since classical methods already exist to find such parameters, a comparison will be needed to have a fully autonomous signal recognition system that can operate at the edge using the minimum resource consumption.

7 Conclusion

This paper investigates the importance of data generation characteristics in the design of Convolutional Neural Network (CNN)-based classification estimators, with a focus on edge deployment. An experimental dataset comprising M-ary Quadrature Amplitude Modulation (QAM) signals with diverse characteristics is presented to evaluate the influence of specific signal features on CNN training performance. The results reveal that overlooked factors, such as the oversampling ratio (OSR), can significantly impact the inference capability of CNN-based models. Comprehensive evaluations considering both the number of samples and the number of examples per modulation order demonstrate that achieving optimal performance requires careful consideration of these data characteristics. Consequently, real-world-oriented datasets should explicitly document signal generation parameters and support trade-off analyses aligned with the design choices explored in this work.

Acknowledgments. This work was funded by the PRR - Plano de Recuperação e Resiliência and by the NextGenerationEU funds at Universidade de Aveiro, through the scope of the Agenda for Business Innovation "Agenda Microeletránica" (Project no.14 with the application C644916358-00000028). We acknowledge that ChatGPT was used to proofread the final draft of the article's text.

References

1. Pihlajasalo, J., et al.: Deep learning based OFDM physical-layer receiver for extreme mobility. In: 2021 55th Asilomar Conference on Signals, Systems, and Computers, pp. 395–399 (2021)
2. Zhang, F., Luo, C., Jialang, X., Luo, Y., Zheng, F.-C.: Deep learning based automatic modulation recognition: models, datasets, and challenges. Digital Signal Process. **129**, 103650 (2022)
3. Shea, T.J.O., Roy, T., Charles Clancy, T.: Over-the-air deep learning based radio signal classification. IEEE J. Sel. Topics Signal Process. **12**(1), 168–179 (2018)
4. Orlic, V.D., Dukic, M.L.: Automatic modulation classification algorithm using higher-order cumulants under real-world channel conditions. IEEE Commun. Lett. **13**(12), 917–919 (2009)
5. Sathyanarayanan, V., Wagner, M., Gerstoft, P.: Over the air performance of deep learning for modulation classification across channel conditions. In: 2020 54th Asilomar Conference on Signals, Systems, and Computers, pp. 157–161 (2020)
6. He, K., Zhang, X., Ren, S., Sun, J.: Deep residual learning for image recognition. In: 2016 IEEE Conference on Computer Vision and Pattern Recognition (CVPR), pp. 770–778 (2016)
7. de Lima Luiz, A., Zimmer, A., Brandmeier, T., Assump o Lolis, L.H.: Performance analysis of CNN speed and power consumption among CPUs, GPUs and an FPGA for EU GDPR 2016/679 compliant automotive applications. Transp. Res. Procedia **72**, 3046–3053 (2023). TRA Lisbon 2022 Conference Proceedings Transport Research Arena (TRA Lisbon 2022), 14th-17th November 2022. Lisboa, Portugal
8. Ya, T., Lin, Y., Haoran Zha, J., Wang, Z.Y., Gui, G., Mao, S.: Large-scale real-world radio signal recognition with deep learning. Chin. J. Aeronaut. **35**(9), 35–48 (2022)
9. Jiang, J., Wang, Z., Zhao, H., Qiu, S., Li, J.: Modulation recognition method of satellite communication based on CLDNN model. In: 2021 IEEE 30th International Symposium on Industrial Electronics (ISIE), pp. 1–6 (2021)
10. Lin, C., Yan, W., Zhang, L., Wang, W.: A real-time modulation recognition system based on software-defined radio and multi-skip residual neural network. IEEE Access **8**, 221235–221245 (2020)
11. Rosa, J., et al.: BACALHAUNET: a tiny CNN for lightning-fast modulation classification. ITU J. Future Evol. Technol. **3**, 252–260 (2022)

Advanced Processes of Mathematics and Computing Models in Complex Data-Intensive Computational Systems (AMCM 2025)

Empirical Analysis for Future Excellence Tourism Policies: The Case of Arzachena (Sardinia, Italy)

Brunella Brundu[1](✉), Sonia Malvica[2], and Donatella Carboni[2]

[1] Department of Economics and Business, University of Sassari, 07100 Sassari, SS, Italy
brundubr@uniss.it
[2] Department of Humanities and Social Sciences, University of Sassari, 07100 Sassari, SS, Italy

Abstract. Coastal areas have historically served as hubs of human activity. Accordingly, the development of port infrastructure has driven strategies for nautical tourism, which can significantly influence the regional economic landscape and foster synergistic collaborations among tourism-related stakeholders. While research on ports and seaside tourism is well established, studies investigating the connection between coastal and inland areas through port facilities remain limited. In the Mediterranean context, Sardinia (Italy) represents a case of highly seasonal tourism and is a prime destination for nautical tourism. In line with the Regional Strategic Plan, the enhancement of the island's inland heritage has been encouraged to promote deseasonalization strategies. Acknowledging the prominent role of nautical tourism in Sardinia, this study is intended as a contribution to a broader research initiative focused on mapping the island's nautical infrastructure. The analysis centers on the municipality of Arzachena (Province of Sassari), which hosts significant infrastructure for large vessels and luxury tourism. Through field research, cartographic analysis, and the application of isochrones, the study investigated the accessibility between local ports and Arzachena's cultural assets. The results suggested a potential for proximity-based and day tourism, enabling nautical tourists to explore inland historical and cultural sites. Overall, further research could support the integrated valorization of coastal and inland resources, highlighting the potential of a territorial approach to nautical tourism planning beyond the coastline. This integrated perspective may yield long-term governance benefits, employment opportunities, and socio-economic development for inland Sardinia through enhanced use of marina facilities.

Keywords: Nautical Tourism · Marina · Cultural Asset · Isochrone analysis · Governance

1 Introduction

Over 70% of the Earth's surface is covered by oceans and seas [1], underscoring the pivotal role of water for humanity and their settlements. Coastal areas have historically served as hubs of human activity, intricately linked to development and progress, and consistently playing a significant economic role [2–4]. Their potential extends beyond the seaside tourism, offering opportunities for recreational and leisure activities [5, 6]. Such pattern is related to nautical activities port infrastructures' development [5].

As primary venues for accommodating boaters and their vessels [4], tourist ports are strongly connected with nautical tourism [5, 7–14]. The expansion of nautical tourism requires the development and availability of appropriate infrastructures [15], which entail substantial investments and synergistic collaboration among involved stakeholders [16–18]. Tourist ports offer a wide array of services [19, 20], including tourism, accommodation, food service, mooring and assistance facilities. These complex structures are fundamental to the reputation of a destination [7] and stimulate various stakeholders, like producers who market their products to boaters [14, 20]. In line with the critical role of investment, construction, and operation in tourist ports, these should be designed and enhanced in accordance with the characteristics of their location [14]. Thus, tourist ports could be related to luxury tourism [21], so they have a role in strengthening and optimizing nautical supply, including the enhancement of specialized services often lacking in existing infrastructures [22].

The notion of ports serving as gateways to inland territories remains a generalized assumption, lacking substantial evidence of concrete interventions [23, 24]. This weakness primarily could be connected with the nautical tourists essence, whose choices are predominantly influenced by a preference for the sea and nature, leading to a strong desire to spend more time at sea rather than on the beach. The aim of this study was to highlight the potential of tourist ports in Sardinia (Italy) by viewing nautical tourism as an opportunity to rediscover the cultural identity of the beyond the coast. Sardinia is, in fact, a Mediterranean island renowned for beach tourism and notable for nautical tourism, retains its unique spirit, or genius loci, particularly in areas beyond the coastal scenery. As part of a broader research project analyzing regional tourist ports, this contribution presents the case of Arzachena territory (in the province of Sassari), identifying tourist ports for large vessels (i.e., yachting) as key elements for integrating offerings that support the cultural identity of the territory.

2 Materials and Methods

2.1 The Case Study

Situated in the heart of the Mediterranean, Sardinia boasts over 1,800 km of coastline, making it a prime destination for nautical tourism. This appeal is largely attributed to its territorial features, with beaches, minor islands, marine reserves, and national parks, offering a varied tourist experience. Sardinia actually captivates tourists with a heritage distinct from the Italian Peninsula's one. Such a uniqueness should serve as a significant economic asset, with tourism contributing substantially to revenue and employment.

Located in the northeastern quadrant of the island, the territory of Arzachena (230.85 sq km) encompasses major port facilities situated in its hamlets. The environment includes various protected and ecologically significant areas: the Special Protection Area (SPA) of the La Maddalena Archipelago; sites of phytogeographic interest such as the Cannigione Ponds, Monti della Muvra Coste delle Saline, and the Portisco Petra

Ruja area; coastal wetlands; the Monte Moro site within the Regional Park System; and the permanent wildlife protection oasis of Paduli Saloni (Fig. 1).

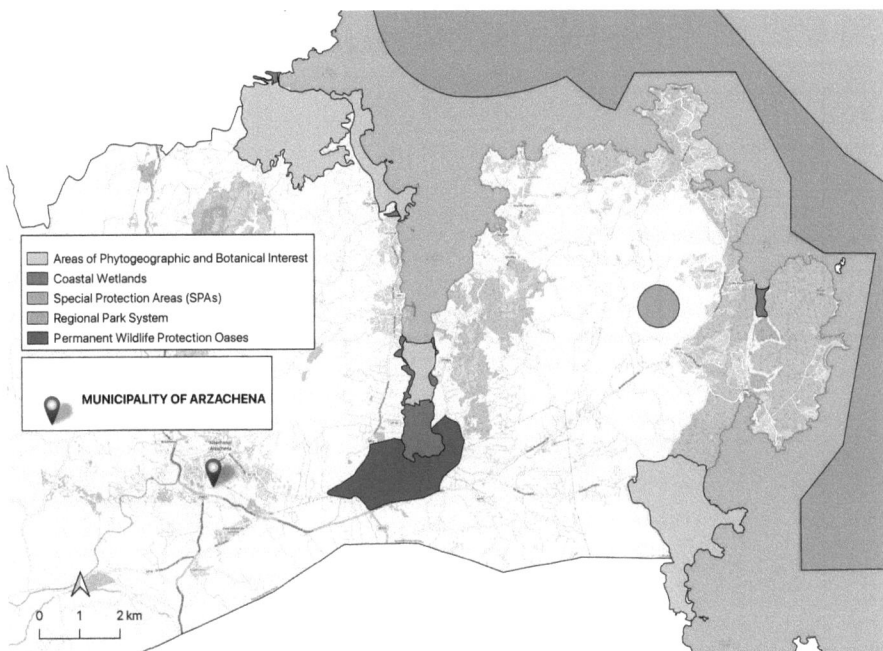

Fig. 1. Arzachena, cartographic representation highlighting key environmental features. Data extracted from [25]. (Authors' elaboration)

Arzachena hosts historical and cultural assets as well [26]. Among its archaeological complexes, approximately 10 km from the Gulf, lies the Necropolis of Li Muri, one of the oldest megalithic burial sites in the region, dating back to the Neolithic period. In the locality of Capichera, the Nuragic Complex of La Prisgiona stands as a testament to Nuragic civilization, with construction phases spanning from the 14th to the 9th century BCE. Further evidence of the area's prehistoric heritage includes the Temple of Malchittu and the Giants' Tombs of Coddu Ecchju, Li Lolghi, and Moru. These funerary structures underscore the significance of ancestor worship in Nuragic societies. The Nuraghe Albucciu, with artifacts suggesting usage from the late Middle Bronze Age, adds to the archaeological tapestry of the region. Arzachena's historical narrative is further enriched by institutions such as La Scatola del Tempo (i.e., an exhibition center guiding visitors through local history) and the Museum of Science, Earth, and Man, which offers natural and anthropological insights. The cultural landscape is complemented by sites contributing to the region's identity and imagery, including the Church of Stella Maris (i.e., an elegant sacred building overlooking the sea) and the Hotel Cala di Volpe (i.e., a hospitality structure completed in 1963). Both are exemplary of the so-called Mediterranean style architecture characteristic of Porto Cervo and, more broadly, the

Costa Smeralda project, which has significantly transformed the historical-geographical landscape of Gallura (Fig. 2).

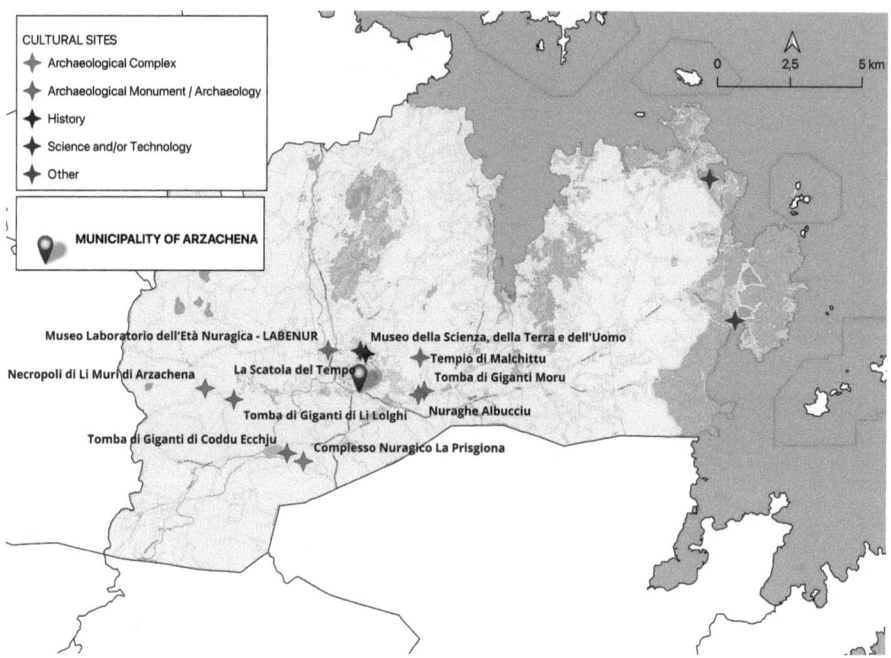

Fig. 2. Arzachena, cultural sites as data extracted from [25]. (Authors' elaboration)

2.2 Field Survey and GIS Analysis

A comprehensive inventory of landing points across the region, with a specific focus on Arzachena, was conducted to identify potential sites of interest for the yachting sector and, more broadly, for recreational boating. In accordance with Legislative Decree No. 171 of 18 July 2005, Article 3, a distinction was made between ports for recreational craft (< 25 m) and ports for large pleasure vessels (≥ 25 m), with the latter considered for coastal-inland integration in Arzachena territory. Among official sources, the focus was to the documents and annexes of the Regional Plan for the Network of Tourist Ports developed by the Autonomous Region of Sardinia [27]. To support the collected data, contacts were established with various stakeholders of the tourist ports.

To verify the accuracy of the gathered data, validations were carried out through: on-site interviews; remote interviews; questionnaires administered to port managers. The identified ports were subsequently analyzed based on the potential advantages of their geographical location. The study aimed to understand the extent to which a potential tourist, once ashore, could benefit from hospitality resources and cultural attractions. To achieve this, in addition to geolocating the reference ports, the research proceeded with the identification of restaurants and agritourism establishments in Arzachena municipality through field data collection. Finally, using OpenRouteService (ORS) Tools in QGIS software, a cartographic analysis was conducted based on the representation of temporal isochrones to evaluate the distance between the identified ports and Arzachena's cultural assets following a perspective of proximity and/or day tourism. Pedestrian routes (30 min) and vehicular routes (15 min) from the tourist ports were then considered to assess accessibility to cultural points of interest, dining establishments, and agritourism facilities within the territory, in order to understand the spatial reach of the Arzachena's ports for large pleasure vessels as nodes for diverse local tourist experiences.

3 Results and Discussion

3.1 Sardinian Scenario and Arzachena's Ports for Large Pleasure Vessels

Results suggested that the distribution of ports in Sardinia could closely be linked to the diverse nature of its coastlines across the island's provinces. In certain instances, significant distances separate these ports; for example, approximately 40 nautical miles (64 km) lie between the port of Alghero and that of Stintino. This diversity is evident not only in the allure of the rugged coasts and the beauty of the sea but also in the challenges posed by constructing port infrastructures along high cliffs or low-lying shores featuring ponds and lagoons.

A substantial portion of port facilities is concentrated along the northeastern, southeastern, and southwestern coasts, whereas the northwestern coast has fewer such structures. Such an imbalance could be related to distances between port facilities and their concentration in specific coastal areas and geographical disparities. Specifically, the northeastern quadrant (province of Sassari) stands out for its number of berths and its capacity to accommodate larger recreational vessels. Consequently, this area is distinguished by having the most functional port infrastructures for hosting maxi-yachts, while other areas possess only one of these characteristics. Following this, the northwestern quadrant (province of Sassari) ranks next in terms of the number of berths, and the southeastern quadrant (metropolitan city of Cagliari) follows regarding the capacity to accommodate larger recreational vessels. Considering individual port facilities, the port of Alghero (in the northwestern quadrant) holds the record for the number of berths, followed by the Marina of Villasimius (in the southeastern quadrant, province of South Sardinia). These facilities also offer a diverse range of services for recreational boating (Fig. 3).

In the case of Arzachena, the identified ports were Porto Cervo Marina, Poltu Quatu Marina dell'Orso, Cala Bitta Baja Sardinia, and Cannigione. Among the most important port facilities in Sardinia, the Marina of Porto Cervo (in the tourist area of Costa Smeralda) is particularly oriented towards the yachting tourism segment. It is therefore configured as a tourist port, active throughout the year. It is divided into: Old Port, which is located closer to the luxury shopping area; New Port, for accommodating a greater number of boats. Overall, Porto Cervo can host up to 720 boats, including those up to 160 m in length. Also, it has a depth ranging from 1.7 m up to 7 m. Poltu Quatu is located in the homonymous hamlet of the municipality of Arzachena, developing at the edge of a long inlet hidden and protected by rocky reliefs, a condition from which its name

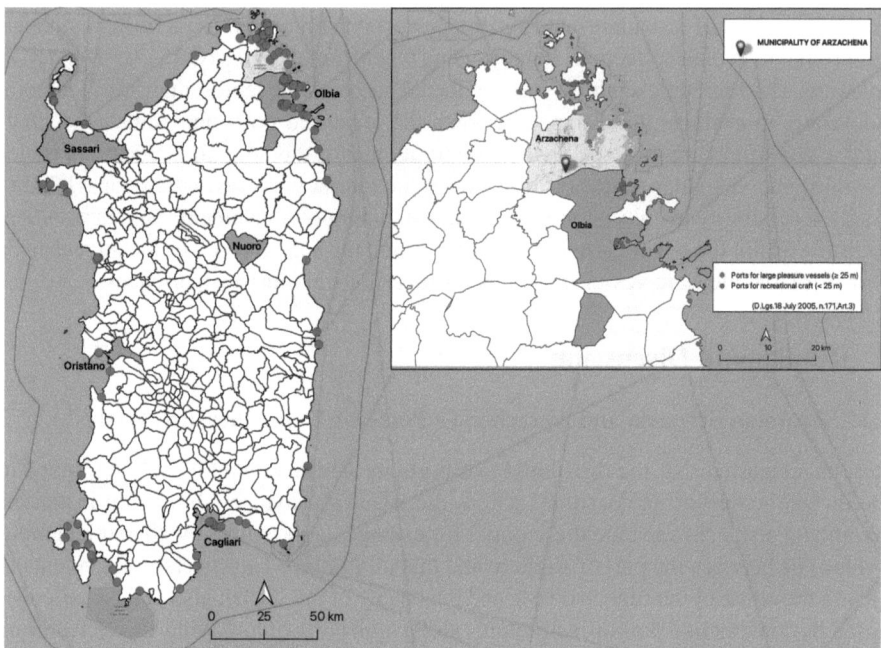

Fig. 3. Distribution of maritime ports in Sardinia, categorized by vessel accommodation capacity. The municipality of Arzachena, located in the northeastern area, is highlighted. (Authors' elaboration)

derives. The location of the port and the distinctive features of the village of Poltu Quatu confer an exclusive character to the port facility. This tourist landing, whose activity takes place throughout the year, has 305 berths and is capable of hosting boats up to 50 m. Finally, it has a minimum depth of 2 m and a maximum of 3 m. The port of Cala Bitta - Baja Sardinia is in the hamlet of Cala Bitta and is configured as a modestly sized facility consisting of a few piers. It has 183 berths and can accommodate boats with a maximum length of 27 m. This port facility falls into the category of tourist ports, with seasonally activity and a seabed that varies from 1.5 to 3 m. Finally, the port of Cannigione is located at the end of the Gulf of Arzachena and develops along the coast of the homonymous hamlet with, in addition, an arm that partially shelters much of the port and is configured as a complex of piers managed by multiple companies, some of which have formed the Marina di Cannigione consortium. This port facility is recognized as a tourist landing with year-round use and is mainly used for fishing, tourism, recreational boating, and nautical shipbuilding activities. Despite its extension, its seabed does not have a particularly high depth, as the minimum is 0.5 m, while the maximum is only 3.2 m. However, it is suitable for accommodating boats with a maximum length of 35 m and guarantees a total of about 800 berths. The port also has a buoy field, which can host 34 recreational units and offers the same services as the port (Table 1).

Table 1. Selected nautical infrastructures in the Arzachena area (northeastern Sardinia), including the main categories of port typology, prevailing functions, and patterns of seasonal or year-round use. (Authors' elaboration)

Name	Typology	Fruition time
Porto Cervo Marina	Marina	Annual
Poltu Qualtu Marina dell'Orso	Tourist berth; Multipurpose port	Annual
Cala Bitta – Baja Sardinia	Marina	Seasonal
Cannigione	Tourist berth; Functional port; Buoy field	Annual

3.2 Isochrones Analysis

The accessibility analysis was based on isochrone generated with ORS Tools in the afternoon of April 1st, 2025, then using OpenStreetMap routing data. The spatial pattern of port typologies and functions in the Arzachena area suggested significant implications for both accessibility and territorial integration. The aggregated 30-min foot-walking isochrone (Fig. 4) revealed a distinctly coastal pattern, with limited coverage towards the south and inland areas. As a result, potential tourists on foot are likely to concentrate around services located in the immediate vicinity of the ports, such as restaurants. In

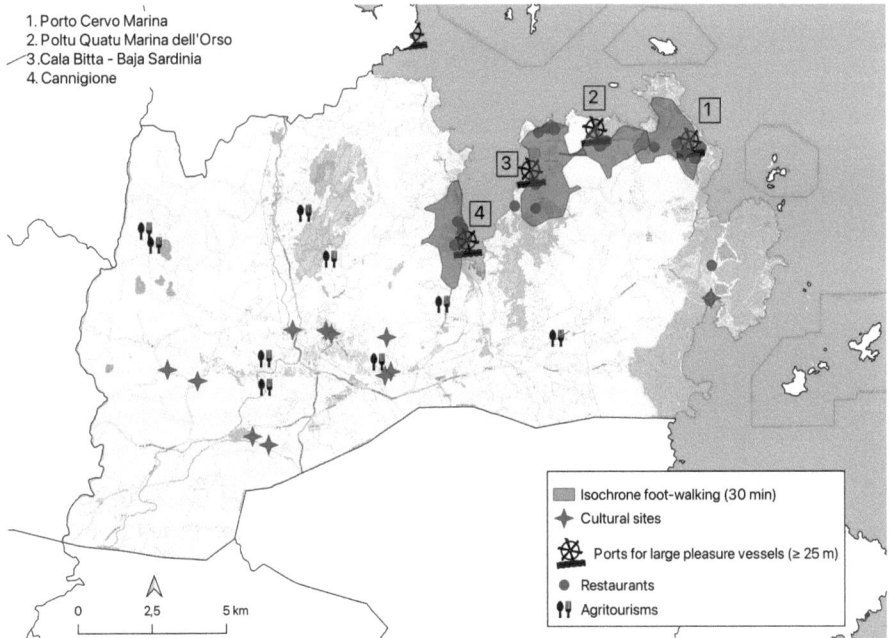

Fig. 4. Arzachena: map showing 30-min foot-walking isochrones from tourist harbors equipped to accommodate yachts with a length overall of 25 m or more. Results may differ over time due to data updates. (Authors' elaboration, April 1st, 2025)

contrast, agritourism facilities and most cultural sites would remain largely inaccessible without additional means of transport. So, it was reported a significant and functionally relevant disconnect between the port network and Arzachena's cultural assets, which are predominantly located in non-coastal areas. It is therefore recommended that the port system be suitably integrated with rental or mobility services that could encourage visitors to move beyond the coastal zone [28–30].

On the contrary, the driving-car isochrone analysis reported a broader spatial coverage for cultural tourism. Porto Cervo (Fig. 5) and Poltu Quatu (Fig. 6) exhibit relatively limited inland reach, serving primarily the northeastern coastal zone. In comparison, the isochrones from Cala Bitta (Fig. 7) and Cannigione (Fig. 8) demonstrated a significant capacity to extend toward the hinterland. Accordingly, Cannigione could be considered as a strategic node in terms of widespread accessibility to rural and cultural assets. Its broader and more articulated spatial coverage includes areas with the highest concentration of agritourism establishments and heritage sites. For this reason, the selected port could be a key access point for enhancing the integration of the coastal port system with inland tourism resources [31].

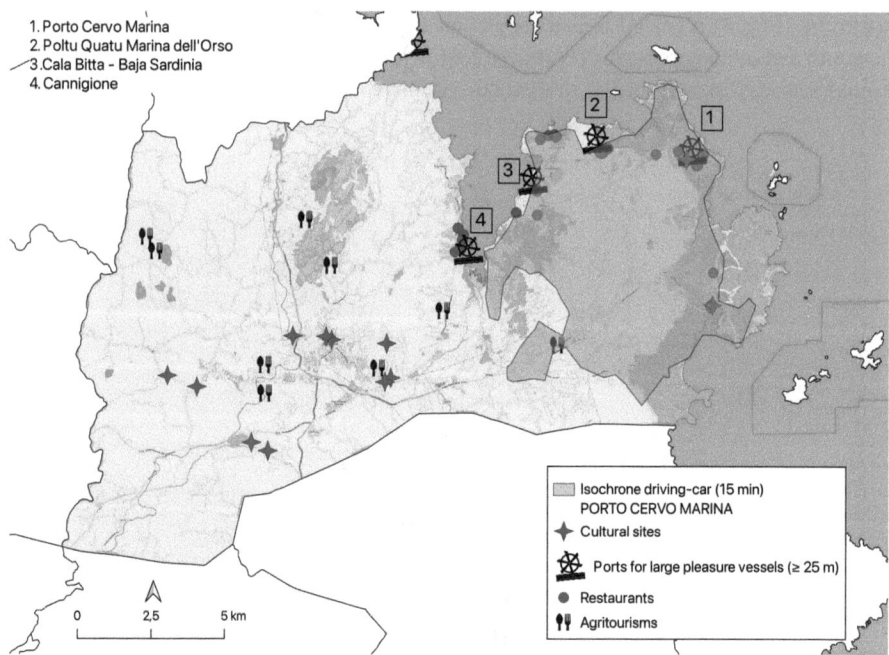

Fig. 5. Arzachena, map showing the 15-min car-driving isochrone from Porto Cervo Marina, which is equipped to accommodate yachts with a length overall of 25 m or more. Results may differ over time due to data updates. (Authors' elaboration, April 1st, 2025)

In sum, results suggested that on-foot tourist flows are likely to concentrate around port-adjacent services (e.g., restaurants), whereas inland facilities and cultural sites remain largely undiscovered. Such a spatial mismatch is especially relevant in the case

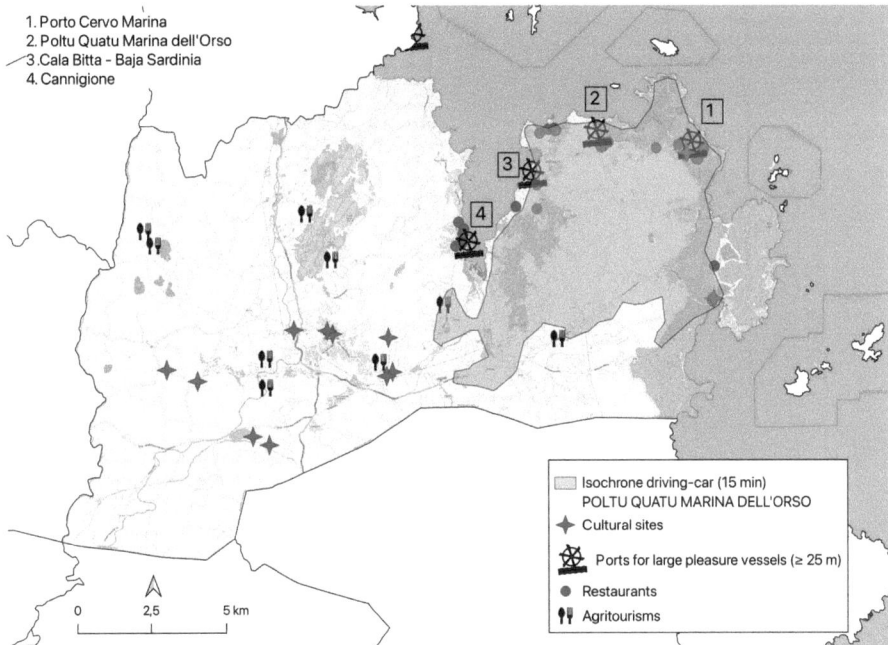

Fig. 6. Arzachena, map showing the 15-min car-driving isochrone from Poltu Qualtu Marina dell'Orso, which is equipped to accommodate yachts with a length overall of 25 m or more. Results may differ over time due to data updates. (Authors' elaboration, April 1st, 2025)

of Porto Cervo and Poltu Quatu, which, despite operating year-round, showed short inland coverage. Cala Bitta, despite showing a meaningful connection with the inland territory, operates on a seasonal basis, thus limiting its role as a year-round territorial access point. Conversely, Cannigione (classified as a multipurpose node with functional and buoy infrastructure) emerged as a strategic port due to its broader inland connectivity. Its catchment area potentially includes the highest density of rural and cultural assets, positioning it as a key hub for integrated tourism development. In addition, its year-round activity and the presence of a mooring field further strengthen its profile as a reference point for integrated nautical tourism. So, whilst Porto Cervo and Poltu Quatu are clearly oriented toward high-end yachting and luxury tourism, Cannigione could offer greater functional versatility and a more articulated infrastructural and socioeconomic role. Although it lacks deep-water berths, it can still accommodate mid-high-sized vessels, confirming its potential adaptability within the regional port network.

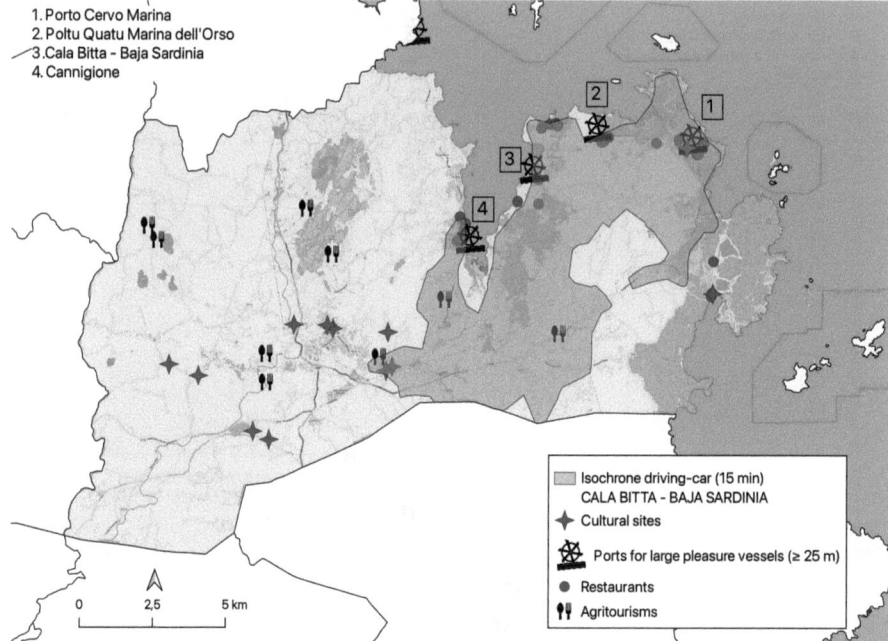

Fig. 7. Arzachena, map showing the 15-min car-driving isochrone from Cala Bitta – Baja Sardinia, which is equipped to accommodate yachts with a length overall of 25 m or more. Results may differ over time due to data updates. (Authors' elaboration, April 1st, 2025)

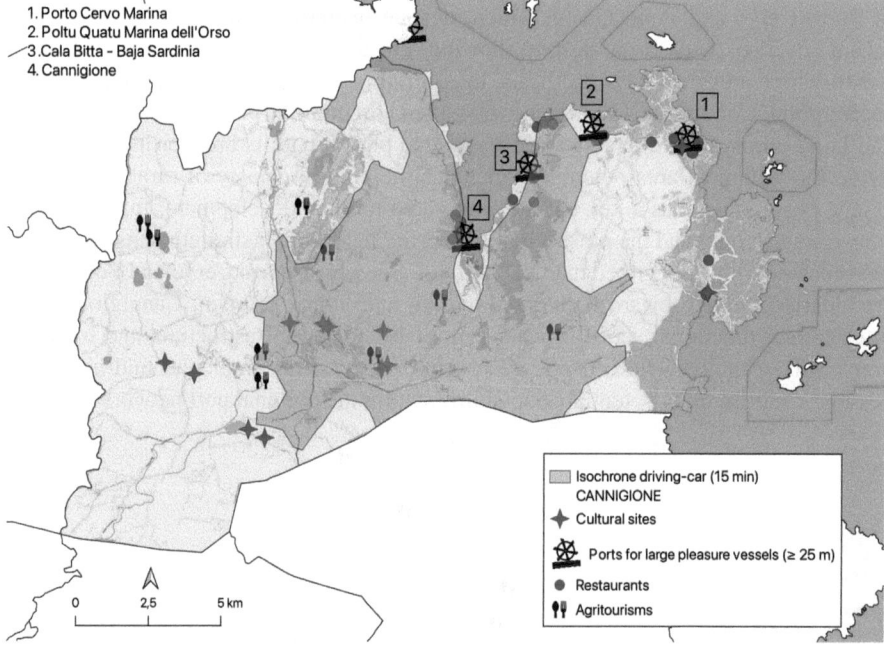

Fig. 8. Arzachena, map showing the 15-min car-driving isochrone from Cannigione, which is equipped to accommodate yachts with a length overall of 25 m or more. Results may differ over time due to data updates. (Authors' elaboration)

4 Conclusion

In an era where even luxury tourism must respond to users' growing sensitivity towards sustainability [32], it is recommended that nautical tourism be linked to the rediscovery of the territory identity. Overall, the present study on Arzachena territory suggested the need for a more structured intermodal approach to tourism infrastructure planning. Integrating the port network with targeted mobility services (e.g., rental vehicles, shuttle connections) could foster spatial integration and encourage tourist flows beyond the immediate coastline. Focusing Cannigione as a multimodal access point could enhance inland heritage resources, aligning port functionality with broader territorial development goals. The analysis of accessibility in Arzachena revealed a dual modality of territorial utilization driven by nautical tourism: (1) a functional coastal proximity, characterized by commercial services that are easily accessible on foot; (2) an access to cultural and rural resources situated inland necessitates private transportation, reflecting a deeper and more meaningful engagement with the territory. This dichotomy underscored critical challenges related to sustainability and modal integration, highlighting the imperative to enhance internal connectivity between the port infrastructure and the hinterland of Gallura. Arzachena's coastal environment offers tangible expressions of Sardinian identity through a diverse array of cultural sites, inviting even seasonal and luxury-oriented tourists to rediscover the island's essence. This scenario presents an opportunity to develop multi-tiered tourism strategies that valorize widespread rural hospitality. Implementing integrated port governance could facilitate the creation of itineraries that seamlessly combine coastal and inland experiences, promoting a more sustainable and evenly distributed tourist flow.

This study has limitations that should be acknowledged. First, the isochrones used to evaluate driving accessibility were performed with QGIS' ORS Tools, so real-time traffic data was not incorporated, considering instead average travel times. This is a significant constraint in the context of coastal Sardinia, where traffic congestion can be intense during the high tourist season. As a result, the actual travel times to inland cultural and rural sites could be longer than those estimated by the model. Then, since isochrones generated are subject to variations due to updates in the underlying data, changes in calculation parameters, time-specific requests, or server-side modifications, the results should be interpreted as indicative and intended for general understanding and exploratory objectives. Future research with integration of dynamic traffic data or time-dependent network analysis during the summer season is then strongly recommended, in order to provide a more accurate and realistic representation of seasonal accessibility patterns for tourist objectives.

Acknowledgements. The authors would like to extend special appreciation to research fellows Valentina Arru, Giovanni Demurtas, and Riccardo Todda for their valuable contribution to the project.

Authors' Contribution. Conceptualization: BB; Methodology: BB, DC; Investigation: all authors; Data Curation: SM; Formal Analysis: SM; Visualization: SM; Writing – original draft: BB, DC; Writing – review and editing: BB, SM. This study was carried out within the framework of the project "Osservazioni e analisi regionali dello yachting e dei porti turistici della Sardegna" (CUP E79I23000860002).

Disclosure of Interests. The authors have no competing interests to declare that are relevant to the content of this article.

References

1. Koundouri, P., Giannouli, A.: Blue growth and economics. Front. Mar. Sci. **2**(94), 1–6 (2015)
2. Cardoso, L., et al.: Features of nautical tourism in Portugal—projected destination image with a sustainability marketing approach. Sustainability **15**(11), 1–30 (2023)
3. Jennings, G.: Water-based tourism, sport, leisure, and recreation experiences. In: Jennings, G. (ed.) Water-Based Tourism, Sport, Leisure, and Recreation Experiences, pp. 1–16. Elsevier, Oxford (2007)
4. Silveira, L., Santos, N., Perna, F.: Yachts passing by the west coast of portugal what to do to make the marina and the destination of Figueira da foz a nautical tourism reference? Pomorstvo **32**(2), 182–190 (2018)
5. Martínez-Vázquez, R.M.: Nautical tourism: a bibliometric analysis. J. Spat. Organ. Dyn. **8**(4), 320–330 (2020)
6. Payeras, M., Jacob, M., García, M.A., Alemany, M., Alcover, A., Martínez-Ribes, L.: The yachting charter tourism SWOT: a basic analysis to design marketing strategies. Tourismos **6**(3), 111–134 (2011)
7. Benevolo, C., Spinelli, R.: The quality of web communication by Italian tourist ports. Tourism: Int. Interdisc. J. **66**(1), 52–62 (2018)
8. Jolić, N., Perko, N., Kavran, Z.: Development of nautical tourism: islands development motivator. WIT Trans. Ecol. Environ. **130**, 267–273 (2010)
9. Kasum, J., Božić-Fredotović, K., Vidan, P.: How nautical tourism ports affect the environment. WIT Trans. Ecol. Environ. **127**, 123–133 (2009)
10. Peres-Labajos, C.Á., et al.: The leisure nautical sector in the Atlantic area. J. Marit. Res. **11**(1), 87–97 (2014)
11. Poljičak, A.-M., Ljubić Hinić, M., Kalac, A.: Nautical tourism case study in the Republic of Croatia. LOGI Sci. J. Transp. Logistics **13**(1), 73–83 (2022)
12. Russo, F., Rindone, C.: Nautical tourism and regional population: the Italian case. WIT Trans. Built Environ. **187**, 251–263 (2019)
13. Vantola, R., Luoma, E., Parviainen, T., Lehikoinen, A.: Sustainability manifesting as a multi-material and sited network effect: how boat-sourced sewage management facilities serve as governance artefacts advancing sustainability in Nautical tourism. Mar. Pollut. Bull. **173**(Part B), 1–10 (2021)
14. Zubak, A., Jugović, A., Stumpf, G.: Analysis and evaluation of the nautical tourism in the Republic of Croatia and its impact on destination development. In: Vranešević, T., Peručić, D., Seabra, C., Hudina, B., Mandić, M., Plantić Tadić, D. (eds.) 3rd International M-Sphere Conference for Multidisciplinarity in Business and Science, p. 19 (2014)
15. Kovačić, M., Bošković, D., Favro, S.: Possibilities and limitations of spatial, technical and technological development of a port of nautical tourism. Naše More **53**(1–2), 54–62 (2006)
16. Gladkikh, T., Séraphin, H.: Conclusion: what is the impact of luxury yachting on the well-being of consumers and relevant stakeholders? Worldwide Hospitality Tourism Themes **15**(4), 451–455 (2023)
17. Gračan, D., Zadel, Z., Pavlović, D.: The stakeholders of nautical tourism process in destination network: topological positions and management participation. Naše more: Znanstveno-stručni časopis za more i pomorstvo **65**(3), 151–156 (2018)

18. Podovac, M., Drpić, D., Perić, G.: Analysis of the current state of nautical tourism in the function of improving the tourist offer of the city of Belgrade. In: IV International Applied Social Sciences Congress, pp. 288–302 (2020)
19. Ivanić, K., Perić Hadžić, A., Mohović, Đ: Nautical tourism: generator of croatian economy development. Pomorstvo **32**(1), 59–66 (2018)
20. Jugović, A., Kovačić, M., Hadžić, A.: Sustainable development model for nautical tourism ports. Tourism Hospitality Manage. **17**(2), 175–186 (2011)
21. Thirumaran, K., Eijdenberg, E.L., Wong, C.: A scoping review of luxury yachting and wellness: study trends and research prospects. Worldwide Hospitality Tourism Themes **15**(4), 371–385 (2023)
22. Bove, A., Mazzola, E.: Social aspects in small ports tourism sustainability. TeMA. J. Land Use Mobility Environ. **16**(1), 67–82 (2023)
23. Benevolo, C.: Turismo nautico. una sfida per il destination management. Riv. Sci. del Turismo **1**(3), 105–129 (2010)
24. Benevolo, C.: Problematiche di sostenibilità nell'ambito del turismo Nautico in Italia. Impresa Progetto Electr. J. Manage. **2**, 1–17 (2011)
25. Sardegna Geoportale. https://www.sardegnageoportale.it. Accessed 09 Apr 2025
26. Sardegna Cultura. https://www.sardegnacultura.it. Accessed 09 Apr 2025
27. Regione autonoma della sardegna: piano regionale della rete della portualità turistica (2020). https://delibere.regione.sardegna.it/it/visualizza_delibera.page;jsessionid=1F631D8C2A824CAD37D56FA911B6F371.app4?contentId=DBR52224. Accessed 13 Apr 2025
28. Favro, S., Kovačić, M., Gržetić, Z.: Nautical tourism the basis of the systematic development. Pomorstvo: Sci. J. Marit. Res. **22**(1), 31–51 (2008)
29. Lopes, E.R., et al.: Nautical tourism: contribution to sustainable tourism development. J. Tourism Res. **26**, 123–143 (2021)
30. Ugolini, G.M.: Infrastrutture portuali e turismo nautico: un nodo da sciogliere a scala regionale. Geotema **40**, 110–118 (2010)
31. Brundu, B., Battino, S., Manca, I.: The sustainable tourism organization of rural spaces. the island of Sardinia in the era of "staycation". In: Proceedings of the International Cartographic Association, vol. 4, pp. 1–8 (2021)
32. Ansaloni, G.M.M., Bionda, A., Ratti, A.: The evolution of yacht: from status-symbol to values' source. In: Zanella, F., et al. (eds.) Multidisciplinary Aspects of Design. Objects, Processes, Experiences and Narratives, Design! OPEN 2022, Springer Series in Design and Innovation, vol. 37, pp. 177–186. Springer, Cham (2024)

Data-Driven Time Series Modeling with Hurst Exponent for Nonlinear Indexes' Forecasting by Artificial Neural Networks

Yeliz Karaca[1,2]($\boxtimes$) and Osvaldo Gervasi[3]

[1] University of Massachusetts Chan Medical School (UMASS), Lake Avenue North, Worcester, MA 01655, USA
yeliz.karaca@ieee.org
[2] Massachusetts Institute of Technology (MIT), Massachusetts Avenue, Cambridge, MA 02139, USA
[3] University of Perugia, Department of Mathematics and Computer Science, Perugia, Italy
osvaldo.gervasi@unipg.it

Abstract. Neural networks reveal the benefit of requiring less formal statistical training owing to their capability of detecting complex nonlinear relationships between dependent and independent variables implicitly. Machine learning, artificial neural networks (ANN) and deep learning, on the other hand, show their upper hands in forecasting and prediction processes involved in various domains, including the analyses concerning financial indexes among other ones. Besides these advances and applications, time series models based on financial data expressed by financial theories may form as a basis for forecasting a series of data. When theories may not directly be applicable to predict the market values with external impacts, ANNs can be applied as a prediction tool for forecasting the market value series. Due to its robustness as a statistical means for examining sequential data over time, time series analyses examine financial stock market indices by identifying trends, predictive details and changing patterns toward accurate and efficient analyses in dynamic and nonlinear markets. Accordingly, the current study aims at forecasting based on the daily values of FCHI (France) and GSPC (India) indexes. Hurst exponent is applied to the dataset consisting of the Open, High, Low and Close values of the FCHI and GSPC indexes. Modeling for the purpose of the study is carried out by feed-forward backpropagation (FFBP) algorithm which is among the ANNs. The forecasting accuracy obtained from the modeling of the index values based on the past daily close attributes of 20 days is compared with respect to Mean Squared Error, and the results have validated the forecasting of indexes. As the steps, Hurst exponent is initially applied to the daily values (Open, High, Low, Close) of FCHI and GSPC indexes, leading to the generation of the dataset with more attributes. As the following step, the dataset with more attributes consisting of the FCHI and GSPC daily values are split into training dataset and test dataset for forecasting the indexes. Subsequently, the model constructed is used to compare the two datasets.

The forecasting accuracy of the index values' modeling based on the daily close values of 20 days is compared by Mean Squared Error. Lastly, modeling through the FFBP algorithm application to the new dataset generated and the FCHI and GSPC indexes enables the comparison and performing of forecasting with regard to these indexes. In addition, interpolation method is employed for managing missing data in the dataset. This approach is intended to a new mode of scheme and implementation tactics in an extended form to reveal the interaction between time series analysis, predictive modeling and indices. Thus, the models to be constructed can be evaluated regarding comprehensive outlooks that are concerned with decision-making, investment strategies' optimization and risk mitigation in various domains with accurate, reliable and data-driven aspects.

Keywords: Data-driven modeling · Nonlinear forecasting · Time series analysis · Hurst exponent · ANN · FFBP algorithm · Data interpolation method · Complexity modeling · Max-min normalization · Financial indexes

1 Introduction

Modeling based on predictive aspects builds on time series analysis by employing past data for the forecasting of future outcomes, and thus, correlations and causations concerning data enable to make informed decisions, strategic planning and management. Time series analysis in mathematical modeling addresses data points gathered sequentially over time, which allows for the capturing trends, fluctuations and/or patterns that are critical for the interpreration of past behaviors as well as for the forecasting of future events. Producing a numeric score based on inputs including a variety of asset prices, a financial index can be used to follow up the performance of assets and securities in a standardized way. In that respect, indixes have key roles in the summarizing and normalizing of data, providing a consolidated metric to represent dynamic datasets. For instance, stock market indices track the performance of a group of securities. When time series and predictive models are integrated, indices will enhance the capabililty of interpretability and provide a clearer level of understanding by which trends as well as forecasts can effectively be monitored and communicated.

A statistical measure is used to classify time series and infer the level of difficulty in predicting and choosing an appropriate model for the series at hand [24]. Predicting changes of indexes long term trend is an important problem for validating strategies of investment to the financial instruments. Changes in this characteristic can enable one to predict the turning point of indexes value long term trend. In finance, stocks represent a certain portion of a company's capital [24]. They offer returns to their investors and stockholders while enabling companies to grow and gain recognition by providing them with resources [13,23,24]. While investigating the fractal nature of financial markets – specifically, the tendency of a time series to regress strongly to its mean or to cluster in a direction introduced to fractal geometry, as Hurst's generation, the term Generalized Hurst Exponent [23]. The Hurst exponent is employed as a measure of the long-term memory of a time series, and long-term correlation memory refers to the interdependences existing among observation periods of the time series even if these periods are separated. In case of examination of long-term dependencies of the indexes, the investors could have better opportunities for informed decision-making processes related to daily data (open, low, high, close). The level of indexes' inefficiency and long-term correlation memory can be measured by applying several statistical and econometrical indicators, one of the most extensively-used measures being the Hurst exponent. These indicators are designed in a way that can measure the level of efficiency of the indexes' information without having knowledge concerning the underlying causal factors. To cite some work from literature, the following indicators have been used fort he analzing of the indexes. Kannan et al. [5], Roman et al. [18] and Ake et al. [1] performed financial index forecast applications with the data mining methods, while Inaoka [4], Evertsz [2], Moyano et al. [12] and Qian [16] conducted financial time series analysis with fractal and multifractal methods. In addition, Sakalauskas [19] applied index trading strategies with Shannon entropy and Hurst exponent indicators. Fuwape et al. [14], on the other hand, used fractal and entropy analysis for share indexes and domestic products, and Rejichi et al. [17] used test Hurst exponent behaviour for index efficiency purposes. Furthermore, machine learning, artificial neural networks (ANN) and deep learning have provided significant advances in forecasting and prediction in various domains, including the analyses concerning financial indexes. Machine learning addresses the development of algorithms enabling the systems to learn from data and thus to improve their performance by offering sound frameworks for identifying patterns and in big datasets. ANNs are adaptive to tasks that require nonlinear modeling and feature extraction which are assets that make ANNs effective for analyzing complex financial datasets. Deep learning algorithms are capable of recognizing patterns that are sequential and significant for purposes like predicting time series data such as economic indicators and stock market trends. The employment of machine learning and deep learning can allow researchers and practitioners to unravel nuanced insights and differences so that predictive models can be built toward anticipating future market behaviors [26]. The use of neural network models and hybrid models is proposed in a study which evaluates the effectiveness of neural network models that are acknowledged to be effective and dynamic in stock-market predictions. The models are analyzed by multi-layer perceptron, dynamic artificial neural network as well as hybrid neural networks using generalized autoregressive conditional heteroscedasticity for extracting new input variables with real exchange daily rate values belonging to the index of NASDAQ Stock Exchange [3]. The use of natural language processing (NLP) models in financial mathematics is also at stake in a work which used a mathematical-based sentiment analysis and deep learning models for forecasting the S&P 500 Index based on the summary text data to calculate sentiment scores [10]. Forecasting the shifts in stock indices plays a critical role for validating the potential strategies of monetary mechanisms, which is examined in a study characterizing complexity and self-similarity based on fractal and entropy analyses for stock market forecast modeling. The authors applied these methods to demonstrate the critical significance of Hurst exponent (HE) computed by Rescaled Range (R/S) fractal analysis when used as indicator along with Shannon entropy (SE) and Renyi entropy (RE) concerning the stock indices' capability of future forecasting [9]. For the purposes of effective data selection and robust prediction, complexity and self-similarity characterization is addressed in another study which obtained analyses based on fractal analysis and wavelet entropy via the seven recognized indexes and formed the forecasting model by applying the ANN algorithms to the datasets [6]. The aim of forecasting stock indices by ANN algorithms is done through the comparison of two Hölder regularity functions forecasting accuracy by characterizing self-similar patterns in time series. The application of the ANN algorithms reveals how the most significant attributes are identified by Hölder functions in finance datasets [8].

Time series models based on financial data conveyed by financial theories may form as a basis for forecasting a series of data. At times such theories might not directly be applicable to predict the market values with external impacts. Notwithstanding, ANNs are preferred to be applied as a prediction tool for forecasting market value series. Time series analysis owing to its robustness as a statistical means for examining sequential data over time comes with its applications in the examination of financial stock market indices by identifying trends, predictive insights and seasonal patterns toward accurate and efficient analyses in dynamic markets. The current study aims to produce forecasting based on the daily values of FCHI (France) and GSPC (India) indexes between 2020 and 2024. Hurst exponent is applied to the dataset consisting of the Open, High, Low and Close values of the FCHI and GSPC indexes, which has made it possible to identify 16 new indicators. The modeling is performed by feed-forward backpropagation (FFBP) algorithm, which is as one of the ANNs proves to be among the widely implemented neural network topologies. The forecasting accuracy obtained from the modeling of the index values based on the past daily close attributes of 20 days is compared with respect to Mean Squared Error (MSE) whose result has validated the forecasting of indexes, showing the importance of Hurst exponent method.

The remainder of the paper is organized as follows: Sect. 2 presents the materials, methods and methodology with Hurst Exponent and FFBP, while Sect. 3 addresses experimental results. The last section is the conclusion, discussion and future directions.

2 Materials and Methods

2.1 Nonlinear Dynamic Time Series Data

Nonlinear dynamic time series data depict the sequences of observations in which the relationship between variables changes in a complex and nonlinear manner over time. When compared with linear time series, nonlinear dynamic time series data have the capability of capturing nuanced details and behaviors observed in real-world phenomena, one of which is those in financial markets. The aim in the end is to reveal underlying patterns and predict future outcomes with higher accuracy levels. The dataset of the current study involves the daily values of FCHI and GSPC indexes based on the close levels at American dollar as the currency between April 2, 2020 and December 29, 2024. The dataset belonging to the stocks has been retrieved from the web address of the World Bank [25]. Table 1 provides information on the nonlinear dynamic time series data including the indexes, parameters and dataset size.

Table 1. Nonlinear Dynamic Time Series Data.

Indexes	Parameters	Dataset Size
FCHI	Open	1280×32
	High	
	Low	
	Close	
GSPC	Open	1280×32
	High	
	Low	
	Close	

Figure 1 depicts the flow chart concerning the application of Hurst exponent to the financial time series on the financial time series index dataset.

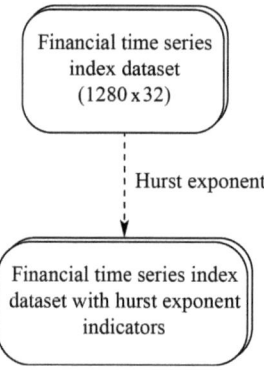

Fig. 1. Time Series Index Dataset with the application of Hurst Exponent.

The indexes belong to FCHI and GSBC stocks being traded for five weekdays within a week, and for the missing data in the dataset, interpolation method has been applied.

2.2 Methods and Methodology

Hurst Exponent. The Hurst exponent referring to the index of dependence or index of long-range dependence quantifies the relative tendency of a time series. The Hurst exponent, H, is defined with respect to the asymptotic behaviour of the rescaled range as a function of the time span of a time series [15].

For a time series $X = X_1, X_2, \ldots, X_n$, R/S analysis method steps are provided in the following mannner:

Step (1): The mean of the m value is calculated according to Eq. 1.

$$m = \frac{1}{n} \sum_{i=1}^{n} X_t \qquad (1)$$

Step (2): The Z time series is calculated based on Eq. 2.

$$Y_t = X_t - m, \quad t = 1, 2, \ldots, n \qquad (2)$$

Step (3): The cumulative deviation of the Z is calculated as per Eq. 3.

$$Z_t = \sum_{i=1}^{t} Y_i, \quad t = 1, 2, \ldots, n \qquad (3)$$

Step (4): The range series is calculated in line with Eq. 4.

$$R_t = \max(Z_1, Z_2, \ldots, Z_t) - \min(Z_1, Z_2, \ldots, Z_t) \quad t = 1, 2, \ldots, n \qquad (4)$$

Step (5): The calculation of the standard deviation of the S series is according to Eq. 5.

$$S_t = \sqrt{\frac{1}{t} \sum_{i=1}^{t} (X_i - u)^2} \quad t = 1, 2, \ldots, n \qquad (5)$$

u value is the mean value from X_1 to X_t. Its mean is found in the regions of $[X_1, X_t], [X_{t+1}, X_{2t}]$ up to $[X_{(m-1)t+1}, X_{mt}]$. $m = $ floor (n/t), and for the calculation in application, a t value that can be divided by n is chosen to use all the data [6]. Given these, Hurst exponent is employed for evaluating long-term correlation memory and classifying the time series. It equals to 0.5 if the analyzed time series is completely random. In this study, HE = 0.55 and its value approaches to 1, so it can be noted that the analyzed time series is persistent and has particular trend is not likely to show variations.

Artificial Neural Network (ANN). Neural networks have the ability to detect complex nonlinear relationships between dependent and independent variables implicitly. Since they require less formal statistical training, they are employed for detecting all the possible interactions between predictor variables. Furthermore, the significance of ANNs comes to the fore as they enable machines to learn from data and to make intelligent decisions on real time basis. This capability of ANNs makes them applicable for the solution of problems with changing data while allowing for making the required adjustments as new variables and developments emerge. This adaptability is important in data-driven modeling strategies and methods, providing robustness in accuracy through a variety of nonlinear time series models [11].

Feed-Forward Back Propagation Algorithm (FFBP). Feed-forward back propagation has the aim of learning and mapping the relationships between inputs and outputs with the learning rule employed to adjust the system's weight values and threshold values to attain the minimum error [21]. It is also used to convey the complex relationship between the input and output values in a network set with each node or neuron having a value determined by the input received from the other units of the network system [20]. FFBP algorithm shows further benefits when compared with conventional methods considering the error percentage renders the program to extend on different types of field data [7]. Accordingly, each unit in the middle and output layers has a transfer function that transfers the signal it receives. The input layer units do not have a transfer function, but they are used to distribute input signals to the network. In addition to this, each connection has a numerical weight, which modifies the signals that pass through it. A three-layer feedforward network with a single output unit, k middle layer units and n input units is provided in Fig. 2.

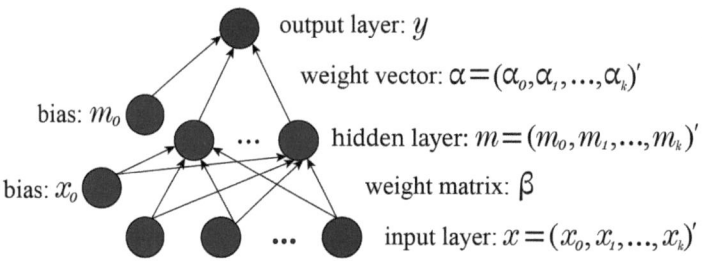

Fig. 2. The general structure of the FFBP algorithm.

The input layer can be represented by a vector. $X = (x_1, x_2, \ldots, x_n)'$ the hidden layer can be represented by a vector $M = (m_1, m_2, \ldots, m_n)'$, and y is the output. Any middle layer unit receives the weighted sum of all inputs and a bias term (denoted by x_0, x_0 always equals one) and produces an output signal.

$$m_j = F\left(\sum \beta_{ij} x_i\right) = F(X'B_j), j = 1, 2, \ldots, k, i = 0, 1, 2, \ldots, n \qquad (6)$$

In Eq. 6, F is the transfer function, x_i is the i_{th} input signal, and β_{ij} denotes the weight of the connection from the i_{th} input unit to the $f h$ hidden layer unit.

In the same way, the output unit receives the weighted sum of the output signals of the middle layer units, and produces a signal.
As Eq. 7, shows:

$$y = G\left(\sum a_j m_j\right), j = 0, 1, 2, \ldots, k \tag{7}$$

G refers to the transfer function, e_j is the weight of the connection from the j_{th} middle layer unit to the output unit, and j = 0 indexes a bias unit m_0 which always equals to one.

$$y = G\left(a_0 + \sum_{j=1}^{k} a_j F\left(\sum \beta_{ij} x_i\right)\right) = f(X, \theta) \tag{8}$$

In line with Eq. 8, X is the vector of inputs, and

$$\theta = (a_0, a_1, \ldots, a_k, \beta_{01}, \beta_{02}, \ldots, \beta_{0k}, \beta_{11}, \beta_{12}, \ldots, \beta_{1k}, \beta_{n1}, \beta_{n2}, \ldots, \beta_{nk})$$

is the vector of network weights. It is possible for F and G to take several functional forms, such as the threshold function which produces binary (0/1) output, the sigmoid (or logistic) function which produces output between 0 and 1. Equation (8) can be interpreted as a nonlinear function which represents the described three-layer feedforward neural network.

3 Experimental Results

Forecasting analysis of information efficiency and long-term correlation memory has been addressed in this study (see Table 1 for dataset details and parameters). The modeling has been done with the daily values (Open, High, Low, Close) of FCHI and GSPC indexes. Hurst exponent and FFBP algorithm have been used for the future forecasting of the indexes and comparison of the indexes. Linear interpolation method has been employed for the generation of the index values whose daily close values are missing. For these purposes of this study, the following steps (Fig. 3) have been implemented:

(i) The dataset made up of the Open, High, Low, and Close values of each of the FCHI and GSPC indexes included 32 attributes. Hurst exponent was applied to the daily values (Open, High, Low, Close) of FCHI and GSPC indexes, which led to the generation of the dataset with 48 attributes.
(ii) The dataset (with 48 attributes) consisting of the FCHI and GSPC daily values was split into training dataset and test dataset with 75% and 25%, respectively, for the indexes' forecasting purposes.
(iii) The model constructed was used to compare the dataset with 32 attributes and the one with 48 attributes (training and test dataset). The forecasting accuracy of the index values' modeling based on the daily close values of 20 days was compared by using Mean Squared Error (MSE), which shows the significance of the Hurst exponent in forecasting the indexes.

(iv) Modeling through the application of FFBP algorithm, one of the ANN algorithms, to the new dataset generated and to FCHI and GSPC indexes enabled the conducting and comparison of forecasting for these two indexes.

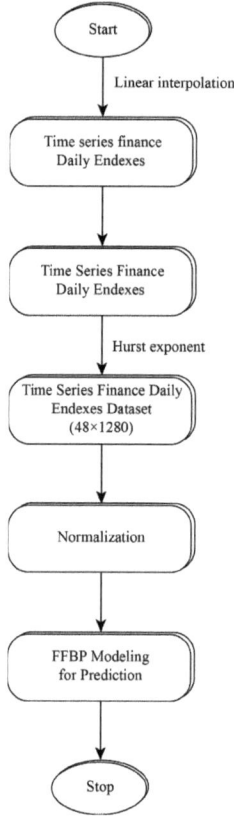

Fig. 3. Flowchart of the proposed time series financial dataset modeling.

All the computations, figures and related analyses were conducted by Matlab [22].

3.1 Data-Driven Time Series Modeling with FFBP Algorithm

Data-driven modeling approaches with the application of ANNs are beneficial for employment in various applications including those related to finance. ANNs, as being nonlinear nonparametric models, allow one to thoroughly utilize the data, through which the structure and parameters of a model are determined. Additionally, the dataset (1280×48) is normalized by max-min normalization method for this method based on the daily values of FCHI and GSPC indexes in this study. The modeling in this study has been done by FFBP algorithm by taking the corresponding output values related to the close values of 20 days concerning FCHI and GSPC indexes. This is depicted in Fig. 4, accordingly.

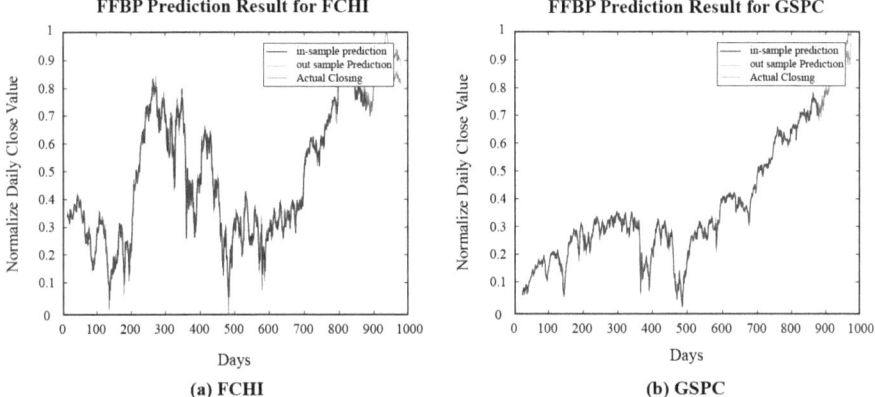

Fig. 4. Modeling of FCHI and GSPC indexes with FFBP algorithm.

Figure 4 provides the trends FCHI and GSPC indexes with the daily close values in the dataset (1280 × 48) based on past data. 75% and 25% make up the training dataset and test dataset, respectively. Modeling is achieved by FFBP algorithm and MSE results have been obtained, as presented in Table 2 and Fig. 4.

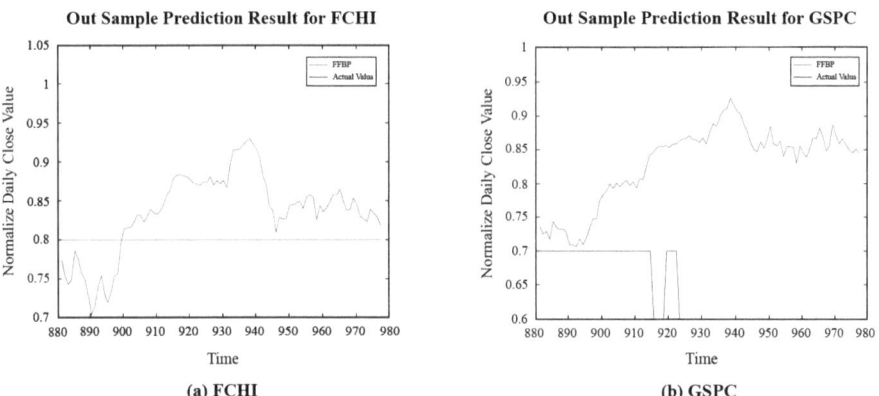

Fig. 5. Analysis results of the constructed model with FFBP and MSE.

Table 2. Numerical results of the time series indexes' modeling with FFBP and MSE.

Index	FFBP
FCHI	7.5155×10^{-4}
GSPC	6.4477×10^{-4}

The comparison of the FCHI and GSPC indexes as presented in Table 2 based on the forecasting processes of FFBP algorithm and MSE yield 7.5155×10^{-4} for FCHI index and 6.4477×10^{-4} for GSPC index (Fig. 5).

4 Conclusion, Discussion and Future Directions

Predictive modeling building upon time series analysis entails the employment of past data for the forecasting of future outcomes, which has the aim of making informed decisions with high levels of accuracy. Time series analysis in mathematical modeling deals with data points collected sequentially over time, and it enables one to capture patterns, varying trends and fluctuations that may prove to be critical to interprerat past behaviors and forecast future events. Along with these considerations, forecasting stock exchange rates is acknowledged to be an important financial problem, which marks the aim of the current paper whose aim is to generate forecasting based on the daily values of FCHI (France) and GSPC (India) indexes between 2013 and 2017 time periods. Hurst exponent has been applied to the dataset consisting of the Open, High, Low and Close values of the FCHI and GSPC indexes, which has made it possible to identify 16 new indicators. The modeling is performed by one of the ANN algorithms, namely feed-forward backpropagation (FFBP) algorithm. The forecasting accuracy obtained from the modeling of the index values based on the past daily close attributes of 20 days is compared with respect to Mean Squared Error (MSE) whose result has validated the forecasting of indexes and demonstrated the importance of Hurst exponent method. To these ends, the following steps have been implemented. Firstly, the dataset made up of the Open, High, Low and Close values of each of the FCHI and GSPC indexes includes 32 attributes, and Hurst exponent has been applied to the daily values (Open, High, Low, Close) of FCHI and GSPC indexes, which has led to the generation of the dataset with 48 attributes. Secondly, the dataset with 48 attributes consisting of the FCHI and GSPC daily values have been split into training dataset and test dataset with 75% and 25% portions, respectively for the forecasting purposes of the indexes. Subsequently, the model constructed has been used to compare the dataset with 32 attributes and the dataset having 48 attributes (training and test dataset). The forecasting accuracy of the index values' modeling based on the daily close values of 20 days has been compared by Mean Squared Error (MSE) which has shown the importance of Hurst exponent in forecasting of the indexes. Finally, modeling has been achieved through the FFBP algorithm application to the new dataset generated and to the FCHI and GSPC indexes, which have enabled the comparison and performing of forecasting regarding these indexes. Furthermore, the interpolation method has been used to manage missing data in the dataset. The use of sample data can provide a new mode of approach and implementation strategies for future studies in an extended form to illustrate the interaction between time series analysis, predictive modeling and indices. The models to be constructed can be evaluated based on comprehensive outlooks regarding decision-making, investment strategies' optimization and risk mitigation in various domains with orientations and transition from reactive to proactive schemes with the support of accurate, reliable, robust as well as data-driven approaches and practices.

References

1. Ake, B., Ognaligui, R.: Financial stock market and economic growth in developing countries: the case of Douala stock exchange in Cameroon. Int. J. Bus. Manag. **5**(5) (2010)
2. Evertsz, C.J.: Fractal geometry of financial time series. Fractals **3**(03), 609–616 (1995)
3. Guresen, E., Kayakutlu, G., Daim, T.U.: Using artificial neural network models in stock market index prediction. Expert Syst. Appl. **38**(8), 10389–10397 (2011)
4. Inaoka, H., Ninomiya, T., Taniguchi, K., Shimizu, T., Takayasu, H., et al.: Fractal network derived from banking transaction-an analysis of network structures formed by financial institutions. Bank Jpn. Work Pap. **4**, 1–32 (2004)
5. Kannan, K.S., Sekar, P.S., Sathik, M.M., Arumugam, P.: Financial stock market forecast using data mining techniques. In: Proceedings of the International Multiconference of Engineers and computer scientists. vol. 1, pp. 1–5 (2010)
6. Karaca, Y., Baleanu, D.: A novel R/S fractal analysis and wavelet entropy characterization approach for robust forecasting based on self-similar time series modeling. Fractals **28**(08), 2040032 (2020)
7. Karaca, Y., Cattani, C.: Computational methods for data analysis. Walter de Gruyter GmbH & Co KG (2018)
8. Karaca, Y., Cattani, C.: A comparison of two hölder regularity functions to forecast stock indices by ANN algorithms. In: International Conference on Computational Science and Its Applications, pp. 270–284. Springer (2019)
9. Karaca, Y., Zhang, Y.D., Muhammad, K.: Characterizing complexity and self-similarity based on fractal and entropy analyses for stock market forecast modelling. Expert Syst. Appl. **144**, 113098 (2020)
10. Kim, J., Kim, H.S., Choi, S.Y.: Forecasting the S&P 500 index using mathematical-based sentiment analysis and deep learning models: a FinBERT transformer model and LSTM. Axioms **12**(9), 835 (2023)
11. Lee, J.: A neural network method for nonlinear time series analysis. J. Time Series Econ. **11**(1), 20160011 (2019)
12. Moyano, L., De Souza, J., Queirós, S.D.: Multi-fractal structure of traded volume in financial markets. Phys. A **371**(1), 118–121 (2006)
13. Nystrup, P., Madsen, H., Lindström, E.: Long memory of financial time series and hidden markov models with time-varying parameters. J. Forecast. **36**(8), 989–1002 (2017)

14. Ogunjo, S., Fuwape, I., Temiye, M.: Impact of global financial crisis on the complexity of emerging markets: case study of the Nigerian stock exchange. Pramana **95**(4), 206 (2021)
15. Qian, B., Rasheed, K.: Hurst exponent and financial market predictability. In: IASTED conference on Financial Engineering and Applications, pp. 203–209. Proceedings of the IASTED International Conference. Chicago Cambridge, MA (2004)
16. Qian, X.Y., Liu, Y.M., Jiang, Z.Q., Podobnik, B., Zhou, W.X., Stanley, H.E.: Detrended partial cross-correlation analysis of two nonstationary time series influenced by common external forces. Phys. Rev. E **91**(6), 062816 (2015)
17. Rejichi, I.Z., Aloui, C.: Hurst exponent behavior and assessment of the MENA stock markets efficiency. Res. Int. Bus. Financ. **26**(3), 353–370 (2012)
18. Roman, J., Jameel, A.: Backpropagation and recurrent neural networks in financial analysis of multiple stock market returns. In: Proceedings of HICSS-29: 29th Hawaii International Conference on System Sciences. vol. 2, pp. 454–460. IEEE (1996)
19. Sakalauskas, V., Kriksciuniene, D.: Tracing of stock market long term trend by information efficiency measures. Neurocomputing **109**, 105–113 (2013)
20. Shaik, N.B., Pedapati, S.R., Taqvi, S., Othman, A., Dzubir, F.: A feed-forward back propagation neural network approach to predict the life condition of crude oil pipeline. Processes **8**(6), 661 (2020)
21. Tan, Z.X., Thambiratnam, D.P., Chan, T.H., Gordan, M., Abdul Razak, H.: Damage detection in steel-concrete composite bridge using vibration characteristics and artificial neural network. Struct. Infrastruct. Eng. **16**(9), 1247–1261 (2020)
22. The MathWorks, Inc.: MATLAB 2023 version 9.12.0 (R2023a), Software, Natick, MA, (2023)
23. Titman, S., Keown, A.J., Martin, J.D.: Financial management: Principles and applications. Pearson (2018)
24. Tsay, R.S.: Analysis of Financial Time Series. John Wiley & Sons (2005)
25. World Bank: World bank (2025). https://www.worldbank.org. Accessed 03 Apr 2025
26. Zhang, G.P.: Time series forecasting using a hybrid Arima and neural network model. Neurocomputing **50**, 159–175 (2003)

Fractal and Multifractal Analysis in Cancer Diagnosis and Segmentation with MRI Data

Bengü Karaca[1] and Fatma Aslan-Tutak[2(✉)]

[1] Bilfen Çamlıca Schools, Istanbul, Turkey
[2] Faculty of Education, Mathematics and Science Education, Bogazici University, Istanbul, Turkey
fatma.tutak@bogazici.edu.tr

Abstract. Fractal and multifractal analysis methods are employed to find scale invariance, irregularity and self-similarity of computerized images and signals. Mathematical modeling solutions in cancer cases enable the comprehension of the biological complexity of cancer, optimization of treatment and development of approaches personalized for each patient. Diagnosis of cancer relies on the degree of accuracy, which depends on the development of parameter identifications against the measured data concerning observed phenomena as the parameters in biomedical models. Symmetry and symmetry-breaking notions of biology and physics may be applied to cancer whose features are examined in relation to symmetry breaking, among which tumor heterogeneity, fractal geometric and information structure, along with functional interaction networks can be addressed. To this end, this study has focused on the mathematical examination of the significant role of multifractal analysis methods in their application to medical images. 2D multifractal pumping method is applied to colon cancer MRI data. For these purposes, local regularity calculation (use of multifractal), Hölder exponent calculation, denoising and transformation with inverse wavelet have been performed analyzing all the pixels from the MRI images. All the pixels, namely matrices, have been calculated on the MRI images of colon cancer patients through computerized applications. The calculations and analyses have shown that computerized applications with technological foundation can facilitate diagnosis, treatment and management for patients with cancer and / or other complex dynamic diseases.

Keywords: Fractal analysis · Fractal dimension · Multifractal analysis · MRI Images · 2D Multifractal pumping method · Hölder regularity · Inverse wavelet transform · Denoising · Noise reduction · Colon cancer · Pattern recognition · Symmetry · Fractal patterns

1 Introduction

Multifractal systems, being common in nature, is known as a generalization of a fractal system where a single exponent or fractal dimension is not adequate to describe its dynamics [1]. Multifractality dates back to sequential or time series data ascribed to mathematical convergence effects and other geometric models [2]. On the other hand, multifractal analysis is employed for investigating large datasets, frequently along with other fractal methods, which requires distorting datasets obtained from patterns for the generation of multifractal spectra depicting the way scaling changes across the dataset. It has been utilized to interpret the generating rules and functionalities of complex networks [3]. With these attributes, multifractal analysis has been applied in practical instances such as the interpretation of images or prediction of earthquakes [4–6].

Multifractal methods can provide robust analytical means to understand and characterize the behaviors and patterns of complex dynamic systems in different fields of science. The multifaceted scaling properties can be captured by those systems with multifractal analysis being able to reveal the underlying irregularities as well as patterns which traditional methods could oversee. This means that the application of multifractal analysis and multifractal methods can enable researchers to understand the interconnection of complex dynamic systems' components, which can result in higher levels of accuracy in predictions, forecasting and risk models so that more robust and optimal models can be designed and implemented.

The advancements in biological discoveries have led to paradigm changes in modeling, which applies for the concept of cancerization field with mathematical propositions being infused with biological as well as genetic details and attributes [7]. Cancers, as complex adaptive diseases, are regulated by nonlinear feedback systems across environmental signals, instabilities, cellular protein flows, and so on. For these reasons, it is important to understand the cybernetics of cancer which necessities the incorporation of information dynamics along multidimensional spatial and temporal scales, which may include various networks from metabolic to epigenetic. Consideration of these multiple dynamics provides a perspective which cultivates the significance of computational systems oncology with regard to nonlinear dynamics, inverse problems, information theory, and complexity, to name some [8]. In view of these perspectives and approaches, it has become evident that mathematical modeling and computer simulations play a remarkable role in solving complex problems which emerge in different scientific disciplines including biomedical sciences by ensuring support to experimental and clinical practices within an interdisciplinary framework. While dealing with these sorts of applications, the generation and development of mathematical models and efficient numerical simulation means are of preliminary importance. Furthermore, accurate estimation techniques rely on the development of parameter identifications against the measured data concerning observed phenomena as the parameters in biomedical models show specific scientific interpretations. Amid all these developments, computational mathematics opens the way for validating mathematical models and investigating related problems [9]. When the relationship between fractal and medical progresses is in question, recent studies have demonstrated that fractal geometry, which entails the irregular shapes' terminology, is beneficial to describe tumors' pathological architecture, providing insights into the mechanisms of tumor growth and angiogenesis complementing the ones captured through modern molecular methods [10].

The importance of mathematical biology (or biomathematics) in cancer research in terms of mathematical modeling (with formulas and techniques) is increasingly recognized in the current times. Mathematical modeling has become an indispensable tool for understanding and controlling complex biological systems such as cancer, predicting the dynamics of 3 these systems and developing treatment strategies. Mathematical modeling solutions in cancer research with the aid of mathematics enable one to comprehend the biological complexity of cancer, optimize treatment and develop approaches personalized and customized for each patient since cancer course varies from patient to patient. In addition, genetic diversity and environmental factors have effects on the success of treatments. Thus, patient-based mathematical models offer more effective and personalized treatment schemes, plans and strategies by simulating individual genetic profiles and treatment responses. All of these solutions have the potential to improve patients' life quality along with their survival rates by supporting advancements in cancer research and clinical practice [11].

Human body is made up of a multitude of very complex structures, and mathematical concepts of fractals which are marked by broken and irregular objects having details on all scales of observation control the structures at all levels of the human body owing to their organization and characteristics. On the other hand, Euclidean geometry has been proven to fail in analyzing irregularities in such complex structures. The use of fractal hypothesis was addressed in a study where statistical distributions of fractal dimensions were examined in the case of mammary cancer and mastopathy. The approach used made it possible to detect significant differences in the underlying distribution between the two groups besides conducting a multifractal analysis on the basis of a wavelet. The study provided directions regarding alternative cancer therapy and cancer prevention [12]. To give another example from literature, applications of fractals in medicine were examined in the diagnosis of diabetic retinopathy by calculating the fractal dimensions of normal and pathological samples of retinal images. Through the fractals' application, it was possible to make the distinction between normal retinas and pathological ones [13].

It can be stated that the interest of fractal geometry originates from its capability to describe fragmented or irregular patterns of natural features along with other complex objects. This feature is frequently conveyed by time-domains or spatial aspects in the behaviors of real-world physical systems, which ensures a geometrical interpretation that is simple and often encountered in different fields such as biology, fluid mechanics, geophysics, among other ones. Regarding the applicability of fractal geometry in medical image analysis is justified due to the fact that self-similarity can hardly be verified in biological objects that are imaged by a finite resolution. This means images are complex on spectral and spatial grounds, and what is more, objects generally display particular similarities at different spatial scales. At this point, it is observed that fractal geometry enables the description and characterization of the images' complexity. Fractal analysis evaluates the fractal dimension to have a global description of the images' inhomogeneities, and its efficiency is revealed in experiments regarding classification and segmentation, in which it was used as an additional texture parameter in addition to being used on its own characterizing healthy and pathological states [4].

With further strands, it has been noted that symmetry and symmetry breaking notions of biology and physics may be applied to cancer based on three categories, which are combinatorial, geometric and functional. Relevant cancer features are examined in relation to symmetry breaking, among which tumor heterogeneity, fractal geometric and information structure besides functional interaction networks can be addressed. Symmetry concepts hold their importance regarding the origin, spread, treatment and resistance for generating solutions to cancer [14]. From this point onwards, the studies using combined methodologies with integrative approaches can be noted, too. For instance, Hidden Markov model (HMM) and multifractal method with predictive quantization complexity models were applied for the differential prognosis and differentiation of a complex disease Multiple Sclerosis (MS) [15]. This integrative proposed model revealed the critical and determining significance of predictive quantization in dynamic complexity while analyzing the dynamic and transient states in varying complex systems. In addition, the use of computational methods, namely Viterbi algorithm enabled optimal maximization and uncovering of the most probable hidden sequence states. Another study highlights the importance of magnetic resonance imaging (MRI) as a sensitive method to detect nervous systems' diseases, and Brownian motion Hölder regularity functions for 2D image along with multifractal methods were applied to brain images to identify the distressed regions in the brain more conveniently in the case of MS. The study provides the classification of MS disease based on multifractal method through the integration of Self-Organizing Map (SOM) algorithm and cluster analysis which included the identification of pixels from distressed regions by means of multifractal methods to diagnose MS subgroups based on artificial neural networks (ANNs) [16]. Many natural phenomena exhibit recurring self-similar patterns, and when a pattern appears to repeat itself, fractal is to be employed. The map put forth by Benoit B. Mandelbrot did not only have applications and impact on mathematics but also on various domains such as physical chemistry, medicine and biology, having a close relationship with a new geometrical system [17].

The applications of fractal and multifractal methods are extensive applications in neurosciences, for example, which require the examination of fractal properties like self-similarity in the brain, an organ characterized by complex structure. Since medical data analysis allows for analyses at various levels of observation, these abovementioned methods are foregrounded by capturing the subtle details which may be overlooked by physicians. In the case of stroke, which could be a life-threatening disease, one paper using a multifarious and integrated methodology identified the self-similar, significant and efficient attributes to attain high rates of classification accuracy for the subtypes of stroke implementing two approaches. The first one was the use of fractal and multifractal methods to identify the self-similar, regular and significant attributes from the dataset with box-counting dimension as well as Wavelet transform modulus maxima. The second approach was Feed Forward Back Propagation (FFBP) for stroke subtype classification. The comparative analyses yielded results concerning sensitivity and specificity for the three datasets in the study which provided contributions by identifying the significant, self-similar and regular attributes from the datasets, revealing the multifractional nature of complex dynamic systems and structures and showing a way to interpret them accurately and sensitively [18].

Concerning multifractal analysis and imaging, one study identified primary cancer in metastatic bone disease by classifying the shape of tissue cells from microscopis images. The study provided contributions through its results of computer-aided analyses [19]. Another work is concerned with the comparative multifractal analysis of dynamic infrared thermograms and X-ray mammograms. The authors a 2D wavelet-based multifractal method for analyzing the spatial fluctuations of breast density in the X-ray mammograms [20]. One other work demonstrates the use of fractal/multifractal analysis for the detection of the melanoma patients' responses to treatment. The analysis proposed by the study showed its advantage of being operator independent, providing new diagnostic directions when compared to more laborious approaches of visual locating or manually contouring of lesions in images [21]. Consequently, advances in high-resolution biomedical imaging that focus on the properties of cells and issues including morphological, electrical and biochemical aspects and tissues have provided improvements in cancer diagnosis. In addition, multiscale imaging has revealed high complexity requiring further and advanced data processing methods of multifractal analysis [22]. Given these, multifractal analysis perceived as an extension of fractals proves to be an effective tool in identifying complex and irregular patterns and structures, so they are utilized for differentiating different tissues on the medical imaging processes. Multifractals can be, and a multi-fractal object is more complex as it is all the time invariant by translation.

Studies on cancer have been on the rise for the identification and treatment of the disease besides the rigorous attempts for developing applicable approaches. Biology and geometry should be perfectly aligned while utilizing technological devices for the purpose of diagnosing cancer. The utilization of different imaging technologies is for the detection of cancerous tissues and structures located in the internal organs of patients. For colon cancer in particular, it is important the scientists and researchers from different disciplines cooperate due to accessibility challenges between internal organs and imaging limitations. Colon cancer is a type of cancer which does not display symptoms at the early stage, and yet if diagnosed at an early stage, it can often be treated through surgical intervention [23]. The accurate and proficient use of magnetic resonance imaging (MRI) does not require the cutting of the skin or installing a device into the body, so this technique with its high-resolution capabilities has become a vital one for the diagnosis of the tumors [24]. In view of these capabilities, this study involves the examination of images obtained by medical technologies and makes use of fractals for the diagnostic aspect. When further studies are examined, one inquires the use of multifractal analysis methods in cancer diagnosis [22]. Concerning colon cancer, another study used the fractal dimension analysis over optical microscopic images to detect the different stages of cancer. The method in question examines the fractal features of density distributions obtained by light transmittance. In this way, the heterogeneous and complexity changes in the tissues with the advancing of cancer can be evaluated quantitatively [2].

The extensive applications of fractal and multifractal methods stem from the nature of multifractal systems being common in nature and being a generalization of a fractal system in which a single exponent or fractal dimension is not adequate to describe its dynamics. The examination of the previous studies in literature shows that there are limited number of studies concerning colon cancer and use of multifractal approaches for the early detection and diagnosis of the disease. Therefore, the aim of this study is to conduct mathematical examinations of the multifractal analysis techniques for segmenting the tissues in medical images. 2D multifractal pumping method is applied to colon cancer MRI data. For early detection of colon cancer, two approaches are employed: i) numerical calculations are conducted for one image of colon cancer patient taken as a sample, with the pixel value $(x, y) = (80, 90)$. . ii) 2D multifractal pumping method is applied for all the pixels in the entire MRI data. For these purposes, local regularity calculation (use of multifractal), Hölder exponent calculation, denoising and transformation with inverse wavelet are carried out analyzing all the pixels from the MRI images. It is the first time that numerical analysis concerning 2D multifractal pumping method has been performed on the MRI of a colon cancer patient for single pixel. Another novelty is that all the pixels, namely matrices, are calculated on the MRI images of colon cancer patients through computerized applications. All these calculations and analyses have demonstrated that computerized applications with technological foundation facilitate diagnosis, treatment and management concerning patients having cancer and / or other complex diseases. Moreover, such approaches enable prompt and accurate outcomes that can reveal subtleties and significant structures like tumors and lesions more distinctly. Thus, this paper is organized as follows: Sect. 2 addressing Methods and Methodology. Section 3 providing experimental results, while Sect. 4 presenting the application of noise reduction of a 2D signal with multifractal pumping method to the UW-Madison GI Tract Image Dataset. Section 5 concludes the study with conclusion, discussion and future directions.

2 Methods and Methodology

Noise Reduction of a 2D Signal with multifractal pumping method is a processing technique that employs a multifractal approach in order to eliminate noise while preserving significant features of the signal such as textures, edges as well as fine details. In this process, noise reduction is performed by using the multifractal pumping method (MFP).

2.1 Fractal Geometry and Multifractals

Fractal geometry and multifractals have a fundamental denominator with respect to their capability at describing and analyzing complex irregular structures as well as patterns that occur across multiple scales. Fractal geometry is focused on objects marked by self-similarity and fractional dimensions, while multifractals extend this notion through capturing the variability in scaling properties within these structures. With these features, it is possible that multifractals ensure a more nuanced comprehension of various systems that have varying regions with diverse scaling behaviors.

The examination of cancer cells with fractals has brought about the need to define a new dimension, referred to as the "fractal dimension" which is represented by rational numbers. The dimensions of fractals are usually not expressed in whole numbers but are measured using fractional values. Fractals are defined by structures repeating themselves at every scale, whereas multifractals are a generalization of fractals. Fractals exhibit similarity across all scales, while multifractals allow this similarity to change across different scales. This can also mean that multifractals may be identical at one scale but exhibit varying complexity at another. However, as multifractals display these properties only in certain regions, a multifractal can have different fractal dimensions in different regions [26]. The multifractal spectrum of a multifractal signal shows the distribution of fractal dimensions across different scales, allowing the modeling of complexity in various areas of the signal at multiple levels. With these characteristics, multifractals have been employed in scientific research, specifically in cancer diagnosis studies.

The analysis of multifractals in studies concerning identification involves fractal dimensions. Yet, it is required to conduct computations in the diagnostic process so that decision making process can be initiated after data obtained geometrically are converted into numerical data. At this particular stage, multifractal spectrum is formed by using Hölder exponent (α) which shows how smooth or complex a signal is in a certain region. The distribution of exponents constitutes the multifractal spectrum of the signal [27]. Multifractal analysis constitutes the signals from which noise is eliminated, so it provides important advantages in terms of obtaining high accuracy rates owing to its capability of maintaining the complex structures of the signal [28]. Wavelet transforms are generally employed in multifractal analysis as wavelet transforms allow for the examination of the signal in different frequencies and resolutions. This upper hand is significant for identifying the signal's structural properties. The multiple resolution level of the signal's wavelet transform is used for differentiating the properties and structures of the signal at different scales. It is possible to differentiate the noisy (high-frequency) and core structure (low-frequency) components via wavelet transform. Subsequent paragraphs, however, are indented.

2.2 Multifractal Pumping Method (MFP)

Calculation of Local Regularity. Multifractal pumping method (MFP) is a special technique employed for noise reduction in the signal [29]. By benefiting from the multifractal nature of the signal, this method enhances the signal with the following approach:

Initially, with multifractal spectrum analysis, the signal is analyzed using multifractal scaling laws. The complexity of the signal at different scales is determined based on the fractal dimension and scaling properties. The next approach is noise identification. Noise with a less complex and more regular structure often has different scaling properties than the real signal it often has. Therefore, these kinds of regions are detected by multifractal analysis, and the noise is separated from the meaningful signal. Finally, signal pumping describes the process of amplifying signal components that comply with multifractal properties while weakening components that belong to noise. This method is known to enhance meaningful signal properties while filtering out components, namely noise that do not comply with multifractal properties.

Theoretical and Mathematical Foundations of Multifractal Denoising Method. This method aims to preserve the multifractal structure of the image while the image is denoised. Within the scope of this study, this method can be examined in the following three steps:

1. Local Regularity Calculation (use of Multifractal): A 2D signal, for example an image or time-series data, is differentiated by means of a method like multifractal wavelet transform. This process captures the scale-related properties of a signal at different resolutions.

The signal is modeled as a noisy original signal according to Eq. 1:

$$S(x, y) = F(x, y) + N(x, y) \quad (1)$$

In Eq. 1, S refers to signal, F denotes the multifractal structure and N means noise. As for the processes, the multifractal properties of the image (signal) are identified. These properties represent significant structures in the signal such as edges and textures, and they are determined by the changing of the fractal dimensions at different scales.

2. *Hölder Exponent Calculation:* Wavelet transform is used to calculate the regularity level (Hölder exponent) at each point of the signal. The Hölder exponent is used to measure the local regularity of the signal and is derived from the scaling properties of the wavelet transform coefficients.

Wavelet transform is employed to calculate the regularity level (Hölder exponent) at each point of the signal. Hölder exponent is used to measure the local regularity of the signal. The function estimates the Hölder exponent $(h(x, y)h(x, y))$ at each point:

Noise: Low Hölder exponent values $(h < 0.2)$.

Multifractal structure: High and variable Hölder exponent values.

Denoising, on the other hand, is another step. After identifying the multifractal features, the noise signal is differentiated. This can be achieved by attenuating the components that have a more linear or flat structure and do not comply with the signal's multifractal structure weaker. The regions with low regularity (generally noise) are suppressed, while the areas where the clean signal's structure has been preserved are restructured.

This method is applied through the following processes outlined below:

i. Thresholding: In the areas where the Hölder exponent is low (noisy areas) wavelet coefficients are suppressed. The coefficients are preserved in the areas with high Hölder exponent.

ii. Redistribution of energy: The coefficients applicable to multifractal spectrum are rescaled, which reinforces the original multifractal features of the signal.

3. *Transformation with inverse wavelet:* Pumping mechanism: These related steps are repeated multiple times, and in each step, the multifractal structure of the signal becomes more pronounced, and the noise is further reduced. For the signal reconstruction, after the noise is filtered out, the remaining clean multifractal components are combined to reconstruct the signal. This step creates a noise-free signal while preserving important structures. Following the identifying of the multifractal features, the noise signal is distinguished. This can be done by attenuating the components that do not conform to the multifractal structure of the signal and have a flatter structure.

- The wavelet coefficients in regions with a low Hölder exponent (noisy) are suppressed.
- The coefficients in regions with a high Hölder exponent are preserved.

This method with three steps is implemented for each pixel, and it is repeated until the image (signal) reaches the desired level of regularity. This kind of an iterative step is referred to as pumping. At each step, the multifractal structure of the signal becomes more pronounced, and noise is reduced further. Finally, the remaining clean multifractal components are restructured by combining the multifractal components after the image has been filtered. This step is beneficial by creating a signal that has been denoised by protecting its important structures. Computer applications enable the pumping and signal reconstruction processes. This study focuses on the examination of the mathematical process made up of three stages as outlined above.

3 Experimental Results: Numerical Calculations and Computerized Applications

3.1 Numerical Calculation: Computation of the Noise Reduction Steps with Multifractal Pumping Method

The first process applied at this stage is to define the 2D visual with the use of fractals and multifractals. Subsequently, the data obtained geometrically are converted into numerical data and the analysis needs to be carried out. This process involves three steps, which are local regulatory calculation (multifractal use), Hölder exponent calculation and inverse wavelet transform.

For computerized applications, MathLab [30] and FracLab [31] software tools have been used for the analyses and figures in this study.

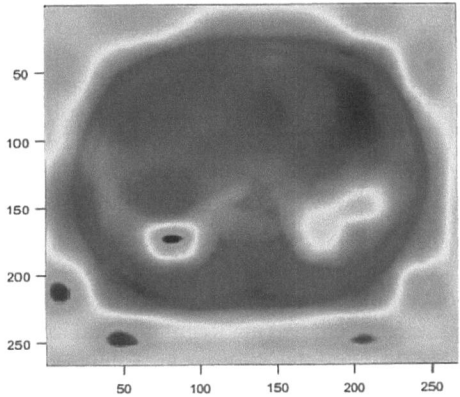

Fig. 1. Colon cancer image with jet coloring after the MFP method has been applied

Reducing noise of a 2D signal by means of MFP method increases regularity and denoising by subjecting each pixel to the mathematical operations presented below. This process allows the MRI image to become clearer and more suitable for segmentation. In the following calculations, the transformation of a pixel's value, for example, the value 5746 located at the 80 × 90 index, into the value of 4801.176 is realized according to the following mathematical operations.

Application of Local Regularity Calculation (Multifractal use) and Wavelet Transform. Wavelet transform allows for the analysis of each pixel in an MRI image in terms of local details and general trends. Daubechies-10 wavelet was used in the application of this method. This wavelet decomposes the signal according to different scales (a) and positions (b) [18, 29]. This is expressed in Eq. 2.

$$T(a, b) = \sum_{\{x,y\}} S(x, y) \cdot \psi_{a,b}(t) \quad (2)$$

Here,

$T(a, b)$ is the wavelet transform coefficient.

$S(x, y) = t$ denotes the pixel value in the input image (i.e. $S(80,90) = 5746$).
$\psi_{a,b}(x)$: Wavelet function refers to the high-frequency components of the signal.

$$\psi_{a,b}(x) = \frac{1}{\sqrt{a}} \psi\left(\frac{t-b}{a}\right) \tag{3}$$

According to Eq. 3, the following points can be explained:
Scale parameter controls the width or frequency of the wavelet.
a>1: The wavelet widens, analyzing low-frequency components (general trends).
a<1: The wavelet compresses, analyzing high-frequency components (fine and subtle details)
Position parameter indicates where the wavelet is shifted along the signal.
$\frac{1}{\sqrt{a}}$: Normalization factor for energy conversation. It keeps the total energy of the wavelet independent from the scale.
ψ: Core wavelet function. **Daubechies-10** includes a scaling function and has the prosperity of 10 vanishing moments.

$$\phi(t) = \sum_{k=0}^{N-1} h_k . \phi(2t - k), N = 10 \tag{4}$$

As Eq. 4 shows, $g_k = (-1)^k . h_{\{N-1-k\}}$: is the modified version of the scaling coefficients. ($g_0 = h_9, g_1 = -h_8, g_2 = h_7, g_3 = -h_6, g_4 = h_5, g_5 = -h_4, g_6 = h_3, g_7 = -h_2, g_8 = h_1, g_9 = -h_0$).

The multiplication operations implemented for each pixel to obtain the T(a,b) wavelet transform coefficient need to be summed up. Regularity and irregularity features around the pixels are analyzed by obtaining the $T(a,b)$ value at this stage. For example, wavelet coefficient corresponding to the value of 5746 is calculated based on a specific scale and location. For a pixel with $(x, y) = (80, 90)$ indices, let input value be $t = 5746$, $a = 4$ and $b = 5000$. The continuing steps of application are presented in the following section:

By identifying the noise regions as regions with a low Hölder exponent ($h < 0.2$), these regions are suppressed, and regions with a high Hölder exponent ($h > 1.0$), which are more regular regions, are enhanced.

The regions with a low Hölder exponent ($h(x, y) < 0.2$) resulting from noise are suppressed, and more regular regions ($h(x, y) > 1.0$) are enhanced. The thresholding process is performed as follows:

The thresholding process is performed in the way described below:

$$T'(a, b) = \begin{cases} T(a, b), & h(x, y) < 0.2 \text{ if satisfies the threshold value} \\ T(a, b) \cdot f(h(x, y)), & \text{in other conditions} \end{cases}$$

In this expression, $f(h(x, y))$ is a weight function suitable for the multifractal spectrum. In this example, we have $T'(a, b) = T(a, b) \cdot (1 + RegularityIncrease)$, and the regularity increase is set to 0.5. This process enhances the coefficients in regular regions while suppressing the coefficients in irregular regions. In this particular step, the processed coefficient of the pixel corresponding to the value 5746 is obtained based on the regularity threshold value.

3.2 Hölder Exponent Calculation

By using the coefficient obtained from the wavelet transform, the Hölder exponent of ($h(x, y)$) each pixel is calculated. This expresses the local regularity of the pixel [16, 29].

$$h(x, y) \sim \log\left(\frac{T(a, b)}{a}\right)$$

$$h(80, 90) \sim \log\left(\frac{T(a, b)}{a}\right) \quad (5)$$

$$= \log\left(\frac{4160.104}{4}\right) = \log(1040.026) = 6.947$$

Equation 5 shows the calculation for the pixel with $(x, y) = (80, 90)$. The regularity of the pixel that the value **5746** corresponds to can be analyzed with the start level analysis.

3.3 Inverse Wavelet Transform

Inverse (Reconstruction). After the wavelet coefficients are rearranged, the signal is reconstructed by inverse wavelet transform:

$$S'(x, y) = \sum_{\{a,b\}} T'(a, b) \cdot \psi_{a,b}(x)$$

In this step, 5746 input pixels are transformed into the value of 0.2008 using adjusted coefficients and inverse transformation. Each pixel is denoised and its regularity is enhanced by making it subjected to the mathematical operations given above. This process enables the MRI image to become clearer and more appropriate for the purpose of segmentation. For example, the indices are $(x, y) = (80, 90)$ and the input value is $t = 5746$, $a = 4$ and $b = 5000$.

Wavelet Transform

$$T(4, 5000) = S(80, 90) \cdot \psi_{(4,5000)}(5746)$$

The calculation processes of the wavelet function (ψ) is an iterative process which is extremely hard to conduct manually. The following result is achieved as obtained regarding the function:

$$T(4, 5000) = 5746 \frac{\psi(1436.5)}{2}$$

$$= 5746 \times 0.7240$$

$$= 4160.104$$

The final step in the noise reduction of a 2D Signal with MFP method is the suppression of regions according to the Hölder exponent value by using inverse wavelet transform for the analyzed pixel. This process enables imaging to become usable and applicable by utilizing medical technology. Regions with low Hölder exponents ($h(x, y) < 0.2$) due to noise are suppressed, and more regular regions ($h(x, y) > 1.0$) are enhanced. The thresholding process is performed as follows [29].

- *Noisecondition*($h(x, y) < 0.2$)

$$U(a, b) = T(a, b)$$

- *Inotherconditions*

$$U(a, b) = T(a, b) \cdot f(h(x, y))$$

In this expression, $f(h(x, y))$ is the weight function suitable for multifractal spectrum. The example is identified as $T\prime(a, b) = T(a, b) \cdot (1 + RegularityIncrease)$, and regularity increase is identified as 0.5.

This process enhances coefficients in regular regions while suppressing coefficients in irregular regions. Returning to the example in which calculations above were done, the processed coefficient of the pixel corresponding to the value 5746 is obtained based on the regularity threshold value.

Pumping

Since $h > 1.0$, regularity increase coefficient is used.

$$T'(a, b) = T(a, b) \cdot f(h(x, y)) = 4160.104 * (1 + 0.5)$$

$$T'(a, b) = T(a, b) \cdot f(h(x, y)) = 6240.156$$

After the wavelet coefficients are rearranged, the signal is reconstructed using the inverse wavelet transform.

Inverse Wavelet Transform

$$S'(80, 90) = \sum_{\{4, 5000\}} T'(4, 5000) \cdot \psi_{4,5000}(6240.156)$$

$$S'(80, 90) = \sum_{\{4, 5000\}} T'(4, 5000) \cdot \psi_{4,5000}(6240.156)$$

$$= 6240.156 \times 0.7694$$

$$= 4801.176$$

Hölder exponent calculation and corrected value after pumping is:

$$4.801176 \times 10^3 \simeq \mathbf{4801.176}$$

Noise reduction of a 2D Signal with MFP method is explained with a numerical example. While diagnosing cancer, it is not possible to manually perform this process repetitively for a cross-sectional image made up of 266x266 pixels. One area in medicine where technology is used is data analysis using programming languages. To demonstrate the way noise reduction of a 2D Signal with MFP method is used, an example which shows how the image presented in Fig. 1 (including the pixel analyzed manually above) is analyzed with the relevant computer application [30, 31].

4 Application of Noise Reduction of a 2D Signal with Multifractal Pumping Method to the UW-Madison GI Tract Image Dataset

4.1 UW-Madison GI Tract Image Dataset

Applying the multifractal image processing method to the UW-Madison GI Tract Image dataset can prove to be useful, particularly in terms of better identification of the intestinal tissue boundaries, detailed analysis of tissue structures as well as increased segmentation accuracy. This application enables segmentation operations to produce clearer and more reliable results without being impacted by noise.

The UW-Madison Carbone Cancer Center is a leading center in MR-Linac (Integrated magnetic resonance imaging (MRI) and linear accelerator systems (MR-Linac)) based radiotherapy. The center has been applying MRI-guided radiotherapy based on the daily anatomies of patients since 2015. The UW-Madison GI Tract Image dataset consists of anonymized MRIs of patients receiving treatment at the UW-Madison Carbone Cancer Center. Mask files in PNG format are provided for each image, and these masks contain pixel values corresponding to different tissues in the image. The masks were prepared by expert radiologists, which makes the dataset clinically reliable.

The dataset includes the segmentation images of organ cells, and it is in the form of masks encoded as **RLE (Run-Length Encoding)**. The images are in 16-bit grayscale PNG format. The names of the image files contain 4 numbers (e.g. 276_276_1.63_1.63.png). These four numbers express the following:

- The first two numbers (e.g., 276_276) indicate the slice's width/height (integers in pixels).
- The last two numbers (e.g. 1.63_1.63) record the pixel interval spacing (width/height) as physical dimensions (decimal numbers in millimeters).

The first two numbers define the resolution of the slice. The last two numbers indicate the physical size of each pixel [32].

4.2 The Application Steps of 2D MFP Method on the MRI Data

The initial image of the application of the noise reduction of a 2D Signal with MFP method using MathLab [30] and FracLab [31] is provided in the upper left side of Fig. 2. As can be observed in the initial image, the dark regions may be cancerous areas, but it is nearly impossible to make a decision based merely on this image due to the low clarity of the image. The images resulting from the application of the three steps mentioned in the study to this colon image analyzed using FracLab [31] (Example 1: slice_0065_266_266_1.50_1.50.png) are presented in Fig. 2.

Figure 2 shows the initial image (original image) located in the upper left side The image in the lower right side is the visual obtained as a result of the steps applied as the noise Reduction of a 2D signal with MFP which have been performed iteratively. The cancerous tissue can be seen in a clearer way in this last visual depiction.

This code enhances an MRI image by using multifractal denoising method (as you can see Table 1). The output generated shows the original image and mask on the top side and the input image as well as the denoised output image on the bottom side. Figure 3

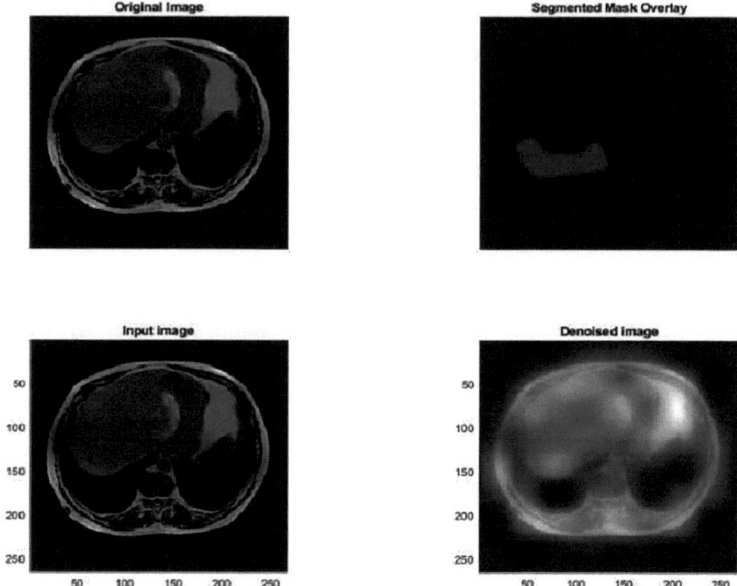

Fig. 2. Noise reduction steps with multifractal pumping method (a) original MRI data (raw data), (b) segmented mask overlay, (c) input image and (d) denoised image

Table 1. Application of the Code: Noise Reduction of a 2D Signal with Multifractal Pumping Method.

```
x = imread('slice_0082_266_266_150_150.png');
(the parts for printing the mask by decoding have been removed.)
QMF = MakeQMF('daubechies',6);
y = mfdpumping2d(x,QMF);
figure; subplot(1,2,1); imagesc(x); title('Input image'); axis image;
subplot(1,2,2); imagesc(y); title('Denoised image'); axis image;
colormap(gray);
```

depicts the colon cancer MRI image with the image mode of the MRI data with jet coloring and the mash mode of the MRI data with pink and copper coloring.

Overall, this method is an effective tool for denoising images in complex structures like MRI images. The preservation of the multifractal structure ensures that the essential information of the image is not lost, and thus this increases its applicability in further analyses.

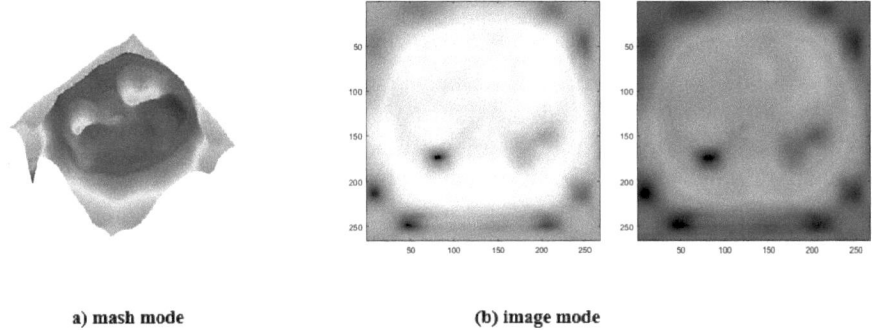

Fig. 3. Colon cancer MRI image (a) image mode of the MRI data with jet coloring and (b) Mash mode of the MRI data with pink and copper coloring

5 Conclusion, Discussion and Future Directions

Fractal and multifractal geometries offer application benefits in various medical signal analyses including but are not limited to texture analysis, pattern recognition and segmentation. The application of this geometry depends on estimation of the fractal features, and fractal analysis is applied in many fields of science from computer graphics to image compression through medicine. Furthermore, the multifractal properties of tumor tissue in MRI images can be used for automatic segmentation. To this end, this study has focused on the mathematical examination of the significant role of multifractal analysis methods in their application to medical images. Specifically, the application of the Multifractal Pumping Method (MFP) for noise reduction in a signal as has been the case in this study can provide a remarkable transformation by encouraging the use of innovative and advanced methods in medical imaging. This study has been the first one in which numerical analysis concerning 2D multifractal pumping method has been carried out on the MRI of a colon cancer patient for single pixel. Another novel point is that all the pixels, namely matrices, are calculated on the MRI images of colon cancer patients through computerized applications. All these calculations and analyses demonstrate that computerized applications with technological foundation facilitate diagnosis, treatment and management concerning patients having cancer and / or other complex diseases. Such approaches with computerized applications can facilitate the processes for achieving prompt and accurate outcomes.

High-quality images free of noise with preserved multifractal properties have significant effects on both diagnostic and treatment processes. It supports a better understanding of complex diseases such as cancer and the development of early diagnosis tools. Through these means, medical innovations can contribute to a higher quality of life worldwide and upgrade the general level of healthcare services. Last but not least, these kinds of advanced image processing methods developed using multifractals optimize existing diagnostic and treatment processes while bringing a new perspective to medical research. It has been observed how mathematics is addressed in different disciplines with such a method that could not be achieved without mathematical modeling. The use of multifractal analysis can support a better understanding of complex diseases such as cancer and the development of early diagnosis tools. In these ways, medical innovations can contribute to a higher quality of life worldwide and elevate the general level of healthcare services.

As directions for future research, fractal and multifractal analyses can be extended with the combination of other advanced methods based on mathematical foundations as well as computerized applications to reveal their potential as objective measure of seemingly random structures and as means for examining the origins of pathological, cancerous and / or damaged forms. The advantages of the protection of edges, adaptive filtering and processing of complex structures can be employed for tissues or structures resembling fractals.

Acknowledgments. The authors would sincerely like to express their thanks to Professor Yeliz Karaca, from University of Massachusetts for her orientation, guidance and validation throughout the stages and processes of the study.

References

1. Harte, D.: Multifractals: Theory and Applications. Chapman and Hall/CRC (2001)
2. Jørgensen, B., Kokonendji, C.C.: Dispersion models for geometric sums (2011)
3. Xiao, X., Chen, H., Bogdan, P.: Deciphering the generating rules and functionalities of complex networks. Sci. Rep. **11**(1), 22964 (2021)
4. Lopes, R., Betrouni, N.: Fractal and multifractal analysis: a review. Med. Image Anal. **13**(4), 634–649 (2009)
5. Moreno, P.A., et al.: The human genome: a multifractal analysis. BMC Genomics **12**, 506 (2011)
6. Atupelage, C., Nagahashi, H., Yamaguchi, M., Sakamoto, M., Hashiguchi, A.: Multifractal feature descriptor for histopathology. Anal. Cell. Pathol. **35**(2), 123–126 (2012)
7. Kimmel, M.: Evolution and cancer: a mathematical biology approach. Biol. Direct **5**, 1–3 (2010)
8. Uthamacumaran, A., Zenil, H.: A review of mathematical and computational methods in cancer dynamics. Front. Oncol. **12**, 850731 (2022)
9. Bretti, G., Natalini, R., Palumbo, P., Preziosi, L. (Eds.): Mathematical Models and Computer Simulations for Biomedical Applications, vol. 33. Springer Nature (2023)
10. Baish, J.W., Jain, R.K.: Fractals and cancer. Can. Res. **60**(14), 3683–3688 (2000)
11. Murray, J.D.: Mathematical biology: I. An introduction (Vol. 17). Springer Science & Business Media (2007)
12. Stehlik, M., Hermann, P.: Fractal based cancer modelling. REVSTAT-Stat. J. **14**(2), 139–155 (2016)
13. Uahabi, K.L., Atounti, M.: Applications of fractals in medicine. Ann. Univ. Craiova-Math. Comput. Sci. Ser. **42**(1), 167–174 (2015)
14. Frost, J.J., Pienta, K.J., Coffey, D.S.: Symmetry and symmetry breaking in cancer: a foundational approach to the cancer problem. Oncotarget **9**(14), 11429 (2017)
15. Karaca, Y., Baleanu, D., Karabudak, R.: Hidden markov model and multifractal method-based predictive quantization complexity models vis-á-vis the differential prognosis and differentiation of multiple sclerosis' subgroups. Knowl.-Based Syst. **246**, 108694 (2022)
16. Karaca, Y., Cattani, C.: Clustering multiple sclerosis subgroups with multifractal methods and self-organizing map algorithm. Fractals **25**(04), 1740001 (2017)
17. Mandelbrot, B.B.: The fractal geometry of nature/Revised and enlarged edition. New York (1983)

18. Karaca, Y., Moonis, M., Baleanu, D.: Fractal and multifractional-based predictive optimization model for stroke subtypes' classification. Chaos Solitons Fractals **136**, 109820 (2020)
19. Vasiljevic, J., Reljin, B., Sopta, J., Mijucic, V., Tulic, G., Reljin, I.: Application of multifractal analysis on microscopic images in the classification of metastatic bone disease. Biomed. Microdevice **14**, 541–548 (2012)
20. Gerasimova-Chechkina, E., et al.: Comparative multifractal analysis of dynamic infrared thermograms and X-ray mammograms enlightens changes in the environment of malignant tumors. Front. Physiol. **7**, 336 (2016)
21. Breki, C.M., et al.: Fractal and multifractal analysis of PET/CT images of metastatic melanoma before and after treatment with ipilimumab. EJNMMI Res. **6**, 1–16 (2016)
22. Huynh, P.K., Nguyen, D., Binder, G., Ambardar, S., Le, T.Q., Voronine, D.V.: Multifractality in surface potential for cancer diagnosis. J. Phys. Chem. B **127**(31), 6867–6877 (2023)
23. Rodrigo, L. (Ed.): Colorectal Cancer: From Pathogenesis to Treatment. BoD–Books on Demand (2016)
24. Chaudry, M.A., Nicholls, R.J.: Handbook of Colorectal Cancer. Springer (2016)
25. Elkington, L., Adhikari, P., Pradhan, P.: Fractal dimension analysis to detect the progress of cancer using transmission optical microscopy. Biophysica **2**(1), 59–69 (2022)
26. Olsen, L.: Multifractal geometry. In: Fractal Geometry and Stochastics II, pp. 3–37. Birkhäuser Basel (2000)
27. Feder, J.: Fractals. Springer Science+ Business Media, LLC (1988)
28. Legrand, P., Lutton, E., Olague, G.: Evolutionary denoising based on an estimation of Hölder exponents with oscillations. In: Workshops on Applications of Evolutionary Computation, pp. 520–524. Springer, Berlin, Heidelberg (2006)
29. Jaffard, S., Lashermes, B., Abry, P.: Wavelet leaders in multifractal analysis. In Wavelet analysis and applications, pp. 201–246. Birkhäuser Basel (2007)
30. The MathWorks, Inc., MATLAB 2023 version 9.12.0(R2023a), Software, Natick, MA (2023)
31. Vehel J.L.: Fraclab (2025), project.inria.fr/fraclab, 5 November 2024
32. https://www.kaggle.com/competitions/uw-madison-gi-tract-image-segmentation/data, 2 Dec 2024

A Review of Artificial Intelligence's Impact on Cybersecurity in the Big Data Era

Esra Çakir and A Çağrı Tolga

Galatasaray University, Çırağan Cad. No .36, 34357 Istanbul, Turkey
{ecakir,ctolga}@gsu.edu.tr

Abstract. This study explores the imperative role of artificial intelligence (AI) for enhancing cybersecurity in the big data environment. With the limitations of traditional cybersecurity approaches in keeping up with the increasing volume, sophistication, and complexity of cyber-attacks, AI and big data analytics (BDA) present viable options for real-time detection, adaptive response, and proactive defense mechanisms. The study discusses the usage of AI technologies like machine learning and deep learning in the most significant cybersecurity tasks such as threat detection, risk analysis, incident response, and protection of critical infrastructure. While the utilization of AI enhances the effectiveness and efficiency of cybersecurity operations, it also poses serious challenges. Some of these challenges include data privacy risks, ethical problems, and vulnerabilities to adversarial AI attacks with the ability to exploit or manipulate intelligent systems. This paper comprehensively discusses these challenges and proposes viable strategies to mitigate the associated risks. With an in-depth analysis of the strengths and weaknesses of AI-powered cybersecurity, the manuscript provides important insights for researchers, policymakers, and practitioners. It concludes by outlining potential research directions and practical implications for the use of AI and big data analytics in designing more advanced and intelligent cybersecurity systems. The findings underscore the capability of AI to transform cybersecurity frameworks in a digitized and data-driven world.

Keywords: Artificial Intelligence (AI) · Big Data Analytics (BDA) · Cybersecurity · Review · Threat Detection · Transformative Impact

1 Introduction

The advent of the age of the digital era has ushered in unparalleled advancements that have transformed communication, business, and access to information. Along with this era came increasingly complex cybersecurity threats. The requirement for the security of data online has increased manifold as people and organizations are threatened by different types of threats, from basic viruses and worms to complex hacking and distributed denial-of-service (DDoS) attacks [4]. Early on, cybersecurity was mainly reliant on rule-based systems and signature identification, which were effective against known threats. However, the traditional cybersecurity methods often prove to be insufficient when faced with rapidly evolving threats, polymorphic malware, and zero-day exploits [2]. These emerging attack techniques are specifically designed to evade signature-based systems, rendering the traditional solutions ineffective in today's dynamic and increasingly adversarial cyber landscape.

In addition, the exponential increase in data—so-called "big data"—has added complexity to the cybersecurity environment. This constantly increasing flow of structured and unstructured data provides rich information on user activity and possible threats but also inundates conventional systems that were not built for this volume [7]. Amidst this, artificial intelligence (AI) has become a game-changing force in combating cybercrime. AI enables real-time threat detection, predictive analysis, and rapid, automated responses to incidents—capabilities that are critical when dealing with the speed and complexity of modern cyberattacks [2, 8]. AI-driven big data analytics (BDA), leveraging techniques such as machine learning (ML), deep learning (DL), and natural language processing (NLP), allows cybersecurity systems to identify unusual patterns and respond to potential threats with unprecedented accuracy and speed [2, 4, 7].

This paradigm has particular significance to the security of critical infrastructure systems, including energy networks, financial systems, health care systems, and transportation systems, which are becoming more networked and susceptible to cyber-attacks [2, 3]. With those critical infrastructures being digitalized, the danger of weaknesses to cybersecurity issues increases, thereby rendering AI-boosted defensive mechanisms not only useful but essential. BDA and AI enable a more resilient, self-upgrading, and adaptive security solution that enhances the overall capacity of organizations to sense, detect, and neutralize threats in real time. Moreover, increasing reliance on AI in industries like marketing, customer care, and logistics necessitates a similar emphasis on safeguarding sensitive data [1]. Security of such information not only includes aspects of cybersecurity but also involves the public trust, adherence to regulatory requirements, and fulfillment of ethical responsibilities. Hence, the use of AI-driven big data analytics is transforming the cybersecurity paradigm. By transitioning from a purely reactive posture to the adoption of intelligent, predictive, and automated responses, organizations have enhanced abilities to deal with the dangers of an ever-changing digital ecosystem. The modern security paradigm acknowledges the limitations of traditional tools and integrates cutting-edge technologies to protect the future of digital infrastructures in different industries. The combination of artificial intelligence, big data analytics, and cybersecurity represents a turning point—one that enables the creation of a more secure and robust digital age.

This study discusses the deep influence of artificial intelligence on cybersecurity in the era of big data. It discusses the application of AI in a wide range of areas in cybersecurity, such as threat detection, risk analysis, incident handling, and critical infrastructure protection. Further, the challenges associated with artificial intelligence-driven cybersecurity solutions—such as data privacy concerns and ethical considerations, the threat of adversarial AI, and the impact of cyberattacks on data integrity—are discussed, along with possible mitigation strategies [1, 5, 6].

The rest of this paper is structured as follows: Sect. 2 outlines the role of AI and big data analytics in cybersecurity, thus highlighting their pivotal role in modern defense strategies. Section 3 deals with particular applications of AI and BDA, including threat detection, risk analysis, and infrastructure protection. Section 4 discusses concerns such as data privacy, ethical issues, and adversarial AI, suggesting proposed solutions. Section 5 discusses future directions for research and implementation of AI in cybersecurity. Finally, Sect. 6 concludes by summarizing major findings and outlining the trans-formative potential of AI and BDA for enhancing cybersecurity.

2 Artificial Intelligence and Big Data Analytics in Cybersecurity

Artificial intelligence (AI) has become a transformative force in the domain of cybersecurity with the potential to improve security solutions and bring in new defense mechanisms against cyber-attacks [2, 7, 8]. The area of AI encompasses creating computational systems with the ability to execute tasks traditionally needing human intellectual capabilities, including learning, problem-solving, and decision-making. Artificial intelligence (AI) is used in the area of cybersecurity to scrutinize large data sets, detect recurring patterns and enable the automation of security actions [2, 6]. Major AI approaches that are of special relevance to cybersecurity include machine learning (ML), deep learning (DL), and natural language processing (NLP) [4, 7, 8].

Machine Learning (ML) algorithms enable systems to learn from experience without explicit programming. Supervised learning, unsupervised learning, and reinforcement learning are forms of ML applied in cybersecurity. Logistic Regression and Gaussian Naive Bayes are a few of the models applied in addressing classification problems where the result of a categorical dependent variable is to be estimated [4, 7].

Deep Learning (DL), as a subset of Machine Learning (ML), employs artificial neural networks with many layers to process intricate data. This emerging technology has been a primary driving force in revolutionizing the domain of cybersecurity and has been employed to bolster security controls, detect threats, and minimize risks in various industries [4, 8].

Natural Language Processing (NLP) enables computers to comprehend, analyze, and process human language [8]. NLP, in the domain of cybersecurity, can be applied to the analysis of text-based information, i.e., security reports and threat intelligence, in a bid to glean pertinent information and detect possible threats [4].

AI enhances traditional cybersecurity measures by increasing threat detection, automating incident response, and enabling predictive analysis [2, 8]. The era of digital information has witnessed an exponential proliferation of data, commonly referred to as "big data" [2, 6]. Big data, as characterized by its volume, velocity, and variety, presents both risks and opportunities to cybersecurity. Big data analytics involves the process of collecting, storing, and analyzing these huge volumes of data to gain insightful knowledge [6].

In cybersecurity, the application of big data analytics is at the heart of enhancing artificial intelligence (AI) systems [8]. Through large datasets analysis, AI algorithms are able to detect anomalies, uncover advanced cyber threats, and enhance the quality of risk analysis [2, 6]. The application of AI-driven big data analytics (BDA) presents a cutting-edge method for enhancing cybersecurity architectures through real-time threat detection, predictive analytics, and automated response actions [2].

AI-powered cybersecurity solutions integrate AI techniques and big data analytics to provide efficient security solutions. These solutions typically consist of modules such as threat intelligence platforms, security information and event management (SIEM) systems, and response systems [2, 6]. Data flow and decision-making in these solutions include data collection and preprocessing, AI-powered analysis, threat detection and alerting, and automated or human-based response [8].

3 Application Areas of Artificial Intelligence and Big Data in Cybersecurity

In cybersecurity, big data analytics (BDA) and artificial intelligence (AI) are key technologies in most application domains. These technologies are most prominent in applications like threat detection and mitigation, risk assessment and management, incident response, and protection of critical infrastructures.

Threat Detection and Prevention: Another critical use of artificial intelligence in the realm of cybersecurity involves the detection and prevention of threats. AI has the ability to scan vast amounts of data in real-time, thus detecting unusual patterns or anomalies that could indicate potential cyber threats. By identifying anomalies in usual patterns of behavior, artificial intelligence is able to identify intrusions, like unauthorized access attempts or malicious behavior, in advance before they can inflict serious damage [9]. This enables earlier response and mitigation of eventual threats. AI-driven tools also better detect malware by monitoring its behavior, as opposed to purely signature-based detection techniques, which may lag behind in identifying new variants [12]. Confronted with advanced persistent threats (APTs), the capacity of artificial intelligence (AI) to manage large amounts of data and to ingest data from emerging attack vectors continuously enables it to identify even highly elaborate cyber threats. In addition, AI is employed to create sophisticated defense mechanisms, like automated firewalls, intrusion detection systems, as well as response mechanisms, that can successfully thwart threats in real-time. AI's capacity to constantly evolve with new attack strategies also ensures that security controls are efficient in the face of emerging threats.

Risk Management and Analysis: AI and BDA are revolutionizing risk management and analysis with the ability of automatic risk discovery and prioritization of potential cybersecurity threats. Traditional risk analysis is time-consuming and typically fails to account for the scale and complexity of modern cyber space. Computer algorithms, however, can consider massive amounts of information and can provide a more accurate analysis of cybersecurity vulnerabilities and threats that might otherwise have gone undetected. This enables companies to make more informed decisions about which threats need to be overcome right away and others that can be managed over time [11, 15, 19]. AI is also capable of discovering vulnerabilities in system protocols and architectures, pointing out the areas that should be patched or reinforced to prevent future attacks [10, 16]. AI can predict the likelihood of specific types of attacks occurring through machine learning and data-driven analysis, giving organizations the chance to implement proactive security measures. The transition from reactive to proactive security measures allows for improved planning and resource distribution, thereby lessening the impact of cyber events. Additionally, artificial intelligence can strengthen national cybersecurity systems by allowing for a greater understanding of emerging threats and vulnerabilities on a larger scale [9].

Incident Response: During the occurrence of a cyberattack or security incident, artificial intelligence has the potential to significantly enhance incident response time and the efficacy of remedial measures. AI-enabled systems can automatically detect and react to security incidents, thereby decreasing the time interval between threat detection and mitigation. This aspect is particularly crucial for circumstances where cyber threats are ephemeral in nature and demand real-time intervention. In addition, AI accelerates post-incident analysis by quickly examining large volumes of data to determine the cause and scope of the breach, allowing valuable intelligence to guide future defense strategies. By automating some aspects of incident management, AI reduces the workload for cybersecurity teams, allowing them to focus on high-priority tasks and strategic decision-making. Additionally, artificial intelligence facilitates the sharing and collective use of threat intelligence across different organizations and industries, thus enhancing overall security measures. Leveraging AI-powered tools makes it possible to share threat intelligence instantly, which speeds up response times to large-scale cyberattacks and helps identify patterns or tactics that attackers may use on several networks.

Protection of Critical Infrastructures: Protection of critical infrastructures—e.g., those in the energy, transportation, and healthcare sectors—is one domain where AI and BDA are especially vital. These sectors are increasingly reliant on digital systems, making them attractive targets for cyberattacks that can have catastrophic consequences for public safety and national security. Artificial intelligence may be employed to improve the security of such systems by observing their activities round the clock, identifying possible vulnerabilities, and taking action against threats in real time [10, 18, 23]. Artificial intelligence is especially crucial for securing smart cities and the Internet of Things (IoT), which are being progressively incorporated into cities and everyday life. IoT device expansion has widened the attack surface for hackers, yet AI can provide real-time monitoring and automatic defense systems to secure these devices. With the ability to process enormous amounts of data from connected devices, AI has the capability to detect anomalies that could indicate a breach or attack on critical infrastructure [13]. Additionally, artificial intelligence can enhance the national security systems' defense strategies by identifying and eliminating potential threats to essential sectors such as energy infrastructures or transportation systems, which are often targeted by sophisticated adversaries [14, 22].

4 Challenges and Solution Alternatives

Artificial Intelligence (AI) and Big Data Analytics (BDA) hold immense potential in revolutionizing cybersecurity. However, the deployment of these technologies is accompanied by numerous challenges that need to be addressed to ensure their effective and ethical application. This section outlines the primary challenges and presents solution proposals, supported by recent literature.

Data Privacy and Security Issues: The integration of AI and BDA into cybersecurity requires access to and processing of extensive volumes of sensitive data. This data aggregation increases vulnerability to breaches, unauthorized access, and misuse [24–26]. Compliance with privacy laws such as the General Data Protection Regulation

(GDPR) further complicates these processes, demanding stringent controls over data handling [27–29]. Recent works highlight how data security frameworks, encryption protocols, and secure federated learning can mitigate these concerns [30, 31].

Algorithmic Bias and Ethical Concerns: AI systems trained on biased datasets risk perpetuating discrimination and unfair practices [32, 33]. In cybersecurity, this can result in disproportionate surveillance or misclassification of threat actors based on flawed data inputs [34, 35]. Furthermore, the opacity of certain AI models—often termed the "black box" problem—limits interpretability and accountability [36, 37]. Addressing these issues demands transparent AI design, bias auditing, and inclusive datasets [38].

Potential for Attackers to Misuse AI (AI vs. AI): While AI enhances defensive capabilities, it also empowers adversaries. Malicious actors are leveraging AI to develop polymorphic malware, automate phishing, and craft advanced social engineering attacks [39–41]. This escalating "AI arms race" necessitates the development of proactive AI systems capable of countering AI-driven threats in real-time [42, 43].

AI and BDA offer powerful tools for cybersecurity, but their implementation comes with various challenges that need to be addressed to ensure their effective and ethical use. Proposed solutions to these challenges are supported by recent literature. Federated learning enhances privacy by allowing decentralized model training without the need to share raw data [30, 33]. Similarly, blockchain technology is being employed to ensure data immutability, traceability, and secure transactions within cybersecurity contexts [27, 38, 42]. To manage the ethical and legal aspects of AI usage in cybersecurity, robust data governance policies are essential. These policies should include clear standards for data collection, processing, and consent, as well as frameworks for organizational accountability [24, 31]. Adhering to international standards such as the GDPR and establishing independent oversight bodies can help ensure compliance and ethical integrity [28, 29]. Given the evolving nature of cyber threats, AI models must undergo continuous learning. This involves regular retraining with up-to-date threat intelligence and feedback loops to improve performance [40, 41]. Dynamic threat modeling and adaptive security architectures are crucial for resilience. AI should augment, not replace, human expertise. Integrating human-in-the-loop mechanisms ensures critical oversight and fosters trust [32, 34]. Collaborative ecosystems that combine machine efficiency with human judgment are key to comprehensive cybersecurity defense. In conclusion, while AI and BDA offer powerful tools for cybersecurity, their benefits must be balanced with ethical and technical safeguards. Implementing the proposed solutions can help mitigate challenges and enhance the security posture of digital infrastructures.

5 Future Perspectives

The future cybersecurity environment will be significantly influenced by the ongoing development of Artificial Intelligence (AI) and Big Data Analytics (BDA). With the growing sophistication of cyber threats, next-generation AI technologies and novel computational paradigms will assume an ever more vital function in the protection of digital infrastructures. This section explores the future trajectory of AI and BDA in cybersecurity, namely the emergence of generative AI, the potential impact of quantum computing, and the importance of international collaboration and standards.

AI and BDA have transformed the landscape of cybersecurity already by improving threat detection, risk management, and incident response. However, the speed with which the technology is evolving guarantees even greater development in the years to come. The future of AI for the domain of cybersecurity is the continued development of more and more advanced machine learning algorithms as well as neural networks that are capable of processing massive and com-plex data sets. These technologies will enable more accurate threat predictions, faster responses to cyber-attacks, and enhanced system resilience [9, 10, 12]. BDA will play a pivotal role in collecting and analyzing data from varied sources, facilitating real-time monitoring and better-informed decision-making. As artificial intelligence models continue to advance to learn from various types of data, not only will they enhance current cybersecurity frameworks, but they also will allow for the creation of new, proactive defense systems that can foresee and fend off cyber-attacks before they materialize [11, 19].

A significant advancement in the field of artificial intelligence is the creation of generative AI, which has the ability to transform the domain of cybersecurity. Such AI, comprising models like GPT (Generative Pre-trained Transformer) and other deep learning techniques, can generate original content or replicate intricate scenarios founded on existing knowledge. Within cybersecurity, the technology can be utilized to create synthetic data to train artificial intelligence models, facilitate the creation of simulated cyberattack scenarios to test defensive measures, and even develop sophisticated countermeasures to new threats. The application of generative AI has the potential to improve the capacity of cybersecurity systems to evolve with new and unfamiliar attack vectors, thereby rendering them more resilient to unexpected threats [12, 13]. Still, this circumstance also rings alarm bells since generative AI can also be utilized by adversaries to synthesize more complex and misleading attacks, for example, deepfakes or malware. Consequently, while the immense potential that generative AI embodies is greatly significant, its dual nature must be controlled and monitored rigorously to avert its misuse [9, 14].

Quantum computing is another emerging technology that is set to transform the cybersecurity landscape. Quantum computers use concepts of quantum mechanics to solve problems that are currently unsolvable by conventional computers. Quantum computing in cybersecurity can potentially enhance security, as well as pose significant challenges. On the positive side, quantum cryptography has the potential to enable very secure communications methods through quantum key distribution (QKD), which is theoretically immune to unauthorized eavesdropping. This development can signal a revolutionizing era for secure communications, particularly with regard to transmitting sensitive data [13]. However, the threat posed by quantum computing towards existing encryption methods is significant. Quantum algorithms, such as Shor's algorithm, can potentially weaken widely used cryptographic protocols like RSA and ECC (Elliptic Curve Cryptography) by efficiently factoring large numbers. This capability poses a significant risk to current encryption systems and could force a wholesale change of worldwide cybersecurity protocols [18, 19]. Hence, the development of quantum-resistant encryption methods is increasingly becoming a top agenda item for cybersecurity experts and organizations worldwide.

The growing sophistication and scope of cyber threats demand more international collaboration and the formulation of international cybersecurity standards. Cyberattacks are borderless, and their impact can be experienced in various nations and sectors, thus necessitating international collaboration in fighting cybercrime and securing digital infrastructures. It is important to have international forums for information sharing, threat intelligence, and joint response mechanisms in order to create a more secure cyber ecosystem [18]. The role played by organizations such as the European Union Agency for Cybersecurity (ENISA) and the Global Forum on Cyber Expertise (GFCE) in bringing people together and standardizing is critical. In addition, bringing countries together and aligning cybersecurity law and regulations, including respecting standards like the General Data Protection Regulation (GDPR), is critical in building a single global cybersecurity framework [22, 23]. In the years ahead, international co-operation and agreements on issues such as cybercrime, critical infrastructure protection, and digital sovereignty will become ever more important as digital transformation continues to accelerate.

6 Conclusion

In conclusion, the convergence of Artificial Intelligence (AI) and Big Data Analytics (BDA) within the realm of cybersecurity has been a significant change in how organizations identify, respond to, and neutralize cyber threats. As the frequency and complexity of cyberattacks continue to rise, conventional methods of cybersecurity have found it challenging to keep up. Nonetheless, AI and BDA present enhanced analysis and prediction capabilities that have transformed the effectiveness of contemporary cybersecurity systems. These technologies allow organizations to transition from reactive to proactive defense mechanisms, enabling the anticipation and prevention of threats before they inflict damage. Real-time monitoring, anomaly detection, intelligent threat classification, and automated response mechanisms are some of the innovations that AI and BDA drive, giving rise to a stronger and more effective cybersecurity posture.

The strategic significance of AI and BDA for securing critical infrastructure and digital assets has become increasingly evident. Sectors such as healthcare, finance, energy, transportation, and government infrastructures now rely on data-driven insights for operational security and continuity. AI-powered cybersecurity solutions, with the ability to handle vast amounts of structured and unstructured data at speed, are able to identify subtle patterns of threats that could evade detection by human analysts. In addition, such systems allow for adaptive learning, which makes them evolve according to the new threat vectors. With the digital landscape becoming more and more interconnected and complex, the need for scalable and smart cybersecurity solutions is likely to increase, making AI and Big Data Analytics key components of any successful cyber defense strategy.

For all their potential to revolutionize, the use of AI and BDA in cyberse-curity also introduces new issues that need to be carefully managed. Among the most important of these is the interpretability of AI models. In order for cybersecurity practitioners to make sound decisions, AI systems need to provide transparency and explainability in their reporting. Without good visibility into how models reach their conclusions, trust and accountability can be undermined. XAI research is thus crucial in filling this gap and improving the performance of AI-based cybersecurity solutions.

Furthermore, the regulatory and ethical aspects of the use of AI and BDA cannot be ignored. Compliance with data protection and privacy laws, as well as adherence to ethical requirements, is imperative for the responsible deployment of these technologies. With AI systems accessing sensitive information and making decisions with high implications, it is imperative that their conformity to human rights and societal values is guaranteed through stringent governance and supervision. Moreover, concern is increasing around adversarial artificial intelligence, whereby malicious actors cause AI models to deceive or breach cybersecurity. To make AI systems more resilient to these attacks involves ongoing innovation and the incorporation of adversarial training and strong validation procedures.

Looking ahead, future research should emphasize the development of transparency in artificial intelligence models, the integration of ethical frameworks, and the exploration of the convergence of artificial intelligence with other emerging technologies, such as quantum computing, blockchain, and generative artificial intelligence. These synergies have the potential to radically change the face of cybersecurity, bringing new paradigms to encryption, authentication, and threat detection. In addition, interdisciplinary efforts among computer scientists, cybersecurity experts, ethicists, and policymakers will be important in guiding the development of secure and ethically sound AI-based systems.

Ultimately, as cybersecurity threats evolve, so too will the technologies and strategies that counter them. AI and BDA will be at the forefront of this evolution, offering powerful tools to secure digital environments from an ever-more varied array of threats. Through investments in innovation, regulation, and education, stakeholders can ensure the future of cybersecurity is both effective and ethical.

Acknowledgements. "This work has been supported by the Scientific Research Projects Commission of Galatasaray University."

References

1. Alhitmi, H.K., Mardiah, A., Al-Sulaiti, K.I., Abbas, J.: Data security and privacy concerns of AI-driven marketing in the context of economics and business field: an exploration into possible solutions. Cogent Bus. Manage. **11**(1), 2393743 (2024)
2. Maharjan, P.: The role of artificial intelligence-driven big data analytics in strengthening cybersecurity frameworks for critical infrastructure. Glob. Res. Perspect. Cybersecurity Gov. Policy Manage. **7**(11), 12–25 (2023)
3. Salako, A.O., Fabuyi, J.A., Aideyan, N.T., Selesi-Aina, O., Dapo-Oyewole, D.L., Olaniyi, O.O.: Advancing information governance in AI-driven cloud ecosystem: Strategies for enhancing data security and meeting regulatory compliance. Asian J. Res. Comput. Sci. **17**(12), 66–88 (2024)
4. Salem, A.H., Azzam, S.M., Emam, O.E., Abohany, A.A.: Advancing cybersecurity: a comprehensive review of AI-driven detection techniques. J. Big Data **11**(1), 105 (2024)
5. Vadisetty, R.: The effects of cyber security attacks on data integrity in AI. In: 2024 International Conference on Intelligent Computing and Emerging Communication Technologies (ICEC), pp. 1–6 (2024)

6. Wickramasinghe, A.: An evaluation of big data-driven artificial intelligence algorithms for automated cybersecurity risk assessment and mitigation. Int. J. Cybersecurity Risk Manage. Forensics Compliance **7**(12), 1–15 (2023)
7. Weng, Y., Wu, J.: Leveraging artificial intelligence to enhance data security and combat cyber attacks. J. Artif. Intell. Gen. Sci. (JAIGS) ISSN: 3006–4023, **5**(1), 392–399 (2024)
8. Al Siam, A., Alazab, M., Awajan, A., Faruqui, N.: A comprehensive review of AI's current impact and future prospects in cybersecurity. IEEE Access (2025)
9. Tatar, Ü., Çalik, O., Çelik, M., Karabacak, B.: A comparative analysis of the national cyber security strategies of leading nations. In: International Conference on Cyber Warfare and Security. Academic Conferences International Limited, p. 211 (2014)
10. Yang, J., Huang, L., Ma, H., Xu, Z., Yang, M., Guo, S.: A 2D-graph model-based heuristic approach to visual backtracking security vulnerabilities in physical protection systems. Int. J. Crit. Infrastruct. Prot. **38**, 100554 (2022)
11. Khan, R.S., Sirazy, M.R.M., Das, R., Rahman, S.: An AI and ml-enabled framework for proactive risk mitigation and resilience optimization in global supply chains during national emergencies. Sage Sci. Rev. Appl. Mach. Learn. **5**(2), 127–144 (2022)
12. Liu, Z., Zheng, J., Wang, S., Muhammad, A.: A novel deep learning based security assessment framework for enhanced security in swarm network environment. Int. J. Crit. Infrastruct. Prot. **38**, 100540 (2022)
13. Nadir, I., Mahmood, H., Asadullah, G.: A taxonomy of IoT firmware security and principal firmware analysis techniques. Int. J. Crit. Infrastruct. Prot. **38**, 100552 (2022)
14. Boyko, S.M.: Political and legal framework of the international information security system: Russian approaches and initiatives. Russ. J. World Politics Law Nations **1**(1–2), 4–22 (2023)
15. Seumo Ntsiepdjap, B.: Ph.D. in cyber security administration: dynamic risk assessment for critical infrastructures under attack. Int. J. Adv. Res. (Indore) **10**(09), 868–908 (2022)
16. Kaul, D., Khurana, R.: AI to detect and mitigate security vulnerabilities in APIs: encryption, authentication, and anomaly detection in enterprise-level distributed systems. Eigenpub Rev. Sci. Technol. **5**(1), 34–62 (2021)
17. Donnelly, P., Abuhmida, M., Tubb, C.: The drift of industrial control systems to pseudo security. Int. J. Crit. Infrastruct. Prot. **38**, 100535 (2022)
18. Khurana, R.: Fraud detection in ecommerce payment systems: The role of predictive AI in real-time transaction security and risk management. Int. J. Appl. Mach. Learn. Comput. Intell. **10**(6), 1–32 (2020)
19. Kure, H.I., Islam, S., Mouratidis, H.: An integrated cyber security risk management framework and risk predication for the critical infrastructure protection. Neural Comput. Appl. **34**(18), 15241–15271 (2022)
20. Di Feo, M., Martino, L.: Public–private partnership (PPP) in the context of European union policy initiatives on critical infrastructure protection (CIP) from cyber attacks. In: Governing Complexity in Times of Turbulence. Edward Elgar Publishing, pp. 54–79 (2022)
21. Gasztold, A., Akrap, G.: Introduction to the special issue: critical infrastructure protection—the challenge of resilience. Secur. Defence Q. **39** (2022)
22. Heino, O.: Intelligent terrorism as a security threat to critical infrastructure. Secur. Defence Q. **39**(3), 33–44 (2022)
23. Putro, P.A.W., Sensuse, D.I.: Review of security principles and security functions in critical information infrastructure protection. Int. J. Saf. Secur. Eng. **12**(4), 459–465 (2022)
24. Manea, O.A., Zbuchea, A.: The convergence of artificial intelligence and cybersecurity: innovations, challenges, and future directions. In: Economic and Political Consequences of AI: Managing Creative Destruction, pp. 321–350. IGI Global Scientific Publishing (2025)
25. Chen, N.: Data security issues and countermeasure suggestions for financial big data: a literature review. Adv. Econ. Manage. Political Sci. **41**, 55–60 (2023)

26. Akpabio, E., Narad, S.: Artificial intelligence and cybersecurity: challenges, opportunities, and defensive. ICT Syst. Sustain. Proc. ICT4SD 2024 **6**, 291 (2024)
27. Yanamala, A.K.Y., Suryadevara, S.: Navigating data protection challenges in the era of artificial intelligence: a comprehensive review. Rev. Inteligencia Artif. Med. **15**(1), 113–146 (2024)
28. Folorunso, A., Adewumi, T., Adewa, A., Okonkwo, R., Olawumi, T.N.: Impact of AI on cybersecurity and security compliance. Glob. J. Eng. Technol. Adv. **21**(01), 167–184 (2024)
29. Chukwunweike, J.N., Yussuf, M., Okusi, O., Oluwatobi, T.: The role of deep learning in ensuring privacy integrity and security: applications in AI-driven cybersecurity solutions. World J. Adv. Res. Rev. **23**(2), 2550 (2024)
30. Ghimire, B., Rawat, D.B.: Recent advances on federated learning for cybersecurity and cybersecurity for federated learning for internet of things. IEEE Internet Things J. **9**(11), 8229–8249 (2022)
31. Ferrag, M.A., Friha, O., Maglaras, L., Janicke, H., Shu, L.: Federated deep learning for cyber security in the internet of things: concepts, applications, and experimental analysis. IEEE Access **9**, 138509–138542 (2021)
32. Chitimoju, S.: Ethical challenges of AI in cybersecurity: bias, privacy, and autonomous decision-making. J. Comput. Innovation **3**(1) (2023)
33. Mmaduekwe, U.: Bias and fairness issues in artificial intelligence-driven cybersecurity. Curr. J. Appl. Sci. Technol. **43**(6), 109–119 (2024)
34. Sarfraz, M., Sumra, I.A., Khalid, B., Fatima, E.: AI-driven predictive threat detection and cyber risk mitigation: a survey. J. Comput. Biomed. Inf. **8**(02) (2025)
35. Radanliev, P., Santos, O.: Adversarial attacks can deceive AI systems, leading to misclassification or incorrect decisions. ACM Comput. Surv. (2023)
36. Kuppa, A., Le-Khac, N.A.: Black box attacks on explainable artificial intelligence (XAI) methods in cyber security. In: 2020 International Joint Conference on Neural Networks (IJCNN), pp. 1–8 (2020)
37. Zhang, Z., Al Hamadi, H., Damiani, E., Yeun, C.Y., Taher, F.: Explainable artificial intelligence applications in cyber security: State-of-the-art in research. IEEe Access **10**, 93104–93139 (2022)
38. Usman, Q., Jackson, M.: Ethical AI in cybersecurity: addressing bias and fairness in automated threat detection systems (2022)
39. Olutimehin, A.T., Ajayi, A.J., Metibemu, O.C., Balogun, A.Y., Oladoyinbo, T.O., Olaniyi, O.O.: Adversarial threats to AI-driven systems: exploring the attack surface of machine learning models and countermeasures. SSRN 5137026 (2025)
40. Begou, N., Vinoy, J., Duda, A., Korczyński, M.: Exploring the dark side of ai: Advanced phishing attack design and deployment using chatgpt. In: 2023 IEEE Conference on Communications and Network Security (CNS), pp. 1–6 (2023)
41. Kolluri, V.: Revolutionary research on the AI sentry: an approach to overcome social engineering attacks using machine intelligence. Int. J. Adv. Res. Interdiscip. Sci. Endeavours **1**(1), 53–60 (2024)
42. Waizel, G.: Bridging the AI divide: the evolving arms race between AI-driven cyber attacks and AI-powered cybersecurity defenses. In: International Conference on Machine Intelligence & Security for Smart Cities (TRUST) Proceedings, vol. 1, pp. 141–156 (2024)
43. Syed, S.A.: Adversarial AI and cybersecurity: defending against AI-powered cyber threats. Iconic Res. Eng. J. **8**(9), 1030–1041 (2025)

Facial Stress and Fatigue Recognition via Emotion Weighting: A Deep Learning Approach

Amirkia Rafiei Oskooei[1](✉)[iD], Eren Caglar[2], Sehmus Yakut[1], Yusuf Taha Tuten[1], and Mehmet S. Aktas[1][iD]

[1] Yildiz Technical University, Department of Computer Engineering, Istanbul, Turkey
{amirkia.oskooei,sehmus.yakut,taha.tuten}@std.yildiz.edu.tr,
aktas@yildiz.edu.tr
[2] Aktif Bank, R&D Center, Istanbul, Turkey
eren.caglar@aktifbank.com.tr
https://www.aktifbank.com.tr

Abstract. This research addresses the gap in direct facial expression-based detection of complex emotional states like stress and fatigue. We propose a novel methodology employing a weighted summation of basic emotion probabilities, outputted by deep learning models, to calculate continuous stress and fatigue scores. Crucially, these emotion weights are empirically justified and grounded in established psychological and neuroscientific literature. Evaluating CNN, hybrid (DDAMFN), and Transformer-based (ViT, BEiT) architectures, our results demonstrate the superior performance of Transformer models, particularly ViT, in aligning with human-annotated ground truth data for stress and fatigue. ViT achieved "almost perfect" Cohen's Kappa ($\kappa = 0.81$) for stress and "substantial" ($\kappa = 0.72$) for fatigue, validating the human-relevance of our emotion-based formulation. This study highlights the effectiveness of Transformer architectures and literature-informed emotion weights for direct and accurate stress and fatigue detection from facial expressions, paving the way for real-world applications in monitoring and well-being.

Keywords: Facial Expression Recognition (FER) · Computer Vision · Deep Learning · Emotion Recognition · Image Processing

1 Introduction

The analysis of human emotions has become increasingly critical in our technology-driven world, permeating diverse fields from human-computer interaction and healthcare to security and automotive safety. Facial Emotion Recognition (FER), powered by advances in deep learning, particularly neural networks, has emerged as a prominent area within affective computing. Neural networks, with their capacity to learn intricate patterns from visual data, have enabled significant strides in automatically recognizing basic emotions like happiness, sadness, anger, fear, disgust, and surprise from facial expressions. This progress has fueled a wide array of applications, including personalized user interfaces, mental health monitoring tools, and enhanced driver assistance systems designed to detect driver drowsiness or distraction.

Despite these advancements in recognizing fundamental emotions, a significant gap remains in the direct detection of more complex and nuanced emotional states such as stress and fatigue. While current FER systems excel at identifying sub-emotions like anger or sadness, they do not inherently provide a direct measure of overarching states like stress or fatigue, which are crucial indicators of well-being and performance in various real-life scenarios. This limitation stems from the fact that stress and fatigue are not singular, basic emotions, but rather complex constructs often manifested through combinations of subtle facial cues and underlying emotional patterns. Therefore, simply identifying basic emotions, while valuable, is insufficient for directly assessing an individual's stress or fatigue level.

This paper addresses this critical literature gap by introducing a novel weighting-based formulation to predict stress and fatigue levels directly from facial expressions. Our approach leverages the outputs of existing FER models, specifically the predicted probabilities or percentages of basic emotions, and combines them using empirically derived weights. These weights, crucially, are not arbitrarily assigned but are informed by a comprehensive review of psychological, neurological, and sociological literature that elucidates the relationship between basic emotions and the complex states of stress and fatigue. By systematically assigning weights to emotions such as anger, fear, sadness, happiness, surprise, disgust, and neutral, we create a quantifiable method to translate the sub-emotion outputs of FER models into meaningful stress and fatigue scores. This formulation allows us to move beyond the recognition of isolated basic emotions and towards a more holistic understanding of emotional state as it relates to stress and fatigue. To rigorously evaluate the effectiveness of this approach, we conduct a comparative study employing various deep learning models, including both Convolutional Neural Networks (CNNs) and Transformer-based architectures. These models, when integrated with our weighting formulation, are assessed against a ground truth dataset of facial expressions annotated for stress and fatigue. This evaluation allows us to determine not only the validity of our proposed formulation but also to benchmark the performance of different deep learning architectures in the context of complex emotional state prediction.

Specifically, this research seeks to answer the following key questions: How effectively can a weighting-based formulation, utilizing sub-emotion outputs from FER models, predict complex emotional states like stress and fatigue? Which deep learning architectures, when combined with this formulation, demonstrate superior performance in facial expression-based stress and fatigue detection? And to what extent are empirically derived weights, grounded in psychological literature, valid in capturing the relationship between basic emotions and stress/fatigue as manifested in facial expressions?

To address these questions, our primary objectives are to develop and validate this novel weighting formulation, to rigorously evaluate the performance of diverse deep learning models within this framework, and to provide a comparative analysis of their effectiveness.

The key contribution of this paper lies in bridging the gap between basic emotion recognition and the direct assessment of complex emotional states. We present a novel, literature-informed, and empirically validated method for predicting stress and fatigue from facial expressions, offering a practical and interpretable approach that enhances the utility of existing FER technologies for real-world applications in health monitoring, safety, and well-being. Furthermore, our comparative evaluation of different deep learning architectures provides valuable insights into the optimal model selection for facial expression-based stress and fatigue detection, advancing the field towards more nuanced and practically relevant emotion analysis.

2 Related Works

Facial Emotion Recognition (FER) has emerged as a significant field within affective computing, driven by the increasing need for systems that can understand and respond to human emotions in diverse applications such as human-computer interaction, healthcare, and automotive safety [6,25]. The advent of deep learning, particularly Convolutional Neural Networks (CNNs), has revolutionized FER, enabling automated systems to achieve remarkable accuracy in recognizing a range of basic emotions from facial expressions [23]. Early successes focused primarily on classifying emotions such as anger, happiness, sadness, fear, disgust, and surprise, using datasets like FER-2013 and AffectNet to train and benchmark models [23,27]. CNN-based architectures, including ResNet [14] and VGGNet [43], became the dominant approach, demonstrating robust performance in extracting spatial features relevant to emotion recognition.

More recently, Transformer architectures, originally developed for natural language processing, have shown exceptional promise in computer vision tasks, including FER [3,8]. Vision Transformers (ViTs) and related models leverage attention mechanisms to capture long-range dependencies within images, a capability hypothesized to be particularly beneficial for understanding nuanced facial expressions where emotional cues can be distributed across the face [20,32]. Hybrid models, combining the strengths of CNNs for local feature extraction and Transformers for global context modeling, have also emerged as a promising direction in FER research [46]. Complementary to the analysis of facial expressions in FER, the field of Talking Head Generation is also rapidly advancing, focusing on the synthesis of realistic and emotionally expressive facial animations. These generative approaches, as exemplified by recent work in deep learning-based talking head systems [34], further underscore the growing importance of understanding and modeling the nuances of facial expressions and their underlying emotional content, albeit from a synthesis perspective [35].

Despite these advancements in recognizing basic emotions, a critical gap persists in the direct and robust detection of more complex emotional states such as stress and fatigue from facial expressions. While existing FER systems can identify sub-emotions that may be correlated with stress or fatigue (e.g., sadness, anger), they do not inherently provide a direct measure of these overarching states, which are crucial for many real-world applications, particularly in safety-critical and well-being monitoring contexts [12,18]. Research on stress and fatigue detection has often relied on physiological measures or contextual data, with limited exploration of methods to directly infer these complex states from facial expressions alone using advanced deep learning techniques [42,45].

Recent research has investigated diverse aspects of distributed systems, user modeling, and data representation. The authors of [1] proposed fault-tolerant information services for Grid and Web infrastructures, emphasizing scalable access to dynamic collections. The authors of [38] conducted a systematic review of verification strategies for mobile applications, identifying key quality assurance challenges. In the domain of user interaction data, the authors of [29,30] introduced embedding-based methods to represent clickstream sequences for behavioral modeling. The authors of [44] presented a provenance-aware data collection platform for environmental simulations, enhancing traceability in scientific workflows. Additionally, the authors of [2,28] explored collaborative grid services and complexity-aware performance environments for computational material science applications. While these studies provide valuable insights into systems engineering and representation learning, none of them address the direct quantification of complex emotional states like stress and fatigue from facial expressions using empirically weighted emotion formulations, which is the core contribution of our study.

3 Methodology

This study proposes a novel methodology for detecting stress and fatigue from facial expressions by leveraging advanced deep learning models and a weighted emotion-based formulation. Our approach builds upon the capabilities of state-of-the-art Facial Expression Recognition (FER) models to identify basic emotions, and subsequently, utilizes a scientifically grounded emotion correlation module to infer stress and fatigue levels. This section details the deep learning models employed, the datasets utilized for training and evaluation, and the formulation for deriving stress and fatigue scores.

3.1 Models

To accurately capture the nuances of facial expressions, we employed a suite of deep learning models encompassing both Convolutional Neural Networks (CNNs) and Transformer-based architectures, each selected for their proven efficacy in image recognition and, increasingly, in facial expression analysis. These models serve as the foundational emotion recognition module, providing the necessary sub-emotion probabilities upon which our stress and fatigue detection framework is built.

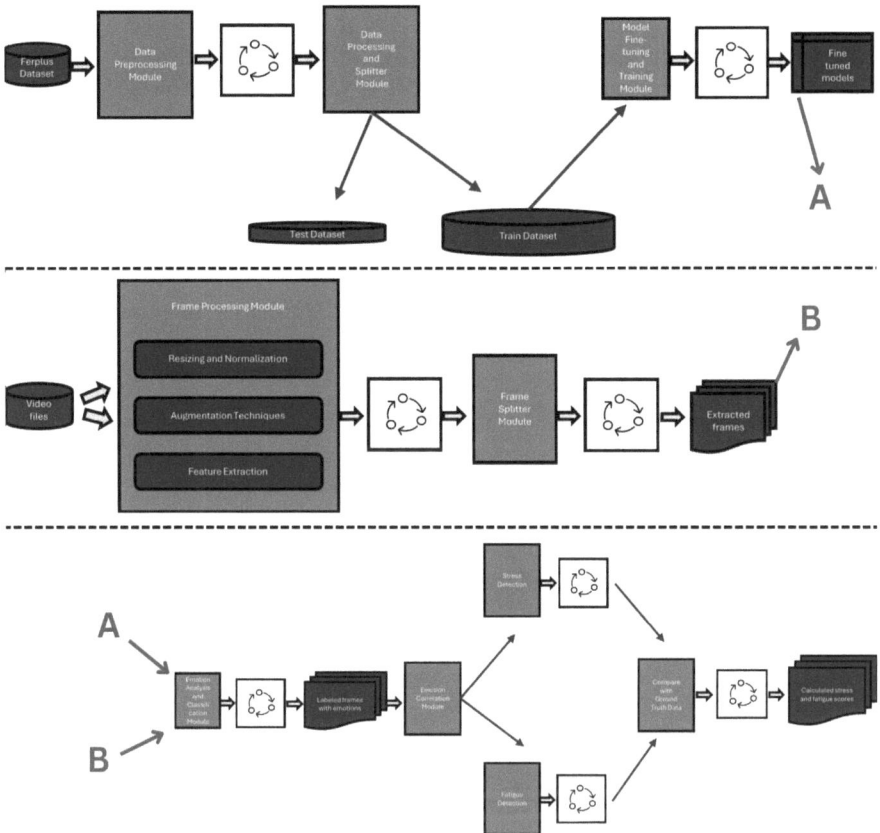

Fig. 1. Proposed system architecture for stress and fatigue detection from videos.

ResNet-50 (CNN). As a representative of traditional CNN architectures, we incorporated ResNet-50, a model renowned for its deep residual learning framework [15]. ResNet-50 addresses the vanishing gradient problem in very deep networks through the introduction of residual connections, or skip connections, which allow gradients to flow more directly through the network. This architecture is composed of multiple residual blocks, where each block learns residual functions with reference to the block's input, rather than trying to learn direct mappings. The ResNet-50 architecture has demonstrated remarkable success in various visual recognition tasks, including facial expression classification, due to its ability to learn hierarchical features effectively and manage the complexities of deep networks. In our study, ResNet-50 serves as a benchmark CNN model to compare against more recent Transformer-based architectures.

DDAMFN (Dual-Direction Attention Mixed Feature Network). To explore hybrid approaches that combine the strengths of CNNs and Transformers, we utilized the Dual-Direction Attention Mixed Feature Network (DDAMFN) [46]. DDAMFN is a specialized architecture designed for facial expression recognition that integrates both CNN and Transformer layers. It leverages a dual-direction attention mechanism to capture both local and global dependencies within facial expression features. The "mixed feature network" aspect refers to its ability to fuse features extracted by both CNN and Transformer components, aiming to leverage the local feature extraction capabilities of CNNs and the long-range dependency modeling of Transformers. DDAMFN is designed to handle complex and multidimensional facial expression data, potentially offering superior generalization capabilities compared to purely CNN or Transformers.

ViT (Vision Transformer). As a pioneering Transformer-based architecture for image recognition, we incorporated the Vision Transformer (ViT) [8]. ViT departs from traditional CNN paradigms by directly applying the Transformer architecture, originally developed for natural language processing, to images. ViT segments an input image into patches, treats these patches as tokens, and feeds them into a standard Transformer encoder. The core innovation of ViT lies in its ability to leverage the attention mechanism to learn relationships between different image patches, effectively capturing long-range dependencies across the entire facial image. This global context awareness is hypothesized to be particularly beneficial for facial expression recognition, where subtle emotional cues can be distributed across different facial regions. We selected ViT to assess the performance of a pure Transformer in our stress and fatigue detection framework.

BEiT (Bidirectional Encoder Representations from Image Transformers). Further exploring Transformer-based models, we included Bidirectional Encoder Representations from Image Transformers (BEiT) [3]. BEiT extends the application of Transformers to image recognition by employing a masked image modeling pre-training approach, inspired by masked language modeling in BERT for natural language processing. BEiT is pre-trained by randomly masking patches of images and training the model to reconstruct these masked patches. This pre-training encourages the model to learn rich, bidirectional representations of visual context. Like ViT, BEiT leverages the Transformer architecture and attention mechanisms to capture global dependencies in images. We included BEiT to evaluate another state-of-the-art Transformer model with a distinct pre-training strategy in the context of facial expression-based stress and fatigue detection, expecting its robust feature representations to enhance performance.

For all models, the initial task was to accurately classify facial expressions into the eight emotion categories provided by the FERPlus dataset: anger, contempt, disgust, fear, happiness, neutral, sadness, and surprise. The output of these models, specifically the probability distribution over these eight emotions, serves as the input to our stress and fatigue detection module.

To adapt the selected deep learning models for facial emotion recognition, fine-tuning and training procedures were implemented using the FERPlus dataset. This module focused on optimizing the performance of each model for emotion classification as a foundation for subsequent stress and fatigue detection. For the Transformer-based models, ViT and BEiT, fine-tuning was performed to adapt them to the FERPlus dataset. Given that ViT and BEiT are pre-trained Transformer models, the fine-tuning process was limited to one epoch for each model. This approach leverages the pre-existing knowledge embedded in these models while allowing for specific adaptation to the facial expression data in FERPlus. For the CNN-based ResNet-50 model, fine-tuning was also employed. However, recognizing that CNN architectures may require more extensive adaptation for optimal performance on a new dataset, ResNet-50 was fine-tuned for 10 epochs. This longer fine-tuning period aimed to ensure that ResNet-50 effectively learned relevant features from the FERPlus dataset for facial emotion recognition. In contrast to fine-tuning, the DDAMFN model was trained from scratch. Due to its unique hybrid architecture, training DDAMFN from scratch for 40 epochs was undertaken to allow the model to fully learn from the FERPlus dataset without relying on pre-trained weights. This approach was chosen to harness the full potential of the DDAMFN architecture for facial expression recognition.

The training and fine-tuning configurations for each model, including the number of epochs and the corresponding time taken, are detailed in Table 1. These configurations reflect the specific requirements and characteristics of each model architecture in adapting to the FERPlus dataset for emotion recognition.

Table 1. Model Training Time and Epoch Number

Model Name	Epoch	Time
ViT	1	1.5 h
BEiT	1	1.5 h
ResNet-50	10	12 h
DDAMFN	40	3.5 h

3.2 Datasets

This research utilized the FERPlus dataset for training and fine-tuning our deep learning models for facial emotion recognition. To evaluate the performance of our stress and fatigue detection system, a separate ground truth dataset was created through human annotation.

FERPlus. The FERPlus dataset [36] is an augmented version of the original FER-2013 dataset, widely used in the facial expression recognition community. FERPlus consists of grayscale facial images, each sized at 48×48 pixels, categorized into eight distinct emotions: anger, contempt, disgust, fear, happiness, neutral, sadness, and surprise. The augmentation in FERPlus addresses some limitations of FER-2013, particularly regarding ambiguous or noisy labels, by providing re-annotated labels with improved inter-rater reliability. This dataset is favored for research due to its challenging nature, representing facial expressions in a controlled yet diverse set of conditions. The use of grayscale images in FERPlus enhances model generalization by reducing sensitivity to variations in color and lighting, focusing the models on structural facial features relevant to emotion. We selected FERPlus as our primary dataset for emotion recognition model training and evaluation due to its relevance to our task, its established use in the field, and the availability of eight emotion categories that are pertinent to inferring stress and fatigue.

Ground Truth Dataset for Stress and Fatigue Validation. To evaluate the accuracy of our stress and fatigue detection methodology, we constructed a ground truth dataset using human evaluators. This dataset was derived from video footage, from which 138 frames were extracted at 5-second intervals across two distinct videos. These extracted frames represented diverse facial expressions in varying contexts. Three independent human evaluators, with background knowledge in emotion recognition and psychology, were recruited to annotate each frame. Evaluators were provided with clear definitions of stress and fatigue, drawing upon established psychological and physiological descriptions of these states. Specifically, stress was defined as a state of mental or emotional strain or tension resulting from adverse or demanding circumstances, characterized by expressions of worry, tension, or agitation. Fatigue was defined as a state of pronounced tiredness, reduced physical or mental energy, often accompanied by expressions of weariness, lack of focus, or drooping features.

For each frame, evaluators independently judged and assigned binary labels for both stress (stressed/not stressed) and fatigue (fatigued/not fatigued). To mitigate subjectivity inherent in human emotion perception and to establish a robust ground truth, a majority voting scheme was employed. For each frame and each dimension (stress and fatigue), the label assigned by at least two out of the three evaluators was taken as the ground truth label. This process ensured a consensus-based and more reliable ground truth dataset against which the performance of our computational stress and fatigue detection system could be rigorously evaluated.

3.3 Emotion-Based Formulation

The core innovation of our approach lies in the development of a novel emotion-based formulation to derive stress and fatigue scores from the sub-emotion probabilities predicted by the deep learning models. This formulation is based on the premise that stress and fatigue, while complex states, are significantly influenced by and correlated with basic, recognizable emotions expressed facially. We developed a weighted summation approach, where each of the eight emotions recognized by our models (anger, contempt, disgust, fear, happiness, neutral, sadness, surprise) is assigned specific coefficients that reflect its empirically and theoretically informed contribution to stress and fatigue levels.

Weight Assignment and Justification. To determine the coefficients for each emotion's contribution to stress and fatigue, we conducted a thorough review of existing literature in psychology, neuroscience, and affective computing. The assigned coefficients, ranging from 0 to 1, are not arbitrary but are systematically derived based on established scientific understanding of the relationship between specific emotions and physiological and psychological markers of stress and fatigue. Table 2 details the empirically calculated coefficients used in our formulation, with justifications provided below:

Table 2. Empirically Calculated Coefficients for Stress and Fatigue Correlations of Emotions

Emotion	Stress Coefficient	Fatigue Coefficient
Angry	0.6	0.05
Contempt	0.1	0.05
Disgust	0.3	0.05
Fear	0.5	0.05
Happy	0.05	0.05
Neutral	0.05	0.4
Sad	0.4	0.8
Surprise	0.1	0.05

Anger (Stress Coefficient: 0.6, Fatigue Coefficient: 0.05): Anger is widely recognized as a strong indicator of stress, activating the sympathetic nervous system and the hypothalamic-pituitary-adrenal (HPA) axis, leading to increased cortisol levels and physiological arousal. Research has demonstrated that facial expressions of anger are directly correlated with heightened neuroendocrine and cardiovascular stress responses. While anger is energetically demanding, its direct contribution to immediate fatigue is less pronounced, hence a lower fatigue coefficient. [13,22,39] Fear (Stress Coefficient: 0.5, Fatigue Coefficient: 0.05): Fear, similar to anger, is a negative emotion associated with stress responses. LeDoux's work on fear circuitry in the brain highlights its role in triggering rapid physiological stress responses. Fear expressions often accompany states of anxiety and heightened alertness, key components of stress. Like anger, fear's immediate impact on fatigue is considered lower compared to its stress-inducing effect [21,26,47]. Sadness (Stress Coefficient: 0.4, Fatigue Coefficient: 0.8): Sadness exhibits a dual relationship with both stress and fatigue. While sadness contributes to stress, particularly chronic stress, it is also strongly linked to fatigue. Research on burnout and emotional exhaustion demonstrates that prolonged sadness and negative affect are significant predictors of fatigue. Research also note the association of sadness with decreased energy levels and reduced physiological arousal, characteristic of fatigue states. The high fatigue coefficient reflects sadness's strong correlation with exhaustion and reduced vitality. [5,33,45] Neutral (Stress Coefficient: 0.05, Fatigue Coefficient: 0.4): A neutral facial expression, while seemingly benign, can indicate different underlying states. In the context of stress and fatigue, prolonged neutral expressions, especially in demanding environments, can reflect disengagement or passive fatigue. While neutral expressions do not directly induce stress, they can be indicative of underlying fatigue, particularly mental fatigue associated with monotonous tasks or lack of stimulation. The moderate fatigue coefficient reflects this potential link to passive fatigue [4,16,19]. Surprise (Stress Coefficient: 0.1, Fatigue Coefficient: 0.05): Surprise is typically a transient emotion triggered by unexpected events. While surprising events can induce a short-lived stress response due to the need for rapid adaptation and cognitive re-appraisal, as described by appraisal theories of emotion, its overall contribution to sustained stress or fatigue is minimal. The low coefficients reflect its short-term impact and less direct link to chronic stress or fatigue [7,31,40]. Disgust (Stress Coefficient: 0.3, Fatigue Coefficient: 0.05): Disgust, as an emotion related to aversion and rejection, can contribute to stress, particularly in contexts involving unpleasant or threatening stimuli. Panksepp's affective neuroscience framework suggests disgust is linked to basic survival mechanisms and can activate stress-related neural circuits . However, disgust is not a primary driver of fatigue, hence the low fatigue coefficient [7,31,37]. Contempt (Stress Coefficient: 0.1, Fatigue Coefficient: 0.05): Contempt, while a negative emotion, is considered to have a less direct and potent link to physiological stress responses compared to emotions like anger or fear. Its contribution to fatigue is also minimal. The low coefficients reflect its relatively weaker association with both stress and fatigue in the context of facial expressions [9,10,17]. Happiness (Stress Coefficient: 0.05, Fatigue Coefficient: 0.05): Happiness, a positive emotion, is generally associated with reduced stress levels and increased well-being. Research in positive psychology, such as Fredrickson's Broaden-and-Build theory, suggests that happiness promotes resilience and buffers against stress. Shang et al. (2023) also note the stress-reducing effects of positive emotions like happiness. Happiness is not considered a contributor to fatigue; in fact, it is more likely to be associated with reduced fatigue and increased energy. The minimal coefficients for both stress and fatigue reflect happiness's stress-buffering and non-fatiguing nature [11,24,41].

Stress and Fatigue Score Calculation. Utilizing these empirically justified coefficients, stress and fatigue scores are calculated for each facial expression frame using a weighted summation approach. For each frame, the emotion recognition model outputs a probability (or logit, which is subsequently converted to probability via softmax) for each of the eight emotions. The stress score is computed as the weighted sum of these emotion probabilities multiplied by their corresponding stress coefficients, as shown in Eq. 1:

$$\text{Stress Score} = \sum_{i=1}^{8}(\text{Probability of Emotion}_i \times \text{Stress Coefficient}_i) \quad (1)$$

Similarly, the fatigue score is calculated as the weighted sum of emotion probabilities multiplied by their respective fatigue coefficients as shown in Eq. 2:

$$\text{Fatigue Score} = \sum_{i=1}^{8}(\text{Probability of Emotion}_i \times \text{Fatigue Coefficient}_i) \quad (2)$$

where i iterates over the eight emotions (anger, contempt, disgust, fear, happiness, neutral, sadness, surprise), and the coefficients are as defined in Table 2. This formulation yields continuous stress and fatigue scores for each analyzed facial expression frame, providing a quantitative measure of these complex emotional states derived from facial cues and informed by established emotion-stress/fatigue relationships. These scores are then used for subsequent analysis and evaluation of our proposed methodology.

3.4 Thresholding for Stress and Fatigue Classification

To enable binary stress and fatigue classification (stressed/not stressed, fatigued/not fatigued) for evaluation and application, we employed thresholding of the calculated continuous scores. Following an empirical approach, optimal threshold values were determined for each model and for both stress and fatigue. This empirical thresholding involved adjusting the decision boundaries to categorize the continuous stress and fatigue scores into binary classifications. The aim was to find thresholds that effectively separated instances of stress from non-stress, and fatigue from non-fatigue, based on the model's output scores.

For each model and for both stress and fatigue, we empirically tested a range of threshold values. The selection of these values was guided by the goal of achieving a practical and effective classification performance in distinguishing stress and fatigue states from facial expressions. The reported threshold values in the Tables 3 and 4 reflect this empirical determination, representing thresholds that provided a reasonable and usable classification for each model. These

Table 3. Logit Sum Threshold Values for Stress Detection Models

Model	Threshold
CNN	22
DDAMFN	33
ViT	35
BEiT	25

empirically-derived thresholds are essential for converting the continuous stress and fatigue scores into binary categories, allowing for quantitative performance evaluation using standard metrics for classification tasks. It is important to recognize that these thresholds are empirically set and reflect a pragmatic approach to achieving binary stress and fatigue detection from the continuous output of our emotion-based scoring system.

Table 4. Logit Sum Threshold Values for Fatigue Detection Models

Model	Threshold
CNN	22
DDAMFN	19
ViT	45
BEiT	30

4 Experiments and Results

This section presents the experimental results evaluating our proposed methodology for stress and fatigue detection from facial expressions. The evaluation is structured to first assess the baseline sub-emotion recognition performance of the deep learning models using the FERPlus dataset, and subsequently, to validate the effectiveness of our emotion-based formulation for stress and fatigue detection using a human-annotated ground truth dataset.

4.1 Results of Sub-Emotion Recognition Using FERPlus

Prior to evaluating stress and fatigue detection, we assessed the baseline performance of each deep learning model in recognizing sub-emotions using the FERPlus dataset. The FERPlus test set, comprising approximately 3,000 images, was used to measure the accuracy of each model in classifying the eight basic emotions: anger, contempt, disgust, fear, happiness, neutral, sadness, and surprise. Table 5 presents the emotion recognition accuracy achieved by each model on the FERPlus test set.

As shown in Table 5, the hybrid DDAMFN model achieved the highest sub-emotion recognition accuracy on the FERPlus dataset, indicating its strong baseline capability in classifying facial expressions into basic emotion categories. Transformer-based models (ViT and BEiT) also demonstrated high accuracy, outperforming the CNN-based ResNet-50 in sub-emotion recognition.

Table 5. FERPlus Test Accuracies: Sub-Emotion Recognition Performance

Model	Accuracy (%)
CNN	76.15
DDAMFN	84.19
ViT	82.68
BEiT	82.37

4.2 Results of Stress and Fatigue Detection on Ground Truth Dataset

To evaluate the effectiveness of our emotion-based formulation for stress and fatigue detection, we assessed the performance of each model when applied to a human-annotated ground truth dataset. This dataset, comprising 138 frames labeled by human evaluators for stress and fatigue, provides a direct validation of our approach in aligning with human perception of these complex emotional states. Tables 6 and 7 present the Precision, Recall, and F1-scores for stress and fatigue detection, respectively, as evaluated on this ground truth dataset using empirically determined thresholds for each model.

Table 6. Stress Detection Performance on Ground Truth Dataset

Model	Precision (%)	Recall (%)	F1 Score (%)
CNN	61.05	55.9	57.3
DDAMFN	50.6	49.1	48.3
ViT	82.1	79.95	81.0
BEiT	81.5	64.05	71.65

Table 7. Fatigue Detection Performance on Ground Truth Dataset

Model	Precision (%)	Recall (%)	F1 Score (%)
CNN	57.65	52.45	52.6
DDAMFN	67.5	81.6	73.6
ViT	73.65	75.85	74.75
BEiT	69.95	74.55	72.2

The results in Tables 6 and 7 demonstrate the effectiveness of our emotion-based formulation when combined with different deep learning architectures for stress and fatigue detection, as validated against human judgments. Notably, ViT consistently achieves the highest F1-scores for both stress and fatigue detection on the ground truth dataset, indicating superior performance in aligning with human perception of these complex emotional states.

4.3 System Validation: Cohen's Kappa and Agreement with Human Annotations

To further validate the system's performance and quantify the level of agreement with human evaluators, we employed Cohen's Kappa coefficient (κ). This metric assesses the inter-rater reliability between the model predictions and human annotations on the ground truth dataset, accounting for the possibility of agreement by chance. Table 8 presents the Cohen's Kappa values for each model in stress and fatigue detection, providing a measure of the system's validity in capturing human-perceived stress and fatigue from facial expressions.

Table 8. Cohen's Kappa Coefficient for Model Predictions on Ground Truth Dataset

Model	Stress Detection (κ)	Fatigue Detection (κ)
BEİT	0.78 (Substantial)	0.64 (Moderate)
VİT	0.81 (Almost Perfect)	0.72 (Substantial)
DDAMFN	0.74 (Substantial)	0.62 (Moderate)
CNN	0.69 (Substantial)	0.57 (Moderate)

As detailed in Table 8, ViT achieves the highest Cohen's Kappa values for both stress and fatigue detection, demonstrating "almost perfect" agreement for stress and "substantial" agreement for fatigue with human evaluators. This high level of agreement, particularly for ViT, validates the human-relevance and effectiveness of our proposed emotion-based formulation and the strong performance of Transformer-based architectures in detecting complex emotional states from facial expressions in alignment with human perception. The substantial to almost perfect agreement levels achieved by ViT, BEiT, and DDAMFN in stress detection, and moderate to substantial agreement in fatigue detection, indicate a promising level of validity for our system in real-world applications involving human emotion recognition and assessment.

5 Discussion

This study addressed a critical gap in the existing literature on facial expression recognition: the limited direct detection of complex emotional states such as stress and fatigue. While prior research has extensively explored the recognition of basic emotions, systems capable of directly and accurately assessing stress and fatigue from facial expressions have remained underdeveloped. Our primary research questions centered on the effectiveness of a novel weighting-based formulation for predicting stress and fatigue from sub-emotion outputs of FER models, the optimal deep learning architectures for this task, and the validity of empirically-derived, literature-informed emotion weights.

To answer these questions and achieve our objectives, we introduced a novel methodology that leverages a weighted summation of sub-emotion probabilities, derived from state-of-the-art deep learning models, to calculate continuous stress and fatigue scores. Crucially, the weights assigned to each sub-emotion were not arbitrary but systematically derived and justified based on a comprehensive review of psychological, neurological, and affective computing literature, grounding our formulation in established scientific understanding of emotion-stress/fatigue relationships. We rigorously evaluated this approach using a comparative framework, testing CNN-based, Transformer-based, and hybrid deep learning architectures.

Our experimental results provide compelling evidence for the effectiveness of our proposed methodology. Firstly, the superior performance of Transformer-based models, particularly ViT and BEiT, in stress detection, consistently across both FERPlus and human-annotated ground truth datasets, strongly suggests that these architectures are better suited for capturing the subtle and complex facial cues indicative of stress. This superiority can be attributed to the inherent capabilities of Transformers in modeling long-range dependencies and nuanced feature interactions within facial expressions, aspects potentially missed by traditional CNNs. Secondly, the consistently positive F1-scores and substantial to almost perfect Cohen's Kappa values achieved by Transformer-based models, especially ViT, when validated against human judgments, demonstrate a significant degree of human-relevance and practical validity for our emotion-based formulation. This validation against human-annotated data underscores that our system is not merely detecting statistical patterns in a dataset, but is capturing aspects of facial expressions that are perceptually meaningful and indicative of stress and fatigue to human observers.

The empirical justification of our emotion weights, grounded in established psychological and neuroscientific literature, further strengthens the theoretical foundation and interpretability of our approach. By explicitly linking each emotion's contribution to stress and fatigue to existing scientific knowledge, we move beyond a purely data-driven method and offer a more transparent and theoretically defensible framework for complex emotion state assessment. This literature-informed weighting scheme, combined with the robust performance of Transformer-based models, represents a significant step towards bridging the gap in direct, facial expression-based stress and fatigue detection. Our findings highlight the potential of leveraging advanced deep learning architectures, particularly Transformers, in conjunction with scientifically grounded emotion-based formulations, to create more accurate, reliable, and human-relevant systems for monitoring and understanding complex emotional states in diverse real-world applications.

6 Conclusion

In conclusion, this study effectively demonstrates the considerable potential of transformer-based deep learning models, specifically Vision Transformer (ViT) and Bidirectional Encoder Representations from Image Transformers (BEiT), for the nuanced task of detecting stress and fatigue through facial expression recognition. Our experimental results consistently highlight the superior performance of these models, when integrated with our novel emotion-based formulation, in comparison to traditional CNN-based architectures like ResNet-50 and hybrid models such as DDAMFN. This advantage underscores the critical role of architectures adept at capturing complex, long-range dependencies within facial expressions for accurate and subtle emotion analysis, particularly for complex states like stress and fatigue. The primary contribution of this research lies in successfully bridging the existing gap between basic emotion recognition and the direct, computationally efficient assessment of complex emotional states through a literature-informed and empirically validated methodology.

Despite the promising findings, this study acknowledges certain limitations that point towards avenues for future research. Firstly, the reliance on the FER-Plus dataset, while a standard benchmark, represents a controlled environment and may not fully capture the variability of real-world facial expressions encountered in unconstrained settings. Secondly, our methodology currently focuses solely on facial expressions as a modality. Future work should explore the integration of multi-modal data, such as physiological signals (e.g., heart rate, electrodermal activity) and contextual information, to enhance the robustness and accuracy of stress and fatigue detection, particularly in noisy, real-world scenarios. Finally, further investigation is needed to refine the empirically derived emotion-weighting formulation and to explore adaptive or personalized thresholding techniques to optimize the system's performance across diverse populations and contexts.

Future research directions should prioritize validating the system's effectiveness in ecologically valid, real-world applications, such as workplace monitoring, driver safety systems, and telehealth platforms. Exploring the generalizability of our findings to more diverse datasets, encompassing varied demographics and environmental conditions, is also crucial. Furthermore, investigating the integration of temporal dynamics of facial expressions and exploring more advanced techniques for handling subtle and ambiguous facial cues could lead to further improvements in the accuracy and reliability of facial expression-based stress and fatigue detection. As deep learning methodologies advance, continued research in this direction promises to unlock the full potential of emotion-aware technologies for enhancing human well-being and operational safety in increasingly complex and demanding environments.

Acknowledgments. This research paper has utilized Generative AI tools solely for the purpose of enhancing the readability and clarity of the manuscript. The AI was employed to refine sentence structure and improve grammatical flow, without altering the original content, introducing new ideas, or impacting the research findings. The authors retain full responsibility for the accuracy and integrity of the presented work. This research was made possible by the collaborative environment provided by **Aktif Bank**. The authors extend their appreciation for their support.

References

1. Aktas, M.S., Fox, G.C., Pierce, M.: Fault tolerant high performance information services for dynamic collections of grid and web services. Futur. Gener. Comput. Syst. **23**(3), 317–337 (2007)
2. Aydin, G., Aktas, M.S., Sayar, A.: SERVOgrid complexity computational environments CCE integrated performance analysis. In: 2005 6th International Workshop on Grid Computing (GRID), pp. 256–261 (2005)
3. Bao, H., Dong, L., Wei, F.: BEiT: BERT pre-training of image transformers. CoRR arxiv:abs/2106.08254 (2021). https://arxiv.org/abs/2106.08254
4. Boksem, M., Meijman, T.F., Lorist, M.M.: Effects of mental fatigue on attention: an ERP study. Cogn. Brain Res. **25**(1), 107–116 (2005). https://doi.org/10.1016/j.cogbrainres.2005.04.011
5. Bower, J.E., Irwin, M.R.: Mind–body therapies and control of inflammatory biology: a descriptive review. Brain Behav. Immun. **51**, 1–11 (2016). https://doi.org/10.1016/j.bbi.2015.06.012
6. Chin Kit, N., Ooi, C., Tan, W., Tan, Y., Cheong, S.: Facial emotion recognition using deep learning detector and classifier. Int. J. Electr. Comput. Eng. (IJECE) **13**(6), 3375 (2023)
7. Curtis, V., Aunger, R., Rabie, T.: Evidence that disgust evolved to protect from disease. Proc. R. Soc. B: Biol. Sci. **271**, S131–S133 (2004). https://doi.org/10.1098/rsbl.2003.0144
8. Dosovitskiy, A., et al.: An image is worth 16x16 words: Transformers for image recognition at scale. CoRR arxiv:abs/2010.11929 (2020). https://arxiv.org/abs/2010.11929
9. Ekman, P., Friesen, W.V.: A new pan-cultural facial expression of emotion. Motiv. Emot. **10**(2), 159–168 (1986). https://doi.org/10.1007/BF00992253
10. Fischer, A.H., Roseman, I.J.: Beat them or ban them: the characteristics and social functions of anger and contempt. J. Pers. Soc. Psychol. **93**(1), 103–115 (2007). https://doi.org/10.1037/0022-3514.93.1.103
11. Fredrickson, B.L.: The broaden-and-build theory of positive emotions. Philos. Trans. R. Soc. B: Biol. Sci. **359**(1449), 1367–1377 (2004). https://doi.org/10.1098/rstb.2004.1512
12. Gao, H., Yüce, A., Thiran, J.P.: Detecting emotional stress from facial expressions for driving safety. In: 2014 IEEE International Conference on Image Processing (ICIP), pp. 5961–5965. IEEE, Paris, France (2014). https://doi.org/10.1109/ICIP.2014.7026203
13. Harmon-Jones, E., Harmon-Jones, C.: Anger: motivation for approach and avoidance, with implications for affective–behavioral links. Emot. Rev. **8**(3), 255–262 (2016). https://doi.org/10.1177/1754073916639664
14. He, K., Zhang, X., Ren, S., Sun, J.: Deep residual learning for image recognition. arXiv preprint arXiv:1512.03385 (2015)
15. He, K., Zhang, X., Ren, S., Sun, J.: Deep residual learning for image recognition. CoRR arxiv:abs/1512.03385 (2015). http://arxiv.org/abs/1512.03385

16. Hockey, R.: The psychology of fatigue: work, effort, and control. Cambridge Univ. Press (2013). https://doi.org/10.1017/CBO9781139026474
17. Hutcherson, C., Gross, J.: The moral emotions: a social–functionalist account of anger, disgust, and contempt. J. Pers. Soc. Psychol. **100**(4), 719–737 (2011). https://doi.org/10.1037/a0022408
18. Jia, C., Jianping, L., Changrun, C., Lixi, C.: A review of driver fatigue detection based on facial expression recognition. In: 2023 20th International Computer Conference on Wavelet Active Media Technology and Information Processing (ICCWAMTIP), pp. 1–6. IEEE, Chengdu, China (2023). https://doi.org/10.1109/ICCWAMTIP60502.2023.10387098
19. Lazarus, R.S.: Emotion and adaptation. Oxford University Press (1991)
20. Le Ngwe, J., Lim, K.M., Lee, C.P., Ong, T.S., Alqahtani, A.: PAtt-Lite: Lightweight patch and attention MobileNet for challenging facial expression recognition. IEEE Access (2024)
21. LeDoux, J.E.: Emotion: clues from the brain. Annu. Rev. Psychol. **46**(1), 209–235 (1995). https://doi.org/10.1146/annurev.ps.46.020195.001233
22. Lerner, J.S., Keltner, D.: Fear, anger, and risk. J. Pers. Soc. Psychol. **81**(1), 146–159 (2001). https://doi.org/10.1037/0022-3514.81.1.146
23. Li, S., Deng, W.: Deep facial expression recognition: a survey. IEEE Trans. Affect. Comput. **13**(3), 1195–1215 (2022)
24. Lyubomirsky, S.: The How of Happiness: A New Approach to Getting the Life You Want. Penguin Books (2008)
25. Mishra, P., Verma, A.S., Chaudhary, P., Dutta, A.: Emotion recognition from facial expression using deep learning techniques. In: 2024 IEEE 9th International Conference for Convergence in Technology (I2CT), pp. 1–6. IEEE (2024)
26. Mobbs, D., Hagan, C.C., Dalgleish, T., Silston, B., Prévost, C.: The ecology of human fear: survival optimization and the nervous system. Front. Neurosci. **9**, 55 (2015). https://doi.org/10.3389/fnins.2015.00055
27. Mollahosseini, A., Hasani, B., Mahoor, M.H.: AffectNet: a database for facial expression, valence, and arousal computing in the wild. IEEE Trans. Affect. Comput. **10**(1), 18–31 (2017)
28. Nacar, M.A., Aktas, M.S., Yuen, D.A.: VLab: collaborative grid services and portals to support computational material science. Concurrency Comput. Pract. Experience **19**(12), 1717–1728 (2007)
29. Olmezogullari, E., Aktas, M.S.: Representation of click-stream data sequences for learning user navigational behavior by using embeddings. In: 2020 IEEE International Conference on Big Data (Big Data), pp. 3173–3179 (2020)
30. Olmezogullari, E., Aktas, M.S.: Pattern2Vec: representation of clickstream data sequences for learning user navigational behavior. Concurrency Comput. Pract. Exp. **34**(9) (2022)
31. Panksepp, J.: Affective Neuroscience: The Foundations of Human and Animal Emotions. Oxford University Press (2004)
32. Pecoraro, R., Basile, V., Bono, V., Gallo, S.: Local multi-head channel self-attention for facial expression recognition. CoRR arxiv:abs/2111.07224 (2021). https://arxiv.org/abs/2111.07224
33. Van der Ploeg, M.M., Kleber, R.J., Defares, P.B.: Acute and chronic job stressors and burnout. Psychol. Rep. **97**(3), 825–832 (2005). https://doi.org/10.2466/pr0.97.3.825-832
34. Rafiei Oskooei, A., Aktaş, M.S., Keleş, M.: Seeing the sound: multilingual lip sync for real-time face-to-face translation. Computers **14**(1), 7 (2024)

35. Rafiei Oskooei, A., Yahsi, E., Sungur, M., S. Aktas, M.: Can one model fit all? An exploration of Wav2Lip's lip-syncing generalizability across culturally distinct languages. In: International Conference on Computational Science and Its Applications, pp. 149–164. Springer (2024)
36. Roy, A.K.: FERPlus (2024). https://www.kaggle.com/datasets/arnabkumarroy02/ferplus. Accessed 06 Nov 2024
37. Rozin, P., Haidt, J., McCauley, C.: Disgust, vol. 3. The Guilford Press (2008)
38. Sahinoglu, M., Incki, K., Aktas, M.S.: Mobile application verification: a systematic mapping study. In: Gervasi, O., et al. (eds.) ICCSA 2015. LNCS, vol. 9159, pp. 147–163. Springer, Cham (2015). https://doi.org/10.1007/978-3-319-21413-9_11
39. Sapolsky, R.M.: Why Zebras Don't Get Ulcers: The Acclaimed Guide to Stress, Stress-Related Diseases, and Coping. Holt Paperbacks (2004)
40. Schützwohl, A.: Surprise and schema strength. J. Exp. Psychol. Learn. Mem. Cogn. **24**(5), 1182–1199 (1998). https://doi.org/10.1037/0278-7393.24.5.1182
41. Shang, Y., other authors: the influence of happiness on stress regulation. J. Positive Psychol. **18**(3), 432–450 (2023). https://doi.org/FILLINDOI
42. Shang, Y., Yang, M., Cui, J., Cui, L., Huang, Z., Li, X.: Driver emotion and fatigue state detection based on time series fusion. Electronics **12**(1), 26 (2023). https://doi.org/10.3390/electronics12010026
43. Simonyan, K., Zisserman, A.: Very deep convolutional networks for large-scale image recognition. arXiv preprint arXiv:1409.1556 (2014)
44. Tufek, A., Gurbuz, A., Aktas, M.S.: Provenance collection platform for the weather research and forecasting model. In: 2018 14th International Conference on Semantics, Knowledge and Grids (SKG), pp. 17–24 (2018)
45. Verma, A., Goyal, A., Kaur, D.: Fatigue detection. CoRR arxiv:abs/1911.10629 (2019). https://arxiv.org/abs/1911.10629
46. Zhang, S., Zhang, Y., Zhang, Y., Wang, Y., Song, Z.: A dual-direction attention mixed feature network for facial expression recognition. Electronics **12**(17), 3595 (2023). https://www.mdpi.com/2079-9292/12/17/3595
47. Öhman, A.: The role of the amygdala in human fear: automatic detection of threat. Psychoneuroendocrinology **30**(10), 953–958 (2005). https://doi.org/10.1016/j.psyneuen.2005.03.019

Apache Spark Implementation of the Constrained K-Means Clustering Algorithm

Nguyen Quang Huy[1], Vu Thu Diep[2], and Phan Duy Hung[1](✉)

[1] FPT University, Hanoi, Vietnam
huy23mse13113@fsb.edu.vn, hungpd2@fe.edu.vn
[2] HaNoi University of Science and Technology, Hanoi, Vietnam
diep.vuthu@hust.edu.vn

Abstract. The essential task of extracting useful patterns from large datasets enables multiple industries to implement data-driven decisions throughout the current significant data era. Unsupervised machine learning contains clustering as one vital technique which identifies data similarities through shared common features to produce groupings. Traditional efficient algorithms such as K-Means struggle to handle complex datasets because distance-based relationships do not describe all pertinent data associations. The proposed study implements Constrained K-Means because its algorithm utilizes must-link and cannot-link constraints to preserve domain-specific relationships in cluster groupings. We conducts tests of the proposed algorithm through Apache Spark platform due to its ability to maximize distributed processing capabilities for large-scale datasets. Experimental results demonstrate that the Constrained K-means algorithm achieves better clustering performance and interpretability and marks superior results compared to K-means when dealing with constraint-aware data sets on synthetic and real-world datasets. The studied combination of constraint-based clustering and distributed computing systems demonstrates potential to create stronger yet scalable machine learning solutions for big data environments.

Keywords: Clustering · Constrained Clustering · Big Data Clustering · Apache Spark

1 Introduction

1.1 Problem and Motivation

In the field of exploratory data analysis in many fields solving the task of the unsupervised classification of patterns into clusters, which is of interest and of wide utility [1]. Generally, clustering aims to divide a set of patterns to the clusters such that patterns remain within clusters more than patterns within the different clusters. This methods uses wordless patterns, and provide them data and then gives a category label to this patterns. Clustering is a very general activity, which is used wherever we use pattern analysis, grouping, decision making or even machine learning in data mining, document retrieval, image segmentation, etc.

However, there are four general types of traditional clustering methods [2], including Partitioning methods, Hierarchical Clustering, Density-based Clustering, and Model based clustering. Yet, these existing methods are commonly used across multiple disciplines due to their lack of capability to utilize prior domain knowledge, or to incorporate specific form of data restrictions. There are many real life cases in which there is extra information or prior knowledge which provides extremely important addition to the problem of demand, forcing researchers to come with methods of clustering processes that take the constraints into account as a part of the clustering [3].

Constrained clustering has emerged as a powerful data grouping methodology since it puts user defined constraints to assign the partitioning process in accounting with more contextually relevant, use case specific credible values of clustering. Previous studies have shown that the much more domain specific clusters can be achieved leveraging prior information in the form of must link and cannot link constraints [3]. In the past years, various constrained clustering algorithms have been introduced in order to enhance the clustering performance on structured and semi structured data. Specific among these approaches are COP-KMeans [4], MPCK-Means [5], and PCCC (Pairwise-Confidence-Constraints-Clustering) [6] as they all have distinguished methods for solving constraints within the cluster improvement strategy. However, by applying constraint based guidance in the clustering process, these algorithms provide improved accuracy and flexibility in a dataset where relationship among data entities contributes to define the effective cluster structure in these datasets.

Nevertheless, traditional constrained clustering algorithms have proved to be scalable only for datasets that exponentialally increase [3]. There are requirements for processing enormous amounts of data such that applications often involve big data and real time processing and the related frameworks are Hadoop and Spark in such applications. It also allows running algorithms in a matter of milliseconds, better resource usage, and scales to millions of records [7]. In this work, we deal with Constrained K-Means, a constrained clustering algorithm which is adapted in such a way to make it an efficient algorithm for a big data setting, so that it can be applied to a large number of large real world problems.

1.2 Related Works

The conventional K-Means [8] is a popular clustering algorithm, where K represents the number of clusters that are found by minimizing the sum of the square of distances between the data points and the cluster centroid. This will conclude the first step of our entire iterative process initialization, assignment, and centroid update until convergence. But K-Means is not without its drawbacks, despite being simple and efficient. Many issues arise like it is sensitive to initial placement of centroids, it has difficulties with non-spherical clusters, and it has not taken constraints into account which eliminates its usage in structured clustering problems [9].

We conclude by identifying how each of these limitations has been collectively addressed in the successive evolution of constrained clustering algorithms. Figure 1 illustrates in a simple way how constrained clustering works.

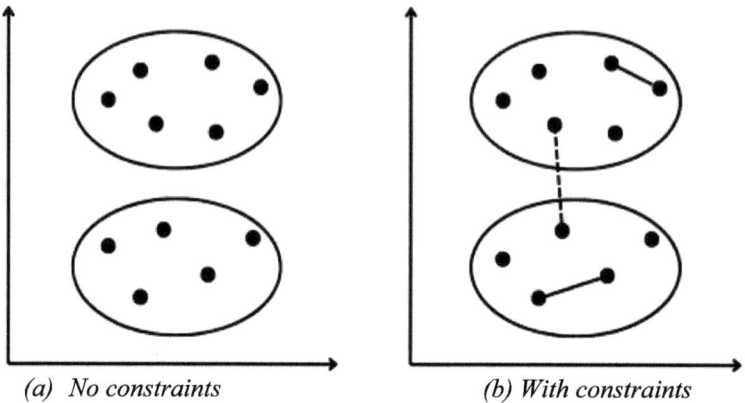

Fig.1. Hard pairwise constraints: must-link and cannot-link constraints are indicated by solid and dashed lines respectively.

A noticeable foundational approach is COP-Kmeans from Wagstaff et al. (2001) [4]. The traditional KMeans algorithm is extended with pairwise constraints, or must link and cannot link relationships that specify if instance pairs should be in the same cluster or in different clusters, with the consequent addition of the COP-Kmeans algorithm. In this more refined approach, it is required that this constraint is strictly enforced in the assignment phase such that an instance is assigned to a cluster only if none of the constraints are violated by it. Although this strict constraint satisfaction guarantees that constraints are satisfied when the constraints are dependable, it may lead to the algorithm being unable to converge to a feasible or optimal solution when the constraints contradict, conflict with the underlying data distribution. Additionally, COP-Kmeans is very sensitive to noisy constraints, which implies just a few erroneously placed constraints can adversely affect clustering performance as much as an order of magnitude. However, COP-Kmeans is still useful when constraint satisfaction is essential, especially if background knowledge is trusted.

Advances constrained clustering is based on metric learning within K-Means concepts that were built upon ideas by Bilenko, Basu, Mooney (2004) [5]. An innovative integration of such distance metric with unlabeled data and pairwise constraints allows the algorithm to adapt such metric as a function of unlabeled data and pairwise constraints. The main idea consists in warping the data space so as to force closer the observations in any same cluster and at the same time keep the distances between different clusters. MPCK-Means iteratively updates distance metric in clustering, and modifies it to assure better constraints satisfaction and better cluster cohesion. It also learns metrics per cluster and is able to accommodate different shapes and orientations of the data which is especially important for the data distribution with more complicated shapes and orientations. MPCK-Means finds better accuracy and robustness to noisy constraints under learned metrics than COP-KMeans, by minimizing an objective function that penalizes constraint violation for a small coefficient, while encouraging lower cluster dispersion by the other coefficient under the learned metrics. On the other hand, the iterative metric learning process brings more computational complexity in high dimension dataset.

By applying it to hard and soft constraints, with associated confidence values, a cellular Pairwise-Confidence-Constraints-Clustering, PCCC as it is called in [6] by Baumann and Hochbaum, provides an elegant way to increase the flexibility and scalability of constrained clustering. Both types of constraints are trained by PCCC in modeling object assignment problem as an integer program to minimize the within cluster sum of squares. The hard constraints that need to be satisfied are separated from the soft constraints on which we have penalties for violation with this framework. Every soft constraint has associated confidence value that multiplies violation penalty, weighting more reliable constraints. Furthermore, PCCC reduces model size by moving nodes to clusters of their q's nearest, while PCCC also adds to its moves for nodes around cluster centres a variant of multi start approach. The flexibility and scalability of the algorithm is expanded in all of these approaches as PCCC can be employed in an area where the reliability of the constraint is a very very loose or very tight. PCCC is in general computationally expensive, but model size reduction strategies are employed to reduce this cost, and PCCC is thus a promising constrained clustering task solver.

As the data continues to grow rapidly in the modern application, there is a demand for scalable clustering methods that are able to manage large scale datasets. Due to its iterative structural nature, traditional clustering (and constrained clustering) methods, such as K-means, suffer from high computational demands (especially in the case of high dimensions and vast numbers of features) [10]. In today's Big data world, Apache Spark has come up as one of key distributed computing platform with the preferred in memory computation model that is also fault tolerant. Spark [7] defines the Resilient Distributed Dataset (RDD) abstraction which provides the ability to execute parallel jobs and Spark MLlib [11] provides the implementation of several machine learning algorithms such as clustering, which can scale. K-Means‖ [12] which builds upon K-Means + + [9] to embed parallelism into the initialization phase and reducing the number of sequential passes, is the fastest among distributed approaches and is efficient in case of large datasets. Nonetheless, still Kmean remains susceptible to issues resulting from a sensitive centroid initialization as well as problem associated with identifying clusters that are not convex or uneven sized, primarily, we see the development of some adaptive clustering methods in Spark. To address these problems, thus various enhanced clustering algorithms have been integrated in the Spark's ecosystem. For example, Jędrzejowicz et al. (2016) [14] provided a Fuzzy C-Means classifier that has been parallelized by the use of RDD based computations to obtain better scalability and efficiency, and distance measures among the kernel and eigenvalue based cluster detection to have better performance at large scales. Parallel to that, Gaussian Mixture Model (GMM) is used in distributed soft clustering, and is applied to pair with entropy driven feature selection to analyze the spread of Zika virus [16] to deal with large dataset and to find epidemiological results. Han et al. (2018) [15] uses a scalable parallel DBSCAN on Spark with improvements to overcome the problems of fault tolerance (e.g., job rescheduling), workload balancing, and merging overheads exposed in MPI or Hadoop. To perform rapidly neighbor searches the authors use kd-tree, the method based on partitioning that balances sub-domains, and a new merging framework, that logically combines partial cluster, showing obvious scaling advantages for wide ranged clustering tasks. Taken together, they show that Apache Spark is a workable and flexible distributed computing platform that is also scalable and capable of high performance in a number of data intensive domain.

Spark-based clustering has been advanced well, but it does not have the mechanisms to meet must-link or cannot-link constraints. Such major drawbacks hinder the applicability into areas where users need to retain existing relations or structured relationships. A comprehensive survey of existing studies shows that existing methods either do not address the problem of integrating constraints into K-Means under the Spark framework, or they only address part of the problem, hence indicating a significant research gap to fill. Therefore this work proposes a Constrained K-Means algorithm that runs within Spark, where must-link and cannot-link constraints can be embedded in the clustering process. The focus of this study will be centered on augmenting K-Means by the ability of constraint enforcements but keeping the scalability and efficiency of Spark and the interpretability as well as the involvement of domain experts.

1.3 Contribution

In this work, we propose and implement a Constrained K-Means clustering algorithm over Apache Spark framework for processing large scale data with the aim to process the data in the most effective way while taking care of processing the must-link and cannot-link constraints. In this study, we develop such an algorithm that is scalable and retains the study criteria within Spark's MLlib framework. Upon spark distributed data structures and spark parallel processing capabilities are applied, whole things gets optimized, and spark dramatically improves the algorithm performance. Besides, the proposed Constrained K-Means algorithm is also evaluated in terms of its performance as compared to the best clustering methods considered namely K-Means and K-Means|| in respect to accuracy, convergence time and computation speed.

2 Methodology

The Constrained K-Means algorithm is created for the system and based on a structured workflow of four phases, called preprocessing, initialization, assignment and iterative constraint validation, executed on top of Apache Spark. Sections 2.1 to 2.4 give detailed explanation on each step of the proposed method, and Algorithms 1 to 4 give high level pseudocode for the method.

We have given input of n objects of d-dimensions feature vector $x_i \in R^d$ and number of clusters k assigned to each of the object. This algorithm is like the standard K-Means algorithm, but to preserve referred to by the domain knowledge, this algorithm uses must link (ML) and cannot link (CL) constraints such that some of the points stuck or stuck together. Because Spark DataFrames can be efficiently processed in parallel and optimized for query with Spark Catalyst optimizer, we use Spark DataFrames to process the underlying data. This algorithm begins with preprocessing in where superpoints is fed in to reduce computationally the number of useful data points, and after that it is computationally efficient by using in to superpoints. The super points are stored in Spark DataFrames so that data transformations can be done efficiently between Spark DataFrame and Spark context, and also cluster centroid initialization can be parallelized with the help of Spark's distributed execution model using the K-Means‖ algorithm. It is the projection of cluster assignment to original data points and being consistent with must link constraints in the third phase. In the last phase, we finally enforce the cannot link constraints using Spark DataFrame operation as an iterative constraint enforcement. For breaking cluster assignments, this algorithm will yield to this, and when a violating data point touches any constraint, it relegates it to another cluster. We have reassignments and no violation is possible at this stage, and the iteration continues to converge to that. It also uses checkpointing and caching to stop doing redundant computations.

2.1 Preprocessing

In the preprocessing phase of the Constrained K-Means, we apply must-link constraints that join connected data points by grouping them into superpoints, prior to clustering (Algorithm 1). Formally, given a dataset $D = \{x_1, \ldots, x_N\}$ and a set of must-link constraints $ML = (x_i, x_j)$ with x_i and x_j must belong to the same cluster, the algorithm represents D as a graph $G = (V, E)$ using GraphFrames [21], where each $x_i \in D$ is a node in V, and edges in $(x_i, x_j) \in E$ exists if $(x_i, x_j) \in ML$. The method applies a connected components algorithm to G, extracting point groups that needs to be from the same cluster, associating a unique root ID as a reference for each group. Its runs through all connected components and generates one superpoint for each connected component by aggregating all the member feature vectors. This extracts $\tilde{D}$, which reduces the size of the data without losing must-link constraints. These constraints are applied during pre-processing so there are no must-link violations in the subsequent steps and the algorithm is scalable to large datasets by using distributed processing.

Algorithm 1: Preprocessing
Input: Dataset $D = \{x_1, \ldots, x_N\}$, must-link constraints ML
Output: Reduced dataset $\tilde{D}$ with superpoints
1.   Represent dataset as a graph $G = (V, E)$
2.   Apply connected components algorithm to G
3.   Assign a unique root ID to each connected component
4.   Aggregate feature vectors of each component (compute centroid)
5.   Construct reduced dataset $\tilde{D}$
6.   **return** $\tilde{D}$

2.2 Initialization

In the initialization step (Algorithm 2), the cluster initialization is performed over the superpoints $\tilde{D}$ that are preprocessed, and it keeps must-link constraints already present from the outset. In this case, the algorithm uses parallelized seeding to pick centroids via K-Means‖ over $\tilde{D}$ with the goal of finding centroids more effectively than random initialization. The superpoints are clustered and consequentially give rise to initial cluster assignments for these superpoints. Subsequent steps will repeat this procedure in adjusted updates and constrained enforcement (including cannot-link conditions) of the clustering solution in all subsequent updates. The use of K-Means‖ makes the algorithm more stable as it improves the cluster level, such that the final clustering solution is computationally efficient while complying with must-link and cannot-link constraint.

Algorithm 2: Initialization
Input: Superpoints $\widetilde{D}$, number of clusters k
Output: Initial cluster assignments
1.   K-Means‖ on $\widetilde{D}$ to initialize cluster centroids
2.   **return** Initial clusters

2.3 Assignment

After the initialization of clusters on superpoints, we propagate these assignments to the original data points with the guarantee that must link constraints are satisfied (Algorithm 3). Since preprocessing merged mustlinked points into superpoints, all data points in the same superpoint therefore have to inherit the cluster assignment of its root ID, it means the constraint consistency is preserved. This is made possible by mapping the assigned cluster of each superpoint to its root ID and joining with the original data, whereby each data point can be assigned independently. Because the number of superpoints is much lower than the original dataset, this is conducted as broadcast joins to avoid communication overheads in a distributed environment. In the next phase, the algorithm finishes the initial clustering step after all data points have been labeled to a cluster and checks if must-link constraints are strictly enforced; then, it proceeds to the constraint validation. An early enforcement helps ensuring convergence of the algorithm, sustaining the structural consistency, and promotes satisfaction of the constraint based clustering objectives.

Algorithm 3: Assignment
Input: Superpoints $\widetilde{D}$ with assigned clusters, original dataset D
Output: Cluster assignments for all data points
1.   Map each superpoint's cluster assignment to its root ID
2.   Join this mapping with the original dataset D
3.   Assign each data point the cluster of its corresponding superpoint
4.   Optimize using broadcast joins to minimize communication overhead
5.   **return** Cluster assignments for all data points

2.4 Constraint Validation

Algorithm 4: Constraint Validation
Input: Cluster assignments, ML constraints, CL constraints.
Output: Refined cluster assignments
1.   **repeat**
2.   Compute cluster centroids
3.   Detect cannot-link violations (same cluster for forbidden pairs)
4.   **if** no violations exist **then**
5.   Terminate process
6.   **else**
7.   Reassign violating points to valid clusters
8.   **end if**
9.   **until** converge or max iterations reached
10.   **return** Final cluster assignments

The iterative constraint validation step ensures that cannot-link constraints are strictly enforced by continuously refining cluster assignments until convergence (Algorithm 4). Let the dataset $D = \{x_1, \ldots, x_N\}$ be given, where each data point $x_i \in R^D$ is initially assigned a cluster label $\hat{k}(x_i) \in \{1, \ldots, K\}$. In the iterative constraint validation process, the first step is to compute the centroids of the clusters. For each cluster j (with $j = 1, \ldots, K$), let

$$C_j = \{x_i \in D \mid \hat{k}(x_i) = j\}$$

denote the set of data points in cluster j. The centroid of cluster j is then calculated as

$$c_j = \frac{1}{|C_j|} \sum x_i \in C_j x_i.$$

These centroids serve as the reference points for reassigning data points that violate cannot-link constraints. The cannot-link constraints are defined by the set $CL = (x_i, x_j)$ with x_i and x_j must not belong to the same cluster.

A violation occurs when, for any pair $(x_i, x_j) \in CL$, the condition $\hat{k}(x_i) = \hat{k}(x_j)$ is true. For each data point x_i involved in a violation, the algorithm computes the Euclidean distance to every centroid c_m for $m \neq \hat{k}(x_i)$:

$$d(x_i, c_m) = \sqrt{\sum_{p=1}^{D} (x_{i,p} - c_{m,p})^2}.$$

The algorithm then selects the closest alternative cluster for x_i by determining:

$$r = \arg\min_{m \neq \hat{k}(x_i)} \left\{ d(x_i, c_m) \mid \forall (x_i, x_j) \in CL, \hat{k}(x_i) \neq m \right\},$$

and updates the cluster assignment $\hat{k}(x_i) \leftarrow r$. This step of reassigning is repeated iteratively; recomputing centroids, and reassigning any remaining violating points, until there are no more cannot link violation or a predefined maximum number of iterations is reached.

It is noted that must-link constraints are already satisfied, since in preprocessing we first form superpoints to guarantee that all substances of a must-link group are assigned to the same set. As all these operations are done in distributed manner, we are rapidly converging onto probable solution to K-Means clustering problem since the algorithm can be run iteratively until the centroid values stop changing. The result is a constrain compliant clustering solution of dataset D that preserves the structure of must-link constraints and the constrain compliance, while being scalable clustering result.

3 Experiments and Results

3.1 System Environment

The experiments are conducted in MacBook Pro 14-inch equipped with Apple M1 Pro chip and 16 GB unified memory on macOS Sonoma 14.6.1. To prepare the virtual environment, Oracle VirtualBox was used to set up the virtual machine; an Ubuntu 64-bit (ARM) virtual machine that had 8GB RAM, 10 virtual processor, 50GB storage. Standalone mode of Apache Spark was deployed and used system hardware resources for the distributed data processing.

3.2 Datasets

In this study, the datasets are adopted from the work of Baumann and Hochbaum [6] which lists a broad range of classification datasets with predefined ground truth labels. These datasets span across a number of domains, such as biological, medical, and synthetic, which gives rise to different level of complexities for assessing how a method performs in clustering. Thanks to the availability of ground truth labels, one may use objective external validation metrics based on the Adjusted Rand Index (ARI) [20], for clustering accuracy assessment. Also, the constraint sets are produced based on the methodology presented by González-Almagro et al. (2020) [19]. The constraints represent must-link pairs of data points that have the same ground truth class and cannot-link pairs of data points that have different classes. Table 1 summarizes the characteristics of the datasets, i.e., the number of instances, attributes, and classes, as did in the experiments.

3.3 Experiments and Results

Experiments with real and synthetic datasets that evaluate the performance of the proposed algorithm by means of the Adjusted Rand Index (ARI) and by comparison with the MLlib K-Means‖ algorithm are performed.

Results from the Table 2 show that, at most ratio of constraints to unlabelled instances, Constrained K-Means offers better clustering accuracy than MLlib KMeas‖. The results improve substantially on the ARI across breast cancer, new thyroid, and moons datasets,

Table 1. Structure of the datasets

Dataset	Instances	Attributes	Classes
Breast Cancer	569	30	2
Ecoli	336	7	8
Ionosphere	351	33	2
Monk-2	432	6	2
Moons	300	2	2
Newthyroid	215	5	3
Sonar	208	60	2
Spectfheart	267	44	2
Spiral	300	2	2
Vehicle	846	18	4

especially where the constraints are set at approximately 15% or 20% (perfect match with the ground truth labels). This again confirms that constraints effectively guide the clustering by encoding meaningful relations among the data points. Additionally, in datasets like Monk-2 and Moons, accuracy is increased and computation time is reduced by a well formed constraint set. For instance, in Monk-2, ARI increases from 0.12 (5%) to 1.0 (20%) while execution time decreases from 46s to 33.79s, which indicates that an effective must-link formation eliminates redundancies and speeds up convergence.

However, the execution time of Constrained K-Means increases with the increase of constraints and the cost of the computation of Constrained K-Means is higher than the one of MLlib K-Means||. This is expected because verifying must-link and cannot-link constraints involves forming superpoints, validating constraints, and reassigning when violations are found. For example, in Ecoli, execution time grows from 46.33s (5%) to 76s (15%) and the same pattern is observed in Newthyroid, and Monk-2. It was also run in a pseudo distributed environment which could have added to longer runtimes because of local communication overhead. However, execution time is not guaranteed to scale linearly with constraint levels and benefits are achieved when must link constraints are well formed so that they can allow less active data points and partially offset constraint enforcement cost.

This confirms that further constraint levels increase the accuracy of clustering, but at the cost of additional execution time as more constraint processing is involved. In addition, consideration of constraints, most especially must links, can contribute to accuracy and computational efficiency, thus demonstrating how constrained clustering over well structured sets of constraints may achieve high quality results.

Table 2. Performance evaluation of the proposed constrained K-Means algorithm and the K-Means‖ algorithm from MLlib with different constraint ratios

Dataset	Constraint Set (%)	Constrained Kmeans		MLlib Kmeans‖	
		ARI	Time (s)	ARI	Time (s)
Breast Cancer	5	0.77	54.2	0.65	1.73
Breast Cancer	10	0.06	67.6	0.65	1.73
Breast Cancer	15	1	37.7	0.65	1.73
Breast Cancer	20	1	37	0.65	1.73
Ecoli	5	0.55	46.33	0.39	1.98
Ecoli	10	0.65	54.22	0.39	1.98
Ecoli	15	0.69	76	0.39	1.98
Ecoli	20	0.86	56.5	0.39	1.98
Ionosphere	5	0.2	50.68	0.17	1.89
Ionosphere	10	0.57	58.7	0.17	1.89
Ionosphere	15	0.044	58	0.17	1.89
Ionosphere	20	1	31.79	0.17	1.89
Monk-2	5	0.12	46	−0.0023	1.78
Monk-2	10	0.004	56.75	−0.0023	1.78
Monk-2	15	1	30.28	−0.0023	1.78
Monk-2	20	1	33.79	−0.0023	1.78
Moons	5	0.56	46.69	0.47	1.37
Moons	10	0.76	48.43	0.47	1.37
Moons	15	0.92	45.25	0.47	1.37
Moons	20	1	28.52	0.47	1.37
Newthyroid	5	0.73	33.75	0.58	1.47
Newthyroid	10	0.89	44.99	0.58	1.47
Newthyroid	15	0.85	47.29	0.58	1.47
Newthyroid	20	1	38.73	0.58	1.47
Sonar	5	0.02	48.14	0.01	1.82
Sonar	10	0.07	50.23	0.01	1.82
Sonar	15	0.65	54.95	0.01	1.82
Sonar	20	0.98	41.77	0.01	1.82
Spectfheart	5	0.0036	52.98	−0.1	1.92
Spectfheart	10	0.053	56.9	−0.1	1.92
Spectfheart	15	0.25	57.88	−0.1	1.92

(*continued*)

Table 2. (*continued*)

Dataset	Constraint Set (%)	Constrained Kmeans		MLlib Kmeans‖	
		ARI	Time (s)	ARI	Time (s)
Spectfheart	20	1	44.65	−0.1	1.92
Spiral	5	0.058	50.52	0.008	1.68
Spiral	10	0.42	52.36	0.008	1.68
Spiral	15	0.95	45.9	0.008	1.68
Spiral	20	0.99	48.69	0.008	1.68
Vehicle	5	0.058	51.15	0.09	1.93
Vehicle	10	0.063	57.49	0.09	1.93
Vehicle	15	0.15	62.92	0.09	1.93
Vehicle	20	1	28.87	0.09	1.93

4 Conclusions and Perspectives

This paper shows the way in which Constrained K-Means algorithm can be used to deal with the larger problem of must link and cannot link constraints when working on large scale clustering problems on Apache Spark. We propose a method that makes use of the Spark distributed architecture to generate valid solutions while the process of constraints can be preserved and they retain scalability and efficiency. On standard K-Means, advantages in terms of constraint handling to produce tighter clusters and possible higher interpretability are shown experimentally. Moreover, clustering accuracy also enhances with the enhancement of constraint level which indicates that the clustering process is predicated on the well structured constraint. These features can be offered, but with the cost of additional execution time which implies that there should be no naive solution to handing constraints.

Consequently, the current approach is proven vindicated with positive results which create more room for more work on this approach. The key priority of improving the constraint validation phase aims to minimize computational overhead especially in the setting where there are many constraints. Improving the formation of the superpoint mitigates redundancy and is seen to reduce computation and as well as enhance performance and scalability. However, we can also parallelize the constraint verification process in such a way that it does not impart an extra load on runtime from Constrained K-Means to deal with large data. We also extend the algorithm with soft constraints that eventually gave rise to the confidence values that we later apply to become more agile to various clustering scenarios. On the massive data's, the efficiency and scalability of it is tested finally on a multi node Spark cluster environment. Finally, the approach will consume the real world data to find out further deep insights of how does the approach works for the real big data clustering. If all these problems are solved, constrained clustering algorithms will be proven effective for use in big data environments. The work can be applied when dealing with time-series data such as biomedical signals [23, 24], insurance expenditures [25, 26], etc.

References

1. Jain, A.K., Murty, M.N., Flynn, P.J.: Data clustering. ACM Comput. Surv. **31**(3), 264–323 (1999). https://doi.org/10.1145/331499.331504
2. Madhulatha, T.S.: An overview on clustering methods. arXiv (2012). https://doi.org/10.48550/arxiv.1205.1117
3. Basu, S., Davidson, I., Wagstaff, K.: Constrained clustering: Advances in Algorithms, Theory, and Applications. CRC Press (2008)
4. Wagstaff, K., Cardie, C., Rogers, S., Schrödl, S.: Constrained K-means Clustering with Background Knowledge. In: International Conference on Machine Learning, pp. 577–584 (2001). https://web.cse.msu.edu/~cse802/notes/ConstrainedKmeans.pdf
5. Bilenko, M., Basu, S., Mooney, R.J.: Integrating constraints and metric learning in semi-supervised clustering. In: Proceedings of the Twenty-First International Conference on Machine Learning (ICML '04), p. 11. Association for Computing Machinery (2004). https://doi.org/10.1145/1015330.1015360
6. Baumann, P., Hochbaum, D.S.: PCCC: the pairwise-confidence-constraints clustering algorithm. arXiv (2022). https://doi.org/10.48550/arxiv.2212.14437
7. Zaharia, M., et al.: Resilient distributed datasets: a fault-tolerant abstraction for in-memory cluster computing. In: Networked Systems Design and Implementation, 2 (2012). http://cobweb.cs.uga.edu/~squinn/mmd_s15/papers/nsdi12-final138.pdf
8. Lloyd, S.: Least squares quantization in PCM. IEEE Trans. Inf. Theory **28**(2), 129–137 (1982)
9. Arthur, D., Vassilvitskii, S.: K-means++: the advantages of careful seeding. Symp. Discrete Algorithms **1027–1035**,(2007). https://doi.org/10.5555/1283383.1283494
10. Kozyriev, A., Norkin, V.: robust clustering on high-dimensional data with stochastic quantization. arXiv (2024). https://doi.org/10.48550/arxiv.2409.02066
11. Meng, X., et al.: MLLIB: Machine learning in apache spark. arXiv (2015). https://doi.org/10.48550/arxiv.1505.06807
12. Bahmani, B., Moseley, B., Vattani, A., Kumar, R., Vassilvitskii, S.: Scalable K-Means++. arXiv (2012). https://doi.org/10.48550/arxiv.1203.6402
13. Blömer, J., Lammersen, C., Schmidt, M., Sohler, C.: Theoretical analysis of the k-means algorithm a survey. arXiv (2016). https://doi.org/10.48550/arxiv.1602.08254
14. Jędrzejowicz, J., Jędrzejowicz, P., Wierzbowska, I.: Apache spark implementation of the distance-based kernel-based fuzzy c-means clustering classifier. In: Smart Innovation, Systems and Technologies, pp. 317–324 (2016). https://doi.org/10.1007/978-3-319-39630-9_26
15. Han, D., Agrawal, A., Liao, W., Choudhary, A.: Parallel DBSCAN algorithm using a data partitioning strategy with spark implementation. In: Proceedings of the IEEE International Conference on Big Data (Big Data), pp. 305–312 (2018). https://doi.org/10.1109/bigdata.2018.8622258
16. Lavanya, K., Banu, J.S., Jain, P.: Clustering of Zika virus epidemic using gaussian mixture model in spark environment. Biomed. Res. **30**(1) (2019). https://doi.org/10.35841/biomedicalresearch.30-18-1132
17. Apache Software Foundation. Hadoop (2010). https://hadoop.apache.org
18. Dean, J., Ghemawat, S.: MapReduce. Commun. ACM **51**(1), 107–113 (2008). https://doi.org/10.1145/1327452.1327492

19. González-Almagro, G., Luengo, J., Cano, J., García, S.: DILS: constrained clustering through dual iterative local search. Comput. Oper. Res. **121**, 104979 (2020). https://doi.org/10.1016/j.cor.2020.104979
20. Hubert, L., Arabie, P.: Comparing partitions. J. Classif. **2**, 193–218 (1985)
21. Dave, A., Jindal, A., Li, L.E., Xin, R., Gonzalez, J., Zaharia, M.: Graphframes: an integrated api for mixing graph and relational queries. In: Proceedings of the fourth international workshop on graph data management experiences and systems, pp. 1–8 (2016)
22. The Constrained K-Means algorithm code is available on GitHub. https://github.com/huynqcharles/spark-constrained-kmeans
23. Hung, P.D.: Detection of central sleep apnea based on a single-lead ECG. In: Proceedings of the 5th International Conference on Bioinformatics Research and Applications (ICBRA '18), pp. 78–83. Association for Computing Machinery, New York, NY, USA (2018)
24. Hung, P.D.: Central sleep apnea detection using an accelerometer. In: Proceedings of the 1st International Conference on Control and Computer Vision (ICCCV '18), pp. 106–111. Association for Computing Machinery, New York, NY, USA (2018)
25. Hai, P.N., Hieu, H.T., Hung, P.D.: An empirical examination on forecasting VN30 short-term uptrend stocks using LSTM along with the ichimoku cloud trading strategy. In: Sharma, H., Shrivastava, V., Kumari Bharti, K., Wang, L. (eds.) Communication and Intelligent Systems. Lecture Notes in Networks and Systems, vol. 461. Springer, Singapore (2022)
26. Dat, D.Q., Hung, P.D.: Improvement for time series clustering with the deep learning approach. In: Luo, Y. (eds.) Cooperative Design, Visualization, and Engineering. CDVE 2021. Lecture Notes in Computer Science(), vol. 12983. Springer, Cham (2021)

Computational Linguistics and Media News: Linguistic Features and Lexical Choices with Time-frequency Statistical Analysis

Ahu Dereli Dursun[1,2]

[1] Institute of Social Sciences, Communication Studies, Istanbul Bilgi University, Istanbul, Turkey
ahu.dereli.dursun@bilgiedu.net
[2] Istanbul Ticaret University, Istanbul, Turkey

Abstract. Media has a critical role in shaping attitudes and public understanding toward mental health. The handling of news on mental health conditions in media comes with intrinsic challenges, some of which are due to the use of language. Language, lexical choices and contexts which the lexical items are attributed to can bring about different effects like stigmatizing and otherizing perceptions or trivializing severe mental health conditions. Hence, language used in media is influential, particularly in health communication which is targeted toward public with the source being represented by health communicators and journalists. In view of these aspects, the present study aims to examine the use of language in print media based on the lexical analyses, including the use of adjectives, nominalizations and connotations, based on theoretical and quantitative dimensions, which are content analysis regarding linguistic features and time-frequency statistical analysis. The dataset contains 725 newspaper articles on mental health and psychological problems, published in six different Turkish national newspapers over a six-year period. The results of the computational linguistic-based analyses belonging to the proposed model show that negative descriptions, attributions and connotations regarding people with mental health disorders outnumber the positive ones. Another aim of the study concerns whether reporting language on mental health conditions is consistent with what has been suggested by the American Psychiatric Association (APA). The results obtained reveal that some lexical choices, particularly certain adjectives and nominalized phrases used in the reporting language, are not in agreement with APA's recommendations. In brief, it has been aimed at pinpointing reporting language in journalistic practices using accurate, responsible and empathic language for mental health reporting and more balanced press coverage concerning mental problems and individuals with mental conditions. This aim can further be oriented towards other media where various genres and styles of language are used across different disciplines.

Keywords: Media Language · Computational Linguistics · Mental Health News · Mental Health Reporting · Media Texts · Linguistic Features · Stigmatizing and Derogatory Language · Lexical Choices · Lexical Variations · Journalistic Practice · Time-frequency Statistical Analysis · Observation Probability · Psycholinguistic Features · Content Analysis

1 Introduction

Media language has been one of the most focal aspects addressed and examined in the domain of linguistics. These domains cover particularly applied linguistics that is concerned with the identification of and solution to language-related real-life problems as well as sociolinguistics which is the study of the interaction between language and society through the investigation of how language is used and how it varies in varying social contexts considering the cultural norms, context, expectations, and so forth. The interest in media language is stated to be due to the accessible feature of the media as a source of language data, its quality as a linguistic institution people are exposed to by hearing and reading on a daily basis, the interesting ways the media linguistically use language in their own right and the media's position as an important social institution [1]. Two decades before, the examination of the languages of journalism was stated to be a relatively novel phenomenon, with an interest sustained by scholars over the last three decades back then [2]. The examination of language in the context of media constitutes multiple layers, which are the formal features of language and less formal ones. While lexical (word) choice, syntax and grammar make up the former mentioned features, textual patterns, formulaic narratives and frames are considered to belong to the latter category. The progress of journalism toward complicated systems of information relay has consequently brought about the growth of journalistic language.

The fact that the system of information relay through language is multi-layered is due to the messages in journalistic contexts encoding broader messages about life beyond the actions' sequencing making up a news event [2]. Thus, the messages conveyed cannot be stated to be simplistic or transparent, and the output of reading a text yields a socially contingent and negotiated process of constructing meaning, which requires the nuanced investigation of a text's adjustment in relation to a broader context including social, political, economic, cultural and cognitive elements. These aspects of journalism languages' study with the emergence of sociolinguistics are acknowledged based on the premise that the study of language is a means of building, maintaining and mediating social relationships [3]. Along with these aspects, it is observed that language also encompasses the skills concerning the news producers that need to be possessed, some of which include but are not limited to news writing, interviewing and copy editing in line with the valued objectives of providing balance, brevity, objectivity, clarity, precision as well as accuracy [4–6]. Linguistic features characteristic of newspaper writing and functions of these linguistic features in news discourse along with the variations existing in the news writing process are other important points of analysis [7]. The syntactic and lexical features can be associated with the communicative context or situational characteristics distinguishing news discourse [8, 9]. Regarding lexical items which are common in newspaper writing, nouns frequently act as premodifiers of other nouns. Likewise, nominalizations, attributive adjectives premodifying nouns and prepositional phrases that follow the nouns are also stated to be common. Noun phrases are a basis to evaluate and label sources and news actors, allowing for a maximum packaging of meaning in minimum space possible, which is a linguistic aspect observed in news story as a whole and headlines in particular.

Language as the medium of communication plays a critical role in shaping societal attitudes, and media platforms including traditional outlets such as newspapers and television, as well as digital platforms like social media, serve as conduits for disseminating information about mental health. Even though the role of media in the public attitudes, beliefs and behaviors intended is acknowledged, it is still a concern that representations in the press about mental health problems are known to be disproportionately negative [10]. This concern extends across a global basis [11], some examples including the US [12], Canada [13], Japan [14] and Türkiye [15]. For the UK, the picture demonstrated by research shows a slightly more positive trend between 2008 and 2016 when the number of articles coded with danger to other people reduced by 4%, from 21 to 17 [16]. This change, interpreted to be modest [11] toward a positive trend is attributed to the increases in accounts to support readers in having a better understanding of mental health [17].

Mental health issues within the press are reported to be of a negative nature with stereotypes being reinforced. Dangerousness, violence and criminality [18, 19] are among the elements of such negativity, while some other common ones are unpredictability [20], bizarreness, vulnerability and dependency [21]. One of the key problems arising from negative coverage in the news is the impact on people who live with and experience mental health problems. A report by Mind surveying 515 individuals with mental health issues in England showed that negative depictions of media made those people's mental health problems worse. One third reported that they felt more depressed and anxious due to bad press, while one twelfth stated they felt suicidal as a result [22]. The primary messages the report revealed emphasized the poor balance of press coverage, reinforcing stigmatizing portrayals and perpetuating social exclusion as consequences, which also point toward the fact that sensationalizing of news items lack responsibility or sensitivity. In addition to the prevailing negativity in the coverage of the news on mental illness, there are some variations among the types of disorders. The theory of cyclical relationship between the press and its readers [23] within a circle of press influencing its readers and the desire of the readers about consuming negative stories is used to explain the pressure on the newspapers to produce such negative accounts. On social media, in the case of the sphere of Twitter, this desire of the users is stated to be reflected by the retweeting process of the news items supported by the readers. Yet, in such support, different disorders are shown to be represented more or less sympathetically [11]. To illustrate, schizophrenia has a more negative representation, while depression is inclined to be represented in a more sympathetic way [17, 24]. A similar finding is shown in another study which aimed to examine schizophrenia-related stigma on social media (Chinese microblogging website) [25]. For this purpose, the authors conducted a human-based content analysis on collected posts to identify if the posts conveyed stigma or not. Another purpose was to find out if schizophrenia-related stigma could be distinguished from stigma regarding other mental illnesses, namely depression-related stigma, in terms of psycholinguistic style. Through the use of their linguistic inquiry and word count software, the extracted posts were analyzed with respect to their psycholinguistic features. The results of the analysis showed that the proportion of posts which indicated stigma related to depression was much lower than the proportion of posts suggesting stigma related to schizophrenia. The level of sympathy is also shown to vary depending on the type of the newspaper. This point is analyzed in the newspapers of the UK where broadsheets are inclined to adopt a less stigmatizing attitude [17], while red-top tabloids are prone to presenting a stigmatizing outlook [26]. This clear contrast is conveyed as the sensational, dramatic and easily accessible tabloid style versus the less subjective and more contemplative broadsheet approach [27].

Communication's reliance on shared knowledge that comprises knowledge of language and of the world reveals context along with the intention of the language user. This is critical to grasping the meaning that lies behind the utterances. This framework by Searle [28] suggests that it is not possible to understand fully what the speaker intends to convey unless these elements are considered. Distinctive from the intended illocutionary force, what the speaker wants to accomplish with his / her words and an utterance in language could have a literal meaning. This example underlines the way communication is reliant on shared knowledge as well as situational factors to be able to derive deeper meanings. It is posited that language used for people with mental illness constitutes an important aspect of stigma. Use of stigmatizing labels or derogatory terms is one way of communicating stigma to the person who has various mental problems. Data from research suggest that stigmatizing labels bring about distress, a feeling of rejection and self-stigma in people with mental illness [29, 30]. Appropriate labels given to patients with mental problems, in contrast, have been shown to improve behaviors concerning seeking help [31]. One related study aimed to examine the extent of stigma concerning treatment avoidance among 14-year-old school students in England in relation to the way they refer to people having mental illness [30]. The data of the qualitative cross-sectional study consisted of the enumeration of the words and terms used to refer to mental illness based on the answers of the students to the question what kinds of words or phrases the student might use to describe someone that experiences mental health problems. The words and terms used were clustered in terms of their connotative and denotative meanings in line with the grounded theory approach, and labels were subsequently derived to capture the key themes attached by the students to the concepts of mental illness. Among the five themes identified from the data of the study, 'popular derogatory terms' (116 items) accounted for almost half of the words examined, while the use of psychiatric diagnoses (15 items) and terms related to violence (9 items) were unexpectedly infrequent. Another related study, motivated by the research gap concerning the commonly used derogatory adjectives for people with mental illness in India, found out that patients having psychotic disorders encountered more derogatory adjectives compared to ones having affective disorders [32]. The study further revealed that 60% of the patients and about 40% were teased by their family members and friends / colleagues, respectively by the use of various derogatory adjectives. Moreover, poor functioning was linked with the significantly higher number of derogatory labels.

The words and context which the words are attributed to are said to foster stigma and prejudice toward individuals with mental health conditions besides trivializing serious ones and experiences accompanying them. Accordingly, reporters have been advised that some words including 'crazy', 'nuts', 'lunatic', 'psycho', and so forth should never be used in reporting. This aspect was addressed in one study which analyzed 14 common terms in everyday language through Twitter data having the potential for stigmatizing mental illnesses in society. Drawing on annotation methods generally used in natural language processing (NLP), the authors focused on evaluating if awareness of mental illnesses could help discourage impulsive uses of the pejorative senses of the words and identified the terms' uses, some of which were expressive, clinical and stigmatizing [33]. A subset of language features was investigated in another study to determine discriminatory characteristics for subreddits on online social media Reddit that became an important resource to share. The results suggested that there were discriminatory linguistic features among subreddits, including sentence complexity or vocabulary usage [34].

Health communication is an area represented by all journalistic genres, whether they be oral (i.e. television, Internet, and so forth) or written (i.e. reports, magazines, newspapers, and so on) [35]. As health communication is targeted towards general public with the source being represented by journalists or health communicators, the information conveyed in health communication is the output of a sort of intra-language translation, which enables the original medical language transformation into a common language [36]. Mental health and psychological issues are one of the most sensitive human conditions, and their handling in the news comes with certain challenges, some of which derive from the use of language. In this respect, attributive adjectives may be used to construe negative connotations and labelling that could lead to stigmatizing and otherizing perceptions for those with mental health problems. The use of adjectives and discrimination is a topic worthy of investigation to paid keen attention to, which was addressed by the World Psychiatric Association (WPA) in 2010 through a detailed document for the purpose of reducing stigma-discrimination towards people who meet the criteria of a mental disorder [37]. Accordingly, the Task Force established in 2009 would examine evidence regarding stigmatization of psychiatry and psychiatrists, providing recommendations about action that could be taken by national psychiatric societies and professionals in order to prevent or reduce their disciplines' stigmatization along with averting its despicable consequences. The World Psychiatric Association (WPA), as a result, recommended avoiding adjective diagnoses for mental disorders since that is the process which is marked as a first step in stigmatization. To put it differently, discrimination is told to start in the language, and thus, phrases like "people with …", "people who suffer from …", "people who have …", "people who meet the criteria for the diagnosis of …" or "people who live with …" were recommended to be used instead of the adjectives [37]. Pertaining to stigma-discrimination complex (SDC) which includes stigma, prejudice, stereotype and discrimination, authors and editors are recommended to use an inclusive language in all contexts so that the negative social impact of SDC in people that meet the criteria for a mental disorder could be reduced [38].

Regarding news media portrayal of people with mental disorders, the number of studies for Türkiye context is limited. One research focuses on journalism ethics in Türkiye concerning media portrayals of people with mental disorders [39]. Another one is a retrospective scanning study on schizophrenia in Turkish newspapers [40] and one work shows forensic elements, criminalization and victimization as the dominant themes in Turkish newspaper articles [41]. Grammatical analysis of language use concerning active - passive verb voice use and framing related to the representation of individuals that experience mental health problems as well as episodic and thematic framing approaches are analyzed in the other studies, respectively [42, 43]. Motivated against this background and to contribute to this area of research in the particular context, this study addresses the use of language in the news as a unit of analysis based on the lexical analyses of the dataset that comprises a total of 725 newspaper articles on mental health and psychological problems published in six different Turkish newspapers over a six-year period (2014–2019). Based on the fact that mass media act as a significant contributor to the dissemination of information that might influence stigma related to mental disorders and illnesses, the present study analyzes newspaper stories and articles on mental health and people with mental issues. Particular emphasis is placed on the use of adjectives to describe people with mental problems along with the positive and negative connotations surrounding the particular problem. Thus, the study aims to contribute to the existing knowledge on the use of language and lexical aspects, addressing adjectives, attributions, nominalizations and connotations in print news media on the theme of mental disorders and people living with such health issues in the context of Türkiye which is a country with a rapidly changing political, economic and social agenda concerning the news and breaking out thereof. The developments in social context make up one of the significant causes of mental distress in a country, so Türkiye context in a constant state of flux is a good showcase of these themes and issues. This constitutes the other motivation and subordinate aim of the paper which also attempts to show the changes over the time period of analysis. A related further aim is to provide insights into journalistic practices in news media supportive of the correct use of language that is sensitive about avoiding phrases, collocations and / or adjectives provoking stigma and discrimination, which can help enhance perception and public knowledge regarding mental distress and people with mental disorder(s).

The rest of the paper is organized as follows: Sect. 2 presents the materials and methods, while Sect. 3 provides the experimental results. Section 4 addresses discussion, conclusion and future directions.

2 Materials and Methods

2.1 Mental Health Print News Dataset

Newspaper articles addressing mental health and mental illness-related themes selected from search with the key words of mental health, mental distress, mental disorder, mental illness, depression, depressive, bipolar disorder and affective disorder make up the dataset of this study. The newspaper articles were retrieved from the electronic sites of six daily national newspapers published in Türkiye between 2014–2019. The dataset used for the present study belongs to the dissertation thesis entitled *News Media Portrayal of Mental Health and Psychological Problems: An Analysis of Daily Newspapers in Türkiye* [44]. The total number of news articles in the dataset analyzed is 725 (*Hürriyet* ($n = 218$), Sabah ($n = 168$), *Milliyet* ($n = 158$), *Sözcü* ($n = 110$), *Cumhuriyet* ($n = 38$) and *Posta* ($n = 33$)). Table 1 provides the breakdown of the news articles by newspaper. The selected newspapers are popular and highly circulating ones in the country, with *Cumhuriyet* having a critical orientation. Thus, it can be noted that the dataset constitutes a representative sample in terms of the newspapers chosen.

Table 1. The corresponding number of newspaper articles by newspapers.

Newspaper	Total number of news articles
Hürriyet	218
Sabah	168
Milliyet	158
Sözcü	110
Cumhuriyet	38
Posta	33

2.2 Methods

Qualitative and quantitative content analysis was conducted to analyze the linguistic features used in the texts of the newspaper articles whose main themes were mental health, mental problems and people with mental health conditions. The newspaper articles were analyzed with respect to the use of language, particularly of attributive adjectives. Statistical Package for the Social Sciences (SPSS) software program (IBM SPSS Version 26.0) was used for the descriptive, frequency and statistical analyses of this study [45].

The aim was to identify connotations (positive, negative) revealed through the adjectives used to describe people with mental health problems and whether the use of reporting language on mental health conditions was in line with what had been suggested by APA [46]. The evaluation to achieve the stated aims of this study was made in two dimensions based on theoretical and quantitative elements including content analysis regarding linguistic features and time-frequency statistical analysis, respectively.

2.2.1 Theory of Computational Linguistics: Lexical Analysis

Computational linguistics, as a scientific and engineering discipline, is oriented toward understanding written and / or spoken language in view of a computational perspective. This sort of computational understanding of language provides vision into thinking and intelligence [47]. Formulating grammatical and semantic frameworks to characterize languages for enabling computationally manageable implementations regarding syntactic and semantic analysis, discovering processing techniques and learning principles that make use of structural and distributional, or statistical, features of language are among the theoretical goals of computational linguistics [48]. This study addressed the lexical aspects (including the use of adjectives, nominalizations and connotations) in national print news media in Türkiye. The themes of the news articles of the dataset are mental disorders and individuals with such health issues. Regarding lexical aspects, denotation refers to the straightforward and literal definition of a word with no additional emotional or cultural associations. Thus, denotation of a word or expression with its direct meaning represents the objective meaning that remains consistent regardless of the context. Connotation, on the other hand, consists of the ideas or meanings associated with it or suggested by it [49]. A positive connotation refers to a non-literal framing of an object or term that intends to add a "good" association [50]. Positive connotations are used in writing to add levity to situations, communicate courtesy and express optimism. In contrast, a negative connotation refers to a word, sign or object regarded with a "bad" association. As a result, negative connotations have the function of evoking "bad" feelings [51, 52].

To help reduce stigma, the American Psychiatric Association (APA) suggests that the words be carefully chosen while writing about mental health. These suggestions are to focus on the person rather than on the condition as the mental health condition is only one aspect of an individual's life. Thus, it should not be reflected as a defining characteristic. For this reason, instead of using a statement like "He is schizophrenic.", "He is a person with schizophrenia." is preferred. Another point to pay attention to is to be specific, so specific disorders should be used whenever possible: "She was diagnosed with bipolar disorder." is to be preferred over "She was mentally ill." Finally, derogatory language needs to be avoided. To illustrate, "He has a mental health illness. He has a substance use disorder." is a statement to be preferred over this one which is suggested to be refrained from: "He suffers from mental illness. He is a drug abuser." [46].

2.2.2 Computational Linguistics: Lexical Analysis and Time-Frequency Statistical Analysis

Time-frequency is employed for understanding the distribution of data in the time-frequency domain to detect and separate the components of signals with non-overlapping, compact components, as well as to observe the prevalence of certain categories and identify possible imbalances in the dataset. A new time-frequency analysis technique applicable to the nature of the dataset has been developed in this study.

The most accurate way of classification is the frequency table where the observed data are clustered into classes. The table obtained gives the observation number in each class. When an experiment is done n times and event A happens f times, the f/n ratio is named relative frequency of event A. Let n increase and f/n relative frequency approaches a limit, this limit is named as the probability of A. For n with big numbers the probability of A is calculated through f/n. For known causes, it is known as the frequency definition of probability [53].

$$RelativeFrequency = Frequency of a particular event / Sample size$$

The following steps are followed to prepare the frequency table:

1st step: The number of observations is identified. n denotes the number of observation ($50 \leq n$ is preferred).

2nd step: Maximum and minimum values are found. Range is obtained when the difference between them is calculated.

$$range = max - min$$

3rd step: The number of classes is found.

$$\sqrt{n} \leq k, \ (k = integer)$$

$classnumber = k$ [53].

3 Experimental Results

This study has addressed the lexical aspects (including the use of adjectives, nominalizations and connotations) on the scale of time-frequency of different years in national print news media in Türkiye. The themes of the news articles of the dataset are mental disorders and individuals with such health issues. The results of the content and lexical analyses reveal that 35 items (4.8%) in 725 of the dataset contain positive descriptions, attributions and connotations regarding people with mental health disorders mentioned in the news articles analyzed. The number of negative descriptions, attributions and connotations is 134 (18.48%), and a higher number amounting to 353 (48.68%) is observed for neutral descriptions. In line with the number of news articles in each newspaper, *Hürriyet* was the newspaper with the highest number of positive ($n = 10$) and negative ($n = 43$) descriptions as well as neutral expressions ($n = 118$). These findings based on computational linguistic analyses by the newspapers are depicted in Figs. 1, 2 and 3.

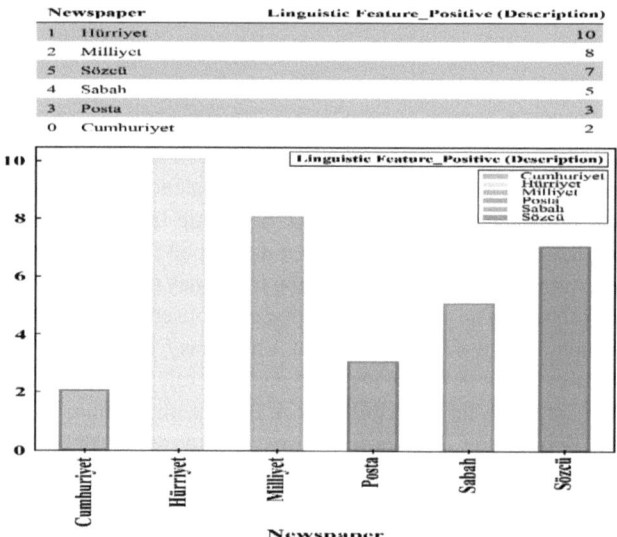

Fig. 1. Positive descriptions by the newspapers

When the analysis over the years is in question, the year 2015 included the highest number of positive descriptions ($n = 11$) followed by 2018 ($n = 8$). The year with the least positive descriptions observed in the news items is 2019 ($n = 2$). The results concerning negative descriptions peaked in 2019 ($n = 39$) followed by 2015 ($n = 27$) and saw the lowest rate in 2014 ($n = 15$) and 2018 ($n = 15$). Neutral descriptions were encountered at their highest rate in 2019 ($n = 89$), with 2018 ($n = 65$) and 2017 ($n = 64$) following at similar frequencies. The lowest number of neutral descriptions was observed in 2016 ($n = 36$) which was also the year when negative descriptions were seen the most. Computational linguistic-based analyses by the years are presented in Figs. 4, 5 and 6.

Computational Linguistics and Media News: Linguistic Features and Lexical Choices 235

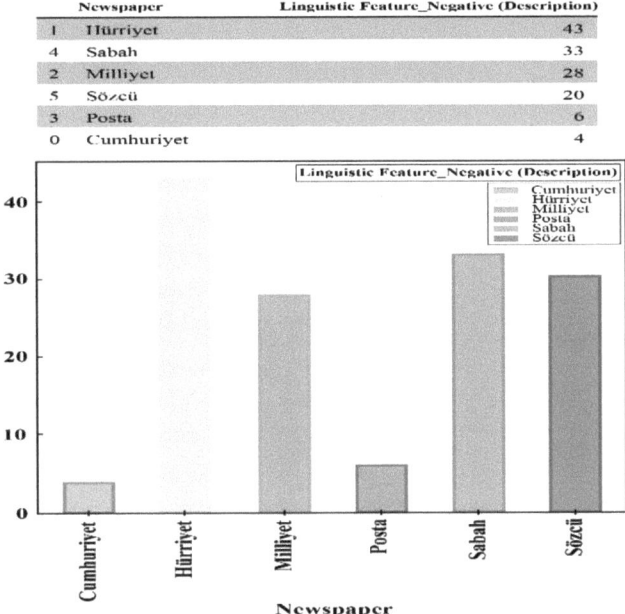

Fig. 2. Negative descriptions by the newspapers

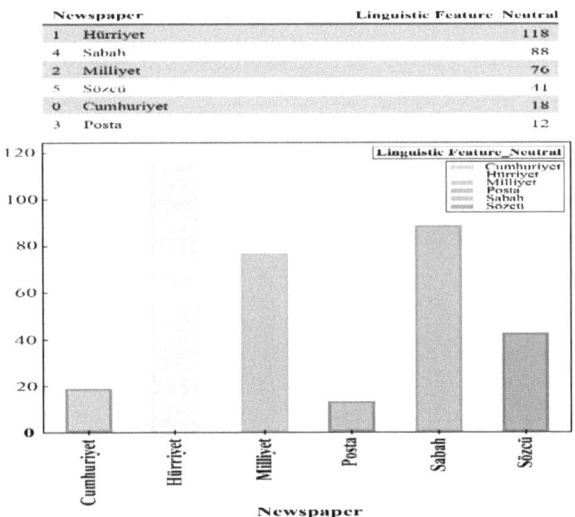

Fig. 3. Neutral descriptions by the newspapers

As for changes over the years, no stable increase or decrease is observed in terms of the use of positive-negative connotations, neutral expressions and linguistic elements.

The use of positive language has been found in 35 (4.8%) of the news items within the dataset, which represents a significantly low number given the total number of the

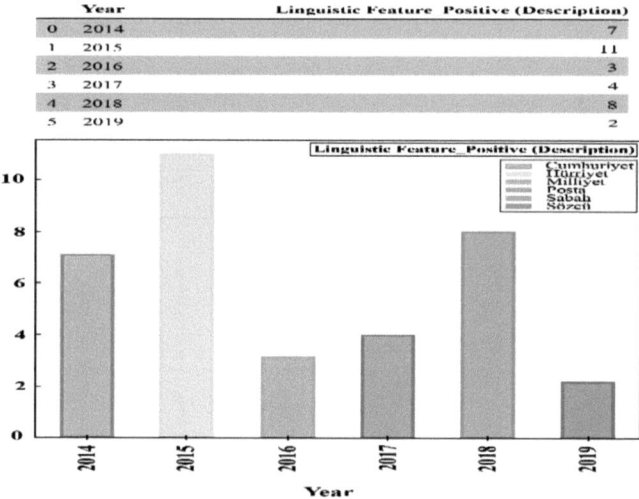

Fig. 4. Positive descriptions by the years

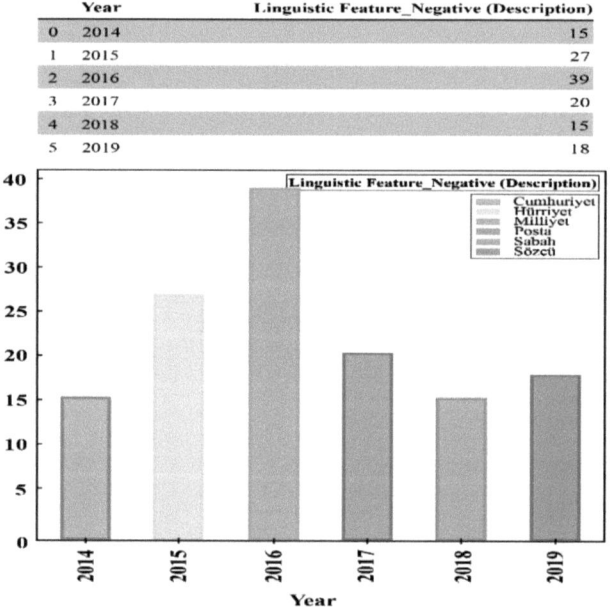

Fig. 5. Negative descriptions by the years

news articles analyzed ($N = 725$). Some selected examples of salient positive language use to describe people with mental conditions can be provided as follows: connection between creativity and having a psychotic disorder or mental distress, individual depicted as doing his/her job successfully and being proficient at work, able to recover, being smart, having superior qualities, celebrities not concealing their mental condition,

Computational Linguistics and Media News: Linguistic Features and Lexical Choices 237

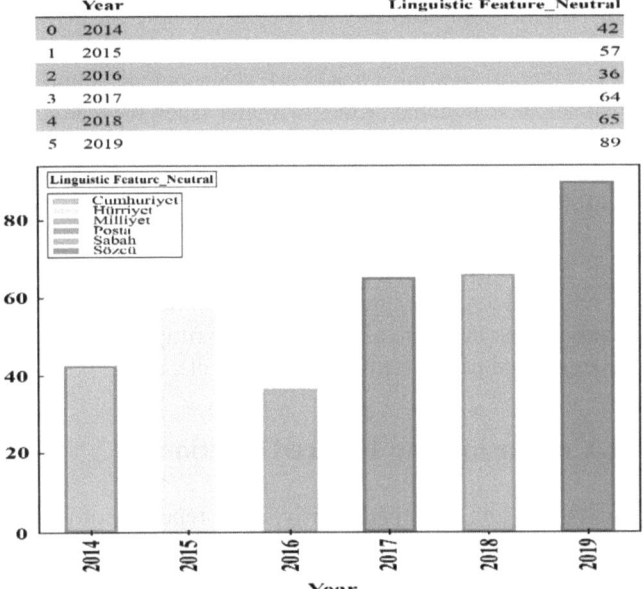

Fig. 6. Neutral descriptions by the years

being a legendary actor, being a role-model for the society, being snip-snap, a valuable name in Turkish literature, pioneer of feminism, engaging in successful artwork and achieving (re)integration with one's society. These positive descriptions supported by language and choice of lexical items underline success, recovery, creativity and favorable personality traits. When compared to the positive use of language and adjectives with positive connotations, the use of negative lexical features is much higher, with 134 of the news articles containing elements of negative attributions. Some selected examples from salient negative language use for the description of mental problems and people with mental conditions are as follows: drug addict, falling into the grip of alcoholism, being worse than before, not what he/she used to be, murdering his wife, an individual who intends to end his/her life, killer mother, talentless, spoilt, suffering from psychological problems, psychopath, patients with severe chronic mental illness, patricide actor, rapist woman, bizarre disorders, a group difficult to deal with, the woman who killed her mother, the defendant who killed her mother, the assailant who kicked the nurse wearing shorts, the kicking assailant, the suspect who killed his neighbor, the one (citing the name and surname) who killed her mother by strangling her, the defendant who killed his wife with an adze, yokel (citing the name and surname) who kicked a young woman on the bus, G. who is a bipolar patient (citing the name), stark mad (for severe schizophrenia), manic depressive juvenile, the psychopath who killed his neighbor, the footballer who committed suicide, the woman with axe who attacked the statue, the assailant on the minibus, mad person, the actress coming to the fore due to alcohol problem (citing the name and surname), the defendant who killed the famous writer, a patient group not normal psychologically, racist man, the one (citing the name and surname) who murdered his girlfriend with 11 bullets, the woman who tried to strangle her baby, imprinted on the memories with her constant alcoholic, messy and miserable appearance, the bipolar woman who attacked the girl wearing a headscarf, schizophrenic kamikaze judge, not having good mental health, that mother, Kung fu fighter killer, the man (citing the name and surname) detained and hospitalized at psychiatric service due to having stabbed his mother 40 times, murder suspect who killed two people five years apart, serial killer, airport agitator, killing 18-year-old pregnant woman and dreadful illness (referring to Virginia Woolf's health problem).

As the negative depictions supported by negative language use and connotations show, unusual behaviors, violent acts, aggression, vulnerability, dependency, bizarreness and lack of self-care are the most prominent images portrayed by the descriptions of mental health challenges and people with mental health disorders.

4 Discussion, Conclusion and Future Directions

Positive connotations in health news particularly in the reporting of mental health are important as has been explained previously. Positive language can help reduce stigma about mental health issues, so if mental health problems are framed in a constructive way with hope elements, individuals with those conditions can seek help without the overwhelm of judgment [54, 55]. Closely related to this point, positive connotations are important for promoting wellbeing and recovery while encouraging behaviors oriented toward help-seeking [54]. Lastly, the use of positive language can result in a more informed public having empathy, which could show its repercussions in social support and policy implementations considering media's role in shaping societal attitudes and sharing public perception [55]. For the present paper, the results of the analyses show that about 5% of the newspaper articles carried positive descriptions, expressions, adjectives and connotations. In contrast, negative descriptions, derogatory language, stigmatizing phrases and attributions are found in about 19% of the newspaper articles, as exemplified in the experimental results. Contrary to the positive effects that could be benefited by the use of positive language, the use of negative language could cause the reinforcement of stigma, resulting in discrimination and social exclusion [56, 57]. Self-stigma is another potential negative impact concerning self-perception [56]. Furthermore, help-seeking behaviors may be hampered, public misunderstanding could arise, and negative consequences may emerge against the promotion of mental health awareness.

Being careful in word choice while writing about mental health can help reduce stigma in line with the suggestions posited by APA [46], which include focusing on the person instead of on the condition as the mental health condition is only one aspect of an individual's life. The results obtained from this study's analyses show that the negative descriptions reinforced by nominalized phrases and attributive adjectives along with the derogatory labels (exemplified in experimental results) used for people with mental conditions may reflect the problem as a defining characteristic of the person. While it is recommended that "He is a person with schizophrenia." could be preferred to "He is schizophrenic.", some phrases used in some newspaper articles like 'stark mad', 'psychopath', 'schizophrenic kamikaze', 'manic depressive juvenile' have been found not to adhere to these suggestions. Related to this point, some adjectives to describe mental problems have been found to convey a tone of fear and uncertainty. For example, the use of following adjectives 'dreadful illness' and 'bizarre condition' may evoke unrealistic interpretations for ones who are not familiar with the conditions or cannot make sense out of such descriptions. Another point recommended by APA is to be specific, so specific disorders should be used whenever possible: "She was diagnosed with bipolar disorder." can be preferred to "She was mentally ill." This recommendation seems to be applicable in neutral descriptions (in the newspaper articles mentioning the specific diagnosis of the mental disorder) demonstrated by this study's findings. However, the use of expressions with negative implications and connotations such 'a group difficult to deal with' is broad and generalizing. The last recommendation of APA is related to avoiding the use of derogatory language. For instance, it is suggested that "He has a substance use disorder." can be a preferred mode of statement. Yet, the results of the current research have revealed that the use of labeling and descriptions like 'drug addict', 'rapist woman', 'yokel' and adjectives such as 'constant alcoholic, messy and miserable appearance', 'talentless' and 'spoilt' can be deemed derogatory and inappropriate based on APA's suggestions on mental health reporting.

On the whole, language used in media is influential, particularly in health communication that is targeted toward general public with the source being represented by health communicators and journalists. Among a myriad of health conditions, mental health distress is one of the most sensitive human conditions. The handling of news on these themes in the media, therefore, comes with its intrinsic challenges, some of which are due to the use of language. One problematic in this regard is the use of attributive adjectives, stigmatizing words or derogatory language which may result in the construing of negative connotations and labelling. This could further lead to stigmatizing and otherizing perceptions for those with mental health problems among other potential outcomes of hindering help-seeking behaviors, policy changes, reinforcing stigma, shaping public perception in a wrong direction, and so forth. Even though there has been a growing body of research in the news media portrayal of people having mental disorders, the number of studies concerning Türkiye is relatively limited. Hence, to contribute to this particular area of research, this study has examined the use of language in the news based on lexical analyses (including the use of adjectives, nominalizations and connotations) of the dataset comprising a total of 725 newspaper articles on mental health and psychological problems published in six different Turkish national newspapers on the scale of time-frequency of different years (2014–2019). Emphasis has been placed on the use of adjectives to describe people with mental problems along with the positive, negative and neutral use of language surrounding the problem. The results of the content analysis have shown that 35 of the newspaper articles (4.8%) out of 725 ones within the dataset include positive descriptions, attributions and connotations regarding people with mental health disorders. While positive descriptions are low in number, the number of negative descriptions, attributions and connotations is much higher, which is 134 (18.48%). 353 (48.68%) newspaper articles have been observed to include neutral descriptions. Another point of analysis concerns whether the reporting language on mental health conditions is consistent with what has been suggested by APA [46]. Literature review reveals that APA's changes in recommendations are an appropriate response to appeals by concerned bodies, and yet there is relatively little scientific research on the topic [59]. Based on this gap, it has been found that some lexical choices, especially some adjectives and nominalized phrases used in the reporting language are not in line with the recommendations of APA since some derogatory labels, generalized conditions and misleading adjectives are observed in the texts of the news articles analyzed.

These observations could point to further future work which may carry out in-depth analyses through larger datasets over more extended periods of time by relating the findings to social contexts and significant developments (i.e. political, economic and cultural) encountered during the period of analysis. This direction can further be oriented towards other media in which various genres and styles of language are used across different disciplines. Furthermore, some principles concerning non-stigmatizing language may not be consistent between groups and communities, which need to be directly engaged with due to shifting language norms so that it can be understood what the particular communities prefer [60]. Taken together, the ultimate aim is to generate and implement journalistic practices with the use of accurate, responsible sensitive and inclusive language in mental health reporting in view of the changing norms in language and sensitivities of different communities.

References

1. Bell, A.: Language and the media. Annu. Rev. Appl. Linguist. **15**, 23–41 (1995)
2. Zelizer, B.: Taking journalism seriously: News and the academy. (2004)
3. Glasgow University Media Group (GUMG): More Bad News. Routledge and Kegan Paul, London (1980)
4. Bell, A.: The Language of News Media. Blackwell, Oxford (1991)
5. Richardson, J.E.: Analysing Newspapers: An Approach from Critical Discourse Analysis. Palgrave Macmillan, Houndmills/New York (2007)
6. Cotter, C.: News Talk: Investigating the Language of Journalism. CUP, Cambridge (2010)
7. Bednarek, M., Caple, H.: News discourse (Vol. 46). A&C Black (2012)
8. Biber, D., Conrad, S.: Register. Genre and Style. Cambridge University Press, Cambridge (2009)
9. Bednarek, M.: Emotion Talk Across Corpora. Palgrave Macmillan, Houndmills/New York (2008)
10. Bowen, M., Lovell, A.: Representations of mental health disorders in print media. Br. J. Ment. Health Nurs. **2**(4), 198–202 (2013)
11. Bowen, M., Lovell, A.: Stigma: The representation of mental health in UK newspaper Twitter feeds. J. Ment. Health (2021)
12. McGinty, E.E., Kennedy-Hendricks, A., Choksy, S., Barry, C.L.: Trends in news media coverage of mental illness in the United States: 1995–2014. Health Aff. **35**(6), 1121–1129 (2016)
13. Whitley, R., Wang, J.: Good news? A longitudinal analysis of newspaper portrayals of mental illness in Canada 2005 to 2015. Can. J. Psychiatr. **62**(4), 278–285 (2017)
14. Ottewell, N.: Newspaper reporting of mental illness. J. Public Ment. Health **16**(2), 78–85 (2017)
15. Bilkay, H.İ, Yaman, Ö., Gürhan, N., Yilmaz-Bingöl, T.: A study on the representation of mental disorders in Turkish newspapers. J. Ment. Health **33**(2), 185–192 (2024)
16. Anderson, C., Robinson, E.J., Krooupa, A., Henderson, C.: Changes in newspaper coverage of mental illness from 2008 to 2016 in England. Epidemiol. Psychiatr. Sci. 1–8 (2018)

17. Goulden, R., Corker, E., Evans-Locko, S., Rose, D., Thornicroft, G., Henderson, C.: Newspaper coverage of mental illness in the UK, 1992–2008. BMC Public Health **11**, 796 (2011)
18. Chen, M., Lawrie, S.: Newspaper depictions of mental and physical health. BJPsych Bulletin **41**(6), 308–313 (2017)
19. Dursun, A.D.: Time Series Based Frequency Analysis of Violence and Criminalization Related Dynamic Mental Health Media News. In: International Conference on Computational Science and Its Applications, pp. 416–424. Springer International Publishing, Cham (2022)
20. Stuart, H.: Media portrayal of mental illness and its treatments: what effect does it have on people with mental illness? CNS Drugs **20**, 99–106 (2006)
21. Wahl, O.F.: Media Madness: Public Images of Mental Illness. Rutgers University Press, US (1995)
22. Mind: Counting the Cost: A Survey of the Impact of Media Coverage on the Lives of People with Mental Health Problems. Mind Publications, London (2000)
23. Morris, G.: Mental Health Issues and the Media: An Introduction for Health Professionals. Routledge, London, United Kingdom (2006)
24. Rhydderch, D., Krooupa, A.-M., Shefer, G., Goulden, R., et al.: Changes in newspaper coverage of mental illness from 2008 to 2014 in England. Acta Psychiatr. Scand. **134**(446), 45–52 (2016)
25. Li, A., Jiao, D., Liu, X., Zhu, T.: A comparison of the psycholinguistic styles of schizophrenia-related stigma and depression-related stigma on social media: content analysis. J. Med. Internet Res. **22**(4), e16470 (2020)
26. Clement, S., Foster, N.: Newspaper reporting on schizophrenia: A content analysis of five national newspapers at two time points. Schizophr. Res. **98**(1–3), 178–183 (2008)
27. Morris, J.: The news media. In: Smith, J. (ed.) Mental Health Issues and the Media, pp. 45–60. Academic Press, US (2022)
28. Searle, J.: A Taxonomy of Illocutionary Acts. In: Gunderson, K. (ed.) Language, Mind and Knowledge, vol. 7, pp. 344–369. University of Minnesota Press, Minneapolis (1975)
29. Angermeyer, M.C., Matschinger, H.: The stigma of mental illness: Effects of labelling on public attitudes towards people with mental disorder. Acta Psychiatr. Scand. **108**(4), 304–309 (2003)
30. Rose, D., Thornicroft, G., Pinfold, V., Kassam, A.: 250 labels used to stigmatise people with mental illness. BMC Health Serv. Res. **7**, 1–7 (2007)
31. Yap, M.B., Wright, A., Jorm, A.F.: The influence of stigma on young people's help-seeking intentions and beliefs about the helpfulness of various sources of help. Soc. Psychiatry Psychiatr. Epidemiol. **46**, 1257–1265 (2011)
32. Grover, S., Shouan, A., Sahoo, S.: Labels used for persons with severe mental illness and their stigma experience in North India. Asian J. Psychiatr. **48**, 101909 (2020)
33. Hwang, J.D., Hollingshead, K.: Crazy mad nutters: The language of mental health. In: Proceedings of the Third Workshop on Computational Linguistics and Clinical Psychology, pp. 1–63 (2016)
34. Gkotsis, G., Oellrich, A., Hubbard, T., Dobson, R., Liakata, M., Velupillai, S., Dutta, R.: The language of mental health problems in social media. In: Proceedings of the Third Workshop on Computational Linguistics and Clinical Psychology, pp. 63–73 (2016)
35. Daniele, F.: The centrality of language in health communication. Eur. Sci. J. **17**(30), 24–37 (2021)
36. Maurer, M., et al.: Lessons Learned from Developing Plain Language Summaries of Research Studies. Health Literacy Research and Practice (2021)
37. Sartorius, N., Gaebel, W., Cleveland, H.R., Stuart, H., et al.: WPA guidance on how to combat stigmatization of psychiatry and psychiatrists. World Psychiatry **9**(3), 131 (2010)

38. Campo-Arias, A., Herazo, E.: Discrimination starts with adjectives. Journal of Public Health Research **10**(4), jphr-2021 (2021)
39. Becerikli, S., Bozkurt, N.: Media Portrayals of People with Mental Disorders: A Research on Journalism Ethics in Turkey. In: Can, C., Kilimci, A. (Eds.) Social Sciences and Humanities: A Global Perspective, pp. 139–167. Detay Yayincilik, Ankara (2016)
40. Boke, O., Aker, S., Aker, A.A., Sarısoy, G.: Schizophrenia in Turkish newspapers: Retrospective scanning study. Soc. Psychiatry Psychiatr. Epidemiol. **42**, 457–461 (2007)
41. Aci, O.S., Ciydem, E., Bilgin, H., Ozaslan, Z., Tek, S.: Turkish newspaper articles mentioning people with mental illness: A retrospective study. Int. J. Soc. Psychiatry **66**(3), 215–224 (2020)
42. Dursun, A.D.: A Computational Content Analysis on Representation in Mental Health News Media with Global Perspectives. In: International Conference on Computational Science and Its Applications, pp. 105–115. Springer Nature Switzerland, Cham (2023)
43. Dursun, A.D., Tunç, A.: Mental Health News Coverage in Turkish National Newspapers with Respect to Episodic and Thematic Framing: A Retrospective Content Analysis. In: International Conference on Computational Science and Its Applications, pp. 59–71. Springer Nature Switzerland, Cham (2024)
44. Dursun, A.D.: News media portrayal of mental health and psychological problems: An analysis of daily newspapers in Türkiye (2024)
45. IBM Corp.: IBM SPSS Statistics for Windows, Version 26.0. IBM Corp, Armonk, NY (2019)
46. American Psychiatric Association: Words matter: Reporting on mental health conditions (2015)
47. Clark, A., Fox, C., Lappin, S.: The Handbook of Computational Linguistics and Natural Language Processing. John Wiley & Sons, Hoboken (2013)
48. Schubert, L.: Computational Linguistics, The Stanford Encyclopedia of Philosophy (Spring 2020 Edition), In: Zalta, E.N. (ed.), (2020). https://plato.stanford.edu/archives/spr2020/entries/computational-linguistics/, last accessed 2025/3/27
49. Finch, G.: Linguistic Terms and Concepts. Palgrave, New York (2000)
50. White, P.: Feelings and JEA Sequences. Psychol. Metaphys. **315** (2017)
51. Yule, G.: The Study of Language. Cambridge University Press, Cambridge (2022)
52. Saeed, J.I.: Semantics, vol. 25. John Wiley & Sons, US (2015)
53. Gómez, P.C.: Statistical Methods in Language and Linguistic Research, pp. 1–273. Equinox, UK (2013)
54. Slade, M.: Mental illness and well-being: The central importance of positive psychology and recovery approaches. BMC Health Serv. Res. **10**, 1–14 (2010)
55. Zhang, H., Firdaus, A.: What Does Media Say about Mental Health: A Literature Review of Media Coverage on Mental Health. Journalism and Media **5**(3), 967–979 (2024)
56. Angermeyer, M.C., Matschinger, H.: Causal beliefs and attitudes to people with schizophrenia: Trend analysis based on data from two population surveys in Germany. Br. J. Psychiatry **186**(4), 331–334 (2005)
57. Ahad, A.A., Sanchez-Gonzalez, M., Junquera, P.: Understanding and addressing mental health stigma across cultures for improving psychiatric care: A narrative review. Cureus **15**(5) (2023)
58. Corrigan, P.W., Watson, A.C.: The paradox of self-stigma and mental illness. Clin. Psychol. Sci. Pract. **9**(1), 35 (2002)
59. Mallinson, M.G., Giannakopoulou, A., Clements, A.J.: The impact of linguistic form of labels on desire for social distance in mental health. Int. J. Ment. Heal. Addict. **22**(4), 1947–1963 (2024)
60. Volkow, N.D., Gordon, J.A., Koob, G.F.: Choosing appropriate language to reduce the stigma around mental illness and substance use disorders. Neuropsychopharmacol. **46**(13), 2230–2232 (2021)

Arabic Sign Language Recognition Using Image-Based Deep Learning and Edge User-Centered Interface

Ahmad Alzu'bi[1(✉)], Amjad Albashayreh[2], and Lojin Bani Younis[1]

[1] Department of Computer Science, Jordan University of Science and Technology, Irbid, Jordan
`agalzubi@just.edu.jo, lhbaniyounis19@cit.just.edu.jo`
[2] Faculty of Information Technology, Applied Science Private University, Amman, Jordan
`a_albashayreh@asu.edu.jo`

Abstract. A growing trend in assisted living involves the use of machine learning techniques to recognize hand gesture patterns tailored for people with disabilities. However, in recognition systems, the limited availability of sign language data gives rise to both data scarcity and privacy concerns. In this paper, a federated deep learning architecture is proposed for Arabic sign language recognition, aimed at addressing the challenge of deciphering the meanings conveyed by image-based hand gestures. The distributed client-server paradigm of federated learning is based on a distributed stochastic gradient descent (SGD) optimizer with a federated averaging mechanism. In addition, an interactive user interface is designed to manage distributed learning on smartphones through a client-server model, where several edge nodes collaborate to jointly learn the discriminating features of confidential data without breaching its privacy. This interactive interface improves accessibility for people with deafness or impairment using image gestures and navigation panels. Several deep learning backbones were employed in the procedure of transfer learning to fit the optimum fine-tuning setup while maximizing recognition accuracy. The experimental results show the effectiveness of the proposed FL model, achieving an accuracy of 98.80% by the FL-VGG19 configuration. There is also a significant reduction in the number of training epochs and rounds, resulting in a decrease in the computational complexity for convergence. This demonstrates the model's capabilities in recognizing Arabic sign language and improving the communication experience for people with disabilities.

Keywords: Federated deep learning · Arabic sign recognition · Smartphone accessibility · Gesture user interface · Communication disabilities

1 Introduction

Sign language (SL) is a visual communication method utilizing gestures, facial expressions, and body movements used by individuals with disabilities, such as deaf or hard-of-hearing individuals, to convey meaning. Because sign language is the primary mode of communication for millions of people worldwide, there is a lot of interest in the potential applications of robust sign language recognition (SLR) tools [1]. Considering the broad range of possibilities, such assisted living solutions could go beyond only translation by facilitating accessible sign language broadcasts, fostering the development of responsive devices that operate seamlessly via sign language commands, and even pioneering sophisticated systems specifically designed to assist individuals with impairments in performing daily tasks more independently. In recent years, there has been a significant focus on the SLR domain with various approaches [2–4] proposed to address the communication challenges faced by people with disabilities. Deep neural networks (DNNs) have emerged as a promising technological advancement for researchers, poised to change the SLR [5]. These networks offer the potential for ground-breaking advances in the automated recognition of hand gestures and signals used in interactions between people who have difficulty speaking or hearing.

However, there are challenges along the way to develop SLR tools that are useful and broadly applicable. Maintaining the accuracy, dependability, and speed of the interpretation algorithms remains a top priority. Errors or delays in interpretation can prevent effective communication and usability; therefore, achieving a delicate balance between precision and real-time processing is critical. Advances in technology and research endeavors are facilitating the ongoing exploration of novel approaches, datasets, and model architectures to improve the performance of SLR systems [6–8]. Collaboration among experts in linguistics, computer vision, and machine learning is crucial to advance this field [9]. Additionally, the presence of extensive databases that encompass a diverse array of sign language gestures is vital for the accurate training and evaluation of SLR systems.

Federated learning (FL) is an emerging paradigm of machine learning associated with decentralized methods, which is shown to be an effective approach to training shared global models [10,11]. FL methods entail coordinating the training of a central model from a collection of participating devices. When training data is sourced from user interactions with mobile applications, for example, a significant application scenario for FL arises [10]. In this context, FL enables mobile phones to collectively learn a shared prediction model while retaining all training data on the device, effectively separating the machine learning capability from the requirement of storing data in the cloud. Instead of storing training data in the cloud, it is kept on users' mobile devices, which act as intelligent edge nodes, performing computations on their local data to update a global model. This approach goes beyond the use of local models for mobile device predictions by bringing model training to the device level.

FL has enormous potential to transform the development of SLR systems. In the context of SLR, this approach provides a promising solution to the challenges of privacy preservation, data diversity, and model adaptability [12]. Individuals in the deaf and hard-of-hearing communities may be hesitant to share their information due to the sensitivity of sign language data. FL addresses this issue by allowing model training to take place locally on the devices of users or decentralized servers. Furthermore, FL allows for the creation of more diverse datasets without the need to centralize data from multiple sources. SLR models trained using federated learning are expected to benefit from decentralized data from a variety of geographic locations, cultural backgrounds, and signing styles. This could make the SLR systems more reliable, allowing them to take into account variations in sign language gestures and expressions effectively.

Arabic sign language (ArSL) encompasses a rich vocabulary and intricate structures. Much like other languages, it involves the combination of hand shapes, orientations, motion, and facial expressions to convey various meanings. To improve the accuracy of Arabic sign language recognition, ElBadawy et al. [13] emphasized the effectiveness of a behavior-based feature extractor and 3D CNN for recognizing gestures in ArSL using depth map data. Zakariah et al. [14] tested different pre-trained models on the ArASL2018 dataset [15]. Saleh and Issa [16] also used transfer learning and fine-tuning of pretrained CNN models, including VGG16 and ResNet152. Similarly, Kamruzzaman [17] proposed a vision-based method to recognize Arabic hand sign-based letters and translate them into spoken Arabic using deep CNNs. Alawwad et al. [18] examined a faster RCNN framework with VGG-16 and ResNet-18 networks, achieving an accuracy of 93.4%. Hayani et al. [19] presented a CNN-based model to identify ArSL characters, including both the alphabet and numerical digits with 2030 images of numbers (from 0 to 10) and 5839 images of letters. Aldhahri et al. [20] developed a model to recognize Arabic letters using MobileNet. Several 3D-based SLR systems [21–23] used the depth and motion information captured in the three-dimensional space, showing efforts to improve communication accessibility for individuals who rely on sign language.

Although various deep learning algorithms have been applied to recognize Arabic sign language, prior studies did not employ federated learning architectures. Their reliance on centralized data storage and processing mechanisms may limit them in meeting the growing demand for decentralized, privacy-preserving, and scalable solutions in ARSL model development. This motivated us to address this gap by using and investigating a federated deep learning model to recognize the Arabic sign language, ensuring privacy for individuals with disabilities, and providing high performance with low time complexity. The primary contribution of this research lies in the introduction of an efficient federated deep learning pipeline for Arabic sign language recognition based on still images. In addition, an interactive use interface is designed to improve accessibility for individuals with communication disabilities and to facilitate federated deep learning of ArSL data through smartphones, serving as intelligent edge nodes. This allows model training to take place locally on the local devices of users or decentralized servers. This method will also ensure that sensitive data remains on users' devices and that only model updates are transmitted to a central server, protecting the privacy of confidential information. Therefore, this approach enables for more accurate and robust recognition of gestures in diverse environments and conditions. Finally, optimization of training time complexity is achieved through comprehensive analytical experiments that utilize transfer learning with various deep learning backbones.

The remaining part of this paper is organized as follows. Section 2 introduces the methodology of the FL-based framework, Sect. 3 presents the experimental results, Sect. 4 discusses the main findings, and Sect. 5 concludes this paper.

2 Methodology

The method we adopted begins by processing the ArSL images. Then, the architecture of federated deep learning is constructed, leveraging several pretrained deep learning backbones. An interactive user interface is designed for the FL-based ArSLR model to facilitate the user experience and enhance the online learning of extracted gesture features through smartphones. The performance of the proposed FL-based model is finally evaluated using several standard metrics in various setups. These phases are detailed in the following subsections.

2.1 Dataset Preparation

The benchmarking dataset used in this work is the Arabic Alphabet Sign Language (ARASL) dataset [15] that comprises 54,049 images of hand gestures representing the Arabic alphabets, designed to aid the deaf in comprehending the language and freely expressing their thoughts and emotions. This dataset includes 32 classes corresponding to Arabic letters, each class containing a specific number of images, as detailed in Table 1. A sample of ARASL hand-gesture images is shown in Fig. 1.

In the data preparation phase, the collections of hand gesture images have been further processed to be suitable for the configuration of federated learning architecture. The image processing procedure includes the use of a custom dataset module to simplify the transfer learning process. This module initializes the data and outlines images and labels, ensuring efficient data preparation. The data undergo a transformation pipeline consisting of three stages: image resizing, tensor conversion, and normalization. Resizing ensures uniform dimensions for all images, while tensor conversion converts data into a multidimensional array suitable for deep learning frameworks. The normalization process sets pixel values to a consistent scale between 0 and 1, handling explosive gradients during training, and improving the model's resilience to fluctuations in pixel intensity and color across different images. Finally, the image collection is divided into 70% for training, 10% for validation, and 20% for testing. The three evaluation splits are further subdivided into multiple subsets for each processing node, an essential phase for emulating distinct datasets on decentralized clients within the federated learning framework.

Table 1. The classes and images of Arabic alphabet signs in the ASASL dataset.

#	Letter in English Script	Letter in Arabic Script	Images	#	Letter in English Script	Letter in Arabic Script	Images
1	Alif	(ألف) أ	1672	17	Za	(ظاء) ظ	1723
2	Ba	(باء) ب	1791	18	Ain	(عَين) ع	2114
3	Ta	(تاء) ت	1838	19	Ghayn	(غَين) غ	1977
4	Tha	(ثاء) ث	1766	20	Fa	(فاء) ف	1955
5	Jim	(جيم) ج	1552	21	Qaf	(قاف) ق	1705
6	Ha	(حاء) ح	1526	22	Kaf	(كاف) ك	1774
7	Kha	(خاء) خ	1607	23	Lam	(لام) ل	1832
8	Dal	(دال) د	1634	24	Mim	(ميم) م	1765
9	Dhal	(ذال) ذ	1582	25	Nun	(نون) ن	1819
10	Ra	(راء) ر	1659	26	Ha	(هاء) ه	1592
11	Zay	(زاي) ز	1374	27	Waw	(واو) و	1371
12	Sin	(سين) س	1638	28	Ya	(ياء) ئ	1722
13	Shin	(شين) ش	1507	29	Taa	(ة) ة	1791
14	Sad	(صاد) ص	1895	30	Al	(ال) ال	1343
15	Dad	(ضاد) ض	1670	31	Laa	(لا) لا	1746
16	Ta	(طاء) ط	1816	32	Yaa	(ياء) ياء	1293

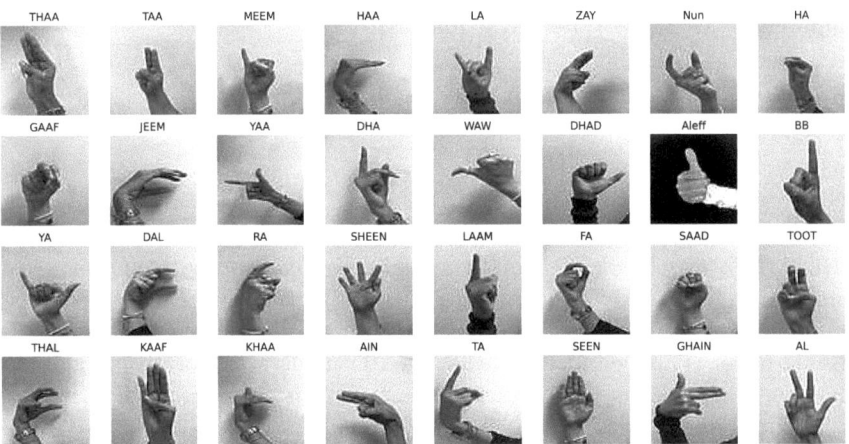

Fig. 1. Sample images from the ARASL dataset with the corresponding Arabic letters.

2.2 Federated Deep Learning Architecture

As can be observed in Fig. 2, the generic pipeline of federated deep learning consists of two main components which are a central server with a global model and multiple clients (M clients) with multiple local models. Each client (indexed from 0 to M) possesses a subset of hand-gesture images D_i consisting of n_i labeled samples drawn from a distribution D_i over input space X and label space Y. The learning model $h_\theta : X \rightarrow Y$ is parameterized by $\theta \in \mathbb{R}^D$. The loss of the model on a sample $(x,y) \in X \times Y$ is denoted by '$(h_\theta(x), y)$, in which we used cross-entropy loss. The loss of the model parameters θ in the i-th client is the average loss of the model h_θ in the samples in D_i, calculated as $f_i(\theta) = \frac{1}{n_i} \sum_{j=1}^{n_i} l(h_\theta(x_{i,j}), y_{i,j}))$, where $(x_{i,j}, y_{i,j})$ represents the j-th sample in D_i. This server configuration aims to leverage data from all clients to identify models that minimize loss $f_i(\theta)$ for each client. To do this, the typical method entails choosing a single model θ that minimizes the average of client losses weighted by the number of samples as follows:

$$\min_\theta \frac{1}{N} \sum_{i=1}^{N} \frac{1}{n_i} \sum_{j \in \hat{D}_i} `(h_\theta(x_{i,j}), y_{i,j})), \tag{1}$$

where $N = \sum_{i=1}^{M} n_i$. Due to communication and privacy constraints, clients cannot share their local data $\hat{D}_i$. Upon receiving θ_t, each client performs local computations as follows:

$$\theta_{t,i,s+1} = \theta_{t,i,s} - \alpha g_{t,i,s}(\theta_{t,i,s}) \tag{2}$$

for $s = 1, \ldots, \tau - 1$, where τ represents the number of local steps, $\theta_{t,i,0} = \theta_t$, $g_{t,i,s}(\theta_{t,i,s})$ is the stochastic gradient of f_i evaluated at $\theta_{t,i,s}$ using b samples from $\hat{D}_i$. The clients then transmit $\theta_{t,i,\tau}$ back to the server. Finally, the server computes the next global iterate as follows:

$$\theta_{t+1} = \frac{1}{N_t} \sum_{i \in I_t} n_i \theta_{t,i,\tau}, \tag{3}$$

where $N_t := \sum_{i \in I_t} n_i$.

In this paper, federated averaging (FedAvg) [24] is applied for federated learning with a network of five clients. The FedAvg approach improves communication efficiency by performing multiple ($\tau \geq 2$) local updates between communication rounds in distributed stochastic gradient descent (D-SGD). The training phase is applied in 10 epochs and 10 rounds with iterative model modifications. This learning procedure entails thorough data preparation, followed by an equal distribution of transformed data among the five clients. In each iteration t, a subset I_t of $m \leq M$ clients is uniformly sampled by the server. These selected clients receive the current global parameters θ_t and perform multiple stochastic gradient descent (SGD) steps on their local data starting from

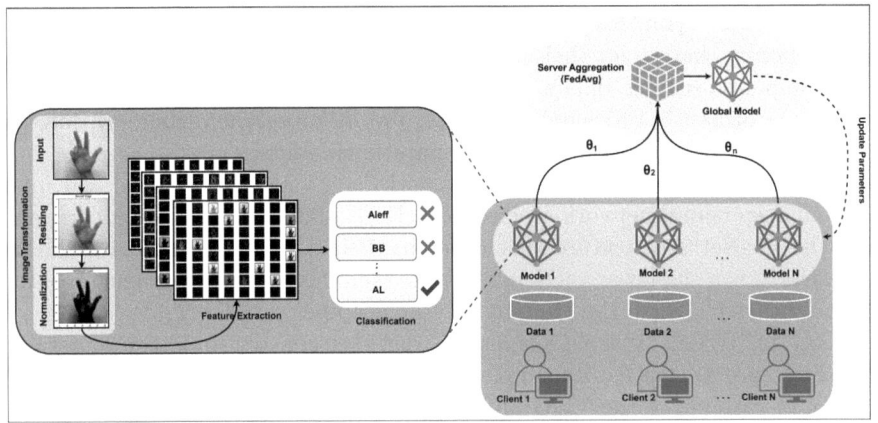

Fig. 2. The pipeline of the proposed FL-based ArSL Recognition.

θ_t. With this setup, we maintain that local training occurs on individual client nodes without the need to share raw image data of people with disabilities.

In addition, the performance of deep convolutional models is evaluated during training using validation datasets split equally between clients to assess accuracy and generalization capability. Each client then transmits its model updates in the form of gradients to the central server. These updates represent the gradients of the local model's parameters concerning the loss function, illustrating how the model's parameters should be adjusted to minimize the steepest increase in the loss function. The server computes the subsequent global parameters θ_{t+1} as a weighted average of the client updates. This procedure harmonizes the local contributions of each client, resulting in an improved global hand-gesture image classification. The global model re-transmits its updates to all local models on the client side. The ten-round federated learning cycle includes local training, model modifications, aggregation, and distribution. This iterative approach enables the global image classification model of Arabic signs to converge on optimal performance, incorporating knowledge from various client datasets.

2.3 Deep Learning Backbones

The procedure of transfer learning adopted for the FL-based Arabic sign recognition model is initialized with seven distinct deep learning backbones, which are: EfficientNet-B, EfficientNet-B1, EfficientNet-B2, ResNet32, ResNet50, VGG16, and VGG19. These models were incorporated into the federated framework to facilitate the training and evaluation process on a federated network of participating client devices. Each model variation was distributed among the client devices to take advantage of their local subset of hand-gesture images for fine-tuning and updating the global model. The main characteristics of the pre-trained deep convolutional architectures are as follows:

- **EfficientNet** [25]: EfficientNet is a family of convolutional neural network architectures known for their efficiency and accuracy. These models are based on compound scaling, balancing network depth, width, and resolution to optimize performance. EfficientNet B0, B1, and B2 represent variants within this family, with varying depths and computational efficiency.
- **ResNet** [26]: ResNet (Residual Network) is a widely recognized and influential deep neural network architecture. ResNet32 and ResNet50 are variants of the ResNet architecture that differ in their depth and number of layers. ResNet32 is a shallower version, while ResNet50 is deeper, leveraging residual blocks that facilitate the training of very deep networks.
- **VGG** [27]: VGG (Visual Geometry Group) is a convolutional neural network architecture known for its simplicity and effectiveness. VGG16 and VGG19 refer to variants of the VGG architecture, differing in the number of layers. VGG16 has 16 layers, and VGG19 has 19 layers, both employing small 3×3 convolutional filters and max-pooling layers.

2.4 Edge User-Centered Interface

Within the federated learning paradigm designed for ArSL recognition, there is a demand to ensure optimal accessibility on edge nodes, or clients. This objective aims to ensure that applications are accessible to a wide range of individuals, regardless of their expertise, skills, or technical specifications of the devices they use. The user-centered approach needs to be followed to design a mainstream solution that performs its intended function; otherwise, there is a chance that a solution will need to be re-engineered to accommodate the unique demands of a certain set of individuals [28], such as people with disabilities.

When discussing the incorporation of a decentralized learning model and assistive technologies, it is important to note the potential benefits of integrating accessibility features into everyday applications. Some solutions proposed by researchers include the use of IoT ([29] to facilitate assistance and technology integration, thereby enhancing quality of life and connectivity. However, in this work, we aim to provide a user-centered interface design for facilitating the procedure of the new data collection and processing on the client side, i.e., an online learning of Arabic sign language. Therefore, improving accessibility in mobile devices will make ArSL recognition applications accessible to as many people as possible. Accessibility is a sub-characteristic of usability [30], and this requirement will be met by the interactive FL-based interface that we build, which enables users with communication impairments to communicate with the recognition system through edge devices such as smartphones.

Figure 3 shows the design of the processing interface offered to the clients involved in the proposed FL-based ArSL recognition system. It demonstrates the generic communication procedure initiated from the server side by broadcasting the global model to all participating edge devices. Each edge device, e.g., smartphone, confirms joining the training phase and therefore permits the application of the recognition model on the local data, i.e., sign images. The progress

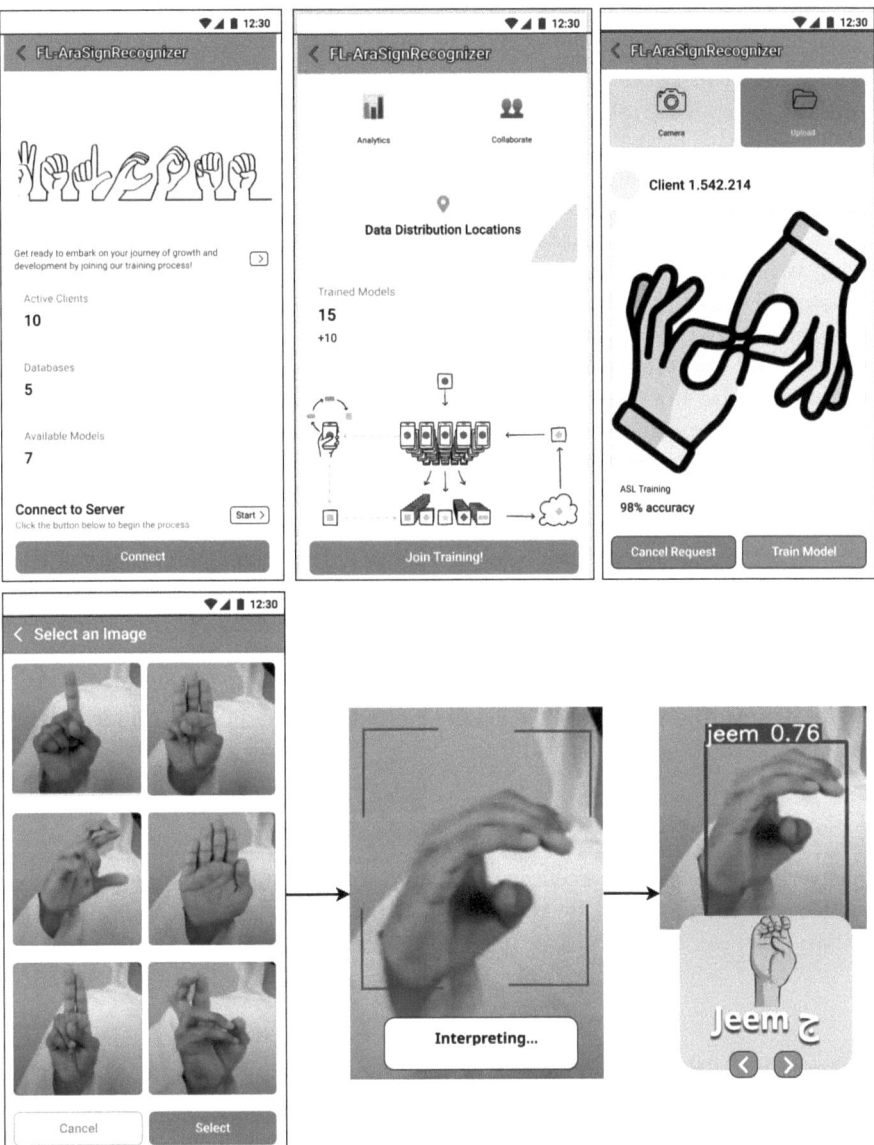

Fig. 3. The user-centered interface proposed for the FL-based ArSL Recognition.

of training is shown on the client's device, and the central server aggregates the results by which it updates the global model and broadcasts it again in the next training round. On the client side, there is the ability to submit and recognize a sign image with the final trained model. Finally, the interactive interface shows the recognition result of any Arabic sign image submitted to the system.

2.5 Evaluation Metrics

A range of performance metrics are used to assess the proposed FL-based deep model to recognize Arabic sign gestures. This comprehensive evaluation offers insights into the model's performance across diverse classification characteristics, ensuring its accuracy and capability to handle various scenarios and classes. The primary metric obtained in this work is the classification accuracy of ArSL images. A high level of accuracy suggests that the model performs well in identifying various hand movements and generating fewer classification errors. True Positive (TP) in ASL recognition occurs when the model accurately predicts the letter represented by a sign gesture. For example, if the sign gesture represents the letter "A" and the model correctly classified it as "A", it is considered a true positive. A False Positive (FP) occurs when a model predicts a letter that does not represent the sign gesture. For example, if the sign gesture represents the letter "A" but the model predicts "B", it is classified as a False Positive. True Negative (TN) occurs when the model accurately predicts that a sign gesture does not represent a specific letter. For instance, if the sign gesture does not correlate with any letter, the classification result will be a True Negative. Finally, a False Negative (FN) occurs when a model fails to accurately predict the correct letter represented by a sign gesture, such as predicting "A" instead of "K" or predicting a different letter, resulting in a false negative. Based on these essential metrics, the accuracy, precision, recall, and F1-Score are calculated.

Accuracy: this measures the number of correct predictions divided by the total number of predictions, and it is calculated as follows:

$$Accuracy = \frac{TP + TN}{TP + TN + FP + FN} \qquad (4)$$

Precision: it is the percentage of true positive predictions among all positive occurrences predicted by the model, which determines how many detected positive cases are truly positive. It can be calculated as follows:

$$Precision = \frac{TP}{TP + FP} \qquad (5)$$

Recall: it is the percentage of true positive predictions, calculated by determining how many positive instances the model correctly predicted. It can be calculated as follows:

$$Recall = \frac{TP}{TP + FN} \qquad (6)$$

F1-Score: this metric balances precision and recall with the best value at 1 and the worst value at 0, and it is calculated as follows:

$$F1 - score = \frac{2 * Precision * Recall}{Precision + Recall} \qquad (7)$$

3 Results

3.1 Experiments Configuration

All experiments were carried out in a cloud-based environment using a PyTorch implementation. Seven different deep learning models were used as part of the federated deep learning framework. Several experiments were performed to identify the optimal hyperparameters for the models, ensuring a fair and consistent environment to evaluate their performance based on average time, accuracy, precision, recall, and F1-score. The models were compared under identical conditions and using identical hyperparameters. Each experiment uses 64 data samples, involving five clients trained over ten epochs. The federated averaging method aggregates gradients on the server side, while categorical cross entropy is used as a loss function. Softmax is used as an activation function, and stochastic gradient descent is used as a primary optimizer with a learning rate of 0.01. Table 2 provides a summary of the hyperparameters used for the deep FL models.

Table 2. The experimental hyperparameters.

Hyperparameter	Value
Aggregation Method	FedAvg
No. of Clients	5
No. of Epochs	10
No. of Rounds	10
Entropy	Categorical Cross-Entropy
Activation Function	Softmax
Optimizer	SGD
Learning Rate	0.01
Batch Size	64

3.2 Experimental Results

Seven experimental setups have been carried out using three versions of EfficientNet (b0, b1, and b2), two versions of ResNet (ResNet32 and ResNet50), and two versions of VGG (VGG16 and VGG19). The performance of each model has been evaluated under a consistent configuration with identical hyperparameters. Figures 4 and 5 depict the validation and testing accuracies for each model over ten rounds. The VGG models show consistent improvement from the initial to the final round, whereas the EfficientNet models demonstrate slower progress initially but show significant improvement after the fourth round.

Table 3 summarizes the performance results of all FL-based models. This evaluation procedure provides a detailed understanding of the model's performance across various classification characteristics, ensuring its correctness and

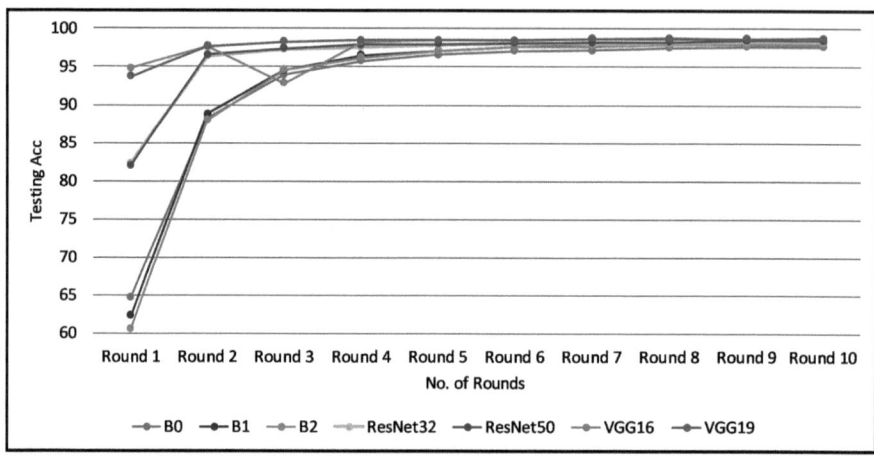

Fig. 4. The testing accuracy per round achieved by the FL-based ArSL classifiers.

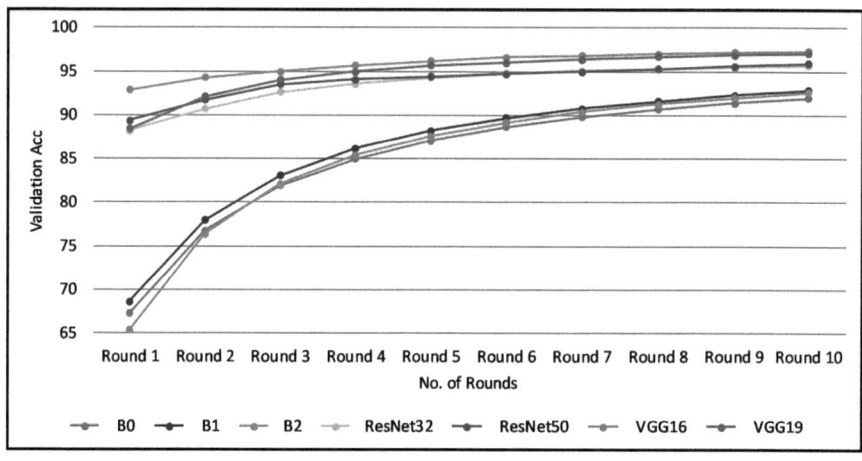

Fig. 5. The validation accuracy per round achieved by the FL-based ArSL classifiers.

ability to handle various scenarios and classes in the dataset. However, due to the imbalanced nature of the Arabic sign language dataset, the model's performance is assessed using accuracy and macro-averaging metrics. In imbalanced circumstances, macro-averaging is very useful since it treats all classes equally without being affected by the majority class. The FL-VGG19 has the highest testing performance, achieving an accuracy of 98.8%, a precision of 98.79%, a recall of 98.78%, and an F1-score of 98.78%. However, FL-VGG16 and FL-VGG19 showed comparable performance in all metrics. FL-VGG16 achieved slightly higher validation accuracy, with a marginal difference of 0.2%, underscoring the minor discrepancies between the performance of the two models.

Table 3. The Performance results of the proposed deep FL Models in 10 rounds.

Model	Val Acc	Test Acc	Precision	Recall	F1-Score	Client Time[1]	Round Time[2]
FL-B0	92.00	97.70	97.74	97.72	97.72	44	3.67
FL-B1	92.90	98.10	98.16	98.14	98.14	55	4.58
FL-B2	92.60	98.00	98.02	98.00	98.00	57	4.75
FL-ResNet32	95.70	98.30	98.28	98.26	98.27	**33**	**2.75**
FL-ResNet50	95.90	98.50	98.46	98.46	98.46	60	5
FL-VGG16	**97.30**	98.70	98.72	98.71	98.71	60	5
FL-VGG19	97.10	**98.80**	**98.79**	**98.78**	**98.78**	65	5.41

[1] Training time per client in *seconds*.
[2] Training time per round in *minutes*.

In addition to the accuracy rates reported in the training phase, we show the time taken on average to train each client and train the whole model in every round. In the validation and testing stages, all FL-EfficientNet models demonstrate high accuracy rates; however, FL-B0 performs marginally worse than FL-B1 and FL-B2. This could be due to architectural variations and hyperparameter optimization. B1 and B2 have greater depth and width, allowing them to capture more intricate patterns in Arabic sign images. However, FL-B0 achieved the classification results in 44 s and 3.67 min on average for the epochs training time and the rounds training time, respectively. Likewise, FL-ResNet23 demonstrated the shortest training times compared to all other FL-based models under the same experimental setups.

4 Discussion

An important finding concluded from the experimental results is that when deploying real-time applications across distributed execution environments, it is essential to weigh the trade-off between the computational complexity and the accuracy of the model.

We also discuss the performance results in the context of previous related work. Table 4 presents a comparison of the performance of our proposed federated deep learning model with related Arabic Sign Language (ArSL) approaches evaluated on the ARASL2018 dataset. It outlines the key features and performance results documented during the testing phase. As can be observed, the proposed FL-VGG19 model outperforms the other approaches in both the accuracy rates and the training time. In this regard, FL-ResNet32 also demonstrates the ability to accurately recognize Arabic sign language, achieving an accuracy of 98.3% with an average training time of 33 s over 10 epochs. Additionally, it requires approximately 28 min on average to train the entire model over 10 rounds with 5 distributed clients, i.e., edge nodes.

It should be noted that some other related studies have evaluated and reported the accuracy of ArSL tasks; however, specifically in the training and

Table 4. A comparison of test accuracy with the related works on ArASL2018.

Work	Method	Model	Test Acc.	Prec.	Recall	F1-score	Epochs
[17]	Transfer Learning	CNN	0.900	N/A	N/A	N/A	100
[20]	Transfer Learning	Mobile-Net	0.945	0.984	0.983	0.984	15
[14]	Transfer learning	EfficientNetB4	0.950	0.956	0.962	0.950	30
ours	Federated Learning	FL-VGG19	0.988	0.987	0.987	0.987	10
ours	Federated Learning	FL-ResNet32	0.983	0.982	0.982	0.982	10

validation phases. Bani Baker et al. [31] suggested using deep transfer learning using ResNet50V2 and InceptionV3 to classify Arabic signs and reported an accuracy of 100% during the training and validation phases. Saleh and Issa [16] also demonstrated the training and validation accuracy rates obtained by transfer learning, achieving a validation accuracy of 99.57% for ResNet152. However, no accuracy results were provided for the testing phase, which is the appropriate performance indicator for unseen Arabic sign language images.

As artificial intelligence developers continue advancing sign language recognition technologies, human-computer interaction (HCI)researchers need to initiate exploration of future interaction possibilities of this technology. Specifically, there is a necessity to comprehend users' desires regarding this technology and to devise optimal interaction designs. Therefore, the sophisticated design of an interactive interface should align with the HCI standards. For example, while native mobile applications offer numerous advantages, not all are accessible, which means that they do not facilitate easy navigation for users [32], particularly those with disabilities or diminished visual capabilities over the years. Further accessibility improvements for people with disabilities could be achieved by facilitating mobility assistance systems in public environments [33], and establishing guidelines to mitigate the emergence of accessibility barriers when designing FL-based recognition systems on edge devices [34].

As a result, the proposed federated deep learning solution stands out as being very successful among the methods discussed. It achieved the best accuracy while maintaining the crucial practice of preserving patient data privacy, a feature that is absent in other techniques. This collaborative distributed learning approach enables efficient model training across remote devices, addressing current concerns about data privacy in data-driven applications. When initialized with several pre-trained deep neural architectures, the federated learning model demonstrated its capability to recognize Arabic sign images, surpassing the state-of-the-art in terms of recognition accuracy and computational complexity.

5 Conclusion

This paper introduces a federated deep learning model aimed at improving communication for people with disabilities by recognizing Arabic sign language and interpreting the meanings of image-based hand gestures. The experimental results revealed that the proposed FL-based framework achieves robust performance with diverse deep learning models, demonstrating efficiency in terms of training time and recognition accuracy. FL-VGG19 achieved the highest test accuracy of 98.8%, with an average training time of 5 min per round across 5 clients, and approximately 65 s per 10 epochs. However, FL-ResNet32 achieved the best time complexity by minimizing the average time for each client per epoch and the total time per round. The further investigation aims to improve recognition and interpretation of Arabic sign language gestures by integrating multimodal data sources, which could improve collaborative learning of sign expressions.

References

1. Al-Qurishi, M., Khalid, T., Souissi, R.: Deep learning for sign language recognition: current techniques, benchmarks, and open issues. IEEE Access **9**, 126917–126951 (2021)
2. Aly, S., Aly, W.: DeepArSLR: a novel signer-independent deep learning framework for isolated Arabic sign language gestures recognition. IEEE Access **8**, 83199–83212 (2020)
3. Shin, J., et al.: Korean sign language recognition using transformer-based deep neural network. Appl. Sci. **13**, 3029 (2023)
4. Al-Hammadi, M., Muhammad, G., Abdul, W., Alsulaiman, M., Bencherif, M., Mekhtiche, M.: Hand gesture recognition for sign language using 3DCNN. IEEE Access **8**, 79491–79509 (2020)
5. Cui, R., Liu, H., Zhang, C.: A deep neural framework for continuous sign language recognition by iterative training. IEEE Trans. Multimedia **21**, 1880–1891 (2019)
6. Rastgoo, R., Kiani, K., Escalera, S.: Sign language recognition: a deep survey. Expert Syst. Appl. **164**, 113794 (2021)
7. Alaftekin, M., Pacal, I., Cicek, K.: Real-time sign language recognition based on YOLO algorithm. Neural Comput. Appl. **36**, 7609–7624 (2024)
8. Cheok, M., Omar, Z., Jaward, M.: A review of hand gesture and sign language recognition techniques. Int. J. Mach. Learn. Cybern. **10**, 131–153 (2019)
9. Bragg, D., et al.: Sign language recognition, generation, and translation: an interdisciplinary perspective. In: Proceedings of The 21st International ACM SIGACCESS Conference on Computers and Accessibility, pp. 16–31 (2019)
10. Pei, J., Liu, W., Li, J., Wang, L., Liu, C.: A review of federated learning methods in heterogeneous scenarios. IEEE Trans. Consum. Electron. (2024)
11. Kairouz, P., et al.: Advances and open problems in federated learning. Found. Trends® Mach. Learn. **14**, 1–210 (2021)
12. Li, T., Sahu, A., Talwalkar, A., Smith, V.: Federated learning: challenges, methods, and future directions. IEEE Signal Process. Mag. **37**, 50–60 (2020)
13. ElBadawy, M., Elons, A., Shedeed, H., Tolba, M.: Arabic sign language recognition with 3D convolutional neural networks. In: 2017 Eighth International Conference on Intelligent Computing and Information Systems (ICICIS), pp. 66–71 (2017)
14. Zakariah, M., Alotaibi, Y., Koundal, D., Guo, Y., Mamun Elahi, M., et al.: Sign language recognition for Arabic alphabets using transfer learning technique. Comput. Intell. Neurosci. **2022** (2022)

15. Latif, G., Mohammad, N., Alghazo, J., AlKhalaf, R., AlKhalaf, R.: ArASL: Arabic alphabets sign language dataset. Data Brief **23**, 103777 (2019)
16. Saleh, Y., Issa, G.: Arabic sign language recognition through deep neural networks fine-tuning. International Association of Online Engineering (2020)
17. Kamruzzaman, M., et al.: Arabic sign language recognition and generating Arabic speech using convolutional neural network. Wirel. Commun. Mob. Comput. **2020** (2020)
18. Alawwad, R., Bchir, O., Ismail, M.: Arabic sign language recognition using faster R-CNN. Int. J. Adv. Comput. Sci. Appl. **12** (2021)
19. Hayani, S., Benaddy, M., El Meslouhi, O., Kardouchi, M.: Arab sign language recognition with convolutional neural networks. In: 2019 International Conference of Computer Science and Renewable Energies (ICCSRE), pp. 1–4 (2019)
20. Aldhahri, E., et al.: Arabic sign language recognition using convolutional neural network and MobileNet. Arab. J. Sci. Eng. **48**, 2147–2154 (2023)
21. Boukdir, A., Benaddy, M., Ellahyani, A., Meslouhi, O., Kardouchi, M.: 3D gesture segmentation for word-level Arabic sign language using large-scale RGB video sequences and autoencoder convolutional networks. Signal Image Video Process. **16**, 2055–2062 (2022)
22. Ahmed, M., Zaidan, B., Zaidan, A., Salih, M., Al-Qaysi, Z., Alamoodi, A.: Based on wearable sensory device in 3D-printed humanoid: a new real-time sign language recognition system. Measurement **168**, 108431 (2021)
23. Sharma, S., Kumar, K.: ASL-3DCNN: American sign language recognition technique using 3-D convolutional neural networks. Multimedia Tools Appl. **80**(17), 26319–26331 (2021). https://doi.org/10.1007/s11042-021-10768-5
24. McMahan, B., Moore, E., Ramage, D., Hampson, S., Arcas, B.: Communication-efficient learning of deep networks from decentralized data. Artif. Intell. Stat. 1273–1282 (2017)
25. Tan, M., Le, Q.: EfficientNet: rethinking model scaling for convolutional neural networks. Int. Conf. Mach. Learn. 6105–6114 (2019)
26. He, K., Zhang, X., Ren, S., Sun, J.: Deep residual learning for image recognition. In: Proceedings of the IEEE Conference on Computer Vision and Pattern Recognition, pp. 770–778 (2016)
27. Simonyan, K., Zisserman, A.: Very deep convolutional networks for large-scale image recognition. ArXiv Preprint arXiv:1409.1556 (2014)
28. Nierling, L., João-Maia, M., Bratan, T., Kukk, P., Cas, J., Capari, L., et al.: Assistive Technologies For People With Disabilities–Part III: Perspectives, Needs and Opportunities: European Parliamentary Research Service (EPRS) (2018). [cited 2021 March 4]. (2018)
29. Žilak, M., Car, Ž, Čuljak, I.: A systematic literature review of handheld augmented reality solutions for people with disabilities. Sensors **22**, 7719 (2022)
30. Iso, I.: IEC 25010: 2011 systems and software engineering–systems and software quality requirements and evaluation (square)–system and software quality models. Int. Organ. Stand. **34**, 208 (2011)
31. Bani Baker, Q., Alqudah, N., Alsmadi, T., Awawdeh, R., et al.: Image-based Arabic sign language recognition system using transfer deep learning models. Appl. Comput. Intell. Soft Comput. **2023** (2023)
32. Acosta-Vargas, P., Salvador-Acosta, B., Salvador-Ullauri, L., Villegas-Ch, W., Gonzalez, M.: Accessibility in native mobile applications for users with disabilities: a scoping review. Appl. Sci. **11**, 5707 (2021)

33. Chang, I., Castillo, J., Montes, H.: Technology-based social innovation: smart city inclusive system for hearing impairment and visual disability citizens. Sensors. **22**, 848 (2022)
34. Zaina, L., Fortes, R., Casadei, V., Nozaki, L., Paiva, D.: Preventing accessibility barriers: guidelines for using user interface design patterns in mobile applications. J. Syst. Softw. **186**, 111213 (2022)

Comparing Emerging Technologies in Image Classification: From Quantum to Kolmogorov

Fabio Napoli(✉), Mariarosaria Castaldo(✉), Stefano Marrone(✉), and Lelio Campanile(✉)

Dipartimento di Matematica e Fisica, Università della Campania "Luigi Vanvitelli", Caserta 81100, Italy
{fabio.napoli,mariarosaria.castaldo,stefano.marrone, lelio.campanile}@unicampania.it

Abstract. The rapid evolution of Artificial Intelligence has led to significant advancements in image classification, with novel approaches emerging beyond traditional deep learning paradigms. This paper presents a comparative analysis of three distinct methodologies for image classification: classical Convolutional Neural Networks (CNNs), Kolmogorov-Arnold Networks (KANs) and KAN-based CNNs and Quantum Machine Learning using Quantum Convolutional Neural Networks. The study evaluates these models on the Labeled Faces in the Wild dataset, implementing the different classifiers with existing, well-assessed technologies. Given the fundamental differences in computational paradigms, performance assessment extends beyond traditional accuracy metrics to include computational efficiency, interpretability, and, for quantum models, gate depth and noise.

As a summary of the results, the proposed Quantum Convolutional Neural Network (QCNN) model achieves an accuracy of 75% on the target images classification task, indicating promising performance within current quantum computational limits. All the experiments strongly suggest that Convolutional Kolmogorov-Arnold Networks (CKANs) exhibit increased accuracy as image resolution decreases, QCNN performance meaningfully changes in relation to noise level, while CNNs still keeping strong discriminative capabilities.

Keywords: Kolmogorov-Arnold Networks · Quantum Convolutional Neural Networks · Image Classification

1 Introduction

Image classification is a cornerstone of Computer Vision (CV) and Machine Learning (ML), with applications spanning numerous fields, from medical diagnosis to autonomous driving. Classical CNNs have consistently achieved state-of-the-art performance in image classification tasks [8,18]. Their ability to learn hierarchical features from raw pixel data has revolutionized image recognition.

However, the computational demands of training deep CNNs, especially for complex datasets, remain a significant challenge. Furthermore, classical CNNs can be vulnerable to adversarial attacks, raising concerns about their robustness and reliability [8].

Hence, CNNs' limitations have spurred research into alternative architectures. Quantum Machine Learning (QML) offers a potential avenue for enhancing or even surpassing classical methods. QCNNs leverage quantum phenomena, such as superposition and entanglement, to potentially speed up computation and improve feature extraction. Another class of networks—the KANs—offers an alternative approach to Deep Learning (DL). They construct a hierarchical representation of the data by composing simple functions.

Comparing these different architectures—classical CNNs, QCNNs, and KANs—presents several key challenges.

- Fair Comparison: Establishing a fair comparison framework across diverse architectures requires careful consideration of factors such as dataset complexity, computational resources, and evaluation metrics.
- QCNNs are increasingly studied as candidates for image classification tasks, yet achieving both scalability and efficiency in their design remains nontrivial. The introduced limitations are well analysed by [18]. Moreover, the constraints imposed by present-day quantum hardware significantly affect how these architectures can be structured and realized in practice.
- KAN Applicability to Image Data: while KANs have shown promise in other domains, their effectiveness for image classification requires further investigation. Adapting KANs to handle the high dimensionality and spatial structure of image data presents a unique challenge.
- Interpretability and Explainability: Understanding the inner workings of both QCNNs and KANs, especially in the context of image classification, is crucial for gaining insights into their decision-making processes and building trust in their predictions.

This paper aims to provide a comprehensive comparison of classical CNNs, QCNNs, and KANs for image classification. We will evaluate their performance on benchmark datasets, analyse their computational complexity, and investigate their robustness to noise and adversarial perturbations. By systematically exploring the strengths and weaknesses of each architecture, this research contributes to a better understanding of their capabilities and limitations for image recognition tasks. More concretely, this study evaluates three models—CNNs, QCNNs, and CKANs—on the Labelled Faces in the Wild (LFW) dataset, implementing the different classifiers with existing well-assessed technologies and software libraries. The models are compared against classical performance indices, i.e., accuracy and loss.

The paper is structured as follows: Sect. 2 reports related scientific papers; Sect. 3 describes the architecture of the chosen models and some technical details; Sect. 3.5 reports the results of the experiments that are discussed in Sect. 4; Sect. 5 ends the paper drawing conclusions and future work.

2 Related Works

Image classification has significantly evolved, with classical CNNs establishing themselves as the benchmark approach over the last decade. CNNs use hierarchical structures to efficiently extract spatial features and achieve superior performance across various benchmarks, especially in face recognition tasks such as the LFW dataset [7]. Landmark CNN architectures such as AlexNet [11], VGGNet [17], and ResNet [6] have progressively enhanced classification accuracy and generalization. Recent studies [5,14] remark on CNNs strengths, including their capability to model complex visual patterns, alongside ongoing challenges such as computational cost and vulnerability to adversarial attacks [4].

KANs, recently proposed in [13], represent an innovative alternative to conventional neural networks by employing spline-based univariate functions that significantly improve interpretability and computational efficiency. Although primarily validated in numerical and scientific contexts [13], recent works have begun applying KAN structures within convolutional frameworks CKANs, demonstrating promising results in remote sensing [1] and general CV tasks. These studies suggest CKANs could achieve competitive accuracy compared to classical CNNs, with the additional benefits of improved interpretability and reduced model complexity.

QML, and in particular QCNNs, provide a distinct computational paradigm exploiting quantum mechanics for enhanced data processing [16]. QCNNs, first outlined in [2], exploit quantum circuits for convolution-like operations, demonstrating promising classification capabilities even on current noisy quantum hardware [9,18]. Studies comparing QCNNs with classical CNNs suggest potential quantum advantages in efficiency and parameter reduction, although noise robustness remains a significant limitation [8].

Direct comparative studies of these advanced ML methodologies—CNN, KAN, and QCNN—remain scarce. However, isolated comparisons suggest each approach offers unique advantages: CNNs excel in absolute accuracy and maturity, KANs provide enhanced interpretability and efficiency, and QCNNs offer promising future potential subject to hardware advancements [1,18]. The present study aims to bridge this gap systematically by evaluating these methodologies under unified experimental conditions, thus contributing to a comprehensive understanding of their relative strengths and applicable domains.

3 Methodology and Experimentation

3.1 Dataset Description

The LFW dataset is a fundamental resource for the study of unconstrained face recognition [7]. Created in 2007, it contains over 13,000 images collected from the web, each labelled with the name of the depicted subject.

This dataset provides greyscale images at a low resolution (62×47 pixels), making it easy to explore and experiment with ML algorithms.

The dataset has supported the development of numerous face recognition techniques, including models based on convolutional networks, Support Vector Machine (SVM), and Principal Component Analysis (PCA). Data can be tailored to specific computational needs, enabling time-quality tradeoffs.

The dataset's inherent diversity in terms of illumination, facial expressions, and poses has made it a useful tool for comparing different methods and is an ideal dataset for academic research on facial verification. However, it has some weaknesses: the demographic representation is unbalanced, and it does not support extreme photographic conditions. These shortcomings make it less suitable for operational scenarios that require robustness to low-light conditions or significant occlusions [7].

LFW has two main advantages: the first is the integration with Scikit-learn, which simplifies the entire experimental workflow, allowing developers to directly test their models; the second is the presence of metadata associated with the images that helps analyze the performance of different approaches. With these advantages, LFW represents a solid starting point for facial recognition research in the broader Artificial Intelligence (AI) field.

3.2 The CNN Model

CNNs are a class of feedforward neural networks commonly used to process and make predictions on different types of data such as text, images, video, and audio [12].

Thanks to their architecture that makes them particularly effective in image classification and object detection [12], they can capture spatial relationships from the data as they are characterized by convolution filters that analyze the characteristics of the input data to provide answers.

They are formed by an input layer, an output layer, and hidden layers, some of which perform convolutions. The layers are distinguished as:

- the *convolutional layer* applies filters to identify local features in the data, such as edges and textures [3];
- the *pooling layer* reduces the spatial dimensions of the input images through operations such as max pooling, which improves the robustness and generalization capabilities of the network [3];
- the *fully connected layer* processes the features extracted from the previous layers, obtaining a final classification using an activation function: the softmax function is often used [3].

The construction of this type of network involves an initial phase of data pre-processing; after defining the parameters for the network structure and by using non-linear activation functions, such as Rectified Linear Unit (ReLU), the training can learn the complex relationships between data.

Subsequently, the optimization phase is planned using algorithms such as Adam and regularization techniques such as dropout and batch normalization to prevent the overfitting phenomenon [10,15];

3.3 KAN and CKAN Network

KANs are a promising alternative to Multilayer Perceptrons (MLPs), developed to efficiently and interpretably approximate multivariate functions. They are based on the Kolmogorov-Arnold theorem, which shows that a continuous multivariate function on a bounded domain can be written as a finite composition of continuous functions of a single variable, and on the binary addition operation [13]. Thanks to this theorem, the KANs architecture is particularly suitable for applications that require high precision.

These neural networks have a fully connected structure like MLPs, but unlike the latter, KANs apply activation functions on the edges of the network; therefore, they do not use linear weight matrices, since each weight parameter is replaced by a spline function [13]. Each function is defined by spline coefficients and a grid of control points that dynamically adapts to the data during training, thus improving the accuracy of the [13] model. In addition, splines can also be used with activation functions—e.g., Sigmoid Linear Unit (SiLU)—in the case of complex relationships. The nodes of KAN networks are classified into:

- *additive nodes* that add the outputs of the spline functions of the previous layers [13];
- *multiplicative nodes* that multiply the contributions to capture nonlinear relationships between the data [13].

These types of nodes can be combined in different ways to improve the capacity of the network. [13].

An important aspect of KANs is their ability to integrate symbolic components that allow them to explicitly represent already known mathematical functions, such as logarithms or powers [13]. In this way, KANs offer a level of interpretability that other deep learning models struggle to achieve, making them particularly suitable for contexts where transparency and model understanding are key requirements [13].

The learning process in KANs uses automatic optimization by differentiation, an approach that allows flexible combinations of different objectives: starting from a Mean Squared Error (MSE), L1 regularization elements and entropy-based penalties are added, with the aim of pushing the network to generate simpler and more readable models [13].

KANs can be trained with common optimizers like Adam, but it also supports more sophisticated methods, like Limited-memory BFGS (LBFGS), which are particularly effective when working with limited datasets [13].

Another interesting aspect is the possibility of simplifying the network by removing unimportant nodes that do not contribute, through pruning techniques, to reduce the computational load without compromising performance [13].

These networks are also characterized by an automatic saving system that allows to keep track of any changes made to the model, storing the state of the network after the application, for example, of the pruning technique or the redefinition of the spline grid. This mechanism simplifies the management of experiments and protects against possible data loss [13].

KANs are particularly suitable for modeling physical phenomena, forecasting time series, or scientific applications where the quality of interpretation is as important as numerical accuracy, representing an advanced and versatile solution in the landscape of artificial intelligence and machine learning [13].

The Pykan library[1] is a framework designed for implementing and training KANs [13]. Experiments were conducted using CKAN networks, an architecture that incorporates KANs, as they have demonstrated superior performance in image classification tasks.

The CKAN architecture represents a fusion of the CNNs and KANs networks: convolutional layers extract spatial features from input images, while KAN layers replace traditional fully connected layers with spline functions [1].

This hybrid architecture achieves an optimal balance between computational efficiency and representation power, making it ideal for advanced computer vision applications [1].

3.4 Quantum Machine Learning

In this part, we describe the approach used to design and evaluate the QCNN architecture for image classification. The process consists of several essential steps, including data preprocessing, mapping classical data into quantum states, constructing the quantum convolutional layers, and incorporating realistic noise models to reflect hardware imperfections. These experiments have been conducted using `PennyLane` to simulate quantum circuits, while `Scikit-learn` is used for the preparation and handling of classical data. This methodology aims to explore both the strengths and current limitations of QCNNs in ideal conditions and under the influence of quantum noise, following core principles of quantum machine learning as discussed in prior literature [16]

As described in Sect. 3.1, we adopt the LFW dataset [7] for our experiments. To ensure a balanced and computationally feasible task, we focus on a binary classification problem distinguishing between the identities "Colin Powell" and "George W. Bush", selecting only those classes with at least 200 images. All images are converted to greyscale and normalized to the $[0, 1]$ range before quantum encoding.

To adapt the dataset to the constraints of current quantum hardware, the dimensionality is reduced by using PCA. This transformation projects the data onto a lower-dimensional subspace while preserving the most significant features. Mathematically, this is expressed as in Eq. 1,

$$X_{\text{PCA}} = X \cdot W_{\text{PCA}}, \tag{1}$$

where X denotes the original data matrix and W_{PCA} contains the eigenvectors corresponding to the largest eigenvalues of the covariance matrix of X. For quantum encoding, we use angle embedding to map classical data vectors $x \in \mathbb{R}^d$ (after PCA) into quantum states via rotations around the X-axis, as in Eq. 2,

---

[1] The library is available on GitHub at https://github.com/KindXiaoming/pykan.

$$|\psi\rangle = \prod_{i=1}^{d} R_X(x_i)|0\rangle, \tag{2}$$

where $R_X(x_i)$ is a single-qubit rotation gate parameterized by the i-th feature. This approach ensures that the input data is efficiently represented in the quantum Hilbert space.

The QCNN architecture is built from repeated layers of parameterized gates and entangling operations. Each layer consists of a sequence of single-qubit rotations and Controlled NOT (CNOT) gates, described by the unitary transformation:

$$U_{\text{layer}}(\theta) = \prod_{i=1}^{d} \text{CNOT}(i, (i+1) \bmod d) \cdot \prod_{i=1}^{d} R_Z(\theta_{i,1}) R_Y(\theta_{i,2}) R_Z(\theta_{i,3}), \tag{3}$$

where $\theta_{i,j}$ are trainable parameters. To improve generalization and prevent overfitting, a dropout is integrated into the quantum circuit by applying depolarizing channels after each layer. The effect of dropout on a quantum state ρ is modelled as in Eq. 4.

$$\mathcal{E}_{\text{dropout}}(\rho) = (1-p)\rho + \frac{p}{2^n} I, \tag{4}$$

where p is the dropout probability, n is the number of qubits, and I is the identity matrix.

To simulate real-world hardware imperfections, we also included depolarizing and phase damping noise channels after each layer. These are given by Eq. 5 and Eq. 6,

$$\mathcal{E}_{\text{depolarizing}}(\rho) = (1-p)\rho + \frac{p}{3}(X\rho X + Y\rho Y + Z\rho Z), \tag{5}$$

$$\mathcal{E}_{\text{phase damping}}(\rho) = (1-p)\rho + pZ\rho Z, \tag{6}$$

which model decoherence and environmental effects in noisy intermediate-scale quantum devices. We adopt a cost function that combines MSE with Norm L2 (L2) regularization as in Eq. 7,

$$\mathcal{L}(\theta) = \frac{1}{N} \sum_{i=1}^{N} (y_i - f(x_i; \theta))^2 + \lambda \|\theta\|_2^2, \tag{7}$$

where y_i is the true label, $f(x_i; \theta)$ is the model prediction, and λ is the regularization coefficient. Optimization is performed using the Adam algorithm with a decaying learning rate, defined at epoch t by 8,

$$\eta_t = \frac{\eta_0}{\sqrt{t}+\epsilon}, \tag{8}$$

where η_0 is the initial learning rate and ϵ is a small constant for numerical stability.

This methodology constitutes a complete pipeline for the development and evaluation of QCNNs in both ideal and noisy environments. The inclusion of noise models and dropout mechanisms provides insights into the feasibility and robustness of deploying quantum models on real hardware.

Figure 1 shows the structure of a single QCNN layer, from angle embedding through trainable gates and noise injection.

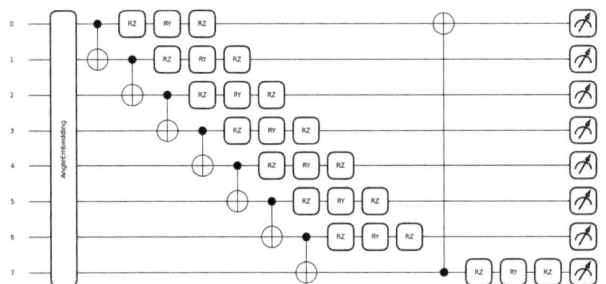

Fig. 1. Quantum circuit representation of a single QCNN layer.

3.5 Experimentation

This section analyses and compares three distinct approaches to image classification, evaluating the performance of a CNN, a hybrid architecture integrating CNN with KAN layers (CKAN), and a QCNN. The objective is to assess the effectiveness of each model in feature extraction and processing, highlighting the advantages and limitations of each methodology.

The CNN implementation was carried out using the LFW dataset, preprocessed with images resized to a scale of 0.4 and normalized based on the dataset's mean and standard deviation.

The images were reshaped into the format (n_samples,1,h,w) to explicitly include the channel and preserve spatial structure, ensuring compatibility with CNN requirements.

The model architecture consists of three convolutional blocks with 3×3 kernels, followed by batch normalization, ReLU activation, MaxPooling, and dropout (0.25). The number of filters in the convolutional blocks progressively increases to extract hierarchical image features. The convolutional output is then flattened and passed through two fully connected layers, with ReLU activation in the first layer and an output dimension corresponding to the number of classes.

Training was conducted using the *CrossEntropyLoss* function and the Adam optimizer (lr=0.001), with a dataset split into 70% training and 30% testing. The process was run for up to 100 epochs, with early stopping based on validation loss. Accuracy and loss metrics were monitored (Fig. 2) to evaluate model performance, ensuring a thorough analysis of the network's behaviour.

The experiment was also conducted on an architecture that combines a CNN with KAN layers (Fig. 3), designed to model advanced nonlinearities using spline-based transformations.

The images were normalized, resized to explicitly include the channel, and split into training (70%) and test (30%) sets. The data was then converted into tensors and loaded using *DataLoader*.

The implemented CKAN model consists of two convolutional layers followed by max pooling operations, progressively reducing spatial dimensionality. The convolutional output, transformed into a linear format, is processed by KAN layers, enabling the model to learn complex data relationships. The output size after pooling is dynamically computed to ensure compatibility with subsequent layers.

This combination of CNN and KAN leverages the CNNs feature extraction capabilities along with the flexibility of spline-based transformations, making the model more interpretable and suitable for analysing structured and complex data.

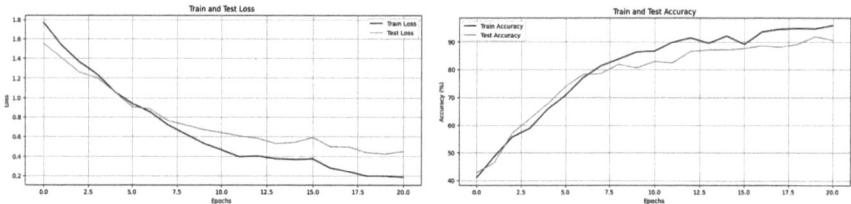

Fig. 2. CNN: training and test loss (left) and accuracy (right).

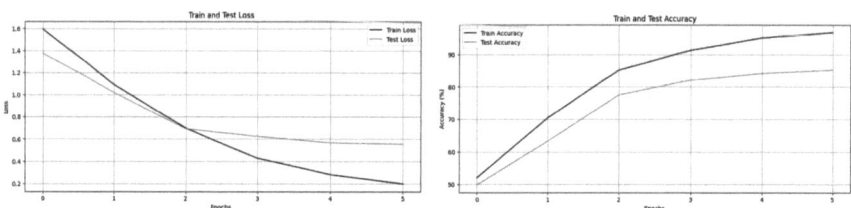

Fig. 3. CKAN: training and test loss (left) and accuracy (right)

Complementing the classical and hybrid approaches, the QCNN was evaluated under both noise-free (Fig. 4) and noisy (Fig. 6) conditions to explore the capabilities and current limitations of quantum-enhanced models.

The LFW dataset was preprocessed using Scikit-learn by normalizing pixel values and flattening images into feature vectors. PCA was applied to retain eight principal components, scaled for quantum embedding. The data was split into training (60%) and testing (40%) sets, maintaining class balance.

QCNNs were implemented in PennyLane using ten layers, each composed of parameterized single-qubit rotations and CNOT entanglement. Angle embedding mapped each 8-dimensional input to quantum states, and Pauli-Z expectation values were used for output measurement.

Training used the Adam optimizer with a learning rate of 0.05. The cost function combined MSE and L2 regularization. Simulations were run for both 5 and 10 epochs using the `default.qubit` (ideal) and `default.mixed` (noisy) backends. The noise model included depolarizing (0.01) and phase damping (0.02) channels.

Each noiseless layer used 40 gates, totaling 240 parameters. In the noisy setting, two additional noise operations per qubit increased the gate count to 72 per layer.

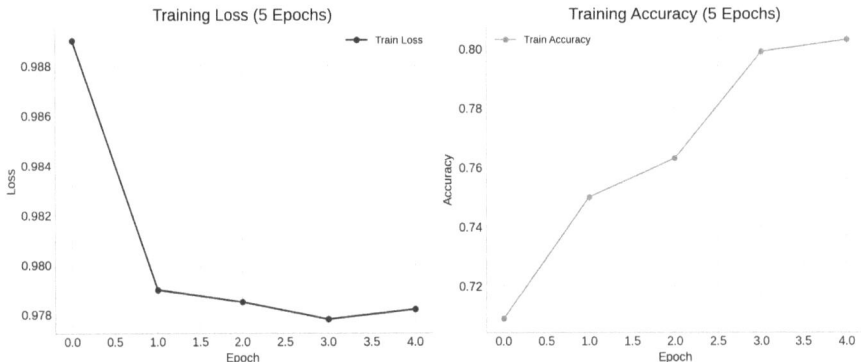

Fig. 4. Noise-free QCNN: training loss (left) and accuracy (right) after 5 epochs.

The full implementation of all models discussed in this work, including the QCNN, CNN, and CKAN architectures, is available on GitHub[2].

4 Discussion

The comparative analysis of classical, hybrid, and quantum neural network models applied to the LFW offers a multifaceted perspective on model behaviour, learning dynamics, and practical trade-offs. As expected, CNNs exhibit strong

---
[2] https://github.com/fabionpl/ICCSA25.

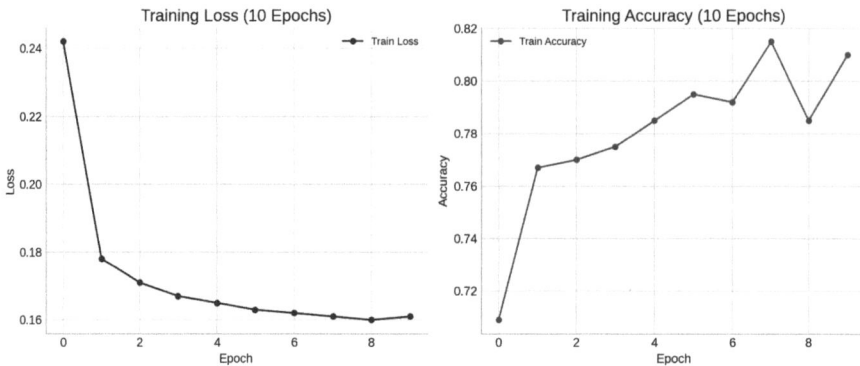

Fig. 5. Noise-free QCNN: training loss (left) and accuracy (right) after 10 epochs.

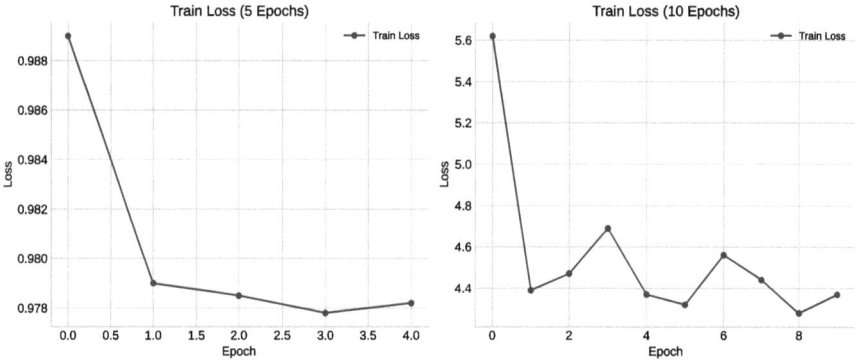

Fig. 6. Noisy QCNN: training loss after 5 epochs (left) and training loss after 10 epochs (right).

discriminative capabilities, consistently reaching high levels of test accuracy. However, this performance often comes at the cost of longer training times and susceptibility to overfitting, especially when training is prolonged or input dimensions are increased. The integration of KAN within a convolutional architecture, as realized in the KAN-CNN model, provides an intriguing alternative. When evaluated across different image resizing settings, KAN-CNN maintains stable test losses while exhibiting improved accuracy as image resolution decreases. This counterintuitive trend suggests that the model benefits from reduced input complexity, perhaps due to a better alignment between its functional decomposition and the compressed visual features. Furthermore, its significantly shorter training times and faster convergence, compared to the classical CNN, reinforce its applicability in contexts where computational efficiency is essential. Although the CNN outperforms KAN-CNN in absolute terms, especially with medium-resolution inputs, the hybrid model remains competitive, particularly when accuracy must be balanced with inference speed and resource constraints.

Turning to the quantum domain, the QCNN introduces a fundamentally different paradigm. In the absence of noise, the QCNN is capable of learning non-trivial representations, achieving a training accuracy of approximately 75%.

Although the quantum model did not surpass the performance of classical networks, its outcomes remain significant considering the nascent state of quantum hardware and its current limitations. However, the presence of quantum noise substantially impacts learning, resulting in minimal improvement in accuracy and erratic loss patterns across epochs. This clear disparity between noiseless simulations and realistic conditions highlights a major hurdle in quantum machine learning: the urgent need for architectures and training methods that can tolerate noise effectively. In general, the comparison reveals a nuanced balance between strengths and weaknesses. Although CNNs continue to lead in raw predictive power, hybrid approaches like KANs-CNNs demonstrate strong potential in scenarios requiring efficient training and adaptability to lower resolution input. Quantum networks, albeit still in development, represent an exciting frontier, with their full utility likely to emerge alongside advancements in hardware. Ultimately, choosing the appropriate model depends on the specific requirements of the task, whether that be accuracy, explainability, computational efficiency, or future scalability.

5 Conclusion and Future Directions

This work offers a comparative analysis of three innovative approaches to image classification: CNNs, CKANs, and Quantum Neural Networks (QNNs), applied to the well-known LFW dataset. CNN-based models confirmed their effectiveness and maturity, consistently achieving high accuracy and proving suitable for real-world deployment. In contrast, KAN-based architectures, particularly CKANs, demonstrated notable advantages in computational efficiency and model interpretability, making them appealing in scenarios where transparency and reduced computational cost are critical.

On the other hand, QCNNs offered intriguing potential, demonstrating their capabilities under ideal, noiseless scenarios, but highlighting notable limitations under realistic, noisy quantum conditions.

These results have significant practical implications. CNNs remain the benchmark for applications requiring maximum predictive performance and proven reliability, especially in real-world environments. CKAN architectures offer efficient training and improved interpretability without significantly compromising accuracy. QCNNs, still constrained by hardware limitations and noise sensitivity, offer significant future value as quantum hardware evolves, potentially providing computational advantages in more complex or high-dimensional tasks.

Future research efforts should focus on several key areas. Optimizing KAN-based architectures and exploring their scalability to larger and more complex datasets can further validate their practicality. At the same time, improving the robustness of QCNNs to noise and hardware imperfections is essential, possibly through the development of novel quantum error mitigation strategies. In addition, broader comparative analyses of different data sets, such as medical or multispectral imaging, could further clarify the application domain of each technology. Investigation of hybrid architectures that strategically combine CNN, KAN, and quantum elements could provide synergistic benefits by leveraging their individual strengths.

Acknowledgments. This work was funded by the European Union - NextGenerationEU under the project NRRP (i)"National Centre for HPC, Big Data and Quantum Computing (HPC)" CN00000013 (CUP D43C22001240001) [MUR Decree n. 1031-17/06/2022] - Cascade Call launched by SPOKE 10 POLIMI: "QML-NTED" project, (ii) "National Quantum Science & Technology Institute (NQSTI)" PE00000023 (CUP B53C22004180005) [MUR Decree n. 341 15/03/2022] – Cascade Call launched by SPOKE 8 CNR: "QUANTIC" project. EU-FESR, PON Ricerca e Innovazione 2014–2020-DM 1062/2021.

The experiments have been performed by using the computing resources operated by the Department of Mathematics and Physics of the University of Campania "Luigi Vanvitelli", Caserta, Italy, within the VALERE Program.

References

1. Cheon, M.: Kolmogorov-arnold network for satellite image classification in remote sensing. arXiv preprint arXiv:2406.00600 (2024)
2. Cong, I., Choi, S., Lukin, M.D.: Quantum convolutional neural networks. Nat. Phys. **15**(12), 1273–1278 (2019)
3. Goodfellow, I.: Deep learning (2016)
4. Goodfellow, I.J., Shlens, J., Szegedy, C.: Explaining and harnessing adversarial examples. arXiv preprint arXiv:1412.6572 (2014)
5. Gupta, P., Saxena, N., Sharma, M., Tripathi, J.: Deep neural network for human face recognition. Int. J. Eng. Manuf. (IJEM) **8**(1), 63–71 (2018)
6. He, K., Zhang, X., Ren, S., Sun, J.: Deep residual learning for image recognition. In: Proceedings of the IEEE Conference on Computer Vision and Pattern Recognition, pp. 770–778 (2016)
7. Huang, G.B., Mattar, M., Berg, T., Learned-Miller, E.: Labeled faces in the wild: a database for studying face recognition in unconstrained environments. In: Workshop on Faces in'Real-Life'Images: Detection, Alignment, and Recognition (2008)
8. Huang, S.Y., An, W.J., Zhang, D.S., Zhou, N.R.: Image classification and adversarial robustness analysis based on hybrid quantum–classical convolutional neural network. Optics Commun. **533** (2023). https://doi.org/10.1016/j.optcom.2023.129287
9. Hur, T., Kim, L., Park, D.K.: Quantum convolutional neural network for classical data classification. Quantum Mach. Intell. **4**(1), 3 (2022)
10. Kingma, D.P.: Adam: a method for stochastic optimization. arXiv preprint arXiv:1412.6980 (2014)
11. Krizhevsky, A., Sutskever, I., Hinton, G.E.: ImageNet classification with deep convolutional neural networks. In: Advances in Neural Information Processing Systems, vol. 25 (2012)
12. LeCun, Y., Bengio, Y., et al.: Convolutional networks for images, speech, and time series. The Handbook of Brain Theory and Neural Networks **3361**(10), 1995 (1995)

13. Liu, Z., et al.: KAN: Kolmogorov-Arnold Networks. arXiv preprint arXiv:2404.19756 (2024)
14. Rawat, W., Wang, Z.: Deep convolutional neural networks for image classification: a comprehensive review. Neural Comput. **29**(9), 2352–2449 (2017)
15. Rumelhart, D.E., Hinton, G.E., Williams, R.J.: Learning representations by back-propagating errors. Nature **323**(6088), 533–536 (1986)
16. Schuld, M., Petruccione, F.: Machine Learning With Quantum Computers, vol. 676. Springer (2021). https://doi.org/10.1007/978-3-030-83098-4
17. Simonyan, K., Zisserman, A.: Very deep convolutional networks for large-scale image recognition. arXiv preprint arXiv:1409.1556 (2014)
18. Smaldone, A.M., Kyro, G.W., Batista, V.S.: Quantum convolutional neural networks for multi-channel supervised learning. Quantum Mach. Intell. **5**(2) (2023). https://doi.org/10.1007/s42484-023-00130-3

Analyzing the Impact of Visual and Listing Features in Real Estate Listings

Serra Nur Bayrak[1(✉)], Gülfem Işıklar Alptekin[1], Günce Keziban Orman[1], and Afra Arslan[2]

[1] Galatasaray University, Istanbul, Turkey
serranursarii@gmail.com, {gisiklar,korman}@gsu.edu.tr
[2] iLab Research and Development Center, Istanbul, Turkey
aarslan@ilab.com.tr

Abstract. This study investigates the relationship between the visual and listing features of real estate listings and their corresponding Click-Through Rates (CTR). Several machine learning methods were used to identify the key attributes influencing CTR, including Decision Tree, Linear Regression, Random Forrest and XG-Boost. The models were trained and evaluated using a dataset comprising 3000 real estate listings. Visual features were extracted from listings' cover images, while listing-related features – such as price, number of rooms, and district, were derived. Our findings indicate that visual image features and listing features have impact on CTR. In the study we also isolate the visual image and listing features and observed their individual contribution to CTR.

Keywords: Image feature extraction · CTR · image quality · feature selection · machine learning · real estate

1 Introduction

In recent years, real estate platforms have become the primary channels through which individuals search for properties. These platforms offer rich and detailed listings that combine textual information with visual content, such as cover images. Given their widespread use, understanding what drives user engagement on these platforms is of significant interest—both from a user experience perspective and for optimizing platform performance.

A widely used metric to quantify user engagement is the Click-Through Rate (CTR), which measures how frequently users click on a property listing after viewing it. Identifying the factors that influence CTR can help improve both listing effectiveness and user satisfaction.

This study aims to identify the relationship between various listing and image attributes and their impact on CTR. To achieve this, we analyzed a dataset of 3,000 listings. The dataset was obtained from a real estate website operated by iLab Holding, one of Turkey's leading digital advertising groups. iLab is well known for its strong presence in Turkey's digital ecosystem. Its group companies collectively reach 65% of the country's internet audience and employ over 2,000 people.

iLab's advertising strategies involve a comprehensive approach, including social media analysis, marketing mix modeling, and brand tracking tools.

Property listings, examining two types of features:

i. Listing features, such as price, price, transaction type (sale/rent), property type (apartment/ mansion/ villa/ summer house/ residence), district, neighborhood, floor number, gross square meters, number of rooms, number of days on the platform, search count (number of listing is up), web/mobile usage ratio, and weighted position in listing results.
ii. Visual image quality features, including low-level quality features (e.g. warm hue, saturation, brightness, contrast of brightness, image clarity, rule of thirds, diagonal dominance, texture and area differences, visual balance of intensity and color).
iii. High-level image content features, (e.g. predicted scene type (interior/exterior), second prediction/room type (kitchen/bedroom/ building façade/floor plan), presence of scenery, windows, sunlight, furniture; perceived clutter, modernity, and luxury.

To determine the most influential features, several feature selection techniques were applied. The selected features were then used as inputs to a set of machine learning models, including Decision Tree, Linear Regression, Random Forrest, and XG-Boost. The performance of these models was compared to evaluate the predictive power of different feature sets in relation to CTR.

This research contributes the following findings:

- Listing features and visual image features contributes CTR.
- Observing listing and visual image features contribution on CTR shows that visual image features have slightly greater impact.

The remainder of this paper is organized as follows: Sect. 2 reviews related works on image aesthetic assessment and the use of CTR as a measure of user engagement. Section 3 describes the datasets used in this study and details the extracted image quality features. Section 4 presents experimental results, including model performance evaluations. Finally, Section 5 concludes the paper by summarizing key findings, offering recommendations, and identifying open issues for future research.

2 Related Work

2.1 Image Aesthetic Assessment

The topics of image quality assessment and image aesthetic assessment have attracted significant research interest in recent years. These studies use a variety of image quality features and machine learning algorithms to evaluate and predict image quality.

A widely used dataset in this domain is AVA (Aesthetic Visual Analysis), a public dataset introduced by Murray, Machicote and Perronnin in 2012 [4]. It contains over 250,000 user-scored photos, with aesthetic scores ranging from 1 to 10.

Zhang, Lee, Singh and Srinivasan [1] thoroughly investigated how image quality affects the property demand on Airbnb platform. The dataset comprised 13,000 listings and 510,000 images. In order to label the images, the authors sed Amazon Mechanical Turk (a popular crowdsourcing platform for human tasks), classifying images as either 'high quality' or 'low quality'. The study revealed that 12 interpretable image attributes scored significantly higher in images taken by professional Airbnb photographers, referred to as verified images. Moreover, the study demonstrated that property demand is influenced by multiple factors, including price, location, room type (private room vs. entire home), super-host status, number of reviews, star rating, and description content. To isolate the effect of image quality, comparisons were made between listings with similar attributes but differing in image verification status. The findings indicated that listing with verified images had higher occupancy rates. Additionally, the 12 interpretable image quality attributes were found to significantly contribute to increased demand.

In a separate work, Deng, Loy and Tang [2] introduced an experimental survey on image aesthetic quality assessment, focusing particularly on deep learning methods. Their analysis emphasizes the shift from traditional handcrafted features (e.g. rule of thirds, contrast) to advanced deep learning-based aesthetic classifiers. The authors demonstrated that deep learning approaches consistently outperform classical feature-engineered models. The models were evaluated using various metrics, including overall accuracy, balanced accuracy, ROC curve, and mean average precision.

Uçan [3] applied deep learning approaches to the domain of real estate images. The study highlighted AVA dataset do not cover real estate specific characteristics. Therefore, the study introduced a new dataset: the Real-Estate Aesthetics Assessment Dataset (RAAD). RAAD includes 2,071 real estate images, each rated by users on a 1–10 scale. Scores of 6 or above were labeled as aesthetic, while those below 6 were considered non-aesthetic. Initially, handcrafted features such as hue, saturation, brightness and energy were extracted, but no significant correlation was found between these features and the user scores. Subsequently, classical classification algorithms were tested, with multi-class regression performing best in the 10-class setting and SVM performing best in the binary classification setting. For deep learning-based feature extraction and classification, models such as VGG16, DenseNet121, and Vision Transformer were evaluated, with Vision Transformer achieving the highest performance.

2.2 Click Through Rate (CTR)

CTR is a critical metric used to evaluate user engagement with search results, content, or listings. While CTR is commonly employed in web search and e-commerce platforms, it also plays a significant role in real estate listing platforms.

Chapelle and Zhang [5] introduced a Dynamic Bayesian Network Click Model to enhance the estimation of CTR and relevance in web search rankings. This technique incorporates both perceived relevance and actual relevance to provide a more nuanced understanding of user behavior. Unlike earlier CTR models, which relied primarily on position bias and limited user actions such as one click, The Dynamic Bayesian Network approach overcomes these limitations and offers a more robust and reliable method for CTR estimation.

3 Methodology

The proposed methodology of this research is explained in the Fig. 1. The process begins with data collection, where we collect different types of data which we believe has an impact on CTR. Following this step, feature extraction process begins and feature selection methods were applied. After selecting the top 15 features, machine learning models were employed. Finally, their performance evaluation was discussed.

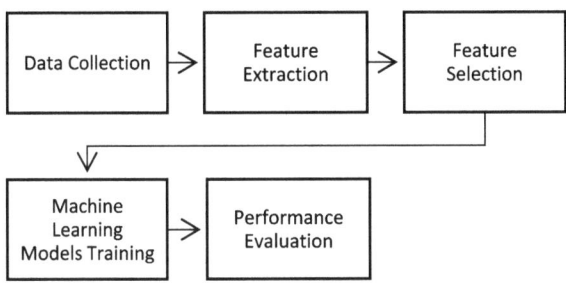

Fig. 1. The flowchart of the proposed methodology

3.1 Dataset Description

The dataset used in this study consists of 3000 real estate listings obtained from a real estate website operated by iLab Holding based in Turkey. Each listing has a cover image and listing features such as listing price, gross square meter, location, floor and other features. From dataset cover images various visual features have been extracted. In order to analyze user interaction CTR is used.

Listing Features. Listing features included in our data frame are listed below:

Transaction type: Indicates whether the property is for rent or sale.

Property type: Specifies the type of the property such as apartment, mansion, villa, summer house or residence.

District: Indicates the district where the property is located.

Neighborhood: Denotes the neighborhood where the property is located.

Floor: Indicates which floor the property is located in the building.

M2 gross: Represents the gross square meter area of the property.

Number of rooms: Indicates the total number of rooms of the property.

Price: Specifies the listed price of the property.

Listing Age: Represents the number of days the listing has been active.

Search count: Indicates how many listings appeared in user's search result.

Web mobile ratio: Refers to the distribution of user's usage web platform over mobile platform.

Weighted position: Indicates the position of the listing in the search results.

Visual Image Quality Features. In order to explore the relationship between image quality and user engagement in real estate, we employed a feature extraction methodology inspired by Zhang, Lee, Singh and Srinivasan [1] Their study shows that mentioned 12 features have an impact on demand which encouraged us to extract these features from the dataset and observe the impact on CTR.

The visual features were extracted from listing cover images which includes warm hue, saturation, brightness, contrast of brightness, image clarity, rule of thirds, diagonal dominance, texture difference, area difference, and color difference, visual balance of intensity and visual balance of color.

Warm hue refers to dominance of warm colors (yellow, orange and red) over cold colors (blue and purple). Warm colors known to have a connection between high excitement levels [6, 7].

Saturation indicates the intensity of colors in an image. Images with high saturation appears to look full of colors, whereas low saturation images look faded [1].

Brightness refers to the whole illumination level of an image and it significantly affects the appeal to viewers. Brighter images seem to be more appealing to the viewers. Adequate illumination enhances the clarity of an image [6–8].

Contrast of brightness denotes to the variation in illumination and indicate if the illumination is uniformly distributed across the image.

Image clarity is affected by the brightness levels in the Hue Saturation Value color space and saturation. Images with low image clarity often have desaturated colors or has near-zero hue intensities. These images can look unclear and hazy [1].

Rule of thirds indicates an image can be divided into nine equal sections using horizontal and vertical lines. This rule suggests that key objects in the image should be on these lines or close to the intersections.

Diagonal dominance can be expressed as visual elements being near to the diagonal lines from corner to corner which is the longest lines in the images [9].

Texture difference refers to the difference between the figure and the ground in terms of texture.

Area difference refers to the area difference between the figure and the ground.

Color difference refers to the color difference between figure and the ground.

Visual balance of intensity and visual balance of color can be explained as the symmetry of visual elements in an image. Symmetry and visual balance are positively correlated [10].

High-Level Image Content Features. Predicted scene type: Indicates whether the image represents an indoor or outdoor setting.

Second prediction/ room type: Indicates the type of room or structure shown in the image such as kitchen, bedroom, building or floor plan.

Presence of scenery: Indicates whether scenic elements are visible in the image such as natural landscapes, views.

Eye catching objects is present: Identifies whether the image features any visually striking or attention capturing object.

Windows: Indicates whether windows are present in the image.

Sunlight: Specifies whether sunlight is present in the image.

Furniture: Indicates whether furniture is present in the image.

Perceived clutter: Assesses whether the furniture is neat or cluttered.
Modernity: Indicates whether the furniture in the image is modernly decorated.
Luxury: Specifies whether the furniture in the image is luxurious.

3.2 Machine Learning Algorithms

We deployed several machine learning algorithms in order to model the relationship between the selected features and CTR. These machine learning algorithms are Decision Tree Regressor, Linear Regression, Random Forest Regressor and XG-Boost Regressor. First, we have detected the top 15 features using different methods then we built our models using these selected features.

Decision Tree Regressor is a tree-based model which employs a recursive partitioning approach to reduce prediction errors. At each step data is partitioned based on a selected feature and every leaf node represents a final prediction class. It is an efficient algorithm for modeling non-linear relationships. This algorithm can comprehend complex interactions and conditional dependencies.

Linear Regression is a supervised learning algorithm which assumes there is a linear relationship between features and the label. This algorithm is straightforward and simple but it may not capture the complex non-linear relationships.

Random Forest Regressor is based on multiple decision trees that aggregates their predictions for improved robustness and generalization. Compared to single decision trees, overfitting risk is reduced. This algorithm is suitable for analyzing complex interactions.

XG-Boost Regressor is based on gradient-boosted decision trees. Every tree is taught to correct the previous mistakes which causes progressively improved accuracy. This algorithm is known for its high performance and ability to handle complex feature interactions.

4 Experimental Results

CTR is commonly known as Click Through Rate which can be used to understand how attractive a content is to its viewers. It's a crucial metric to measure user engagement. In our dataset there are various features which can affect CTR. In this section we have employed different feature selection methods and applied several machine learning algorithms to observe the impact of these features on CTR.

4.1 Feature Selection Results

Feature selection is a key point in order to improve the model performance. In this study we have listing features, image quality features and extracted image features. Various feature selection methods have been used and their performances were compared. ANOVA F-test, Mutual Information Regression, Lasso and Pearson correlation.

Table 1 shows the selected 15 features for every feature selection method can be observed. Several features can be seen in the multiple selection methods. Luxury, brightness, sunlight and price occur in every feature selection method.

Presence of scenery, web mobile ratio, texture difference, image clarity, saturation, diagonal dominance and visual balance of color occur in three models.

Table 1. Top 15 Selected Features by Feature Selection Methods

Anova (F-Test)	Mutual Information	Lasso	Pearson Correlation
luxury	m2 gross	price	luxury
image clarity	price	m2 gross	image clarity
rule of thirds	furniture	listing age	rule of thirds
brightness	eye catching objects is present	search count	brightness
presence of scenery	texture difference	web mobile ratio	presence of scenery
texture difference	search count	weighted position	texture difference
visual balance of color	diagonal dominance	presence of scenery	visual balance of color
visual balance of intensity	brightness	eye catching object is present	visual balance of intensity
color difference	sunlight	windows	color difference
area difference	visual balance of color	sunlight	area difference
web mobile ratio	windows	furniture	web mobile ratio
saturation	luxury	luxury	saturation
price	warm hue	warm hue	price
sunlight	contrast of brightness	saturation	sunlight
diagonal dominance	image clarity	brightness	diagonal dominance

4.2 Prediction Results for CTR with Selected Features

In this section, machine learning algorithms performances with selected features are discussed. From the conducted feature selection methods, top 15 features have been selected and machine learning models have built with these features.

Decision Tree Regressor. Decision tree showed modest performance predicting CTR compared to other machine learning models. For fine tuning process, the grid search approach is used to select the depth and minimum sample split hyper parameters. For all feature selection methods, max depth 5 and minimum sample split is 10.

The following Table 2 includes the results of Decision Tree Regressor Model. Lasso feature selection method demonstrated slightly better performance with Decision Tree Regressor Model.

Linear Regression. Linear regression has the weakest performance among the algorithms that are used. The reason that linear regression is not adequate can be the relationships between CTR and the features may not be linear.

Table 3 consists of the results of Linear Regression Model. Anova (F-test) and Pearson correlation feature selection methods demonstrated slightly better performance with Decision Tree Regressor Model.

Table 2. Decision Tree Regressor Performance Evaluations

Feature selection	R2 Score	RMSE	MAE	Pearson's Correlation Coefficient
ANOVA (F-test)	0.28627	0.04427	0.03137	0.53917
Mutual Info	0.28627	0.04427	0.03137	0.53917
Lasso	0.28839	0.04421	0.03164	0.54223
Pearson Corr	0.28627	0.04427	0.03137	0.53917
ANOVA (F-test)	0.28627	0.04427	0.03137	0.53917

Table 3. Liner Regressor Performance Evaluations

Feature selection	R2 Score	RMSE	MAE	Pearson's Correlation Coefficient
ANOVA (F-test)	0.02389	0.05178	0.0386	0.17749
Mutual Info	0.00755	0.05221	0.03903	0.13025
Lasso	0.00411	0.0523	0.03911	0.12226
Pearson Corr	0.02389	0.05178	0.0386	0.17749
ANOVA (F-test)	0.02389	0.05178	0.0386	0.17749

Random Forest Regressor. Table 4 includes the performance evaluation of Random Forest Regressor. Random Forest Regressor have reached the highest overall performance. Random forest regressor can deal with complex feature interactions. CTR is also a very complex measure that depends on countless features.

For fine tuning process, the grid search approach is used to select the depth and minimum sample split hyper parameters. For all feature selection methods, max depth = 5, minimum sample split = 2, n_estimators is 200 for Lasso and 100 for the other feature selection methods. The best feature selection method is mutual information-based feature selection.

Table 4. Random Forest Regressor Performance Evaluations

Feature selection	R2 Score	RMSE	MAE	Pearson's Correlation Coefficient
ANOVA (F-test)	0.31186	0.04347	0.03109	0.562
Mutual Info	0.32993	0.0429	0.03071	0.57802
Lasso	0.32603	0.04302	0.03058	0.57363
Pearson Corr	0.31186	0.04347	0.03109	0.562
ANOVA (F-test)	0.31186	0.04347	0.03109	0.562

XG-Boost Regressor. Table 5 includes the performance evaluation of XG-Boost Regressor which has shown better performance compared to Linear Regression and Decision Tree. Best performed feature selection method is Lasso. XG-Boost regressor is also known for dealing with complex nonlinear relationships that may be the reason that XG-Boost performed better.

The best performance results are taken by setting hyperparameters learning_rate = 0.1, max_depth = 3 and n_estimators = 50. It can be observed that isolating the image quality features causes improvement in the model performance.

Table 5. XG-Boost Regressor Performance Evaluations

Feature selection	R2 Score	RMSE	MAE	Pearson's Correlation Coefficient
ANOVA (F-test)	0.30609	0.04366	0.03111	0.5632
Mutual Info	0.31153	0.04348	0.03043	0.56114
Lasso	0.31922	0.04324	0.03065	0.56702
Pearson Corr	0.30609	0.04366	0.03111	0.5632
ANOVA (F-test)	0.30609	0.04366	0.03111	0.5632

4.3 Prediction Results for Only Image Quality Features

In order to observe the isolated effect of the image quality features on CTR we have set the listing features as control variables such as price, district, number of rooms and other listing features. This enabled us to observe the distinctive contribution of image quality features. The two of the best performed algorithms used in this experiment.

XG-Boost Regressor. XG-Boost Regressor were used to analyze the image quality effect on CTR by setting the other features as control variables.

Table 6 shows the performance evaluation of XG-Boost Regressor for only image features. The best performance results are taken by setting hyperparameters learning_rate = 0.1, max_depth = 5 and n_estimators = 100. It can be observed that isolating the image quality features causes improvement in the model performance.

Table 6. XG-Boost Regressor Performance Evaluations Considering Image Quality Features

Feature selection	R2 Score	RMSE	MAE	Pearson's Correlation Coefficient
ANOVA (F-test)	0.3593	0.0419	0.0296	0.602

Random Forest Regressor. Random Forest Regressor were used to analyze the image quality effect on CTR by setting the other features as control variables.

Table 7 shows the performance evaluation of Random Forest Regressor for only image features. The best performance results are taken by setting hyperparameters max_depth = 15, min_sample_splits = 2 and n_estimators = 200. It can be observed that isolating the image quality features causes even better improvement in the model performance with random forest regressor.

Table 7. Random Forest Regressor Performance Evaluations Considering Image Quality Features

Feature selection	R2 Score	RMSE	MAE	Pearson's Correlation Coefficient
ANOVA (F-test)	0.3819	0.0412	0.0296	0.602

4.4 Prediction Results for Only Listing Features

In this section, we aim to analyze the isolated effect that listing features has on the CTR. We have set the image quality and extracted image features as control variables. This enabled us to observe the distinctive contribution of listing features. The two of the best performed algorithms used in this experiment.

XG-Boost Regressor. XG-Boost Regressor were used to analyze the listing features effect on CTR by setting the other features as control variables.

Table 8 shows the performance evaluation of XG-Boost Regressor for only listing features. The best performance results are taken by setting hyperparameters learning_rate = 0.1, max_depth = 5 and n_estimators = 100. It can be observed that isolating the image quality features causes improvement in the model performance compared to having all the features in the model.

Table 8. XG-Boost Regressor Performance Evaluations Considering Listing Features

Feature selection	R2 Score	RMSE	MAE	Pearson's Correlation Coefficient
ANOVA (F-test)	0.3644	0.0418	0.0295	0.6048

Random Forest Regressor. Rrandom Forest Regressor were used to analyze the listing features effect on CTR by setting the other features as control variables.

Table 9 shows the performance evaluation of Random Forest Regressor for only listing features. The best performance results are taken by setting hyperparameters max_depth = 10, min_sample_splits = 5 and n_estimators = 200. Random forest regressor have very similar results compared to XG Boost regressor.

Considering the experimental results it can be observed that, image quality and listing features has impact on CTR. When evaluated independently the predictive performances of models increased. Isolating the image quality features have even better performance compared to other set of features. According to these results we can say that image quality has impact on user engagement.

Table 9. Random Forest Regressor Performance Evaluations Considering Listing Features

Feature selection	R2 Score	RMSE	MAE	Pearson's Correlation Coefficient
ANOVA (F-test)	0.3643	0.0418	0.0297	0.6047

4.5 Limitations

It should be acknowledged that CTR is a measurement which depends on countless aspects and would be truly challenging to predict. CTR can vary according to user profiles or the listings shown nearby. In the study 3000 listing were used. Models' performances can be improved by using a larger set of listings. The number of features is numerous which increases the complexity of the models.

5 Conclusion

In this research, we analyzed the impact of various listing and image attributes on CTR. To achieve this, we analyzed a dataset of 3,000 listings. A set of visual and listing features were extracted. Several feature selection techniques were employed and top 15 features were selected. Machine learning models were trained with these features and performances are evaluated. Random Forest Regressor had the highest overall performance among all models with mutual information-based feature selection. XG-Boost performance results were similar to Random Forest Regressor with Lasso feature selection method.

This study also investigates the isolated effect of listing and image quality features separately. Both experiments showed that these features have significant contributions to CTR separately. The experiments performed with only image features have slightly better performance. Enhancing image quality might increases CTR. Scope of the study includes certain features that effects CTR which can explain only a part of CTR's variance.

Acknowledgments. The numerical application of the research was conducted in partnership with iLab Holding Inc. I would like to thank Arda Yücel, Doruk Yetki, Hacer Tilbeç, Gürkan Yılmaz, Gizem Güneş and Sena Necla Çetin for invaluable guidance and support throughout this study.

References

1. Zhang, S., Lee, D., Singh, P.V., Srinivasan, K.: What Makes a Good Image? Airbnb Demand Analytics Leveraging Interpretable Image Features, SSRN Electronic Journal, (2019). https://ssrn.com/abstract=2976021
2. Deng, Y., Loy, C.C., Tang, X.: Image aesthetic assessment: An experimental survey. IEEE Signal Process. Mag. **34**(4), 80–106 (2017)
3. Uçan, N.Ö.: Aesthetic quality assessment for real estate images through deep learning methods. M.S. thesis, Dept. Comput. Eng., Middle East Technical Univ., Ankara, Turkey, (2022)

4. Murray, N., Marchesotti, L., Perronnin, F.: AVA: A large-scale database for aesthetic visual analysis. IEEE Trans. Image Process. **21**(3), 2408–2414 (2012)
5. Chapelle, O., Zhang, Y.: A Dynamic Bayesian Network Click Model for Web Search Ranking, In: Proceedings of the 18th International World Wide Web Conference (WWW), Madrid, Spain, pp. 1–10 (2009)
6. Valdez, P., Mehrabian, A.: Effects of Color on Emotions. J. Exp. Psychol. Gen. **123**(4), 394–409 (1994)
7. Gorn, G.J., et al.: Waiting for the Web: How Screen Color Affects Time Perception. J. Mark. Res. **41**(2), 215–225 (2004)
8. Gorn, G.J., Chattopadhyay, A., Yi, T., Dahl, D.W.: Effects of Color as an Executional Cue in Advertising: They're in the Shade. Manage. Sci. **43**(10), 1387–1400 (1997)
9. Grill, T., Scanlon, M.: Photographic Composition. Watson-Guptill (1990)
10. Krages, B.: Photography: The Art of Composition. Allworth Press, USA (2005)

Advanced Numerical Approaches for Assessment and Design of No-Tension Masonry Structures (ANAMS 2025)

Toward a Unified Approach to Torsion-Shear Constraints in Convex Limit Analysis of Masonry

Elham Mousavian[✉]

Edinburgh School of Architecture and Landscape Architecture (ESALA), Edinburgh College of Art, The University of Edinburgh, 20 Chambers Street, Edinburgh EH1 1JZ, UK
emousavi@ed.ac.uk

Abstract. Limit analysis of discrete masonry assemblies, developed from Hyman's theorem, has proven to be an effective and computationally efficient approach for analyzing masonry structures. The convex method builds on this by abstracting the interface between two rigid blocks to a single point—typically the centroid—where internal forces and moments are computed to equilibrate external loads applied to the blocks. These internal actions are constrained to prevent different types of failure, including torsion-shear failure, which defines the maximum combined tangential force and torsional moment an interface can resist. Several studies based on the convex method have formulated torsion-shear constraints, though all are limited to rectangular interfaces. Those formulations address both dry frictional contacts between blocks and cohesive interfaces within blocks, where failure can occur due to finite tensile and shear strength. In both cases, the torsion-shear constraint is highly sensitive to the geometry of the interface. To overcome this, researchers have proposed general approximation methods for torsion-shear constraints that apply across rectangular interfaces with varying aspect ratios. This paper, for the first time, explores the extension of the convex method—specifically its torsion-shear constraints—to arbitrary planar interfaces bounded by convex closed polylines. It investigates whether a single approximate constraint can be established to cover diverse geometries. The proposed formulation includes both zero-tension frictional interfaces and internal discontinuities with finite shear and tensile strength. Given the proven accuracy and efficiency of the convex method, this work represents a key step toward its application in complex assemblies with diverse interface geometries.

Keywords: Torsion-shear yield function · arbitrary planar interfaces · dry and cohesive interfaces · discrete assemblies

1 Introduction

The limit analysis of rigid blocks, as formulated by Heyman [1], is based on modeling a masonry discrete structure as an assembly of rigid blocks. In this approach, external forces applied to the structure are balanced by internal stresses distributed along the interfaces between the blocks. When these stresses exceed their limits, failure occurs at the corresponding interfaces.

Adopting this theorem, an abstraction method introduced by Livesley [2] that first represents an interface between rigid blocks as one or more 'contact points' distributed along the surface and then computes the internal forces at these points to balance the external forces. Two major models extending this approach are known as the convex and concave models [3].

The convex model simplifies an interface to a single representative point and seeks to determine the internal normal and tangential forces, along with bending (flexural) and torsional moments, to characterize the interface behavior [3]. In contrast, the concave model represents the interface using multiple points and calculates the internal normal and tangential forces at each point to maintain equilibrium with the external forces. Similar to the convex model, these forces are subject to constraints, and when these constraints are reached, the interface reaches its limit state before failure occurs [2].

The evolution of constraints in both the convex and concave approaches will be discussed in more detail below. However, as a general observation, the convex approach has proven capable of producing more accurate results, whereas the concave approach offers greater flexibility in modeling assemblies with complex block geometries and, consequently, more varied interface configurations. In other words, while the convex model has primarily been applied to assemblies with rectangular interfaces, the concave model has been explored for interfaces with a wide range of polygonal boundaries as well as linear or nonlinear surfaces [4, 5]—albeit with an expected reduction in accuracy.

This reduction in accuracy is particularly evident in the shear-torsion capacity of the interface, which reflects the resistance of an interface under a combination of tangential force and torsional moment. Casapulla and Maione [3] demonstrated that the torsion-shear capacity predicted by the concave model is significantly higher than the experimental results. In the case of pure torsion, the estimated capacity can reach about 1.8 times the actual torsional strength of a rectangular interface with a width-to-length ratio of 1.5. In contrast, the same study showed that the convex model provides a much closer match to experimental data for the same interface geometry.

Given this observed accuracy—particularly in simulating torsion-shear constraints—this paper explores the potential extension of the convex model to non-rectangular planar interfaces. This approach can lead to more accurate form-finding and the innovative design of a new generation of stone assemblies characterized by non-rectilinear geometries. The reintroduction of stone construction has been strongly advocated in [6–9], and exhibitions like [10] and [11], who refers to this shift as a "New Stone Age." This resurgence is largely driven by global concerns over embodied carbon and resource depletion, which have prompted a renewed interest in natural materials requiring minimal processing compared to industrialized materials. Among both organic and inorganic natural materials, stone and other earth-derived substances hold particular promise. Unlike organic materials such as wood and bamboo, stone and other earth-born materials typically involve lower embodied water and have a reduced environmental impact on forests and vegetation. To support the revival of geo-sourced material construction—an approach increasingly pursued in manufacturing and building practices as highlighted by [11, 12]—it is essential to develop advanced computational tools and numerical models for early-stage form-finding. These tools are critical for exploring structurally optimized geometries, ensuring both precision in design and computational efficiency.

As will be shown later, the torsion-shear yield surface exhibits a high degree of nonlinearity, strongly influenced by the geometry of the interface. This paper investigates a simplified linearized method that is both extendable and applicable to a wide range of arbitrary planar interface geometries.

In the remainder of the introduction, a review of the development and evolution of the constraints—including torsion-shear—governing internal forces in both the convex and concave models will be presented, as discussed in various studies. The constraints should be defined based on the expected behavior at the interface between rigid bodies. Traditionally, failure discontinuity from which a discerte assembly can fail was considered the dry (mortar less) interfaces between the rigid block. Such interfaces are typically considered fully plastic [13], carrying no tensile strength, while their tangential behavior is governed by frictional resistance along the interface. This abstraction model was later extended to account for cohesive (inner) interfaces within blocks—interfaces along which block fracture may occur—alongside the dry interfaces between blocks, forming what is known as a multi-surface plasticity approach [13]. Portioli et al. [14] developed a method in which both inner and dry interfaces were modeled as plastic, differing primarily in their tangential cohesion. Mousavian et al. [15] and Iannuzzo et al. [16] proposed a convex model in which dry and inner interfaces follow distinct failure criteria: while dry interfaces are frictional, following Coulomb's law and carrying no tensile forces, inner interfaces can carry tension, and their tangential behavior is governed by the material's shear strength. Yet, the behaviour of both inner and dry faces have been considered plastic. To the best knowledge of the author, the only work that has attempted to incorporate combinations of different elasto-plastic failure modes at the interfaces is [17], though this approach has so far been limited to 2D cases.

Considering purely plastic behaviour at an interface means to prevent flexural hinges at a face with zero tensile strength, it must be ensured that, in the convex model, the internal normal force remains within the interface boundary. Instead in the concave model, the internal normal force at each point cannot be negative, as a negative value would indicate tensile forces.

Defining constraints that govern tangential failure at an interface is inherently more complex. Tangential failure can take several forms: pure shear, where the interface is subjected solely to a tangential force acting at the centroid; pure torsion, where only a torsional moment is applied at the interface centroid; torsion-shear, where the entire interface is subjected to both a tangential force and a torsional moment; and finally, torsion-shear-flexure interaction, which arises when the normal force is not applied at the centroid—resulting in a non-uniform normal stress distribution across the interface. In this latter case, it is assumed that the normal force is uniformly distributed only over a portion of the interface, known as the effective area [13], while the remaining part of the interface carries no normal force. The torsion-shear interaction is then considered to occur within this effective area.

In the concave model for a frictional (dry) interface, representing all types of tangential failure listed above requires assuming that the ratio between the tangential and normal force at each contact point does not exceed the friction coefficient [18]. For an inner interface, however, the tangential force must not exceed a certain proportion of the total shear resistance, which is determined by multiplying the material's shear strength by the interface area [19]. The resulting constraints are highly dependent on the number and placement of contact points on the interface. For example, Casapulla and Maione [3] demonstrated that when contact points are positioned at the corners of a rectangular interface, the computed torsion-shear and torsion-shear-flexural resistance is overestimated up to close two times compared to actual experimental results. They suggest shifting the contact points inward from the boundary using a specific formula, in order to obtain a more realistic estimate of the interface resistance. However, this solution mainly improves torsion-shear accuracy. Shifting contact points inward leads to underestimating bending capacity, since in plastic behavior, rotational hinges form at the boundary where eccentric normal forces act—suggesting contact points are better placed along the edges. Mousavian and Casapulla [19] and Casapulla et al. [20] investigated different numbers and placements of contact points on a rectangular inner face to determine the most accurate shear-torsion resistance. However, the question remains open, as the ideal number and positioning of contact points vary depending on the interface geometry.

In contrast, the convex model calculates the torsion-shear resistance of the interface by summing the torsional resistance at each point on the interface. Adopting the method proposed by Casapulla and Portioli [21], this approach will be detailed in Sect. 2. The torsion-shear yield graph for rectangular interfaces exhibits a high degree of non-linearity yet consistently maintains a convex shape, though the degree of convexity varies depending on the width-to-length ratio (see Sect. 2 for further details). Ultimately, the final results demonstrate the highest compatibility with experimental tests for both dry and inner interfaces [3, 20], leading to the conclusion that the convex model provides more accurate results than the concave model when the contact points in the concave model are placed at the corners of the interface boundary.

As mentioned above, the torsion-shear yield surface is highly non-linear, with this non-linearity strongly influenced by the aspect ratio of the rectangular interface. Orduña and Lourenço [13], Casapulla and Portioli [21], and Portioli et al. [22] investigated a wide range of aspect ratios from zero to infinite values to determine upper and lower bounds for the torsion-shear yield surface and proposed various linearized approximations, independent of aspect ratio. These approximations will be introduced in the Sect. 3.

Building on the reasoning behind these approximations, this paper explores whether a generalized linear approximation can be developed—one that is valid not only for rectangular interfaces but also for arbitrary planar geometries. Section 2 presents the method for determining the actual torsion-shear yield surface for any arbitrary geometry. Section 3 reviews existing linearization methods and examines whether a general approximation can be applied across different interface shapes. Section 4 concludes the findings.

2 Torsion-Shear Yield Function

The convex method of limit analysis is based on abstracting the interface between two blocks to a single point—typically the interface centroid—and computing the internal forces, bending moments, and torsional moment at that point to equilibrate the external forces applied to the block's centroid [3]. These internal components include a normal force N, two orthogonal tangential forces (T_u and T_v), two corresponding bending moments M_u and M_v (whose axis of moment is parallel to T_v and T_u, respectively), and a torsional moment M_t whose axis of moment is aligned with the normal vector N.

For an arbitrary interface ς with boundary β, when no bending moment is applied at the centroid, the entire interface is uniformly compressed, meaning the full surface engages in plastic tangential interaction. In this case, if only a tangential force T_v acts at the centroid, the interface experiences pure shear along the V direction. Assuming the maximum tangential stress that can be imposed on an arbitrary point **P** of the interface is denoted by τ_0, in the pure shear case all τ_0 vectors are parallel and aligned with the v direction (see Fig. 1), the maximum allowable tangential force in the V direction, referred to as $T_{v0\text{-pure shear}}$, is equal to:

$$T_{v0-pureshear} = \tau_0 \int_{u_{min}}^{u_{max}} du \int_{b(u)}^{t(u)} dv \qquad (1)$$

This double integral equation involves integrating a function of two variables (u and v) in two steps: first integration is done with respect to v, while u is treated as constant (e.g., u_1) (Fig. 1). For this, the bottom and top points on the interface boundary corresponding to $u = u_1$ are identified, and the moment of τ_0 about the centroid is integrated at all points between these two points.

To determine the bottom and top points for a given u, the interface boundary is divided into two functions, **b(u)** and **t(u)**. If the boundary is curved, it should first be simplified into a piecewise polyline. Then, the points with minimum and maximum u values (u_{min} and u_{max}) are located, and the boundary is split into two open polylines. Each polyline is defined as a piecewise linear function—**b(u)** and **t(u)**—composed of linear segments over specific intervals (Fig. 1). For any u between u_{min} and u_{max}, the corresponding v on **b(u)** and **t(u)** can be found.

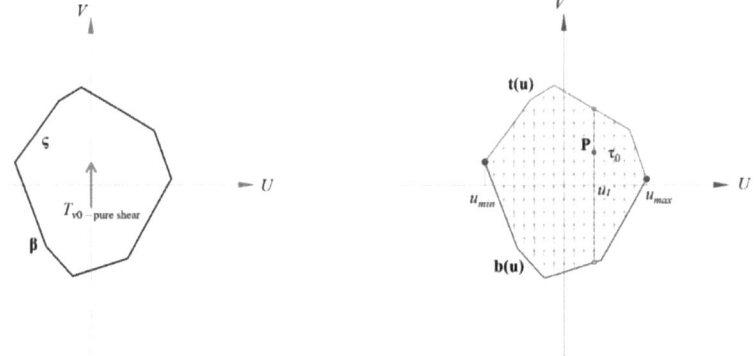

Fig. 1. Pure shear modelling of an arbitrary interface.

After the first integration, the result is integrated with respect to u, from u_{min} to u_{max}. In fact, in the simple case of pure torsion along the V direction, this double integral simplifies to the interface area. Evidently, when both T_u and T_v act at the centroid, the interface experiences pure shear inclined with respect to the U axis, forming an angle of $\alpha = arctan\,(T_v\,/\,T_u)$. In this case, maximum value of T_u and T_v, i.e., $T_{u0\text{-pure shear}}$ and $T_{v0\text{-pure shear}}$ are simply equal to:

$$T_{u0-pureshear} = T_{0-pureshear}.\cos(\alpha) \qquad (2)$$

$$T_{v0-pureshear} = T_{0-pureshear}.\sin(\alpha) \qquad (3)$$

On the other hand, when only a torsional moment is acting at the centroid—known as pure torsion interaction—the maximum value M_t can take, denoted as M_{T0}, corresponds to the stress distribution pattern depicted in Fig. 2, in which τ_0 is tangential to a circle centered at the centroid of rotation, which in this case coincides with the interface centroid. Extending the formulation developed by Casapulla and Portioli [21], $M_{T0\text{-pure torsion}}$ can be found as:

$$M_{T0-puretorsion} = \tau_0 \int_{u_{min}}^{u_{max}} du \int_{b(u)}^{t(u)} \sqrt{u^2 + v^2} dv \qquad (4)$$

In this formula, the centroid is considered the origin of a local coordinate system whose axes are U and V.

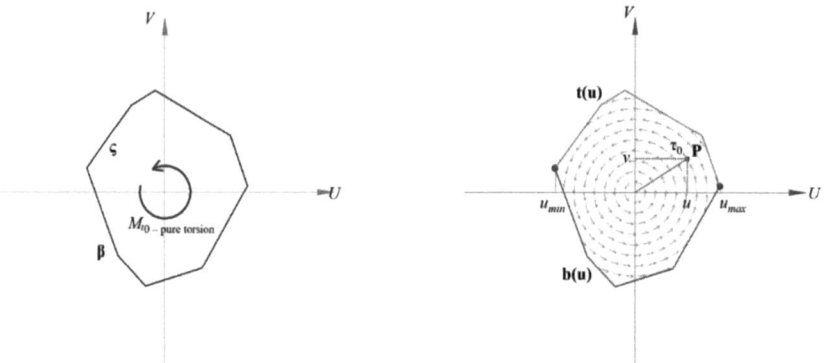

Fig. 2. Pure torsion modelling of an arbitrary interface.

When T_u and T_v act in combination with a torsional moment M_t at the centroid, the circular stress distribution pattern observed in pure torsion remains the same; however, the center of these circles—known as the center of rotation—shifts away from the interface centroid, as shown in Fig. 3. In this case, the maximum possible T_u and T_v denoted as T_{u0} and T_{v0} are equal:

$$T_{v0} = \tau_0 \int_{u_{min}}^{u_{max}} du \int_{b(u)}^{t(u)} \frac{u}{\sqrt{u^2 + v^2}} dv \qquad (5)$$

$$T_{u0} = \tau_0 \int_{u_{min}}^{u_{max}} du \int_{b(u)}^{t(u)} \frac{v}{\sqrt{u^2 + v^2}} dv \qquad (6)$$

And the moment acting on the center of rotation which is in fact equal to $M_{t0} + T_{u0} \cdot s_v + T_{v0} \cdot s_u$ can be given by:

$$M_{t0} + T_{u0} \cdot s_v + T_{v0} \cdot s_u = \tau_0 \int_{u_{min}}^{u_{max}} du \int_{b(u)}^{t(u)} \sqrt{u^2 + v^2} dv \tag{7}$$

where s_u and s_v are distances of the center of mass and the interface centroid in the U and V directions, respectively.

τ_0, introduced as the maximum tangential stress that can be sustained at any point of an interface, is defined differently depending on the interface type. For dry interfaces, τ_0 is equal to $\mu \cdot n$, where n is the normal stress uniformly distributed over the interface (i.e., $n = N / A$, with A being the interface area). For inner (cohesive) interfaces, τ_0 corresponds to the material's shear strength.

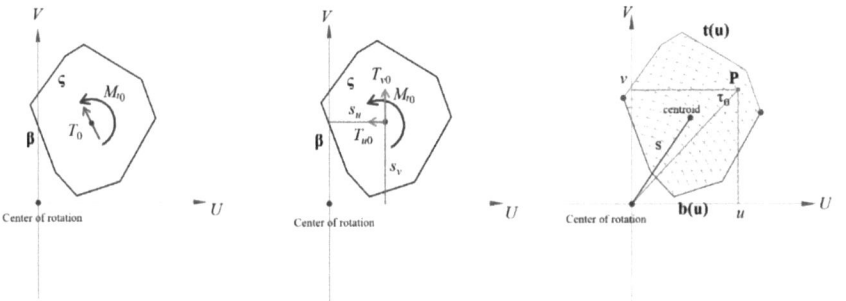

Fig. 3. Combined torsion-shear interaction of an arbitrary interface.

A visual representation of Eq. 7—which defines the torsion-shear yield curves—is provided in Fig. 4. It illustrates two cases: (1) a rectangular dry interface between two blocks (30 × 20 cm) with a normal force N of 467 N acting at the interface centroid, and a friction coefficient $\mu = 0.64$; and (2) a rectangular inner interface within a block (10 × 3 cm) with a shear strength of 0.08 kN/m, both subjected to combined T_v and M_t. These two graphs were produced by the author and are fully detailed in [3, 20].

These two graphs are concave downward and decreasing. As shown by Orduña and Lourenço [13], Casapulla and Maione [3], for any aspect ratio—from zero to infinity—of a rectangular interface, the yield curve maintains the same general shape, although its degree of convexity varies with the aspect ratio. Based on this observation, several approximation methods have been proposed [13, 21, 22], which will be discussed in the next section.

3 Torsion-Shear Yield Function Approximation

By obtaining the torsion-shear yield curves for a wide range of rectangular interfaces with aspect ratios from zero to infinity, Orduña and Lourenço [13], Casapulla and Portioli [21], and Portioli et al. [22] developed three different approximation methods. These approximations are essential, as the high degree of non-linearity in the exact yield curves unnecessarily complicates both the expressions and the computational effort.

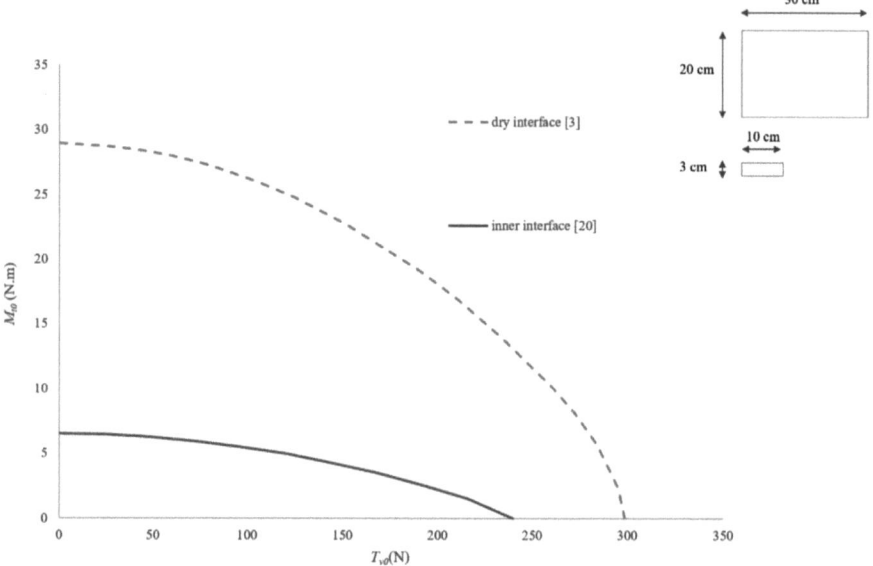

Fig. 4. Torsion-shear yield curve for a dry and an inner cohesive rectangular face.

Orduña and Lourenço [13] proposed a piecewise approximation consisting of three segments: a horizontal segment with $M_{t0} = M_{t0\text{-pure torsion}}$, an inclined middle section, and a vertical line with $T_0 = T_{0\text{-pure shear}}$ (Fig. 5). This piecewise graph is based on the average shape of yield curves across the full range of aspect ratios between zero and infinity, as their influence was found to be relatively minor.

In contrast, Casapulla and Portioli [21] aimed to develop an approximation based on the minimum envelope of all possible yield curves, ensuring that the torsion-shear resistance of any rectangular interface remains above this lower bound. They observed that the yield curves of rectangular interfaces always lie above a parabolic shape, which they adopted as the lower-bound curve. This was then linearized into a two-piece approximation (see Fig. 5).

The simplest yet effective approach is a straight-line approximation connecting the two extremes—pure torsion and pure shear (Fig. 5). This function in case T_v and M_t are acting on the interface centroid can be written as:

$$\frac{M_{t0}}{M_{t0\text{-puretorsion}}} + \frac{T_{v0}}{T_{v0\text{-pureshear}}} = 1 \qquad (8)$$

This method, also based on the minimum curve principle, was adopted by Portioli et al. [22] and validated through application to various configurations, including single brick wall panels, corner panels, and U-shaped brick wall assemblies. The results confirmed its effectiveness for practical masonry analysis.

Adopting the last linear approximation concept (Eq. 8), this paper investigates whether the approach can be extended to arbitrary interface geometries. Based on the principle of constructing a minimum curve, it must first be established whether the

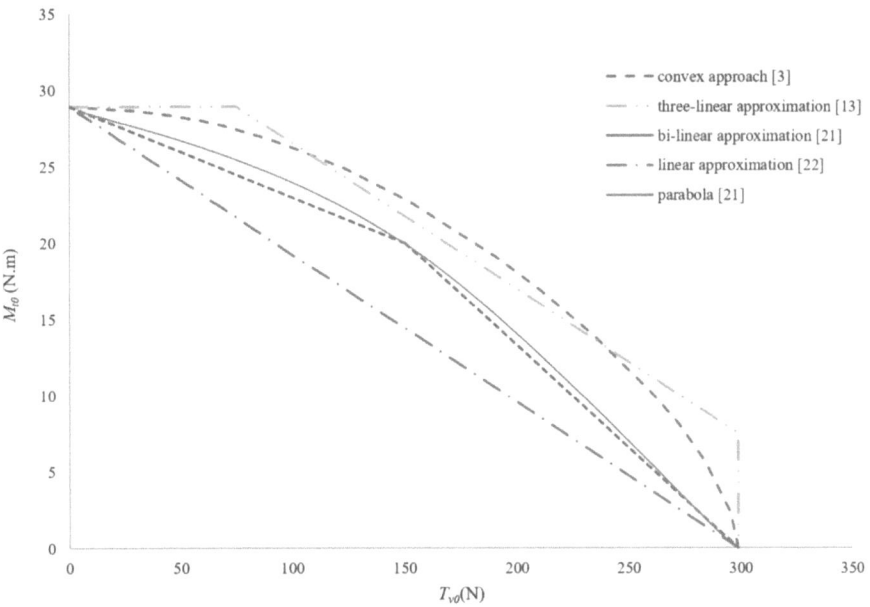

Fig. 5. Various approximations of torsion-shear yield curve.

torsion-shear yield curve (with endpoints corresponding to the maximum pure torsion and pure shear capacities—computed by Eqs. 1 and 2, respectively) is always concave downward, descending. In other words, it must be verified that the torsion-shear curve does not take on a different shape, such as a concave upward or non-monotonic form. If such cases exist, a linear approximation connecting the extremes of pure shear and pure torsion would no longer be valid. If not, this linear approximation can be confidently assumed as a lower bound that the torsion-shear yield curve can never fall below.

To this aim, this paper tracks the geometric variations along the graph, which by convention starts from the left (starting point corresponding to the pure torsion case) and ends on the right (ending point corresponding to the pure shear case).

In the case where T_v and M_t act on the interface centroid, with $M_t = T_v \cdot ecc$, where ecc represents the eccentricity along the U direction from the centroid, the variation along the torsion-shear yield curve—from left to right—can be analogized to the change in ecc. At the leftmost point of the curve (representing pure torsion), ecc is close to infinite. Moving rightward along the curve corresponds to a gradual decrease in ecc, approaching zero at the rightmost point (representing pure shear).

Similarly, this analogy can be extended to the distance between the center of rotation and the interface centroid, s_u. At the leftmost point of the curve, s_u is zero; as we move toward the right, s_u increases, becoming nearly infinite in the pure shear case (see Fig. 6).

In this case, where T_v and M_t act on the interface centroid, Eq. 7 can be rewritten as:

$$M_{t0} = -s_u . T_{v0} + \tau_0 \int_{u_{min}}^{u_{max}} du \int_{b(u)}^{t(u)} \sqrt{u^2 + v^2} dv \qquad (9)$$

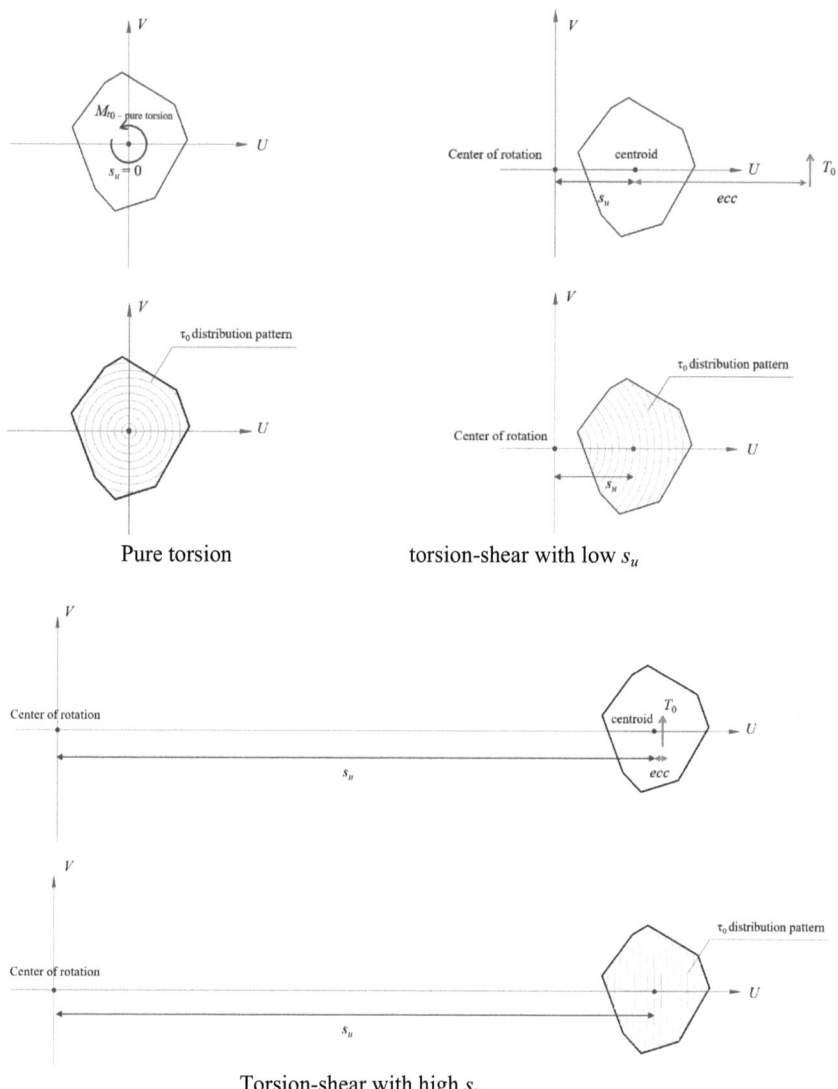

Fig. 6. Stress distribution pattern for various distance between the center of rotation and the interface centroid.

For the torsion-shear yield curve, $-s_u$ in this equation can be interpreted as the slope of the curve. As mentioned above, moving from left to right along the curve, this slope increases from zero to near infinity. This observation directly supports the conclusion that the torsion-shear yield curve is always concave downward and decreasing. Looking more closely, we can also see that in the case of pure torsion—when the expression $-s_u.T_{v0}$ equals zero—Eq. 9 reduces to Eq. 2. Similarly, in the case of pure shear, Eq. 9

can be rewritten as:

$$T_{v0} = \tau_0 \frac{\int_{u_{min}}^{u_{max}} du \int_{b(u)}^{t(u)} \sqrt{u^2 + v^2} dv}{S_u} = \tau_0 \int_{u_{min}}^{u_{max}} du \int_{b(u)}^{t(u)} \frac{\sqrt{u^2 + v^2}}{S_u} dv \quad (10)$$

Since the center of rotation is assumed to be very far from the interface in the case of pure shear, the stress distribution lines become almost parallel. As a result, the term $\frac{\sqrt{u^2+v^2}}{S_u}$ can be approximated as 1, and the equation simplifies to:

$$T_{v0} = \tau_0 \int_{u_{min}}^{u_{max}} du \int_{b(u)}^{t(u)} dv \quad (11)$$

Which is a double integral equal to the interface area, as observed in Eq. 1.

This clearly shows that the torsion-shear yield surface for any arbitrary planar interface with a convex boundary is concave downward and descending, with two extremes corresponding to pure torsion and pure shear. Therefore, the linear constraint proposed by Portioli et al. [22] (Eq. 8) can be considered a valid approximation, enabling us to extend the convex method to any arbitrary block—and consequently, any interface geometry—when this approximation is incorporated.

4 Conclusions and Future Works

This paper investigated whether a unique approximation can be found to serve as the torsion-shear yield function for any arbitrary planar interface with a convex boundary. A general method was first presented to analyze the actual torsion-shear behavior at such interfaces. Given the high degree of non-linearity in the torsion-shear yield function, the paper then explored whether a simplified approximation can be valid across all possible interface geometries between blocks. This investigation is based on determining whether the yield curve can ever take a form that is not concave downward and decreasing. By demonstrating that such a case is not possible, the paper proposed using a linear yield function—bounded by the two extremes of pure shear and pure torsion—as a general approximation. This enables the extension of the convex method to analyze complex masonry assemblies with arbitrary block and interface geometries.

While the proposed linear torsion-shear approximation was guaranteed to serve as a lower bound, the degree of underestimation—depending on the actual convexity of the yield function—requires further investigation. Also, this paper did not address the combined torsion-shear-flexure interaction at the interface, where the primary challenge lies in determining the effective area for interfaces of arbitrary geometry.

Disclosure of Interests. The author has no competing interests to declare that are relevant to the content of this article.

References

1. Heyman, J.: The stone skeleton. Int. J. Solids Struct. **2**(2), 249–279 (1966)
2. Livesley, R.K.: A computational model for the limit analysis of three-dimensional masonry structures. Meccanica **27**, 161–172 (1992)
3. Casapulla, C., Maione, A.: Modelling the dry-contact interface of rigid blocks under torsion and combined loadings: Concavity vs. convexity formulation. Int. J. Non-Linear Mech. **99**, 86–96 (2018)
4. Frick, U., Van Mele, T., Block P.: Decomposing three-dimensional shapes into self-supporting, discrete-element assemblies. In: Modelling Behaviour: Design Modelling Symposium 2015, pp. 187–201. Springer International Publishing (2015)
5. Kao, G.T-C., Iannuzzo, A., Thomaszewski, B., Coros, B., Van Mele, T., Block, P.: Coupled rigid-block analysis: stability-aware design of complex discrete-element assemblies. Computer-Aided Design **146** (2022)
6. Boote, S., Lynes, A.: Stone as a structural material, Part 1: Mechanical properties. The Physics Teacher **98**(3), 20–25 (2020)
7. Boote, S.: Stone as a structural material, Part 2: Traditional and reinforced stone stairs. Struct. Eng. **98**(6), 18–23 (2020)
8. Boote, S., Lynes, A.: Stone as a structural material, Part 3: Posttensioned stone structures. Struct. Eng. **98**(8), 22–28 (2020)
9. Boote, S.: Stone as a structural material, Part 4: Contemporary loadbearing stone buildings. Struct. Eng. **98**(10), 28–33 (2020)
10. AAU Anastas: Official Website, https://www.aauanastas.com/, last accessed 2025/05/08
11. Webb Yates Engineers: The New Stone Age, https://webbyates.com/projects/the-new-stone-age/, last accessed 2025/05/08
12. Dezeen: Tavs Jorgensen develops cob bricks for low-carbon construction. Dezeen, https://www.dezeen.com/2024/10/29/tavs-jorgensen-cob-bricks-low-carbon/, last accessed 2025/05/08
13. Orduña, A., Lourenço, P.B.: Three-dimensional limit analysis of rigid blocks assemblages, Part I: Torsion failure on frictional interfaces and limit analysis formulation. Int. J. Solids Struct. **42**, 5140–5160 (2005)
14. Portioli, F., Cascini, L., Casapulla, C., D'Aniello, M.: Limit analysis of masonry walls by rigid block modelling with cracking units and cohesive joints using linear programming. Eng. Struct. **57**, 232–247 (2013)
15. Mousavian, E., Kibriya, G., Bagi, K., Iannuzzo, A.: multi-surface plasticity model for analysis of complex interlocking assemblies, In: 6th International Conference on Structures and Architecture, Antwerp, Belgium (2025)
16. Iannuzzo, A., Herczeg, M. Bagi, K., Mousavian, E.: Equilibrium analysis of 2D complex dis-crete assemblies modelled using cracking blocks with non-dilatant interfaces. In: Iványi, P., Kruis, J., Topping, B.H.V. (ed.), Proceedings of the Fifteenth International Conference on Computational Structures Technology, pp. 1–14. Civil-Comp Press (2024)
17. Ramaglia, G., Lignola, G.P., Prota, A.: Collapse analysis of slender masonry barrel vaults. Eng. Struct. **117**, 86–100 (2016)
18. Gilbert, M., Casapulla, C., Ahmed, H.M.: Limit analysis of masonry block structures with non-associative frictional joints using linear programming. Comput. Struct. **84**(13–14), 873–887 (2006)
19. Mousavian, E., Casapulla, C.: Structurally informed design of interlocking block assemblages using limit analysis. J. Comput. Des. Eng. **7**(4), 448–468 (2020)
20. Casapulla, C., Mousavian, E., Argiento, L., Ceraldi, C., Bagi, K.: Torsion-shear behaviour at the interfaces of rigid interlocking blocks in masonry assemblages: experimental investigation and analytical approaches. Mater. Struct. **54**(3) (2021)

21. Casapulla, C., Portioli, F.: Experimental and analytical investigation on the frictional contact behavior of 3D masonry block assemblages. Constr. Build. Mater. **78**, 126–143 (2015)
22. Portioli, F., Casapulla, C., Cascini, L., D'Aniello, M., Landolfo, R.: Limit analysis by linear programming of 3D masonry structures with associative friction laws and torsion interaction effects. Arch. Appl. Mech. **83**, 1415–1438 (2013)

Experimental and Numerical Study of SRG-to-Masonry Joints

Salvatore Verre[1], Sam Cocking[2], Alessio Cascardi[3], Raimondo Luciano[4], Francesco Fabbrocino[5], and Carlo Olivieri[5(✉)]

[1] Department of Theoretical and Applied Sciences (DiSTA), eCampus University, Novedrate Como, Italy, via Isimbardi 10, Novedrate, CO, Italy
[2] Department of Engineering, Cambridge, UK
[3] Department of Civil Engineering, University of Calabria, Arcavata di Rende, Italy
[4] Parthenope University, Naples, Italy
[5] Department of Engineering, Pegaso Telematic University, Centro Direzionale ISOLA F2, Naples, Italy
carlo.olivieri@unipegaso.it

Abstract. Steel reinforced grout (SRG) – in which steel fiber strips are embedded in an inorganic mortar – is a promising strengthening methodology for the retrofitting of reinforced concrete (RC) or masonry structures. While its effectiveness has been established in various applications, delamination (debonding) at the fiber-mortar or mortar-substrate interfaces may dramatically affect its mechanical performance when a premature failure occurs. Bond tests can provide crucial insights by evaluating debonding forces versus slip relationships. The performance of SRG interventions depends on factors including the fiber and mortar types, reinforcement layers, bonded length, substrate properties, and environmental conditions. To address the current lack of knowledge regarding these criteria, this paper presents experimental and numerical studies of SRG-to-masonry bonds. Specifically, Finite Element (FE) analysis is used to model typical SRG-to-masonry joints, leveraging results from a previous campaign of laboratory tests. The results showed satisfactory accuracy of the experimental/numerical comparison, in terms of constitutive bond laws.

Keywords: FRCM · SRG · Masonry · shear bond tests · Finite Element Model FEM

1 Introduction

Unreinforced masonry buildings offer a good structural capacity when they have been well designed [1–12], even when currently in a deformed configuration due to external boundary conditions [13–16], or in the case of slender structures [17]. However, due to damage or mechanical decay to the masonry over time, strengthening may become necessary [18]. Enhancing existing structures, to enable their life extension or reuse with increased load-carrying capacity, has led to a growing interest in composite materials for strengthening. These materials, with reinforcing fibers in organic or inorganic matrices, are bonded to structures to increase performance with minimal invasiveness. Fiber Reinforced Polymers (FRP), Fabric Reinforced Cementitious Matrices (FRCM) and Steel Reinforced Grout (SRG) are among the most popular composite systems used for structural strengthening. Their mechanical performance is dependent on the interaction between the reinforcing fibers and the matrix [19, 20]. In particular, SRG consists of galvanized high-strength steel wires twisted together to form cords that can be arranged at different distances from each other, obtaining different specific density levels [21]. In this way, unidirectional fabrics are created. The diameter of the steel wires ranges from 0.1 to 0.5 mm, and coatings are used to prevent corrosion. This manufacturing approach leads to cord tensile strengths between 2800 and 3200 N/mm^2, with Young's moduli between 180 and 210 N/mm^2. Variation of the cord spacing results in different densities. Typical overall density values for low (LD), medium (MD), and high (HD) density SRG are 600 g/m^2, 2000 g/m^2, and 3300 g/m^2, respectively.

Recent experimental investigations have studied the mechanical behavior of structural members strengthened in shear [22] or confined [23] with SRGs. The results clearly indicate debonding processes that may occur at both the fiber-mortar and mortar-substrate interfaces. These processes can be analyzed in greater detail by bond tests, including either single- or double-lap direct shear tests. These enable evaluation of local debonding forces, slip laws, and corresponding interface fiber stresses. However, experimental investigations on SRG-to-masonry bond behavior are rarer [24–27], reporting on single-lap shear tests with varying bonded lengths and loading rates.

These tests observed failures occurring through fiber rupture, mixed mode failure, de-bond of the masonry-matrix interface, and inter-laminar failure between the fibers and matrix. The failure type was primarily influenced by the bonded length which, in these tests, varied between 175 and 200 mm. However, high dispersion of textile-to-matrix slippage measurements was also observed. This was ascribed to factors including the non-homogeneous stress distribution among the steel cords and within the filaments in each cord, cords-to-matrix friction, and failure mode developments.

Ascione et al. [26] conducted an extensive experimental study on the bond behavior between SRG and concrete. These tests investigated the influence of the surface roughness of the concrete, the density of the steel fibers (including both LD and MD fiber spacings), the bonded length, and the concrete strength. Failures in the SRG matrix were observed due to both sliding phenomena and cohesive failure, irrespective of strength or surface roughness of the underlying concrete specimens. While the use of a higher number of steel strips in the SRG was correlated with an improved maximum load capacity, a reduced average tensile strength (and hence exploitation ratio) was also observed. The effective bonded length in these tests was between 200 and 300 mm, for the LD and MD steel fibers, respectively.

Additionally, Sneed et al. [27] performed shear bond tests to evaluate the bond performance between SRG composites and concrete. The SRG composites were constructed using MD steel fibers and a mineral mortar. A bonded length of 330 mm was used in these tests, which were performed both with and without an external mortar layer. Failures of the fibers occurred either by slippage within the matrix or direct fracture. There was no post-peak softening seen in the load response.

Beyond the parameters studied to date in the literature, others may influence the behaviour of SRG-reinforced structures. These include the precise specifications of the fiber and mortar types, the number of reinforcement layers, the preparation used for the external substrate, its strength, and environmental conditions. Further work is needed to study the effects of these parameters before a reliable analytical model can be developed for the overall performance of SRG-reinforced structures.

In this paper, numerical and experimental studies on SRG-to-masonry bonds are presented and discussed. Specifically, a series of direct, single-lap shear tests were performed on SRG-reinforced brick masonry specimens. A numerical Finite Element (FE) procedure was then developed, utilizing the well-recognized FE software [28], to predict the global behavior of SRG-to-masonry joints. The following sections outline the experimental and numerical procedures used in this study, before a discussion of the key results and potential avenues for future research.

2 Experimental Investigation

2.1 Materials and Specimen Preparation

Three single-lap shear tests were performed at the University of Calabria laboratory using a push-pull configuration. For full details of these tests, see [29]. Each masonry specimen had cross-sectional dimensions of 120 × 120 mm, a joint length of 510 mm, and was constructed using eight clay bricks. The average brickwork compressive strength, $f_{bc} = 42$ MPa (with a coefficient of variance of 0.0526), was measured by coring four samples of 50 × 50 mm cross section from bricks in the same batch used to build the test specimens. The masonry test specimens were constructed and strengthened with SRG in laboratory conditions. The fiber fabric density of the steel used for SRG reinforcement was 1200 g/m^2. and the cross-sectional area of each cord was 0.538 mm^2 (Fig. 1). The steel fiber consisted of micro cords, each comprising five filaments. Two filaments were used to wrap the remaining three to create each micro cord.

Fig. 1. Medium steel mesh used in SRG reinforcement.

Tensile tests on five typical coupons were used to determine the mechanical properties of the fiber mesh, using the experimental setup shown in Fig. 2a. The length and width of each coupon were 560 mm and 50 mm, respectively. The coupon cross section contains eight steel cords, giving a resultant area of $A_f = 4.30$ mm². The ends of each coupon were fixed to thin steel plates measuring 80 mm in length. The displacement rate for these testss was 1.25 mm/s, and axial strain was recorded using an extensometer of gauge length = 50 mm. Results for the elastic modulus, tensile strength, and ultimate strain are presented in Table 1, while Fig. 2b shows the experimental stress–strain curves.

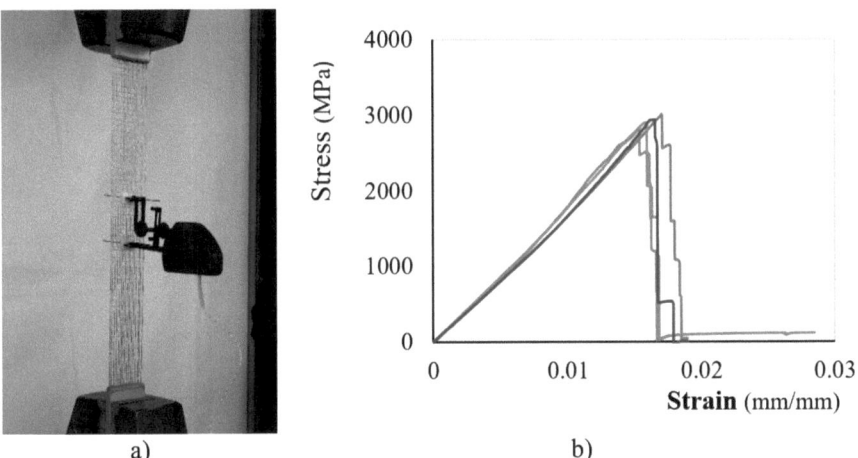

Fig. 2. A) Coupon test setup and b) resulting stress–strain curves.

Table 1. Steel fibre geometry and measured mechanical properties.

	Steel fiber
Elastic modulus	*200 GPa (8%)*
Break deformation	0.020 mm/mm (8%)
Equivalent thickness	*0.169 mm*

To reinforce the masonry specimens, the steel fibers were embedded between two, 5 mm-thick matrix layers and bonded to the specimens, beginning 30 mm from the edge of the top surface. A mold was used to ensure uniform thickness of the composite strip.

3 Results and Numerical Model

This paper presents the results for three specimens, which were subjected to classical, push-pull tests. In these, fibers were pulled while the masonry joint remained fixed in place. Aluminum load tabs were used to apply force to the top of the fibers, while a 100 kN load cell was used to perform measurements. The tab width was identical to that of the specimens (50 mm), while their length was 60 mm. Even attachment to the bare fiber was achieved using epoxy resin, ensuring uniform distribution of pressure during the test. Slip was calculated by averaging recordings from two linear variable displacement transducers (LVDTs), labeled "*a*" and "*b*" (c.f., Fig. 3). These LVDTs were located near to the bonded region of the specimens. The displacement rates for these tests was 0.18 mm/min. Figure 3 shows the experimental setup.

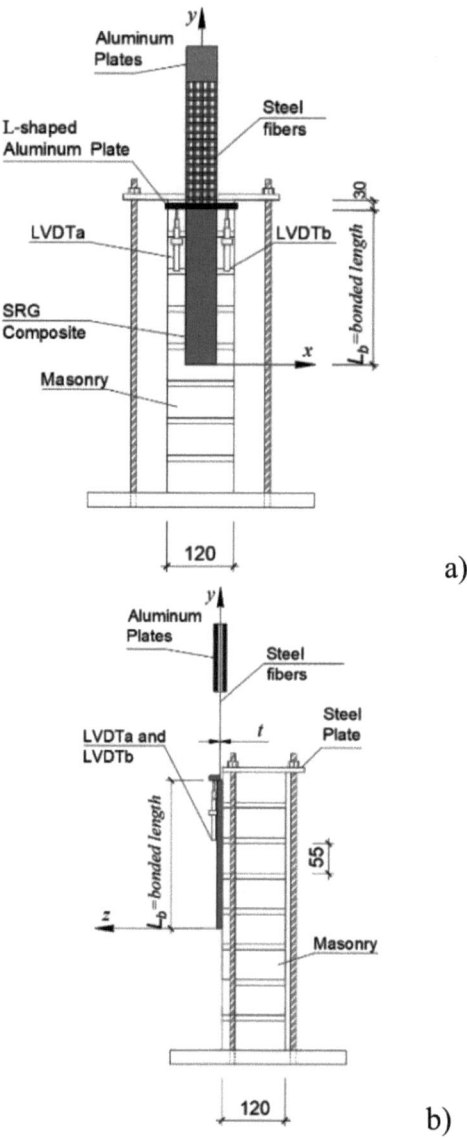

Fig. 3. Experimental setup for the single-lap shear tests: a) front and b) side views.

The naming convention for the test specimens was "*DS_N*," in which "*N*" denotes the specimen number. Table 2 summarizes the maximum applied load (P_{max}) achieved in each test.

Table 2. Maximum applied loads in the direct shear tests.

	P_{max} [kN]	Average [kN]
DS_1	6.46	6.04
DS_2	5.32	
DS_3	6.35	

3.1 Geometrical Modelling and Materials Model

Two modelling techniques were used in the numerical procedure, in the FE software. First, the masonry substrate was modeled using 3D FE elements (C3D4) for macro modeling [30, 31], while the steel fibers and the inorganic mortar were modeled using 2D shell elements (S4). The 3D element presents a tetrahedral geometry with 4 nodes, and was characterized by linear interpolation functions and constant stress. However, 2D shell elements were quadrilinear and presented a membrane strain and a reduced integration with hourglass control. In Fig. 4, the adopted FE mesh is shown. This was obtained after mesh sensitivity analysis, aimed to avoid mesh influence on the results. Vertical and horizontal displacements at the base of the masonry prism were constrained, as well as for the horizontal displacements at the top (*y-z plane*).

The nonlinear behavior of the inorganic matrix was described using the Concrete Damage Plasticity model (CDP). This function is commonly used in the literature, to model the quasi-brittle materials found in masonry or concrete elements [32]. CDP is essentially an extension of the Drucker–Prager model, featuring a modified yield criterion. In the CDP model, the hardening/softening strain branch is influenced by the potential function parameter, which can be set equal to or different from the frictional parameter. The steel fibers were modeled as a homogeneous elastic material up to failure. The input parameters included the density ($\rho = 2.5$ g/cm^3), the elastic modulus as evaluated in Sect. 2.1, and the Poisson's ratio ($\nu = 0.3$).

3.2 Interface Modelling

In SRG systems, debonding is frequently observed at the fibre-mortar interfaces. Assuming that this will be the site of failure, interactions at the substrate-matrix interface are modeled as perfectly bonded. In contrast, interface conditions at the fiber-matrix interfaces (for both the internal and external matrices) were modeled as a cohesive surface through general contact. These contact surfaces are critical components of the SRG system, and are shown in Fig. 5. Relative displacements occurring at these interaction

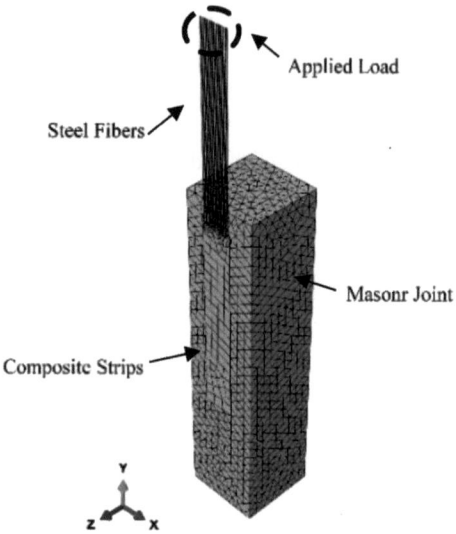

Fig. 4. Geometrical modeling and FE analysis

surfaces are described using the "traction-separation approach" (as specified in the software), applied to these contact surfaces. This internal function follows a bilinear pattern, with an initial linear elastic response followed by softening. The softening phase captures damage progression.

The bond-slip law used in this study is based on the bilinear model proposed in [33] for FRP composites (Fig. 6). This approach utilizes a bilinear function to capture Mode I and Mode II failure modes, as well as the initiation and progression of damage. Initiation of damage occurs at the peak of normal or shear stress. The adopted bond-slip law consists of three linear branches [33] and was proposed for analyzing FRP–concrete joints. Since the load-slip responses of both FRP and SRG systems are similar, the same bond-slip law can be used to analyze the performance of structures reinforced with SRG. The parameters were calibrated specifically for SRG composites using experimental data, resulting in the following estimates: initial stiffness $k_0 = 77.01$ N/mm^3, bond stress reaches $\tau_{max} = 5.93$ MPa, and Fracture Energy $G_f = 0.67$ N/mm.

3.3 Computational Results

The numerical simulations again assumed displacement control conditions for the load tests. Specifically, an enforced displacement (λ_d) was imposed at the top surface of the steel fibers. To obtain nonlinear numerical solutions, a dynamic (i.e., *explicit*) approach was employed. This method is commonly used for quasi-static analyses that involve complex nonlinear effects and contact conditions. Consequently, direct integration of the governing equation of motion was possible using an extended Newmark *β-method*, known as the *Hilber-Hughes-Taylor (HHT)* time-integration operator. It is important to note that the model consists of multiple components (substrate, matrix, and fabric) with different stiffness and mass properties.

These components are addressed separately in the numerical dynamic solution using a scaling method. The main parameters for obtaining the static solution include variable mass scaling, alongside the ratio of kinetic and internal energies. In this study, a variable mass scaling of 0.00005 was applied throughout, and the ratio was constrained below 5% throughout analysis.

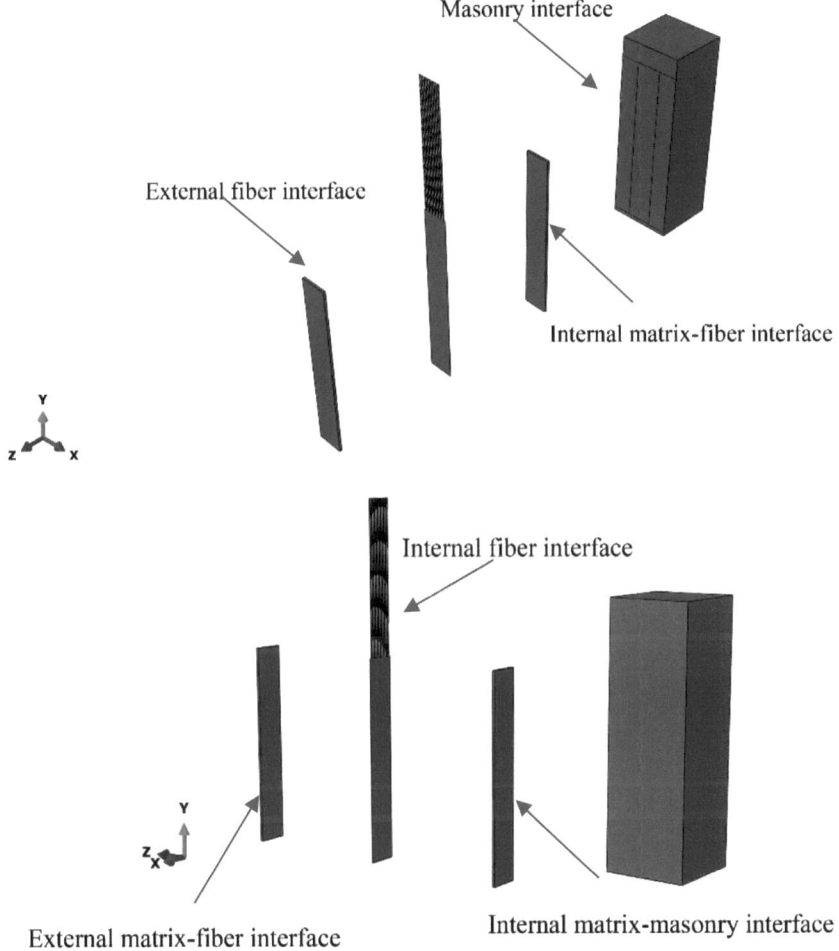

Fig. 5. Interaction surfaces

3.4 Result and Discussion

Figure 7 shows the typical failure mode, while Fig. 8 presents results obtained for the direct shear tests. Initially, the load-response curve (Fig. 8) exhibits a linear segment, corresponding to linear-elastic bond behavior at the fiber-matrix interface. Following this, increases in global slip led to a nearly uniform applied load until sudden failure, characterized by softening in the response. During this stage, micro-damage was observed at the fiber-matrix interfaces.

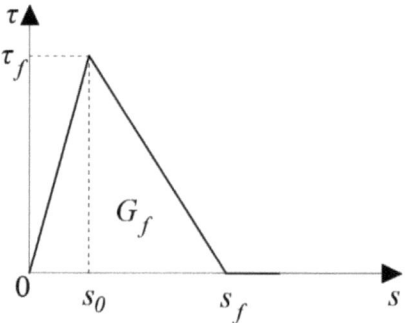

Fig. 6. Bond slip law

Fig. 7. Typical failure mode

The numerical results, as shown in Fig. 8, align well with the experimental data. However, the numerical model slightly underestimated the maximum applied load, reporting a value of 5.73 kN, which corresponds to a 6% error (Fig. 8).

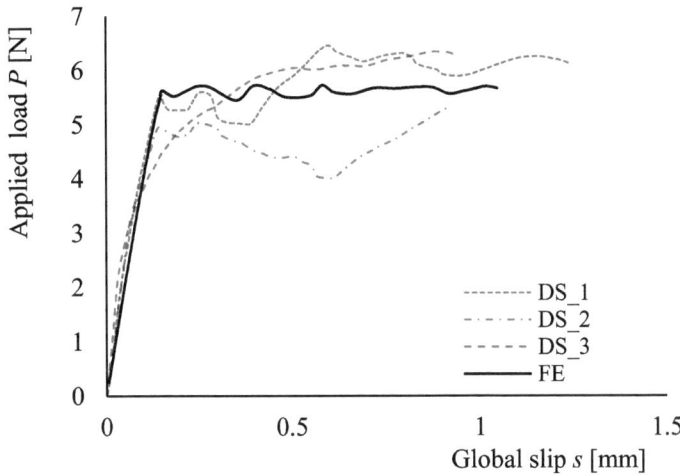

Fig. 8. Comparison of experimental and numerical curves of applied load, P, vs. global slip, s.

4 Conclusions

This paper summarizes results from parallel experimental and numerical studies of the stress-transfer behaviour and matrix-fiber interface performance for masonry substrates reinforced using SRG systems. The following key findings have been observed:

- Debonding of the matrix-fiber interfaces is the key driver of failure, resulting in complete separation and loss of the external reinforcing layer.
- The MD SRG system used in this study has proven to be effective as an avenue for strengthening retrofit. Further details of the performance of this MD SRG system can be found in [29].
- The numerical FE simulations provided a satisfactory prediction of the maximum applied load, and hold promise for prediction of general SRG behaviour.

However, the results obtained are valid only for the tested strengthening system, as variations in fiber sheet density and inorganic matrix can occur with different substrates. Therefore, further experimental investigations are needed to validate these findings, specifically examining the influence of other variables. These variables of interest include the number of steel textile layers used in the reinforcement, the masonry substrate strength, and the curing conditions of the mortar.

Acknowledgments. The authors are grateful for the following financial support from the Italian Ministry of University and Research (MUR): Research Grant PRIN 2020 No. 2020EBLPLS on "Opportunities and challenges of nanotechnology in advanced and green construction materials"; and Research Grant PRIN 2022 No. 2022TN5M7F on "TReE - Supporting the Transition to Ecological Economy in Italian cities Regeneration: circular model tools for reusing architecture and infrastructures".

References

1. Olivieri, C., Fortunato, A., DeJong, M.: A new membrane equilibrium solution for masonry railway bridges: The case study of Marsh Lane Bridge. Int. J. Masonry Res. Innov. **6**(4), 446–471 (2021)
2. Olivieri, C., Adriaenssens, S., Cennamo, C.: A novel graphical assessment approach for compressed curved structures under vertical loading. Int. J. Space Struct. **38**(2), 141–155 (2023)
3. Buonocore, G., Gesualdo, A., Monaco, M., Savino, M.T.: Improvement of Seismic Performance of Unreinforced Masonry Buildings using Steel Frames, In: Civil-Comp Proceedings: 106, B.H.V. Topping and Iványi eds., Civil Comp Press, Kippen, Stirlingshire, U.K (2014)
4. Gesualdo, A., Monaco, M.: Seismic vulnerability reduction of existing masonry buildings. Modelling of retrofitting tecniques. In: Urban Habitat Construction Under Catastrophic Events. **1**, 853–858, London, New York: CRC Press, Taylor & Francis Group (2010)
5. Gesualdo, A., et al.: Seismic retrofitting techniques for masonry arch bridges. Urban Habitat Constr. Catastrophic Events. **1**, 859–864 (2010)
6. Olivieri, C.: FORMERLY-Math: constrained form-finding through membrane equilibrium analysis in Mathematica. Software Impacts **16**, 100512 (2023)
7. Crespino, E., Adriaenssens, S., Fraddosio, A., Olivieri, C., Piccioni, M.D.: A multi-objective optimization approach for novel shell/frame systems under seismic load. Struct. **65**, 106625 (2024)
8. Di Gennaro, L., de Cristofaro, M., Loreto, G., Minutolo, V., Olivares, L., Zona, R., Frunzio, G.: In-situ load testing of an ancient masonry structure using fibre optics. Structures, **70** (2024)
9. Iannuzzo, A., Montanino, A.: A limit analysis-based CASS approach for the in-plane seismic capacity of masonry façades. Int. J. Solids Struct. **289**, 112633 (2024)
10. Fabbrocino, F., Olivieri, C., Luciano, R., Vaiano, G., Maddaloni, G., Iannuzzo, A.: Seismic performance of historic masonry buildings: A comparative analysis of equivalent frame and block-based methods. Alex. Eng. J. **109**, 359–375 (2024)
11. Olivieri, C., Cocking, S., Fabbrocino, F., Iannuzzo, A., Placidi, L., Adriaenssens, S.: Seismic capacity of purely compressed shells based on Airy stress function. Continuum Mech. Thermodyn. **37**(2), 21 (2025)
12. Iannuzzo, A., Mallardo, V.: A novel approach to model differential settlements and crack patterns in masonry structures. Eng. Struct. **323**, 119220 (2025)
13. Pingaro, N., Milani, G.: Simple non-linear numerical modelling of masonry arches reinforced with SRG using elasto-fragile and elasto-ductile truss finite elements. Eng. Struct. **293**, 116637 (2023)
14. Iannuzzo, A., Musone, V., Ruocco, E.: A neural network-based automated methodology to identify the crack causes in masonry structures. Comput.-Aided Civil and Infrastructure Eng. **39**(24), 3769–3785 (2024)
15. Montanino, A., Iannuzzo, A.: A quadrilateral plate-type finite element to model stress singularities in no-tension materials. Comput. Methods Appl. Mech. Eng. **432**, 117433 (2024)
16. D'Altri, A.M., de Miranda, S., Castellazzi, G., Glisic, B.: Numerical modelling-based damage diagnostics in cultural heritage structures. J. Cult. Herit. **61**, 1–12 (2023)
17. Di Gennaro, L., Guadagnuolo, M., Monaco, M.: Rocking Analysis of Towers Subjected to Horizontal Forces. Build. **13**(3) (2023)
18. Massaro, L., Di Gennaro, L., Guadagnuolo, M., Frunzio, G.: Strengthening of Masonry Arches: The "Santa Maria delle Grazie" Church. COMPDYN Proceedings (2023)
19. Carloni, C., Verre, S., Sneed, L.H., Ombres, L.: Open issues on the investigation of PBO FRCM-Concrete debonding. Compos. Struct. **299** (2022)

20. Ombres, L., Aiello, M.A., Cascardi, A., Verre, S.: Modeling of Steel-Reinforced Grout Composite System-To-Concrete Bond Capacity Using Artificial Neural Networks. J. Compos. Constr., **28**(5) (2024)
21. Sneed, L.H., Verre, S., Ombres, L., Carloni, C.: Flexural behavior RC beams strengthened and repaired with SRP composite. Eng. Struct. **258** (2022)
22. Ombres, L., Verre, S.: Influence of the strengthening configuration on the shear capacity of reinforced concrete beams strengthened with SRG (steel-reinforced grout) composites. Fibers **10**(7), 57 (2022)
23. Aiello, M.A., et al.: Masonry columns confined with fabric reinforced cementitious matrix (FRCM) systems: A round robin test. Constr. Build. Mater. **298** (2021)
24. Santandrea, M., Focacci, F., Mazzotti, C., Ubertini, F., Carloni, C.: Determination of the interfacial cohesive material law for SRG composites bonded to a masonry substrate. Engineering Failure Analysis, **111** (2020)
25. Bencardino, F., Nisticò, M., Verre, S.: Experimental Investigation and Numerical Analysis of Bond Behavior in SRG-Strengthened Masonry Prisms Using UHTSS and Stainless-Steel Fibers. Fibers 2020, **8**(8), (2020)
26. Ascione, F., Lamberti, M., Napoli, A., Realfonzo, R.: Experimental bond behavior of Steel Reinforced Grout systems for strengthening concrete elements. Constr. Build. Mater. **232**, 117105 (2020)
27. Sneed, L.H., Verre, S., Carloni, C., Ombres, L.: Flexural behavior of RC beams strengthened with steel-FRCM composite. Eng. Struct. **127**, 686–699 (2016)
28. Abaqus Theory and User's Manual: Version 2025
29. Ombres, L., Iorfida, A., Verre, S.: FRCM/SRG - Masonry Joints: Experimental Investigation and Numerical Modelling. Key Eng. Mater. **817**, 3–8 (2019)
30. Verre, S.: Numerical Strategy for Column Strengthened with FRCM/SRG System. Build. **12**, 2187 (2022)
31. Pingaro, N., Milani, G.: Non-linear 1D 16-DOF finite element for Fiber Reinforced Cementitious Matrix (FRCM) strengthening systems. Comput. Struct. **300**, 107422 (2024)
32. John, S. K., Cascardi, A., Verre, S., Nadir, Y.: RC-columns subjected to lateral cyclic force with different FRCM-strengthening schemes: experimental and numerical investigation. Bullet. Earthquake Eng. 1–30 (2025)
33. Lu, X.Z., Teng, J.G., Ye, L.P., Jiang, J.J.: Bond slip models for FRP sheet/plates bonded to concrete. Eng. Struct. **27**(6), 920–937 (2005)

Geometrical Proportioning of Masonry Arch Bridges

Michela Monaco(✉)

DING - Department of Engineering, University of Sannio, Benevento, Italy
monaco@unisannio.it

Abstract. The design of masonry arches has been based for centuries on empirical rules, and many of the arch bridges currently in use were designed and built according to geometric proportions. All the elements of the bridge, thickness at the springer and at the crown, dimensions of the abutments, height of the abutments, were defined according to methods that were reported for the first time in Renaissance treatises. The structure of geometric relations took on increasingly complex forms in relation to the development of mathematical thought of the time. This article presents a reasoned catalogue of empirical formulas reported in treatises from the Renaissance to the first decades of the twentieth century, together with an evaluation of their reliability using modern calculations.

Keywords: Masonry arch · Collapse mechanism · Empirical rules

1 Introduction

Since the earliest civilizations masonry arches have been the solution to bridge a gap. Before the development of static methods, geometrical rules and empirical methods have been the only source of design methods for arch bridges [1]. Despite their design did not envisage actual heavy traffic loads, several of these bridges are, at this time, a "live" part of the railway and road network. Excellently designed bridges, nowadays in service, can be found everywhere in Europe. For local authorities in charge of masonry arch bridges still in service it is a key problem to understand the "rules" intended in the last centuries to establish the structural shape of the bridge [2-4]. The problem of stability has become a key issue in case of cultural heritage bridges located in seismic areas [5]. To address these needs, a historical-critical analysis taking into account the design methodology can be the first step toward a complete understanding of the construction and a correct methodological approach for planning minimum restoration interventions [6-7]. Thickness at the springing and at the crown, together with the dimensions of abutments, have been determined in the past centuries by means of empirical methods [8-12], based on simple geometrical relations. They were aimed at providing both the dimensions of several bridge components (i.e. span, rise and thickness of the arch, width and height of piers and abutments) and the safety of the structure based on the observation of existing bridges and past experience [13]. The empirical rules continued to be employed until the first half of the 20th century, when the developments of statics and continuum mechanics were consolidated [14] and already in use for framed structures.

Essential parameters like weight and stiffness of the structure (due to arch, fill and spandrels), strength of the materials and problems related with the stability of the arch (snap-thorough) were not considered [1]. In every case, the geometrical approach was widely used and the results of these empirical formulae are in several cases masonry arch bridges actually in perfect conditions, playing until today their role in the traffic network. Recent researches have pointed out the strong link existing among modern formulation and pre-elastic theories, laying stress on the fact that *"the statics of the arch finally escaped from the labyrinth of empirical methods and theoretical conjectures"* [15]. On the contrary, it can be shown that several successful analysis methods, based on limt analysis for masonry arches, do not take into account the "essential parameters" named above.

The most popular and the first "mechanism method", proposed by Heyman in the second half of last century [16-19], is mainly based on the hypothesis of infinite compressive strength, null tensile strength and no-sliding among the voussoirs. Recent researches have in fact assessed that the material strength is not a key point in a stability analysis of an arch bridge [20], even in case of damage [21-22] since major cause of global failure can be envisaged as loss of equilibrium rather than the material failure. In many cases in fact the collapsed blocks are in perfect condition and restoration can be done merely by rebuilding, like in the Mostar bridge. The Heyman approach has recently been applied to the analysis of vaults, with successful and elegant formulations [23-26].

The search for the best shape of the arch that stimulated architects and engineers in the last centuries has produced as a result a lot of empirical formulae whose reliability could be evaluated taking into account the development of assessment methods [27-28]. The most usual method of verifying the adequacy of an arch proportioned according to these empirical methods has been made in the 19th century by means of the static procedures at that time consolidated and based on the line of thrust position. These methods have been successively extended to threedimensional surfaces, in order to analize masonry vaults [29-30]. In every case, a large part of empirical rules, although of doubtful mechanical orgin, has shown to be efficient [31].

In general the empirical approach calculates the crown thickness as a function of the span or the rise, according to the shape chosen for the intrados of the arch (circular, segmental, elliptical [31-34]. The analytical structure of the relations ranges from the simple linear relation proposed since the Renaissance [35] to the complex one given by Baker at the beginning of 20th century [3], according to the development of mathematics. A large part of these relations are reported in the treatises of the time, together with the examples effectively built by the author. Several of them are included in the major part of the tecnical manuals diffused among the engineers until the first half of last century [36-38], even in the code of practice by the Italian National Road Company (A.N.A.S.).

This paper presents a reasoned catalogue of empirical formulas reported in the treatises from the Renaissance to the first decades of the 20th century, together with an evaluation of their reliability by means of modern calculations.

2 Empirical relations

The first step in designing a masonry bridge was the definition of the number of arches and the intrados curve, generally based on hydraulic requirements, for the passage of the water and/or the boats, if the bridge spanned a river or stream [39].

The aesthetic and the stability requirements were strongly connected to these choices, considering that "...masonry bridges are more beautiful. They are more stable. They have durability. They are simple, both to design and to construct" [12].

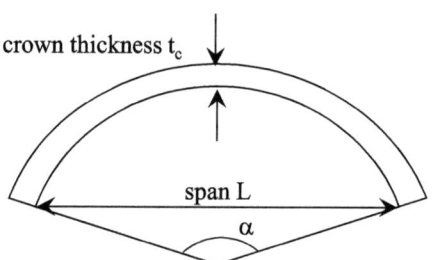

Fig. 1. Geometry of the masonry arch

The following step was the determination of the thickness at the crown, i.e. the depth of the keystone. Great part of the relations express the the crown depth (t_c) as a function of the span L or the radius R of the circle passing through the crown. Some of them are reported in Table 1 [9-11, 40-43].

As it will be shown in the following, the values of thickness obtained by the above relations 1 and 2 are too large for large span, unsafe for small span, while the relations 10 give values of smaller thickness for low-rise arches than for semicircular ones, as a further indication that the increase of flatness do not influence the bridge behaviour.

In this last ones in fact the influence of the rise is totally absent, so that buckling phaenomena for low-rise arches like the snap-through are not taken into account.

A picture of the variation of the crown thickness versus the span length is reported in Fig 2.

The decrease of the arch thickness over the years, especially for the large span arches, can be recognized. This is surely due to the development of masonry techniques and to the increasing trust in the materials strength, thanks to the diffusion of results of laboratory tests.

The red dots in Fig. 2 refer to real masonry bridges proportions, reported by Baker [3]. As it can be noted, several of them, actually in service, present crown thickness in the range under the Perronet formula.

The only particular case of a very low thickness is the footbridge at Pontypridd, Wales. It is not a coincidence that the minimum crown thickness is that of a bridge subjected to its own weight and limited traffic loads, the pedestrian only.

The dark blue dot, which seems in agreement with the Baker formula, refers to the Roman arch bridge in Pont Saint Martin, Italy, a shallow circular footbridge actually in perfect conditions (Fig. 3, left). The light blue dot refers to another Roman arch

Table 1. Empirical formulae for crown thickness.

	te	Author	Deep arch	Low-rise arch
1	XV c.	L.B. Alberti	$t_c = L/10$	
2	XVII c.	(before Perronet)	$t_c = L/15$	
3	1756	Perronet	$t_c = 0.325 + 0.035\,L$	$t_c = 0.325 + 0.0694\,R$
4	1809	Gauthey (L<16m)	$t_c = 0.33 + 0.021\,L$	
5	1809	Gauthey (16m<L<32m)	$t_c = 0.042\,L$	
6	1809	Gauthey (L>32m)	$t_c = 0.67 + 0.021\,L$	
7	1826	Léveillér	$t_c = 0.333 + 0.033\,L$	
8	1828	Déjardin	$t_c = 0.3 + 0.045\,L$	
9	1865	Rankine	$t_c = 0,191\,\sqrt{R}$	
10	1855	Lesguiller	$t_c = 0.10 + 0.20\,\sqrt{L}$	
11	1870	Dupuit	$t_c = 0.20\,\sqrt{L}$	$t_c = 0,15\,\sqrt{L}$
12	1885	Croizette-Desnoyers	$t_c = 0.15 + 0.17\,R^2$	
13	1914	Séjourné	$t_c = 0.15 + 0.15\,\sqrt{2R}$	
14	1920	Baker	$t_c = 0.138\sqrt{R + \frac{L}{2}} + 0.061$	

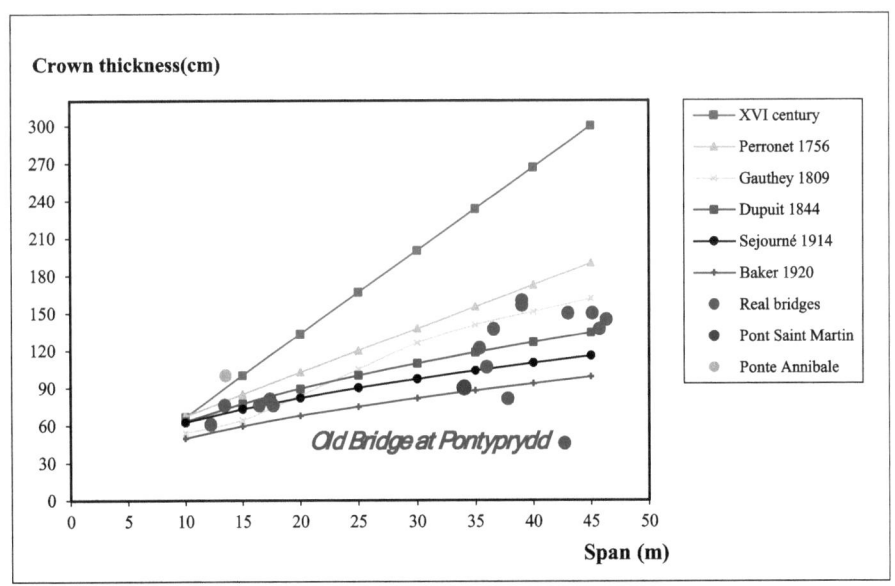

Fig. 2. Variation of the crown thickness with the span

bridge, in San Mango sul Calore, Italy (Fig. 3, right), whose proportions are far above the Renaissance relation.

A small non-scientific note: Roman engineers designed arch bridges according the local workmanship and material availability, so that it is impossible to force their proportions into relations that do not take into account the set of aspects Roman engineers considered. On the contrary, the bridges designed from the Middle Ages onwards were proportioned according to the geometrical relations reported in the treatises of the time.

Fig. 3. The Roman arch bridges in Pont Saint Martin (left) and San Mango sul Calore (right)

In general, bridges with low span show a constant thickness of the arch, while large span bridges present depth increment at springing, and empirical rules for the design of the bridge complete geometry can be found in the same treatises.

According to the Sejourné treatise [12], depth at springing in low-rise arches (angle $\alpha \leq 120°$ in Fig. 1) can be expressed in function of the crown thickness as:

$$t_a = t_c \left(1 + 12 n^2\right)$$

where t_a is the springing depth, t_c is the crown thickness, n is the height at springing with respect to the intrados curve center, so that:

$$n \leq \frac{1}{2\sqrt{3}} \quad (\alpha \leq 120°)$$

while the thickness at springing for deep arches can be designed according the following relation [12]:

$$t_a = t_c \left(1 + 2 n\right)$$

It should be underlined that the thickness calculated according to the previous relation can be given, according to Sejourné, to the sections corresponding to $\alpha=120°$, since, for Sejourné and other French authors, the remaining part of the bridge does not behave like an arch, due in general to the strong backing of the abutments. In every case, with the development of structural mechanics the geometrical approach was not abandoned, but used as predimensioning for design basis [31], until the first half of last century.

3 Kinematic analysis

In the following, a kinematic sensitive analysis has been conducted on semicircular masonry arches designed according the empirical formulae above reported.

The analysis of the arch has been perfomed according classical limit analysis, considering masonry a no-tension material with infinite compressive strength and infinite friction.

The collapse occurs for loss of equilibrium, due to the formation of hinges in the sections where the thrust line touches extrados and intrados curve.

The arch has been considered subjected to the selfweight (supposed constant in all the analyses) and a single point force whose position is defined by the ratio a/L (see Fig. 4).

In all the diagrams the minimum value of the force F that corresponds to incipient collapse (four-hinge mechanism) is reported, in function of the ratio a/L.

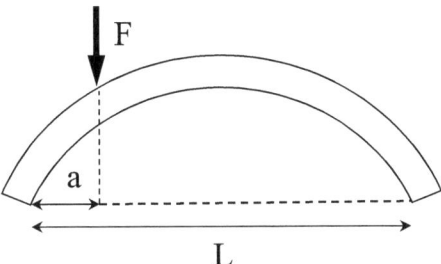

Fig. 4. Position of the point load on the arch

The analysis examines bridges of different spans, proportioned with the empirical relations reported in Table 1, starting from the Renaissance-type formula (Fig. 5). Figures 6-8 make reference to the remaining relations.

Since the Séjourné formula gives a reasonable factor of safety, while the other relations give an overestimation of the crown thickness, especially for large span, all the analyses are related to the upper limit of the Séjourné formula, reported in Figs. 5-8 with red line, in order to have a direct comparison with the famous XIX century formula.

The diffused trust in the geometrical approach should be probably found in this oversizing of the masonry structure.

The safety factor evaluable from the Séjourné formula is somewhat independent on the arch span, as it can be deduced by Fig. 8, while significant differences can be observed in the previous relations.

A summary of the analyses is reported in Fig. 9, in which an analysis of one of the two Roman masonry arch bridges considered, the one with the lower crown/span thickness ratio, is compared with the results of the sensitive analysis. As it can be easily seen, the safety degree obtained in this case is comparable with those obtained by means of the more ancient formulae.

This confirms that the geometrical approach, based on the observation of the realized structures, gives smaller dimensions as time passes by [44].

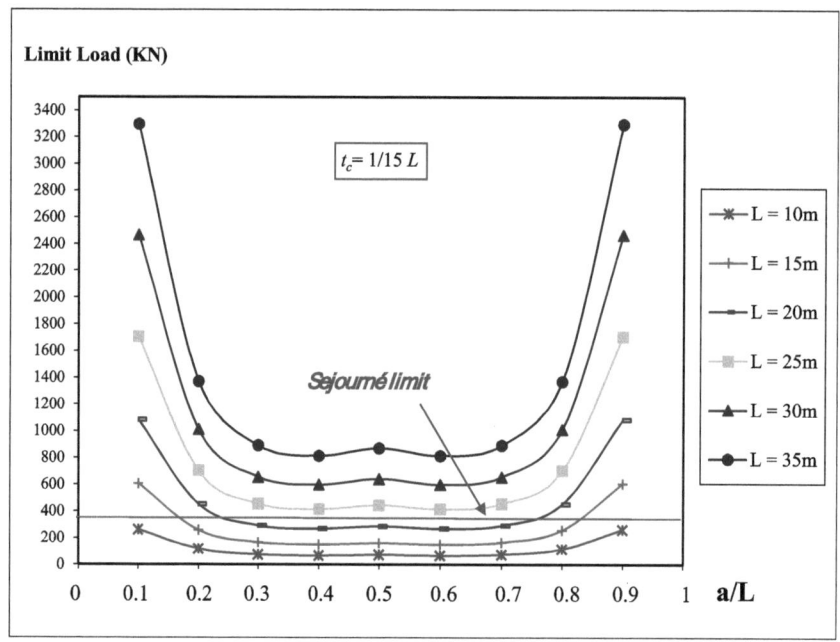

Fig. 5. Limit load vs loading position for different crown thickness according the XVI century formula

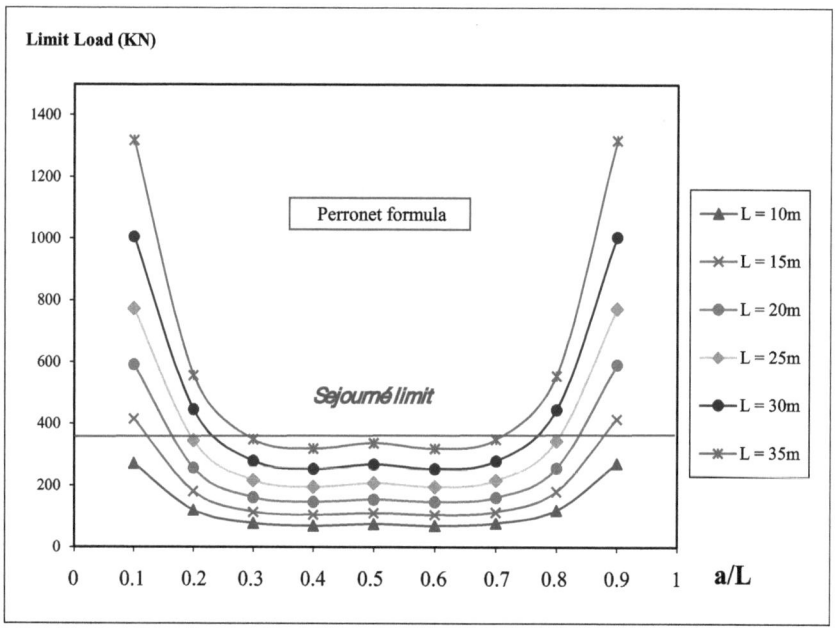

Fig 6. Limit load vs loading position for different crown thickness according Perronet formula

Geometrical Proportioning of Masonry Arch Bridges 321

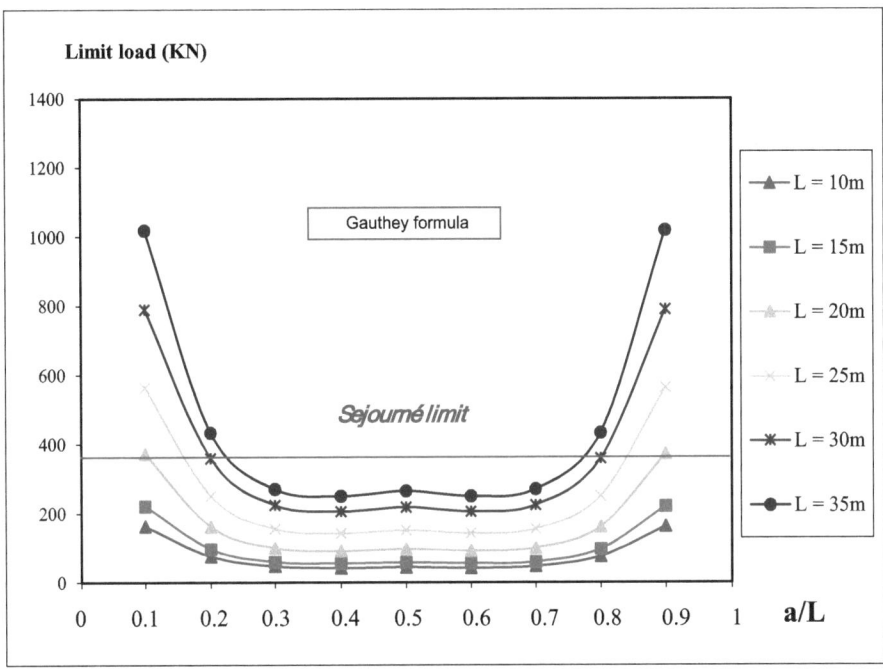

Fig. 7. Limit load vs loading position for different crown thickness according Gauthey formula

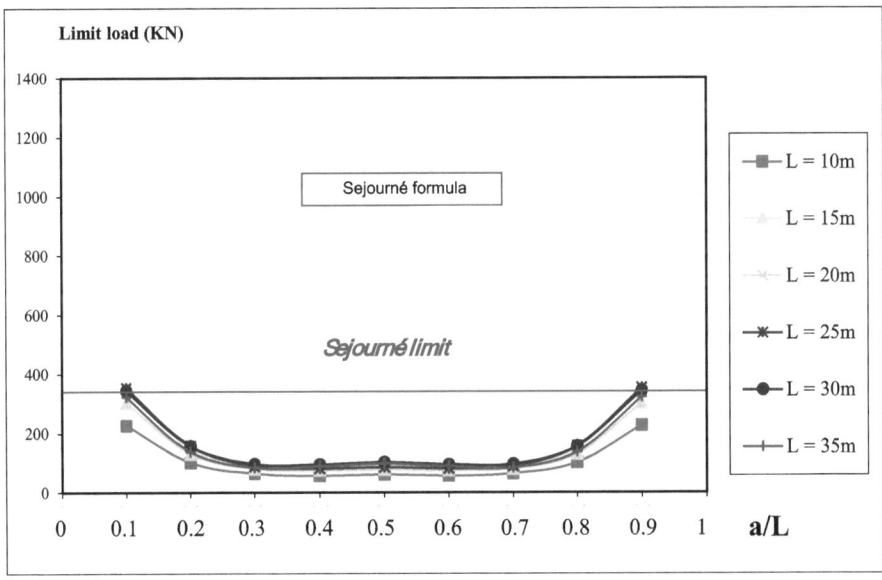

Fig. 8. Limit load vs loading position for different crown thickness according Sejourné formula

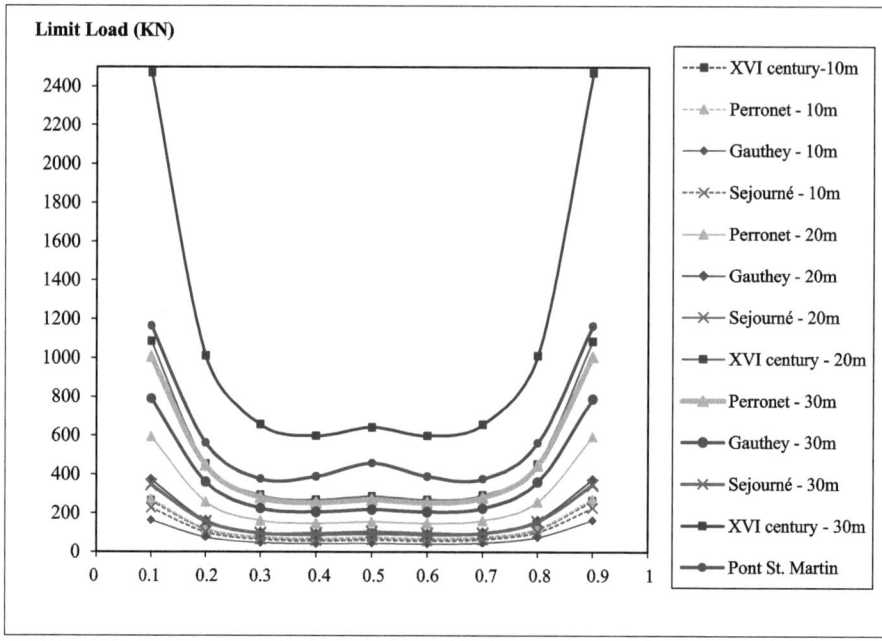

Fig. 9 Limit load vs loading position for different crown thickness according empirical formulae

The experience and tests performed on existing structures [45-46] confirm that good load carrying capacity of the structures can be obtained with a more limited volume of material, although the limits of these formulas have been recognized since the first half of last century [31].

4 Discussion and conclusion

The structural shape of a large part of the masonry bridges actually in service and part of the traffic network has been obtained over the centuries by means of geometrical rules. These empirical relations seem nonconservative in several cases (shallow arches) but they do not take into account the contribution given by spandrels and fill to the good structural performance of the bridge. Nevertheless, maintenance and repair of these bridges should take into account the principles on which the design process was based. This paper reports and discusses a catalogue of historical empirical formulas reported in the treatises from the Renaissance to the first decades of the 20th century, together with an evaluation of the reliability of the geometrical approach after a sensitive analysis.

Disclosure of Interests. The author ha no competing interests to declare that are relevant to the content of this article.

References

Corradi, M.: Empirical methods for the construction of masonry arch bridges in the 19th century. In: *Arch Bridges*, pp. 25-36, CRC Press. (2020)

Huerta, S.: Arch bridge design in eighteenth-century France: The rule of Perronet. Build. Knowl. Constr. Hist. **2**, 773–780 (2018)

Baker, I.O.: A treatise on masonry costruction. Wiley, New York (1910)

Massaro, L., et al.: Understanding past rules of the art in columna-capreoli wood trusses. Dev. Built Environ. **19**, 5 (2024). https://doi.org/10.1016/j.dibe.2024.100472

Olivieri, C., Cocking, S., Fabbrocino, F., Iannuzzo, A., Placidi, L., Adriaenssens, S.: Seismic capacity of purely compressed shells based on Airy stress function. Continuum Mech. Thermodyn. **37**(2), 21 (2025). https://doi.org/10.1007/s00161-024-01350-z

Frunzio, G., et al.: Use of engineered wood for the retrofitting of existing structures. WIT Trans. Built Environ. **210**, 225–236 (2022). https://doi.org/10.2495/ARC220191

Massaro, L. et al.: Strengthening of masonry arches: the "Santa Maria delle Grazie" Church. In: COMPDYN2023 Proceedings, Volume I (2023). https://doi.org/10.7712/120123.10567.20441.

Degrand, E., Resal, J. : Ponts en maçonnerie, (Stabilité des voûtes) In : Baudry, C. (ed.), Paris (in French). (1887)

Dejardin, M.: Routine de l'Etablissement des voûtes. Carilian-Goeury, Paris (1845)

Gauthey, M. : La construction des ponts, F. Didot imprimeur-libraire, Paris (in French) (1809)

Perronet, J.R. : Mémoire sur la recherche des moyens que l'on pourrait employer pour construire de grandes arches de pierre de 200, 300, 400 et jusqu'à 500 pieds d'ouverture qui seraient destinées à franchir de profondes vallées bordées de rochers escarpés, par le citoyen Perronet, Impr. Nationale Exécutive du Louvre, Paris (in French). (1793)

Sejourné, P.: Grandes voûtes, Imprimerie Vve Tardy Pigelet et fils, Bourges (in French) (1914)

Benvenuto, E.: La scienza delle costruzioni e il suo sviluppo storico, Sansoni editore, Firenze (in Italian) (1981)

Benvenuto, E.: An introduction to the history of structural mechanics - Part II: vaulted structures and elastic. Springer-Verlag (1991)

Sinopoli, A., et al.: Modern formulations for pre-elastic theories on masonry arches. J. Eng. Mech. ASCE **123**(3), 204 (1997). https://doi.org/10.1061/(ASCE)0733-9399(1997)123:3(204)

Heyman, J.: The stone skeleton. Int. J. Solids and Struct. **2**, 249–279 (1966). https://doi.org/10.1016/0020-7683(66)90018-7

Heyman, J.: The safety of masonry arches. Int. J. Mech. Sci. **11**, 363–385 (1969). https://doi.org/10.1016/0020-7403(69)90070-8

Heyman, J.: The masonry arch. Ellis Horwood Limited, Chichester, U.K. (1982)

Kooharian, A.: Limit analysis of voussoir (segmental) and concrete arches. J. Am. Concr. Inst. **24**, 317-328 (1952). https://doi.org/10.14359/11822

Olivieri, C., et al.: A new membrane equilibrium solution for masonry railway bridges: The case study of Marsh Lane Bridge. Int. J. Masonry Res. Innov. **6**(4), 446–471 (2021). https://doi.org/10.1504/IJMRI.2021.118831

Montanino, A. et al.: On different discretisation strategies to solve the kinematical and equilibrium problem for masonry-like structures, In: ECCOMAS2022, (2022). https://doi.org/10.23967/eccomas.2022.207

Di Gennaro, L. et al.: Influence of damage on the stability of masonry arches, Int. J. Space Struct. (2025)

Monaco, M., et al.: A no-tension analysis for a brick masonry vault with lunette. J. Mech. Mater. Struct. **13**, 703–714 (2018). https://doi.org/10.2140/JOMMS.2018.13.703

Olivieri, C.: Formerly-math: constrained form-finding through membrane equilibrium analysis in mathematica. Softw. Impac. **16**, 100512 (2023). https://doi.org/10.1016/j.simpa.2023.100512

Olivieri, C., et al.: A continuous stress-based form finding approach for compressed membranes. Int. J. Masonry Res. Innov. **9**(5–6), 585–605 (2024). https://doi.org/10.1504/IJMRI.2024.141665

Montanino, A., Iannuzzo, A.: A quadrilateral plate-type finite element to model stress singularities in no-tension materials. Comput. Methods Appl. Mech. Eng. **432**, 117433 (2024). https://doi.org/10.1016/j.cma.2024.117433

Stabilini, L.: Ponti, Tamburini, Milano (in Italian) (1946)

Page, J.: Masonry arch bridge. HMSO Publications, London, U.K. (1993)

O'Dwyer, D.: Funicular analysis of masonry vaults. Comput. Struct. **73**(1–5), 187–197 (1999). https://doi.org/10.1016/S0045-7949(98)00279-X

Block, P., Ochsendorf, J.: Thrust network analysis: a new methodology for three-dimensional equilibrium. J. Int. Assoc. Shell and Spatial Struct. **48**(3), 167–173 (2007)

Albenga, G.: Lezioni di Ponti, UTET, Torino (in Italian). (1930)

Houard, B.A.: Recueil polytechnique des ponts et chaussées, canaux de navigation, ports maritimes, desséchemens des marais agriculture, manufactures, arts mécaniques et des constructions civiles de France en général..., Goeury et Demoraine, Paris (in French) (1803)

Gay, G.: Ponts en maçonnerie, Paris, (in French). (1924)

Boothby, T.E.: Empirical design of masonry arch bridges. J. Architect. Eng. **26**(1), 02519002 (2020). https://doi.org/10.1061/(ASCE)AE.1943-5568.0000388

Alberti, L.B.: L'Architettura, tradotta in lingua fiorentina da Cosimo Batoli, gentiluomo e accademico fiorentino, appresso Lorenzo Tormentino Impressor Ducale, Firenze (in Italian). (1550)

Jorini, A.F.: Costruzione dei ponti in legno, in ferro, in muratura, Hoepli, Milano (in Italian) (1927)

Campanella, G.: Ponti in muratura, Vallardi, Milano (in Italian) (1928)

Stabilini, L.: La tecnica e la scienza delle costruzioni dal 1877 ad oggi. l'Industria, **43**, 9-10 (1929)

Croizette-Desnoyers, P.: Cours de construction des ponts, V.CH. Dunod Editeur, Paris (in French). (1885)

Leveiller, P.: Note sur les ponts en maconnerie. Lemans (in French) (1826)

Dupuit, J.: Traité de l'équilibre des voutes et de la construction des ponts en maçonnerie, Dunod editeur, Paris (in French) (1870)

Rankine, W.J.M.: A manual of civil engineering. Griffin, London (1865)

Monaco, M., Gargiulo, M.R.: Empirical methods for the proportioning of masonry arches, In: Proc. WONDERMasonry3, Workshop on Design for Rehabilitation of Masonry Structures, Lacco Ameno, 9-11 October, Edizioni Polistampa, Firenze (2012)

Di Gennaro, L., et al.: In-situ load testing of an ancient masonry structure using fibre optics. Struct. **70**, 10 (2024). https://doi.org/10.1016/j.istruc.2024.107567

Fanning, P.J., Boothby, T.E.: Experimentally-based assessment of masonry arch bridges. Proc. Inst. Civil Eng.-Bridge Eng. **156**(3), 109–11 (2003). https://doi.org/10.1680/bren.2003.156.3.109

The Effects of Localised Damage on the Structural Stability of Masonry Arches

Luciana Di Gennaro(✉) , Mariateresa Gaudagnuolo , and Giorgio Frunzio

Department of Architecture and Industrial Design, University of Campania Luigi Vanvitelli, Aversa, CE, Italy
luciana.digennaro@unicampania.it

Abstract. Masonry arches represent a widely adopted structural solution in structure and infrastructure systems, including bridges, viaducts, and architectural constructions. They often exhibit signs of degradation due to ageing, insufficient maintenance, and exposure to natural actions, such as seismic events, soil settlements, and material deterioration. Such factors can significantly compromise structural stability, making the assessment and preservation process more complex. The present study investigates the stability of masonry arches subjected to horizontal loads, with particular attention to the influence of localised damage on the collapse multiplier across different geometric configurations. Arches with different geometry were analysed, ranging from elliptical arches with a quarter-span rise to semicircular (full-centre) arches. Damage was modelled by introducing localised reductions in thickness along the entire intrados to evaluate its impact on the structural response. Moreover, multiple thicknesses were considered for each geometry to assess slenderness's role in undamaged and damaged conditions. The findings identify the most critical damage locations regarding structural capacity loss under the applied loading configuration and provide useful insights for the preliminary assessment and conservation of historic masonry arch structures, particularly in contexts where rapid and simplified evaluations are required.

Keywords: Masonry arch · Collapse mechanism · Limit analysis

1 Introduction

Masonry arch bridges are a significant portion of the infrastructural heritage across Italy and Europe, bearing testimony to the evolution of civil engineering and architectural practice. Since antiquity, efforts have been made to understand and optimise arch geometries to enhance structural performance, developing numerous analytical theories. From the seminal treatises of De La Hire, Mascheroni, and Méry to the mechanical theories of Heyman and Benvenuto [1–5], significant progress has been made in modelling the behaviour of masonry arches. In particular, Heyman's application of limit analysis principles remains a cornerstone in the field [6, 7].

While modern numerical techniques such as the Finite Element and Discrete Element Methods offer accurate assessments [8–10], they require extensive data collection and considerable computational effort, making them less suitable for rapid assessments [11, 12]. Consequently, limit analysis methods—particularly those based on the kinematic theorem—remain valuable for preliminary evaluations, as they demand fewer input parameters while still providing meaningful insights into structural stability [13–19].

Recent experimental investigations have offered valuable insights into the structural behaviour of masonry arches, particularly for assessing their residual strength, identifying failure modes, and evaluating the influence of material degradation on collapse mechanisms [20–23].

A critical factor in such assessments is the presence of defects and damage, often caused by environmental or anthropogenic actions [24, 25]. These can lead to significant, yet difficult to predict, performance losses [26–28], particularly in seismic regions. Although modern surveying techniques enable accurate geometric documentation [29], detailed structural characterisation may be unfeasible in large-scale or urgent assessments [30–32]. In this context, modelling damage as a localised reduction in thickness has emerged as a feasible and effective approach within limit analysis frameworks [33].

This study investigates the structural capacity of masonry arches under horizontal loading through a two-dimensional limit analysis approach. The analysis focuses on elliptical arches with a horizontal major axis and variable geometries. A parametric study is conducted by varying both the rise and the thickness of the arch to explore the influence of these geometrical parameters on structural stability. Damage is modelled as a localised reduction in intradossal thickness, and collapse multipliers are computed to evaluate the loss of load-bearing capacity in each geometrical condition. The proposed methodology offers a rapid yet effective way of assessing damaged masonry arches' structural vulnerability, supporting conservation and maintenance strategies.

2 The Geometry of the Arch

The arches analysed in this study were idealised as two-dimensional structures with intrados profiles derived from a single geometrical family: elliptical curves with a horizontal major axis. This formulation allows for a continuous and systematic variation of the rise-to-span ratio while maintaining the typical structural and geometric characteristics of historical masonry arches. The intrados geometry was defined by the upper half of an ellipse governed by the equation:

$$\frac{x^2}{a^2}+\frac{y^2}{b^2} = 1, x \in [-a, a] \qquad (1)$$

where $a = L/2$ is the semi-span, and $b = h$ represents the rise. The span L was kept constant in all analyses, while the rise h was parametrically varied to explore different arch shapes. A rise equal to half the span ($b = h = L/2$) yields a semicircular profile, which corresponds to the special case commonly referred to as a full-centered arch.

In all configurations, the arch was assumed to have a constant thickness t along the profile. This thickness was also treated as a variable parameter in the analysis, in order to investigate its influence on the structural response under horizontal loading.

The elliptical parametrisation here adopted ensures a smooth and symmetric geometry, suitable for discretisation into rigid blocks and fully compatible with the assumptions of kinematic limit analysis. Moreover, it enables a unified treatment of both flatter and more curved profiles within a consistent mathematical framework.

3 Background and Theoretical Framework

The mechanical behaviour of masonry arches has long been studied through simplified models that capture their essential structural characteristics. Among these, Heyman's theory [3, 34] provides a foundational framework by idealising masonry as a material with no tensile strength, infinite compressive strength, and no sliding between blocks. Despite its simplicity, the model captures the essential features of masonry behaviour and has been widely employed and further developed in recent decades [35, 36]. These assumptions naturally lend themselves to the framework of limit analysis, which allows the evaluation of the ultimate load-bearing capacity without detailed stress computations. In particular, the kinematic theorem of limit analysis states that a structure is unstable if a compatible collapse mechanism exists for which the internal energy dissipation is lower than the external work [37–39]. This principle forms the basis of the kinematic approach, which is especially suited to the study of masonry as an assemblage of rigid blocks.

Through the kinematic method, possible failure mechanisms can be explicitly modelled, and upper-bound estimates of collapse loads can be obtained by evaluating virtual work equilibria.

Within the framework of limit analysis, damage may be introduced through geometric simplifications, such as a localised reduction in thickness, which has been adopted in several recent studies as a pragmatic proxy for crack patterns, voids, or material loss. This modelling strategy enables evaluation how damage influences structural capacity while maintaining computational efficiency. Despite its simplicity, the kinematic approach remains a valuable tool for preliminary assessment, particularly when limited geometric and material data are available. It provides a rational basis for early-stage engineering decisions and for prioritising further detailed investigations.

4 Methodology

The structural behaviour of the masonry arch is investigated under a system of increasing horizontal loads superimposed on the constant self-weight of the structure. The horizontal actions are expressed through a dimensionless load multiplier, denoted by λ, which governs the proportional increase in lateral loading.

According to established literature [40–42], this loading scenario typically induces the development of a four-hinge failure mechanism, which is characteristic of masonry arches subjected to dominant horizontal forces (Fig. 1). The arch is divided into four rigid blocks, separated by plastic hinges. The first block, adjacent to the springing on the left, remains constrained at the support, while the remaining three blocks rotate about the hinges as the mechanism evolves. Hinges typically form in a defined sequence: the first and third at the intrados and the second and fourth at the extrados.

Experimental and analytical studies have shown that the angular positions of the hinges—denoted as θ_1, θ_2, and θ_3—tend to fall within specific intervals, which depend on the geometry and loading conditions of the arch [41]. These admissible ranges are defined as:

$$\Omega_{\theta 1} = [15°, \ 75°], \Omega_{\theta 2} = [30°, \ 90°], \Omega_{\theta 3} = [90°, \ 165°] \tag{2}$$

The kinematics of the collapse mechanism are fully described by a Lagrangian parameter, α, which governs the relative rotation of the rigid blocks. Each block rotates around a defined centre—C_1, C_2, and C_4 for the first, second, and third block, respectively—as illustrated in Fig. 1.

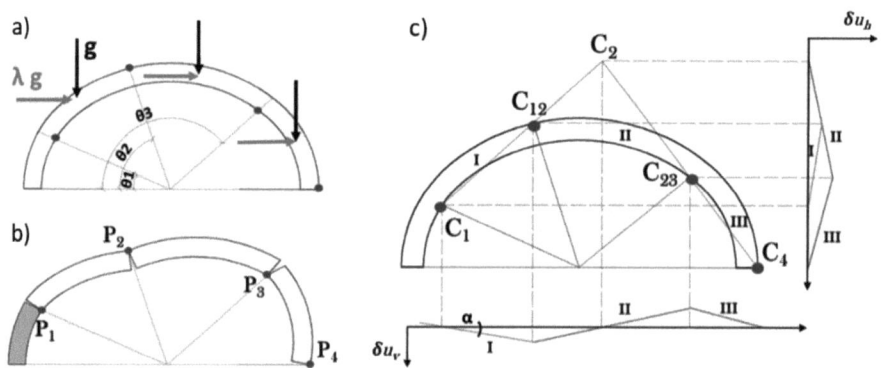

Fig. 1. a) Load condition and angular hinge position; b) Schematic representation of the four-hinge mechanism; c) Collapse mechanism and displacement profiles.

The structure remains in equilibrium under the load system $\mathbf{g} + \lambda \mathbf{g}$, where g denotes the self-weight and λg the increasing horizontal forces, provided the Principle of Virtual Work is satisfied. This condition is expressed as:

$$\langle \mathbf{g}, \ \delta u_v \rangle + \langle \lambda \mathbf{g}, \ \delta u_h \rangle \leq 0; \quad \forall \ \delta u \in \mathbf{M} \tag{3}$$

At the onset of collapse, the system reaches a limit state where the virtual work of external actions vanishes along the kinematically admissible mechanism **M**, leading to the equality:

$$\langle \mathbf{g}, \ \delta u_v \rangle + \langle \lambda \mathbf{g}, \ \delta u_h \rangle = 0; \quad \forall \ \delta u \in \mathbf{M} \tag{4}$$

From this, the collapse multiplier λ can be computed explicitly as:

$$\lambda = -\frac{\langle \mathbf{g}, \ \delta u_v \rangle}{\langle \mathbf{g}, \ \delta u_h \rangle} \tag{5}$$

The multiplier λ is a function of the hinge angles ($\theta 1, \theta 2, \theta 3$). Each block's geometry, mass and centre of gravity are calculated for each admissible triplet, allowing for the corresponding value of λ to be evaluated. According to the kinematic (upper bound) theorem of limit analysis, the critical multiplier corresponds to the minimum value of λ across all admissible configurations, beyond which equilibrium cannot be maintained.

A constrained optimisation problem is formulated to identify this minimum. The domain of admissible configurations Ω is defined as the Cartesian product of the angular intervals:

$$\Omega = \Omega_{\theta 1} \times \Omega_{\theta 2} \times \Omega_{\theta 3} \qquad (6)$$

Further constraints are imposed to ensure the physical plausibility of the mechanism, notably:

$$\theta 2 - \theta 1 \geq 15°, \quad \theta 3 - \theta 2 \geq 15° \qquad (7)$$

The resulting admissible set $\overline{\Omega}$ is thus defined as:

$$\overline{\Omega} = \begin{cases} \Omega = \Omega_{\theta 1} \times \Omega_{\theta 2} \times \Omega_{\theta 3} \\ \theta 2 - \theta 1 \geq 15° \\ \theta 3 - \theta 2 \geq 15° \end{cases} \qquad (8)$$

The collapse multiplier is then obtained by solving:

$$\lambda = \min_{(\theta 1, \theta 2, \theta 3) \forall \overline{\Omega}} \lambda(\theta 1, \theta 2, \theta 3). \qquad (9)$$

This procedure allows for systematically identifying the most unfavourable hinge configuration, providing an upper-bound estimate of the load capacity under horizontal actions.

4.1 Analysis Parameters

A parametric analysis was performed by varying the rise (h) and the thickness (t) of a masonry arch with a fixed span (L = 3 m) to evaluate the influence of geometry on the collapse multiplier λ. The applied load condition corresponds to the increasing horizontal forces system described in Eq. 9.

The rise h, defined as the vertical distance between the crown and the springing line, was varied between a quarter of L and half of L, discretised into five equally spaced values, each of them representative of typical historical configurations:

$$h_1 = \frac{1}{4}L; \; h_2 = \frac{5}{16}L; \; h_3 = \frac{3}{8}L; \; h_4 = \frac{7}{16}L; \; h_5 = \frac{L}{2} \qquad (10)$$

The arch thickness t was defined according to the empirical formula suitable for small-span bridges [41]:

$$t = A\left(1 + \sqrt{L}\right) \qquad (11)$$

where the coefficient A ranges from 0.15 to 0.18. Five discrete thickness values were derived accordingly.

For each (h, t) combination, the collapse multiplier was computed through constrained minimisation over the hinge angle domain ($\theta 1, \theta 2, \theta 3$), discretised with 5° increments and subjected to geometric constraints. The procedure was implemented in Wolfram Mathematica© [43], allowing for systematic evaluation of λ across all admissible configurations.

4.2 Damage Modelling

Localised damage was introduced into the model using three key parameters:

- Thickness Reduction (I): the defect was modelled as a uniform local decrease in thickness, set to one-third of the original value.
- Damage Extension (E): the angular extent of the damaged region was kept constant along the intrados, with a fixed radial spread equal to 15°.
- Damage Position (P): the position of the defect was defined by its initial angular coordinate φi, which varied from 15° to 165° in 5° increments, resulting in 31 discrete locations.

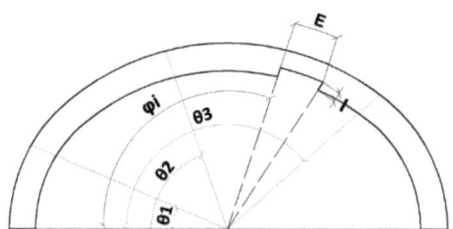

Fig. 2. Representation of damage

This parameterisation enabled the systematic assessment of how defect placement affects the collapse multiplier λ in arches subjected to horizontal loading (Fig. 2).

In this context, the reduction in thickness is intended to represent a localised loss of material at the intrados, such as that caused by erosion, detachment, or mechanical degradation [44, 45]. The assumption enables a simplified yet physically meaningful representation of damage effects within the analytical framework.

5 Results

5.1 Undamaged State

The collapse behaviour of the undamaged masonry arch was examined by evaluating the collapse multiplier λ across a range of geometric configurations. The analysis was conducted with a constant span L = 3 m and considered systematic variations of the rise (h) and thickness (t), as previously defined. The masonry was assumed to have a unit weight $\gamma = 16$ kN/m3.

The objective was to assess the sensitivity of the structural capacity to these parameters and to investigate the potential presence of nonlinear trends in the collapse response. Table 1 reports the computed values of λ for each (h, t) combination.

The results reveal that increasing the thickness t leads to a systematic rise in the collapse multiplier λ across all configurations, thereby confirming that thicker arches are more resistant to horizontal forces. In contrast, an increase in the rise h is associated with a reduction in λ, indicating that flatter arches perform better in terms of structural capacity under lateral actions. Although the effect of increasing thickness appears

Table 1. Collapse multiplier for each (h, t) combination – undamaged state.

	t_1	t_2	t_3	t_4	t_5
h_1	0.482	0.539	0.593	0.644	0.692
h_2	0.334	0.375	0.414	0.450	0.486
h_3	0.253	0.285	0.315	0.342	0.370
h_4	0.204	0.231	0.253	0.276	0.299
h_5	0.171	0.193	0.214	0.233	0.251

approximately linear, its influence is more pronounced in arches with lower rise. As the rise increases, the benefit of additional thickness becomes less significant, suggesting a nonlinear interaction between the two parameters (Fig. 3).

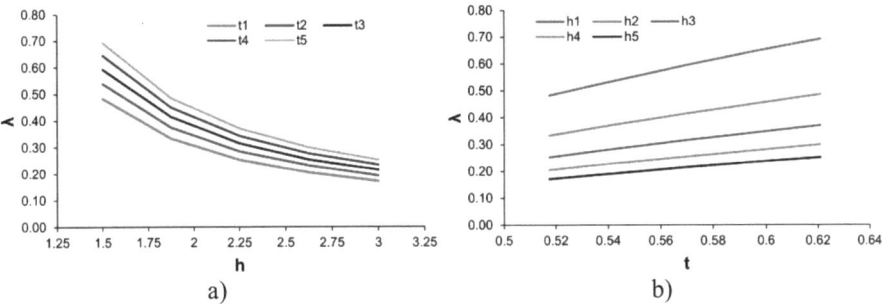

Fig. 3. Undamaged condition. a) h versus λ graph, b) t versus λ graph

5.2 Damaged State

The influence of localised damage on the collapse behaviour of masonry arches was assessed by evaluating the collapse multiplier λ as a function of the damage position φ_i for each combination of rise h and thickness t. Figure 4 presents the results for the low-rise cases, h_1 and h_2, with each curve corresponding to a different thickness (t_1–t_5).

The trends highlight a clear dependence on both geometry and damage location. λ remains relatively high and exhibits moderate variation across the angular domain, indicating a limited sensitivity to damage position. The worst conditions appear near the springs (φ_i equal to 15° and 165°) and in the right part of the arch (φ_i equal to 135° for h_1 and 130° for h_2).

As the rise increases (h_3 to h_5), the influence of damage becomes more pronounced and spatially localised (Fig. 5). In particular, a significant reduction in λ is often observed around $\varphi \approx 115°$–125°, depending on the geometry. These angular positions appear to be especially critical in triggering collapse mechanisms, as indicated by the sharp drop in load-carrying capacity.

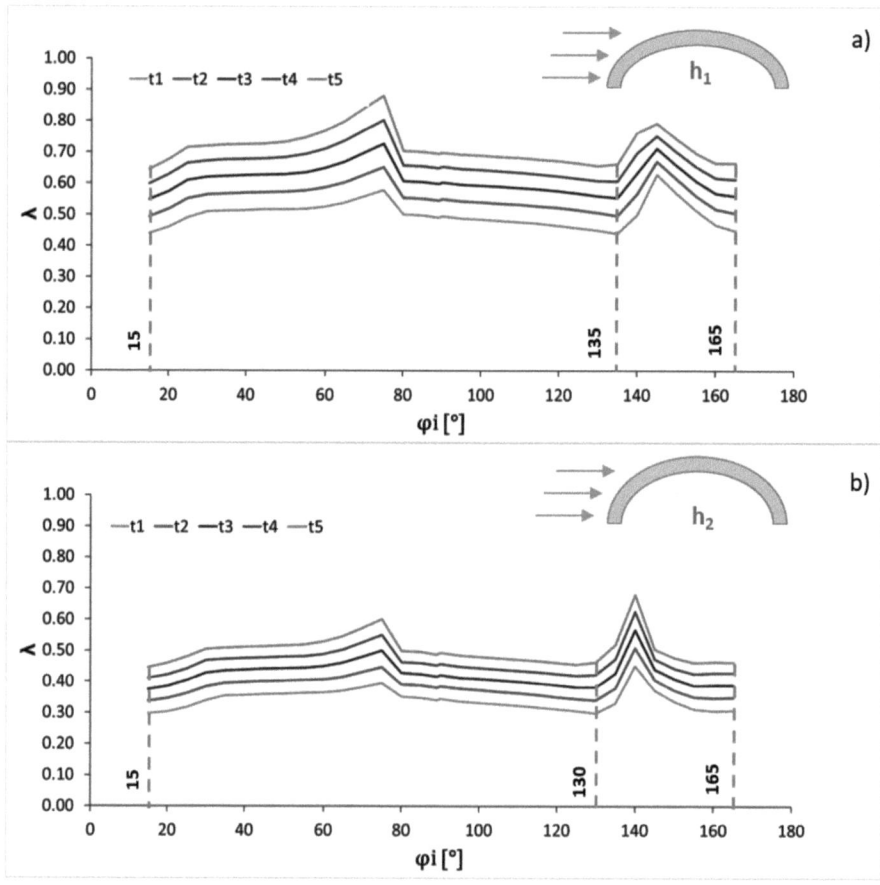

Fig. 4. Collapse multiplier λ as a function of the damage starting angle φi: a) h_1; b) h_2

Interestingly, for φi values immediately following this range (e.g. 135°–145°), λ tends to increase again, suggesting that the arch is less sensitive to damage located in those sectors. The graphical results confirm that even small shifts in the position of the damaged zone can lead to notable variations in structural response. The influence of thickness t is present across all cases, with higher thickness values generally associated with increased collapse multipliers. However, this effect becomes less marked as the rise increases: the curves for different t values tend to converge, suggesting that geometry becomes the dominant factor in structural performance in high-rise configurations.

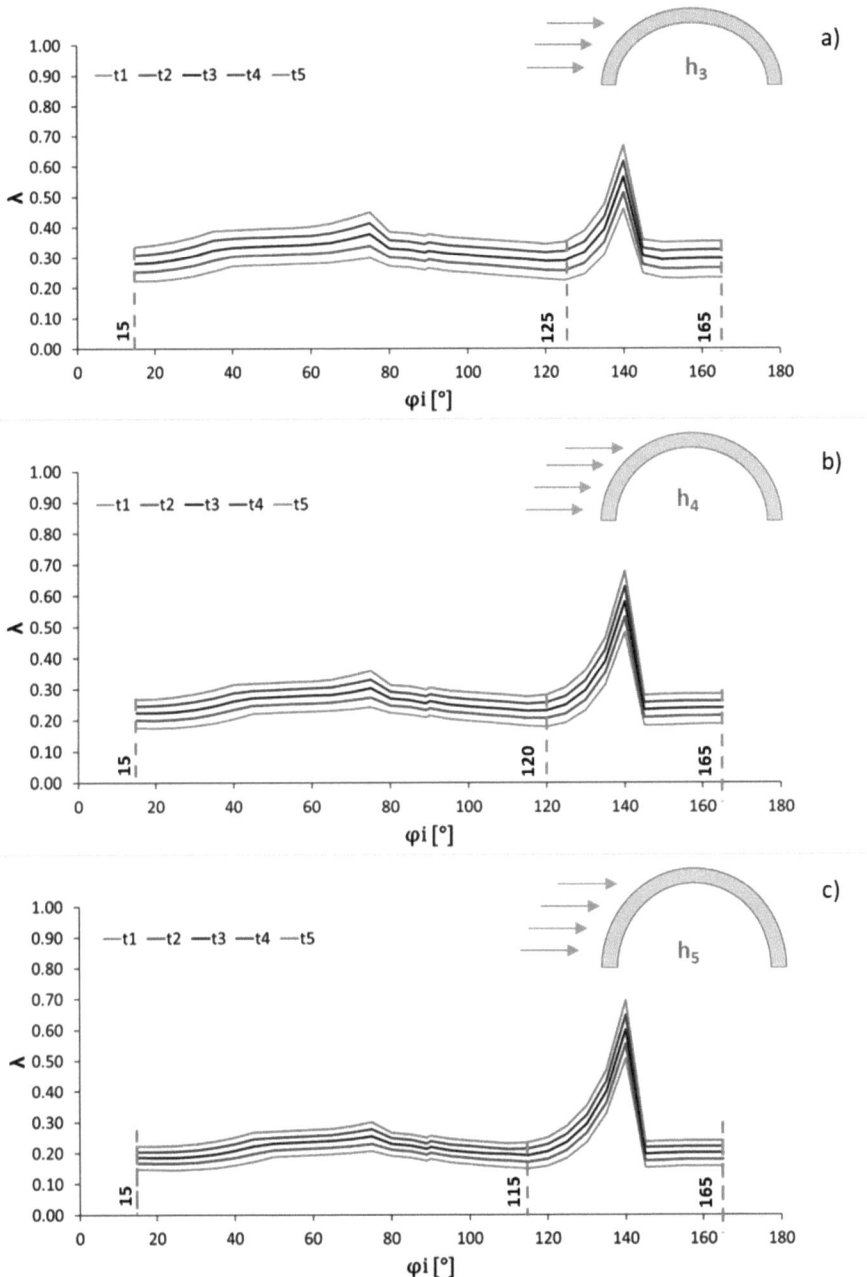

Fig. 5. Collapse multiplier λ as a function of the damage starting angle φi: a) h_3; b) h_4; c) h_5

6 Discussion and Conclusion

This study investigated the stability of masonry arches subjected to horizontal loads, with a specific focus on the effects of localised damage. A parametric approach was adopted to examine how variations in arch geometry, i.e. the rise h, the thickness t, and angular position of damage φi, influence the collapse multiplier λ. Both undamaged and damaged configurations were analysed, allowing for a direct comparison of their structural responses.

In the undamaged state, the analysis confirmed that increasing the arch thickness improves structural capacity, while higher rise values reduce the collapse multiplier. This inverse trend reflects the superior efficiency of flatter arches in resisting horizontal actions. The interaction between rise and thickness is nonlinear: the beneficial effect of thickness becomes less pronounced as the geometry becomes more slender. In the damaged condition, the sensitivity of λ to the angular position of the defect was systematically assessed. The results show that the structural response is strongly dependent on the exact location of the damaged zone. For lower-rise configurations, the variation of λ across the angular domain is relatively smooth, suggesting a more distributed structural response. In contrast, in higher-rise arches, a sharp drop in ultimate capacity is observed when the damage begins within specific angular intervals—particularly between $\varphi \approx$ 115° and 130°, depending on the geometry. Interestingly, neighbouring angular positions, such as $\varphi \approx$ 135°–145°, result in significantly lower reduction of λ, highlighting the importance of precise localisation in damage modelling.

Thickness continues to influence the structural behaviour across all cases; however, its relative impact diminishes with increasing rise as the ratio h/L becomes the dominant factor. These findings suggest that while increasing cross-sectional dimensions may be beneficial, its effectiveness is conditional on both the global shape of the arch and the location of potential damage.

From a practical perspective, the outcomes of this study underscore the importance of assessment strategies that consider not only the extent but also the precise angular position of damage. In particular, for arches with greater rise, localised reductions in thickness—when occurring in structurally sensitive zones—may result in substantial losses in load-bearing capacity. Based on limit analysis and parametric investigation, the methodology adopted provides a rational and computationally efficient tool for the preliminary evaluation of structural vulnerability in masonry arch systems.

Disclosure of Interests. The authors have no competing interests to declare that are relevant to the content of this article.

References

1. Benvenuto, E.: An introduction to the history of structural mechanics - Part II: vaulted structures and elastic. (1991)
2. De La Hire, P.: Traité de Mécanique. (1695)
3. Heyman, J.: The stone skeleton. Int. J. Solids Struct. **2**, 249–279 (1966). https://doi.org/10.1016/0020-7683(66)90018-7

4. Mascheroni, L.: Nuove ricerche sull'equilibrio delle volte. , Bergamo (1785)
5. Méry, E.: Sur l'equilibre des voûtes en berceau. (1840)
6. Clemente, P., Saitta, F., Buffarini, G., Ormando, C.: Masonry Arch Bridges with Finite Compression Strength Subject to Horizontal Longitudinal Seismic Actions. Applied Sciences (Switzerland). **13**, (2023). https://doi.org/10.3390/app13137509
7. Monaco, M., Bergamasco, I., Betti, M.: A no-tension analysis for a brick masonry vault with lunette. J. Mech. Mater. Struct. **13**, 703–714 (2018). https://doi.org/10.2140/JOMMS.2018.13.703
8. Karalar, M., Çufalı, G.: Structural Assessment of Historical Stone Bridges with the Finite Element Method under Dynamic Effects of Arch Shape: The Antik Iscehisar Bridge. Applied Sciences (Switzerland). **13**, (2023). https://doi.org/10.3390/app131910740
9. Malena, M., Angelillo, M., Fortunato, A., de Felice, G., Mascolo, I.: Arch bridges subject to pier settlements: continuous vs. piecewise rigid displacement methods. Meccanica. **56**, 2487–2505 (2021). https://doi.org/10.1007/s11012-021-01397-1
10. Massaro, L., Di Gennaro, L., Guadagnuolo, M., Frunzio, G.: Strengthening of masonry arches: the "Santa Maria delle Grazie." COMPDYN Proceedings. (2023). https://doi.org/10.7712/120123.10567.20441
11. Di Gennaro, L., Zizi, M., Chisari, C., Guadagnuolo, M., Frunzio, G., De Matteis, G.: STRUCTURAL ASSESSMENT OF DAMAGED MASONRY ARCH BRIDGES: A PARAMETRIC STUDY BASED ON LIMIT ANALYSIS. In: 18th WORLD CONFERENCE ON EARTHQUAKE ENGINEERING WCEE2024. , Milano (2024)
12. Alpaslan, E., Yilmaz, M.F., Şengönül, B.D.: Rating and reliability assessment of a historical masonry arch bridge. J Civ Struct Health Monit. **13**, 1003–1021 (2023). https://doi.org/10.1007/s13349-023-00692-7
13. Gaetani, A., Monti, G., Paolone, A., Lourenço, P.B., Milani, G.: Seismic capacity of masonry groin vaults through upper bound limit analysis. In: Structural Analysis of Historical Constructions: Anamnesis, diagnosis, therapy, controls - Proceedings of the 10th International Conference on Structural Analysis of Historical Constructions, SAHC 2016. pp. 1505–1512 (2016)
14. Guadagnuolo, M., Aurilio, M., Faella, G.: Kinematic analysis of historic chimney stacks: the Royal Palace of Carditello. In: Procedia Structural Integrity. pp. 766–773 (2022). https://doi.org/10.1016/j.prostr.2023.01.100
15. Frunzio, G., Di Gennaro, L.: The out of plane behaviour of masonry infilled frames. In: Journal of Physics: Conference Series (2021). https://doi.org/10.1088/1742-6596/2090/1/012148
16. Gesualdo, A., Calderoni, B., Iannuzzo, A., Fortunato, A., Monaco, M.: Minimum energy strategies for the in-plane behaviour of masonry. Frattura ed Integrità Strutturale. **14**, 376–385 (2019). https://doi.org/10.3221/IGF-ESIS.51.27
17. Cennamo, C., Cusano, C.: The gothic arcade of santa maria incoronata in Naples: Equilibrium of gothic arches. International Journal of Masonry Research and Innovation. **3**, 92–107 (2018). https://doi.org/10.1504/IJMRI.2018.092454
18. Cennamo, C., Zuccaro, G., Montanino, A., Angjeliu, G., Cusano, C.: Considerations about the static response of masonry domes: a comparison between limit analysis and finite element method. International Journal of Masonry Research and Innovation. **1**, (2021). https://doi.org/10.1504/ijmri.2021.10037898
19. Perelli, F.L., De Gregorio, D., Montanino, A., Olivieri, C., Maddaloni, G., Iannuzzo, A.: Energy-based modelling of in-plane fragility curves for the 2D ultimate capacity of Italian masonry buildings. Front Built Environ. **9**, (2023). https://doi.org/10.3389/fbuil.2023.1127523
20. Page, J.: Load tests to collapse on two arch bridges at Strathmashie and Barlae. (1989)
21. Taylor, N., Mallinder, P.: Brittle hinge in masonry arch mechanism. Structural engineer London. **71**, 359–366 (1993)

22. Fantilli, A.P., Burello, N.S.: Experimental and numerical analyses of curvilinear masonry structures exposed to high temperatures. International Journal of Masonry Research and Innovation. **9**, 475–497 (2024). https://doi.org/10.1504/IJMRI.2024.141647
23. Liu, B., Drougkas, A., Sarhosis, V., Smith, C.C., Gilbert, M.: Experimental investigation on the shear behaviour of the brickwork-backfill interface in masonry arch bridges. Eng Struct. 292, (2023). https://doi.org/10.1016/j.engstruct.2023.116531
24. Zizi, M., Chisari, C., De Matteis, G.: Influence of uncertain mechanical parameters on the load-bearing capacity of multi-span masonry arch bridges. In: Life-Cycle of Structures and Infrastructure Systems. pp. 1538–1545. CRC Press, London (2023). https://doi.org/10.1201/9781003323020-189
25. Özcan, Z.: Structural assessment and seismic response of the historic Justinian stone arch bridge. Case Studies in Construction Materials. 22, (2025). https://doi.org/10.1016/j.cscm.2025.e04471
26. Augusthus-Nelson, L., Swift, G.: Experimental investigation of the residual behaviour of damaged masonry arch structures. Structures. **27**, 2500–2512 (2020). https://doi.org/10.1016/J.ISTRUC.2020.08.008
27. Tecchio, G., Donà, M., Saler, E., da Porto, F.: Fragility of single-span masonry arch bridges accounting for deterioration and damage effects. Eur. J. Environ. Civ. Eng. **27**, 2048–2069 (2023). https://doi.org/10.1080/19648189.2022.2108504
28. Iannuzzo, A., Mallardo, V.: A novel approach to model differential settlements and crack patterns in masonry structures. Eng. Struct. **323**, 119220 (2025). https://doi.org/10.1016/J.ENGSTRUCT.2024.119220
29. Bouzas, O., Conde, B., Matos, J.C., Solla, M., Cabaleiro, M.: Reliability-based structural assessment of historical masonry arch bridges: The case study of Cernadela bridge. Case Studies in Construction Materials. 18, (2023). https://doi.org/10.1016/j.cscm.2023.e02003
30. Di Gennaro, L., Guadagnuolo, M., Monaco, M.: Rocking Analysis of Towers Subjected to Horizontal Forces. Buildings. 13, (2023). https://doi.org/10.3390/buildings13030762
31. Di Gennaro, L., de Cristofaro, M., Loreto, G., Minutolo, V., Olivares, L., Zona, R., Frunzio, G.: In-situ load testing of an ancient masonry structure using fibre optics. Structures. 70, (2024). https://doi.org/10.1016/j.istruc.2024.107567
32. Homaei, F., Yazdani, M.: Seismic fragility, loss, and resiliency of old railway masonry arch bridges under near-field ground motion. Sustain Resilient Infrastruct. (2025). https://doi.org/10.1080/23789689.2025.2456362
33. Simoncello, N., Zampieri, P., Zizi, M., Rossi, L., Pellegrino, C.: Lateral response of damaged stand-alone arches: Tilting tests and rigid-block analysis. Eng Struct. 268, (2022). https://doi.org/10.1016/j.engstruct.2022.114700
34. Heyman, J.: The masonry arch. (1982)
35. Olivieri, C., Cennamo, C., Cusano, C., Cutolo, A., Fortunato, A., Mascolo, I.: Masonry Spiral Stairs: A Comparison between Analytical and Numerical Approaches. Applied Sciences (Switzerland). 12, (2022). https://doi.org/10.3390/app12094274
36. Maia Avelino, R., Iannuzzo, A., Van Mele, T., Block, P.: Assessing the safety of vaulted masonry structures using thrust network analysis. Comput Struct. 257, (2021). https://doi.org/10.1016/j.compstruc.2021.106647
37. George, J., Menon, A.: Kinematic approach for scour analysis of masonry arch bridges. Eng Fail Anal. 141, (2022). https://doi.org/10.1016/j.engfailanal.2022.106703
38. Pepe, M., Pingaro, M., Trovalusci, P.: Limit analysis approach for the in-plane collapse of masonry arches. Proceedings of the Institution of Civil Engineers: Engineering and Computational Mechanics. **174**, 66–81 (2021). https://doi.org/10.1680/jencm.20.00013
39. Di Carlo, F., Coccia, S.: Collapse state of elliptical masonry arches after finite displacements of the supports. Eng Fail Anal. 114, (2020). https://doi.org/10.1016/j.engfailanal.2020.104593

40. Clemente, P., Occhiuzzi, A., Raithel, A.: Limit Behavior of Stone Arch Bridges. Journal of Structural Engineering. 121, (1995). https://doi.org/10.1061/(asce)0733-9445(1995)121:7(1045)
41. Como, M.: Statics of Historic Masonry Constructions. Springer (2013)
42. Ochsendorf, J.A.: Collapse of Masonry Structures. (2002)
43. Wolfram Company: Wolfram Mathematica, https://www.wolfram.com/mathematica/
44. Zampieri, P., Zanini, M.A., Faleschini, F.: Influence of damage on the seismic failure analysis of masonry arches. Constr. Build. Mater. **119**, 343–355 (2016). https://doi.org/10.1016/j.conbuildmat.2016.05.024
45. Kamiński, T., Bień, J.: Application of kinematic method and FEM in analysis of ultimate load bearing capacity of damaged masonry arch bridges. In: Procedia Engineering. pp. 524–532 (2013). https://doi.org/10.1016/j.proeng.2013.04.067

Seismic Performance of Irregular Buildings Through the CASS Method

Andrea Montanino[1](✉) and Francesco Fabbrocino[2]

[1] International Center for Numerical Methods in Engineering, Carrer del Gran Capità, 08034 Barcelona, Spain
amontanino@cimne.upc.edu
[2] Pegaso Telematic University, Centro Direzionale ISOLA F2, 80143 Naples, Italy
francesco.fabbrocino@unipegaso.it

Abstract. The behavior of masonry structures plays a crucial role in the preservation and conservation of heritage sites, especially in seismically active areas. In this work, the Continuous Airy-based for Stress Singularities (CASS) method is applied to model the response of a masonry façade under different external loading and displacement conditions, including lateral seismic forces.

The formulation of a Boundary Value Problem (BVP) for structures composed of unilateral materials, is briefly recalled, then, the CASS numerical formulation is presented, highlighting its distinctive features, such as its ability to model complex stress distributions, especially dealing with stress concentration over curves. The resulting discrete problem is cast as an optimisation problem with conic discontinuity constraints, which is particularly useful for handling complex geometries, such as those encountered in heritage architecture.

The presented numerical results not only address the calculation of seismic load multipliers—key parameters for evaluating the seismic performance of structures—but help in discussing various numerical aspects, such as convergence issues and the treatment of irregular geometries.

Keywords: Masonry structures · Unilateral materials · Boundary Value Problem · Force-based method

1 Introduction

The preservation and assessment of historic masonry structures, which constitute a significant portion of the world's architectural heritage, have gained increasing attention within the scientific community. Accurate modeling of the mechanical behavior of these structures is essential not only for protecting human lives but also for maintaining the artistic and cultural value they bring, particularly in terms of tourism and historical significance. Given that most of these structures are made from masonry, it is crucial to develop methods that account for the peculiar behavior of this material.

The characteristic of masonry material is its ability of withstanding only compressive forces [19,22,23]. Traditional finite element (FE) methods are often inadequate for modeling this behavior [7,46], which necessitates the development of more advanced approaches [2,40,42–45,47].

The seminal work of Heyman, which framed the mechanics of masonry within modern plasticity theory, led to the development of models such as the Normal, Rigid, No-Tension (NRNT) model, where masonry is treated as a no-tension continuum that can resist compression but not tension. In contrast to previously recalled models, requiring accurate material models and parameter identification [12], Heyman's model does not require the identification of any material parameter [5,20].

A significant challenge in modeling masonry is dealing with stress singularities—lines, or surfaces, where stress concentrates. In the framework of the Heyman material, several strategies have been proposed to capture stress singularities, in the framework of domes and vaults [11,33,38,39], and in the framework of planar masonry buildings, both following displacement-based approaches [16,21,24–27], and force-based approaches [3,6,9,10,29,36,37].

Restricting to masonry façades, the Continuous Airy-based method for Stress Singularities (CASS) has been recently introduced for the mesh-independent identification of stress patterns [30].

A key point of the CASS method is the computation of curvature within Finite Elements, which is not a common theme in the literature. Several possibilities have been presented in the literature, among which the adoption of averaged value across more elements [17,35], or adopting higher-order plate-type elements, as in the case of Isogeometric Analysis (IGA) [15], to improve continuity and reduce computational complexity. The last technique, in particular, introduces an unnecessary continuity for the Airy stress potential which potentially limits the space of possible solutions of the Boundary Value Problem.

A particularly useful characteristic of the CASS approach is its ability to determine in a fast manner the load-bearing capacity of masonry structures [28,34], by identifying the maximum load multiplier for which an equilibrated solution exists. From this point, it is possible to determine the in-plane mechanisms of the structures [1,8,13,14,41].

Building on these insights, this paper recalls the quadrilateral plate-type FE formulation proposed in [31], designed to model complex, curved in-plane masonry structures, such as arches and buttresses. This formulation provides an optimal balance between accuracy and computational efficiency, addressing the limitations of traditional FE methods and enabling the analysis of a broader range of masonry geometries.

The paper is organized as follows: Sect. 2 provides the theoretical background of the proposed formulation; Sect. 3 recalls briefly the numerical formulation for the case of generically-shaped quadrilateral plate-type FE, detailing the computation of curvature components; Sect. 4 validates the method on an irregular masonry façade under permanent and accidental loads, estimating the seismic performance, and discussing several numerical issues. Finally, in Sect. 5, conclusions and future developments are discussed.

2 Boundary Value Problem

In this Section, the Boundary Value Problem for masonry structure is briefly recalled, together with the main ingredients needed to develop the CASS methodology.

A domain $\Omega \in \mathbb{R}^2$, as presented in Fig. 1, is considered, with boundary $\partial \Omega$ partitioned in a loaded part $\partial \Omega_N$ and a constrained part $\partial \Omega_D$, such that $\partial \Omega_N \cap \partial \Omega_D = \emptyset$ and $\partial \Omega_N \cup \partial \Omega_D = \partial \Omega$.

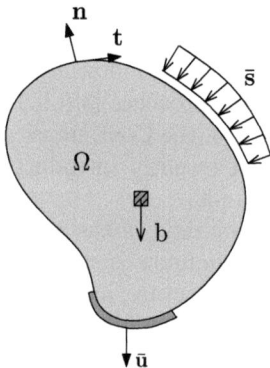

Fig. 1. Domain of the Boundary Value Problem with main notation.

The boundary value problem on Ω is represented by the equilibrium conditions, the kinematic conditions and a constitutive law. The equilibrium equations are

$$\nabla \cdot \mathbf{T} + \mathbf{b} = \mathbf{0} , \qquad \mathbf{x} \in \Omega \qquad (1a)$$
$$\mathbf{T}\mathbf{n} = \bar{\mathbf{s}} \qquad \mathbf{x} \in \partial \Omega_N \qquad (1b)$$

where $\mathbf{T}$ is the stress tensor, $\mathbf{b}$ is the volume load, $\mathbf{n}$ is the boundary outward normal, and $\bar{\mathbf{s}}$ is the assigned boundary load on $\partial \Omega_N$.

The kinematic conditions are

$$\mathbf{E} = \frac{1}{2}(\nabla \mathbf{u} + \nabla \mathbf{u}^T) , \qquad \mathbf{x} \in \Omega \qquad (2a)$$
$$\mathbf{u} = \bar{\mathbf{u}} \qquad \mathbf{x} \in \partial \Omega_D \qquad (2b)$$

being $\mathbf{E}$ the strain tensor, $\mathbf{u}$ the displacement field, and $\bar{\mathbf{u}}$ the prescribed displacement at the constrained boundary $\partial \Omega_D$.

The constitutive relation for the masonry material is represented by the Heyman assumption of a Normal, Rigid, No-Tension (NRNT) material, expressed as

$$\mathbf{T} \in \text{Sym}^- \quad , \tag{3a}$$

$$\mathbf{E} \in \text{Sym}^+ \quad , \tag{3b}$$

$$\mathbf{T} \cdot \mathbf{E} = 0 \quad , \tag{3c}$$

where (3a) expresses the no tension material requirement, (3b) the indeformability in compression, and (3c) the normality condition, that is, the infinite friction condition.

This boundary value problem can be recast into an optimisation problem by introducing the Total Potential Energy

$$\mathcal{E}_p(\mathbf{u}) = \frac{1}{2}\int_\Omega \mathbf{T} \cdot \mathbf{E} d\Omega - \int_{\partial\Omega_N} \bar{\mathbf{s}} \cdot \mathbf{u} dA - \int_\Omega \mathbf{b} \cdot \mathbf{u} d\Omega \tag{4}$$

or the Total Complementary Energy

$$\mathcal{E}_c(\mathbf{T}) = \frac{1}{2}\int_\Omega \mathbf{T} \cdot \mathbf{E} d\Omega - \int_{\partial\Omega_D} \mathbf{T}\mathbf{n} \cdot \bar{\mathbf{u}} d\Omega \tag{5}$$

From these energies, two different solution strategies can be developed [32]: the minimisation of the Total Potential Energy with respect to the unknown field $\mathbf{u}$ gives rise to a displacement-based approach; the minimisation of the Total Complementary Energy with respect to the stress field $\mathbf{T}$ originates a force- or stress-based approach.

In this work, the latter strategy is considered: the minimisation problem, therefore, is written as

$$\mathcal{E}_c(\mathbf{T}^*) = \min_{\mathbf{T} \in \mathcal{H}} \mathcal{E}_c(\mathbf{T}) \quad , \tag{6}$$

with

$$\mathcal{H} = \left\{ \mathbf{T} \in \text{SBV s.t. } \mathbf{T} \in \text{Sym}^-, \nabla \cdot \mathbf{T} + \mathbf{b} = \mathbf{0}, \mathbf{T}\mathbf{n} = \bar{\mathbf{s}} \right\} \tag{7}$$

the set of admissible stress fields, that is, compliant with the internal and external equilibrium (1), and with the material restriction (3a).

Furthermore, given the normality condition (3c), the objective function

$$\mathcal{E}_c(\mathbf{T}) = -\int_{\partial\Omega_D} \mathbf{T}\mathbf{n} \cdot \bar{\mathbf{u}} d\Omega \tag{8}$$

is a linear functional.

The formulation (6)-(7), in its present form involving directly the stress field, in any discretized version, would bring to a problem with a high number of equality constraints, corresponding to all the evaluations of the equilibrium condition. Therefore, it is useful to rewrite it adopting the Airy stress potential F, that is, a scalar function intrinsically complying with the equilibrium condition. The Airy stress potential is formulated as a scalar function

$$F \in C^0 \quad \text{s.t.} \quad \mathbf{T} = \mathbf{R}^T \mathbf{H}(F) \mathbf{R} + \mathbf{B}_F, \tag{9}$$

with $\mathbf{H}$ the Hessian operator, $\mathbf{R}$ is a skew-symmetric operator representing a counterclockwise rotation of $\pi/2$, and $\mathbf{B}_F$ a tensor accounting for the specific internal load distribution $\mathbf{b}$, such that

$$\nabla \cdot \mathbf{B}_F = -\mathbf{b}. \tag{10}$$

Equations (9) and (10), particularised to the Cartesian reference frame, read in the form

$$T_{xx} = F_{,yy}, \quad T_{yy} = F_{,xx}, \quad T_{xy} = -F_{,xy} + b_y x + b_x y, \tag{11}$$

being T_{xx}, T_{yy}, and T_{xy} the Cartesian components of the stress tensor $\mathbf{T}$, and b_x and b_y the Cartesian components of the internal volume load $\mathbf{b}$. Moreover, a Latin letter following a comma, as a subscript, represents partial derivative. Replacing (11) into the internal equilibrium condition (1a) allows for checking the correct definition of the Airy stress potential.

Therefore, Problem (6)-(7) is reformulated in terms of the Airy stress potential as

$$\mathcal{E}_c(F^*) = \min_{F \in \mathcal{H}_F} \mathcal{E}_c(F), \tag{12}$$

being $\mathcal{H}_F$ the set of admissible Airy stress potentials, univocally determined from $\mathcal{H}$.

The material constraints transform into a condition on the Hessian of the Airy stress potential, specifically

$$\mathbf{R}^T \mathbf{H}(F) \mathbf{R} + \mathbf{B}_F \in Sym^- \tag{13}$$

that is, in a Cartesian reference frame,

$$F_{,xx} + F_{,yy} \leq 0, \quad F_{,xx} F_{,yy} - (-F_{,xy} + b_F)^2 \geq 0. \tag{14}$$

It is worth noting that, in the absence of volume forces, condition (13) has an immediate geometrical meaning, since the Hessian of a function is strictly linked to its curvature. Therefore, the Airy stress potential for a domain composed of a unilateral material must have a negative, semi-definite Hessian in each point, and therefore, be point-wise concave.

Concerning boundary conditions, the Airy-based formulation transforms the boundary equilibrium into

$$\mathbf{R}^T \mathbf{H}(F) \mathbf{R} \mathbf{n} + \mathbf{B}_F \mathbf{n} = \bar{\mathbf{s}}, \tag{15}$$

and, denoting with

$$T_{nn} = \mathbf{n} \cdot \mathbf{T} \mathbf{n}, \quad T_{nt} = \mathbf{t} \cdot \mathbf{T} \mathbf{n}, \tag{16}$$

the normal and tangential components of the emerging stress at the boundary, with $\mathbf{t}$ and $\mathbf{n} = \mathbf{Rt}$ the unit vectors tangent and orthogonal to the boundary itself, the boundary conditions can be finally rewritten as

$$T_{nn} = \bar{\mathbf{s}} \cdot \mathbf{n} = \mathbf{t} \cdot \mathbf{H(F)t} + \mathbf{n} \cdot \mathbf{B_F n} = F_{,tt} - 2b_F t_x t_y \quad (17a)$$

$$T_{nt} = \bar{\mathbf{s}} \cdot \mathbf{t} = -\mathbf{n} \cdot \mathbf{H(F)t} + \mathbf{t} \cdot \mathbf{B_F n} = - F_{,nt} + b_F(t_x^2 - t_y^2) \quad (17b)$$

being t_x, t_y the Cartesian components of $\mathbf{t}$.

3 The Continuous Airy-Based for Stress Singularities

In this Section the main points of the numerical formulation proposed in [31] are recalled, starting from the domain discretisation until the discrete formulation of the optimisation problem (12).

The domain is decomposed in quadrilateral plate-type finite elements, with four nodes in correspondence of its corner, as depicted in Fig. 2b; each node is provided with three degrees of freedom, specifically the unknown function value ϕ and its first derivatives in the Cartesian directions $\phi_{,x}$ and $\phi_{,y}$. This assures the discretisation being C^1-continuous at the nodes, and only C^0-continuous across the element boundary, since this discretisation cannot assure continuity of the normal derivative at the elements' interfaces.

For generalisation purposes, each element is mapped into a square element, referred to as as parent element, in a parent reference frame $\{0, s, t\}$, such that $0 < s < 1$, and $0 < t < 1$, as shown in Fig. 2.

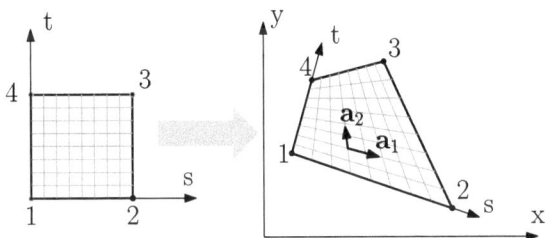

Fig. 2. Mapping between the parent and real geometries.

Since each element is provided with a total of 12 degrees of freedom, the interpolant function $\phi(x(s,t), y(s,t))$ is generated through the scalar product of a coefficient vector $\hat{\mathbf{w}} = [w_1, ... w_{12}]^T$ and a monomial basis

$$\mathbf{p}^T(s,t) = \left[1, s, t, s^2, st, t^2, s^3, s^2t, st^2, t^3, s^3t, st^3\right], \quad (18)$$

such that

$$\phi(x(s,t), y(s,t)) = \mathbf{p}^T(s,t)\hat{\mathbf{w}}, \quad (19)$$

The coefficient vector $\hat{\mathbf{w}}$ can be rewritten in terms of the nodal degrees of freedom

$$\hat{\boldsymbol{\phi}} = [\hat{\phi}^1, \hat{\phi}^1{}_{,x}, \hat{\phi}^1{}_{,y}, ..., \hat{\phi}^4, \hat{\phi}^4{}_{,x}, \hat{\phi}^4{}_{,y}] \tag{20}$$

after a suitable interpolation of $\phi(x(s,t), y(s,t))$, on the original element shape, with the nodal degrees of freedom, represented by 12 conditions in the form

$$\phi\big|^i = \hat{\phi}^i, \quad \phi_{,x}\big|^i = \hat{\phi}^i{}_{,x}, \quad \phi_{,y}\big|^i = \hat{\phi}^i{}_{,y}, \tag{21}$$

with $i = 1, .., 4$, and collected in compact form as

$$\hat{\boldsymbol{\phi}} = \mathbf{B}\hat{\mathbf{w}} \;. \tag{22}$$

By inverting (22) and combining with (19), the final interpolation function is

$$\phi(x(s,t), y(s,t)) = \mathbf{p}^T(s,t)\mathbf{B}^{-1}(\hat{\mathbf{x}})\hat{\boldsymbol{\phi}}. \tag{23}$$

By recalling from Sect. 2 that the curvature of the unknown function is required to compute the stress, first of all, it has to be noticed that the curvature is not continuous at the element nodes, therefore, it must be computed on internal points, referred to as control points. In this work, the points with local coordinates

$$\begin{aligned} \bar{s}_1 &= 0.25, & \bar{t}_1 &= 0.25 \\ \bar{s}_2 &= 0.75, & \bar{t}_2 &= 0.25 \\ \bar{s}_3 &= 0.75, & \bar{t}_3 &= 0.75 \\ \bar{s}_4 &= 0.25, & \bar{t}_4 &= 0.75 \end{aligned} \tag{24}$$

are selected, represented in Fig. 3.

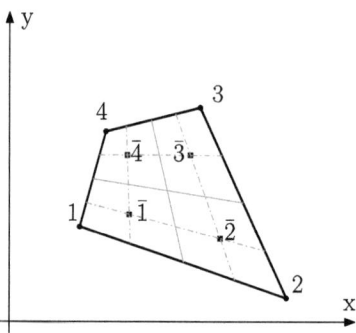

Fig. 3. Position of the control points on a generic element. The control points are placed at the centres of each quadrant in which the element is partitioned.

The Hessian tensor $\mathbf{H}(\phi)$ is expressed, following the curvilinear reference frame adopted of Fig. 2b, as

$$\mathbf{H} = (\nabla \phi)_{,\alpha} \otimes \mathbf{a}^\alpha, \tag{25}$$

with $\mathbf{a}^\alpha$, $\alpha = 1, 2$ the contravariant basis of the curvilinear reference system. Then the Hessian is projected onto the Cartesian directions as

$$H_{ij} = [(\nabla\phi)_{,\alpha} \cdot \mathbf{e}_i](\mathbf{a}^\alpha \cdot \mathbf{e}_j). \tag{26}$$

In Eqs. 25-(26) the derivation with respect to α means partial derivative with respect to the curvilinear directions s, t, respectively.

After some algebra (with details reported in [31]), the final expressions of the Cartesian components of the curvature can be expressed in terms of the nodal unknowns as

$$\begin{aligned}\phi_{,xx} &= \mathbf{h}_{xx}^T \mathbf{B}^{-1}\hat{\phi} \\ \phi_{,yy} &= \mathbf{h}_{yy}^T \mathbf{B}^{-1}\hat{\phi} \\ \phi_{,xy} &= \mathbf{h}_{xy}^T \mathbf{B}^{-1}\hat{\phi}\end{aligned} \tag{27}$$

being $\mathbf{h}_{xx}$, $\mathbf{h}_{yy}$, and $\mathbf{h}_{xy}$ vector functions depending on the curvilinear coordinates and on the element mapping.

3.1 BVP Discretisation

Given the procedure recalled in the previous Section, here some discussion on the discretisation of the BVP is addressed.

In particular, the Total Complementary Energy (8) in terms of the Airy stress potential is given by

$$\mathcal{E}_c(F) = -\int_{\partial\Omega_D} \left(\mathbf{R}^T \mathbf{H}(F)\mathbf{R} + \mathbf{B}_F\right) \mathbf{n} \cdot \bar{\mathbf{u}} ds, \tag{28}$$

which is written in terms of the second derivatives of the Airy stress potential, which are not degrees of freedom in the present formulation. However, by integrating Eq. (28) along the DIrichlet boundary, it comes out, after discretisation, that

$$\begin{aligned}\mathcal{E}_c(\hat{F}) =& [F_{,t}\big|_1 - F_{,t}\big|_2 - 2b_F t_x t_y \Delta s] \bar{u}_n \\ &+ [F_{,n}\big|_2 - F_{,n}\big|_1 - b_F(t_x^2 - t_y^2)\Delta s]\bar{u}_t,\end{aligned} \tag{29}$$

with $\bar{u}_t$ and $\bar{u}_n$ the normal and tangent boundary settlement in tangential $\mathbf{t}$ and normal $\mathbf{n}$ direction, respectively. Equation (29), summed up on all the elements of the Dirichlet boundary, represents the discretised objective function. $F_{,t}$ and $F_{,n}$ can be further rewritten in terms of the Cartesian components of the gradient of the Airy stress potential at the nodes of the discretisation.

The negative semi-definiteness of the stress in the domain is just checked by evaluating the stress in the elements' control points, that is, evaluating (14) through (27). Therefore, the material constraints transform into a set of coninc constraints in the form

$$\begin{aligned}(\mathbf{h}_{xx}^T + \mathbf{h}_{yy}^T)\mathbf{B}^{-1}\hat{F} &\leq 0 \\ (\mathbf{h}_{xx}^T \mathbf{B}^{-1}\hat{F})(\mathbf{h}_{yy}^T \mathbf{B}^{-1}\hat{F}) - ((\mathbf{h}_{yy}^T \mathbf{B}^{-1}\hat{F}) - b(\mathbf{x}))^2 &\geq 0\end{aligned} \tag{30}$$

Relations (30), collected for all the control points, form a set of coninc disequality constraints, that can be written in the form

$$f(\hat{\mathbf{F}}) \geq \mathbf{0} \qquad (31)$$

The last ingredient is the imposition of the boundary conditions (17). Again, here second derivative of the unknown function appears, which are not among the degrees of freedom, therefore, the most convenient step is the integration of emerging stresses across the element boundary, realizing not a point-wise equilibrium on the element side, but an equilibrium of the stress resultant, that can be understood also as an average equilibrium at the elementary level. This formulation, however, converges to the point-wise equilibrium with the reduction of the mesh size.

Therefore, Eqs. (17) are rewritten as

$$\mathbf{R}_n = \int_{\partial\Omega_{el}} F_{,tt} - 2b_F t_x t_y \qquad (32a)$$

$$\mathbf{R}_t = -\int_{\partial\Omega_{el}} F_{,nt} + b_F(t_x^2 - t_y^2) \qquad (32b)$$

with $\mathbf{R}_n$ and $\mathbf{R}_t$ the resultant of the applied load along the element boundary in the normal and tangential directions, respectively.

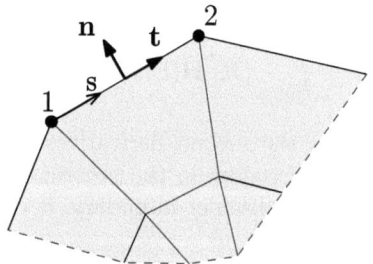

Fig. 4. Geometry of a boundary element and main notation.

After some algebra, and introducing the nodal degrees of freedom, the final boundary conditions at the element boundary are

$$F_{,t}\big|_2 - F_{,t}\big|_1 = T_{nn}\Delta s + \\ -b_y t_x t_y (x_1 + x_2)\Delta s + \\ -b_x t_x t_y (y_1 + y_2)\Delta s \qquad (33)$$

$$F_{,n}\big|_2 - F_{,n}\big|_1 = -T_{nt}\Delta s \\ + \frac{1}{2}b_y(t_x^2 - t_y^2)(x_1 + x_2)\Delta s \\ + \frac{1}{2}b_x(t_x^2 - t_y^2)(y_1 + y_2)\Delta s \qquad (34)$$

where Δs is the element's boundary length, and x_1, x_2, y_1, y_1 are the coordinates of the two extreme points of the element's boundary, as represented in Fig. 4.

Equations (33)-(34) can be written as linear expression of the degrees of freedom, as

$$\mathbf{K}_{\partial\Omega}\hat{\mathbf{F}} = \hat{\mathbf{s}} \tag{35}$$

and finally, by collecting Eqs. (29), (31), and (35), for all the evaluations required, the final, discrete form of the optimisation problem is

$$\begin{aligned} E_c(\hat{\mathbf{F}}^0) &= \min E_c(\hat{\mathbf{F}}) \\ \text{s.t.} \quad & f(\hat{\mathbf{F}}) \leq 0 \\ & \mathbf{K}_{\partial\Omega}\hat{\mathbf{F}} = \hat{\mathbf{s}} \end{aligned} \tag{36}$$

Following the same discretisation strategy, but slightly changing the problem formulation, it is possible to compute the maximum - or minimum - admissible load on a masonry structure by parametrizing the external load through a coefficient λ, such that

$$\hat{\mathbf{s}} = \hat{\mathbf{s}}_0 + \lambda \hat{\mathbf{s}}_v \tag{37}$$

with $\hat{\mathbf{s}}_0$ the permanent loads, and $\hat{\mathbf{s}}_v$ the variable part of the load, related, for example, to a seismic action, or to accidental loads.

In this case, the optimisation problem is reformulated as

$$\begin{aligned} \lambda^0 &= \min \lambda \\ \text{s.t.} \quad & f(\hat{\mathbf{F}}) \leq 0 \\ & \mathbf{K}_{\partial\Omega}\hat{\mathbf{F}} = \hat{\mathbf{s}}_0 + \lambda \hat{\mathbf{s}}_v \end{aligned} \tag{38}$$

4 Numerical Examples

In this Section a non-symmetric structure is considered, under the action of permanent loads, in which the formation of possible load patterns are observed, and under the effect of horizontal loads, to determine the maximum load multiplier and the corresponding seismic performance of the structure.

The geometry of the masonry façade is represented in Fig. 5, with its geometrical dimensions.

The permanent loads on the top side is $q = 25$ kN/m, while the self-weight is of 18 kN/m². Additionally, two variable loads on the vertical sides of the structures are considered, representative of seismic actions.

Effect of Permanent Loads. The analysis under the effect of the load on the top side of the structure, and of the self-weight, reveals the stress patterns, in terms of minimum principal stress, depicted in Fig. 6.

In particular, it may be observed the formation of singularities above the lintel of the window on the right side, as well of a singularity until the lower corners of the façade.

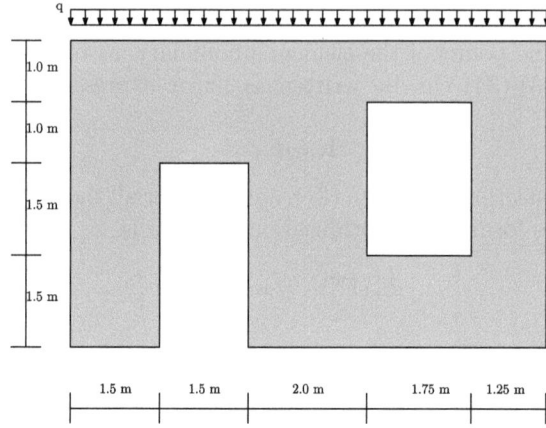

Fig. 5. Unsymmetric façade - geometry and dimensions.

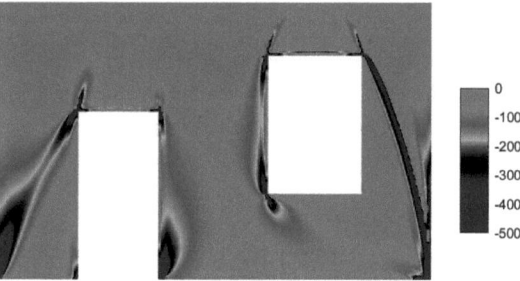

Fig. 6. Unsymmetric façade - stress pattern for the only permanent loads.

The equilibrium of this geometry under the vertical loads is got introducing a precompressive loads on the left and right sides of the structure, in the form of a normal, homogeneous load $q_s = 5.07$ kN/m, corresponding to an horizontal force $F_H = 25$ kN, which is however not relevant, from a practical point of view, with respect to the total vertical load, represented by the combination of the self-weight and the upper load, which sums to $F_V = 750$ kN, being therefore the ratio $F_H/F_V = 0.033$

Seismic Loads. For checking the seismic performance of the structure, an equivalent horizontal load has been simulated at the left and right sides of the structures, and increased until an equilibrated solution is found.

By solving (38) for the case of the seismic load on the left side of the structure, and considering a permanent load $q_{s,l} = 150$ kN/m (that is, the total vertical load acting on the façade), a maximum value for the seismic multiplier is $\lambda = 0.55$, which also stands for the so called Peak Ground Acceleration (PGA), a seismic indicator measuring the maximum soil acceleration that a structure can withstand. The corresponding stress pattern is depicted in Fig. 7, where stress singularities are visible, in the form of preferential stress paths going to the lower, right corners of the structure (against the left side of the door, and of the right part of the façade). This stress pattern also suggests possible rocking mechanisms of the structure. The presence of unloaded zones, or of zones under monoaxial stress patterns, also suggest the possible formation of cracks without loss of energy for the structure.

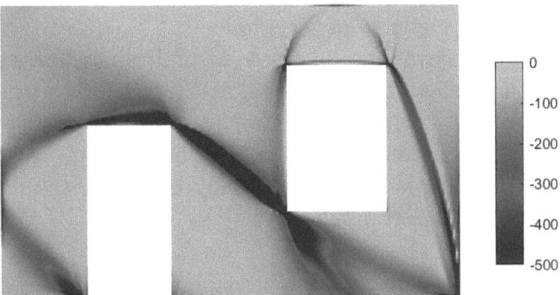

Fig. 7. Unsymmetric façade - stress pattern for the permanent and equivalent seismic load from the left side.

Repeating the simulation for the same variable load, but on the right side, the maximum value of the seismic multiplier is $\lambda = 0.586$, whose corresponding stress pattern is reported in Fig. 8. Also in this case, stress singularities pointing against the lower corners of the structure are present, suggesting the formation of other rocking mechanisms which however are coherent with the imposed load and the structure geometry.

Fig. 8. Unsymmetric façade - stress pattern for the permanent and equivalent seismic load from the right side.

A further comment is proposed concerning the difference between the values of λ in the two cases. This slight difference, already observed in [4], even though for a different type of horizontal load, is due to the unsymmetry of the structure, which naturally leads to different load multipliers.

5 Conclusion

In this paper, the Continuous Airy-based method for Stress Singularities (CASS) is applied to determine the seismic multiplier on unsymmetric façades. After recalling the theorical fundamentals of the Boundary Value Problem, and of the discretisation strategy in the CASS method, with particular focus on the curvature computation on non-rectangular finite elements, the CASS method is applied to a non-symmetric structure to determine possible stress patterns under self-weight, and under the effects of seismic loads.

Specifically, the non-symmetry of the load multiplier, following the unsymmetry of the structure, is evidenced, as well as the need for a suitable numerical prestress at the sides of the structure to simulate the effects of the vertical loads.

Future developments of this work will involve out-of-plane mechanisms, which are well developed with displacement-based approaches [18], but still need to be approached from a force-based perspective.

Disclosure of Interests. There is no competing interest to declare.

References

1. Buzzetti, M., Gandolfi, A., Pingaro, N., Milani, G.: A new advanced and simple procedure for the nonlinear static analysis of curved masonry structures. In: International Conference on Protection of Historical Constructions, pp. 176–183. Springer (2025)
2. Alfano, G., Rosati, L., Valoroso, N.: A numerical strategy for finite element analysis of no-tension materials. Int. J. Numer. Methods Eng. **48**(3), 317–350 (2000). https://doi.org/10.1002/(SICI)1097-0207(20000530)48:3<317::AID-NME868>3.0.CO;2-C
3. Angelillo, M.: Constitutive relations for no-tension materials. Meccanica **28**, 195–202 (1993). https://doi.org/10.1007/BF00989121
4. Angelillo, M., Iannuzzo, A., Montanino, A.: Discretised continuum approaches: from continuum to dis-continuum. In: Discrete Computational Mechanics of Masonry Structures, pp. 95–163. Springer (2023). https://doi.org/10.1007/978-3-031-32476-5_3
5. Angelillo, M. (ed.): Mechanics of Masonry Structures. CICMS, vol. 551. Springer, Vienna (2014). https://doi.org/10.1007/978-3-7091-1774-3
6. Baratta, A., Corbi, O.: Stress analysis of masonry vaults and static efficacy of FRP repairs. Int. J. Solids Struct. **44**(24), 8028–8056 (2007). https://doi.org/10.1016/j.tafmec.2005.09.008
7. Block, P., Ciblac, T., Ochsendorf, J.: Real-time limit analysis of vaulted masonry buildings. Comput. Struct. **84**(29–30), 1841–1852 (2006). https://doi.org/10.1016/j.compstruc.2006.08.002
8. Buzzetti, M., Pingaro, N., Gandolfi, A., Milani, G.: Limit analysis-based approach for the assessment of local failures in masonry aggregates according to Italian standards. In: International Conference on Protection of Historical Constructions, pp. 168–175. Springer (2025)

9. Crespino, E., Adriaenssens, S., Fraddosio, A., Olivieri, C., Piccioni, M.D.: A multi-objective optimization approach for novel shell/frame systems under seismic load. Structures **65**, 106625 (2024)
10. Cuomo, M., Ventura, G.: A complementary energy formulation of no tension masonry-like solids. Comput. Methods Appl. Mech. Eng. **189**(1), 313–339 (2000). https://doi.org/10.1016/S0045-7825(99)00298-4
11. Cusano, C., Montanino, A., Olivieri, C., Paris, V., Cennamo, C.: Graphical and analytical quantitative comparison in the Domes assessment: the case of San Francesco di Paola. Appl. Sci. **11**(8), 3622 (2021). https://doi.org/10.3390/app11083622
12. Di Gennaro, L., et al.: In-situ load testing of an ancient masonry structure using fibre optics. Structures **70**, 107567 (2024)
13. Di Gennaro, L., Guadagnuolo, M., Monaco, M.: Rocking analysis of towers subjected to horizontal forces. Buildings **13**(3), 762 (2023)
14. Fabbrocino, F., Olivieri, C., Luciano, R., Vaiano, G., Maddaloni, G., Iannuzzo, A.: Seismic performance of historic masonry buildings: a comparative analysis of equivalent frame and block-based methods. Alex. Eng. J. **109**, 359–375 (2024)
15. Farahat, A., Verhelst, H.M., Kiendl, J., Kapl, M.: Isogeometric analysis for multi-patch structured Kirchhoff-Love shells. Comput. Methods Appl. Mech. Eng. **411**, 116060 (2023)
16. Ferrero, C., Cusano, C., Yavuzer, M.N., Wu, Y.X., Iannuzzo, A.: When cracks are (not) a structural concern: the case of 'Giovanni Vinciguerra' School in Anagni. Int. J. Masonry Res. Innov. **7**(1–2), 217–232 (2022)
17. Fraternali, F., Angelillo, M., Fortunato, A.: A lumped stress method for plane elastic problems and the discrete-continuum approximation. Int. J. Solids Struct. **39**(25), 6211–6240 (2002)
18. Frunzio, G., Di Gennaro, L.: The out of plane behaviour of masonry infilled frames. J. Phys. Conf. Ser. **2090**(1), 012148 (2021)
19. Guadagnuolo, M., Di Gennaro, L., Basile, A., De Matteis, G.: Simplified methods for the evaluation of mechanical properties of tuff masonry walls in Campania (Italy). Procedia Struct. Integr. **44**, 878–885 (2023)
20. Heyman, J.: The stone skeleton. Int. J. Solids Struct. **2**(2), 249–279 (1966). https://doi.org/10.1016/0020-7683(66)90018-7
21. Hua, Y., Buzzetti, M., Pingaro, N., da Silva, L.C., Milani, G.: A computerized tool for the kinematic limit analysis of 2D masonry structures failing on a tilting table. SoftwareX **30**, 102180 (2025)
22. Huerta, S.: The analysis of masonry architecture: a historical approach: to the memory of professor Henry. J. Cowan. Archit. Sci. Rev. **51**(4), 297–328 (2008). https://doi.org/10.3763/asre.2008.5136
23. Huerta Fernández, S.: Mechanics of masonry vaults: the equilibrium approach (2001)
24. Iannuzzo, A., et al.: Modelling the cracks produced by settlements in masonry structures. Meccanica **53**(7), 1857–1873 (2017). https://doi.org/10.1007/s11012-017-0721-2
25. Iannuzzo, A., Musone, V., Ruocco, E.: A neural network-based automated methodology to identify the crack causes in masonry structures. Comput. Aided Civ. Infrastruct. Eng. **39**(24), 3769–3785 (2024). https://doi.org/10.1111/mice.13311
26. Iannuzzo, A.: Energy based fracture identification in masonry structures: the case study of the church of "Pietà dei Turchini". J. Mech. Mater. Struct. **14**(5), 683–702 (2019). https://doi.org/10.2140/jomms.2019.14.683

27. Iannuzzo, A., Mallardo, V.: A novel approach to model differential settlements and crack patterns in masonry structures. Eng. Struct. **323**, 119220 (2025). https://doi.org/10.1016/j.engstruct.2024.119220
28. Iannuzzo, A., Montanino, A.: A limit analysis-based CASS approach for the in-plane seismic capacity of masonry façades. Int. J. Solids Struct. **289**, 112633 (2024). https://doi.org/10.1016/j.ijsolstr.2023.112633
29. Lucchesi, M., Šilhavỳ, M., Zani, N.: A new class of equilibrated stress fields for no-tension bodies. J. Mech. Mater. Struct. **1**(3), 503–539 (2006). https://doi.org/10.2140/jomms.2006.1.503
30. Montanino, A., De Gregorio, D., Olivieri, C., Iannuzzo, A.: The continuous airy-based for stress-singularities (CASS) method: an energy-based numerical formulation for unilateral materials. Int. J. Solids Struct. **256**, 111954 (2022). https://doi.org/10.1016/j.ijsolstr.2022.111954
31. Montanino, A., Iannuzzo, A.: A quadrilateral plate-type finite element to model stress singularities in no-tension materials. Comput. Methods Appl. Mech. Eng. **432**, 117433 (2024). https://doi.org/10.1016/j.cma.2024.117433
32. Montanino, A., Olivieri, C., De Gregorio, D., Iannuzzo, A., et al.: Two continuous dual strategies to solve the kinematical and equilibrium problem for masonry-like structures. In: WCCM-ECCOMAS CONGRESS. Scipedia SL (2022)
33. Montanino, A., Olivieri, C., Zuccaro, G., Angelillo, M.: From stress to shape: equilibrium of cloister and cross vaults. Appl. Sci. **11**(9), 3846 (2021). https://doi.org/10.3390/app11093846
34. Montanino, A., Perelli, F.L., De Gregorio, D., Zuccaro, G.: Application of the continuous airy-based for stress singularities (CASS) to the load bearing capacity of masonry structures under seismic loads. In: 9th International Conference on Computational Methods in Structural Dynamics and Earthquake Engineering Methods in Structural Dynamics and Earthquake Engineering (2023). https://doi.org/10.7712/120123.10577.21347
35. Nguyen-Xuan, H., Rabczuk, T., Bordas, S., Debongnie, J.F.: A smoothed finite element method for plate analysis. Comput. Methods Appl. Mech. Eng. **197**(13-16), 1184–1203 (2008). j.cma.2007.10.008
36. Nodargi, N.A.: An isogeometric collocation method for the static limit analysis of masonry domes under their self-weight. Comput. Methods Appl. Mech. Eng. **416**, 116375 (2023). https://doi.org/10.1016/j.cma.2023.116375
37. Olivieri, C.: FORMERLY-Math: constrained form-finding through membrane equilibrium analysis in Mathematica. Softw. Impacts **16**, 100512 (2023). https://doi.org/10.1016/j.simpa.2023.100512
38. Olivieri, C., Cocking, S., Fabbrocino, F., Iannuzzo, A., Placidi, L., Adriaenssens, S.: Seismic capacity of purely compressed shells based on Airy stress function. Continuum Mech. Thermodyn. **37**(2), 21 (2025)
39. Olivieri, C., Fortunato, A., DeJong, M.: A new membrane equilibrium solution for masonry railway bridges: the case study of Marsh Lane Bridge. Int. J. Masonry Res. Innov. **6**(4), 446–471 (2021)
40. Paris, V., Gobbin, F., Nannei, V.M., Resmini, M., Mirabella Roberti, G.: Distinct element method analyses for damage assessment: the Northern Spur of Valverde Bulwark in the Venetian Fortress of Bergamo. Int. J. Archit. Herit., 1–15 (2024)
41. Perelli, F.L., De Gregorio, D., Montanino, A., Olivieri, C., Maddaloni, G., Iannuzzo, A.: Energy-based modelling of in-plane fragility curves for the 2D ultimate capacity of Italian masonry buildings. Front. Built Environ. **9**, 1127523 (2023)

42. Petracca, M., Camata, G., Spacone, E., Pelà, L.: Efficient constitutive model for continuous micro-modeling of masonry structures. Int. J. Archit. Herit. **17**(1), 134–146 (2023). https://doi.org/10.1080/15583058.2022.2124133
43. Prosperi, A., Longo, M., Korswagen, P.A., Korff, M., Rots, J.G.: Sensitivity modelling with objective damage assessment of unreinforced masonry façades undergoing different subsidence settlement patterns. Eng. Struct. **286**, 116113 (2023). https://doi.org/10.1016/j.engstruct.2023.116113
44. Rotunno, T., Fagone, M., Ranocchiai, G., Grande, E.: Micro-mechanical FE modelling and constitutive parameters calibration of masonry panels strengthened with CFRP sheets. Compos. Struct. **285**, 115248 (2022). https://doi.org/10.1016/j.compstruct.2022.115248
45. Shadlou, M., Ahmadi, E., Kashani, M.M.: Micromechanical modelling of mortar joints and brick-mortar interfaces in masonry Structures: a review of recent developments. Structures **23**, 831–844 (2020)
46. Shin, H.V., Porst, C.F., Vouga, E., Ochsendorf, J., Durand, F.: Reconciling elastic and equilibrium methods for static analysis. ACM Trans. Graph. (TOG) **35**(2), 1–16 (2016). https://doi.org/10.1145/2835173
47. Xia, Q., Sun, Y., Wu, J., Li, J., Li, Y., Shen, C.: Investigation of compression constitutive relationship of ancient brick masonry. Constr. Build. Mater. **317**, 126093 (2022). https://doi.org/10.1016/j.conbuildmat.2021.126093

FE Upper Bound Limit Analysis for Automated Identification of Collapse Mechanisms in Masonry Structures

Martina Buzzetti[✉], Natalia Pingaro, and Gabriele Milani

Department of Architecture, Built Environment and Construction Engineering, Politecnico di Milano, Milan 20133, Italy
`martina.buzzetti@polimi.it`

Abstract. A finite element method based on upper bound limit analysis is proposed to estimate the collapse acceleration that induces local failure mechanisms in existing masonry structures. The structural assessment follows the Italian building code, with the added flexibility of not relying on predefined failure mechanisms. The structural model is composed of infinitely rigid hexahedron elements interconnected by quadrilateral interfaces, where plastic deformations are concentrated according to a to a failure criterion such as the Mohr-Coulomb model. The limit analysis problem is formulated following the kinematic approach and solved through a well-established linear programming algorithm. This approach allows the automatic detection of the collapse acceleration and the corresponding failure mechanism, depending on the tensile strength. Through an iterative extrapolation procedure, the solution for the no-tension material model is obtained – as required by Italian standards and commonly assumed for masonry structures in the technical literature. The methodology can also account for the presence of tie-rods. Furthermore, an innovative filtering algorithm is introduced to consider only the elements implicated in the failure mechanism, allowing for the evaluation of the collapse spectral acceleration. The methodology is used for the seismic assessment of a portion belonging to complex historical building in Italy.

Keywords: Limit analysis · Masonry constructions · Local failure mechanisms · Seismic assessment

1 Introduction

In many European and Mediterranean countries, much of the built heritage consists of masonry structures and is located in regions with moderate to high seismic hazard [1]. Historic masonry structures often exhibit weak connections between walls, floors, and roofs, as they were originally conceived to support only vertical loads. As a result, when subjected to seismic forces, these structures fail to develop a box-like behavior and instead experience local collapse mechanisms [2]. In some cases, even when connections are adequate, out-of-plane failures may still occur due to the high slenderness of the walls [3].

To ensure the preservation and structural safety of these buildings, it is crucial to determine the accelerations that trigger such failure mechanisms and to develop suitable strengthening strategies. Several analytical and numerical approaches are available for this purpose, including Finite Element Modeling (FEM), Discrete Element Modeling (DEM), and kinematic limit analysis. In addition, recent analytical formulations based on Airy stress functions have been proposed to evaluate the seismic capacity of purely compressed structures [4].

FEM is widely used as it enables the assessment of both global structural behavior and local failure mechanisms [5–7]. However, defining appropriate constitutive models for masonry nonlinear behavior within FEM involves numerous parameters. Among the most commonly used for masonry structures is the Concrete Damage Plasticity (CDP) model, as it can accurately replicate their mechanical behavior when properly calibrated [8, 9]. Nevertheless, this model does not strictly allow for a no-tension material assumption. A low value of tensile strength must be assigned to ensure numerical convergence, which can sometimes lead to an overestimation of the collapse acceleration for out-of-plane failure modes.

DEM, on the other hand, is highly effective in modeling masonry structures since it directly represents the interaction between individual masonry units [10–12]. Despite its accuracy, DEM-based approaches are often computationally expensive and require access to costly commercial software, which can be a limiting factor.

Due to these challenges, the Italian building code requires the safety assessment of out-of-plane local collapses through at least a kinematic linear analysis based on predefined failure mechanisms [13, 14]. While this method is computationally efficient and straightforward, it may either overestimate or underestimate the critical acceleration required to trigger local failures articularly in structures with complex geometries where the affected portion of the structure is not easily identifiable in advance.

The structural safety of complex historical masonry constructions under seismic actions is assessed in this paper with a numerical approach based on the combination of limit analysis with finite elements [15–17], which have proven effective also in evaluating the effectiveness of tie-rod strengthening interventions [18]. The primary objective is to verify out-of-plane local failure mechanisms in accordance with Italian standards while overcoming the previously discussed limitations. The approach proposed follows the upper bound limit analysis approach and has been implemented in MATLAB, following the methodology proposed in [19, 20]. It allows the estimation of the collapse load assuming a no-tension material as required by Italian regulations through a linear extrapolation, accounting also for the presence of eventual tie-rods, as well as the estimation of the failure mechanism and the collapse spectral acceleration one again in agreement with the Italian building code through a filtering algorithm to avoid the overestimation of the structural bearing capacity, proposed for the first time in [21].

The present methodology offers a computationally efficient alternative to DEM while requiring only the definition of the structural geometry and the Mohr-Coulomb failure criterion, thereby overcoming the challenges associated with FEM constitutive models. Additionally, it eliminates the need for predefined failure mechanisms, making it a more flexible and effective tool for assessing seismic vulnerability in historic masonry structures.

2 Upper Bound Limit Analysis-Based Methodology Description

This study presents a numerical methodology that integrates the limit analysis upper bound theorem with finite elements to evaluate the seismic capacity of existing masonry structures. The most frequent failure modes for such types of construction are out-of-plane failures. The approach is consistent with Italian standards [13, 14] and offers the advantage of not requiring predefined failure mechanisms. As described in [19], a classical limit analysis problem can be formulated for any masonry structure if (i) the structure is discretized into hexahedral elements, which are considered infinitely resistant, as depicted in Fig. 1, and (ii) inelastic deformations are lumped only at element interfaces.

The active failure mechanism and collapse load are provided by the limit analysis problem, which can be tackled using either static or kinematic theorem. Given the adopted assumptions, plasticity is lumped into a discrete number of interfaces, ensuring that the kinematic and static solutions converge. As a result, the kinematic approach is preferred in this study for its ease of application, while the static formulation could be derived through a self-dual linear programming problem.

The problem sees six unknowns per hexahedral element, which are the velocities of the centroid along the reference axes (U_x^i, U_y^i, U_z^i) and the rotational rates about the centroid $(\phi_x^i, \phi_y^i, \phi_z^i)$, as illustrated in Fig. 1. External forces are assumed to be solely vertical forces $f_0^{(i)}$, representing self-weight, and horizontal volume forces $f_\Gamma^{(i)}$, dependent on the load multiplier Γ mimicking seismic actions. In agreement with Italian standards [13, 14], two horizontal load distributions can be modelled for $f_\Gamma^{(i)}$. The first, referred to as G1, represents the primary force distribution, which is mass proportional and is directly proportional to the height, forming an inverse triangular pattern. The second, denoted as G2, corresponds to a secondary force distribution, which remains constant along the height while still being mass proportional.

Constraining the velocity jump at element interfaces ensures plastic compatibility, as plastic dissipation is permitted only in these regions. The compatibility conditions are applied to a faceted approximation of the quadrilateral interface, represented by four triangular facets sharing a common vertex at the centroid. Internal actions, velocity jumps, and power dissipation are evaluated in four collocation points, positioned at the corners of the quadrilateral interface. Internal actions are given by the product of the triangle area with the corresponding normal and tangential stresses. These calculations are made referring to an appropriate local reference frame, denoted as $n - q - r$, as shown in Fig. 1.

The jump of velocity at the collocation point C_{P_K} belonging to two adjacent elements (i) and (j), if the versor n is outward from element (i), is computed as:

$$\Delta U_{CPK} = R^{(j)} u^{(j)} - R^{(i)} u^{(i)} \tag{1}$$

where the velocity at the collocation point C_{P_K} for element (i) is evaluated as:

$$U_{CPK}^{(i)} = \begin{bmatrix} n^T \\ q^T \\ r^T \end{bmatrix} \begin{bmatrix} 1 & 0 & 0 & 0 & z_{P1}-z_{GEi} & -(y_{P1}-y_{GEi}) \\ 0 & 1 & 0 & -(z_{P1}-z_{GEi}) & 0 & x_{P1}-x_{GEi} \\ 0 & 0 & 1 & y_{P1}-y_{GEi} & -(x_{P1}-x_{GEi}) & 0 \end{bmatrix} \begin{bmatrix} U^{(i)} \\ \phi^{(i)} \end{bmatrix} = R^{(i)} u^{(i)} \quad (2)$$

With $U^{(i)} = \begin{bmatrix} U_x^i & U_y^i & U_z^i \end{bmatrix}^T$, $\phi^{(i)} = \begin{bmatrix} \phi_x^i & \phi_y^i & \phi_z^i \end{bmatrix}^T$, as well as the coordinates of the collocation point C_{P_K} are identified as x_{Pk}, y_{Pk}, z_{Pk} while $x_{GEi}, y_{GEi}, z_{GEi}$ are the coordinates of the centroid of the element.

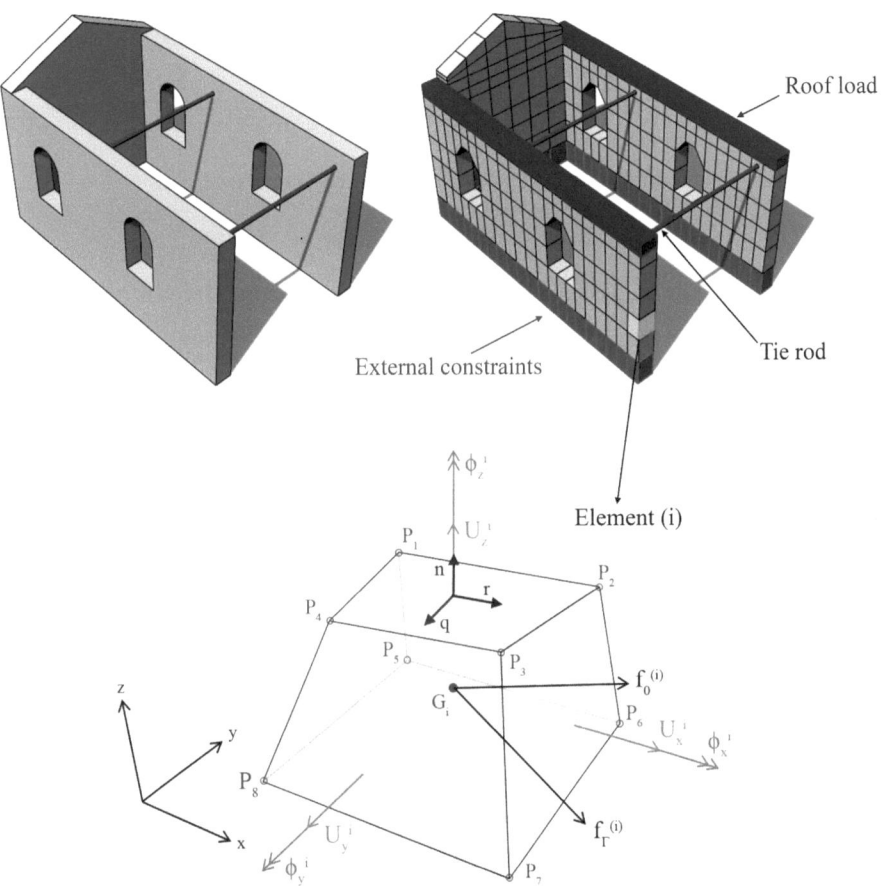

Fig. 1. Structure discretization in hexahedron elements featuring six kinematic variables.

The proposed method enables the consideration of various construction materials for the elements and properties at the interfaces, as visually represented by various colors in Fig. 1. At the interfaces between adjacent elements, a failure criterion such as the Mohr-Coulomb model, with cut-offs in tension and compression, is assumed. It is defined by tensile f_t and compressive f_c strengths, friction angle Φ, and cohesion c. It is supposed in the present approach that cohesion equals the tensile strength. For a detailed insight into this assumption, the reader is referred to [21]. The plastically admissible strength domain can be defined by a set of linear inequalities in the local reference frame $n-q-r$:

$$A_{in}^I \begin{bmatrix} N_I \\ Q_I \\ R_I \end{bmatrix} \leq b_{in}^I \quad (3)$$

In Eq. 3, $N_I = A_I \sigma_I$, $Q_I = A_I \tau_{qI}$, $R_I = A \tau_{rI}$ are the internal actions, whereas $\sigma_I, \tau_{qI}, \tau_{rI}$ are the stresses acting along n, q and r, respectively, and A_I is the area of the quadrilateral interface.

The plastic multipliers $\dot{\lambda}_I$ are linked to the velocity jumps between adjacent elements (i) and (j) due to the associate flow rule assumed:

$$R^{(j)} u^{(j)} - R^{(i)} u^{(i)} - A_{in}^{I\,T} \dot{\lambda}_I = 0 \quad (4)$$

Moreover, plastic multipliers are non-negative at each interface:

$$\dot{\lambda}_I \geq 0 \forall I = 1, \ldots, N_{in} \quad (5)$$

Therefore, the power dissipated by internal actions at the interfaces is given by:

$$P_{in} = \sum_{I=1}^{N_{in}} P_{in}^I = \sum_{I=1}^{N_{in}} \sum_{k=1}^{4} \frac{A_I}{4} b_{in}^{I\,T} \dot{\lambda}_{Ik} \quad (6)$$

While the power associated with external volume forces is calculated as:

$$P_0 = \sum_{i=1}^{N_e} V_i f_0^{(i)T} U^{(i)} \quad (7)$$

$$P_\Gamma = \Gamma \sum_{i=1}^{N_e} V_i f_\Gamma^{(i)T} U^{(i)} \quad (8)$$

The normalization condition allows for the selection of the collapse mechanism from the infinite set of homothetic failure modes. It is assumed that the power expended by the loads dependent on the load multiplier is unitary when $\Gamma = 1$.

From the internal and external powers balance, the load multiplier Γ is estimated. By maximizing the power balance according to the kinematic theorem, the collapse load multiplier is found.

External boundary conditions are translated as velocity constraints for those elements externally constrained:

$$A_{bc}^{(h)} U^{(h)} = 0 \quad (9)$$

In Eq. 9, the apex (h) identifies the constrained element while the dimension of the matrix $A_{bc}^{(h)}$ changes according to the constraint type.

The present method considers the tie-rods as rigid truss elements. This is translated into velocity constraints on the elements (k) and (l) connected by the ties:

$$A_{tr}^{(k)}U^{(k)} - A_{tr}^{(l)}U^{(l)} = 0 \qquad (10)$$

Finally, the classic limit analysis formulated as follows is solved through a linear programming algorithm in the software Matlab.

$$\min\left\{\Gamma = \sum_{I=1}^{N_{in}}\sum_{k=1}^{4}\frac{A_I}{4}b_{in}^{I\,T}\dot{\lambda}_{Ik} - \sum_{i=1}^{N_e}V_i f_0^{(i)T}U^{(i)}\right\} \qquad (11)$$

$$\text{s.t.} \begin{cases} R^{(j)}u^{(j)} - R^{(i)}u^{(i)} - A_{in}^{I\,T}\dot{\lambda}_I = 0 \forall I = 1,\dots,N_{in} \\ \sum_{i=1}^{N_e}V_i f_1^{(i)T}U^{(i)} = 1 \\ A_{bc}^{(h)}U^{(h)} = 0 \forall h \in \text{b.c.} \\ A_{tr}^{(k)}U^{(k)} - A_{tr}^{(l)}U^{(l)} = 0 \forall k,l \in \text{tie rods} \\ \dot{\lambda}_I \geq 0 \forall I = 1,\dots,N_{in} \end{cases} \qquad (12)$$

2.1 Results Extrapolation for NTM (No-Tension Materials)

Regarding the masonry strength domain, it is important to highlight that assuming zero tensile strength, namely a no-tension material, is a well-established hypothesis in classical literature. Moreover, Italian regulations require the assessment of the acceleration that activates local collapses considering masonry with vanishing tensile strength. However, enforcing null tensile strength can lead to spurious sliding between adjacent elements or cause numerical convergence issues.

To address this, the iterative procedure based on limit analysis, originally introduced by [20] for determining failure loads under no-tension material conditions, is implemented. This approach relies on two key assumptions: (i) only minimal sliding between adjacent elements is permitted, and (ii) the estimation of the collapse load for a material with null tensile strength is based on a failure mechanism that is not significantly influenced by spurious sliding due to an excessively low tensile strength.

According to [21], the load multiplier Γ is linear in f_t and in any mechanical parameter that quantitatively defines the homothetic contraction or expansion of the strength domain. Performing limit analysis iteratively while gradually decreasing f_t enables the generation of $\Gamma - f_t$ plots while simultaneously identifying the corresponding failure mechanisms. The $\Gamma - f_t$ relationship remains linear within all ranges of f_t where the same failure mechanism remains active.

2.2 Spectral Acleration Estimation

Performing a standard safety assessment from limit analysis, essential for practical design, requires careful consideration, especially for local failure mechanisms. These mechanisms often occur in buildings with weak floor stiffness and poor wall interlocking, involving significantly less mass than global failure scenarios. Additionally, upper-floor mechanisms may experience amplification effects. Overestimating structural capacity by considering the entire mass is a common issue, which occurs together with the selection of pre-determined collapse mechanisms suggested by Italian standards. To address this, a filtering procedure is necessary to accurately capture complex, unforeseen failure mechanisms by isolating critical structural portions.

According to Italian standards [13, 14], the acceleration triggering the local failure mechanism is equal to the spectral acceleration a_0^*:

$$a_0^* = \frac{\alpha_0 \cdot g}{e^* \cdot FC} \tag{13}$$

In Eq. 13, α_0 represents the load multiplier at collapse, g is the acceleration of gravity, FC is the confidence factor, defined according to [13, 14], and e^* is the effective mass ratio.

$$e^* = \frac{g \cdot M^*}{\sum_{i=1}^{n+m} P_i} \tag{14}$$

In Eq. 14, $n + m$ defines the total number of self-weights P_i that contribute to horizontal forces acting on the elements of the kinematic chain because of the seismic action, while M^* is the participating mass.

$$M^* = \frac{\left(\sum_{i=1}^{n+m} P_i \delta_{x,i}\right)^2}{g \cdot \sum_{i=1}^{n+m} P_i \delta_{x,i}^2} \tag{15}$$

In Eq. 15, $\delta_{x,i}$ is the horizontal virtual velocity of the point where the i-th weight P_i is applied. To avoid the overestimation of a_0^*, only the elements of the structure featuring a velocity $\delta_{x,i}$ greater than a predefined limit (20% of the maximum one, as found in [21]) are considered for evaluating the participating mass M^*.

Furthermore, the real distribution of horizontal forces acting on the construction is properly considered by substituting the collapse load α_0 in Eq. 13 with the quantity $a_g/g = \frac{baseshear}{verticalload}$. Indeed, for the evaluation of local mechanisms, Italian standards assume only a G2 horizontal load distribution, resulting in a drawback for the method presented here.

Finally, a local mechanism is not triggered if:

$$a_0^* \geq \frac{a_g S}{q} \tag{16}$$

In Eq. 16, a_g denotes the maximum ground acceleration at the bedrock at the location site, S is a coefficient accounting for the soil type and topography class, while q denotes the behavior factor (fixed at 2 according to [14]).

To assess the reliability and accuracy of the proposed method, it has been benchmarked against experimental results available in the literature from the dynamic testing of a simple U-shaped wall on a shaking table. A detailed description of the proposed numerical procedure, as well as the comparison with the experimental results, are provided in [21].

3 Case Study: Implementation of the Approach

The methodology described in the previous section is applied to a real case study, named the old monastery of Santa Maria della Pace, Piacenza (Italy). The monastery was constructed in the 16th century. Significant structural changes were not made on the portion of the structure that still stands nowadays [5, 22]. The old monastery features a cloister layout developed on two levels, as illustrated in Fig. 2. The cloisters and the corridors on the first floor feature a vaulted ceiling with cross vaults, while pavilion vaults constitute the covering of most of the rooms, only a few of them have timber floors. The pitched timber roof varies in height, adapting to the building elevation geometry. The portion of the structure analyzed is highlighted in green in Fig. 2. It is one of the most vulnerable parts. Indeed, it features a basilica layout architecture with one of the longitudinal walls supported by a cloister vault covering a big room on the ground floor, as shown in Fig. 2.

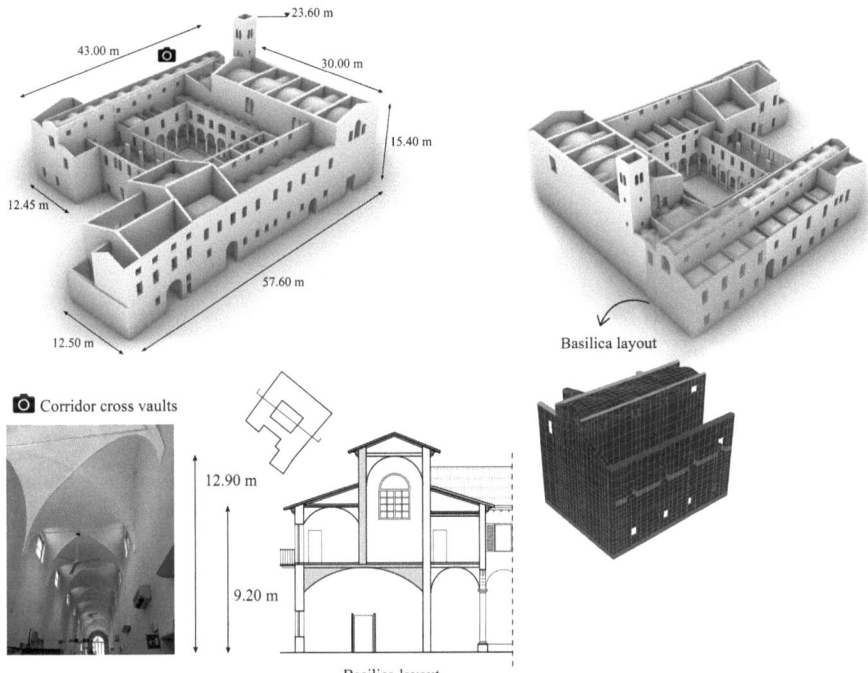

Fig. 2. Santa Maria della Pace Monastery: overview and numerical model of the analyzed portion.

The local failure mechanisms triggered by the spectral acceleration a_0^* are studied under two horizontal load distributions (G1 and G2) acting perpendicular to the longitudinal walls of the basilica layout. The structural performance of this portion of the monastery is verified against the seismic design acceleration prescribed by the regulation for the site of Piacenza for the life safety (SLV) limit state. The design acceleration is characterized by a 475-year return period T_R and a bedrock PGA a_g equal to 0.092 g. According to Italian regulations and the site stratigraphy, the soil type is classified as

C while the topography class is T1. Consequently, the coefficient S is equal to 1.5. Therefore, in agreement with Eq. 16, the failure mechanism is not activated if:

$$a_0^* \geq \frac{a_g S}{q} = 0.677 \, m/s^2 \quad (17)$$

The collapse accelerations a_g/g at progressively decreased tensile strength are depicted in Fig. 3. The analyses are performed under horizontal forces with G1 and G2 distributions orthogonal to the longitudinal walls, exhibiting the highest vulnerability under out-of-plane loading. The collapse acceleration a_g/g for a no-tension material ($f_t = 0 MPa$) is estimated by means of a linear extrapolation of the results. During the linear extrapolation process, collapse accelerations linked to collapse mechanisms influenced by spurious sliding of the elements are excluded.

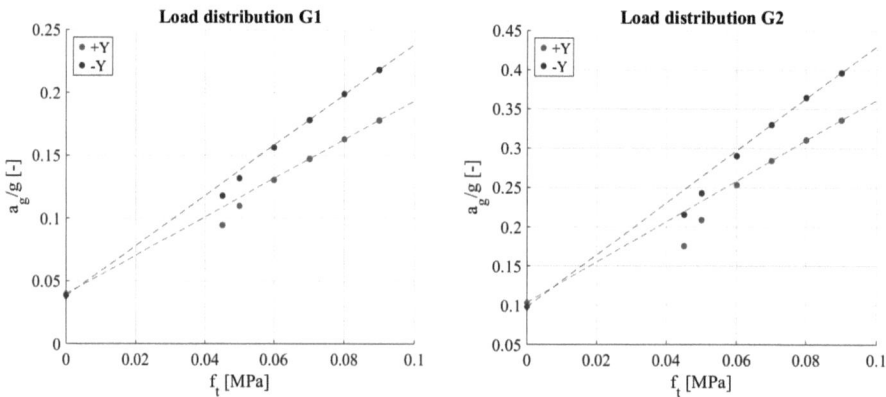

Fig. 3. Seismic assessment of the Basilica Layout: collapse acceleration vs tensile strength.

The spectral acceleration that activates the local collapse mechanism is evaluated based on the collapse acceleration a_g/g, estimated for a material with zero tensile strength, and is compared with the design value defined in Eq. 17. Figure 4 presents the estimated spectral accelerations and the active local collapse mechanisms of the structure under the G1 and G2 horizontal load distributions, for both the positive and negative Y directions. The G2 load distribution leads to a collapse spectral acceleration greater than the design value, indicating that the structure is verified. In contrast, for the G1 load distribution, the structure is not verified against the design seismic acceleration, as the spectral acceleration is lower.

Since the construction is not verified for the G1 load distribution, the contribution of existing tie-rods to the structural load-bearing capacity is assessed. The disposition of tie rods is shown in Fig. 5. Three tie rods are placed on the ground floor in correspondence with the cloister vault, and four ties are placed in the corridor on the first floor under the cross vaults. The collapse accelerations a_g/g for reduced values of tensile strength are shown in Fig. 6, together with the results for the same structure without tie-rods.

The collapse mechanism and the collapse spectral acceleration of the strengthened structure, computed assuming zero tensile strength, are depicted in Fig. 7. The chains give a significant improvement of the structural load-bearing capacity when the load acts in the Y-positive direction (about 44%). Indeed, a different collapse mechanism is triggered with respect to the structure without tie-rods (see Fig. 4). Instead, the increment is negligible (about 11%) when the structure is loaded in Y negative direction. The failure mechanism is quite the same for both the reinforced and unreinforced structure. However, for both loading directions, the structure is not verified, and the design acceleration is greater than the collapse spectral acceleration.

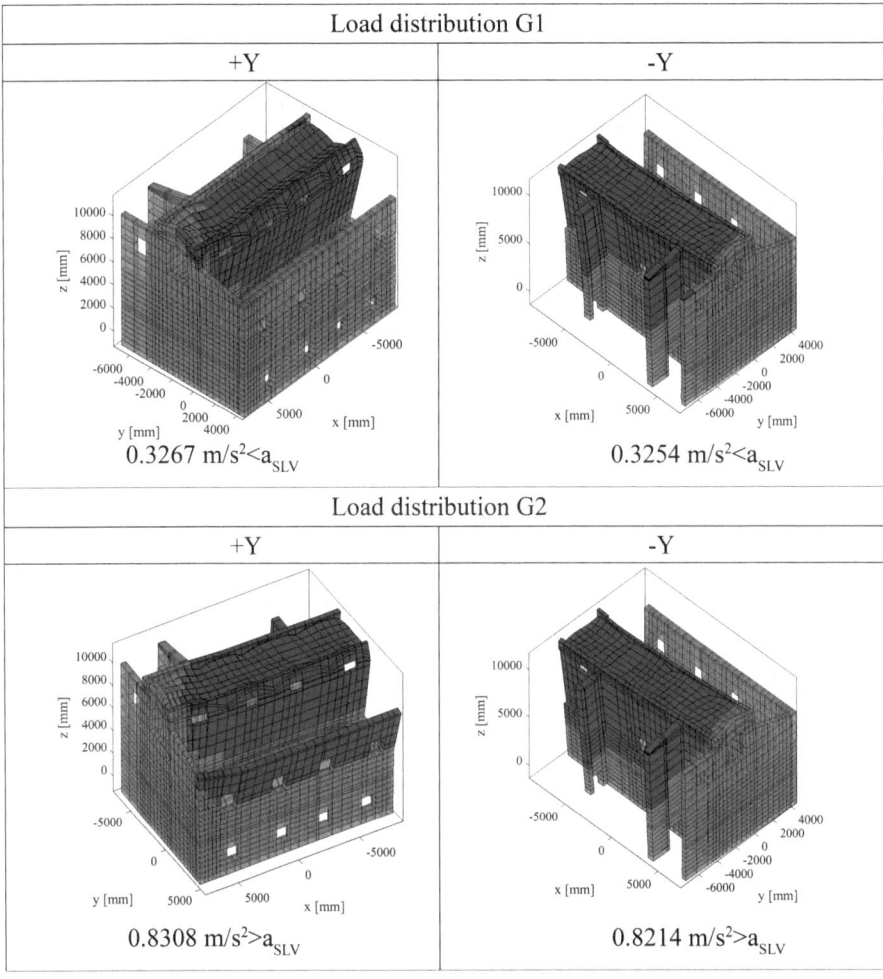

Fig. 4. Seismic assessment of the Basilica Layout: failure mechanisms and spectral accelerations.

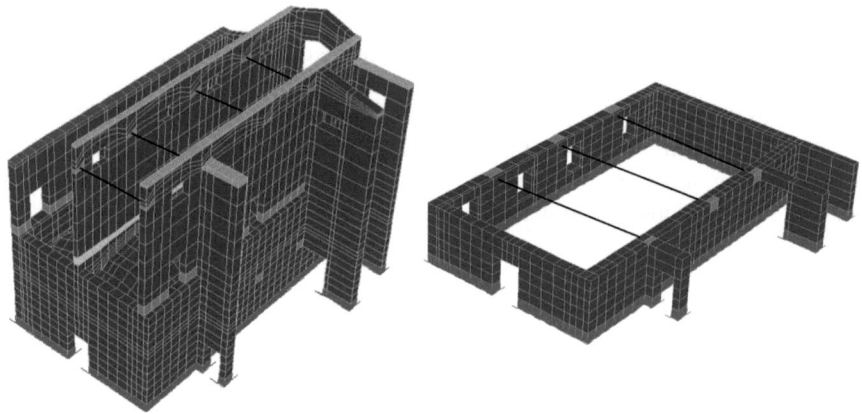

Fig. 5. Disposition of the tie-rods.

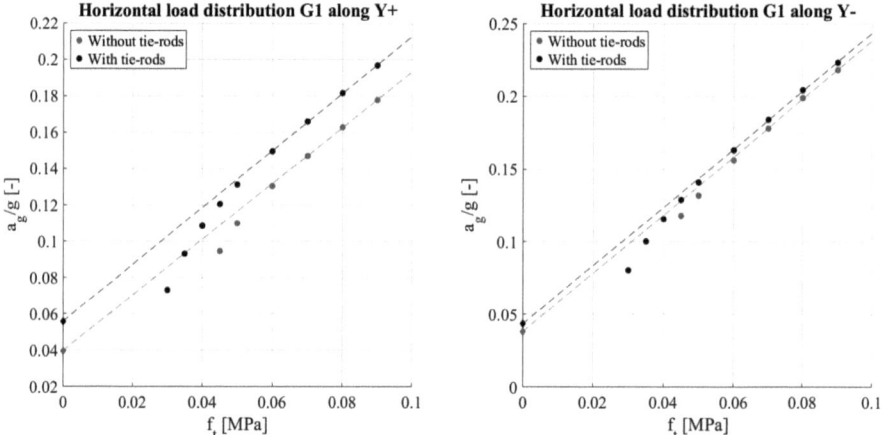

Fig. 6. Seismic assessment of the Basilica Layout with tie-rods: collapse load vs the tensile strength.

4 Conclusions

This study introduces an upper-bound finite element limit analysis approach, incorporating a velocity filtering routine to evaluate the seismic safety of masonry structures with complex geometries, while also accounting for the presence of eventual chains. The method aligns with Italian standards while eliminating the need for predefined failure mechanisms. The structure is discretized into infinitely resistant hexahedral elements, with plasticity lumped to their interfaces, making the upper and lower bounds of the limit analysis problem coincide.

Solving the classic limit analysis problem formulated following the kinematic theorem through a linear programming problem, the collapse acceleration and failure mechanisms are found. Internal actions are computed from the static dual linear programming problem.

Since Italian standards prescribe negligible tensile strength without sliding, the collapse acceleration is indirectly determined through linear extrapolation, preventing premature algorithm failure and spurious sliding. The MATLAB-based implementation requires only the mesh definition and Mohr-Coulomb strength parameters, facilitating rapid analysis. Additionally, an automated filtering strategy identifies elements significantly contributing to the collapse mechanism, ensuring an accurate evaluation of the collapse acceleration for ultimate limit state verifications.

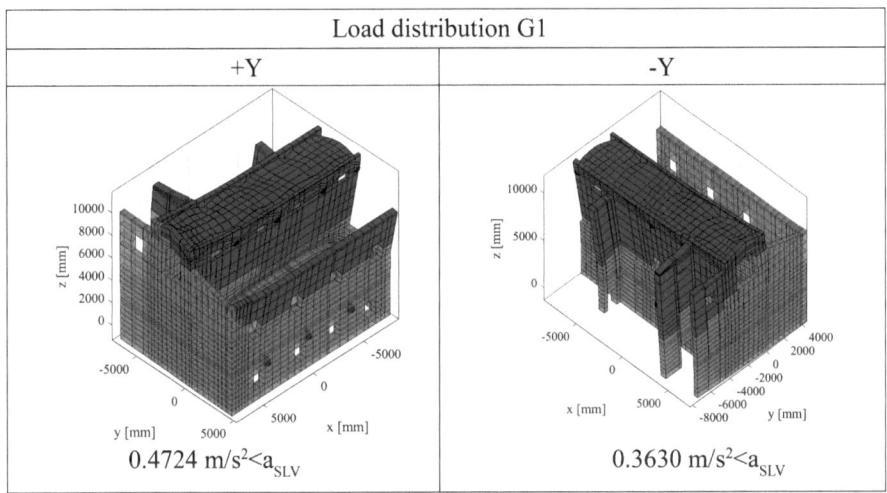

Fig. 7. Basilica Layout with tie-rods seismic assessment: failure mechanisms and collapse spectral accelerations under G1 horizontal load distribution.

The methodology is applied to a real case study in Piacenza, Italy, namely the former Monastery of Santa Maria della Pace. The structure features a complex geometry, making standard analysis methods unreliable. The most critical portion of the structure is studied, which is characterized by a basilica layout. The results highlight the necessity of strengthening interventions, as local collapses could be triggered by the design seismic action specified in the Italian building code, even if the existing tie-rods are accounted for.

Acknowledgments. The study was partially developed within the research activities carried out in the frame of 2024–2026 ReLUIS Project – WP10 masonry structures (Coordinator – Prof. Guido Magenes), specifically by means of the research carried out in WP10.1.1 and WP10.2 Masonry Structures (Task Coordinators – respectively Prof. Serena Cattari and Prof. Sergio Lagomarsino).

The Italian Department of Civil Protection has funded such a project.

Finally, the study was partially developed with the financial support of the Italian Ministry of Scientific Research MUR within the research project PRIN-2022 (https://www.dabc.polimi.it/en/progetto/advanced-mechanical-models-and-computational-methods-for-large-scale-3d-printing-of-innovative-concrete-structures/) titled "Advanced mechanical models and computational methods for large-scale 3D printing of innovative con crete structures (COM^3D-CREATE)" (National PI: Prof. Andrea Chiozzi, Local PI: Prof. Gabriele Milani). Finanziato dall'Unione europea Next Generation EU, Missione 4 Componente 1 CUP D53D23004070006.

Disclosure of Interests. The authors have no competing interests to declare that are relevant to the content of this article.

References

1. Shabani, A., Kioumarsi, M., Zucconi, M.: State of the art of simplified analytical methods for seismic vulnerability assessment of unreinforced masonry buildings. Eng. Struct. **239**, 112280 (2021)
2. Acito, M., Buzzetti, M., Chesi, C., Magrinelli, E., Milani, G.: Failures and damages of historical masonry structures induced by 2012 northern and 2016–17 central Italy seismic sequences: critical issues and new perspectives towards seismic prevention. Eng. Fail. Anal. **149**, 107257 (2023)
3. Sorrentino, L., D'Ayala, D., de Felice, G., Griffith, M.C., Lagomarsino, S., Magenes, G.: Review of out-of-plane seismic assessment techniques applied to existing masonry buildings. Int. J. Architectural Heritage **11**, 2–21 (2017)
4. Olivieri, C., Cocking, S., Fabbrocino, F., Iannuzzo, A., Placidi, L., Adriaenssens, S.: Seismic capacity of purely compressed shells based on airy stress function. Continuum Mech. Thermodyn. **37**, 21 (2025)
5. Acito, M., Buzzetti, M., Cundari, G.A., Milani, G.: General methodological approach for the seismic assessment of masonry aggregates. Structures **57**, 105177 (2023)
6. Clementi, F., Gazzani, V., Poiani, M., Lenci, S.: Assessment of seismic behaviour of heritage masonry buildings using numerical modelling. J. Build. Eng. **8**, 29–47 (2016)
7. Milani, G., Valente, M.: Comparative pushover and limit analyses on seven masonry churches damaged by the 2012 Emilia-Romagna (Italy) seismic events: possibilities of non-linear finite elements compared with pre-assigned failure mechanisms. Eng. Fail. Anal. **47**, 129–161 (2015)
8. Acito, M., Bocciarelli, M., Chesi, C., Milani, G.: Collapse of the clock tower in Finale Emilia after the Emilia Romagna earthquake sequence: numerical insight. Eng. Struct. **72**, 70–91 (2014)
9. Castellazzi, G., D'Altri, A.M., de Miranda, S., Chiozzi, A., Tralli, A.: Numerical insights on the seismic behavior of a nonisolated historical masonry tower. Bull. Earthq. Eng. **16**, 933–961 (2018)
10. Schiavoni, M., Giordano, E., Roscini, F., Clementi, F.: Advanced numerical insights for an effective seismic assessment of historical masonry aggregates. Eng. Struct. **285**, 115997 (2023)
11. Azevedo, J., Sincraian, G., Lemos, J.V.: Seismic behavior of blocky masonry structures. Earthq. Spectra **16**, 337–365 (2000)
12. Oktiovan, Y.P., Messali, F., Pulatsu, B., Lemos, J.V., Rots, J.G.: A contact-based constitutive model for the numerical analysis of masonry structures using the distinct element method. Comput. Struct. **303**, 107499 (2024)

13. Ministero delle Infrastrutture e dei Trasporti: Decreto 17 gennaio 2018 Aggiornamento delle "Norme tecniche per le costruzioni". Gazzetta Ufficiale Della Repubblica Italiana (2018)
14. Ministero delle Infrastrutture e dei Trasporti: Circolare 21 gennaio 2019 n.7: Istruzioni per l'applicazione dell'Aggiornamento delle "Norme Tecniche per le Costruzioni" di cui al decreto ministeriale 17 gennaio 2018. Gazzetta Ufficiale Della Repubblica Italiana (2019)
15. Chiozzi, A., Grillanda, N., Milani, G., Tralli, A.: UB-ALMANAC: an adaptive limit analysis NURBS-based program for the automatic assessment of partial failure mechanisms in masonry churches. Eng. Fail. Anal. **85**, 201–220 (2018)
16. Lo Monaco, A., et al.: Seismic assessment of Romanian Orthodox masonry churches in the Banat area through a multi-level analysis framework. Eng. Fail. Anal. **153**, 107539 (2023)
17. Aita, D., Bruggi, M., Garavaglia, E.: Collapse analysis of masonry arches and domes considering finite friction and uncertainties in compressive strength. Eng. Fail. Anal. **163**, 108462 (2024)
18. Fabbrocino, F., Olivieri, C., Luciano, R., Vaiano, G., Maddaloni, G., Iannuzzo, A.: Seismic performance of historic masonry buildings: a comparative analysis of equivalent frame and block-based methods. Alex. Eng. J. **109**, 359–375 (2024)
19. Wang, P., Milani, G.: Specialized 3D Distinct element limit analysis approach for a fast seismic vulnerability evaluation of massive masonry structures: Application on traditional pagodas. Eng. Struct. **282**, 115792 (2023)
20. Wang, P., Milani, G.: Seismic vulnerability prediction of masonry aggregates: iterative finite element upper bound limit analysis approximating no tensile resistance. Eng. Struct. **293**, 116595 (2023)
21. Buzzetti, M., Pingaro, N., Milani, G.: Automatic detection of local collapse mechanisms in historical masonry buildings: fast and robust FE upper bound limit analysis. Eng. Fail. Anal. **170**, 109310 (2025)
22. Pingaro, N., Buzzetti, M., Milani, G.: Advanced FE nonlinear numerical modeling to predict historical masonry vaults failure: assessment of risk collapse for a long span cloister vault heavily loaded at the crown by means of a general-purpose numerical protocol. Eng. Fail. Anal. **167**, 109070 (2025)

Airy-Based Form-Finding of Purely Compressed Masonry Shells Under Vertical and Horizontal Loads

Sam Cocking[1]($\boxtimes$), Luigi Sibille[2], Sigrid Adriaenssens[3], Americo Cunha Jr[4,5], Francesco Fabbrocino[6], and Carlo Olivieri[3,6]

[1] Department of Engineering, University of Cambridge, JJ Thomson Avenue 7a, Cambridge CB3 0FA, UK
sc740@cam.ac.uk

[2] Department of Ocean Operations and Civil Engineering, Norwegian University of Science and Technology, 4th Floor, A-block, Larsgårdsvegen 2, 6009 Ålesund, Norway
luigi.sibille@ntnu.no

[3] Department of Civil and Environmental Engineering, Princeton University, Princeton, NJ 08544, USA
sadriaen@princeton.edu

[4] National Laboratory of Scientific Computing – LNCC, Petrópolis, Brazil
americo@lncc.br

[5] Rio de Janeiro State University – UERJ, Rio de Janeiro, Brazil
americo.cunha@uerj.br

[6] Department of Engineering, Pegaso Telematic University, Centro Direzionale ISOLA F2, 80143 Naples, Italy
{francesco.fabbrocino,carlo.olivieri}@unipegaso.it

Abstract. The assessment and design of masonry vaulted structures in seismic regions presents challenges to the designer. Typical form-finding methods for compression-only shells may not directly consider horizontal loading, leading to uncertainty regarding structural performance during earthquake events. In the case of new design, this can result in inefficient structures and material overuse, while historic structures may be condemned or damaged through inappropriate interventions. Direct consideration of the static horizontal force capacity - the threshold at which hinge formation triggers dynamic, rocking-like mechanisms in the vault - would allay these concerns, and is primarily a product of the structural geometry. Recent work by the authors has presented a methodology for form-finding compression-only shells under combined vertical and horizontal loading, which is based on the theories of Limit Analysis and Membrane Equilibrium Analysis. However, this method relies on the constrained optimisation of a concave stress potential, which can result in computational challenges. Solutions may be further complicated in the case of vaults containing either cracking damage or intentional geometric discontinuities, such as cross vaults. This paper outlines the key challenges in refinement and implementation of the new form-finding methodology and presents two potential computational solutions, utilising non-convex optimisation and machine learning methods.

Keywords: Vault · Shell · Masonry · Form finding · Airy stress function · seismic

1 Introduction

Compression-only shells, such as unreinforced masonry or concrete vaults, offer elegant structural forms and are often found throughout historic architecture. The duality between form and force means that form-finding methods not only enable the design of new shells of this type, under defined loading conditions, but also offer a means of assessing existing vaulted structures. Under vertical gravity loads, there are a variety of techniques available to perform this task [33]. However, when horizontal forces must also be considered, such as in seismic regions, this analysis becomes more complex. Methods such as Tilted Thrust Line Analysis indirectly consider the effect of horizontal body forces (e.g., as in [15]). Recently, a method based on Membrane Equilibrium Analysis (MEA) has been proposed which directly includes these horizontal forces in the equilibrium formulation [25].

Understanding the horizontal force capacity of compression-only shells is critical when they are proposed for construction in seismic regions. While this type of construction is resource-efficient, typically utilising a small structural depth and eschewing modern reinforcement techniques, the topography of elements such as bricks or tiles can nonetheless be tailored to achieve an adequate structural capacity [28]. Specifically, the static horizontal force capacity of compression-only shells, before activation of rocking mechanisms through hinge formation [7,8,11,27], is of interest. Dynamic behaviour following this point is highly sensitive to both the structural response and the specific characteristics of the earthquake, such as the spectral characteristics and maximum ground acceleration. However, the behaviour up to this static limit is largely governed by geometry.

The methodology adopted in this paper, for direct calculation of the static horizontal force capacity of compression-only shells, is based on MEA [1,4,14], the Safe Theorem of Limit Analysis (LA), and the no-tension hypothesis for masonry-like materials proposed by Heyman [16] and adopted by other authors to model unilateral materials [19,20]. It was first presented in [25], in which a typical masonry sail vault was analysed. It has previously been shown [10,26] that, under vertical forces, MEA offers a less conservative and more accurate safety factor than can be achieved by other LA methods based on classical Thrust Line Analysis (TLA) [17,18,22,31], since these alternative approaches consider the shell to be an arch structure and consequently do not include the beneficial effects of biaxial membrane behaviour.

As described fully in [25], the method used here adopts a parametric description of a concave Airy Stress Function (ASF) alongside a finite-element formulation of equilibrium that directly accounts for vertical and horizontal loads. By ensuring concavity of the ASF, the behaviour of the shell remains purely compressive. However, this can result in computational challenges during implementation of the method. This paper discusses these challenges and introduces two potential solution strategies: Machine Learning techniques to identify optimum ASFs and non-convex optimisation techniques based on the cross-entropy method [9] to improve computational performance.

2 Membrane Equilibrium Analysis Under Vertical and Horizontal Loads

By adopting Heyman's no-tension hypothesis for masonry-like materials, the equilibrium of a compression-only shell can be expressed in terms of geometry, without the need for mechanical properties. MEA extends the familiar concept of a thrust line [16] to that of a thrust membrane, which must lie within the thickness of the shell in order to prevent collapse. Since the membrane must be purely in compression, its generalised stresses must be negative semi-definite. MEA expresses the equilibrium of this membrane in Pucher form [5,29], in terms of two unknown scalar functions for the stress potential and height, i.e., shape, of the membrane, throughout its extent. The choice of an ASF then reduces these equilibrium equations to transverse equilibrium only.

Pucher stresses are the primary variables in these membrane equilibrium equations. These stresses represent the projections of the generalised stresses onto the planform – i.e., the 2D projection of the shell as viewed from above [5,29]. For general shells, the shell geometry and its vertical projection onto the planform can be conveniently expressed in terms of a Monge patch. The natural vector basis associated with this Monge description can be used to transform the generalised membrane stress components in Pucher stresses. For more details of this approach, readers are directed to [2,3]. Here, the third basis vector in the triad is chosen to be normal to the surface of the shell.

Since the two equations related to Pucher stresses describe both the stresses and shape of the shell membrane, either may be chosen as an unknown. For instance, in the assessment of historic structures, the shape is known while the associated load capacity is sought. For the purposes of form-finding, however, the shell's form is chosen as the unknown and expressed in terms of geometric parameters to be optimised. Constrained optimisation is then performed to identify the shell geometry with the highest horizontal load multiplier, under the unilateral constraints of the masonry material.

For more details of the method summarised below, readers are directed to [25].

2.1 Geometry and Loads

Under the action of self-weight and horizontal body forces defined by a load factor $\lambda = \{\lambda_1, \lambda_2\}$, a general shell is shown in Fig. 1 [25]. A membrane surface S contained within the thickness of this shell can be described by a Monge patch, expressed here using the orthonormal triad for a given Cartesian frame $\{O; x_1, x_2, x_3\}$:

$$\{x = x_1 + x_2 + f(x_1, x_2), (x_1, x_2) \in \Omega\}, \tag{1}$$

where $f(x_1, x_2)$ is an arbitrary continuous function of its arguments (x_1, x_2) and defines the shape of the membrane. Ω is the planform of S on the x_1-x_2 plane, having boundary $\partial\Omega$.

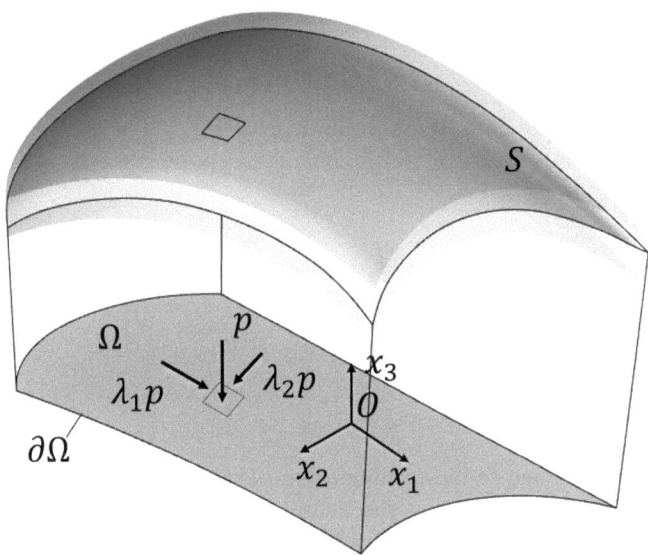

Fig. 1. A general compression-only shell under combined vertical and horizontal body forces. The membrane surface S, fully in compression, lies within the shell thickness and projects onto the planform domain Ω with boundary $\partial\Omega$. The general force components acting on a region of S, form the basis of the membrane equilibrium formulation (from [25]).

Figure 1 shows the general surface forces acting on the shell, per unit projected area of S. These body forces need not be uniform and can be expressed as:

$$p = \{\lambda_1 p, \lambda_2 p, -p\}, \tag{2}$$

where $p = \rho J$ is the self-weight of the shell per unit projected area, given in terms of ρ, the material specific weight, and J, the Jacobian determinant that describes the ratio between surface area on S and projected area on Ω.

2.2 Forces and Equilibrium

Using subscript comma notation (e.g., $\blacksquare_{,ij}$) to represent general derivatives – in this case, subsequent differentiation with respect to the i-th and j-th coordinates

- membrane equilibrium under loads p can be described through a Differential Geometry formulation [3] based on the Pucher stresses [29]. This results in the following three scalar equations:

$$S^{11}_{,1} + S^{12}_{,2} + \lambda_1 p = 0, \tag{3}$$

$$S^{21}_{,1} + S^{22}_{,2} + \lambda_2 p = 0, \tag{4}$$

$$S^{11} f_{,11} + S^{22} f_{,22} + 2 S^{12} f_{,12} + f_{,1} \lambda_1 p + f_{,2} \lambda_2 p - p = 0. \tag{5}$$

where S^{ij} is the ij Pucher stress component for $i,j = 1,2$. By solving these equilibrium equations using a continuous stress potential, the ASF $F(x_1, x_2)$, the following are obtained:

$$S^{11} + \int \lambda_1 p \, dx_1 = F_{,22}, \tag{6}$$

$$S^{22} + \int \lambda_2 p \, dx_2 = F_{,11}, \tag{7}$$

$$S^{12} = S^{21} = -F_{,12}. \tag{8}$$

$F(x_1, x_2)$ is assumed to be continuous, as discussed in more detail in [21,24]). Adapting these equations, using the definition $h_i = \int \lambda_i p \, dx_i$ with $i = 1, 2$, a single linear equation is obtained in which the ASF is unknown:

$$(F_{,22} - h_1) f_{h,11} + (F_{,11} - h_2) f_{h,22} - 2 F_{,12} f_{h,12} - f_{h,1} \lambda_1 p - f_{h,2} \lambda_2 p - p = 0. \tag{9}$$

As described in [25], this second-order PDE may be elliptic, parabolic, or hyperbolic. Here, we assume that Eq. (9) is elliptic and can be formulated as a Boundary Value Problem (BVP), supplemented by conditions on the stress function or on its normal slope with respect to the boundary. In formulating this BVP, either Dirichlet-type boundary conditions, specifying the value of f along the boundary, or Neumann-type, specifying the derivative of f along the outward unit normal $\mathbf{n}$ on the boundary, or a combination of both types, may be used. It is often convenient to use Dirichlet-type conditions to define f along the boundary, based on an initial architectural design for the shell that is being form-found.

2.3 Constitutive Restriction and Requirements of Continuity

As described in [25], the constitutive restriction for a no-tension material such as masonry can be expressed as follows:

$$\mathbf{T} \in \text{Sym}^-, \quad \mathbf{E} \in \text{Sym}^+, \quad \mathbf{T} \cdot \mathbf{E} = 0, \tag{10}$$

Here, **T** is the Cauchy stress tensor, **E** is the infinitesimal strain tensor, and Sym^+ and Sym^- are the spaces of symmetric positive and negative semidefinite tensors, respectively. In terms of the ASF, this constitutive restriction can also be expressed as follows:

$$F_{,11} + F_{,22} \leq 0, \quad F_{,11}F_{,22} - F_{,12}^2 \geq 0, \tag{11}$$

Consequently, the curvature tensor of the ASF must be negative semi-definite. In other words, an admissible stress surface must be concave at all points within the domain of interest. The curvature tensor is defined by the Hessian matrix $\mathbf{H}_F$, as follows:

$$\mathbf{H}_F = \begin{bmatrix} F_{,11} & F_{,12} \\ F_{,12} & F_{,22} \end{bmatrix}. \tag{12}$$

Here, the diagonal terms correspond to curvature along the x_1 and x_2 directions, while the off-diagonal terms relate to coupling between these directions.

Furthermore, for single patch shells, C^1-continuity is enforced throughout the domain and at the boundaries. Consequently, no singularities are modelled in the stress field, such as may arise in vaults suffering from cracking damage or which have an inherently discontinuous form, such as cross vaults. In such multi-patch scenarios, the specification of C^1-continuity throughout the domain necessitates additional constraints to enforce this continuity at the patch interfaces.

2.4 Expression of Equilibrium in the Weak Form

The PDEs governing membrane equilibrium (Eqs. (5) and (9)) are numerically solved using the finite element method (FEM). In this paper, this step has been implemented with the Python package FEniCS [6]. Previous work has utilised FEM approaches in Mathematica to demonstrate the feasibility of this approach [23]. FEM requires discretisation of the continuous surface S into finite mesh elements, forming the computational domain in which the PDE is solved. FEniCS supports various mesh element types, such as triangles, quadrilaterals, tetrahedra, and hexahedra for 2D and 3D problems.

FEM necessitates reformulation of the governing PDEs in their weak form [13], to accommodate solutions with lower regularity and reduce the continuity requirements on the approximate solution. To obtain the weak form, the PDE is multiplied by a test function v, belonging to the same function space as the sought solution, and integrated over the planform domain Ω. The standard Galerkin method, used in FEniCS, requires the PDE to contain only first-order derivatives. Hence, integration by parts is applied to reduce the derivative order, resulting in additional boundary terms that vanish due to the Dirichlet boundary conditions.

Following these steps, the equilibrium equation under horizontal loads (Eq. (9)) becomes as follows:

$$\int_\Omega [(F_{,22} - h_1(\lambda_1)) f_{,1}v_{,1} + (F_{,11} - h_2(\lambda_2)) f_{,2}v_{,2} - 2F_{,12}f_{,1}v_{,2} - f_{,1}\lambda_1 pv - f_{,2}\lambda_2 pv - pv] \,d\Omega = 0. \tag{13}$$

3 Discontinuities in the Masonry Shell - Example of a Cross Vault

As alluded to in Sect. 2.3, it may be desired to generalise the form-finding method to multi-patch scenarios when considering inherent discontinuities in the form of a proposed shell. Cross vaults are a simple and common example of such discontinuity. Inspired by the cross vaults of Kings College Chapel in Cambridge, UK, Fig. 2 shows an initial design with discontinuities along both lines of mirror symmetry in its planform.

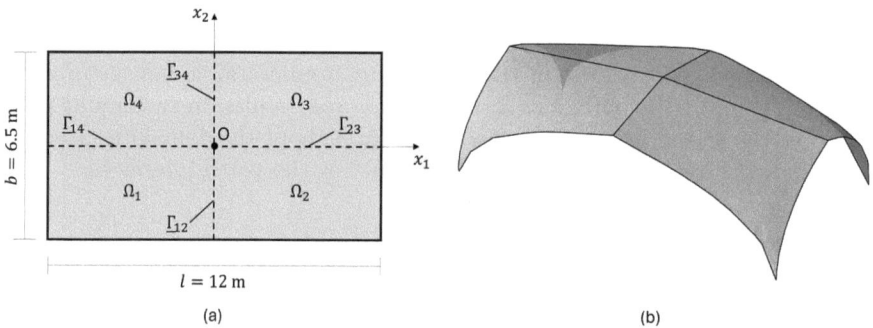

Fig. 2. (a) A rectangular planform domain and (b) the corresponding shell geometry, featuring discontinuities along both lines of mirror symmetry, partitioning the domain into four subdomains $\Omega_{1,\,2,\,3,\,4}$ separated by interfaces $\Gamma_{12,\,23,\,34,\,14}$.

3.1 Airy Stress Function Definition

One appropriate family of ASFs for the multi-patch membrane shown in Fig. 2 can be defined piecewise as follows:

$$\mathcal{F}(\sigma, \alpha, \gamma) = \begin{cases} F_2(\sigma, \alpha, \gamma), & \text{in } \Omega_1 \text{ and } \Omega_3, \\ F_1(\sigma, \alpha, \gamma), & \text{in } \Omega_2 \text{ and } \Omega_4. \end{cases} \tag{14}$$

where F_1 and F_2 are given by:

$$F_1(\sigma, \alpha, \gamma) = \frac{\gamma}{2b^2}\left(\frac{b^2}{4} - x_2^2\right) + \frac{\sigma - \gamma}{2l^2}\left(\frac{l^2}{4} - x_1^2\right), \tag{15}$$

$$F_2(\sigma, \alpha, \gamma) = \frac{\alpha}{2l^2}\left(\frac{l^2}{4} - x_1^2\right) + \frac{\sigma - \alpha}{2b^2}\left(\frac{b^2}{4} - x_2^2\right). \tag{16}$$

Here, l and b are constants defining the size of the planform (c.f., Fig. 2), x_1 and x_2 are spatial coordinates, σ, α, and γ are parameters, and Ω_i are the domains of the piecewise regions.

4 Challenges of this Approach

Parameterisation of the family of ASFs requires the use of multiple parameters, posing notable challenges during the form-finding optimisation process, particularly in ensuring concavity of the ASF. Greater sophistication of the family of ASFs can be achieved by increasing the number of parameters. However, this leads to a high-dimensional parameter space, making it more onerous to interpret whether a continuous domain or specific region within the parameter space exists in which concavity is consistently maintained. Concavity is of paramount importance, as it guarantees a purely compressive stress state within the shell in alignment with the no-tension hypothesis commonly assumed for masonry-like materials.

The inherent nonlinearity of the governing equilibrium equations further complicates the numerical solution process. Specifically, the equations relating the parameters of the ASF to the membrane geometry are nonlinear. This creates challenges in achieving convergence and numerical stability, which may result in a poor solution, sensitivity to local minima, or failure of the solver.

These challenges are amplified when the shell structure exhibits singularities, such as geometric discontinuities (see Fig. 2). In these cases, the shell problem is decomposed into multiple patches, each described by separate Airy stress parameters. In this multi-patch approach, continuity of the ASF along the boundary lines between patches must also be enforced. This continuity is essential to maintaining accurate stress transfer and significantly increases both the complexity and computational burden of the overall form-finding process.

Faced with these challenges, it is not straightforward to computationally implement the method outlined above in Sect. 2. Traditional optimisation packages have been trialled in Python and have struggled to perform adequately. In contrast, a tool that utilises these methods will only be of value to practitioners if it can achieve reliable results in efficient run-times. To combat these challenges, the following Sect. 5 outlines potential strategies to improve computational performance and reliability.

5 Potential Solutions and Directions for Future Work

Form-finding with a multi-parameter Airy Stress Function can be approached via two broad strategies: data-driven machine learning (ML) and non-convex optimisation. Each approach aims to identify parameter values that satisfy the equilibrium conditions represented by the governing PDE for a given design scenario, under the constraints that the chosen ASF is concave and that the form-found membrane must lie within the thickness of the shell.

Within ML approaches, regression-based methods employ supervised learning to predict optimal Airy stress parameters. A dataset of solved examples is generated by varying the parameter set within ranges that guarantee concavity, and recording the optimum membrane solution obtained from the equilibrium equation. Regression algorithms then learn patterns from these datasets without explicitly embedding the underlying physics. Frequently used regression techniques include ensemble methods such as random forests [30], Gaussian process (GP) regression [34], and instance-based methods such as k-nearest neighbours (k-NN) [12].

However, regression-based methods present certain limitations. A notable drawback is their black-box nature, meaning they depend heavily on the quality and diversity of the dataset. They generally perform well within the range covered by training data but may struggle with extrapolation, as they do not inherently respect physical constraints beyond observed scenarios [32]. For example, random forests are confined to predictions within the bounds of their training data [30]. Consequently, if a new scenario significantly differs from those encountered during training, these methods risk providing non-physical or unstable parameter sets.

An alternative ML strategy is the use of Physics-Informed Neural Networks (PINNs), which integrate governing physical equations directly into the training process. Unlike traditional regression models, PINNs embed the equilibrium PDE into their loss function. In this strategy, a neural network (e.g., a feed-forward deep network) is constructed to represent the ASF over the domain [32]. This method allows the PDE itself, supplemented with appropriate boundary conditions, to drive network training without relying exclusively on extensive datasets.

Despite these advantages, PINNs present their own challenges. Training such networks is computationally demanding, requiring iterative adjustment of potentially very many parameters (representing weights and biases in the network) until the PDE residual is successfully minimised. The high dimensionality and non-convex nature of the optimisation pose significant convergence challenges, necessitating careful and extensive tuning [32]. Moreover, since each new design scenario requires training a new network from scratch, unless the network architecture explicitly accommodates multiple cases, the computational overhead can be substantial. Thus, while PINNs enhance physical accuracy and consistency compared to purely data-driven regression methods, they inherently trade off computational efficiency and simplicity for these advantages.

Aside from ML methods, the second major strategy for solving the form-finding problem is direct optimisation using non-convex methods. In contrast to convex optimisation, non-convex methods are better suited to handling local minima. However, this is often associated with a heavier computational cost. While techniques for non-convex optimisation are often black-box in nature, the use of control variables in some methods such as Cross-Entropy (CE) Optimisation [9] provides improved transparency. The CE method uses rare event estimation to iteratively update a probability distribution over the solution space, converging efficiently to the global optimum. Its flexibility and robustness make it well-suited for handling the multiple constraints and parameters in the form-finding method.

In ongoing work, both ML regression (utilising random forest, gradient boosting, and k-NN) and the CE method are being trialled as implementation routes for the form-finding methodology. Evaluated alongside more traditional optimisation strategies and packages, these approaches show promise for improved reliability and computation time.

6 Conclusions

This paper has summarised a methodology for the form-finding of compression-only shells, which directly considers both vertical and horizontal applied loading. The method is of practical relevance in the design of new shells where horizontal loading is appreciable – such as in seismic areas or regions of high wind loading. Through the use of the Pucher stress formulation, alongside a parametric, concave ASF, optimum thrust membrane geometries can be obtained for various load combinations and used to establish an ideal final structural form. This provides a more effective and intuitive workflow to the designer, compared to other methods which only consider horizontal loading indirectly.

However, the sophistication of the solution is linked to the number of parameters used to define the ASF which, in turn, increases the computational challenge of implementing this method. The inability of no-tension materials such as masonry to sustain tensile stresses manifests in this method in the requirement for the ASF to be concave, further constraining the solution procedure. Moreover, for designs such as cross vaults that exhibit inherent discontinuities of form, the need to achieve continuity of the ASF along the boundaries of a multi-patch solution adds further complexity.

Strategies to overcome these computational challenges have also been outlined in this paper. These can be grouped into two key categories: non-convex optimisation strategies, and Machine Learning techniques which can be trained to achieve viable solutions in place of direct optimisation. Both categories are the focus of ongoing work, as part of the implementation of this form-finding methodology.

Acknowledgments. The authors gratefully acknowledge the financial support of: The Italian Ministry of University and Research (MUR), Research Grant PRIN 2020 No. 2020EBLPLS on "Opportunities and challenges of nanotechnology in advanced and green construction materials"; The Italian Ministry of University and Research (MUR), Research Grant PRIN 2022 No. 2022TN5M7F on "TReE - Supporting the Transition to Ecological Economy in Italian cities Regeneration: circular model tools for reusing architecture and infrastructures"; and the United Kingdom Engineering and Physical Sciences Research Council (EPSRC) and Department for Transport (Research Grant No. EP/Y024257/1).

References

1. Angelillo, M., Montanino, A., Pandolfi, A.: On the connection between geometry and statically determined membrane stresses in the human cornea. J. Biomech. Eng. **142**(5), 051006 (2020). https://doi.org/10.1115/1.4044742
2. Angelillo, M., Babilio, E., Fortunato, A.: Singular stress fields for masonry-like vaults. Continuum Mech. Therm. **25**, 423–441 (2013). https://doi.org/10.1007/s00161-012-0270-9
3. Angelillo, M., Fortunato, A.: Equilibrium of masonry vaults. In: Novel Approaches in Civil Engineering, pp. 105–111. Springer (2004)
4. Angelillo, M., Fortunato, A., Montanino, A., Lippiello, M.: Singular stress fields in masonry structures: Derand was right. Meccanica **49**, 1243–1262 (2014). https://doi.org/10.1007/s11012-013-9842-z
5. Angelillo, M., Iannuzzo, A., Montanino, A.: Discretised continuum approaches: from continuum to dis-continuum. In: Discrete Computational Mechanics of Masonry Structures, pp. 95–163. Springer (2023). https://doi.org/10.1007/978-3-031-14934-9_4
6. Baratta, I.A., et al.: DOLFINx: the next generation fenics problem solving environment (2023). https://doi.org/10.5281/zenodo.10447666
7. Bisegna, P., Coccia, S., Como, M., Nodargi, N.A.: A novel impact model for the rocking motion of masonry arches. Meccanica **58**(10), 2079–2093 (2023). https://doi.org/10.1007/s11012-023-01675-3
8. Castellano, A., Elia, I., Fraddosio, A., Olivieri, C., Piccioni, M.D.: A new experimental approach for small-scale dynamic tests on masonry arches aimed at seismic assessment. Int. J. Mason. Res. Innov. **7**(1–2), 89–112 (2022). https://doi.org/10.1504/IJMRI.2022.119865
9. Cunha Jr, A., Issa, M.V., Basilio, J.C., Telles Ribeiro, J.G.: CEopt: a MATLAB package for non-convex optimization with the cross-entropy method. PrePrint arXiv:2409.00013 (2024). https://doi.org/10.48550/arXiv.2409.00013. https://ceopt.org
10. Cusano, C., Montanino, A., Olivieri, C., Paris, V., Cennamo, C.: Graphical and analytical quantitative comparison in the domes assessment: the case of San Francesco di Paola. Appl. Sci. **11**(8), 3622 (2021). https://doi.org/10.3390/app11083622
11. De Lorenzis, L., DeJong, M., Ochsendorf, J.: Failure of masonry arches under impulse base motion. Earthq. Eng. Struct. Dyn. **36**(14), 2119–2136 (2007). https://doi.org/10.1002/eqe.719
12. Fix, E.: Discriminatory Analysis: Nonparametric Discrimination, Consistency Properties, vol. 1. USAF school of Aviation Medicine (1985)
13. Fletcher, C.A.J.: Galerkin Finite-Element Methods, pp. 86–154. Springer, Heidelberg (1984). https://doi.org/10.1007/978-3-642-85949-6_3

14. Fraternali, F., Angelillo, M., Fortunato, A.: A lumped stress method for plane elastic problems and the discrete-continuum approximation. Int. J. Solids Struct. **39**(25), 6211–6240 (2002). https://doi.org/10.1016/S0020-7683(02)00479-3
15. Galassi, S., Tempesta, G.: Safety assessment of masonry undamaged and damaged arches subjected to gravitational loads and horizontal forces. a numeric procedure to identify the optimal thrust line. Int. J. Solids Struct. **301**, 112943 (2024). https://doi.org/10.1016/j.ijsolstr.2024.112943
16. Heyman, J.: The stone skeleton. Int. J. Solids Struct. **2**(2), 249–279 (1966). https://doi.org/10.1016/0020-7683(66)90018-7
17. Huerta, S.: Galileo was wrong: the geometrical design of masonry arches. Nexus Netw. J., 25–51 (2006). https://doi.org/10.1007/978-3-7643-8188-2_4
18. Huerta Fernández, S.: Geometry and equilibrium: the gothic theory of structural design. Struct. Eng. **84**(2), 23–28 (2006)
19. Iannuzzo, A., Mallardo, V.: A novel approach to model differential settlements and crack patterns in masonry structures. Eng. Struct. **323**, 119220 (2025)
20. Montanino, A., Iannuzzo, A.: A quadrilateral plate-type finite element to model stress singularities in no-tension materials. Comput. Methods Appl. Mech. Eng. **432**, 117433 (2024)
21. Montanino, A., Olivieri, C., Zuccaro, G., Angelillo, M.: From stress to shape: Equilibrium of cloister and cross vaults. Appl. Sci. **11**(9), 3846 (2021). https://doi.org/10.3390/app11093846
22. Nodargi, N.A., Bisegna, P.: Thrust line analysis revisited and applied to optimization of masonry arches. Int. J. Mech. Sci. **179**, 105690 (2020). https://doi.org/10.1016/j.ijmecsci.2020.105690
23. Olivieri, C.: FORMERLY-Math: constrained form-finding through membrane equilibrium analysis in Mathematica. Softw. Impacts **16**, 100512 (2023). https://doi.org/10.1016/j.simpa.2023.100512
24. Olivieri, C., Angelillo, M., Gesualdo, A., Iannuzzo, A., Fortunato, A.: Parametric design of purely compressed shells. Mech. Mater. **155**, 103782 (2021). https://doi.org/10.1016/j.mechmat.2021.103782
25. Olivieri, C., Cocking, S., Fabbrocino, F., Iannuzzo, A., Placidi, L., Adriaenssens, S.: Seismic capacity of purely compressed shells based on Airy stress function. Continuum Mech. Thermodyn. **1**(1), 1 (2025)
26. Olivieri, C., Fortunato, A., DeJong, M.: A new membrane equilibrium solution for masonry railway bridges: the case study of marsh lane bridge. Int. J. Mason. Res. Innov. **6**(4), 446–471 (2021). https://doi.org/10.1504/IJMRI.2021.118831
27. Oppenheim, I.J.: The masonry arch as a four-link mechanism under base motion. Earthq. Eng. Struct. Dyn. **21**(11), 1005–1017 (1992). https://doi.org/10.1002/eqe.4290211105
28. Paris, V., Pizzigoni, A., Adriaenssens, S.: Statics of self-balancing masonry domes constructed with a cross-herringbone spiraling pattern. Eng. Struct. **215**, 110440 (2020). https://doi.org/10.1016/j.engstruct.2020.110440
29. Pucher, A.: Uber den Spannungszustand in gekrümmten Flächen. Beton und Eisen **33**(19), 298–304 (1934)
30. Segal, M.R.: Machine learning benchmarks and random forest regression (2004)
31. Stockdale, G.L., Sarhosis, V., Milani, G.: Seismic capacity and multi-mechanism analysis for dry-stack masonry arches subjected to hinge control. Bull. Earthq. Eng. **18**(2), 673–724 (2020). https://doi.org/10.1007/s10518-019-00741-4

32. Vahab, M., Haghighat, E., Khaleghi, M., Khalili, N.: A physics-informed neural network approach to solution and identification of biharmonic equations of elasticity. J. Eng. Mech. **148**(2), 04021154 (2022)
33. Veenendaal, D., Block, P.: An overview and comparison of structural form finding methods for general networks. IJSS **49**(26), 3741–3753 (2012)
34. Williams, C., Rasmussen, C.: Gaussian processes for regression. Adv. Neural Inf. Process. Syst. **8** (1995)

Insights into the Collapse of the Asciello Masonry Bridge in Benevento

Antonino Iannuzzo[1(✉)], Giuseppe Matarazzo[2], Concetta Cusano[3], Mario Ferraro[3], and Giuseppe Maddaloni[1]

[1] Department of Engineering, University of Sannio, Piazza Roma, 28, 82100 Benevento, Italy
{aniannuzzo,maddaloni}@unisannio.it
[2] University of Sannio, Benevento, Italy
g.matarazzo2@studenti.unisannio.it
[3] Independent Professional Architect, Benevento, Italy
concetta.cusano@archiworldpec.it, mf@mattereconomy.it

Abstract. This contribution focuses on detecting the causes of the collapse of the Asciello Bridge, located in Cautano, in the Benevento area, Italy. The bridge was built in the 1860s. Towards the end of World War II, it was demolished during the retreat of the German Nazist army and subsequently rebuilt in the early post-war years. In the 1960s, the bridge collapsed, likely due to a landslide, and was never reconstructed.

This study investigates the bridge collapse using the discrete element method. The numerical analysis was conducted on a 2D geometry reconstructed from a point cloud obtained via laser scanning. The bridge geometry was carefully discretised using rigid elements with unilateral contact, featuring Mohr-Coulomb friction at the interfaces. The arch geometry was reconstructed following an in-depth geometrical and damage analysis. Specifically, the portion of the bridge still standing was directly derived from laser scanner data, whereas the collapsed section was hypothesised by referring to engineering principles outlined in post-war technical treatises and, importantly, in analogy with its "twin bridge" built near it. A parametric kinematic investigation was performed for several imposed increasing settlements simulating a landslide affecting an abutment of the bridge. The parametric study confirmed that the collapse was caused by differential settlement, characterised by a horizontal displacement component of approximately 90 cm, with an inclination on the horizontal plane between 15 and 25°.

Keywords: Masonry structures · Masonry Bridges · Foundation settlements · Displacement capacity · Distinct element method · Rigid blocks

1 Introduction

The masonry arch has been used for several thousand years. As early as 3500 BC, the Sumerians had developed the technique of assembling stones into an arch shape to construct roofs for their buildings [15]. Although proper arches existed, the Romans were the first to recognise their potential for bridge construction [5]. The expansion and effective governance of the Roman Empire across Europe and the Mediterranean region relied on the use of bridges to develop transport infrastructure for military mobility, trade, communication, and urban water supply. From that period up to the 19th century, numerous masonry arch bridges, tunnel linings, and viaducts were built to support transport infrastructure development throughout Europe. The introduction of new construction materials such as iron, steel, and reinforced concrete in the early 1900s led to a decline in the construction of masonry arch bridges. Nevertheless, many thousands of stone and brick masonry arch bridges still exist across Europe, most built between the second half of the 19th century and the early decades of the 20th century. Many of them are still a key infrastructural asset in the European system. Indeed, in the UK, approximately 40,000 bridges (40% of the total) are still in use [49], while in Spain, the railway network contains over 3,000 masonry arch bridges, accounting for 45% of the total [36]. In Italy, the railway network alone contains nearly 10,000 masonry arch bridges. Of these, around 20% have a span of 2 to 5 m, 11.5% range between 5 and 10 m, and 8.5% exceed 10 m. Most of these bridges were built after the establishment of the Kingdom of Italy, that is, between 1860 and 1920 [12].

Since the seminal work of Heyman [27,28], it was understood that cracks are not a structural concern [18,45] as arched structure can experience large deformation till the collapse as demonstrated in experimental tests [10,17] or through numerical analyses on digital models [14,19,33]. Because of this, several methods were developed to assess the stability of masonry structures, using revised version of the graphic statics [6–8,43,48], rigid blocks [29,44], or continuous approach [11,20,34,39,41,42], finite element approaches based on limit analysis [4,52,53], or adopting complex constitutive relations [9,13,21,26,37]. Numerical solutions based on limit analysis for masonry arch and bridges experiencing pier settlements are proposed in [16,22–25,30], or considering the direct interaction among soil and structure as in [32]. Restricting to real arch bridges, several scientific studies regarding masonry bridges were proposed for evaluating the load-carrying capacity of masonry arch bridges subjected to traffic loads [33,57] or assessing their performance under earthquake loading [51]. However, only a few numerical simulations investigate the vulnerability of masonry arch bridges to pier settlements. In particular, path-following analyses conducted on 2D or 3D finite element models of multi-span masonry bridges subjected to scour-induced settlement are presented in [35,56,58,59] or in [48] using Airy stress potential [1,40,46,47]. In [31], the authors propose a novel artificial intelligence-based approach to assess the stability and identify the causes of cracks in masonry structures, with a real-case application to the Deba masonry bridge in Spain. The reader is referred to [55] for a detailed review.

The present paper presents a real-case study of the Asciello Bridge in Benevento, Italy, which collapsed more than 60 years ago, most likely due to a

Fig. 1. The remaining of the Asciello Bridge, Benevento, Italy.

landslide (Fig. 1). In this study, the Distinct Element Method (DEM) [2,3,50] is adopted to identify the causes behind its collapse.

2 Asciello Bridge: Historic Information

The remaining part of the Asciello Bridge is located southwest of Cautano, a small village in the Benevento province, Italy (Fig. 2). It was built over the Ienga stream in a depression that facilitated the connection between Cautano and the village of Tocco Caudino. The area surrounding the bridge lacks significant

Fig. 2. The blue dashed rectangle highlights the Asciello Bridge structure. The yellow line represents the new road alignment, while the red dashed line indicates the route served by the bridge until the 1960s. (Color figure online)

natural plains, instead featuring artificially created terraces used for agriculture and other anthropogenic settlements. The slopes around the bridge are steep.

The territory of Cautano is characterised by a complex geological evolution, reflecting the interaction between sedimentary processes and, to a lesser extent, volcanic influences related to the regional structure of Campania. The forma-

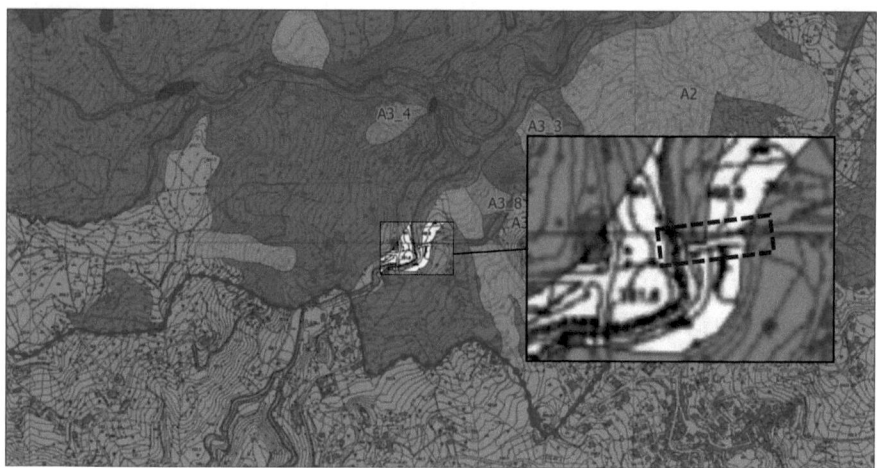

Fig. 3. Geological maps produced by the Cautano administration, with a zoom-in on the Asciello Bridge, show that the right pier (from the viewer's perspective) is founded on an area affected by a landslide.

Fig. 4. Image of the twin bridge (a) and zoom-in on its masonry texture (b), which is identical to that of the Asciello Bridge (c).

tions in the area consist mainly of sedimentary deposits, including clayey and calcarenitic materials, which accumulated during the Neogene in environments alternating between fluvial and marine conditions. In some locations, volcanic materials linked to the Campanian area have contributed to diversifying the local stratigraphy, as evidenced by studies conducted by the National Institute of Geophysics and Volcanology and the University of Naples Federico II.

All information on the historical reconstruction of the Asciello Bridge comes from interviews with local people and technicians, as no official plans or additional documentation related to its construction or collapse have been found. The bridge was built around the 1860s, shortly after the establishment of the Kingdom of Italy. It was blown up during the German army's retreat at the end of World War II. Rebuilt in the early postwar period, it collapsed in the early 1960s. The most widely accepted hypothesis of the collapse is a failure caused by a landslide, confirmed by local testimony and geological maps. Other factors, such as hydrogeological instability or neglect, have been ruled out. Indeed, during one of the many inspections, the bed of the Ienga stream was examined, and the bridge foundations were found to be in good condition, showing no signs of scavenging or erosion, thus excluding the possibility of hydrogeological instability. Regarding the risk of landslides in the study area, reference was made to geological maps produced by the Cautano administration as part of the zone of the municipal urban plan, as reported in Fig. 3. As shown in Fig. 3, there is a landslide movement behind and adjacent to the right side of the bridge, which, as demonstrated in this paper, is the primary cause of the collapse. In 2015, the Ienga stream overflowed, causing additional damage to the remnants of the historic bridge under study.

It is worth noting that a few hundred meters north of the Asciello Bridge, there is a "twin" bridge (see Fig. 4). This bridge was likely built around the same period as the Asciello Bridge and has undergone subsequent structural rehabilitation works after World War II. Figure 4 shows a photo of the twin bridge, where the rehabilitation works are visible, particularly the construction of a reinforced concrete arch. The masonry texture is the same as that of the Asciello Bridge, as shown in 4. The bridge is currently operational.

3 Geometry Reconstruction

The Fig. 5 shows the 3D point cloud of the Asciello Bridge obtained through laser scanning. The southern and northern paraments are shown in the orthophotos in Fig. 6. The southern parament is the focus of the 2D analysis presented in this paper. The stone blocks were extracted from the nearby Campoli quarry. As can be observed, the masonry texture is regular, consisting of roughly shaped stones and regular joints, both vertical and horizontal. As depicted in Fig. 6, the left side of the bridge shows a sub-vertical transverse crack. This crack is present on both the southern parament, which is the subject of the study, and the northern one, although less pronounced. The reconstruction shown in Fig. 7 highlights that the sub-vertical crack identifies an area that has rigidly rotated

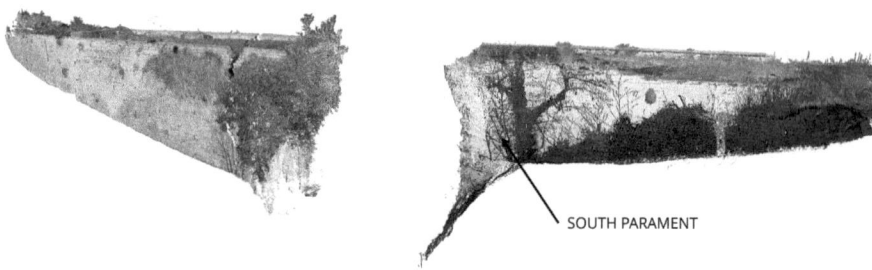

Fig. 5. 3D Point cloud reconstruction of the Asciello Bridge obtained through laser scanning highlights the southern parament, which is the focus of the 2D analysis presented in this paper.

Fig. 6. Orthophoto of the north and south parament of the bridge.

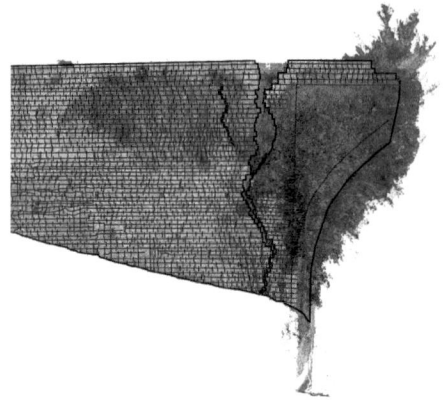

Fig. 7. Zoom-in on the reconstruction of the left abutment of the southern parament. The sub-vertical crack delineates a macroblock that has rotated approximately 2° clockwise. This rotation most likely occurred after the collapse.

by approximately 2° clockwise from the viewer's perspective, likely triggered after the collapse. The whole bridge geometry was derived using laser scanner data for the still-standing portion, while the collapsed one was reconstructed by referring to engineering principles outlined in post-war technical treatises and, importantly, in analogy with the twin bridge (see Fig. 8).

4 Numerical Investigation

This section reports the main steps followed to set the numerical model and perform the subsequent numerical investigation. In particular, Sect. 8 illustrates the model considered for the numerical campaign performed and summarised in Sect. 4. The DEM investigation is performed considering rigid blocks and lumping all block and joint stiffness properties into the normal and tangential stiffnesses of the contact interfaces following the procedure reported in [38]. The contact between blocks was modelled with the Mohr-Coulomb friction law defined by zero cohesion and a friction angle of 35°. The arch geometry was reconstructed following an in-depth geometrical and damage analysis.

4.1 Discretisation

The parametric investigation was performed using Itasca's 3DEC software. In particular, because of the complexity of the bridge and the related computational demand, the investigation was conducted on a 2D interlocked discretisation. The growing need to work with digital stereotomies that closely reflect real geometries is well recognised and supported by several studies. For further details, readers may refer to [54]. Moreover, to balance the results' accuracy and computational demand, the bridge was modelled using mainly prismatic blocks with dimensions equal to 0.50 m × 0.35 m and unit extrusion depth rather than the real stereotomy. This choice was made so that each block of the model corresponded to approximately 4 real blocks. They are staggered by half a brick between one row and the next. For geometric needs, blocks with a trapezoidal or triangular footprint were used where necessary. Indeed, from a technical point of view, it was necessary to model the stereotomy and interlocking between the stones accurately; while, from a numerical point of view, an excessive number of blocks was avoided, as this would have made the parametric analysis inefficient on several selected scenarios due to the high computation times.

It is worth noting that the stereotomy on the left side, undisturbed by the landslide body, is made with horizontal and vertical mortar joints. The right side of the bridge instead has a counter slope of a couple of degrees, even opposite to that of the road axis. The upper parapet of the bridge was also modelled by placing trapezoidal stones that allow the stereotomy to change slope from horizontal to inclined with a counterclockwise rotation.

4.2 DEM Identification of the Collapse Cause

The DEM analysis is conducted on a reduced model, as shown in Fig. 9. The structural geometry is divided into five different zones based on a hypothetical transverse stiffness that accounts for the material stratification between purely structural elements (arch and piers) and the areas with filling, with a decreasing degree of compaction towards the top, up to the blue parament - not considered in the present analysis. All blue slender blocks of Fig. 9 simulate supports, representing the contacts between the bridge and the soil. In particular, all supports

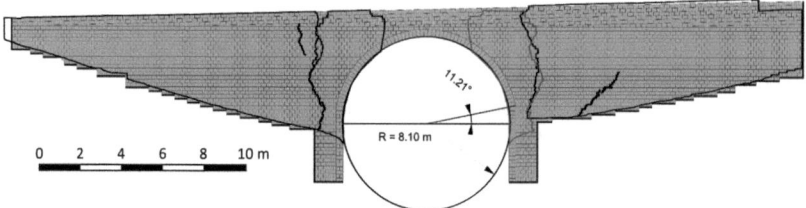

Fig. 8. Bridge geometric reconstruction and digital model with rigid blocks measuring 0.50 m × 0.35 m.

on the right side of the bridge will be used to apply foundation movements, simulating the landslide. The supports on the left side will be considered fixed. As the reader may notice, the left vertical edge of the bridge is not subjected to support conditions to avoid overconstraining the structure. Specifically, the vertical edge on the left part of the boundary, highlighted by the rectangle in Fig. 9, is subjected to surface forces, including a triangular pressure distribution simulating the transmission of the earth's at-rest pressure. The passive earth pressure was not considered for safety reasons. Before performing the parametric analysis, a two-step model calibration was carried out to reduce computational time while minimising errors. The first step focused on the displacement speed of the right supports during settlement. It was observed that speed steps of 0.10 m/s did

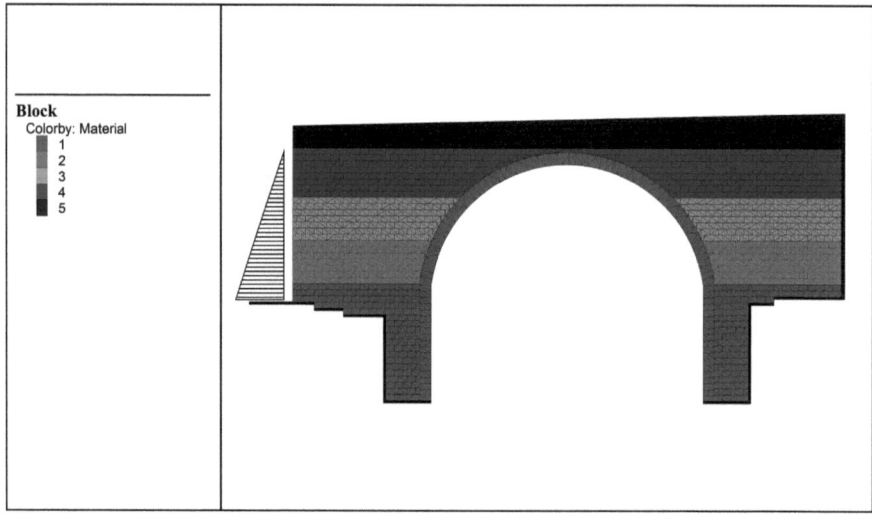

Fig. 9. Reduced geometry considered in the analysis using distinct element software, with subdivision into five structural zones based on the transverse material properties. The area in blue represents the parapet, which will not be included in the DEM numerical campaign. All blue slender blocks represent supports, simulating the contacts between the bridge and the soil. (Color figure online)

not affect the maximum allowable displacement. Consequently, the movement speed of the right support was set to 0.10 m/s. The second step considered the proportional reduction of contact stiffness to decrease computation time. All stiffness values were reduced by 10^3, which did not affect the final displacement but decreased the calculation time by approximately one-third, reducing it from 3 h to 1 h on a laptop equipped with an i7-8700hq Intel processor. The parametric investigation was conducted by varying the inclination of the foundation settlements from 45° to 15° in steps of 5°. The maximum allowable displacement ranged from 1.88 m to 0.95 m. Figures 10 and 11 show the collapse mechanism obtained from the incremental analysis, caused by the right side of the bridge being subjected to an incremental foundation settlement inclined at 45° and 20° with respect to the horizontal plane, respectively.

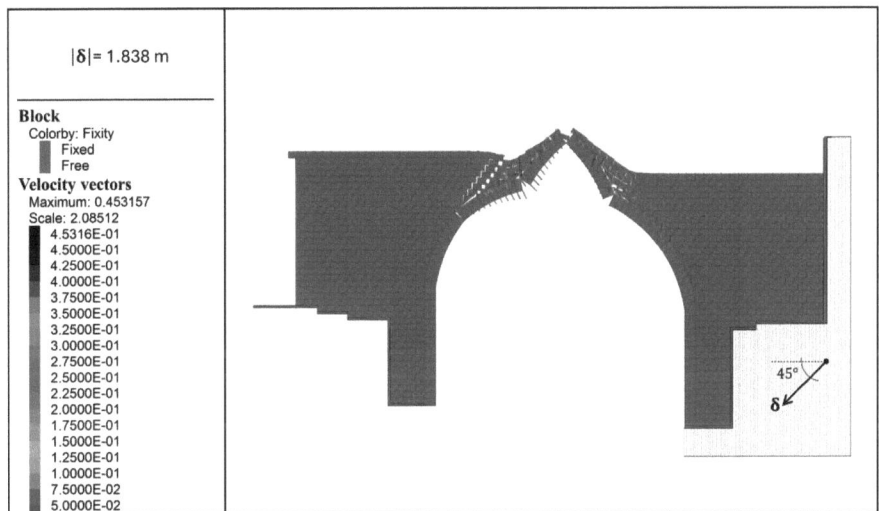

Fig. 10. Onset of the collapse mechanism due to incremental foundation settlement inclined at 45° with respect to the horizontal plane, involving the right side of the bridge. The collapse occurs with a displacement δ of magnitude equal to 1.84 m.

5 Discussion

The main finding is that the collapse was likely caused by a landslide with an average inclination of approximately 20° relative to the horizontal plane, as confirmed by the current overall reciprocal position of the left and right piers. Additionally, it is observed that the reconstructed geometric ratio between the thickness and the internal radius of the arch (t/r) is approximately 1/12. Even considering a non-zero springing angle, this ratio appears too small to guarantee adequate stability for the bridge. This assessment is further supported by

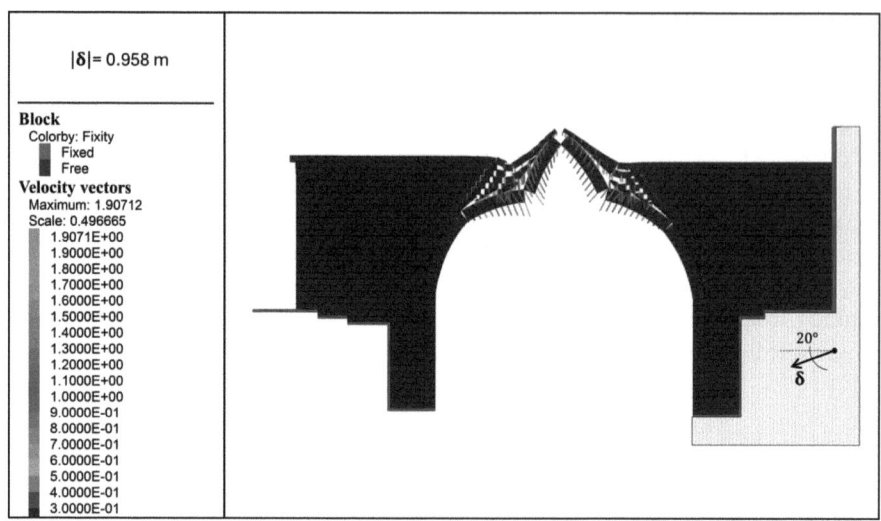

Fig. 11. Onset of the collapse mechanism due to incremental foundation settlement inclined at 45° with respect to the horizontal plane, involving the right side of the bridge. The collapse occurs with a displacement δ of magnitude equal to 0.96 m.

Fig. 12. Overlay of the remaining part related to the left abutment resulting from the incremental displacement analysis with 20° and the current geometry. Although it would need an additional clockwise rotation of 2°, the virtual geometry matches the existing geometry very well.

the fact that the twin bridge underwent rehabilitation works involving the central arch with reinforced concrete, indicating that the Asciello Bridge arch was likely undersized as well. As demonstrated by the numerical analyses, the reduced arch thickness resulted in a low maximum allowable displacement, approximately ranging from $\frac{1}{8}r$ to $\frac{1}{4}r$ of the inner radius for subhorizontal and 45° inclined settlements, respectively. This displacement capacity is about half that of semi-circular arches with t/r ratios of 0.15 or 0.20.

Lastly, the geometry of the existing left part of the bridge coincides, except for small motions that occurred in the following decades, with the one coming from the numerical analysis of the digital model as shown in Fig. 12.

6 Conclusions

The main objective of this contribution was to investigate and identify the causes of the collapse of the Asciello Bridge over the Ienga stream in Benevento, Italy.

The parametric investigation demonstrated that the collapse that occurred during the 1960s was due to a landslide affecting one abutment, confirming testimonies collected from the people and technicians of Cautano. Moreover, the proposed study demonstrated that the overall inclination of the landslide should be approximately 15°–25°. The geometry reconstructed through point cloud data and using information from the twin bridge showed that the Asciello Bridge arch was most likely undersized. This resulted in a low displacement capacity, estimated at around 1 m. The study also demonstrates how integrating data from laser scanners and digital image processing enables detailed and in-depth model analysis, providing valuable insights into the development and stratification of the construction techniques used throughout the bridge's history.

However, the analysis presented in this paper cannot be considered exhaustive since, from a structural perspective, further steps would require three-dimensional modeling of the existing geometry and a more accurate survey of the bridge piers. These operations were made impossible by the presence of debris and vegetation in the riverbed. In situ investigations would also be necessary to define the characteristics of the foundation structures and the ground. Despite these limitations, the analysis conducted allowed us to determine, with a good degree of approximation, the cause of the collapse.

Acknowledgments. This research is funded by the Italian Ministry of University and Research through the Programme "Rita Levi Montalcini for Young Researchers" (FFO 2020). The authors gratefully acknowledge Itasca for providing the 3DEC software under the 'Educational Discount Agreement'.

References

1. Angelillo, M., Iannuzzo, A., Montanino, A.: Discretised continuum approaches: from continuum to dis-continuum. In: Discrete Computational Mechanics of Masonry Structures, pp. 95–163. Springer (2023). https://doi.org/10.1007/978-3-031-32476-5_3
2. Bagi, K., Angelillo, M.: Discrete Computational Mechanics of Masonry Structures, vol. 609. Springer (2023). https://doi.org/10.1007/978-3-031-32476-5
3. Bruun, E.P., Oval, R., Al Asali, W., Gáspár, O., Paris, V., Adriaenssens, S.: Automating historical centering-minimizing masonry vaulting strategies: applications to cooperative robotic construction. Dev. Built Environ. **20**, 100516 (2024). https://doi.org/10.1016/j.dibe.2024.100516
4. Buzzetti, M., Pingaro, N., Milani, G.: Automatic detection of local collapse mechanisms in historical masonry buildings: fast and robust FE upper bound limit analysis. Eng. Fail. Anal. **170**, 109310 (2025). https://doi.org/10.1016/j.engfailanal.2025.109310
5. Como, M.: Statics of Historic Masonry Constructions, vol. 1. Springer (2016). https://doi.org/10.1007/978-3-319-24569-0
6. Cusano, C., Angjeliu, G., Montanino, A., Zuccaro, G., Cennamo, C.: Considerations about the static response of masonry domes: a comparison between limit analysis and finite element method. Int. J. Mason. Res. Innov. **6**(4), 502–528 (2021). https://doi.org/10.1504/IJMRI.2021.118835
7. Cusano, C., Montanino, A., Cennamo, C., Zuccaro, G., Angelillo, M.: Geometry and stability of a double-shell dome in four building phases: the case study of Santa Maria Alla Sanità in Naples. Int. J. Archit. Herit. **17**(2), 362–388 (2023). https://doi.org/10.1080/15583058.2021.1922954
8. Cusano, C., Montanino, A., Olivieri, C., Paris, V., Cennamo, C.: Graphical and analytical quantitative comparison in the Domes assessment: the case of San Francesco di Paola. Appl. Sci. **11**(8), 3622 (2021). https://doi.org/10.3390/app11083622
9. Cutolo, A., Guarracino, F., Olivieri, C., Mascolo, I.: Nonlinear FE analysis of a masonry spiral staircase in Nisida: a refined numerical case study. Int. J. Multiscale Comput. Eng. **20**(5) (2022). https://doi.org/10.1615/IntJMultCompEng.2022042413
10. Daponte, P., De Vito, L., Iannuzzo, A., Monaco, M., Neyestani, A., Picariello, F.: Low-cost marked tracking monitoring system for 3D-scaled masonry models. In: 2024 IEEE International Workshop on Metrology for Living Environment (MetroLivEnv), pp. 172–177. IEEE (2024). https://doi.org/10.1109/MetroLivEnv60384.2024.10615826
11. De Chiara, E., Cennamo, C., Gesualdo, A., Montanino, A., Olivieri, C., Fortunato, A.: Automatic generation of statically admissible stress fields in masonry vaults. J. Mech. Mater. Struct. **14**(5), 719–737 (2019). https://doi.org/10.2140/jomms.2019.14.719
12. De Santis, S., de Felice, G.: Overview of railway masonry bridges with a safety factor estimate. Int. J. Archit. Herit. **8**(3), 452–474 (2014). https://doi.org/10.1002/eqe.2416
13. Di Gennaro, et al.: In-situ load testing of an ancient masonry structure using fibre optics. Structures **70**, 107567 (2024). https://doi.org/10.1016/j.istruc.2024.107567
14. Di Gennaro, L., Guadagnuolo, M., Monaco, M.: Rocking analysis of towers subjected to horizontal forces. Buildings **13**(3), 762 (2023). https://doi.org/10.3390/buildings13030762

15. Favre, R., De Castro San Roman, J.: The arch: enduring and endearing. Struct. Concr. **2**(4), 187–200 (2001). https://doi.org/10.1680/stco.2.4.187.40359
16. Ferrero, C., Calderini, C., Portioli, F., Roca, P.: Large displacement analysis of dry-joint masonry arches subject to inclined support movements. Eng. Struct. **238**, 112244 (2021). https://doi.org/10.1016/j.engstruct.2021.112244
17. Ferrero, C., Calderini, C., Roca, P.: Experimental response of a scaled dry-joint masonry arch subject to inclined support displacements. Eng. Struct. **253**, 113804 (2022). https://doi.org/10.1016/j.engstruct.2021.113804
18. Ferrero, C., Cusano, C., Yavuzer, M.N., Wu, Y.X., Iannuzzo, A.: When cracks are (not) a structural concern: the case of 'Giovanni Vinciguerra' School in Anagni. Int. J. Mason. Res. Innov. **7**(1–2), 217–232 (2022). https://doi.org/10.1504/IJMRI.2022.119866
19. Ferrero, C., Portioli, F., Calderini, C.: Lateral load response of a dry-joint masonry arch subject to vertical support displacements by rigid block analysis. Meccanica, 1–18 (2025). https://doi.org/10.1007/s11012-024-01927-7
20. Fortunato, A., Gesualdo, A., Mascolo, I., Monaco, M.: P-Bézier energy optimisation for elastic solutions of masonry-like panels. Int. J. Mason. Res. Innov. **7**(1–2), 113–125 (2022). https://doi.org/10.1504/IJMRI.2022.119857
21. Frunzio, G., Gennaro, L.D., Guadagnuolo, M.: Palazzo Ducale in Parete: remarks on code provisions. Int. J. Mason. Res. Innov. **4**(1–2), 159–173 (2019). https://doi.org/10.1504/IJMRI.2019.096826
22. Galassi, S.: An alternative approach for limit analysis of masonry arches on moving supports in finite small displacements. Eng. Fail. Anal. **145**, 107004 (2023). https://doi.org/10.1016/j.engfailanal.2022.107004
23. Galassi, S., Misseri, G., Rovero, L.: Capacity assessment of masonry arches on moving supports in large displacements: numerical model and experimental validation. Eng. Fail. Anal. **129**, 105700 (2021). https://doi.org/10.1016/j.engfailanal.2021.105700
24. Galassi, S., Misseri, G., Rovero, L., Tempesta, G.: Failure modes prediction of masonry Voussoir arches on moving supports. Eng. Struct. **173**, 706–717 (2018). https://doi.org/10.1016/j.engstruct.2018.07.015
25. Galassi, S., Zampieri, P.: A new automatic procedure for nonlinear analysis of masonry arches subjected to large support movements. Eng. Struct. **276**, 115359 (2023). https://doi.org/10.1016/j.engstruct.2022.115359
26. Gesualdo, A., Monaco, M.: Constitutive behaviour of quasi-brittle materials with anisotropic friction. Lat. Am. J. Solids Struct. **12**, 695–710 (2015). https://doi.org/10.1590/1679-78251345
27. Heyman, J.: The stone skeleton. Int. J. Solids Struct. **2**(2), 249–279 (1966). https://doi.org/10.1016/0020-7683(66)90018-7
28. Heyman, J.: The safety of masonry arches. Int. J. Mech. Sci. **11**(4), 363–385 (1969). https://doi.org/10.1016/0020-7403(69)90070-8
29. Hua, Y., Buzzetti, M., Pingaro, N., da Silva, L.C., Milani, G.: A computerized tool for the kinematic limit analysis of 2d masonry structures failing on a tilting table. SoftwareX **30**, 102180 (2025). https://doi.org/10.1016/j.softx.2025.102180
30. Iannuzzo, A., Gesualdo, A., Olivieri, C., Montanino, A., et al.: 3D exploration of internal stresses due to lateral loads and foundation movements in a semicircular arch. In: Computational Methods in Structural Dynamics and Earthquake Engineering, pp. 2476–2491. National Technical University of Athens (2023)
31. Iannuzzo, A., Musone, V., Ruocco, E.: A neural network-based automated methodology to identify the crack causes in masonry structures. Comput. Aided Civ. Infrastruct. Eng. **39**(24), 3769–3785 (2024). https://doi.org/10.1111/mice.13311

32. Iannuzzo, A., Mallardo, V.: A novel approach to model differential settlements and crack patterns in masonry structures. Eng. Struct. **323**, 119220 (2025)
33. Iannuzzo, A., Mele, T.V., Block, P.: Stability and load-bearing capacity assessment of a deformed multi-span masonry bridge using the PRD method. Int. J. Mason. Res. Innov. **6**(4), 422–445 (2021). https://doi.org/10.1504/IJMRI.2021.118842
34. Iannuzzo, A., Montanino, A.: A limit analysis-based CASS approach for the in-plane seismic capacity of masonry Façades. Int. J. Solids Struct. **289**, 112633 (2024). https://doi.org/10.1016/j.ijsolstr.2023.112633
35. Malena, M., Angelillo, M., Fortunato, A., de Felice, G., Mascolo, I.: Arch bridges subject to pier settlements: continuous vs. piecewise rigid displacement methods. Meccanica **56**(10), 2487–2505 (2021). https://doi.org/10.1007/s11012-021-01397-1
36. Martin-Caro, J.: Puentes de fabrica. Los puentes ferroviarios dentro del patrimonio industrial [Fabrica bridges. The railway bridges within the industrial heritage]. Madrid: ADIF (2013). (in Spanish)
37. Massaro, L., Di Gennaro, L., Guadagnuolo, M., Frunzio, G., et al.: Strengthening of masonry arches: the "santa maria delle grazie" church. In: COMPDYN Proceedings, vol. 1, pp. 2380–2393. National Technical University of Athens (2023). https://doi.org/10.7712/120123.10567.20441
38. McInerney, J., DeJong, M.: Discrete element modeling of groin vault displacement capacity. Int. J. Archit. Herit. **9**(8), 1037–1049 (2015). https://doi.org/10.1080/15583058.2014.923953
39. Monaco, M., Bergamasco, I., Betti, M.: A no-tension analysis for a brick masonry vault with lunette. J. Mech. Mater. Struct. **13**(5), 703–714 (2019). https://doi.org/10.2140/jomms.2018.13.703
40. Montanino, A., Iannuzzo, A.: A quadrilateral plate-type finite element to model stress singularities in no-tension materials. Comput. Methods Appl. Mech. Eng. **432**, 117433 (2024). https://doi.org/10.1016/j.cma.2024.117433
41. Montanino, A., Olivieri, C., De Gregorio, D., Iannuzzo, A., et al.: Two continuous dual strategies to solve the kinematical and equilibrium problem for masonry-like structures. In: WCCM-ECCOMAS CONGRESS. Scipedia SL (2022)
42. Montanino, A., Olivieri, C., Zuccaro, G., Angelillo, M.: From stress to shape: equilibrium of cloister and cross vaults. Appl. Sci. **11**(9), 3846 (2021). https://doi.org/10.3390/app11093846
43. Nodargi, N.A., Bisegna, P.: Thrust line analysis revisited and applied to optimization of masonry arches. Int. J. Mech. Sci. **179**, 105690 (2020). https://doi.org/10.1016/j.ijmecsci.2020.105690
44. Nodargi, N.A., Bisegna, P.: A unifying computational approach for the lower-bound limit analysis of systems of masonry arches and buttresses. Eng. Struct. **221**, 110999 (2020). https://doi.org/10.1016/j.engstruct.2020.110999
45. Ochsendorf, J.A.: Collapse of masonry structures (2002)
46. Olivieri, C.: FORMERLY-Math: constrained form-finding through membrane equilibrium analysis in Mathematica. Softw. Impacts **16**, 100512 (2023). https://doi.org/10.1016/j.simpa.2023.100512
47. Olivieri, C., Cocking, S., Fabbrocino, F., Iannuzzo, A., Placidi, L., Adriaenssens, S.: Seismic capacity of purely compressed shells based on airy stress function. Continuum Mech. Thermodyn. **37**(2), 21 (2025). https://doi.org/10.1007/s00161-024-01350-z
48. Olivieri, C., Fortunato, A., DeJong, M.: A new membrane equilibrium solution for masonry railway bridges: the case study of Marsh Lane Bridge. Int. J. Mason. Res. Innov. **6**(4), 446–471 (2021). https://doi.org/10.1504/IJMRI.2021.118831

49. Page, J.: Masonry arch bridges: state-of-the-art-review. HM Stationery Office (1993)
50. Paris, V., Gobbin, F., Nannei, V.M., Resmini, M., Mirabella Roberti, G.: Distinct element method analyses for damage assessment: the northern spur of Valverde Bulwark in the Venetian Fortress of Bergamo. Int. J. Archit. Herit., 1–15 (2024). https://doi.org/10.1080/15583058.2024.2345701
51. Pelà, L., Aprile, A., Benedetti, A.: Seismic assessment of masonry arch bridges. Eng. Struct. **31**(8), 1777–1788 (2009). https://doi.org/10.1016/j.engstruct.2009.02.012
52. Pingaro, N., Buzzetti, M., Milani, G.: Advanced FE nonlinear numerical modeling to predict historical masonry vaults failure: assessment of risk collapse for a long span cloister vault heavily loaded at the crown by means of a general-purpose numerical protocol. Eng. Fail. Anal. **167**, 109070 (2025). https://doi.org/10.1016/j.engfailanal.2024.109070
53. Pingaro, N., Cardani, G., Coronelli, D., Milani, G.: On the stability of masonry arches through limit analysis and a nonlinear finite element-based method. In: International Conference on Protection of Historical Constructions, pp. 201–208. Springer (2025). https://doi.org/10.1007/978-3-031-87316-4_25
54. Pourfouladi, M., Pingaro, N., Valente, M.: Polibrick plugin as a parametric tool for digital stereotomy modelling. Comput. Struct. **311**, 107722 (2025). https://doi.org/10.1016/j.compstruc.2025.107722
55. Sarhosis, V., De Santis, S., de Felice, G.: A review of experimental investigations and assessment methods for masonry arch bridges. Struct. Infrastruct. Eng. **12**(11), 1439–1464 (2016). https://doi.org/10.1080/15732479.2015.1136655
56. Scozzese, F., Ragni, L., Tubaldi, E., Gara, F.: Modal properties variation and collapse assessment of masonry arch bridges under scour action. Eng. Struct. **199**, 109665 (2019). https://doi.org/10.1016/j.engstruct.2019.109665
57. Tubaldi, E., Minga, E., Macorini, L., Izzuddin, B.: Mesoscale analysis of multi-span masonry arch bridges. Eng. Struct. **225**, 111137 (2020). https://doi.org/10.1016/j.engstruct.2020.111137
58. Tubaldi, E., Macorini, L., Izzuddin, B.A.: Three-dimensional mesoscale modelling of multi-span masonry arch bridges subjected to scour. Eng. Struct. **165**, 486–500 (2018). https://doi.org/10.1016/J.ENGSTRUCT.2018.03.031
59. Zampieri, P., Zanini, M.A., Faleschini, F., Hofer, L., Pellegrino, C.: Failure analysis of masonry arch bridges subject to local pier scour. Eng. Fail. Anal. **79**, 371–384 (2017). https://doi.org/10.1016/j.engfailanal.2017.05.028

FEMANOLA v3.0 as a Tool to Predict Settlement-Induced Cracks in Masonry Walls

Natalia Pingaro(✉) [ID] and Gabriele Milani [ID]

Department of Architecture, Built Environment and Construction Engineering, Politecnico di Milano, 20133 Milan, Italy
`natalia.pingaro@polimi.it`

Abstract. This paper introduces a finite element tool (FEMANOLA v3.0) developed for the nonlinear analysis of masonry walls subjected to ground settlements. The approach, specifically conceived for masonry structures, uses a heterogeneous modeling technique, i.e. bricks and mortar are meshed separately. In particular, bricks are modeled using elastic four-node elements, while mortar joints are represented as nonlinear interfaces with cohesive-frictional behavior, incorporating softening in tension and compression under the application of shear actions. Mortar interfaces are discretized through isogeometric four-node elements, ensuring that normal stresses along the interface direction are nullified. The reliability and precision of the model are verified by comparing the results obtained with some available in the existing literature, focusing on masonry walls subjected to settlement. These comparisons highlight the model ability to accurately predict the response of masonry walls subjected to ground settlement, including crack initiation, propagation, and failure mechanisms. FEMANOLA v3.0 thus provides a robust and efficient strategy for analyzing masonry structures subjected to settlement, offering key insights into the performance and failure mechanisms of historical masonry walls under various load conditions.

Keywords: Masonry · Settlement · FE analysis · Nonlinear interfaces

1 Introduction

The necessity of preserving historical masonry buildings has heightened interest in studying this type of construction. This has caused the need to develop new and appropriate computational methods to analyze their structural performance. A significant part of this area involves understanding the reasons behind the damage observed in existing structures. Although masonry buildings are highly vulnerable to horizontal forces [1–3], cracks can still be found in structures located in non-seismic regions or areas without a history of seismic activity. Given that the equilibrium state of a masonry structure primarily depends on its geometry [4–8], one of the contributors to damage is the motion of its foundations [9–13]. In many cases, the formation of cracks is attributed to differential settlements. It is important to note that most old masonry buildings were originally constructed on foundations composed of various structural elements, often disconnected from one another. Therefore, when soil motion occurs, the upper structure experiences differential displacements at the base level, leading to a deformed equilibrium configuration.

The existing technical literature provides various studies that address the development of crack patterns due to foundation settlements. Many of these works analyze the issue by performing nonlinear simulations using the Finite Element Method (FEM). In some models, the soil-structure interaction is explicitly included by modeling the soil itself [14]. In [15] the authors propose a 2D semi-coupled FEM model that incorporates this interaction through dedicated soil-structure interfaces. After validating the model through experimental tests [15], they apply it to analyze a façade subjected to settlement caused by tunneling [16]. In general, many studies opt to simplify the modeling of the soil to reduce computational complexity, often simulating settlements by directly applying displacements at the base of the numerical model. Some research uses nonlinear FEM to study the effects of settlements on masonry arch bridges [17] or to assess how structural modifications might influence the occurrence of differential settlements in historical masonry buildings [18]. This approach is sometimes enhanced with homogenization techniques [19].

As an alternative to FEM, some studies use the Distinct Element Method (DEM) [20, 21], or iterative analyses on macro-blocks with nonlinear springs at their interfaces [22, 23]. Other studies idealize the masonry structure as an assembly of rigid blocks, identifying crack patterns through limit analysis procedures that are solved using linear and conic programming techniques [24–29]. The latter are particularly suitable for representing the behavior of masonry structures under settlement.

Nevertheless, all the aforementioned numerical procedures are not without drawbacks. Commercial FEM codes can be complex for common users, for whom obtaining reliable results is not a straightforward task, primarily because the material models available in the standard libraries of commercial software—potentially adaptable to handle such sources of nonlinearity—are typically designed for other application contexts. At the same time, DEM models, while requiring fewer parameters than FEM and concentrating cracks at the interfaces between blocks, do not allow for heterogeneous modeling, and nonlinear static analyses are, in fact, slow dynamic analyses. Finally, limit analysis, while being the most suitable for a settlement-induced cracking problem in masonry, overestimates the ultimate load-bearing capacity, classical limit analysis does not account for sliding and, if yes, it is associated, and the blocks are rigid therefore the deformed shape is all inelastic. Consequently, limit analysis becomes predictive only in proximity to the development of a well-defined kinematic chain.

Unfortunately, dedicated software still appears to be lacking in the literature, and the present paper aims to fill this gap. FEMANOLA v3.0, which stands for Finite Element MAsonry NOn Linear Analysis, is a 2D Finite Element homemade code implemented to carry out nonlinear static analyses for masonry structures subjected to plane loads. The material behavior is represented through a heterogeneous approach, with nonlinearity concentrated in the joints, modeled as interfaces. A key feature of the code is that the joints can be meshed with either their actual thickness or an almost negligible thickness (to represent interfaces or dry joints). In both cases, the joints are represented using four-node isoparametric elements, with the elastic modulus in their direction assumed to be zero. The blocks are considered elastic and are discretized again using standard four-node isoparametric elements. The software is capable of handling both plane deformation and plane stress analyses. The material model for the joints incorporates coupled shear and normal stress behavior. A cohesive frictional model is applied for shear, with the joint undergoing progressive damage once the peak shear stress is reached. The post-peak tangential behavior is governed by a user-defined Mode II fracture energy, which is assumed to depend on the current normal stress. A residual strength, also defined by the user concerning the normal stress, can be incorporated as well. The nonlinear solver follows an iterative elastic scheme [30–34], where the stiffness of Gauss points exhibiting softening is penalized using a straightforward return-to-limit-surface algorithm that is entirely explicit. The robustness of the solver is improved in the presence of softening, facilitating rapid nonlinear analyses without the risk of premature failure. The accuracy of the results is ensured when sufficiently small load increments are applied. Since arc length control is not yet available, analyses can be performed under displacement control.

The numerical method proposed offers several advantages over conventional commercial codes, the most notable of which is the wealth of information (particularly at the local level) available during post-processing. Among the numerous case studies used to validate the reliability of the internally developed software, only one is presented here for brevity. This case involves a masonry wall subjected to settlement, previously examined both experimentally and numerically in [35, 36]. Excellent predictive capabilities are demonstrated in replicating experimental tests at both global and local levels.

2 FEMANOLA v3.0 Description

This section aims to present a new in-house developed nonlinear static Finite Element (FE) software (named FEMANOLA v3.0), where the material nonlinearity is managed using a fully explicit iterative elastic approach. For the mortar joints, four-node isoparametric elements are employed, with the normal stiffness in the direction of the joint being set to zero. The joints can be meshed either with their actual thickness or with an almost negligible thickness to simulate interfaces or dry joints. This allows the interfaces, with their specific geometric thickness, to be modeled in the pre-processing phase in the same manner as a standard elastic heterogeneous discretization. The model assumes plane stress conditions, although plane-strain problems can also be analyzed.

Since nonlinearity is addressed through an elastic procedure that progressively reduces the stiffness of damaged Gauss points to account for softening, it is useful to refer to the elastic case directly, where **D** represents the elastic stiffness of the mortar joint.

Consider a local coordinate system for each mortar joint, as shown in Fig. 1, where x' and y' correspond to the local axes aligned with the direction of the joint and its normal, respectively. It is also assumed that t_E is the out-of-plane thickness of the element (considered constant), **J** is the Jacobian of the transformation from physical to natural coordinates (ξ_1 and ξ_2), and **B** is the matrix that contains the first derivatives of the shape functions. Therefore, the element stiffness matrix in the local coordinate system is given by:

$$\mathbf{K}'_E = \int_{-1}^{1}\int_{-1}^{1} \mathbf{B}^T \mathbf{D} \mathbf{B} |\mathbf{J}| t_E d\xi_1 d\xi_2 \tag{1}$$

A standard integration using four Gauss points is employed, enabling the numerical evaluation of $\mathbf{K}'_E$ as follows:

$$\mathbf{K}'_E = \sum_{i=1}^{4} w_i \mathbf{B}_i^T \mathbf{D}_i \mathbf{B}_i |\mathbf{J}_i| = \text{Gauss Point} \tag{2}$$

where w_i represent the weights of the Gauss points.

Finally, a rotation $\mathbf{R}_{-\vartheta_E}$ is performed to obtain the element stiffness matrix in the global coordinate system:

$$\mathbf{K}_E = \mathbf{R}_{-\vartheta_E}{}^T \mathbf{K}'_E \mathbf{R}_{-\vartheta_E} \tag{3}$$

The elastic stiffness matrix $\mathbf{D}$ of the element is assumed to be diagonal, with the normal component along the direction of the joint set to zero:

$$\mathbf{D}_i = \begin{bmatrix} 0 & 0 & 0 \\ 0 & E^{k,i} & 0 \\ 0 & 0 & G^{k,i} \end{bmatrix} \tag{4}$$

where $E^{k,i}$ and $G^{k,i}$ denote the Young's modulus and shear modulus of the mortar at the i-th Gauss point during the k-th iteration of the loading process, respectively.

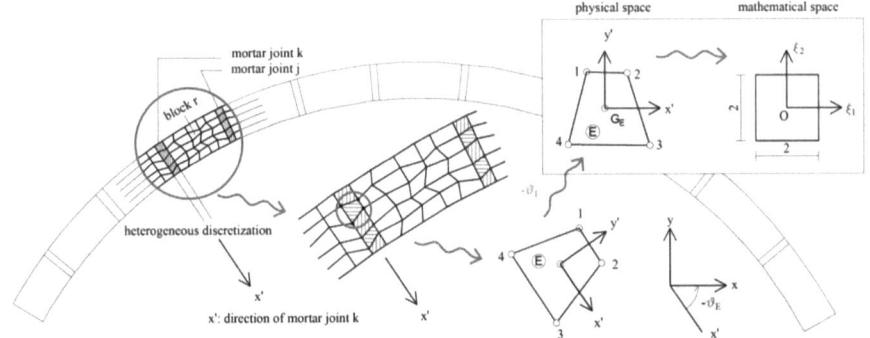

Fig. 1. Heterogeneous finite element discretization of a masonry structure in FEMANOLA v3.0.

Concerning non-linearity, its general aspects are illustrated in Fig. 2, which specifically represents the response of a Gauss point subjected to inelastic tensile stress. Suppose that, at the end of the load iteration k, the i-th Gauss point experiences normal stress $\sigma_{nn}^{k,i}$ that exceeds its tensile strength. Notably, if the Gauss point is already on the softening branch, this strength is lower than its initial undamaged value. In such a case, the elastic modulus for the next iteration $k + 1$ is adjusted according to the return mapping scheme shown in Fig. 2. Since the procedure is fully explicit, no sub-iterations are required, ensuring convergence as long as the external load is applied in sufficiently small increments. Typically, instead of imposing forces, displacements are progressively increased to explicitly capture the structural response in the softening phase.

The constitutive model for the joint distinguishes between tensile, compressive, and shear behavior. This is defined during preprocessing through a user-friendly Excel spreadsheet interface, as depicted in Fig. 3, where the mechanical parameters required to set up the model are shown. The code does not include purely numerical parameters (such as the viscosity one in the CDP model in Abaqus); instead, every property set in FEMANOLA v3.0 corresponds to a clear physical counterpart. It is interesting to point out that the number of mechanical parameters required by a numerical code is directly proportional to the information that can be obtained in the output. Therefore, a greater number of mechanical parameters corresponds to a more detailed representation of the physical behavior in the numerical model.

2.1 Tensile Behavior

The tensile behavior consists of an initial elastic phase (with Young's modulus E and peak tensile strength f_t), followed by an exponential softening governed by fracture energy G_I^f and described by the following equation:

$$\begin{aligned} \varepsilon_{nn} < f_t/E \quad & \sigma_{nn} = E\varepsilon_{nn} \\ \varepsilon_{nn} \geq f_t/E \quad & \sigma_{nn} = f_t e^{-\frac{\varepsilon_{nn}-f_t/E}{G_I^f}} \end{aligned} \quad (5)$$

where ε_{nn} represents the normal strain.

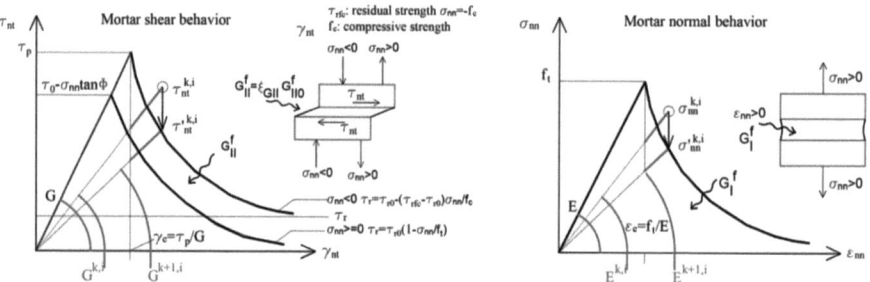

Fig. 2. Penalization scheme for the elastic and shear moduli of a Gauss point undergoing softening in tension (right) and shear (left).

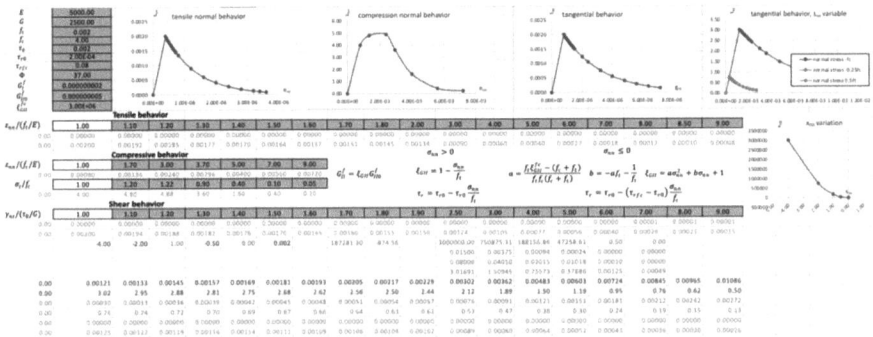

Fig. 3. Excel spreadsheet interface for defining the constitutive behavior of mortar joints (using the data employed to obtain the numerical results in Sect. 3).

2.2 Compressive Behavior

Unlike the tensile behavior, the compressive response is defined through discrete points to accurately capture the typical hardening-softening behavior of a mortar joint under compression. f_c denotes the stress at the elastic limit, while the elastic modulus remains the same as in the tensile regime.

It is important to note that, within the context of FEMANOLA v3.0, it is feasible to study the case of a material with no tensile resistance. Even though zero tensile strength cannot be directly implemented, a very low tensile resistance and similarly low fracture energy can approximate a no tension scenario. As a result, the compressive resistance is not activated. However, there is the possibility to account for joint crushing if needed, but this is not relevant in the current case, as will be demonstrated in the validation section.

2.3 Shear Behavior

The shear behavior is characterized by a linear-exponential $\tau_{nt} - \gamma_{nt}$ relationship (see Fig. 4), coupled with the normal stress σ_{nn} acting on the interface. This interaction is governed by a cohesive frictional law. In Fig. 4, n represents the unit normal vector of the interface, and t refers to the interface direction.

For a given normal stress σ_{nn}, let Φ, τ_0, and τ_{r0} denote the friction angle, tensile peak, and residual strengths at $\sigma_{nn} = 0$, , respectively. The peak (τ_p) and residual (τ_r) tangential strengths for any applied σ_{nn} are given by the following relations:

$$\tau_p = \tau_0 - \sigma_{nn} \tan\Phi$$
$$\sigma_{nn} < 0 \rightarrow \tau_r = \tau_{r0} - (\tau_{rfc} - \tau_{r0})\frac{\sigma_{nn}}{f_c} \quad (6)$$
$$\sigma_{nn} \geq 0 \rightarrow \tau_r = \tau_{r0} - \tau_{r0}\frac{\sigma_{nn}}{f_t}$$

The $\tau_{nt} - \gamma_{nt}$ relationship is hence defined as follows, distinguishing between elastic and inelastic softening phases:

$$\gamma_{nt} < \tau_p/G \qquad \tau_{nt} = G\gamma_{nt}$$
$$\gamma_{nt} \geq \tau_p/G \quad \tau_{nt} = (\tau_p - \tau_r)e^{-\frac{\gamma_{nt} - \tau_p/G}{G_{II}^f}} + \tau_r \quad (7)$$

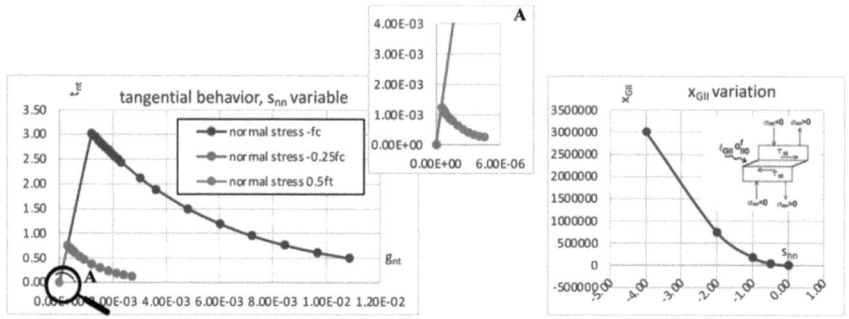

Fig. 4. Shear response of the mortar joints under varying normal stress levels σ_{nn} (left) and the non-dimensional parameter ξ_{GII} used to adjust the Mode II fracture energy at different σ_{nn} levels (right).

where G_{II}^f denotes the Mode II fracture energy, G is the shear modulus, and all other symbols have already been defined. In the model, G_{II}^f is also assumed to be dependent on σ_{nn} as described by the following relationship:

$$G_{II}^f = \xi_{GII} G_{II0}^f \qquad (8)$$

where G_{II0}^f represents the Mode II fracture energy at $\sigma_{nn} = 0$, and ξ_{GII} is a non-dimensional parameter that increases parabolically when $\sigma_{nn} \leq 0$ and decreases linearly when $\sigma_{nn} > 0$, as given by the following formulas:

$$\sigma_{nn} \leq 0 \rightarrow \xi_{GII} = a\sigma_{nn}^2 + b\sigma_{nn} + 1 \text{ where } a = \frac{f_t \xi_{GII}^{fc} - (f_c + f_t)}{f_t f_c (f_c + f_t)} \quad b = -af_t - \frac{1}{f_t}$$
$$\sigma_{nn} > 0 \rightarrow \xi_{GII} = 1 - \frac{\sigma_{nn}}{f_t} \qquad (9)$$

3 FEMANOLA v3.0 Validation on a Masonry Wall Subjected to Settlement

To validate the effectiveness of the proposed approach, experimental and numerical results from the literature are used, as referenced in [35, 36].

The benchmark is a masonry dry-joint wall whose dimensions are 1737 × 605 × 90 mm³. A uniform downward displacement is imposed at the bottom-right corner, over a length equivalent to 190% of a single brick length (as illustrated in Fig. 5).

Figure 6 presents the load-displacement curves plotted for nodes 771, 733, 783, 735, and 212, where unit displacements are applied (as shown in Fig. 5). At nodes 771, 783, and 212, the reaction force is nearly zero, as confirmed by the graph in Fig. 6, where the three corresponding curves overlap almost perfectly at the origin. The most significant reaction forces are observed at nodes 733 and 735, which are approximately located at the centroid of the two blocks (see the zoom provided in Fig. 6). The reaction force at node 735 is larger than that at node 733 because the two forces form a couple, ensuring a constant displacement to prevent rotation as depicted in the zoom provided in Fig. 6.

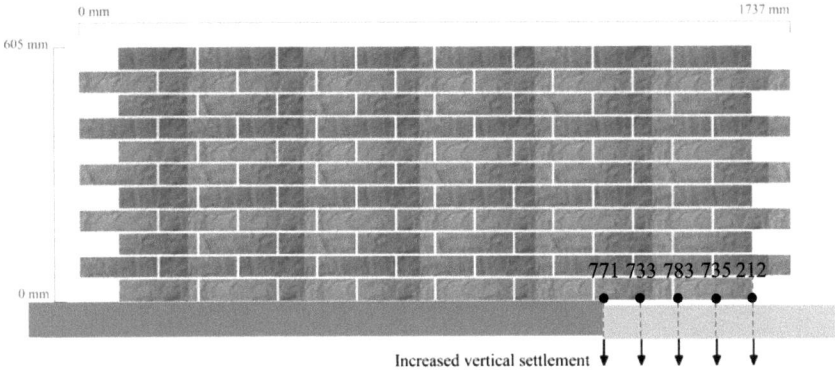

Fig. 5. The masonry wall under study.

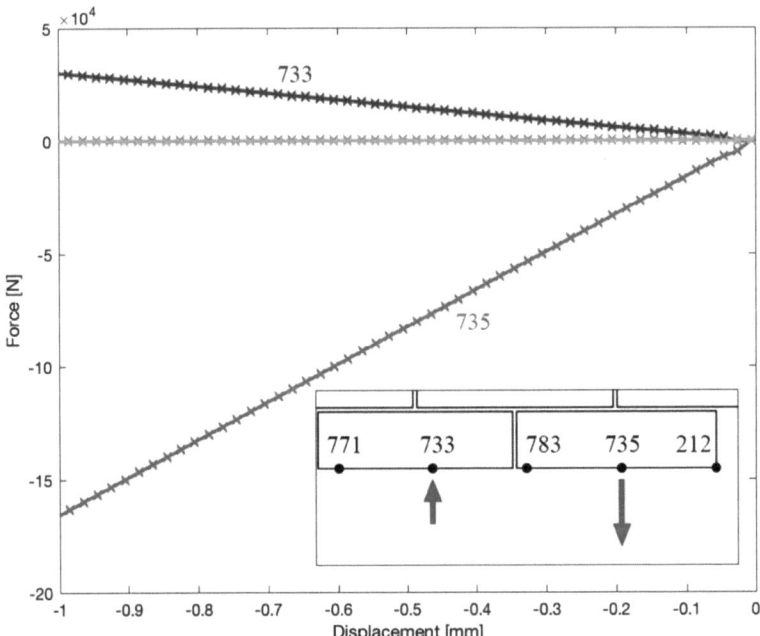

Fig. 6. Force-displacement curves obtained in the five nodes in which the unitary displacements are applied.

Figures 7 and 8 illustrate the local behavior at step 13 out of 50, presenting tangential and normal stresses. Additionally, the shear and tensile damage states are also shown.

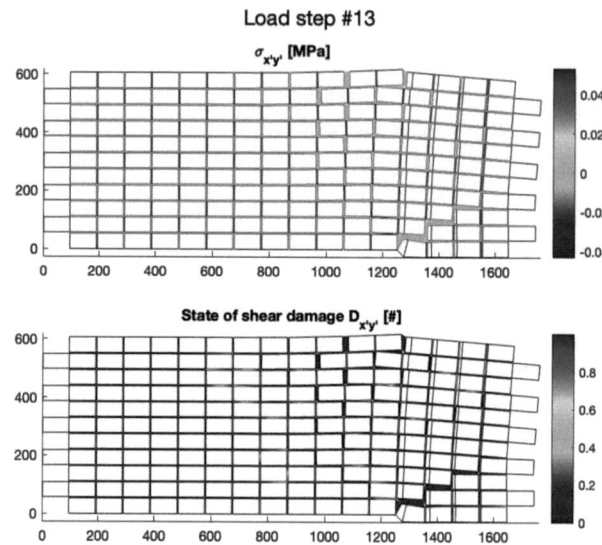

Fig. 7. Local behavior (step #13). Tangential stresses and state of shear damage.

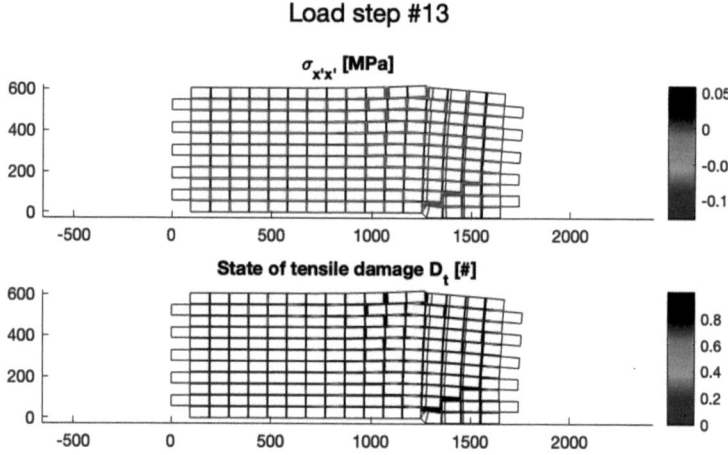

Fig. 8. Local behavior (step #13). Normal stresses and state of tensile damage.

The same results are reported in Figs. 9 and 10 for step 50.

In Fig. 11 a zoom of Fig. 10 regarding the state of tensile damage is shown.

In conclusion, it can be observed that in the figures corresponding to step 13, damage is developing, primarily concentrated in the area where displacements are applied. The evolution of the global failure mechanism becomes evident in step 50 and aligns with the numerical results from limit analysis found in [36] and with experimental evidences [35]. Additionally, Figs. 10 and 12 also illustrate the typical arcuate detachment associated with the settlement problem under investigation (the same finding was also observed

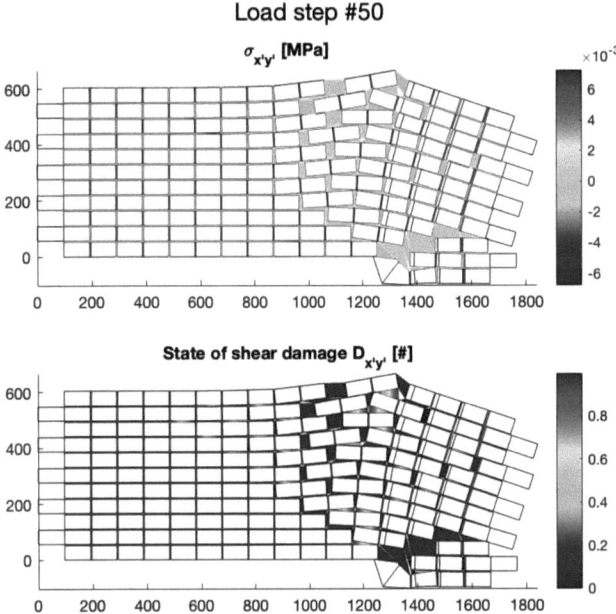

Fig. 9. Local behavior (step #50). Tangential stresses and state of shear damage.

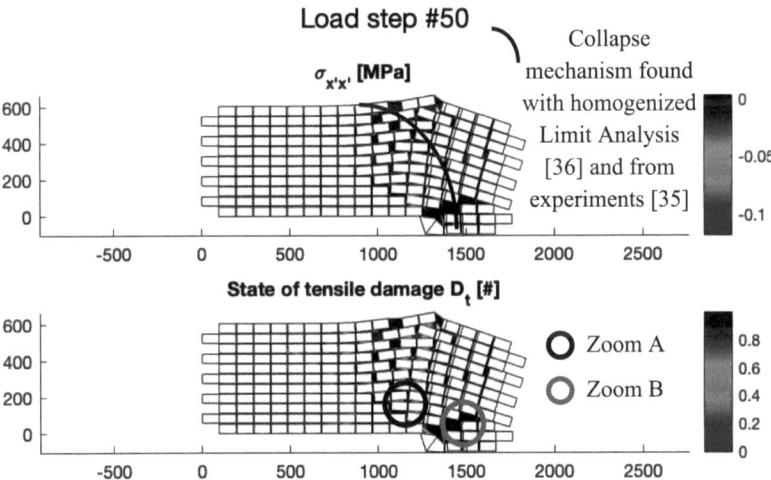

Fig. 10. Local behavior (step #50). Normal stresses and state of tensile damage.

in [35, 36]). Finally, in Fig. 12, zoom B from Fig. 10 is compared with the physical outcome.

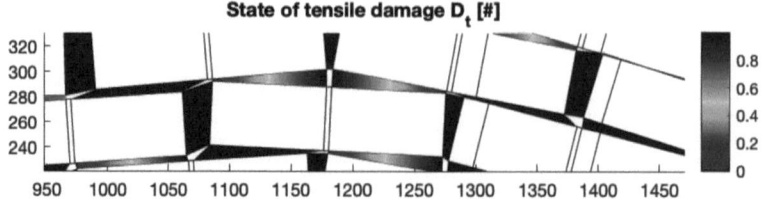

Fig. 11. Local behavior (step #50). State of tensile damage (zoom A, see Fig. 10).

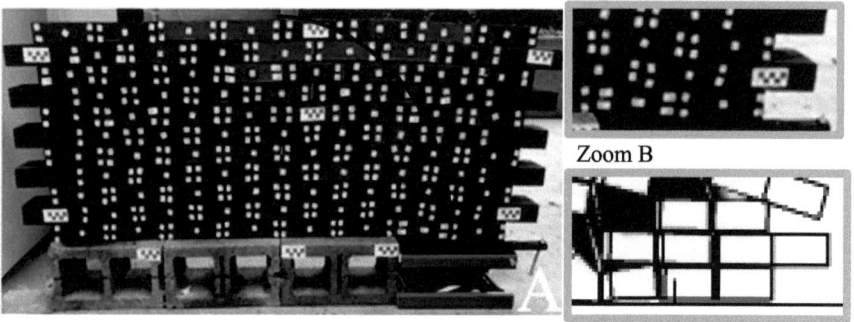

Fig. 12. Experimental results found in [35]. On the right, zoom B is compared with the outcome from [35] (zoom B, see Fig. 10).

4 Conclusions

The preliminary results obtained using FEMANOLA v3.0, an in-house developed non-linear FE software designed for robust anelastic static analyses of in-plane loaded masonry structures, have been presented. The software incorporates several key features that distinguish it from conventional approaches: (i) a heterogeneous modeling strategy that explicitly represents both bricks and mortar joints; (ii) mortar joints represented as interfaces with thickness, where all non-linearity is concentrated; (iii) bricks considered as elastic; (iv) mortar interfaces modeled with a single row of four-noded isoparametric elements, assuming a diagonal stiffness matrix and a vanishing elastic modulus along the interface direction; (v) a constitutive model incorporating a coupling between inelastic shear behavior and normal stress at the interface level.

Non-linearity is handled through a progressive penalization of the elastic moduli at Gauss points exhibiting softening during a given loading step. This approach results in a fully explicit and computationally efficient algorithm, eliminating the need for iterative solvers while maintaining numerical stability. The constitutive behavior follows a sawtooth law, ensuring a clear and controlled evolution of material degradation under loading conditions.

The computational cost required for the case study under investigation is approximately 3 min on a standard laptop. However, it is important to note that comparing computational times can be challenging, as software that generates figures, as the present version does, for example, cannot be directly compared to others that do not offer this feature.

The proposed model provides a significant amount of detailed information, particularly at the local scale, compared to other numerical methods in the literature. This feature is especially useful for capturing crack initiation, propagation, and failure mechanisms in masonry subjected to settlements. The accuracy of the numerical results was validated against both numerical and experimental data available in the literature, with a specific benchmark test involving a masonry wall subjected to soil settlements. The model demonstrated excellent predictive capabilities, effectively replicating both the global structural response and local behavior.

Beyond the specific validation case, FEMANOLA v3.0 represents a promising tool for assessing the structural integrity of masonry buildings affected by 2D loading conditions. Its ability to explicitly model heterogeneous masonry, coupled with a computationally efficient nonlinear solver, makes it a valuable resource for both research and practical engineering applications. Future developments will aim to further enhance the software capabilities, including the integration of arc-length control techniques to improve the robustness of softening simulations and the extension of the methodology to three-dimensional problems. Additionally, the potential coupling of the model with soil-structure interaction analyses could further improve its applicability in engineering practice, offering more comprehensive assessments of masonry behavior under various loading conditions. Moreover, future work will include the development of scaled models fabricated using additive manufacturing techniques, allowing for more controlled experimental validation and deeper insights into the mechanical response of masonry structures. Another important aspect of future development is the creation of a graphical user interface (GUI), which will simplify the interaction with the software and make its use more accessible to engineers and researchers alike.

Acknowledgments. The study was partially developed within the research activities carried out in the frame of 2024–2026 ReLUIS Project – WP10 masonry structures (Coordinator – Prof. Guido Magenes), specifically by means of the research carried out in WP10.1.1 and WP10.2 Masonry Structures (Task Coordinators – respectively Prof. Serena Cattari and Prof. Sergio Lagomarsino). The Italian Department of Civil Protection has funded such a project. Finally, the study was partially developed with the financial support of the Italian Ministry of Scientific Research MUR within the research project PRIN-2022 (https://www.dabc.polimi.it/en/progetto/advanced-mechanical-models-and-computational-methods-for-large-scale-3d-printing-of-innovative-concrete-structures/) titled "Advanced mechanical models and computational methods for large-scale 3D printing of innovative concrete structures (COM^3D-CREATE)" (National PI: Prof. Andrea Chiozzi, Local PI: Prof. Gabriele Milani). Finanziato dall'Unione europea – Next Generation EU, Missione 4 Componente 1 CUP D53D23004070006.

Disclosure of Interests. The authors have no competing interests to declare that are relevant to the content of this article.

References

1. Buzzetti, M., Pingaro, N., Milani, G.: Automatic detection of local collapse mechanisms in historical masonry buildings: Fast and robust FE upper bound limit analysis. Eng. Fail. Anal. **170**, 109310 (2025)
2. Pingaro, N., Tiberti, S., Milani, G.: Automatic CAD kinematic limit analysis approach for the limit analysis of masonry towers. In: Simos T. (ed.) Proceedings of the 17th International Conference of Numerical Analysis and Applied Mathematics, ICNAAM 2019, Rhodes, Greece (2019)
3. Pingaro, N., Milani, G.: Full 3D CAD procedure for the speedy evaluation of the seismic vulnerability of masonry towers. In: In: Simos T. (ed.) Proceedings of the 15th International Conference of Computational Methods in Sciences and Engineering, ICCMSE 2019, Rhodes, Greece (2019)
4. Pingaro, N., Milani, G.: Simple non-linear numerical modelling of masonry arches reinforced with SRG using elasto-fragile and elasto-ductile truss finite elements. Eng. Struct. **293**, 116637 (2023)
5. Pingaro, N., Buzzetti, M., Milani, G.: Advanced FE nonlinear numerical modeling to predict historical masonry vaults failure: assessment of risk collapse for a long span cloister vault heavily loaded at the crown by means of a general-purpose numerical protocol. Eng. Fail. Anal. **167**, 109070 (2025)
6. Gandolfi, A., Pingaro, N., Milani, G.: Simple nonlinear numerical modeling for unreinforced and FRP-reinforced masonry domes. Buildings **14**(1), 166 (2024)
7. Gandolfi, A., Pingaro, N., Milani, G.: Elastic Body Spring Method (EBSM) for the stability analysis of the Global Vipassana Pagoda in Mumbai, India. Buildings **15**, 653 (2025)
8. Pourfouladi, M., Pingaro, N., Valente, M.: PoliBrick plugin as a parametric tool for digital stereotomy modelling. Comput. Struct. **311**, 107722 (2025)
9. Como, M.: Settlement response of masonry constructions. In: Geotechnical Engineering for the Preservation of Monuments and Historic Sites – Proceedings of the 2nd International Symposium on Geotechnical Engineering for the Preservation of Monuments and Historic Sites, Naples, Italy, pp. 265–272 (2013)
10. Iannuzzo, A., Mallardo, V.: A novel approach to model differential settlements and crack patterns in masonry structures. Eng. Struct. **323**, 119220 (2025)
11. Iannuzzo, A., Musone, V., Ruocco, E.: A neural network-based automated methodology to identify the crack causes in masonry structures. Comput. Aided Civil Infrastruct. Eng. **39**(24), 3769–3785 (2024)
12. Prosperi, A., Longo, M., Korswagen, P.A., Korff, M., Rots, J.G.: Sensitivity modelling with objective damage assessment of unreinforced masonry façades undergoing different subsidence settlement patterns. Eng. Struct. **286**, 116113 (2023)
13. Como, M.: Statics of Historic Masonry Constructions, 2nd edn. Springer, Berlin (2013)
14. Burd, H.J., Houlsby, G.T., Augarde, C.E., Liu, G.: Modelling tunnelling-induced settlement of masonry buildings. In: Proceedings of the Institution of Civil Engineers – Geotechnical Engineering, vol. 143, no. 1, pp. 17–29 (2000)
15. Giardina, G., Marini, A., Hendriks, M.A.N., Rots, J.G., Rizzardini, F., Giuriani, E.: Experimental analysis of a masonry façade subject to tunnelling-induced settlement. Eng. Struct. **45**, 421–434 (2012)
16. Giardina, G., van de Graaf, A.V., Hendriks, M.A.N., Rots, J.G., Marini, A.: Numerical analysis of a masonry façade subject to tunnelling-induced settlements. Eng. Struct. **54**, 234–247 (2013)
17. Zampieri, P., Zanini, M.A., Faleschini, F., Hofer, L., Pellegrino, C.: Failure analysis of masonry arch bridges subject to local pier scour. Eng. Fail. Anal. **79**, 371–384 (2017)

18. Alessandri, C., Garutti, M., Mallardo, V., Milani, G.: Crack patterns induced by foundation settlements: integrated analysis on a renaissance masonry palace in Italy. Int. J. Architect. Herit. **9**(2), 111–129 (2015)
19. Reccia, E., Milani, G., Cecchi, A., Tralli, A.: Full 3D homogenization approach to investigate the behavior of masonry arch bridges: the Venice trans-lagoon railway bridge. Constr. Build. Mater. **66**, 567–586 (2014)
20. Lemos, J.V.: Discrete element modelling of masonry structures. Int. J. Architect. Herit. **1**(2), 190–213 (2007)
21. Bui, T.T., Limam, A., Sarhosis, V., Hjiaj, M.: Discrete element modelling of the in-plane and out-of-plane behaviour of dry-joint masonry wall constructions. Eng. Struct. **136**, 277–294 (2017)
22. Zampieri, P., Simoncello, N., Pellegrino, C.: Structural behaviour of masonry arch with no-horizontal springing settlement. Fract. Struct. Integr. **12**(43), 182–190 (2018)
23. Galassi, S., Zampieri, P.: A new automatic procedure for nonlinear analysis of masonry arches subjected to large support movements. Eng. Struct. **276**, 115359 (2023)
24. Portioli, F., Cascini, L.: Assessment of masonry structures subjected to foundation settlements using rigid block limit analysis. Eng. Struct. **113**, 347–361 (2016)
25. Grillanda, N., Mallardo, V.: Compatible strain-based upper bound limit analysis model for masonry walls under in-plane loading. Comput. Struct. **313**, 107743 (2025)
26. Galassi, S.: An alternative approach for limit analysis of masonry arches on moving supports in finite small displacements. Eng. Fail. Anal. **145**, 107004 (2023)
27. Portioli, F., Cascini, L.: Large displacement analysis of dry-jointed masonry structures subjected to settlements using rigid block modelling. Eng. Struct. **148**, 485–496 (2017)
28. Iannuzzo, A., et al.: Modelling the cracks produced by settlements in masonry structures. Meccanica **53**(7), 1857–1873 (2018)
29. Iannuzzo, A., Block, P., Angelillo, M., Gesualdo, A.: A continuous energy-based numerical approach to predict fracture mechanisms in masonry structures: CDF method. Comput. Struct. **257**, 106645 (2021)
30. Pari, M., Van de Graaf, A.V., Hendriks, M.A.N., Rots, J.G.: A multi-surface interface model for sequentially linear methods to analyse masonry structures. Eng. Struct. **238**, 112123 (2021)
31. Yu, C., Hoogenboom, P., Rots, J.: Extension of incremental sequentially linear analysis to geometrical non-linearity with indirect displacement control. Eng. Struct. **229**, 111562 (2021)
32. Pari, M., Swart, W., Gijzen, M., Hendriks, M.A.N., Rots, J.G.: Two van solution strategies to improve the computational performance of sequentially linear analysis for quasi brittle structures. Int. J. Numer. Meth. Eng. **121**, 2128–2146 (2020)
33. Pingaro, N., Milani, G.: A novel analytical model for fiber reinforced cementitious matrix FRCM coupons subjected to tensile tests. Compos. Struct. **327**, 117666 (2024)
34. Pingaro, N., Calabrese, A.S., Milani, G., Poggi, C.: Debonding sawtooth analytical model and FE implementation with in-house experimental validation for SRG-strengthened joints subjected to direct shear. Compos. Struct. **319**, 117113 (2023)
35. Napolitano, R., Glistic, B.: Methodology for diagnosing crack patterns in masonry structures using photogrammetry and distinct element modelling. Eng. Struct. **181**, 519–528 (2019)
36. Tiberti, S., Grillanda, N., Mallardo, V., Milani, G.: A genetic algorithm adaptive homogeneous approach for evaluating settlement-induced cracks in masonry walls. Eng. Struct. **221**, 111073 (2020)

International Workshop on Territorial Planning to integrate Risk Prevention and Urban Ontologies. (IWPRO 2025)

Leveraging Gamification to Strengthen Social Resilience and Climate Resilience

Naghmeh Mohammadpourlima[1(✉)], Mikael Nygård[1], and Mehdi P. Heris[2]

[1] Department of Social Policy, Åbo Akademi University, Rantakatu 2, 65100 Vaasa, Finland
`naghmeh.mohammadpourlima@abo.fi`
[2] Department of Urban Policy and Planning, Hunter College,
City University of New York, 695 Park Avenue, New York, NY 10065, USA

Abstract. Climate change presents challenges to urban areas and vulnerable communities, making resilience strategies crucial. Climate resilience refers to a system's ability to withstand, adapt to, and recover from climate-related stresses while minimizing future vulnerabilities. Social resilience, which relies on strong networks, collective action, and knowledge-sharing, plays an important role in improving climate resilience. However, a theoretical gap exists in linking these concepts within climate change research. This study, through a systematic literature review, explores the relationship between social resilience and climate resilience in urban communities and examines how gamification can enhance resilience-building efforts. The findings present conceptual frameworks that show social resilience strengthens climate resilience by improving governance, fostering knowledge-sharing, and helping communities adapt to climate challenges. The research also highlights that gamification can drive behavior change, improve disaster preparedness, and increase policy engagement, all contributing to social and climate resilience. By integrating gamification into resilience strategies, communities can improve adaptation practices, strengthen social connections, and enhance collective responses to climate challenges.

Keywords: Gamification · Social resilience · Climate resilience · Game App · Gamified Place · Urban Gamification · Sustainable development

1 Introduction

Climate change strains urban environments and society [1] and causes severe impacts on vulnerable communities [2]. Therefore, climate resilience is vital for communities facing climate change crises [3, 4]. Climate resilience encompasses a range of strategies and practices aimed at mitigating the impacts of climate change across various sectors [5–7]. It refers to the capacity of a system to withstand external ecosystem stresses imposed by climate change, enabling it to organize, mobilize, and evolve toward a sustainable configuration that minimizes future climatic impacts and vulnerabilities [8–11]. Based on the concept of climate resilience, social resilience serves as a foundation for enhancing climate resilience, meaning that cities with stronger social networks perform better in responding to environmental crises.

In simple terms, social resilience refers to the capacity of a community to cope with, adapt to, or transform in response to changes, shocks, or stressors [12]. Social resilience is crucial for climate resilience as it enhances community capacity to withstand and recover from climate-related shocks [13]. There remains a theoretical gap in linking the concepts of social, resilience, and climate within climate change research [14]. Since social resilience is influenced by social relations and network structures, institutions and power relations, and knowledge and discourses [15], an innovative tool which effects on these factors can be useful. Gamification has the potential to transform the way cities and communities manage disasters and risks by making resilience strategies more engaging and interactive [16]. Gamification, which originated in marketing, involves using game design elements in non-game contexts to engage and motivate people, with the goal of improving participation, encouraging behavior change, and enhancing learning [17]. By integrating gamification into resilience planning, communities can better prepare for climate-related challenges while promoting inclusive and participatory decision-making. This study explores its role in resilience-building efforts and examines its potential to bridge gaps between social and climate resilience. Based on this approach, it poses two research questions:

- What is the relationship between social resilience and climate resilience in urban communities?
- How can gamification be used to enhance social resilience and contribute to climate resilience?

This study reviews existing research to highlight the importance of social resilience in enhancing climate resilience. Based on these findings, the study emphasizes the need to incorporate gamification into urban planning and resilience strategies to create more sustainable and resilient cities.

2 Methodology

This study will adopt a qualitative research methodology, using a literature review to address the research questions. The approach will focus on secondary data and existing research to understand the relationship between social resilience and climate resilience, as well as the role of gamification in enhancing these resilience aspects.

- Literature Review

A systematic review of existing literature will serve as the primary method for addressing the first and second research questions. The review will focus on academic articles, books, and reports that explore:

The search for relevant articles was conducted in two phases. In the first phase, to address the first research question—examining the relationship between social resilience and climate resilience in urban communities—the search string included the following keywords: (social OR communit*) AND (resilience OR adaptation) AND (climate) AND (urban OR cities OR municipal). In the second phase, to explore the second research question—how gamification can theoretically enhance both social and climate resilience—the search was expanded by adding gamification-related terms to the previous string:

AND (gamification OR game* OR gamif*). To ensure the relevance of the selected studies, a two-step screening process was applied: first, by reviewing the abstracts and then by a full-text analysis.

– Synthesis and Analysis

After reviewing the literature and analyzing studies, the findings will be combined to give a clear understanding of how social resilience, climate resilience, and gamification are connected. This synthesis will help identify important patterns and insights. The goal is to provide practical recommendations for urban planners and decision-makers, helping them use gamification as a tool to improve resilience and create more sustainable cities (Fig. 1).

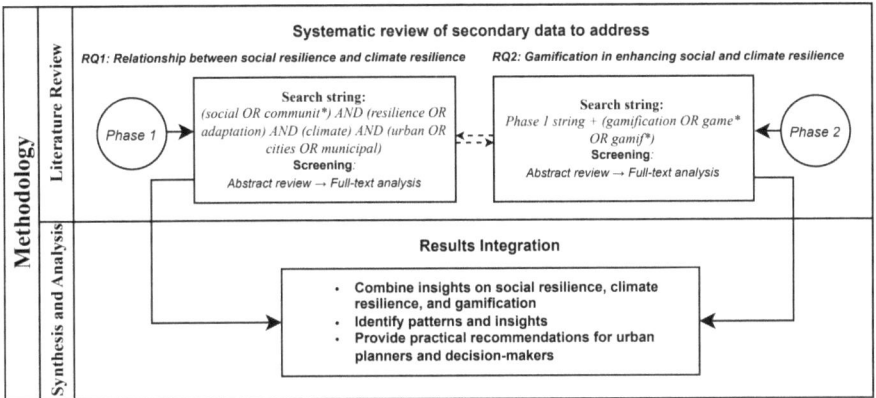

Fig. 1. Research Methodology

3 Understanding the Concepts

3.1 Climate Resilience in Urban Communities

Climate resilience is defined in various ways, reflecting its broad scope and importance in addressing climate-related challenges. It is the ability to anticipate, prepare for, and respond to hazardous climate events, trends, or disturbances [7]. It also refers to how systems, communities, and households absorb shocks, adapt to changes, and recover in ways that improve their conditions [13]. Furthermore, climate resilience involves maintaining critical functions such as food production and well-being while adapting to and transforming in response to climate change [4]. It encompasses the capacity of both human and natural systems to cope with climate-related disasters and extreme events [11]. According to UN Climate Change, climate resilience includes preventing, anticipating, absorbing, adapting, and transforming in response to climate extremes, ensuring sustainable and equitable development [18]. In urban settings, resilience is the ability of a city and its inhabitants to endure, recover, and adapt to environmental stresses while maintaining continuity and progressing toward sustainability [6]. Overall, climate resilience is essential for enabling communities and systems to respond effectively and sustainably to climate challenges.

Climate resilience requires the capacity of interconnected social, economic, and ecological systems to cope with disturbances while maintaining their core functions. It involves adaptive capacity that is negotiated and built through inclusive engagement and consideration of diverse community needs [9]. Table 1 shows the main elements that help cities become more resilient to climate change. Green Infrastructure and Nature-Based Solutions include things like trees, green roofs, and natural spaces that reduce risks, manage water, and support biodiversity. Infrastructure Resilience and Resource Management focus on strong buildings, flood protection, clean energy, and emergency plans to handle climate impacts. Community Engagement and Social Support highlight the need to involve people in planning and building strong social networks for recovery. Climate Adaptation Knowledge and Sharing help communities understand climate risks and make better decisions. Collaborative Risk Assessment and Planning means working together—governments, businesses, and communities—to assess risks and improve climate resilience. These elements, supported by different studies, create a strong foundation for making cities more prepared for climate challenges.

Table 1. Key Elements Contributing to Climate Resilience in Urban Communities

Key Item Group	Description	References
Green Infrastructure and Nature-Based Solutions	Urban greening, green roofs, and nature-based solutions that reduce risks, improve water management, and enhance biodiversity in cities	[4, 18, 19, 20, 21, 22]
Infrastructure Resilience and Resource Management	Resilient infrastructure, including flood protection, renewable energy, and emergency planning, to withstand climate impacts	[4, 18, 21, 22]
Community Engagement and Social Support	Involving local communities in planning and fostering social networks to help recover from climate impacts	[11, 18, 23–26]
Climate Adaptation Knowledge and Sharing	Building community knowledge and awareness about climate risks and adaptation strategies for better decision-making	[1, 18, 21, 26]
Collaborative Risk Assessment and Planning	Collaborative efforts across governments, businesses, and civil society and continuous climate risk assessments	[8, 20, 21, 22, 25]

3.2 Social Resilience in the Context of Climate Change

Social resilience is a relatively new concept that has recently attracted researchers in the social sciences [27]. It has an interdisciplinary nature, which means that its definitions can draw from various fields, including sociology, economics, and environmental science [15]. By adapting Cutter's resilience framework, social resilience can be conceptualized both as a process of capacity building (e.g., disaster planning) and as a post-disaster outcome (e.g., population retention rates after an earthquake) or as a combination of both [28]. In the disaster management context, social resilience is about the ability of communities and social systems to withstand, adapt to, and recover from disasters, emphasizing the importance of social structures and mechanisms throughout the disaster cycle [29]. Almost all definitions relate to social resilience as the ability or capacity to withstand, recover, and maintain [27].

The importance of social resilience lies in its ability to empower communities to respond to crises effectively, adapt to changing circumstances, and transform their social structures for better future preparedness [30]. Accordingly, social resilience is dynamically strengthened over time as people gain new knowledge and skills from past disaster relief activities, enriching the social knowledge system and passing it on to future generations [31]. Building urban social resilience is essential as it reduces patterns of inequality and improves the well-being of the population, which contributes to the community's ability to cope with various stresses and shocks [32].

In the context of climate change, social resilience includes important factors that help communities deal with and recover from challenges. These factors are Social Capital, Networks, and Cohesion, which bring people together through trust, shared values, and cooperation. Knowledge, Adaptability, and Support improve resilience by using local knowledge, technology, and social support to help people cope and find new solutions. Governance, Decision-Making, and Preparedness ensure communities are ready for climate impacts through planning and making decisions together. Economic Resources and Infrastructure help reduce risks by providing financial support and improving resources like insurance. Finally, Inclusive, Cultural, and Psychological Resilience supports vulnerable groups and strengthens psychological well-being by encouraging inclusive planning and respecting cultural values. Table 2 shows these key elements that help build social resilience against climate change.

3.3 Gamification for Social and Climate Resilience

Gamification aims to create engaging experiences that can lead to cognitive and behavioral changes [44]. It involves transforming monotonous tasks, which usually require collaboration and engagement, into more interactive and motivating experiences [45]. In this study, we focus on two aspects of gamification—game apps and gamified places (urban gamification)—in the context of serious games.

Serious games are designed with specific educational, informational, or training objectives, integrating learning directly into the gameplay [46, 47]. Serious games provide immersive experiences that promote active participation, problem-solving, and critical thinking [48]. Unlike serious games, gamification does not necessarily involve a complete game but rather uses game-like elements to achieve specific objectives [49].

Table 2. Key Elements Contributing to Social Resilience in the Face of Climate Change

Key Item Group	Description	References
Social Capital, Networks, and Collective Action	Encompasses trust, social connections, interpersonal relationships, community cohesion, shared values, reciprocity, volunteerism, and interdependence to foster collective action and mutual aid	[2, 11, 27, 33–39]
Knowledge, Technology, and Adaptability	Includes local knowledge, technology development, knowledge co-production, adaptability, social support, family/community backing, and psychological factors to enhance coping and innovation	[11, 23, 27, 33, 37, 40]
Governance, Decision-Making, and Preparedness	Combines participatory decision-making, effective governance, risk-informed strategies, disaster preparedness, proactive adaptation, and climate impact assessments to align responses with community needs	[13, 37, 39–42]
Economic Resources and Infrastructure	Covers resource acquisition, economic diversification, cash transfers, weather-index insurance, sustainable practices, and infrastructure improvement to reduce vulnerability and support resilience	[13, 33, 34, 40, 41]
Inclusive, Cultural, and Psychological Resilience	Integrates tailored approaches for vulnerable groups, addressing disparities, inclusive planning, cultural adherence, psychological resilience, and positive deviance for equitable and meaningful adaptation	[2, 11, 23, 37, 43]

Gamification refers to the application of game design elements in non-game contexts to achieve different aims, like encouraging participation and involvement [17].

Game apps are primarily for entertainment and do not typically provide the educational framework that serious games offer [50], But they can be designed by utilizing gamification for specific aims, such as facilitating community engagement, increasing knowledge, and enhancing decision-making [44, 46]. On the other hand, Urban gamification applies game elements to urban environments to engage citizens in civic activities and enhance public understanding of urban issues [51].

In summary, while gamification and serious games both aim to enhance learning and engagement, they differ in their approach and application. Gamification uses game elements in non-game contexts, whereas serious games are complete games with educational purposes. Urban gamification extends these concepts to civic engagement, while game apps primarily focus on entertainment. The aim of this research, which seeks to use gamification in two types—game Apps and urban gamification—as an innovative tool for enhancing social resilience, falls within the realm of serious games.

Gamification has been successfully applied to enhance social resilience through various mechanisms such as Community Engagement and Participation [17, 44, 52], Education and Awareness [17, 38, 53], and Behavioral Change [52, 54]. Gamification also plays a crucial role in enhancing climate resilience by Promoting Climate Action [52, 54], Supporting Policy and Planning [53, 55], and Enhancing Disaster Preparedness [56]. By incorporating urban gamification (gamified places), key outcomes such as building a sense of ownership, influencing public behavior, and fostering community engagement can be achieved. Similarly, through game apps, intrinsic motivation and scalability can enhance engagement and awareness [17]. In the context of social resilience and climate resilience, especially within specific locations, creating a sense of community and ensuring scalability for use in different places are crucial for sustaining long-term involvement and collective action.

4 Addressing the Research Questions

After reviewing the scholarly literature related to the concepts of our study, we now turn to answering the research questions based on the insights gained in the previous section.

4.1 Relationship Between Social Resilience and Climate Resilience

The relationship between social and climate resilience in urban communities is multifaceted. The connection between social resilience and climate resilience in urban communities is complex. It involves understanding how social systems adapt to and recover from climate challenges. These two types of resilience are closely linked, as both depend on shared resources, governance, and the ability to adjust to change. Social resilience is a community's ability to cope with and adapt to external shocks, like climate change, by using social networks and support systems. Climate resilience, on the other hand, focuses on how urban areas manage and recover from environmental impacts. By fostering social networks, collective action, knowledge-sharing, and psychological well-being, social resilience enhances climate resilience, enabling communities to better prepare for, respond to, and recover from climate disruptions.

The diagram in Fig. 2 visually represents the interplay between social resilience and climate resilience in urban settings. On the right side, social resilience in the face of climate change is highlighted with a purple circle, showing its key elements: Social

Capital, Networks, and Collective Action; Knowledge, Technology, and Adaptability; Governance, Decision-Making, and Preparedness; Economic Resources and Infrastructure; and Inclusive, Cultural, and Psychological Resilience. These components are interconnected, as each influences and reinforces the others.

On the left side, climate resilience in urban communities is displayed with a blue circle, including elements such as Green Infrastructure and Nature-Based Solutions; Infrastructure Resilience and Resource Management; Community Engagement and Social Support; Climate Adaptation Knowledge and Sharing; and Collaborative Risk Assessment and Planning. Like social resilience, these components are also interlinked, collectively strengthening a city's ability to cope with climate-related challenges.

Each element has direct and indirect connections to elements in the other category. For example, Economic Resources and Infrastructure (social resilience) directly support Infrastructure Resilience and Resource Management (climate resilience), while Collaborative Risk Assessment and Planning (climate resilience) reinforces Governance, Decision-Making, and Preparedness (social resilience). Indirectly, improvements in Green Infrastructure and Nature-Based Solutions can enhance psychological resilience, fostering community well-being.

Overall, social resilience and climate resilience affect each other, so improving one also strengthens the other. For example, Collaborative Risk Assessment and Planning depends on strong social networks because communities with high social capital are more likely to work together in decision-making and crisis response. Likewise, Knowledge-Sharing and Technological Adaptability help climate resilience by making sure urban communities have access to the latest climate adaptation strategies. In addition, Community Engagement and Social Support build trust and cooperation, which are important for carrying out sustainability projects and managing resources during crises.

Understanding these relationships enables decision-makers to implement holistic strategies that enhance both social and climate resilience simultaneously, making urban communities more adaptive and sustainable.

4.2 Gamification to Enhance Social and Climate Resilience

The second research question aims to answer how gamification, as an innovative tool, can contribute to enhancing social and climate resilience. This question encompasses the first research question, as shown in Fig. 3, where elements of climate resilience are represented in blue, social resilience in purple, and their connection is indicated by the gray line. These elements are exactly the same as in Fig. 2. In the center of Fig. 3, we have the element of gamification in dark green, with the impact of each element on social and climate resilience shown by the same color. There is a direct connection represented by solid lines and indirect contributions indicated by dotted lines.

The framework in Fig. 3 illustrates how gamification can create direct and indirect connections between different resilience factors, ultimately leading to more adaptive and sustainable communities. Gamification helps build both social and climate resilience by encouraging people to change their behavior, engage with their community, and support better policies. In Fig. 3, gamification is at the center, showing how it affects education, community participation, and policy planning. These elements play a big role in disaster preparedness, governance, and social networks, all of which help communities become

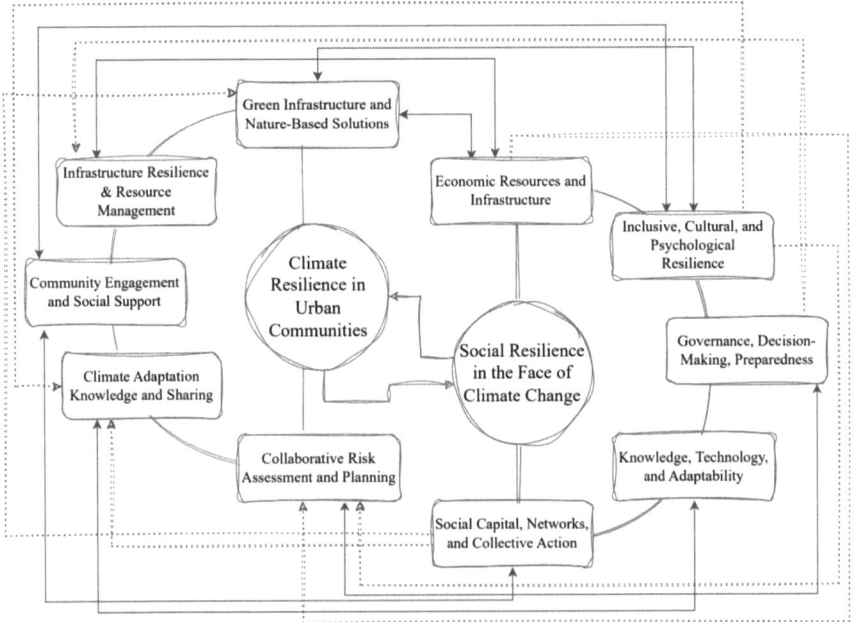

Fig. 2. Interconnections Between Social Resilience and Climate Resilience

stronger. The diagram also shows how infrastructure and resource management improve when people are involved and aware.

One of the main benefits of gamification is that it motivates people to change their behavior in a positive way. By using challenges, rewards, and leaderboards, it encourages actions like preparing for disasters, adopting eco-friendly habits, and working together on climate solutions. These small actions can lead to big improvements in how communities adapt to climate change. Also, gamification makes learning about climate adaptation and disaster response easier and more fun, which helps more people understand these important topics.

Gamification also brings people together and strengthens communities. Games and interactive activities help build trust and cooperation, making people more likely to support each other in tough situations. This idea is represented in Fig. 3 through social capital and networks, which connect directly to governance and preparedness. When communities are more connected and engaged, they can respond faster and more effectively during disasters.

Another important way gamification helps is by supporting policy and planning. It can be used to train people for emergencies, test different solutions, and involve the public in decision-making. For example, serious games and simulations help governments and organizations plan for disasters and develop better infrastructure. These activities support climate adaptation and risk assessment, as shown in the diagram.

Gamified platforms or game apps can simulate disaster scenarios, enabling participants to practice response strategies in a safe, controlled environment. These experiences help people understand the importance of planning, coordination, and swift action during climate-related crises, thus improving the overall resilience of urban communities to extreme weather events or natural disasters. Specifically, Urban gamification can foster a sense of ownership and collective action. By turning urban spaces into gamified zones, people can engage with climate adaptation projects and contribute to solutions like improving green infrastructure or managing water resources. This sense of ownership encourages sustained community involvement and collective decision-making, which are key factors in building both social and climate resilience.

Both game apps and urban gamification in real of gamification are powerful ways to connect social and climate resilience by encouraging action, educating people, strengthening communities, and improving policies. By leveraging gamification strategies, stakeholders can effectively address climate challenges while promoting inclusive, participatory, and resilient societies.

Ultimately, gamification serves as a powerful tool to bridge social and climate resilience by fostering participation, education, and collective action. When incorporated into urban planning and resilience strategies, gamification can make climate adaptation efforts more accessible, engaging, and effective.

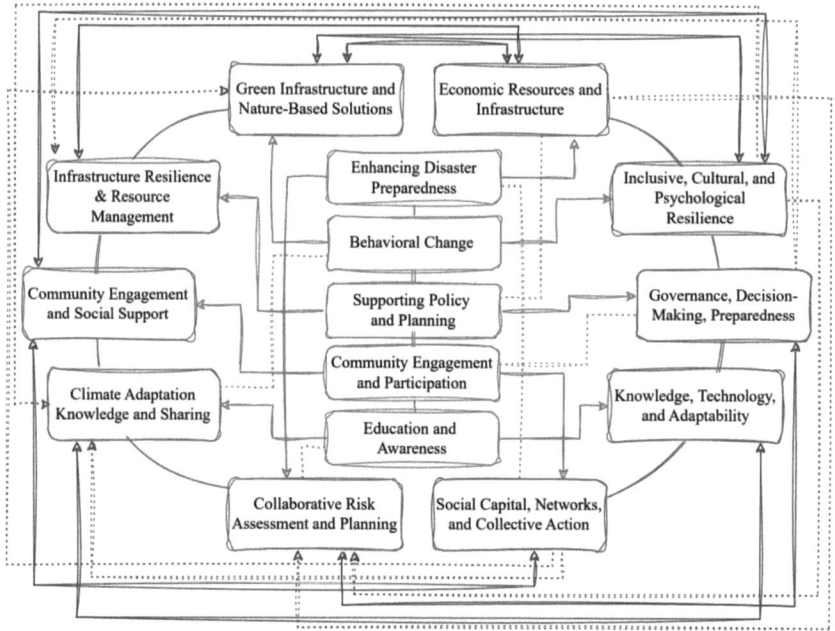

Fig. 3. Gamification for Social and Climate Resilience

5 Conclusion

Climate change puts significant pressure on urban environments and society, often causing severe impacts on vulnerable communities. As cities face increasing climate challenges, climate resilience becomes vital in ensuring they can manage and adapt to the consequences of climate change. It involves strategies and practices that help mitigate these impacts and enable systems to withstand stresses caused by climate change. Social resilience, which refers to a community's ability to cope with and adapt to shocks, plays an essential role in strengthening climate resilience. The more robust the social networks within a community, the better the response to environmental crises. Therefore, improving both social and climate resilience is crucial for sustainable urban development.

This study has shown the strong connection between social resilience and climate resilience in urban communities. Social resilience, which focuses on social networks, collective action, and sharing knowledge, helps improve climate resilience. At the same time, climate resilience, which includes infrastructure, resource management, and climate adaptation, also strengthens social resilience. These two types of resilience are closely linked, meaning that improving one can also help improve the other. Understanding this relationship is important for urban planners and decision-makers to create strategies that support both social and climate resilience, making cities more adaptable and sustainable.

Additionally, the research highlights how gamification can be a valuable tool to strengthen both social and climate resilience. Gamification, through games, challenges, and rewards, encourages people to change their behavior, get involved in their communities, and support better policies. It can motivate people to prepare for disasters, adopt eco-friendly habits, and engage in climate adaptation projects. Gamification also builds trust and cooperation within communities, which is essential in times of crisis. Furthermore, it supports decision-making and planning by allowing people to test solutions and take part in important discussions.

Building on the findings from this study, several areas for future research can further explore the relationship between social resilience, climate resilience, and the role of gamification in enhancing both. While this study offers a conceptual framework for understanding the relationship between social and climate resilience, future research could involve empirical studies to test these connections in real-world urban settings. Research could focus on specific communities that have implemented integrated resilience-building strategies and assess how improvements in one area (e.g., social resilience) lead to measurable benefits in the other (e.g., climate resilience). Longitudinal studies would help understand the dynamic and evolving nature of these interrelationships over time. Additionally, the incorporation of advanced technologies like augmented reality (AR) and virtual reality (VR) could enhance the immersive experience of gamification. Future studies could explore the use of these technologies to simulate climate-related disasters or test different urban resilience strategies in a controlled, virtual environment. This approach could offer communities and urban planners the opportunity to practice crisis management and explore solutions for real-world challenges in a risk-free setting.

In conclusion, gamification offers a powerful way to connect social and climate resilience. By making climate adaptation efforts more engaging and accessible, gamification helps people learn, participate, and take action. When used in urban planning and resilience strategies, gamification can play a key role in building more resilient, sustainable cities.

Acknowledgments. Special acknowledgment is given to the ÅAU Foundation for financial support – ÅAU doctoral research grant 2024.

Declaration of generative AI and AI-Assisted Technologies in the Writing Process. In the process of developing this document, the authors utilized ChatGPT to refine the language and enhance its readability. After employing this technology, the authors meticulously examined and adjusted the text as required, and they bear complete responsibility for the publication's content.

Conflict of Interests. The authors affirm that they have no apparent conflicts of interest, financial or personal, that could have influenced the findings presented in this paper.

References

1. Khoja, A., Felicioni, L., Danylenko, O.: Towards defining climate adaptation literacy in the context of urban resilience. IOP Conf. Ser. Earth Environ. Sci. **1402**, 012069 (2024). https://doi.org/10.1088/1755-1315/1402/1/012069
2. Wambura, S.P.: Building resilient communities: the interplay between climate change and social capital. World J. Adv. Res. Rev. **24**, 1801–1812 (2024). https://doi.org/10.30574/wjarr.2024.24.2.3491
3. Fuentes, M., et al.: Harnessing Network Science for Urban Resilience: The CASA Model's Approach to Social and Environmental Challenges (2024). https://doi.org/10.48550/ARXIV.2411.08015
4. Hachem-Vermette, C.: Enhancing urban climate resistance through the application of selected strategies and technologies. Discov. Cities. **1**, 17 (2024). https://doi.org/10.1007/s44327-024-00018-2
5. Mazhar, S.S., Khan, F.S., Srivastava, P., Khan, A.S.: Resilience & vulnerability: concepts and policy contexts. In: Ghosh, S., Kumari, M., Mishra, V.N. (eds.) Geospatial Technology to Support Communities and Policy, pp. 327–341. Springer Nature Switzerland, Cham (2024). https://doi.org/10.1007/978-3-031-52561-2_18
6. Mohammadpourlima, N., Lü, X., Nygård, M., Girgibo, Nebiyu: The integration of decarbonization and resilience strategies in shaping sustainable cities. In: Gervasi, O., Murgante, B., Garau, C., Taniar, D., Ana, M.A., Rocha, C., Lago, M.N.F. (eds.) Computational Science and Its Applications – ICCSA 2024 Workshops: Hanoi, Vietnam, July 1–4, 2024, Proceedings, Part VI, pp. 291–305. Springer Nature Switzerland, Cham (2024). https://doi.org/10.1007/978-3-031-65285-1_19
7. Fitzpatrick, R., West, H.: Improving Resilience, Adaptation and Mitigation to Climate Change Through Education in Low- and Lower-Middle Income Countries. Institute of Development Studies (2022). https://doi.org/10.19088/K4D.2022.083
8. Yadava, N.: Climate resilient development for discourse the disastrous confront. In: Sheraz Mahdi, S., Singh, R., Dhekale, B. (eds.) Adapting to Climate Change in Agriculture-Theories and Practices, pp. 257–267. Springer Nature Switzerland, Cham (2024). https://doi.org/10.1007/978-3-031-28142-6_11

9. Lonsdale, K., et al.: Climate resilience: interpretations of the term and implications for practice. In: Dessai, S., Lonsdale, K., Lowe, J., Harcourt, R. (eds.) Quantifying Climate Risk and Building Resilience in the UK, pp. 15–23. Springer International Publishing, Cham (2024). https://doi.org/10.1007/978-3-031-39729-5_2
10. Badolo, M.: Improving urban resilience actions efficiency and impact: a multidimensional resilience framework (2024). https://doi.org/10.31219/osf.io/du4a6
11. Motevalli, S., et al.: Resilience on climate change through the literature. Int. J. Educ. Cogn. Sci. **4**, 53–61 (2023). https://doi.org/10.61838/kman.ijecs.4.2.6
12. Shackleton, R.T., Malherbe, W., Biggs, R. (Oonsie): 96: Resilience (2024)
13. Fahrudin, A., Andayani, R.H.R., Albert, W.K.G., Hindarsah, I., Hakim, M.Z., Yusuf, H.: The impact of social protection on community resilience in the context of climate change and natural disaster. J. Ecohumanism **3**, 1424–1431 (2024). https://doi.org/10.62754/joe.v3i8.4824
14. Qamar, A.H.: Social dimensions of resilience and climate change: a rapid review of theoretical approaches. Present Environ. Sustain. Dev. 139–153 (2023). https://doi.org/10.47743/pesd2023171010
15. Mahler, B.: The meaning of social resilience: Interdisciplinary status or a new viewpoint? Szegedi Tudományegyetem Gazdaságtudományi Kar (2024). https://doi.org/10.14232/gtk.gdtgiss.2024
16. Gheorghe, A., Katina, P.: Gamification for Resilience: Resilient Informed Decision-Making. Wiley (2023).https://doi.org/10.1002/9781394157778
17. Mohammadpourlima, N., Nygård, M., Heris, M.P.: Gamification: a catalyst to achieve carbon-neutral cities. In: Gervasi, O., et al. (eds.) Computational Science and Its Applications – ICCSA 2024 Workshops. pp. 226–243. Springer Nature Switzerland, Cham (2024). https://doi.org/10.1007/978-3-031-65285-1_15
18. Resilience – Climate Action Pathway 2021|UNFCCC. https://unfccc.int/climate-action/marrakech-partnership/reporting-tracking/pathways/resilience-climate-action-pathway#Climate-Action-Pathway-2021
19. Fu, Q., Zheng, Z., Sarker, M.N.I., Lv, Y.: Combating urban heat: systematic review of urban resilience and adaptation strategies. Heliyon **10**, e37001 (2024). https://doi.org/10.1016/j.heliyon.2024.e37001
20. World Cities Report 2024: Cities and Climate Action|UN-Habitat
21. Climate Resilience Infographic|UN-Habitat – Metropolis (2022). https://urbanresiliencehub.org/wp-content/uploads/2022/12/4-CLIMATE-RESILIENCE.pdf
22. Resilience – Climate Action Table 2021|UNFCCC. https://unfccc.int/climate-action/marrakech-partnership/reporting-tracking/pathways/resilience-climate-action-pathway#Climate-Action-Pathway-2021
23. Wen, Q., Feng, J., Wei, X., Yang, Y., Haq, S.U.: Climate change resilience: cultural insights from diverse Chinese communities and environmental implications. Pol. J. Environ. Stud. (2024). https://doi.org/10.15244/pjoes/189716
24. Choko, O.P., Schmitt Olabisi, L., Onyeneke, R.U., Chiemela, S.N., Liverpool-Tasie, L.S.O., Rivers, L.: A resilience approach to community-scale climate adaptation. Sustainability **11**, 3100 (2019). https://doi.org/10.3390/su11113100
25. Thomas, V.: Resilience that shapes risk. In: Risk and Resilience in the Era of Climate Change, pp. 53–72. Springer Nature Singapore, Singapore (2023). https://doi.org/10.1007/978-981-19-8621-5_4
26. Hankins, D.L.: Climate resilience through ecocultural stewardship. Proc. Natl. Acad. Sci. U.S.A. **121**, e2310072121 (2024). https://doi.org/10.1073/pnas.2310072121
27. Qamar, A.H.: Social resilience: a critical synopsis of definitions. Corvinus J. Sociol. Soc. Policy. **15**, 129 (2024). https://doi.org/10.14267/CJSSP.2024.1.6

28. Kwok, A.H., Doyle, E.E.H., Becker, J., Johnston, D., Paton, D.: What is 'social resilience'? Perspectives of disaster researchers, emergency management practitioners, and policymakers in New Zealand. Int. J. Disaster Risk Reduct. **19**, 197–211 (2016). https://doi.org/10.1016/j.ijdrr.2016.08.013
29. Saja, A.M.A., Goonetilleke, A., Teo, M., Ziyath, A.M.: A critical review of social resilience assessment frameworks in disaster management. Int. J. Disaster Risk Reduct. **35**, 101096 (2019). https://doi.org/10.1016/j.ijdrr.2019.101096
30. Urban Resilience Enhancer: Social Resilience|UN-Habitat. https://unhabitat.org/urban-resilience-enhancer-social-resilience
31. Yang, L.E., Chen, J., Geng, J., Fang, Y., Yang, W.: Social resilience and its scale effects along the historical Tea-Horse Road. Environ. Res. Lett. **16**, 045001 (2021). https://doi.org/10.1088/1748-9326/abea35
32. Social Resilience Infographic|UN-Habitat – Metropolis (2022). https://urbanresiliencehub.org/wp-content/uploads/2022/12/2-SOCIAL_RESILIENCE.pdf
33. Yang, L.E., Weinelt, M., Unkel, I., Petrie, C.A.: Social resilience to changes in climate over the past 5000 years. Environ. Res. Lett. **19**, 120201 (2024). https://doi.org/10.1088/1748-9326/ad95a3
34. Warrington, M., Fisher, D., Komdeur, J., Pilakouta, N., Griesser, M.: Stronger together? A framework for studying population resilience to climate change impacts via social shielding (2024). https://ecoevorxiv.org/repository/view/8137/. https://doi.org/10.32942/X2QG9C
35. Idajati, H., Damanik, J., Kusworo, H.A., Rindrasih, E.: The role of social capital and individual competence on community resilience of the tourism industry against climate change. IOP Conf. Ser. Earth Environ. Sci. **1366**, 012023 (2024). https://doi.org/10.1088/1755-1315/1366/1/012023
36. Bernados, S., Ocampo, L.: Exploring the role of social capital in advancing climate change mitigation and disaster risk reduction. Community Dev. **55**, 470–490 (2024). https://doi.org/10.1080/15575330.2023.2253316
37. Akuba, T.: The sociological implications of climate change: community adaptation and resilience. J. Adv. Sociol. **5**, 30–42 (2024). https://doi.org/10.47941/jas.1858
38. Cosentino, M., Gal-Oz, R., Safer, D.L.: Community-based resilience: the influence of collective efficacy and positive deviance on climate change-related mental health. In: Coren, E., Wang, H. (eds.) Storytelling to Accelerate Climate Solutions, pp. 319–338. Springer International Publishing, Cham (2024). https://doi.org/10.1007/978-3-031-54790-4_15
39. Khan, A.S., et al.: Social system dynamics and community resilience: a mixed-methods approach. J. Infrastruct. Policy Dev. **8**, 7318 (2024). https://doi.org/10.24294/jipd7318
40. Merino-Benítez, T., Bojórquez-Tapia, L.A., Miquelajauregui, Y., Batllori-Sampedro, E.: Navigating climate change complexity and deep uncertainty: approach for building socio-ecological resilience using qualitative dynamic simulation. Front. Clim. **6**, 1331945 (2024). https://doi.org/10.3389/fclim.2024.1331945
41. Zapanti, T.G., Constantina, S.: Thriving in the anthropocene: building community resilience to combat climate change. Proc. World Conf. Clim. Change Glob. Warm. **1**, 29–43 (2024). https://doi.org/10.33422/ccgconf.v1i1.338
42. Salman, S.A.: Community resilience and climate change: challenges assessing sustainable development objectives. In: Bhaumik, A., Poddar, S., Dadhich, M., Hiran, K.K., Doshi, R. (eds.) Practice, Progress, and Proficiency in Sustainability, pp. 93–108. IGI Global (2024). https://doi.org/10.4018/979-8-3693-6522-9.ch006
43. Pasupuleti, R., Orekanti, E.R.: Resilience nexus with climate change, food security, mental health, and social stability in a changing world: In: Samanta, D., Garg, M. (eds.) Advances in Psychology, Mental Health, and Behavioral Studies, pp. 67–81. IGI Global (2024). https://doi.org/10.4018/979-8-3693-2177-5.ch005

44. Fernández Galeote, D., Rajanen, M., Rajanen, D., Legaki, N.-Z., Langley, D.J., Hamari, J.: Gamification for climate change engagement: review of corpus and future agenda. Environ. Res. Lett. **16**, 063004 (2021). https://doi.org/10.1088/1748-9326/abec05
45. Johansen, A.G., Pedersen, C.B.: Gamified participation: challenging the current participation methods in urban development with Minecraft (2019)
46. Avendano-Uribe, B., Lukosch, H., Milke, M.: Playing with uncertainty: facilitating community-based resilience building. Urban Plan. **7** (2022). https://doi.org/10.17645/up.v7i2.5098
47. Davis, K., Gowda, A.S., Thompson-Newell, N., Maloney, C., Fayyaz, J., Chang, T.: Gamification, serious games, and simulation in health professions education. Pediatr. Ann. **53** (2024). https://doi.org/10.3928/19382359-20240908-06
48. Lamb, R.: Serious games. In: Oxford Research Encyclopedia of Communication. Oxford University Press (2024). https://doi.org/10.1093/acrefore/9780190228613.013.1482
49. Zadeja, I., Bushati, J., University of Shkodra, Faculty of Education Sciences, Shkoder, Albania: gamification and serious games methodologies in education. In: Proceedings – The Eleventh International Symposium GRID 2022, pp. 599–605. University of Novi Sad, Faculty of Technical Sciences, Department of Graphic Engineering and Design (2022). https://doi.org/10.24867/GRID-2022-p66
50. Fischer, S., Göhlich, M., Schmitt, J.: Adapting to climate change through play? Didactically effective elements of a business simulation game. Front. Educ. **9**, 1303107 (2024). https://doi.org/10.3389/feduc.2024.1303107
51. Kim, M., Ahn, J., Park, Y.: Urban Gentri: serious game on learning about gentrification. J. Plan. Educ. Res. (2024). https://doi.org/10.1177/0739456X241280179
52. Lee, J.J., Matamoros, E., Kern, R., Marks, J., De Luna, C., Jordan-Cooley, W.: Greenify: fostering sustainable communities via gamification. In: CHI 2013 Extended Abstracts on Human Factors in Computing Systems, pp. 1497–1502. ACM, Paris France (2013). https://doi.org/10.1145/2468356.2468623
53. Marome, W., Natakun, B., Archer, D.: Examining the use of serious games for enhancing community resilience to climate risks in Thailand. Sustainability **13**, 4420 (2021). https://doi.org/10.3390/su13084420
54. Sillanpää, M., Mauro, A., Hänninen, M., Illingworth, S., Hamza, M.: A collaborative adaptation game for promoting climate action: minions of disruptions™. Geosci. Commun. **7**, 167–193 (2024). https://doi.org/10.5194/gc-7-167-2024
55. Blackett, P., FitzHerbert, S., Luttrell, J., Hopmans, T., Lawrence, H., Colliar, J.: Marae-opoly: supporting localised Māori climate adaptation decisions with serious games in Aotearoa New Zealand. Sustain. Sci. **17**, 415–431 (2022). https://doi.org/10.1007/s11625-021-00998-9
56. Kankanamge, N., Yigitcanlar, T., Goonetilleke, A.: Gamifying community education for enhanced disaster resilience: an effectiveness testing study from Australia. Future Internet. **14**, 179 (2022). https://doi.org/10.3390/fi14060179

Digital Twin as a Tool for Participatory Cultural Heritage Regeneration: The Case of Pavia Historical Urban Center in Italy

Minqing Ni[2(✉)], Tiziano Cattaneo[1], and Lyu Ji[1]

[1] University of Pavia, 27100 Pavia, Italy
[2] Tongji University, Shanghai 200092, People's Republic of China
niminqing@tongji.edu.cn

Abstract. This paper presents ongoing research developed within the project entitled *Digital Modelling to Support the Design of Safe, Sustainable and Resilient Environments* of the Department of Excellence 2023–2027 in the Department of Civil Engineering and Architecture of the University of Pavia. The main aim of this paper is to develop an investigation on the application of digital twins in historical cities to implementing a specific application scenario for the city of Pavia. The adopted method is based on an exploratory qualitative approach that is not only interpretative, but above all proactive and projective. The results obtained highlight the possibility of applying digital twins as an important tool that can combine adaptive regeneration design in medium-small sized historical urban centers such as the city of Pavia, balancing the needs of heritage protection with those of sustainable transformation, participation and inclusiveness.

Keywords: Digital Twin · Cultural Heritage · Urban design · Historical Urban Centers · Environmental design

1 Introduction

Digital twins (DT) have recently undergone a significant evolution, extending the opportunities for their use in the urban context, with relevance in historic centers. In those contexts, characterized by high morphological complexity and cultural heritage, the integration of multisensory data, 3D modeling and predictive techniques opens new perspectives for all the actors involved in the urban development: from urban and architectural design to monitoring and adaptive management of heritage. However, their application raises critical questions about data interoperability, representative accuracy and sustainability of digital workflows. Furthermore, the use of interactive platforms enhances participatory design, but requires new forms of governance and epistemological inclusiveness [1–4].

Although digital twins were initially developed for industrial applications, their use has rapidly extended to the urban environment, attracting growing interest, especially in historic centers, where conservation challenges intertwine with those of adaptation [5].

Therefore, digital twins are establishing themselves as innovative and strategic tools for planning, urban and architectural design, as well as for city management. In short, they can be described as virtual replicas of physical systems, capable of integrating real-time data, simulations and advanced analyses, in order to design processes as well as support decision-making [6].

Nevertheless, the application of digital twins' tools and platforms in historic urban contexts brings specific challenges and opportunities, different from modern urban environments. Historic centers such as the city of Pavia preserve invaluable cultural assets that require targeted approaches for monitoring, conservation, regeneration and adaptive design, supported by intelligent management. Furthermore, integrating heritage protection within digital twin frameworks implies an interdisciplinary collaboration between planners (urban planners, architects, designers), conservation experts, data scientists and local stakeholders [7]. Implementation of digital twins for application in historical urban centers is based on the integration of a structured set of technologically advanced operational tools that consequently involve the adaptation of new operational workflows. Data collection is delivered to high-precision acquisition technologies, such as 3D scans using LiDAR, photogrammetry and geo-radar, which allow obtaining extremely detailed digital representations of historical buildings and urban fabrics, detecting complex geometries and material conditions with high accuracy [8]. In support, IoT sensor networks monitor environmental and structural parameters in real time – such as temperature, humidity, vibrations and tourist flows – using non-invasive methods, which are essential for the protection of architectural heritage [7]. Three-dimensional simulations, based on tools such as computational fluid dynamics, finite element analysis and agent-based modeling, allow us to anticipate the impact of events and interventions on structures [6]. Finally, artificial intelligence and machine learning offer predictive and diagnostic tools for both conceptualization of design strategies and the revealing of anomalies and maintenance management. Furthermore, digital twin applications for cultural heritage offer a wide range of strategic advantages. For example, the permanent monitoring and real-time simulations allows to rapidly identify structural problems, humidity phenomena or material degradation processes [5]. Predictive simulations also allow to evaluate the effects of environmental factors such as climate change, pollution and overtourism pressure, providing effective bases for mitigation strategies [7]. As well as virtual environments allow to test design interventions in a safe way, while high-definition digital models contribute to accumulate endless material for documentation, preservation and so doing the protection of historical memory of a place [6]. Finally, one of the most relevant contributions offered by digital twins is their potentiality to strengthen participatory processes within historical urban contexts. Through interactive visualization platforms, it is possible to actively involve residents, business operators and tourists, offering them direct access to data and scenarios of urban transformation [9, 10]. This approach facilitates the co-creation of knowledge, combining technical skills with local knowledge for a shared and complex reading of the places [11]. Furthermore, decision-making transparency is improved thanks to the possibility of clearly visualizing the consequences of design choices, promoting a more inclusive urban governance [8]. However, it is necessary to keep in mind that the success of such practices requires solid governance, active community involvement and integration with existing practices [12].

Within this framework, the research question might be: How can digital twins contribute to adaptive conservation and design in small-medium sized historical urban centers such as the city of Pavia, balancing the needs of heritage protection with sustainable transformation and inclusive participation?

To answer this research question, this paper proposes to adopt an exploratory qualitative approach, based on a comparative documentary analysis of case studies relating to the use of digital twins in some European and non-European historical cities. The aim is not only interpretative, but above all proactive, aimed at developing a feasible scenario for the city of Pavia. The framework in which this research has been developed is on the one hand the Dorian project (Digital Modeling to Support the Design of Safe, Sustainable and Resilient Environments) which is a project of the Department of Excellence 2023–2027 of DICAr (Department of Civil Engineering and Architecture of the University of Pavia), on the other the experience gained within international collaborations between the University of Pavia and Tongji University and which allowed the authors to directly observe the installation, implementation and application of the CityScope platform jointly developed by the City Science Lab of MIT and the College of Design and Innovation of Tongji University in Shanghai. The full work package developed in the CityScope @Shanghai project is the main background on which the following research phases have been developed: 1) the selection of case studies, 2) the thematic matrix for the comparative analysis of the selected case studies, 3) the scenario design in which a preliminary project proposal for the city of Pavia is developed.

Consequently, this article is set out as follows: first, after a brief introduction, an overview of the MIT-Tongji CityScope Project in Shanghai is developed, summarizing the results and lessons learned but above all the correlations that CityScope can have in historical urban contexts such as Pavia. Second, a comparative synthesis of five international case studies is developed with a particular focus on the contextual adaptations of digital twins in urban and historical contexts. Third, a SWOT analysis of the application of digital twins to historical urban centers is developed. Fourth, based on the entire body of knowledge developed in the previous phases, a proposal of the Digital Twin application to the urban context of Pavia is delivered. Finally, the research outcomes are critically discussed.

Please note that the first paragraph of a section or subsection is not indented. The first paragraphs that follows a table, figure, equation etc. does not have an indent, either.

Subsequent paragraphs, however, are indented.

2 The MIT-Tongji CityScope Project in Shanghai

2.1 Overview of CityScope Shanghai

CityScope Shanghai is a platform developed by MIT City Science Lab and jointly applied at the College of Design and Innovation of Tongji University. It is a pioneering application of interactive digital twins for participatory urban design. Although not specifically designed for historical contexts, the project stands out for both its technical format and the methodologies used, which have a high potential for adaptation to decision-making processes related to the protection and enhancement of cultural heritage.

The platform operates through an interactive augmented reality system, which simulates the impact of emerging urban design solutions and technologies on the built environment. It integrates physical models, projective mapping, sensor networks and advanced computational simulations, configuring a dynamic environment that facilitates shared design experimentation [13].

Its application in the Siping Road district in Shanghai represents a fundamental example of the use of digital twins to support inclusive decision-making processes in urban design and planning. In this context, CityScope has demonstrated a remarkable capacity for integrating physical and digital representations: real-time data, combined with simulation results, are projected onto physical models of the area, thus enhancing the interaction between users and the system. The interface, based on LEGO components, allows stakeholders to physically manipulate urban elements and immediately visualize the effects of changes [14].

The system also uses a complex layering of data that includes real-time traffic flows, building morphologies, land use patterns, socio-economic and environmental indicators (such as air quality and noise levels), as well as energy parameters. This information set allows the modeling of complex urban scenarios, including the management of pedestrian flows, the reconfiguration of public spaces, the optimization of green infrastructures, the modification of transport networks and the experimentation of mixed-use urban development schemes.

CityScope is also configured as a collaborative decision-making space, where public administrators, designers, residents and other stakeholders can discuss design solutions in a shared environment, iteratively improving proposals based on generated data and simulations [15, 16].

2.2 Results and Lessons Learned and Correlation with Historical Urban Contexts

The experience of CityScope applied to the Siping Road urban community has highlighted significant results. The visual and tangible component of the platform has encouraged public participation, overcoming the typical barriers of traditional decision-making processes. The possibility of visualizing the impact of designed project in real time has allowed to revise and implement the project proposals based on evidences, making possible to achieve at least two very important results that we believe are relevant for the purpose of this research: 1) facilitation of solutions partially or totally already discussed and shared with the inhabitants of the community, 2) revision and refinement of the project proposals on visible data, allowing to avoid project compromises that would have reduced the effectiveness of the project itself. This was possible by having the opportunity to visualize and explain the projects to the inhabitants in advance and therefore putting them in a position to evaluate the best available solutions, thus avoiding choices oriented to individual interests. Therefore, CityScope has made clear the importance of integrating advanced digital technologies and the social dimension, highlighting once again how the human component and the active involvement of citizens is essential for the success of digital innovations.

Finally, taking into account the aim and the research question of this study, it is necessary to mention the fact that the morphological, architectural and cultural heritage characteristics of the urban area of Siping Road in Shanghai are different from the historical centers of European cities. Siping Community is a complex, active and thriving urban context. Located in the Midwest of Yangpu district of Shanghai, it is 2.75 square kilometers in area and has a population of over a hundred thousand. Siping community includes one of Shanghai's first workers village called Anshan village. It was built in the 50's of last century and become one of the largest villages in Shanghai at that time. After continuous expansion, it now includes 8 villages. In the community, two thirds of the buildings recognized as an old community due to housing condition, outdated infrastructure, and lacking quality in public space, and the neighborhood looks less vital and strength. But at the same time, there are lots of leftover space and hidden space that are not well used and are ready to be converted [17, 18].

Nevertheless, the solutions and results achieved with the CityScope can also be applied to contexts such as the historical center of Pavia if consciously adapted with respect to at least three themes: 1) the symbolic value and memory of urban spaces and architectural elements, 2) cultural and identity aspects of local communities, 3) the morphological, material, visual and perceptive complexity of the urban environment. Once again, from a design point of view, the context, understood in its broadest expression of a set of physical or environmental elements and meaning, remains of fundamental importance even in the application of digital technologies that do not yet seem to be able to grasp the urban environment semantic as well as its symbolic cultural depth [19].

3 Selected Case Studies: Contextual Adaptations of Digital Twins in Urban and Historical Contexts

The following selected five case studies were chosen with the aim of representing a variety of approaches, scales and purposes in the adoption of digital twins in European and non-European urban contexts. These examples underline complementary application scenarios: from the preservation of cultural heritage in vulnerable historical environments, to the promotion of civic participation, and yet to resilient urban design and planning. This heterogeneity it is not diriment for our research scope but in the contrary allowed us to explore in a comparative method the potential and challenges of transferability of this technology, providing a complex framework useful for adapting the model to the case of Pavia.

In the current wide spectrum of urban applications of digital twins, the city of Venice represents for our study one of the most representative cases in a historical context. The initiative promoted by Venice municipality is motivated by the need to respond to exceptional conservation challenges that characterize Vencie itself, linked to the hydrogeological vulnerability of the city and the pressure exerted by mass overtourism. The developed system integrates a plurality of data in real time: from sea level rise to the structural settlements of buildings and tourist flows. This technological infrastructure has proven to be particularly effective in balancing the needs of heritage protection with those of contemporary fruition, outlining new models of adaptive urban governance [20].

In Herrenberg, a German town located in the metropolitan area of Stuttgart, the use of the digital twin has focused on issues related to urban mobility and air quality. Thanks to an interactive platform that combines digital simulations and immersive virtual environments, the city promoted a participatory decision-making process, actively involving citizens and local stakeholders in the co-creation of scenarios for traffic management and environmental sustainability. The small scale of the context favored a high and quick responsiveness between technologies, communities and urban policies [21].

The Amsterdam Time Machine case instead adopts a deeper historical perspective, developing a digital twin that integrates ancient maps, archival documents sources and three-dimensional models to trace the urban evolution of the city over the time. This "four-dimensional" approach allows not only to explore the urban past, but also to understand how historical dynamics influence the contemporary spatial urban structure. The project is a valuable resource for architects, planners, historians and citizens interested in a layered narrative of urban development [22].

The city of Zurich offers another example of a long-term application of digital twins in the urban sphere. Perhaps the most developed in Europe, since the 1990s, the city has started a progressive process of digitization of spatial data, culminating in 2011 with the creation of an integrated three-dimensional urban model. Currently, the digital twin of Zurich serves as an operational tool to address complex urban planning challenges, modeling future scenarios through the combination of geospatial data, simulations and intuitive visual interfaces [23].

Finally, the project developed in New Orleans after Hurricane Katrina demonstrates the application of digital twins in contexts of climate vulnerability and cultural heritage. Focused on the historic neighborhoods of the French Quarter and the Garden District, the system integrates predictive modeling for floods, structural monitoring of historic buildings and heritage protection strategies. This case study, despite of being not an European case provide a meaningful insights for our study. In fact, the New Orleans platform contributes substantially to the construction of a data-driven urban resilience, oriented towards prevention and safeguarding the city's identity [24].

By deploying a comparative analysis of the five case studies clearly arise how digital twin technologies share a common infrastructural basis – consisting of 3D models, real-time data integration and predictive simulation capabilities – but require careful adaptation to local specificities. The experiences of Venice and New Orleans show an application oriented towards heritage protection in contexts at environmental risk, while Herrenberg and Zurich focus on sustainable planning and urban management through participatory models. Amsterdam, on the other hand, is an outstanding example for its strong historical-cultural and temporal vocation. In all cases, the effectiveness of digital twins depends on their ability to interface with designers, governance, the needs of local communities and the constraints imposed by cultural preservation. The following Tables 1 and 2 represents respectively, highlight of the objectives, technological approaches and distinctive features of the projects analyzed and, the SWOT analysis of the application of digital twins to historic urban centers.

Table 1. Comparative analysis of the five case studies

Case Study City	Main Objectives	Technological Approach	Distinctive Elements
Venice, Italy	Tourism management and adaptation to climate change in a fragile historic context	Integration of real-time data: water levels, structural stability, tourist flows	Holistic system for heritage conservation and environmental monitoring
Herrenberg Germany	Reduction of urban congestion and improvement of air quality	Immersive simulations and virtual reality for co-design	Active citizen involvement in a transparent decision-making process
Amsterdam, Netherlands	Study of historical urban evolution and informed planning	3D modeling and digitized historical maps (4D approach)	Strong archival and temporal component to understand urban changes
Zurich, Switzerland	Support for urban planning and sustainable management	3D urban model with integrated geospatial data	Long-term experience with progressive urban digitization
New Orleans, USA	Strengthening urban resilience in historic neighborhoods after disasters	Predictive simulations for floods and structural monitoring	Focus on protecting cultural heritage in vulnerable areas

4 Application of the Digital Twin to the Urban Context of the City of Pavia

4.1 The Urban Heritage of Pavia: A Layered Context

Located in the Lombardy region, in northern Italy, Pavia is an emblematic case of a medium-small sized European historical city, whose urban settlement reflects a thousand-year-old stratification. Founded as a Roman settlement, the urban morphology in the central area preserves a historical road network characterized by orthogonal blocks, which integrate the medieval layout and subsequent additions. Significant architectural elements include monuments, towers, palaces and the large historical complex of the University – among the oldest in Europe – the Visconti Castle and numerous historic churches. The city also features a strong integration between the urban and natural landscapes, highlighted by the relationship between the historical center and the Ticino River, with iconic elements such as the Ponte Coperto as well as the evident correlation with the surrounding agricultural landscape with the Cascine farmhouse and the water network infrastructure of the hundreds of creeks and the water canal Naviglio Pavese. Along with this physical context the city presents social dynamics embodied by traditional practices, but above all by a lively student population. Considered as a whole,

Table 2. SWOT analysis of the application of digital twins to historic urban centers

Strengths	Weaknesses
– Real-time and holistic monitoring of historic centers, with predictive capabilities and dynamic temporal analysis – Objective decision support, increased transparency, and public participation through interactive visual tools – Integrated management of physical components and cultural practices	– High costs for technologies and specialized skills – Lack of complete historical documentation – Technical integration difficulties among heterogeneous systems – Regulatory limitations for sensor installation and privacy-related issues
Opportunities	**Threats**
– Growing political support and access to European and international funding – Potential to enrich the tourist experience with immersive technologies – Effective tools for climate resilience and adaptive planning – Promotion of interdisciplinary synergies among technology, conservation, and planning	– Risk of marginalizing traditional skills – Digital accessibility barriers for certain segments of the population – Uncertainties about long-term sustainability and data security – Doubts regarding the authenticity of digital representations

these characteristics are imposing specific requirements for the implementation of a digital twin, profoundly different from those of large modern cities [25, 26]. Based on the literature analyzed and international case studies, a modular and progressive approach is proposed for the introduction of a participatory digital twin in the city of Pavia, divided into three main phases: 1) data collection and infrastructure construction, 2) development of an interactive platform, and 3) simulation of scenarios for decision support.

4.1.1 Digital Workflow

The first phase is suggested involves the collection of data on urban heritage using non-invasive IoT sensors, capable of monitoring environmental conditions in historic buildings (temperature, humidity, vibrations), supported by mobile technologies and citizen science tools, to limit direct intervention on protected structures. This is coupled by three-dimensional documentation through photogrammetry and laser scanning, integrated with digitalized historical sources such as maps, photographs and archives. These data feed a multi-level platform that organizes information relating to architectural heritage, environmental context, mobility and land use patterns, as well as management and protection activities. The technological structure is based on a scalable cloud infrastructure, enhanced by edge computing nodes for sensitive areas, and accompanied by Application Programming Interfaces (API) for interoperability with the physical world at local, regional and national systems [27].

4.1.2 Participation and Interactive Design

A key component assumed at the beginning of our research is the implementation and the involvement of local stakeholders, including conservation bodies, public administrations, citizens, universities and tourism operators [28]. The adoption of inclusive participation strategies, with particular attention to potentially excluded groups, is essential to ensure legitimacy and effectiveness. The development of multimodal interfaces aimed at both experts (GIS tools and 3D analysis) and residents and visitors (mobile applications, augmented physical models, virtual and augmented reality experiences) can be visualized as the LEGO model earlier described for the CityScope Shanghai [13]. These tools should ensure accessibility for users with different digital abilities and skills, and promote participation through continuous feedback mechanisms, gamification elements and digital forums integrated with official decision-making processes.

4.1.3 Scenario Simulation and Support for Urban Governance

The platform should integrate advanced simulation capabilities to assess the effects of urban planning and conservation interventions, such as traffic reorganization, tourism management, climate adaptation, restoration and adaptive reuse of buildings, as well as improving the quality of public spaces. The adoption of multi-criteria analysis tools will allow balancing conservation, social, environmental and economic objectives [29]. Furthermore, dynamic dashboards, early warning systems for environmental threats and visual communication tools will allow to translate technical outputs into operational knowledge for public decision makers and citizens.

4.2 Specificity and Adaptation of the Digital Twin for Pavia

As earlier mentioned at the Sect. 2.2, the application of the digital twin in Pavia should take into account some specific characteristics that, in our opinion, should be considered crucial to any urban project:

- The landscape: the origin of the city is fully intertwined to the relationship with the Ticino River. The river represents an essential landscape element but can also represent a vulnerability in hydrogeological and environmental terms.
- The morphological dimension of the historic center, although of great value, is coupled by its limited spatial dimension that requires the adoption of sustainable solutions to be activated progressively also through pilot projects.
- The tourist dimension potentiality is not yet adequately developed. If on the one hand it is hoped to avoid the crystallization of the historic center for purely tourist purposes, on the other hand the application of the digital twin could contribute to greater visibility in the national and international tourist panorama of the city as well as contribute to the adoption of effective and sustainable promotional techniques.
- The presence of the University as an institution – among the oldest in the world – offers humanistic and scientific competences that could be strategic for the sustainable development of the city.

In conclusion, the adoption of a digital twin in Pavia represents an opportunity to combine the preservation of cultural heritage along with technological innovation and social engagement. The approach we propose, which is based on the qualitative interpretation of empirical data acquired from the critical analysis of the best international practices applied to local contexts, has set itself the main objective of enhancing the historical-cultural identity of the city of Pavia through the application of a possible, effective and efficient holistic project capable of addressing contemporary challenges related to sustainability, urban resilience and inclusiveness in its broadest sense [30, 31].

5 Discussion, Critique and Conclusion

This study was developed within the project entitled Digital modelling to support the design of safe, sustainable and resilient environments of the Department of Excellence 2023–2027 of the DICAr (Department of Civil Engineering and Architecture of the University of Pavia). The main purpose of this paper is to develop an investigation on the application of digital twins in European and non-European historical cities aimed at developing a specific application scenario for the city of Pavia. The adopted method can be traced back to an exploratory qualitative approach that is not only interpretative, but above all proactive, based on the experience acquired by the authors in other contexts within the cooperation between the University of Pavia and the Tongji University of Shanghai. The results obtained, which will have to be implemented in the continuation of the research, highlight the possibility of applying digital twins as an important tool that can combine adaptive conservation and design in medium-small sized historical urban centers such as the city of Pavia, balancing the needs of heritage protection with those of sustainable transformation, participation and inclusiveness.

Beside encouraging results achieved in terms of innovation and development prospects, the approach reveals inevitable critical issues and limitations.

First, if on the one hand, it may seem redundant to highlight that the integration of digital twins in small and medium-sized historic urban centers such as Pavia, represents an emerging and fundamental frontier as also affirmed by the EU's Digital Strategies for Smart Cities and Communities in Europe [32] in the field of urban design and planning it pave the way to new perspectives as it integrates multidimensional data, advanced high-quality 3D modeling and predictive techniques to support effective decisions. On the other hand, it is not obvious to highlight again what we can define as the contextual adaptation of technological innovation. In fact, for the city of Pavia, characterized by a layered historical, cultural, morphological complexity, a progressive and modular approach is proposed, based on the structured collection of data, the development of an interactive platform and the simulation of future scenarios fully incorporated into the context, understood in its broadest expression as a set of physical or environmental elements and of identity meaning.

The contextual adaptation of this approach is even more fundamental if the aim is also to adopt inclusive participation practices, which can guarantee a broad social sharing of the proposed solutions.

As a consequence, if this technology opens new perspectives for the management and sustainable development of cities, at the same time it raises crucial questions related to the interoperability of systems, the accuracy of the information collected, the long term sustainability of digital infrastructures and the digital literacy of the broadest spectrum of the population. In this context, the interactive platforms studied and analyzed in other research, such as the CityScope developed by MIT and Tongji University in Shanghai, demonstrate how such integration can facilitate shared decision-making processes and improve the understanding of urban phenomena. However, the transfer of these models to different contexts, such as European historic centers, requires specific adaptations. The analysis of five case studies, four of which are European case, ranging from the conservation of cultural heritage to the promotion of urban resilience, highlights the potential and critical issues of such adaptations. The critical element that emerges from these experiences is the pulverized or ultra-specialized application of these technologies and that in this research it is suggested to avoid for the scenario of the city of Pavia.

In conclusion, for urban realities such as Pavia, the digital twin cannot constitute a tout-court solution that is based exclusively on the application of advanced technologies but rather highlights the need to integrate a set of tools that, if adopted with awareness and competence, can facilitate new opportunities for urban design and planning, participation and sustainable management of the urban and architectural heritage. In this sense, these tools will be able to connect human intelligence and represent a bridge between the memory of the past and the challenges of the future, advancing the construction of more aware, resilient and inclusive historical cities.

Acknowledgments. This study was co-supported by research funding of the Department of Civile Engineering and Architecture of the University of Pavia, and by funding of the College of Design and Innovation of Tongji University.

Disclosure of Interests. The authors have no competing interests to declare that are relevant to the content of this article. Tiziano Cattaneo is faculty member of the Department of Civile Engineering and Architecture, University of Pavia, Italy and research member of the team for the project DORIAN – Digital modelling to support the design of safe, sustainable and resilient environments – ACTION 4 Digital Twin for Built Heritage and Open Spaces. Minqing Ni is faculty member of the College of Design and Innovation of Tongji University and collaborating within the Tongji-MIT City Science Lab @Shanghai. Lyu Ji has received under the supervision of Tiziano Cattaneo a post-doc scholarship (assegno di ricerca) funded under DORIAN project Action 4 from the Department of Civile Engineering and Architecture, University of Pavia.

References

1. Batty, M.: Digital twins. Environ. Plan B: Urban Analyt. City Sci. **45**(5), 817–820 (2018)
2. Dell'Era, C., Magistretti, S., Verganti, R.: Exploring digital twins for urban design: framework and challenges. J. Urban Technol. **27**(1), 3–22 (2020)
3. Holzer, D., Gassner, G.: The digital twin: a framework for design futures in the built environment. Archit. Des. **91**(2), 68–73 (2021)
4. Ponzini, D., Sampieri, L.: Cultural heritage, digitalization and participation: emerging dynamics in historical urban landscapes. Cities **138**, 104305 (2023)
5. Boeri, A., Longo, D., Massari, M., Sabatini, F., Turillazzi, B.: The role of historical city centers in the climate-neutral transition of cities: the digital twin as a tool for dynamic and participatory planning. In: Battisti, A., Baiani, S. (eds.) ETHICS: Endorse Technologies for Heritage Innovation. Designing Environments. Springer, Cham (2024)

6. Ferré-Bigorra, J., Casals, M., Gangolells, M.: The adoption of urban digital twins. Cities **131**, 103905 (2022)
7. Karatzas, S., Lazari, V., Fouseki, K., Pracchi, V.N., Balaskas, E.: Digital twins-enabled heritage buildings management through social dynamics. J. Cult. Herit. Manage. Sustain. Dev. (2024) (ahead-of-print)
8. Liu, Z., Wang, J.: Protection and utilization of historical sites using digital twins. Buildings **14**(4), 1019 (2024)
9. Grugni, F., Voltolina, M., Cattaneo, T.: Use of object recognition AI in community and heritage mapping for the drafting of sustainable development strategies suitable for individual communities, with case studies in China, Albania and Italy. In: Post-carbon. Proceedings of the 27th International Conference on Computer-Aided Architectural Design Research in Asia (CAADRIA 2022). The Association for Computer-Aided Architectural Design Research in Asia (CAADRIA). Conference held in Hong Kong and Sydney, vol. I, pp. 717–726 (2022)
10. Weil, B., Linner, T., Bock, T.: Urban digital twin challenges: a systematic review and research agenda. Sustain. Cities Soc. **97**, 104997 (2023)
11. Corneli, A., Rotilio, M.: Urban centres management: a digital twin approach. In: Proceedings e Report, vol. 137, pp. 10–19. Firenze University Press (2023)
12. Ćosović, M., Maksimović, S.: Digital twins of the built environment: an overview of applications and future research directions. In: Proceedings of the 3rd International Conference on Digital Technologies and Applications (ICDTA 2022), vol. 3266, pp. 89–96 (2022). CEUR-WS.org
13. Alonso, L., et al.: CityScope: a data-driven interactive simulation tool for urban design. Use case Volpe. In Minai, A., Braha, D., Bar-Yam, Y. (eds.) Unifying Themes in Complex Systems IX, pp. 253–261. Springer (2018)
14. Noyman, A.: CityScope: An Urban Modeling and Simulation Platform. Doctoral Dissertation. MIT Media Lab (2022)
15. City Science Lab @ Shanghai – MIT Media Lab Project Overview. https://www.media.mit.edu/projects/city-science-lab-shanghai/overview/. Accessed 25 March 2025
16. CityScope LivingLine Shanghai – MIT Media Lab Project Overview. https://www.media.mit.edu/projects/cityscope-livingline-shanghai/overview/. Accessed 25 March 2025
17. Ni, M., Cattaneo, T.: Design for urban resilience: a case of community-led placemaking approach in Shanghai, China. In: Smith, M.J., Salvendy, G. (eds.) Human-Computer Interaction. Design Practice in Contemporary Contexts. HCI 2019. Lecture Notes in Computer Science, vol. 11569, pp. 207–222. Springer (2019)
18. Cattaneo, T., Ni, M.: Specificity and continuity of spatial structure in urban communities in Shanghai: the case of Siping Road. In: Valentin, V.N. (ed.) Contemporary China. Architectural, Urban Insights, pp. 34–37. Gangemi Editore spa, Roma (2023)
19. Norberg-Schulz, C.: Genius loci: Towards a phenomenology of architecture. Rizzoli (1980)
20. Villani, L., Gugliermetti, L., Barucco, M.A., Cinquepalmi, F.: A digital twin framework to improve urban sustainability and resiliency: the case study of Venice. Land **14**(1), 83 (2025)
21. Dembski, F., Wössner, U., Letzgus, M., Ruddat, M., Yamu, C.: Urban digital twins for smart cities and citizens: the case study of Herrenberg, Germany. Sustainability **12**(6), 2307 (2020)
22. Amsterdam Time Machine. https://www.amsterdamtimemachine.nl. Accessed 25 March 2025
23. Schrotter, G., Hürzeler, C.: The digital twin of the city of Zurich for urban planning. ISPRS Int. J. Geo-Inf. **9**(5), 1–21 (2020)
24. Waguespack, L.J.: Digital Cities: Representations of the City and Urban Space in Science Fiction Film. Doctoral Dissertation. University of New Orleans (2017)
25. De Lotto, R.: Città e pianificazione: la tradizione di Pavia e le opportunità per il future. Maggioli Editore, Santarcangelo di Romagna (RN) (2008)

26. Parrinello, S., Picchio, F., De Marco, R.: Pavia 3D: reading and decomposition of the city for the construction of dynamic databases on heritage/De Marco, R., Parrinello, S., Picchio, F.//Bulletin of the PNRPU. Applied Ecology. Urban Development, 2017 – №1 – pp. 33–45 (2018)
27. Somanath, S., Naserentin, V., Eleftheriou, O., Sjölie, D., Wästberg, B.S., Logg, A.: Towards urban digital twins: a workflow for procedural visualization using geospatial data. Remote Sens. **16**(11), 1939 (2024)
28. Ni, M., Cattaneo, T.: Social impact in design education. In Rau, P.L.P. (ed.) Cross-Cultural Design. Applications in Learning, Arts, Cultural Heritage, Creative Industries, and Virtual Reality. HCII 2022. Lecture Notes in Computer Science, vol. 13312, pp. 92–107. Springer (2022)
29. Ni, M.: Digital participation for inclusive growth: a case study of Singapore's collaborative digital governance model. In: Giorgi, E., Cattaneo, T., Flores Herrera, A.M., Aceves Tarango, V.d.S. (eds.) Design for Vulnerable Communities, pp. 323–337. Springer (2022)
30. Cattaneo, T., Giorgi, E., Flores, M., Barquero, V.: Territorial effects of shared-living heritage regeneration. Sustainability **12**(20), 8616 (2020)
31. Giorgi, E., Cattaneo, T., Serrato Guerrero, K.P.: The Principles of design for vulnerable communities: a research by design approach overrunning the disciplinary boundaries. Buildings **12**(11), 1789 (2022)
32. Digital Strategies for Smart Cities and Communities. https://digital-strategy.ec.europa.eu/en/policies/smart-cities-and-communities. Accessed 25 March 2025

Author Index

A

Adriaenssens, Sigrid 368
Aktaş, Mehmet S. 16
Aktas, Mehmet S. 88, 193
Albashayreh, Amjad 243
Alptekin, Gülfem Işıklar 274
Al-Saidi, Nadia M. G. 70
Alzu'bi, Ahmad 243
Arslan, Afra 274
Aslan-Tutak, Fatma 165

B

Bayrak, Serra Nur 274
Bozoglan, Mehmet Cevheri 88
Brundu, Brunella 139
Buzzetti, Martina 354

C

Caglar, Eren 193
Campanile, Lelio 260
Carboni, Donatella 139
Cascardi, Alessio 302
Castaldo, Mariarosaria 260
Cattaneo, Tiziano 428
Çakir, Esra 182
Cocking, Sam 302, 368
Cornali, Roberto 106
Costantini, Alessandro 35, 51
Coutinho, Fábio D. L. 124
Cunha Jr, Americo 368
Cusano, Concetta 381

D

Di Gennaro, Luciana 325
Diep, Vu Thu 212
Donvito, Giacinto 35

Dursun, Ahu Dereli 226
Duy Hung, Phan 3

F

Fabbrocino, Francesco 302, 338, 368
Faria, João Rodrigo 124
Ferraro, Mario 381
Frunzio, Giorgio 325

G

Gaudagnuolo, Mariateresa 325
Gervasi, Osvaldo 152
Giommi, Luca 35

H

Hung, Phan Duy 212
Huy, Nguyen Quang 212

I

Iannuzzo, Antonino 381

J

Ji, Lyu 428

K

Karaca, Bengü 165
Karaca, Yeliz 70, 152

L

Linh, Nguyen Nhu Hai 3
Luciano, Raimondo 302

M

Maddaloni, Giuseppe 381
Malvica, Sonia 139
Marrone, Stefano 260

Matarazzo, Giuseppe 381
Milani, Gabriele 354, 396
Mohammadpourlima, Naghmeh 413
Monaco, Michela 314
Montanino, Andrea 338
Moreira, Thalles M. 124
Mousavian, Elham 289

N
Napoli, Fabio 260
Ni, Minqing 428
Nygård, Mikael 413

O
Oliveira, Arnaldo S. R. 124
Olivieri, Carlo 302, 368
Orman, Günce Keziban 274
Oskooei, Amirkia Rafiei 88, 193

P
P. Heris, Mehdi 413
Pereira, Samuel S. 124
Pingaro, Natalia 354, 396

R
Ranieri, Domingo 35
Ronchieri, Elisabetta 51, 106

S
Samawi, Venus W. 70
Şafak, Ilgın 16
Savarese, Giovanni 35
Sibille, Luigi 368

T
Taşgetiren, Nail 16
Teixeira, Bruno M. S. 124
Thu Diep, Vu 3
Tolga, A Çağrı 182
Tuan, Ngo Anh 3
Tuten, Yusuf Taha 193

V
Van Hiep, Pham 3
Verdesca, Laura Claudia 51
Verre, Salvatore 302
Vino, Gioacchino 35

Y
Yakut, Sehmus 193
Younis, Lojin Bani 243
Yousif, Suhad A. 70
Yukcu, Selcan 88

Z
Zurlo, Giovanni 106

MIX
Papier aus verantwortungsvollen Quellen
Paper from responsible sources
FSC® C105338

If you have any concerns about our products,
you can contact us on
ProductSafety@springernature.com

In case Publisher is established outside the EU,
the EU authorized representative is:
**Springer Nature Customer Service Center GmbH
Europaplatz 3, 69115 Heidelberg, Germany**

Printed by Libri Plureos GmbH
in Hamburg, Germany